*A. M. Whiton*

# Genealogical Records

## of the

# Families of Antrim,

## New Hampshire

Excerpted from:

*History of the Town of Antrim, New Hampshire,
From its Earliest Settlement, to June 27, 1877,
With a Brief Genealogical Record
of All the Antrim Families.*
Manchester, N.H.: 1880

By

Rev. W. R. Cochrane

## Notice

In many older books, foxing (or discoloration) occurs and, in some instances, print lightens with wear and age. Reprinted books, such as this, often duplicate these flaws, notwithstanding efforts to reduce or eliminate them. The pages of this reprint have been digitally enhanced and, where possible, the flaws eliminated in order to provide clarity of content and a pleasant reading experience.

*Genealogical Records of the Families of*
*Antrim, New Hampshire*

Excerpted from:

*History of the Town of Antrim, New Hampshire,*
*From its Earliest Settlement, to June 27, 1877,*
*With a Brief Genealogical Record of All*
*the Antrim Families*; pages 329-785

Originally published
Manchester, N.H.
1880

Reprinted by:

Janaway Publishing, Inc.
732 Kelsey Ct.
Santa Maria, California 93454
(805) 925-1038
www.janawaygenealogy.com

2011

ISBN: 978-1-59641-176-0

*Made in the United States of America*

## PUBLISHER'S PREFACE

This book has been excerpted from *History of the Town of Antrim, New Hampshire, From its Earliest Settlement, to June 27, 1877, with a brief Genealogical Record of All the Antrim Families*; by Rev. W. R. Cochrane, Manchester, New Hampshire, 1880, and includes pages 329 to 785 of the original volume. This work retains those original page numbers.

Janaway Publishing, Inc.

# GENEALOGIES.

# PREFACE TO GENEALOGIES.

The following family records will explain themselves, for the most part. The arrangement is original with me, and fixed upon as best for our limited requirements, while it would not do for an extended genealogy. The *first* generation born here or identified with Antrim is *numbered*, and everything said about each child or descendants of the same immediately follows within *brackets*. The *next* generation is printed in *Italics*, and immediately after each name follows the record of the same and descendants in *parenthesis*. It will be noted that the parenthesis with its contents is included in brackets. Notices of other generations before and after these two will be given in a form of words needing no explanation. Only the first generation is numbered. This avoids the extensive use of numbers, and all mixtures of Roman and Arabic terms; and is sufficient, as in most cases we have only three or four generations to deal with.

As these records are given in alphabetical order, no index is needed. When several families are of the same name, it has been the rule to mention first the family earliest here. When places OUTSIDE of New Hampshire are mentioned, the initials of the State are given therewith, except in a few cases where it would be needless, as New Orleans, Philadelphia, etc.

It has been the rule, as far as practicable without dividing families unwarrantably, to confine our remarks to those born in Antrim. Dates have been brought down to Centennial Day, June 27, 1877; and but little will be found in these genealogies subsequent to the above point of time, and this only such as has come unsought to my hand. These families are allotted different amounts of space, since some were here but a little while, and some left no information or record behind. I have made it a rule to give all information to the point which I could get. If families would give me but little, they must not complain if but little is said of them here. Most of the old settlers are noticed at some length. Sometimes I have had to decide between conflicting statements by different branches of the same family. Some who had absolutely no records of their own will find notices here which I have picked up from various sources and put together. In making these searches during about five years, I have written fifteen hundred letters and about two thousand postals, — many of them for convenience in our own town. Of families who long since left town, I have often had to write to town clerks and clergymen and others, to find a person who could tell *any-*

*thing;* and then write over and over, inclosing stamps, till sick at heart with it, to get out of him what I wanted. I have tried with entire impartiality to get in all cases what facts I could.

All matters of biography in this book are embodied in the genealogies. Have said but little about the living.

It should be added, that, some items coming in late, I have been obliged to make the additions in a manner out of the usual order. Some of the larger sketches of families I have actually written over four times, to make them correspond with new information, often also unknown to the families themselves. About sixty families have during this period resided in Antrim more or less who are not named in the genealogies, because we have no valid information. Most of these were so little here, or so little identified with us, as not to be greatly missed. The following persons lived here at least one year each before 1810: Joseph Clark, Jonathan Lamson, Daniel Moore, Stephen Reynolds, Thomas Patch, Jonathan Flanders, Thomas Miller, David Carleton, —— Hoyt, William Davidson, William Johnson, and Jesse Rogers. Subsequently, Nathan Cram, Thomas Aucerton, Sampson Reed, Thomas Carleton, Bezaleel Wheeler, Luther Conant, John Edwards, most of them with large families, resided here for a time. More recently, many families have come and gone, whom neither convenience nor interest would justify us in following. These genealogies embrace three hundred and twenty-nine different names, and five hundred and eighty-one different families. I have taken what seemed to me all possible pains to be accurate; yet probably many mistakes will be found, for which I ask in advance the patience of all concerned. The result may seem imperfect; but, scattered through five years, I have spent more than twelve months of steady, close labor on these genealogies alone, and submit them as the best I can do under the circumstances.

I am indebted to Miss Abby C. Morse, of Concord, for much patient and most efficient work in arranging and copying these materials. Clark Hopkins also has been of great service to me, and has been willing to spend much time in my help. Reed P. Saltmarsh has been ui tiring in his efforts to aid me, and has been of great service. To these especially, and to many others, I here put on record my tender of honest thanks.

And among those who have gone out from the town who have aided in this work. I would mention Rev. S. G. Abbott, Hon. George W. Nesmith, Hon. A. H. Dunlap, and, in particular, Hon. Charles Adams, Jr. The last named has taken upon him more actual labor and pains than any other person, and he has been ready both with money and work to forward these investigations.

I may add that I have drawn items from every possible source, without hesitation but thankfully, for which it would take too much room to make separate acknowledgments.

Robert C. Mack, Esq., of Londonderry, has been greatly my helper, as he is always my honored friend, and my fellow-laborer as a genealogist.

No abbreviations are employed except b. for born, m. for married, and d. for died, unless in case of initials of names; the object being to make every page as plain as possible, especially to the aged.

# GENEALOGIES.

## ABBOTT.

REV. SAMUEL ABBOTT was son of Dea. Ephraim and Dorothy (Stiles) Abbott. This Dea. Ephraim was the son of Ephraim, who was the son of Ephraim, who was the son of John, who was the son of George Abbott, who came from Yorkshire, England, and settled in Andover, Mass., 1643. Rev. Samuel Abbott was born in Mont Vernon, 1777, married Sarah, daughter of Rev. John Rand, 1798; was pastor in Middleborough, Bridgewater, and Chester, Mass., and Londonderry, N. H. Was the inventor of "Abbott's window-shades," 1825; came here in 1838, and bought the present estate in Clinton, where he remained till his death in 1853. Mr. Abbott was wholly uneducated in the schools, but had strong native abilities, was a good sermonizer, and an impressive preacher. In style, he was bold, incisive, and logical. As a minister, he was honest and fearless. He never wrote a sermon. An incident will best show the man. He preached for Dr. Whiton one day, and had for a subject: "What must be put out of the church to promote a revival?" After enlarging on several items, he paused and said, "One thing more must go out of the church. [A pause.] Yes, I must mention it, — *Rum* must go out of the church!" And then with great courage and ability he enforced the reasons why. Those were the first days of the temperance excitement, and many of the members had long been accustomed to a daily dram. Many, therefore, were offended and declared they would never hear Mr. Abbott again. The next time Dr. Whiton asked him to preach, he consented on condition that no hint of it be given beforehand. Then, when suddenly he arose to speak and several men started for the door, he was too quick for them, and in a loud voice gave out his text: "And they, being convicted in their own consciences, went out one by one!" And at once they all appreciated the thing, — heard him through, and were ever after good friends! Mr. Abbott's children were thus: —

1. SAMUEL, [d. in infancy.]
2. EPHRAIM, [b. Milford 1801, m. Ann Wallace of Merrimack, lives in Sudbury, Mass.]
3. SARAH G., [b. in Middleborough, Mass., 1804, m. Richard Waldron, and lives in Providence, R. I.]
4. MILLE R., [d. in Antrim 1848, unm., aged 41.]

5. HEPSIBAH N., [b. in Middleborough, Mass., 1809, d. in Antrim 1841.]
6. SAMUEL W., [b. in Bridgewater, Mass., 1812, m. Clarissa P. Claggett of Derry, d. Montreal, Can., 1862. Samuel W. Abbott was the first of the family here. He came in 1835, and bought, in company with Dea. Imla Wright. all the water-power between Holt's and Paige's mills, with a large tract of land. They two built the Abbott mill, 1836. The former bought the Boyd house, 1837, moved it and fitted it up as it now stands. This house was built in 1797, and, when moved. the shingles that had done service forty years were turned over and relaid on the back side, and are doing good service now, having lasted upwards of eighty years.]
7. DOROTHY S., [b. in Bridgewater 1813, m. Rev. Isaac Woodbury 1857, d. in Antrim June, 1873.]
8. JOHN R., [b. in Bridgewater, Mass., Feb. 14, 1817, m. Hannah O. True of Francestown, Dec. 19, 1848; carried on an extensive business in Clinton many years, was a smart and efficient business man, a loving and devout Christian. Died in the prime of life, Dec. 6, 1863, in the State of Pennsylvania, where he had gone in pursuit of health. His widow died June 21, 1875, a noble woman full of prayer and good works. aged 53. Their children are: —

*John G.*, (b. Nov. 3, 1854. He carries on a large business in Clinton, is a most worthy young man and desirable citizen. Is town treasurer, and probably the youngest man that ever held that office in Antrim.)

*Charles S.*, (b. Aug. 16, 1856.)

*Harlan P.*, (b. July 10, 1860.)

*Mary Jane*, (an adopted daughter, niece of Mrs. Abbott, b. July 13, 1857.)]

9. REV. STEPHEN G., [b. in Bridgewater, Mass., Nov. 9, 1819, studied theology at New Hampton, was licensed to preach by the Baptist Church of Antrim, and settled in Needham, Mass., and other places. He m. Sarah B. Cheney of Holderness, in 1846. The degree of A. M. was conferred on Mr. Abbott, by Bates College, in 1870. He has but one child.

*John T.*, (b. in Antrim in 1850, was graduated at Bates College in 1871, m. Alice E. Merriman, and is now a lawyer in Keene.)]

GENEALOGIES. 333

## ADAMS.

[Chiefly from Drake's History of Boston, Folio Edition.]

AP ADAM came to England out of the "Marches of Wales," and twenty-three generations of his descendants in the male line are here given. The earlier generations lived in Lancashire and Devonshire, England, and the later ones in America.

1. Sir John Ap Adam, Knt. Lord Ap Adam, member of Parliament from 1296 to 1307.
2. Sir John Ap Adam.
3. William Ap Adam.
4. Sir John Ap Adam.
5. Thomas Ap Adam.
6. Sir John Ap Adam, Knt.
7. Sir John Ap Adam, alias Adams.
8. Roger Adams.
9. Thomas Adams.
10. John Adams.
11. John Adams.
12. John Adams.
13. Richard Adams.
14. William Adams.
15. Henry Adams, who settled in Braintree, Mass. (now Quincy), and died 1646.
16. Edward Adams, of Medfield, Mass.
17. John Adams, of Medway, Mass.
18. Abraham Adams, of Brookfield, Mass.
19. Jesse Adams, of Brookfield, Mass.
20. Dr. Charles Adams, of Antrim.
21. Hon. Charles Adams, Jr., North Brookfield, Mass.
22 Charles Woodburn Adams, North Brookfield, Mass.
23. Charles Joseph Adams, North Brookfield, Mass.

From Henry Adams (15), who settled in Braintree, descended the presidents. He had a large family besides the Edward named above, and among them a son Joseph, born 1626, who married Abigail Baxter, and died 1694. This Joseph had a son Joseph, born Dec. 24, 1654. Of this second Joseph, the second son was Dea. John Adams of Braintree, who died May 25, 1760. Dea. John married Susanna Boylston of Brookline, Mass., and their oldest son was John Adams, born Oct. 19, 1735, second president of the United States, reaching the age of nearly 91. His oldest son was John Quincy Adams, born July 11, 1767, sixth president, dying Feb. 23, 1848. John Q. Adams married Louisa C. Johnson, and was father of the distinguished Charles Francis Adams.

Dr. Charles Adams, the twentieth generation from Ap Adam of Wales, was son of Jesse and Miriam (Richardson) Adams of Brookfield, Mass., and was born in that place Feb. 13, 1782. His early years were spent on the farm with his father. His education was chiefly acquired in the district school and Leicester Academy. He then taught some two years in Half Moon, N. Y. On return (1803), he commenced the study of medicine with Dr. Asa Walker of Barre, Mass., with whom he remained in practice one year after completing his studies. He came to Antrim and began practice in the early summer of 1807, coming to take the place of Dr. Cleaves, whose death occurred in April of that year. His attention was called to Antrim by Dr. Whiton, who afterwards settled here in the ministry, and at that time had been here enough to know something of the people and their wants. At first Dr. Adams established himself at the Center of the town, where he remained about a year. He bought the place now occupied by Harold Kelsea in South Village, Oct. 31, 1808, and some months after located there, and remained there till his removal from town. This house and the few acres of land attached to it was part of a large tract containing five hundred and ninety-five acres, all which was sold for taxes, Oct. 28, 1778, by James Duncan, constable of the town, to Daniel McFarland, in two lots, for £16. 15s. 2d. McFarland held all this land till 1798, when he sold about twenty acres (now belonging to Kelsea, Alvah Dodge, and many others) to Nehemiah Knight, for eighty dollars, under date of June 7 of that year. Knight sold to Dr. Adams, and Dr. Adams to Moses B. Ferson, June 23, 1832. The succeeding owners were John Dunlap, Ezra Hyde, Mark B. Woodbury, N. W. C. Jameson, and Harold Kelsea. Dr. Adams paid three hundred dollars, in 1808, for what is now worth many thousands. At that time there was on the place a little, low, unpainted house, with a small shop joined on to it, which, having apparently been a shoemaker's shop, now became the doctor's office. Feb. 13, 1809, his twenty-seventh birthday, Dr. Adams married Sarah McAllister, daughter of James and Sarah (McClary) McAllister of Antrim. She was a woman of excellent tastes and talents, of rare patience under trial, and of a sweet and winning Christian spirit, — all which made her a woman conspicuously worthy and attractive. "In her tongue was the law of kindness." "Her children rise up and call her blessed." His practice here was large and laborious, and promised to remain so, suggesting to him the idea of a change; and on the death of Dr. Fobes of Oakham, Mass., near his native town, he determined at once to go there, and made his removal to that place in 1816. He died in that place March 6, 1875. Dr. Adams, in Antrim, was occasionally in town office, was a favorite among the people, and was held to be a successful physician and a man of marked ability. He was a great reader, was full of information, pursued his practice till most of his contemporaries were gone, and even in extreme old age he was sent for in difficult cases. He was the oldest of twelve children, all of whom he survived more than a quarter of a century. Unbroken health was given him all his life long, and he died of old age at last. Dr. Adams had eight children, four of them born in Antrim and the four youngest in Oakham.

1. Hon. Charles, Jr., [b. Jan. 31, 1810. Had his first schooling here, under charge of Daniel M. Christie and Miss Fanny Baldwin. After removal from this town, he was at school six months under Rev. John Bisbee of Brookfield,

Mass.; then studied eight months with Rev. Josiah Clark of Rutland, Mass.; and this was the limit of his opportunity for education. Then, though quite young, he was in a store five or six years, obtaining much practical knowledge in the course of his work. Is what is called a self-made man. Few men can be found better versed than he in literary affairs or political economy. May 8, 1834. he married Eliza, daughter of Dea. Joseph Cummings of Ware, Mass., and settled in North Brookfield, that State, where he has since resided. Was a long time book-keeper, and afterwards partner, in the immense boot and shoe manufacturing establishment of that place, from which he retired just before the war. With singular continuance he has been kept in offices of trust by the people of his town and State. He was clerk of the town ten years; representative, four years; on the Massachusetts executive council, four years; treasurer of the State, five years; and is now (1877) on his fourth year as senator in the Massachusetts legislature. Has been in public life more than a quarter of a century. Is a man of fixed principle and irreproachable character; and is held in honor throughout his adopted State. Has always been greatly attached to his native town, cherishing with unfading love the rocks and the hills upon which he looked in childhood. Was one of the donors of the vestry to the Center Church, with which he subsequently united. He is a Scotch antiquarian of much reading, foreign travel, and patient research. The degree of A. M. was conferred upon him by Dartmouth College, 1878. Has had five children: Joseph Charles, Charles Woodburn, Ellen Eliza, John Quincy, and George Arthur.]

2. AUSTIN, [b. June 23, 1811; m. 1st, Charlotte Noyes, 1845; 2d, Almira Stearns; is a mason by trade, lives in Oakham, Mass.]

3. CHARLOTTE, [b. May 21, 1813, m. John F. Howard of Boston, and died Oct. 14, 1849.]

4. LYMAN, [b. April 1, 1815, m. Sarah Brown of Baltimore, Md., and died at New Orleans, March 18, 1859.]

5. DEA. LEVI, [b. Oakham, March 7, 1817; m. Sarah L. Ward of North Brookfield, Aug. 14, 1845; 2d, Clara M. Dwight of Belchertown, Mass., May 14, 1854. He died Aug. 11, 1860. Was a fine scholar and a superior teacher. He fol-

lowed the profession of teaching nearly twenty years; was a man of early and life-long piety; very able in meetings; greatly loved by all classes; was deacon in Congregational Church of North Brookfield, and his early death was one of great glory and peace. In the struggles of death he said to his pastor, referring to his funeral: " 1 wish you to state that I do not want a Unitarian Savior now, but one that is Almighty!"]

6. HORACE, [d. unm., 1849, aged 30.]
7. CLARINDA R., [b. Nov. 17, 1823, m. George A. Ellis, who is now treasurer of the South Boston Savings Bank. She is a woman of rare sweetness of character and life.]
8. JOHN. [b. April 4, 1827, m. Marietta Pierce, lives in Boston.]

EDWIN T. ADAMS, carpenter by trade, son of John and Betsey (Atkins) Adams, born in Waterbury, Vt., 1836, came here in 1870 into the Ezra Hyde house, which he has greatly enlarged and improved. Married Jennie Davis of Hancock, and has one child, Sadie M.

## AIKEN.

EDWARD AIKEN, ancestor of all the New Hampshire Aikens, came over from the north of Ireland in 1720, the next year after the settlement of Londonderry, and located among his countrymen in that new town. Parker puts the date of emigration in 1722. But near the close of 1720 the general committee of the town were "petitioned to by William Aiken, John Bell, Andrew Todd, John Wallis, and Benjamin Wilson, for the grant of a stream or brook, which commonly goes by the name of Aiken's brook, in order to the setting-up of a saw-mill thereon, and also one acre of land adjoining to said brook, that will be convenient for a yard to said mill." This shows that the Aikens must have been on the ground previous to December, 1720, long enough for the stream to get the name "Aiken's brook." Many of these Aikens were millwrights and mechanics,— the first Aiken in Antrim also having up a saw-mill soon after he got fairly started on his farm.

The emigrant, Edward Aiken, had three sons, all, it seems, born in Ireland; and if he had daughters, we have no note of them. The sons settled on adjoining farms in Londonderry, and hence the neighborhood was called "Aiken's Range."

Nathaniel, oldest son of Edward, was born May 14, 1696; married Margaret Cochran, daughter of James, Dec. 1, 1726, and had children: Edward, John, Eleanor, Nathaniel, Christian, Jane, James, Ninian, William, Susannah, and Thomas. Nathaniel, the father of these, died Dec. 1, 1783, and his wife in 1788. Edward Aiken, the emigrant, was born in Ireland in 1660, married Barby Edwards, and died in Londonderry in 1747.

Edward, the oldest child of Nathaniel, went to Windham, Vt. He was born Sept. 2, 1727; was grandfather of Rev. Dr. Samuel C. Aiken of Ohio.

John, second child of Nathaniel, called Dea. John, married Annis Orr, and removed to Bedford. He was grandfather of Rev. Dr. Silas Aiken of Boston, afterwards of Rutland, Vt., and also of Hon. John Aiken of Andover, Mass., and great-grandfather of Rev. Dr. C. A. Aiken, professor at Princeton. The descendants of Dea. John Aiken are very numerous.

Much might be given of the other children of Nathaniel, but it is beyond the province of this book. James, his seventh child, remained in Londonderry, and had a large family.

Ninian, the eighth child, lived in Deering, and was grandfather of James Aiken, Esq., of Lewisburg, Penn., whose poem appears in the centennial proceedings.

William, the ninth child of Nathaniel, was born Feb. 20, 1743, married Betsey Woodburn, settled in Deering, and died Feb. 19, 1799. He was known as "Dea. William," was an excellent man, and was a leader in the new town where he settled and died. Had ten children, and was grandfather of M. M. Aiken, Esq., a man of note in Peoria, Ill., and of the Gillis family named elsewhere. The descendants of "Dea. William" are many in number and noble in character.

Thomas, youngest child of Nathaniel save a daughter, Harriet, supposed to have died young, was born Feb. 27, 1747. He married Mary Anderson Dec. 31, 1772; was known as "Spinning-wheel Thomas." He settled in the south part of Deering, and there manufactured spinning-wheels for the whole region. Was an officer in the militia. The section where he lived was called Antrim as early as 1770. This was the Thomas Aiken that "lived in Antrim," and brought up the boy Samuel Downing, who became the last survivor of the Revolutionary army. (See Downing.) "Spinning-wheel Thomas" died June 10, 1831, aged eighty-four. Thousands of his spinning-wheels were in use in this region fifty years ago, and a few are still preserved. He had ten children: Joseph, Nancy, John, Thomas, Susanna, Alice, Jennie, Mary, Robert, and Sallie. Inasmuch as he claimed that he "lived in Antrim," his children shall have additional mention here, as follows: —

Joseph was graduated at Dartmouth College, 1799, and died in 1803.
Nancy married Daniel Dane of New Boston.
John married Nancy Moore, and died in Texas, 1846.
Thomas died young.
Susanna married David Lewis of Francestown.
Alice married David Ellinwood of Deering.
Jennie married Peter Clark of Francestown.
Mary married William Langdell of New Boston, and left a large family.
Robert settled in Kingston, Canada, and his descendants are now in that vicinity.
Sallie married Rufus Fuller of Contoocookville, and had a large family.

Walter and J. B. Aiken, manufacturers at Franklin Falls, are descendants of "Spinning-wheel Thomas."

James Aiken, second son of the emigrant Edward, married Jean Cochran, Oct. 26, 1725, probably a sister of Margaret Cochran, named above. They had six children. The oldest, Elizabeth, was born Aug. 13, 1726. The others were Edward, James, Jane, Agnes, and John. —We have no knowledge of Elizabeth: Edward, Jane, Agnes, and John went to Benson, Vt., and were among the best people there. A descendant, James H. Aiken, Esq., now resides there, and many are scattered in the South and West.

James, the other of these six children of James and Jean Cochran, was our "Dea. James," of whom a brief sketch follows here. - In addition to this sketch it may be said that Dea. Aiken served one campaign or more in the Revolutionary army. He lived to see the forest of 1767 turned into a thriving town of thirteen hundred inhabitants. A brief obituary may be found in the "Amherst Cabinet" of Aug. 2, 1817.

DEA. JAMES AIKEN of Antrim was born in Londonderry, June 1, 1731; was out in the French war; was one of the company celebrated as "Rogers's Rangers," who scoured the country and accomplished marvels in the line of bravery and endurance. Dr. Whiton tells us that Dea. Aiken was once on a scout with Maj. Rogers as far west as Lake George, and the party were almost famished with hunger and thirst, nothing remaining but a glass of rum in a soldier's canteen. The major offered him a dollar for the rum. But the soldier, saying, "Major, I love you, but I love myself better," tipped the canteen and swallowed the rum!

That Dea. Aiken was a brave man, is attested by the fact that alone he faced the forest and the savage, and fixed his home here many miles from a human neighbor. He was the second permanent settler of Antrim. He came and made a little opening in 1766, and the next year removed his family here. Their arrival at his cabin was on Aug. 12, 1767, and it stood against a big rock near the house of Robert Dodge at the foot of the hill in South Village, that being, as he said, the first dry spot he came to on this side of the river. It was four years before another settler joined him in that part of the town. Dea. Aiken was a man of remarkable energy and power, was ready to help any one, was intimidated by no hardship, made his house a shelter to the first settlers, and opened his humble door to every wanderer. Some of these, as elsewhere related, found a happy refuge with this family in the wilderness. For many subsequent years, whenever one came to preach to the scattered settlers, Dea. Aiken "took care of the minister." In his barn, September, 1775, was preached the first sermon ever heard in Antrim. At the formation of the Presbyterian Church, 1788, he was the first person chosen elder, and he held the office with great faithfulness till his death, July 27, 1817, aged eighty-six. He died in the old house by the poplar-tree, which house was taken down by Charles McKeen about 1855. His wife was Molly McFarland, a worthy and noble companion of his hardships and perils. They brought with them four children. She died Dec. 3, 1814, aged seventy-eight. _ Besides two that died young, the family was as follows : —

1. JANE, [Was preparing to marry Dea. John Alexander, when she suddenly sickened and died, to the great grief of the people.]
2. BARBARA, [m. John Campbell, 1786, and d. Feb. 1, 1828, aged 63.]
3. KATHERINE, [b. Aug. 10, 1761, m. James Hopkins 1788, and d. Sept. 6, 1820.]
4. MARTHA, [m. Joseph Fayor and went to New Chester, now Hill. Her husband was killed by the fall of a bank of earth upon him, Oct. 13, 1807. She died in Lowell, Mass., more than fourscore years of age.]
5. POLLY, [b. April 15, 1768, first child of the white race born in Antrim; m. Ebenezer Kimball, and d. Dec. 14, 1862. She was mother of the noted Dr. Kimball of Lowell.]
6. JAMES, JR., [b. in the spring of 1772, being the first male of the white race born in this town. He married a daughter of Hugh Orr of Antrim. He built on the farm of his father, just north of the deacon's residence, the large house now (1879) Mr. Whittum's, and previously Gove's and Barrett's. He soon after went to New York with his wife and two children, Fanny and Edward, locating in Locke, now Summerhill. No son of Antrim has been hunted for more eagerly than this one, by the writer, but without avail. It is known, however, that he had several sons after emigration, one of whom was Leonard Aiken, who began life as a lawyer.]
7. PEGGY, [b. Aug. 30, 1776, m. Richard McAllister, and d. leaving several children, March 1, 1813, aged 36.]
8. NANCY, [d. unm., 1814.]

William, the youngest son of Edward the emigrant, married Janet Wilson, and had two sons, Edward and William, the former going to Windham, Vt., and the latter to Truro, Nova Scotia. This Janet Wilson was aunt of that Mary Wilson who was born on board of a pirate ship while her mother was a prisoner, and who was named for the pirate captain's wife, and received valuable presents from him. The whole of the children known were Agnes, Edward, Mary, Jonathan, Martha, and William. Agnes was born Nov. 17, 1726. Other and valuable information concerning the several branches of the Aiken family must be omitted for want of space.

## ALEXANDER.

RANDALL ALEXANDER, no doubt son of Randall and Janet Alexander, who received their lot of land in Nutfield in 1720, came here from Londonderry and began the James Hopkins place (Arthur Miller's) in 1772. Had been a soldier in the French war. Then he seems to be lost sight of on the records till he turns up in this place. When he came here he "squatted" (built a log cabin) on the brick-yard hill, so called, near the present house, but never made any purchase. And not possessing a spirit congenial with his neighbors, the land he claimed was quietly bought by others; and when he resisted removal, he was hustled off without the forms of law. 'Tis said they dragged him down the sand-hill by his heels! Would not this seem a good process to apply at a day as late as the present in certain cases?

Mr. Alexander had the first grindstone in Antrim for several years; and when asked by Aiken, his nearest neighbor, where he got it, said he found it in the jam, the annual collection of drift-wood in the bend of the river east of his camp. Aiken said he knew he lied, but couldn't resist the temptation to use that grindstone! So things went on for a time, until it was found that Alexander had borrowed the grindstone in Peterborough, without the owner's consent, and sent it down the river in a large sap-trough!

Mr. Alexander left town in 1784. Nothing can be ascertained about his family, or where he went. But he came back here in 1823, white-headed, feeble, and forgotten, and was supported by the town till his death in 1826, at the age of ninety-two. Dr. Whiton says, objection was made to tolling the bell for him, because it was the tradition that he saw a beautiful French girl murdered for her beads when he might have prevented it with a word. Very likely there was no truth in the charge; but this circumstance shows that this people were very sensitive to a wrong. And that was the first year they had a bell, and no doubt it seemed a very sacred thing.

DEA. JOHN ALEXANDER, not known to be kin of the above, — of Scotch race, — came here from Londonderry and began the Daniel Holt farm in 1787; married Mary Nevins of Salem, Mass. Sold his farm to Samuel McAdams and moved to the Branch in 1795, into a little house then standing six or eight rods east of Sylvester Preston's. Was chosen elder in the Presbyterian Church in 1800; died in 1812. Left no children. Was a good man. His widow, partially insane, and without friends, survived him many years. Nothing is known of their ancestry.

## ALLDS.

JOHN ALLDS, son of James and Sarah (Hopkins) Allds, came here from Peterborough in 1798; cleared and settled the Jesse Combs place (now Lewis Green's); put up the present buildings in 1800; married Sarah, daughter of Charles Tuttle, in 1803; after many years moved into a house then standing between B. F. Dustin's and the Keene road; moved to Conneaut, Penn., in 1835, and died there, April 11, 1859, aged eighty. Children: —

1. ISAAC W., [b. May 26, 1804, m. Abigail Butters July 19, 1836, lived in west part of Antrim till 1853, when he moved to

GENEALOGIES. 341

Stoddard, and died there April 26, 1876. Had children, all born here: —

*John*, (b. July 15, 1837, d. in infancy.)
*Benton*, (d. Sept. 23, 1842, aged 4.)
*Eliza*. (d. Sept. 28, 1842, aged 2.)
*Sarah Ann*, (b. Aug. 3, 1843, m. Charles S. Fletcher of this town March 25, 1874.)
*Louisa Ellen*, (b. June 25, 1845, m. Cyrus J. Whitney, Jr., Oct. 17, 1875.)
*Isaac Worden*. (b. Nov. 30, 1848, lives in Centralia, Wis.)
*Warren*, (b. June 18, 1850, now of Worcester, Mass.)
*John Langdon*. (b. Oct. 3, 1853, d. June 23, 1861.)]

2. JOHN. [b. March 25, 1806, went to Conneaut, Penn., in 1827, m. Sarah Osmore, now lives in Camp Douglas, Wis.]
3. SARAH A., [twin sister of John, m. Langdon Swett April 25, 1833, was blind many years, d. Dec. 11, 1878.]
4. NANCY H., [b. Jan. 11, 1811, became second wife of Calvin Barrett of Stoddard.]
5. JONATHAN, [b. June 18, 1815, went with his father to Conneaut, Penn., and still lives there; m. Hannah Loomis.]

## ANTHOINE.

NICHOLAS ANTHOINE came over to Marblehead, Mass., about the middle of the last century, and there married Rachel Hawkes. He was of French race, coming from the Isle of Jersey in the English channel, which has long been a possession of England, though once a part of France and retaining its French manners and customs to this day. Nicholas Anthoine and Rachel Hawkes had three children: John, Rachel, and Nicholas, Jr. The latter went to Windham, Me., with many others, who formed a settlement and called it New Marblehead, after their old home, — which name was subsequently changed to Windham.

Nicholas, Jr., married Anna Pettingill, whom he found in his new home in Maine. He was a man of note in his day in that section of the country. He had only six weeks' schooling in all his life, yet was a fine scholar, many years a teacher; was teacher of Latin, and was particularly proficient in astronomy. He had his telescope and library of astronomical works, and used to calculate the various eclipses. He also studied medicine sufficiently to be of great use in that place and day, when physicians were remote.

John Anthoine, son of Nicholas, Jr., married Mary Gilman, and their son, Dr. Isaiah G. Anthoine, was born in Windham, Me., March 25, 1846, and came here as the successor of Dr. Kimball in 1874. He married Kate I. Preston, Jan. 2, 1877. Is superintending school-committee of the town. Dr. Anthoine studied at Stevens' Plains Seminary near Portland, Me.; entered the academic department of Dartmouth College in 1868, leaving at the close of the first year to go out teaching; then studied nearly two years in the Portland School of Medical Instruction ; and was graduated at Bowdoin Medical College in 1874, coming immediately here, and locating in South Village. Has one son, Harry M., b. Oct. 2, 1879.

## APPLETON.

CHARLES APPLETON, grandson of Judge Robert Alcock, who came direct from England to Deering, and son of James and Mary (Stewart) Appleton, was born in Deering, 1825; name was changed from Alcock to Appleton ; married Nancy J. Parker, moved onto the then-called Tennent place, 1859, and still occupies the same. Children : —

1. CLARA A., [b. in Deering Sept. 5, 1853, m. Andrew D. White April 4, 1877.]
2. GEORGE J., [b. in Deering, Feb. 18, 1855.]
3. SCOTT J., [b. in Antrim, June 23, 1862.]

## ATHERTON.

JOSEPH S. ATHERTON, name changed from Witherspoon. See that family.

## ATWOOD.

JOSHUA ATWOOD. Little known of him. Lived awhile in Lempster; was son of Caleb Atwood of Weare; came here and settled the John Barker place, 1790; married Susan Cram, and died in 1829, aged seventy-nine. The five last children were by a second wife, Mrs. Anne (Miller) Dresser of Windsor. He sold his farm to John Barker, in old age, and moved to Washington, but did not long survive the change. The children, except two that died in infancy, are given below. First wife died at the age of thirty-five.

1. WELLS, [m. Betsey Dresser, and moved to Windsor ; went thence to Washington. and d. there years ago.]
2. BETSEY, [m. Samuel Brown, d. on the Dea. Woods farm.]
3. POLLY, [m. John Dresser, moved to Washington, d. there.]
4. JESSE, [m. Betsey Hall of Londonderry, Vt., and lived and d. in that place.]
5. DOLLY, [m. Squire Gove, and moved to Weare.]
6. PETER CLARK, [b. in Lempster Aug. 11, 1795, m. Mary F. Wilkins (" Polly ") of Antrim. They lived here about five years after marriage, moving to Londonderry, Vt., in November, 1820. They had children thus : —

   *Dr. Matthew Whipple*, (b. in Antrim May 22, 1816, m. Fannie W. Burnham of this town Oct. 10, 1843, settled as a physician in New Hudson, N. Y., and d. there, of consumption, Aug. 19, 1847, aged 31. Was a young man of much promise, and his untimely death was the occasion of great sorrow.)

*Mary Almira*, (b. in Antrim Jan. 18, 1818, m. Elisha D. Gearfield Oct. 13, 1836, d. of consumption in Londonderry, Vt., July 5, 1847.)

*Lydia W.*, (b. in Antrim March 5, 1820, m. Alvah W. Pierce May 3, 1841, d. of consumption May 9, 1854.)

*Harriet N.*, (b. in Londonderry, Vt., March 23, 1823; m. 1st, Joel M. Pettengill. Her husband d. at the age of 25; m. 2d, Harvey S. Curtis, Dec. 25, 1850. Home in Kenosha, Wis.)

*Emeline*, (b. March 14, 1825, m. Samuel B. Coffin, lives in Newport.)

*Susan A.*, (b. Oct. 2, 1827, m. Josiah W. Pettigrew, lives in Ludlow, Vt.)

*Sarah F.*, (b. Oct. 11, 1829, m. Thomas P. Davis, lives in Boston.)

*Peter C.*, (b. Jan. 26, 1832, m. Helen Aldrich.)

*Ann E.*, (b. Feb. 18, 1835, m. Prof. Addison P. Wyman, d. Sept. 24, 1871. Her husband followed in six months.)

*James H.*, (b. June 5, 1840, m. Frances Palmer, and lives in Canton, Ill.)]

7. JOSHUA, [m. Alice Sanborn of Unity; went some twenty years ago to Wisconsin; supposed to be dead.]

8. RHODA, [b. May 1, 1800, m. William Gove of Weare.]

9. SALLY A., [m. John Flint of Antrim, Jan. 31, 1822, and now lives a widow at Albany, Wis.]

10. JOHN, [child of second wife, b. Dec. 2, 1807, went into U. S. army in the Mexican war, was badly wounded, from the effects of which he soon died.]

11. JEREMIAH S., [b. Nov. 22, 1809, m. Elisabeth Moore, has children: Hiram G., b. Nov. 2, 1841; Samuel H., b. May 9, 1843; Mary R., b. May 1, 1845; Diantha E., b. May 29, 1846; Martha A., b. July 10, 1850; James M., b. Feb. 20, 1852; Joshua C., b. Aug. 27, 1855; George L., b. Oct. 20, 1857; Abby M., b. Oct. 16, 1859; and John M., b. Aug. 13, 1864.]

12. IRA, [b. July 11, 1813, m. Mary Temple of Claremont, went to New York.]

13. LENORA, [b. Oct. 2, 1816, m. Oscar Lawrence, and went to New York.]
14. LUCETTE, [m. Harrison Andrews of Windsor.]

WILLIAM D. ATWOOD, grandson of Caleb, and son of Philip and Sarah (Dustin) Atwood, was born in Sandwich, 1789, and married Sally Simonds of this town, May 7, 1812; came here in 1810, lived near Lovering's mills; moved to Bridgewater, Vt., in 1823, where he now survives at great age. Children, all but the youngest born here, were thus: —

1. ALEXANDER, [b. in 1813, unm., lives in Pennsylvania.]
2. SARAH. [b. in 1816, m. Cephas Harding of Pomfret, Vt., d. 1854.]
3. LOUISA, [b. in 1818, m. Isaac Angell of Bridgewater, Vt.]
4. LUKE, [b. in 1820, m. Martha Weld, and lives in Barnard, Vt.]
5. HANNAH, [b. in 1823, m. Sylvester Woodward, and has recently come from Deering to this town.]
6. WILLIAM, [b. in 1829, m. Sarah Fairbanks, and lives in Bridgewater, Vt.]

## AUSTIN.

But little is known of the ancestry of the Austins of this town. The father of Nathan, named below, was killed by the Indians, but the time and place cannot be ascertained. The father and son were fording a river, both on one horse, when the savages fired upon them. The father was killed and fell into the river, but the boy and the horse escaped unhurt. This boy was taken to Pelham, and there he was brought up, and there he married; and his posterity are very numerous and respectable.

NATHAN AUSTIN came here from Pelham, and began the Danforth farm, west of the Gould place, in 1780. His wife was Phebe Barker, half-sister to Capt. Peter Barker. Brought with him a large family. Moved to Rochester, Vt., in 1800, and died there very aged in 1840. Their children, besides four little ones buried in Antrim, were: —

1. NATHAN, [m. 1st, Betsey Brown; 2d, Sarah Brown; went with his father to Rochester, Vt., and d. there in 1847, aged 78.]
2. MARENA, [b. 1770, m. John Brown; had one son, Samuel, b. in Antrim, who m. Louisa Ayer, and is now living in Montpelier, Ind. After the birth of Samuel, they moved to Rochester, Vt., and had a large family, one of whom, Thomas Brown, m. his cousin, Lucy Brown of Antrim, in 1829, and lived on what is called the Thomas Brown place, till 1866, when he moved to Hancock. Mrs. Lucy Brown

d. in 1875, aged 74. Marena d. in Goshen, Vt., at the age of 80.]
3. HANNAH, [m. Ezra Washburn and lived and d. in Rochester, Vt. The date of her death was Sept. 6, 1833, and her age 54.]
4. DANIEL, [m. Polly Baker, lived in Rochester, Vt., and d. there May, 1827.]
5. ABIJAH, [went to Potsdam, N. Y., m. Polly Shaw, and d. April 15, 1860, aged 79. His wife d. Feb. 7, 1858, aged 75.]
6. PHINEHAS, [m. "Dicy" Washburne, went to Potsdam, N. Y., and d. there April 15, 1863. His wife d. Aug. 20, 1865, aged 80.]
7. SARAH, [m. Daniel Shaw of Rochester, Vt., went to Potsdam, N. Y., and d. there, Dec. 22, 1834, aged 47. Her husband d. April 20, 1854, aged 73.]
8. ISAAC, [went to Potsdam, m. Mary Field, moved to Hopkinton, N. Y., and d. there, March 1, 1862, aged 72. His wife d. Oct. 4, 1863, aged 69.]

## AVERILL.

PHILIP AVERILL, son of Thomas and Mary Averill, of Windsor, born in Amherst, 1789; married, 1st, Hannah Boutwell, Sept. 16, 1812; 2d, Mary Vose, Sept. 28, 1834; 3d, Hannah G. Barber of Peterborough. Lived many years in a house then standing near Windsor line, on the road above Daniel Swett's: moved thence to Peterborough in 1836, and died there, Sept. 27, 1858. Children : —

1. MARY ANN, [b. Jan. 30, 1815 ; m. 1st, James Boutelle, Jr., Oct. 23, 1834; 2d, Benjamin B. Osmer ; lives in Peterborough.]
2. JOHN, [b. June 29, 1817, m. Elisabeth Puffer of Peterborough.]

## AVERY.

DAVID P. AVERY, born in Greenfield, 1821; married Mary A. Newhall of Nottingham: came here in 1856, and lived where John C. Butterfield now lives; was a carpenter by trade; moved to Rutland, Mass., in 1868; has but one child, now Mrs. Daniel C. Putnam of that place.

## BAILEY.

LEVI P. BAILEY, son of Luther and Betsey (Crombie) Bailey, was born in Troy, Vt., in 1818; married Hannah Morse, and came here into the Champney house, at the Branch, in 1876. Children: —

1. WILLIAM, [b. July 4, 1841.]
2. MARCUS M., [b. Oct. 4, 1843, m. Helen Thompson, and lives in Nelson.]
3. CHARLES, [b. Nov. 26, 1844, m. Abby Quint of Great Falls, and settled in Wilton.]
4. HIRAM S., [m. Mary A. Woodward of Francestown, lived here awhile, where one child, Walter, was b. Nov. 18, 1876.]
5. LEVI E.
6. AMANDA, [m. Richard Woodward, and lives in Francestown.]
7. ALONZO P., [m. Sarah Woodward, sister of above; lived here in 1876. One child, Charles, was b. here in Nov., 1876.]

## BAKER.

The ancestor of Elliot Webster Baker in this country was John Baker, who came from England, and, bringing a large family, settled in Waltham, Mass., in 1738, where he resided six years. Then the father, and probably his younger children, removed to Killingsley, Conn., while the others remained. The youngest son was Richard, who was ten years of age on arrival in this country. In 1757, he purchased a section of wild land in Westminster, Mass., with the intention of settling on the same, but was pressed into the army against the French and Indians for one year. At the close of the year the British officers refused them their discharge. But the whole company, being stationed at Albany, N. Y., determined to leave in a body, and, making themselves snow-shoes, they started across the Green Mountains over the deep snow for their home in Massachusetts. They were safe from pursuit, inasmuch as they could not be followed without snow-shoes, no considerable number of which would be ready. But they lost their way, wandering several days among the mountains, till, after a time, they struck Deerfield river, and followed it to Coleraine, where they found welcome and shelter and food. They slept on the snow, and were nine days without provisions, except a small dog which they killed and ate. Mr. Baker reached his friends in safety, soon after married Mary Sawyer of Lancaster, settled on his land, had a large family of children, and died in good old age. The fourth son of Richard and Mary (Sawyer) Baker was Bezeleel, who was born in Westminster, Mass., 1768. He came to Marlborough, our State, in 1787, and selected a tract of land on which he soon after settled. In 1793, he married Abigail, daughter of Dea. Nathan Wood of his native town. They had several children, among them the late Dea. Abel Baker, deacon of the Congregational Church of Troy, and Asa Baker of Jaffrey. The latter married, first, Hannah Moors; second, Adeline Plummer, daughter of Jesse T. Plummer of Goffstown. The second marriage occurred June 19, 1856. Asa Baker died in Jaffrey, Oct. 12, 1869. His first wife died Dec. 24, 1854.

ELLIOT W. BAKER, son of Asa and Hannah (Moors) Baker, was born in Jaffrey, Sept. 1, 1846. He came here with his step-mother in

1870, into the Ephraim Simonds house in South Village, which house in itself and surroundings he has greatly improved. Mr. Baker is the very careful and obliging insurance agent for this section. He married Julia V. McCoy of Antrim, Feb. 10, 1878.

## BALCH.

JAMES T. BALCH, son of Varion and Mary (Thompson) Balch of Francestown, born there 1817, came here 1840, to work for Dea. Baldwin in the manufacture of hoes; married Lois W. Robbins, 1844; lives in the Robbins house; has children : —

1. CHARLES F., [b. Nov. 29, 1844, m. Ellen O. Fleming Nov. 17, 1870, and lives in Bennington.]
2. GEORGE W., [drowned May 8, 1852, aged 6 years. Went fishing with other boys, and fell into the river near Baldwin bridge.]
3. WILLIAM A., [b. Nov. 4, 1856.]
4. JOHN A., [b. Feb. 28, 1860.]

## BALDWIN.

HENRY BALDWIN of Devonshire, England, was a citizen of Woburn, Mass., as early as 1640. Was selectman and deacon of the church. He married Phebe Richardson of England, Nov. 1, 1649, and had eleven children. He died Feb. 14, 1698. His eighth child, Henry Baldwin, Jr., married Abigail Fisk, May 4, 1692, and had eight children, of whom Isaac, the third in order, was born Feb. 20, 1700. This Isaac married Mary Flagg, March 24, 1726, and had four children : Luke, Jeduthun, Nahum, and Isaac, Jr.

Nahum, known as "Col. Nahum," was born May 3. 1734, and settled in Amherst. This was without doubt the record of the ancestry of the Antrim family, and may be found more full in Savage's Genealogical Dictionary. Some of the descendants of Dea. Henry Baldwin are said to occupy places in Woburn settled by him two hundred and forty years ago. "Col. Nahum Baldwin" was the "village blacksmith" of Amherst, was deacon in the Congregational Church the last fourteen years of his life, and died May 7, 1788.

ISAAC BALDWIN of Antrim was son of Col. Nahum and Martha (Low) Baldwin, and grandson of Isaac Baldwin. The father, Col. Nahum, was an officer of considerable note in the Revolutionary war, was the first treasurer of Hillsborough county, was a man of property, was several times representative of Amherst in the New Hampshire Congress, and took conspicuous place on its committees and in its debates, as appears by the Journal of the House. He was one of the parties in the first case brought before a grand jury in this county. The other party was Jonas Stepleton, who, being brought to the bar, pleaded guilty, and threw himself upon the mercy of the court. It was a queer kind of mercy which was dispensed, according to the old record, thus: "It is ordered that the Stepleton be whipped twenty stripes on the naked back at the public whipping-post between the hours of one and two of the afternoon of this third day of October (1771), and that he pay Nahum Baldwin, the owner of the good stolen, forty-four pounds lawful money, being tenfold the value of the goods stolen (the goods stolen being returned), and that in default of the payment of said tenfold damage and cost of prosecution, the said Nahum Baldwin be authorized to dispose of said Jonas in servitude to any of His Majesty's subjects for the space of seven years, to commence from this day."

Isaac, who came here, was born in Amherst in 1768. He married Bethia Poole of Hollis, before coming here. Came and settled the Baldwin farm on the river in 1793. He was a stirring, earnest, useful man, greatly respected by all. Was one often called to preside in town meetings, and go ahead in important matters. He died in the prime of manhood, in 1821. He raised a large and respectable family as follows below. The marriage of his sister, who settled near him in Antrim, appears in the "Village Messenger" of Amherst, thus: "In Antrim Sept. 1797 Mr. William Starrett to the agreeable Miss. Lucy Baldwin."

1. EMMA. [b. at Amherst July 13, 1792, m. Jabez Youngman March 14, 1809, and now lives in Dorchester.]
2. FANNY, [b. at Antrim Feb. 26, 1794, m. Dr. Israel Burnham Dec. 11, 1817, and d. April 8, 1847.]
3. DEA. ISAAC, [b. Mar. 22, 1796; m. 1st, Sarah Osgood of Nelson, in 1823, who d. in 1831; 2d, Nancy White of Nelson, in 1833, and d. Feb. 9, 1872. He was one of the building committee of the Center Church in 1826, afterwards was deacon in the Congregational Church at Bennington many years. He was a good man, very decided in his convictions and set in his purposes, yet always meaning to be right. Children:—

*Sarah A.*, (b. June 20, 1824, now Mrs. Gideon Dodge of Fairfax, Io.)

*Isaac O.*, (b. Feb. 23, 1826, graduated at Dartmouth College in 1849, m. Elizabeth Means of Ohio, and is a lawyer of note in Clinton, Io.)

*Nathaniel O.*, (m. Mary Clough of Lowell, Mass., d. in New York City in 1859.)

*John W.*, (m. Mary Currier of New York City; had one child, Frank, b. here 1865; is now a merchant in New York City.)

*Abby B.*, (m. Maj Benjamin R. Jenne Oct. 18, 1869, and lives in Brattleboro', Vt.)

*Albert*, (b. in 1837, m. Martha J. Eaton in 1871; is in the insurance business at Brattleboro', Vt.)

*Benjamin B.*, (m. Carrie Cochran, and lives in Clinton, Io.)
*Edward P.*, (now of Fairfax, Io.)]
4. DEXTER, [b. July 5, 1798; graduated from Dartmouth Medical College in 1823, practiced medicine many years in Mount Vernon, Me., afterwards in Boston; retired after practice of nearly forty years, to Framingham, Mass., in 1860, and died there May 27, 1870. Was one of the first "abolitionists" in Maine; a man of strict principles and a helper in every good work; m. 1st. Caroline Peabody of Franklin, 1824, who soon died; 2d, Lavina B. Howard of Winthrop, Me., in 1829. He was a fine specimen of the physical man, pleasant, fearless, and open-hearted. Once in public meeting when the votes were counted and they found one "abolition" vote, they sneeringly shouted, " Dr. Baldwin!" " Dr. Baldwin!" At once he raised himself on tiptoe, and standing high above them all he said: " Yes, gentlemen; and you and I will live to see the day when a vote like *that* will be the rule and not the exception in this town!" And he *was right*. But it was thirty years before the war.]
5. NAHUM, [b. July 13, 1800, d. of spotted fever in 1812.]
6. SAMUEL, [b. June 15, 1802; m. 1st, Betsey G. Bell of Bennington, in 1830; 2d, Mrs. Martha (Gregg) Lear of Manchester, in 1871. Settled in 1832 in North Branch as a blacksmith, moved thence to Bennington in 1836, where he still resides. Has followed business of machinist and manufacturer. Three eldest children were born in Antrim.
*Anna M.*, (b. March 13, 1833, m. Levi Woodbury of Antrim May 21, 1856; a woman whose amiability and good works are often heard mentioned with praise throughout the town. We are indebted to her for some of the views in this book.)
*Samuel Dexter*, (b. June 11, 1834, unm., d. in Bennington, 1879.)
*William K.*, (b. Nov. 1, 1835, m. Nancy E. Barrett of Wilton Sept. 5, 1861; was a merchant in East Wilton many years; d. in the midst of his usefulness, Feb. 12, 1877.)
*Helen P.*, (b. Bennington Feb. 25, 1838, m. Abram A. Ramsay Nov. 28, 1860.)
*Lucretia G.*, (b. May 7, 1840, d. Nov. 27, 1863.)
*Sarah F.*, (b. Aug. 27, 1841, d. Oct. 26, 1873.)
*Augusta J.*, (b. Jan. 16, 1843, m. George A. Whittemore May 2, 1866.)]

7. LUCY, [b. June 12, 1804; m. 1st, Dr. David Flanders, Sept. 20, 1829; 2d, David Watts, 1855; 3d, Aaron Perkins, 1858; 4th, Dea. Fiske of Wilmot, March 15, 1872.]
8. THOMAS J.; [b. Dec. 15, 1806, d. of spotted fever in 1812, aged 6.]
9. WILLIAM, [b. May 15, 1809, m. Abigail R. Kenney of Westbrook, Me.; was a man of energy and large business; d. at Lawrenceville, Ill., 1849. His wife d. 1865, aged 56.]
10. CYRUS, [b. May 14, 1811; studied at New Ipswich, then at Phillips Academy, Andover, Mass.; entered Dartmouth College, 1835, was graduated in class of 1839; went as teacher to Meriden the following year; has been an honored and successful teacher nearly forty years, at Palmyra, N. Y., at Freehold, N. J., and at Providence, R. I., but mostly at Meriden, where he now resides; m. Hannah Shattuck of Meriden, in 1841. Few sons of Antrim have a better record.]
11. HARRIET, [b. April 26, 1814, m. Dr. J. L. Flanders Oct. 15, 1835; moved to Lawrence, Ill., and d. there in 1846.]
12. ESTIMATE R. E., [b. Oct. 22, 1816, m. Dr. Calvin McQuestion Sept. 11, 1844, and went to Hamilton, C. E. Harriet and Estimate once went over the river for the cows, when, being gone some time, the water suddenly rising flooded the road three feet deep. But undismayed, each got on a cow's back and rode through it home!]

JAMES BALDWIN, born in Tyngsborough, Mass., in 1783, son of Jeremiah and —— (Carr) Baldwin, married Abigail Pollard of Greenfield, in 1814; settled in Hillsborough, but moved to the Solomon Hopkins place, Antrim, in 1835, where he lived eighteen years, then moved back to Hillsborough and died there at the age of eighty-eight. Left two children: —

1. ABBY, [b. in 1816, m. Ericson Burnham, and d. in Hillsborough in 1858, leaving two daughters now m. and living in California.]
2. MARIA, [b. in 1821, m. Alonzo Travis, and is now living in Mont Vernon.]

## BALLARD.

BARTHOLOMEW BALLARD came here from Ashby, Mass., 1795. Soon after built what is known as the Henry Hill house, South Village, in one part of which he lived, and in the other part manufactured clocks. His work was quite distinguished in that day. Many of these clocks are in existence now, and occasionally appear on sale. marked, " B. Ballard, Antrim." They were of the old-fashioned kind, standing in the corner of the room. One of these is now in possession of the writer, having run eighty years, — fifty of those years giving the time to one family in Malden, Mass. It is still in good condition and bears marks of delicate workmanship. Mr. Ballard left Antrim, probably in 1806, and went into the same business in Ohio, and died near Columbus, that State, in 1830. He married, first, Rusha Lawrence, in 1796 ; second, Lucinda Lawrence of Ashby, Mass., cousin of the first. Only two children known: —

1. CHRISTIANA. [b. in 1800, daughter of first wife.]
2. LUCINDA, [daughter of second wife, b. 1804, d. unm. 1829.]

## BALL.

JAMES BALL, born in Townsend, Mass., Jan. 1, 1764. was son of Lieut. Jeremiah and Mary (Stevens) Ball, and grandson of Jeremiah Ball, who married another Mary Stevens and settled in Townsend in 1727. This last was son of Nathaniel Ball. This Nathaniel's father was Nathaniel, son of John Ball, who came from Wiltshire, England, and settled in Concord, Mass., in 1640.

James Ball married Rebecca Shattuck of Pepperell, Mass., in 1791; came here about 1796, probably a little earlier. Was one of the refugees from the Shay's Rebellion that escaped into New Hampshire in 1787. Cleared and built about half-way up the west side of Robb mountain, and there after a time he was joined by his wife and their two children. She died on the mountain in 1829. Not long after he went to live with his son Jonas in Nashua; and they two died within a day of each other, August, 1850. Children: —

1. JAMES D., [b. Jan. 28, 1794, m. Mary Farnsworth.]
2. JOHN, [b. June 15, 1796, m. Rebecca Proctor of Stoddard in 1818 ; took the homestead farm, lived here till 1835, when he moved to Washington, where he yet lives. His children were : —

    *Dexter*, (m. Hannah Brockway, lives in Washington.)
    *Nathaniel*, (m. Sylvia J. Perkins, lived in Washington ; killed by a blow from a cart-tongue in 1858.)
    *Worcester H.*, (m. Lydia A. Allen of Nashua, lives in Washington.)
    *Henry M.*, (m. Emily J. Kidder of Walpole, lives in Washington.)
    *Rebecca H.*, (m. Andrew J. Barney, lives in Washington.)
    *Rosanna*, (m. Sumner Fairbanks and moved to the West.)
    *Allen W.*, (m. Frances Bradford.)]
3. NEHEMIAH, [d. in 1817, aged 16.]
4. DAVID, [b. in 1804, m. Julia West of Greenfield, settled in Oregon.]

5. JONAS, [b. July 3, 1807, m. Rosa Nichols of Haverhill, Mass., moved to Marlow, thence to Nashua, where he d. Aug. 14, 1850.]
6. SARAH, [b. April 18, 1810, m. Benjamin Mead of Swanzey March 6, 1834, and lives in that town.]

## BARKER.

NATHAN B. BARKER, son of Daniel and Bathsheba (Blanchard) Barker, was born in Lyndeborough in 1784. His father was lost in the Revolutionary war. Nathan B. was himself an officer in the war of 1812; married Hannah Parker of Peterborough; came with his children from Bennington in 1833, and located on the Adam Dunlap place, where he lived till 1846, when he followed his children to Western New York, and died in Buffalo in 1864. Children: —

1. STEPHEN B., [b. in Greenfield in 1808, m. Abigail Ordway of Deering July 12, 1835. She d. in Lyndeborough July 15, 1850. He lived here several years, then moved to Francestown and d. Feb. 2, 1860. His children (b. in Antrim) are: —

    *Nancy*, (m. Daniel F. Carey, and went to Cedar Rapids, Io.)
    *Clark H.*, (d. unm. March 15, 1861.)
    *Nathan*, (lives unm. at Morton, Ill.)
    *Newton*, (d. quite young.)
    *Stephen N.*, (b. July 19, 1843, m. Mrs. Evelyn S. (Upton) Walker Nov. 27, 1878, and lives in Nashua. He served in the late war both in army and navy, was in Admiral Porter's Mississippi squadron, and was all through the Red-river expedition, and for some time after the close of the war was stationed in the navy-yard at Brooklyn, N. Y.)
    *Hannah M.*, (m. N. T. Hartshorn and lives in Concord.)]

2. PROF. NATHAN B., JR., [b. in Peterborough in 1811, was a teacher all his life after the age of 17. Went to Riga, N. Y., and there m. Minerva N. Morse in 1841, and d. of apoplexy in 1873. At the time of his death he was principal of Buffalo public school; was an able and good man, and left children: Sarah, James W., Ella, Jennie, and Ida.]
3. SARAH, [d. unm. in 1835, aged 21.]
4. REV. SEWALL P., [b. in 1816; is a Methodist minister; ordained at Shelby, N. Y.; m. Eliza Dean and lives in Buffalo. Has been a teacher most of his life.]
5. ABEL P., [m. Esther M. Sargent of Manchester, 1842; lived some years in that city; thence went to New York; thence

eight years in California; now lives in Nashua; has but one son living, Abel W.]

6. PROF. JAMES W., [b. 1824; degree of A. M. conferred upon him by Hillsdale College, Michigan, 1861; m. Amanda Balcom of Lockport, N. Y., 1848; teacher from age of 18 except a short editorial career; was president of New York State Teachers' Association, 1868; has place of high responsibility in Buffalo city schools; is a poet of some eminence, his occasional pieces finding a welcome place in periodicals for many years. The Antrim Centennial Poem was from his pen. He is also editor of "The Buffalo School Journal," a vigorous eight-page paper in that city.]

Peter and Abijah Barker, Revolutionary soldiers and good men, were sons of Zebediah and Deborah (Merrill) Barker of Atkinson.

CAPT. PETER BARKER married Sally Wood and came here in 1789, or a little earlier. They had a child born here that year. He bought the place now Levi Curtis's, and began to clear the same; but, after a time, for reasons not given, exchanged places with Charles Wood, his wife's brother, who had made a beginning on the Moody Barker place. On this last Capt. Peter lived and died, and his descendants still occupy the ground. This exchange of places seems to have been made during the year 1789, and before either party had subdued a great amount of land. Peter Barker was captain of the "Alarm List," of which notice will be found in the military history of Antrim. He died May 23, 1829, aged seventy-four, and his wife in 1843, aged eighty-eight. Children : —

1. SAMUEL, [b. in Atkinson, m. Polly Barker of Hancock, lived several years in a log house a little west of the Artemas Brown place; in 1817 went to Oppenheim, N. Y., and d. there in 1870, aged 87. His wife d. March, 1874, aged 89. Children born here were : —

*Nancy*, (b. Dec. 20, 1805, m. John Warner of Oppenheim, d. 1877.)

*Samuel*, (b. 1807, d. 1812.)

*Peter*, (b. 1809, d. in infancy.)

*Susannah*, (b. 1810, became 2d wife of William Cook.)

*Peggy W.*, (b. 1812, married William Cook, d. 1862.)

*Mary*, (m. Jacob Cook of Oppenheim, and is yet living in that place.)

*Elbridge G.*, (m. Mary Stone, lives on farm adjoining the homestead of his father.)

These seven children were born in Antrim. Afterward five others were born to them whose names are given below : —

*William B.*, (m. 1st, Mercy Haile of Temple; 2d, Mary Hudson; lives in Oppenheim.)

*Samuel*, (m. Eliza J. Foster, d. 1868 aged 48.)

*Sarah*, (m. Benjamin Turney, lives in Johnstown, N. Y.)

*Lucy S.*, (d. 1836, aged 12.)

*Peter*, (m. Adeline Fuller, d. Orwell, N. Y., 1865.)]

2. HANNAH, [b. in Atkinson, m. Daniel McIlvaine Jan. 28, 1808, d. June 14, 1856.]

3. PETER, [b. in Antrim March 14, 1789, m. Maria D. Marsh in St. Albans, Vt., went to Cleveland, O., and died there 1864.]

4. ISAAC, [b. July 2, 1791; brick-maker by trade; m. Nabby Taylor Dec. 25, 1817; settled in Deering, then moved to Charlestown, Mass., thence after a brief sojourn in Antrim he moved to Centre Township, Io., and died there Nov. 26, 1872. His second wife was Abigail Nesmith, whom he married October, 1847. He left five children, three by first wife and two by second, as follows: —

*Hannah T.*, (b. Dec. 20, 1818, m. Zebadiah Kinsley of Somerville, Mass.)

*Isaac*, (b. Oct. 23, 1823, m. Mary O. Giles of Somerville, Mass.; is brick-maker by trade; is an honored and wealthy citizen of San Francisco, Cal.)

*Henry L.*, (unm., lives in San Francisco.)

*John J.*, (b. August, 1848, is railroad engineer in Iowa.)

*Milton R.*, (b. October, 1851, m. Mary Hanna, lives in Mount Vernon, Io.)]

5. THOMAS, [b. 1793, m. Nancy Taylor 1825; settled in Deering, but after the death of his wife came back to Antrim; m. 2d, Pamelia Barker of Sutton, lived at foot of sand-hill and died there 1867. Left no children.]

6. CAPT. MOODY MORSE, [b. May 24, 1795, m. Nancy Bixby of Hillsborough in 1821, and remained on homestead. They lived together till March 24, 1873, when he died, and she followed March 26. They were quiet, unassuming, and Christian in their lives. Children: —

*John B.*, (b. 1822, m. Harriet Newton of Bennington, went to Mexico, and d. there in prime of life.)

*Emily*, (b. 1824, m. Samuel Brown, and lives in Wilton.)

*Adeline*, (b. Sept. 12, 1829, m. Charles Wood of Hillsborough, July 3, 1854.)

*Miles C.*, (b. 1832, m. Sarah J. Carr of Hillsborough, lives in Nashua.)

*Henry M.*, (b. Aug. 24, 1838, m. Mary J. Colburn of New Boston Nov. 30, 1864, lives on homestead settled by his grandfather, and has three sons: Herbert L., b. Aug. 27, 1866; Harry C., b. March 31, 1870; and Fred M., b. May 4, 1871.)]

7. SALLY, [b. Jan. 26, 1797, m. Dea. Asa Bond, now lives a widow in Hancock.]

ABIJAH BARKER, the other son of Zebediah and Deborah (Merrill) Barker that came here, married Susannah Wood, sister of Peter Barker's wife, and moved here in the spring of 1787. Probably these two brothers were here a season or two at work before moving here. He located in the pasture northeast of Alvin Barker's; cleared the land and built the house himself, living in a room of Daniel Nichols's house (now George Turner's) until his humble shelter could be reared. In this house of his own building he raised his family, and lived till 1834, — forty-seven years, — when he went to spend his old age with his children, and died April 22, 1847, aged eighty-seven. His wife died Oct. 28, 1840, aged eighty. She was a woman of great courage and endurance. As an illustration of this, one fact may be given. In the fall of 1791, she went on a visit to Atkinson, upwards of forty-five miles as the bad and crooked roads were then, went through in one day on horseback and alone, and on a man-saddle, and carried her babe Gideon, weighing eighteen pounds, in her arms! What think ye of that, young misses hardly able to walk out to dinner? Who argues for easy carriages any longer?

After Mr. Barker had moved away, the old buildings he had occupied so long dropped to pieces by the decay of years, and now no vestige of them remains; the bridle-path to them is grown over; and few of the living remember the spot. The children of Abijah and Susannah (Wood) Barker were thus: —

1. CHARLES W., [b. Sept. 17, 1787, m. Polly Chapman of Windsor Dec. 17, 1811; lived some years between John Barker place and Cooledge place, in the deep valley, in the Brown house which has been gone near half a century; built the Cooledge house 1823; moved to Henniker, 1829, and there both husband and wife are now living in ripe and honorable old age. Children born in Antrim: —

*John*, (b. April 4, 1813, m. Mary J. McClure, d. in Boston Feb. 15, 1873.)

*Mary C.*, (b. Jan. 13, 1816, m. James M. French, lives in Henniker.)

*Almira A.,* (b. March 19, 1820, m. Joseph Nichols, lives in Manchester.)

*Caroline M.,* (b. June 5, 1823, d. aged 6 years.)

*Charles W.,* (b. June 19, 1828, m. Caroline E. Eaton, d. in Warren, October, 1875.)]

2. ABIJAH, [b. Jan. 7, 1789, m. Jane McIlvaine 1817, and settled on the mountain south of where widow Levi Curtis lives. In 1824 he built, on land bought of Daniel McIlvaine, the house now Alvin Barker's, moving his barn from the farm on the mountain to this place, and occupying most of the homestead of his father; d. August, 1870. Had children : —

*Susan H.,* (b. Oct. 8, 1818, m. Frederick Gray of Bennington April 17, 1847, and d. in that town Sept. 12, 1850.)

*Robert,* (d. in infancy.)

*Minda G.,* (b. March 23, 1823; m. Hartwell Lakin, the jeweler in Bennington, Feb. 25, 1851.)

*Livera O.,* (b. Feb. 26, 1825.)

*Betsey J.,* (b. May 27, 1827, m. William Russell of Greenfield, d. June 23, 1865.)

*Allen,* (d. in childhood.)

*Alvin R.,* (b. Nov. 27, 1831, occupies homestead, m. Mary E. Shattuck June 1, 1859; has children : Willis A., b. June 3, 1860; Allen F., b. Jan. 15, 1862; Junia E., b. March 19, 1863; Nellie M., b. Feb. 4, 1868; and Eugene L., b. May 27, 1870. Part of the rear of Alvin Barker's house was built by Robert McAllister at the foot of Perry's hill, 1793, then after some years was moved up near the Dea. Woods cider-mill and occupied by Samuel Brown; next was moved out east of Campbell's pond, and there occupied some years by same Brown; then was moved to the Kidder place and occupied by Reuben Kidder, and last to the Barker place, where it now abides !)

*Elzaphan I.,* (b. Feb. 22, 1834, m. Elizabeth Wheeler of New Boston Oct. 4, 1859, lived some years on the John Barker place, moved to Nashua 1871.)]

3. GIDEON, [b. in 1791, went to the State of Maine about the age of 21, m. Lavinia Brown near Canaan, that State; served in the army through a large part of the war of 1812, was paid and discharged, and is supposed to have been murdered on the way home.]

4. JOHN, [b. in 1794, m. Mary A. Taft of Deering, lived on the Joshua Atwood place, and d. there March 23, 1872. Left no children.]
5. POLLY, [b. in 1796, m. Joseph Moulton, d. 1872.]
6. SUSANNAH, [b. in 1798, d. unm. 1832.]

## BARNES.

WILLIAM BARNES came here from Hillsborough, and was son of Rev. Jonathan Barnes, first minister of that town, who was born in 1749, graduated at Harvard College in 1770, and married Abigail Curtis 1774, having built the preceding year the house at Hillsborough Center now occupied by his grandson, Samuel G. Barnes, Esq. William, their son, was born Christmas day, 1774. Married Mehitable Miller, and came here and built the famous three-story house on the Gould place, 1802. There he kept tavern several years. This place, which he had bought of John McCoy, he sold about 1812 to William Lawrence. During his stay here, he owned and occupied an extensive stage-line,—a most important business at that day. This three-story hotel was burned in February, 1818. In 1812 Mr. Barnes went back to Hillsborough; thence went to Stanstead, Canada; thence after some years to Mokena, Ill., where he died in 1855, leaving no children.

## BARRETT.

ISAAC BARRETT, son of Isaac and Susan (Page) Barrett, came here from Hudson in 1808, and succeeded Samuel McAdams on the Daniel Holt farm; married Susan, sister of Capt. John Worthley, and died in 1850, aged sixty-nine. Their children were:—

1. POLLY, [b. Nov. 19, 1811, d. aged 20.]
2. ISAAC, [b. July 7, 1813, m. Mary Breed; has lived mostly in Lowell, though he occupied the Aiken or Dea. Burnham place in South Village from 1864 to 1875; has long had a place of trust in the Lowell mills; has but one child, Ida M., b. Oct. 25, 1849, who married, Dec. 10, 1873, Charles E. Adams, a merchant in that city.]
3. NAHUM, [b. in 1815, m. Mary Noyes of Henniker, and went to Nashua.]
4. DUSTIN, [b. Nov. 29, 1816; bought the Dr. Cleaves place in 1858; m. Louisa A. Hall; has children: Levi, b. Jan. 31, 1860; Nellie L., b. Sept. 4, 1864; Isaac, b. May 12, 1869; and Kate A., b. May 13, 1871.]
5. ABEL, [b. Sept. 19, 1824, m. Lemira Blackington of Woburn, Mass., in 1857, and now lives in that place.]

CHARLES A. BARRETT, son of Jesse and Ann (Lawrence) Barrett of Brookline, Mass., was born in 1835, married Mrs. Betsey A. (Butler) Hill; came here in 1857; has spent many years on the sea; children: —

1. NELLIE, [b. in January, 1857.]
2. FRANK A. S., [b. Feb. 22, 1861.]
3. LUVIE E., [b. in March, 1866.]
4. FREDDIE S., [b. in December, 1867.]
5. ANNA E., [b. in June, 1871.]
6. DANIEL S., [b. in January, 1875.]
7. HARRY A., [b. in December, 1877.]

## BARTLETT.

REV. JOSHUA R. BARTLETT, son of William and Maria (Partridge) Bartlett, was born in Templeton, Mass., in 1839, married Martha A. Southworth of North Easton, Mass., came here in 1874 as pastor of the Methodist Church, and moved to Amherst in 1876. This was his first charge, and prospered under his care. Has children: Mary E., Maria H., and Edwin S. One younger child was born and died here.

## BASS.

EBEN BASS, son of David and Mary (Eaton) Bass of Deering, and grandson of Simeon and Hannah (Sawyer) Bass of Sharon, was born May 20, 1823. Married Clara Wilkins (daughter of John and Lucinda (Forsaith) Wilkins, and granddaughter of Bray Wilkins, one of the first settlers of Deering), Nov. 16, 1848. He bought the Dr. Whiton farm in 1854, succeeding Silas Hardy on that place, and has since occupied the same, making extensive improvements in buildings and farm. The large and beautiful trees in the yard were planted by Dr. Whiton, assisted by Clark Hopkins, in 1814. They were given to the minister by Hon. John Duncan, who, though an old man, brought them up in his arms on horseback. This house has been a very popular resort for summer boarders from the city for many years. A second large building was put up for this purpose in 1878. Mr. Bass is one of our live, smart men, diligent in business, has been honored by his townsmen with places of trust, and has had considerable business as auctioneer for years. Children are: —

1. ELLA F., [b. Dec. 5, 1849, m. George F. Newman Nov. 30, 1871, and lives in Somerville, Mass.]
2. CHARLES H., [b. Dec. 9, 1851, m. Jennie Darrah of Bennington Dec. 25, 1877.]
3. CLARA L., [b. March 24, 1857, m. Lucien W. Putney Nov. 25, 1875.]
4. JOHN W., [b. June 24, 1861.]
5. FRANK E., [b. Sept. 4, 1862.]

DAVID BASS, JR., brother of Eben, born in 1821; married Jane Carr of Deering; lived some years in the Cummings house, and for a time run the bedstead-factory, now Dea. E. C. Paige's. Is now engaged in extensive wooden manufactures at Woonsocket, R. I. Children : —

1. MARY A., [b. July 20, 1846, m. Lyman H. Fulton of Bedford May 18, 1870.]
2. JENNIE, [d. aged 16.]
3. LEWIS C., [b. May 29, 1862.]
4. VIOLA, [b. Nov. 4, 1864.]

LEWIS C. BASS, brother of the two above, born in Deering in 1831; married Mary J. Wiggin of St. Albans, Me. Came here in 1867, and bought, in company with David, the Cummings place and mill; but soon divided, retaining the farm, bought the Kendall house adjoining, and still occupies the same.

## BATES.

REV. JOHN H. BATES, son of Moses and Drusilla (Hart) Bates, born in Colchester, Vt., in 1814; fitted for college in Williston, that State, and was a graduate of the University of Vermont, class of 1840. His seminary course was partly at Alleghany City and partly at Union Seminary, New York. Mr. Bates came here, January, 1853. He gave such immediate and full satisfaction that he received a call from the church, Feb. 8, following, and was settled over it (Center Church) March 16. He was a fine scholar, an able preacher, and full of the old doctrines. On exchange he was very welcome in all the pulpits of the vicinity. One sermon, "Righteousness taught by Divine Judgments" (Nov. 27, 1862), was published and extensively circulated. Through the efforts of Mr. Bates the church was remodeled (1857) and the excellent organ procured (1864). Much credit is due to him. Far and wide he had the respect of the people. While an effort was being made to increase his salary, he resigned, July 1, 1866. This was his first and only settlement. After leaving Antrim, he preached awhile in Merrimack. Then, with enfeebled health, he went South; and though in constant service teaching and preaching, he died very unexpectedly, near Charleston, S. C., May 10, 1870. His body lies buried in Magnolia cemetery of that city. Mr. Bates had no children. His wife was Sarah J. Hillyer, a lady of unquestioned refinement and worth, — now Mrs. Roland Mather, of Hartford, Conn.

## BEASOM.

HENRY J. BEASOM, son of Henry and Serena (Williams) Beasom, born in Hudson City, now Jersey City, N. J., Oct. 1, 1851; married Vienna C. Upton of Stoddard, June 3, 1873; came here the next year to work in Parkhurst's mill at the Branch. More recently has lived in South Village. Is foreman in one of the cutlery-shops. His wife was born Feb. 14, 1852. Children : —

1. SUSAN ALORA, [b. Stoddard, March 29, 1874.]
2. DANIEL B., [b. Antrim, May 12, 1876.]

## BELL.

JOHN BELL, son of Joseph and Mary (Houston) Bell of Bedford, born in 1779, came to Antrim in 1799; married Margaret Brown in 1801; built the two-story house now Mr. Conant's, was licensed to keep tavern there in 1802; lived there sixty-four years, was forty years an elder in the Presbyterian Church, and died Oct. 5, 1864. His wife died Jan. 14, 1860, aged eighty-seven. Children: —

1. MARY, [m. Josiah W. Christie May 11, 1830.]
2. JOHN, [d. in childhood.]
3. MARGARET, [b. 1805, m. Dea. Samuel Wood Dec. 24, 1833.]
4. REV. HIRAM, [b. Dec. 15, 1807; united with the Presbyterian Church in 1828; was graduated at Williams College; studied theology at East Windsor, Conn.; was settled in Marlborough, Killingworth, and Westchester, Conn.; preached thirty-seven years, and died in the work at Westchester, Conn., June 18, 1876. Was a strong, sound, and successful pastor. His service was all in another State, but always in demand, and honorable to the town that gave him birth. He married Mary E. Wells and left several children. Rare are the men purer and abler than Rev. Hiram Bell. "Their works do follow them."]
5. LOUISA, [d. in childhood.]
6. MARINDA, [d. in childhood.]
7. JOHN L., [b. June 27, 1815; m. Charlotte E. Root, and lived in Rochester, N. Y., till his wife died in 1861. He then moved to Kansas; went thence into the army, was with Sherman in the famous "march to the sea," and, returning, died June 15, 1869.]

HIRAM BELL was born in Antrim, March 16, 1803. His father, Thomas Bell (son of William Bell of Andover, Mass.), born July 31, 1769, lived at the Branch quite a number of years. Thomas had seven children: Margaret, John, James, Hiram, Hannah, Thomas Jefferson, and Betsey. He moved to Washington and died there, Feb. 25, 1811, aged forty-two. Was buried in Hillsborough. He married Mary Giles of Deering (one report says *Gibbs*), Sept. 8, 1796. Of the children of Thomas Bell, little has been ascertained of any except Hiram, the subject of this sketch, and Jefferson, who lives highly respected at Chicopee Falls, Mass. The most of them, however, were born in Antrim. Margaret, born June 8, 1797, married an overseer in Lowell by the name of Taylor; but after his death she returned to Hillsborough, and died there April 8, 1854. John lived and died in Hillsborough. James died unmarried. Hannah married a Murdough of Hillsborough, and lived and died in that town. Thomas J. (called "Jefferson" by old people), born Dec.

23, 1808, married Emily Dean of Bellows Falls, Vt., and is now spoken of as " enjoying the rest and comfort which a life well-spent deserves."

It is believed that Thomas Bell moved away about 1809. None of the family returned here to live except Hiram, by whom chiefly the family was identified with this town. Hiram Bell returned to North Branch to live in the fall of 1832, and on Dec. 19, of the same year, he married Mary French. She was born in Hancock, Aug. 28, 1813. In 1833, Mr. Bell went into trade at the Branch, in company with Hiram Griffin. But he did not long continue in the business ; and we find he moved to Henniker in March, 1837. He died Feb. 27, 1871. He left three children whose names will be found below.

Mr. Bell was largely noted as a hotel-keeper. He began his career of serving the public in this way by opening a tavern in company with Ira Cochran in the McCoy brick house in Antrim, now Samuel M. Thompson's. This was in 1826, under the "Sign of the Big Pumpkin." He kept a bowling-alley, — the first in this section, it is said. But he came into notice specially as a landlord at the White Mountains. He presided at the Profile House seven seasons ; at the Crawford House for a time; and at the Pemigewasset House, Plymouth, for many years. Was an exceedingly genial and pleasant man, helpful and wide-awake, and everywhere he had a host of friends.

1. GEORGE E., [b. in Antrim May 15, 1834, m. Susan J. Thompson Dec. 4, 1862; was a hotel-keeper in Boston, smart, capable, widely-known, and popular. He died suddenly, April, 1880. Was an alderman of Boston ; was several years in the custom-house, by appointment of the President; was one of those genial men who usually have a host of friends and no enemies. The " Boston Journal " says : " In his private relations he was a most estimable man, and in his official life as a member of the board of aldermen his duties were discharged in a conscientious manner. Although a Democrat in politics, he was not a partisan in deciding matters affecting the interest of the city of Boston, and, although at times differing with his colleagues in this respect, he always had their respect as acting according to his honest convictions."]
2. MARY E., [b. in Henniker Aug. 21, 1837 ; m. Col. Edwin R. Abbott, Feb. 20, 1860. Mr. Abbott went from Bradford, and is now at the head of an immense hotel at Coney Island, N. Y.]
3. ELLEN A., [b. in Henniker May 4, 1845, m. Solon Newman July 1, 1873.]

## BEMAINE.

GEORGE BEMAINE, of English birth, came here in the spring of 1770, and made his home several years with Dea. Aiken. He was a deserter from the British in Boston, and came to this frontier town for concealment. Was a man of fifty years or more, well educated, was a good reader, a superior penman, and was the first teacher in Antrim, and also the first in Hillsborough. His first school in that town seems to have been in the fall of 1771. In early life he had been a school-mate of Dilworth, of spelling-book fame. Here he taught the children in private houses, as there was no school-house, and deserves credit as one very useful in the new settlement. He finally went into the Revolutionary army, and lost his life at the battle of White Plains, Oct. 28, 1776. Nothing can be learned of his ancestry, or connections. He deserves credit as the first teacher in Antrim or vicinity. Made his home at Dea. Aiken's till death, though occasionally absent for purposes of teaching. Seems to have been a very worthy man, and just the one to meet the wants of these pioneer families, giving instruction when otherwise it must have been denied.

## BICKFORD.

DANIEL BICKFORD, an Englishman, one of ten sons, was born on the voyage to this country. His father settled in Exeter. Daniel was a hatter by trade, came here from Pembroke in 1795, and settled a short distance southwest of the Riley or Judge Whittemore place. He married Martha Mann of Pembroke in 1786. Moved to the Scott Moore place, Hillsborough, in 1812, and died there in 1815, aged fifty-five. They had six children, the two youngest born here: —

1. WILLIAM M., [b. in 1787, m. —— Cragin of Charlestown, Mass., and d. in that city in 1825.]
2. ABRAHAM, [m. Jane Stuart of Henniker, and d. in that town in 1872, aged 82.]
3. DANIEL, [b. in 1792, m. Sarah Spring, went to New York and d. 1813.]
4. SALLY P., [b. in 1794, m. Reuben Kidder, d. 1847.]
5. JAMES D., [b. in 1796, a clothier by trade; m. Salome Huntoon of Unity, d. Newport 1842.]
6. POLLY M., [b. in 1798, m. David McCaine of Francestown, d. in that town in 1838.]

## BISHOP.

RICHARD BISHOP, son of John and Mary (Poor) Bishop, and grandson of Thomas Bishop, was born in the county of Kilkenny, Ireland, in December, 1822. He married Mary Flinn, of the same place, and two of his children were born on that side the water. He came to Antrim from Boston in 1857, and lived in what is known as the Bishop house, being that next east of Maplewood Cemetery. Thence he moved to Bennington in 1870, where he now resides. Children : —

1. MARY, [b. March 12, 1851, m. Michael Harrington of Hancock.]
2. ANNE.
3. KATE, [m. Thomas Welch.]
4. ELLEN.

## BLANCHARD.

THOMAS BLANCHARD and his son Samuel came over in 1639, and settled in Charlestown, Mass. They were of Huguenot race, and the name was originally Blanche. Samuel, the son, moved in 1686 to Andover, Mass., and died there in 1707, aged seventy-seven. His son, Samuel Blanchard, Jr., is understood to have been the father of Caleb, who came to Antrim. This second Samuel married Ruth Gould, of Chelmsford, Mass.

Caleb, son of Samuel and Ruth (Gould) Blanchard, was born in Andover, Mass., in 1760, came to Antrim from Dracut, Mass., in 1818 (following his son Joshua who had come here some years before), and bought of Francis Brown what is now known as the Whiteley place. He married Lucy Gould, of Chelmsford, Mass., and had seven children, all born elsewhere, but most of them lived more or less in this town. He fell in the barn and broke his neck, Aug. 7, 1843, aged eighty-three. He was a remarkably vigorous man; walked two miles before breakfast on the day of his death. His widow died in 1852, aged nearly ninety-three. Their children : —

1. JOHN, [b. in Dracut, Mass., July 30, 1788; m. Margaret H. Taylor of New Boston; remained on homestead; d. Nov. 30, 1860. His wife d. June 20, 1866, aged 78. His house was burned Feb. 14, 1842, while all the family were gone to church, and the present house was built in the summer of that year. Mr. Blanchard was many years a teacher, was a great reader, was a man of active memory, strict in his family, very religious, and very decided and unbending in his convictions. His children were : —

    *Betsey H.*, (b. Sept. 22, 1821, m. Edward Whiteley Sept. 15, 1853, remains on homestead.)

    *John N.*, (b. Nov. 11, 1824; rendered partially insane by fit of sickness; has been patiently cared for by his sister many years.)

    *Ephraim T.*, (d. at the age of 11, July 2, 1840.)

    *Lucy G.*, (d. at the age of 18, Aug. 9, 1849.)]

2. JOSHUA, [m. Isabella Harvey of Dracut, Mass.; came here about 1814; bought the Jonas White place (B. C. Butter-

field's); was a blacksmith, and had a shop a little south of the house; was succeeded by his brother Caleb; after a few years moved to Lyndeborough, and d. there in 1821, aged 31. His children were: —

*William G.*, (b. in Antrim, m. Eugenia Morange of New York, lives in Boston.)

*Julia Ann*, (b. in Dracut, Mass., m. Mason Wheaton, lives in Malden, Mass.)

*Harriet N.*, (b. in Lyndeborough, unm., lives in Boston.)

*Jane C.*, (b. in Antrim. m. Henry Chesley, lives in Brighton, Mass.)

*Isabella*, (d. unm. in Boston in 1854.)

*Mary F.*, (m. 1st, George W. Hope; 2d, Daniel Sargent of Sutton.)]

3. RUTH. [m. John Barton of Weston, N. Y.; had five children; all dead but one, and she the widow of Col. Bartlett Dorr, who was killed in battle in the late war. A daughter, Lizzie, was the wife of Rev. Henry C. Fuller. The aged parents are both living.]

4. LUCY, [m. Thomas Knowlton of Dracut, Mass.; had a family of ten children; but now parents and children are all dead, save one son, Charles P. Knowlton, living in the West.]

5. CALEB. JR., [b. May 17, 1795, m. "Millie" Cram July 12, 1821; was blacksmith by trade; succeeded his brother Joshua in shop and farm occupied by him; was there but a short time; had children, Elizabeth W. and Oliver H., born in Antrim, and several after removal from town; went from here to Eden, N. J.; thence to Kansas; and as nothing has been heard from them, it is supposed they were all swept off by the Indians, who made fearful depredations at that time in the State.]

6. AMOS, [b. Nov. 30, 1799; built the Collins Whittemore house in 1819; m. Eunice Flint April 6, 1820; sold in 1824, probably to John Dunlap, and went to Aurora, N. Y.; is still living in Jamestown in that State. Children: —

*Amos A.*, (b. in Antrim in 1821; graduated at Dartmouth College, class of 1845; m. Ruth Tenney of Hanover; is a lawyer of note in Buffalo, N. Y.)

*George G.*, (b. in Antrim in 1822, m. Philinda Keyes of Jamestown, N. Y.; lives in San Francisco; has been attorney-general of California. George A., his only son, is a lawyer in that State, and district-attorney of Sacramento county.)

*Flint,* (b. in Aurora, N. Y., in 1824, m. Sarah J. Allen, lives in Jamestown, N. Y. One son, Henry L. Blanchard, is a lawyer in Port Townsend, Washington Territory, and another son is a physician in Jamestown.)

*William D.,* (m. Sarah Prince of Buffalo in 1856, d. in Jamestown, N. Y., in 1862.)

*Charles,* (graduated at Dartmouth College Medical Department in 1851, m. Cornelia Lampson of Detroit in 1864, is a physician in Buffalo, N. Y. The name appears as Henry Charles on the college record.)

*Mary,* (d. unm. in Jamestown, N. Y., in 1864.)]

7. MARY, [b. May 6, 1802, m. Samuel H. Pratt of Boston Aug. 16, 1827. Mr. Pratt d. Feb. 14, 1862. Children : —

*Henry O.,* (b. in Boston in 1828, unm., lives in Brighton, Mass.)

*Charles O.,* (m. Anna E. Jones, lives in Dorchester, Mass.)

*Mary B.,* (m. James E. Favor and lives in Bennington.)

*Edwin B.,* (m. Harriet A. Hemmenway, lives in Waltham, Mass., was an ensign in the navy during the war.)

*Harriet N.,* (m. Arthur D. Phelps, lives in Boston.)

*Julia Marella,* (five preceding b. in Boston; this b. in Aurora, N. Y., m. D. A. Glidden, lives Boston Highlands.)

*William B.,* (b. in Antrim in 1840, m. Susie Snelling of Boston; was colonel in the army; wounded at Atlanta; lives in St. Louis; is in postal railway service.)

*Caroline E.,* (b. in Boston in 1843, m. William F. Hunt of Roxbury, Mass., lives in Chicago.)]

MRS. CARRIE (FOOTE) BLANCHARD came to South Village in January, 1876, bringing five children, all born in Bennington, viz.: John, born in 1858; Fred, born in 1860; Charles, born in 1867; Minnie, born in 1869; Eugene, born in 1871. John Blanchard, her husband, was killed by the explosion of a powder-mill, Oct. 4, 1870.

## BODWELL.

WILLIAM BODWELL, son of Joshua Bodwell, whose mother was murdered by the Indians in Haverhill, Mass., was born in Methuen, Mass., in 1761, married Rachel French of Atkinson in 1785, settled the Reuben Robinson place west of the pond (Dutton's) in 1789, went to Ohio in 1800, and died there in 1834. The widow afterwards married Alexander Witherspoon, and died April 12, 1837. Children of William Bodwell : —

1. WILLIAM, [b. Sept. 6, 1786, m. Betsey Kimball of Dublin, went to Stow, N. Y., in 1811, and died there in 1816.]
2. SALLY, [b. Sept. 4, 1788, d. 1804.]
3. JOHN, [b. Sept. 5, 1790; moved to Stow, N. Y., in 1811; thence after the death of his brother William he went to Ohio, and nothing more can be learned of him.]
4. HANNAH, [b. Jan. 25, 1793, m. Joseph Knight, moved to Atkinson, and is yet living there.]
5. ANNA, [b. March 24, 1795, m. Dea. Samuel Fletcher, April 20, 1814; is a noble, devoted woman, spending her old age with children at Bunker Hill, Ill.]
6. EDE, [b. July 30, 1797, m. Rev. David Van Alstin, a Universalist preacher, settled in Atkinson in 1818, and she died there in 1831.]
7. PRISCILLA, [b. March 3, 1800, d. Oct. 18, 1803.]

## BOND.

DEA. ASA BOND, adopted son of Dea. Elisha Bond of Gilsum, married, first, Almira Ellis of Sullivan; went from Gilsum to Nashua, and was a machinist there of considerable prominence. His wife died in Nashua in 1842; married, second, Sally Barker of Antrim in 1844; came here in 1846, and bought the Samuel Carr place (now James Richardson's) and lived there till his sudden death, Oct. 30, 1865, at the age of sixty-nine. Mr. Bond was at work repairing machinery at a lathe in the shop now J. A. Bryer's, and dropped dead so suddenly that when found he still held the tools in his hands; was a long time an elder in the Presbyterian Church, and a pure and devoted man. His descendants are all gone from Antrim. He buried six children before coming here, and brought four with him as follows: —

1. WILLIAM L., [b. in Nashua in 1828, m. Jane Pickles, is a physician, lives in Charlestown, Mass.]
2. J. ELLIOT, [b. in Gilsum in 1830, now of Somerville, Mass.]
3. SIBYL E., [b. in Peterborough in 1832, m. James Gordon in 1850, lives in Somerville, Mass.]
4. CHARLES F., [b. in Nashua in 1837, m. Olivia Brown of Antrim Feb. 19, 1857, now lives in Hancock. Their children, — Charles W., b. Dec. 10, 1857; George A., b. Dec. 21, 1859; and Mary A., b. in 1861, d. in infancy, — were all natives of Antrim.]

## BOUTWELL.

REUBEN BOUTWELL was born in Reading, Mass., in 1760; came here in 1783 from Amherst; married Olive Bradford of Mont Vernon;

*Chandler B Boutell*

moved first into a log house a few rods southeast of Daniel Simonds place, in which he lived several years and had three children born, one of whom was Chandler B. Boutwell, Esq., long the oldest person in Antrim. Afterwards lived in Simonds house for a time, then cleared and settled the farm begun by Hutchinson, next west of Daniel Swett's, putting up the buildings there in 1799. These buildings are now gone, and the road to them thrown up. The house was moved to the Branch, was known as the mill-house, and was burned in 1876. Mr. Boutwell died in 1816, and at the burial, March 11, at the cemetery on the hill, the snow was so deep and the cold so intense it was impossible to fill the grave, and they left it to be finished in warm weather. His children that grew up were : —

1. REBECCA, [b. July 25, 1780, m. Asa Robinson Feb. 23, 1804, d. Aug. 13, 1831.]
2. MOLLY, [b. June 19, 1784, m. John Robinson, and d. in early life.]
3. CHANDLER B., [b. March 5, 1786, m. Peggy Carr June 4, 1811, with whom he lived more than sixty-two years. She died Oct. 23, 1873. Bought of John Woodcock the place on which he now resides; built the brick house in 1847; has been always a vigorous, industrious man, of good calculations and simple habits; has acquired large property; been a constant attendant at church all his life; one that the minister was sure to find in his place and one that always supported the gospel with his means. He united with the Presbyterian Church at the age of 88; is now smart and cheerful in his 93d year; has voted seventy-two times in succession at the March meeting, without a break. Since writing the above Mr. Boutwell has died, the event occurring Jan. 27, 1880. At one time they buried all their family of children in a row of four little graves on Meeting-House Hill, but afterwards were born to them as follows: —

    *Roxah*, (b. Dec. 14, 1815; m. Daniel Swett, June 18, 1840; a most excellent woman; d. after lingering sickness and great suffering in August, 1875.)

    *Achsah*, (twin sister of Roxah, m. Sylvester Preston, Dec. 26, 1837.)

    *Margaret*, (b. Jan. 9, 1826, m. William M. Conn April 9, 1854. They occupied the homestead of her father, where she d. very suddenly of diphtheria Feb. 16, 1876.)

    *Elizabeth*, (b. Feb. 11, 1829, m. Charles R. McClary, and lives in Nashua.)]
4. JAMES, [b. March 13, 1788; m. 1st, Lottie Dodge of New Bos-

ton; lived on his father's homestead till the death of the latter; then moved to the Weeks or McCoy place in the east part of the town where the large brick house stands. His wife d. Jan. 17, 1844, aged 53, and he m. 2d, Hepsibeth (Draper) Brooks, widow of William Brooks of Hancock. He d. April 26, 1851, aged 63. His children were: —

*James*, (m. Mary A. Averill Oct. 23, 1834, and moved to Peterborough. He d. in Milford March 27, 1855, aged 44.)

*Achsah*, (m. James Wilson Dec. 25, 1834, and d. July 25, 1863, aged 49.)

*Reuben*, (b. in 1815, m. Hannah Gillis, inherited the homestead, and d. Nov. 15, 1868, leaving two children: Susie E., who m. John M. Blodgett of Newbury, where he died in 1871, and Horace G., b. March 19, 1858.)

*Charlotte*, (d. Feb. 28, 1840, aged 20.)

*Eunice*, (now Mrs. Ziba Crane of Washington.)

*Benjamin*, (m. Frances Emery of Athens, Me., and d. March 20, 1858, aged 32.)

*Sarah M.*, (m. James D. Matthews of Hancock in 1850, and d. in that town.)]

5. HANNAH, [b. May 11, 1791, m. Philip Averill Sept. 26, 1812, d. Nov. 5, 1834.]

6. PATTY, [b. Aug. 25, 1796, m. Walter Jones of Hillsborough Aug. 10, 1815, moved to the West many years ago.]

7. WILLIAM, [b. Jan. 8, 1798, m. Elizabeth Morrison of Windsor Nov. 4, 1817. He lived a short time in Stoddard; bought and built in 1825 where his son William now lives, at the end of the road, south of the Keene road in the west part of this town. Built again about 1830 between the Levi Curtis place and the Keene road; but after a few years bought the Abner Cram place, where he lived till his death in January, 1878, aged a few days over 80 years. His first wife d. Nov. 7, 1862, aged 68, and he m. 2d, Mrs. Hepsibah (Tyler) Rogers, who survives him. This family spell their name Boutelle. The oldest child, Mary, was born in Windsor; the rest in Antrim.

*Mary*, (b. Feb. 29, 1818, m. Albert Frost Feb. 21, 1843, and lives in Peterborough. Has children: George A., Mary E., Eugene L., and Emma Jane.)

*Ann M.*, (b. April 14, 1819, m. John Hutchinson July 4, 1844.)

*William*, (b. May 3, 1823; m. Susan Splaine Oct. 27, 1847; lives in extreme west of the town south of Keene road; was out in the army in the Thirteenth N. H. Regiment; has children: Elizabeth J., b. Aug. 24, 1848, who m. 1st, Rodney D. Wyman, and 2d, Henry Shepherd of Stoddard; William H., b. Nov. 24, 1849, who m. Lottie Wilmot of Rome, Pa., and has children, Mary Belle and Nellie May; Wallace M., b. Sept. 10, 1851, who m. Hattie B. Cram of Nelson Oct. 6, 1875; Augusta S., b. April 16, 1855, who m. Henry Hasling and lives in Lawrence, Mass.; Nancy J., b. May 1, 1857, who m. George H. Buffum June 28, 1873; James E., b. Sept. 16, 1859; Nell S., b. June 17, 1862; and John H., b. Aug. 6, 1865.)

*Jackson*, (b. June 12, 1824; m. Fanny Wier in October, 1853; lives on the Horace Tuttle farm, High Range; was out in the war in the Thirteenth N. H. Regiment; has children: Mary J., b. Oct. 4, 1854; Willie T., b. Dec. 27, 1856; Henry E., b. March 7, 1858; Lilla E., b. Aug. 18, 1861; George E., b. Nov. 15, 1865; Albert L., b. April 21, 1871; and Ada F., b. June 12, 1873.)

*John*, (b. March 12, 1825; went to California in 1858; not heard from since 1861.)

*Nancy O.*, (b. Nov. 25, 1827; m. George W. Baldwin Nov. 6, 1851; lived in Nashua; but his health failing, he came to Antrim and died here, three days after the birth of his youngest child. His death occurred Oct. 3, 1856, at the age of 29. She m. 2d, Col. William Cross of Litchfield, Jan. 1, 1858, who d. Jan. 6, 1867, aged 56. She m. 3d, Aaron Cutler of Londonderry, March 5, 1868, and now resides in Litchfield.)

*Margaret J.*, (b. in 1832; m. Augustus Lovejoy of Hollis Feb. 24, 1853; has children: Nellie Jane, b. in 1857, and Frank H., b. in 1863.)

*Reuben*, (b. May 17, 1835; was out in the war in the Thirteenth New Hampshire Regiment; m. Rose McGue of Nashua; has one son, Fred, b. in September, 1860.)

*David W.*, (b. June 25, 1837; m. Eliza J. Whitney March 20, 1860; lived awhile in Nashua; was out in the war in the Thirteenth New Hampshire Regiment; was disabled by disease, and now draws a pension for support; lives at the Branch; has children: Jennie F., who was b. in Nashua

March 13, 1861, and Charles H., who was b. in Antrim April 25, 1863.)]

## BOUTELLE.

CHARLES M. BOUTELLE, son of Charles and Betsey (Knight) Boutelle of Hancock, born in 1825, was a cabinet-maker; came here to work for Isaac B. Pratt in Clinton in 1848; married Sarah Buckminster in 1850; built the same year the house now Allen Sawyer's (Clinton), but moved to Bear Valley, Minn., in 1859, and died there in 1876. Mr. Boutelle stood in high repute in the community where he died; was postmaster in Bear Valley ten years. Left children:—

1. PROF. CLARENCE M., [b. in Antrim in 1851; now professor of mathematics and physics in the State Normal School at Winona, Minn.]
2. CHARLES H., [b. in 1853, lives in Bear Valley.]

## BOYD.

The ancient family of Boyds "descended from a younger son of the illustrious lord high steward of Scotland." Robert, son of Simon, who was third son of Alan the second lord high steward, was of a very fair complexion, and consequently was named "Boyt," or "Boyd," from the Gaelic, signifying fair. From this Robert Boyt or Boyd, all the Boyds of Scotland descended. Some families by the name of *Boit* claim that as the original name. Robert Boyd died about 1240. His son, Sir Robert Boyd, called in 1262 "Robertus de Boyd," died in 1270. And his son, the third "Sir Robert Boyd," was one of the barons who were forced to swear fealty to King Edward I. of England in 1296. The following year he joined Sir William Wallace, but died soon after. His son, the fourth "Sir Robert Boyd," was one of the most gallant and able friends of Robert Bruce, and was by that king made Lord of Kilmarnoc, and covered with honors. His descendants have been traced in the male line down to the year 1800, and stand high among the dignities of old Scotland. Some of the younger sons from time to time emigrated to Ireland, and thence in subsequent years their children came to America. Much about the Boyds of Scotland must be omitted here from lack of space. In Ireland they kept clear of the natives. William Boyd, Esq., of Foxborough, Mass., who was born in Newtownards, Ireland, in 1800, tells us the word which the grandmother would call out to the "bairns" in the street when the native Irish came along: "Came in, an' stay in till them folks hae a' gane awa', for they're Eerish oot there an' ye maunna gang neer them." William of Foxborough was grandson of Hugh Boyd, who had a brother William born about 1710, or a little later. The names William, Robert, and James occur many times. There is no doubt that Capt. William Boyd, father of the brothers who settled in Antrim, was of this stock. There is little doubt that he was a cousin of "William, born in 1710 or later." But positive proof must be sought in the old records on the other side of the water. I am indebted, for various papers, to Francis Boyd, Esq., of Boston.

CAPT. WILLIAM BOYD, a man of notable courage and force, came to Londonderry among the early settlers of that town, though not for several years after the beginning in 1719. Eight of this name appear on the memorial to Gov. Shute, March 26, 1718, asking encouragement to obtain land in "that very excellent and renowned Plantation" called New England. In his mature years, he signed the "Association Test," April, 1776. Mr. Boyd came over the water fourteen times as captain, bringing Scotch emigrants from Ireland. Married Alice Hunter, and settled permanently in the western part of Londonderry in 1751. Died Nov. 24, 1789, aged 70. His wife died Nov. 26, 1790, aged 60. Children : —

1. DEA. JOSEPH, [came to Antrim in 1774 and began the D. H. Goodell farm ; m. Mary McKeen, — "Molly Boyd," as she was called; had the reputation of being " peculiarly kind, tender-hearted, and generous." Joseph Boyd was a very efficient elder in the Presbyterian Church from 1800 until his death. It was said that nobody ever knew him do an unfair thing; was eminently sincere and honorable; was a man patiently laborious and industrious. His death, Dec. 20, 1816, was occasioned by his being thrown from a carriage just below the old meeting-house on return from worship. His age was 64. His wife, Mary, who d. May 3, 1828, aged 73, was a woman of great force and courage. At one time her husband was absent in Londonderry, and she was left with two or three small children in their log house in the woods, when a bear attacked her pigs. They had a small barn, one cow, a pair of oxen, and two pigs. This was all their stock. The bear broke into the inclosure some way, and her first notice of it was by the terrible squealing of the pigs. One of them ran by the door in a fright, and as the other kept up the squealing, she went down near the barn and found a bear hugging it nearly to death. Quick as a flash she grabbed a stake, one end of which was on fire, and struck bruin such a fearful blow that he dropped the pig, ran off about two rods, set up on his haunches, and looked at her as if deliberating what to do ! She used to say that he looked more like the devil than anything else she ever saw ! She got between him and the pig and drove the bleeding thing into the pen and shut it in. Then she ran for Daniel McFarland, the nearest man

(at N. W. C. Jameson's), to come and shoot the bear. McFarland hurried up, and just then her husband came, but the bear was gone. But they made a trap, baited it with part of the mangled pig, and caught the old fellow that night. He weighed over three hundred pounds! The children of Dea. Joseph and Mary Boyd, besides five little ones laid long ago in the grave, were as follows : —

*Robert*, (b. Nov. 7, 1778, m. Betsey Paige in 1800. His father gave him the Whiteley farm, which he occupied for a time. Afterwards he lived on the homestead of his father. He was found dead in the woods on the John Moore Duncan farm, September, 1837. He left a family of eight children, thus: William, who was b. Sept. 24, 1801, and died in childhood; Betsey, who was b. Nov. 2, 1803, m. James W. Wilder, and lives in Providence, Penn.; Joseph, who was b. Aug. 11, 1807, m. Mary G. Bemis of Boston, was long time in the provision business in that city, amassed wealth, and lives in Somerville, Mass., having but one surviving child, Frances A., unm.; William, who d. in infancy; Mary, who died in March, 1812; David, who was b. April 9, 1813, m. Abbie S. Butler of Bolton, Mass., and now lives in Plymouth, Vt.; and Mary, b. June 30, 1815, now living with her brother Joseph. The mother of these died in Providence, Penn., May 5, 1869. David buried his wife, Abbie Butler, in 1878, but has two children, William D. and Mary Alice.)

*Alice*, (b. June 24, 1780, m. Mark Woodbury. A woman of rare attractions and unusual ability and force. She d. April 15, 1858.)

*David*, (b. Nov. 17, 1782; never m.; lived on the old homestead till all the rest of the family were dead or gone, then boarded here and there in town till his death, Sept. 2, 1859.)

*John C.*, (never m.; went into the army in the war of 1812, and d. in the service at Portsmouth, March 18, 1813, aged 27. His body was brought to Antrim and buried on the hill.)]

2. WILLIAM, [came to Antrim as early as 1777, and selected a tract of land of which the original deed is appended: —

Know all men by these presents : That George Jaffrey of Portsmouth . . . . for and in consideration of one hundred and fifty pounds, lawful money of said state, to him in hand, paid before the delivery hereof, by William Boyd of Londonderry .... yeoman, the receipt whereof I do hereby acknowledge .... do by these presents give, grant, bargain, sell, alien, release, convey and confirm to him the said William Boyd, all my right, title and estate of, in, and to, a certain lot of land, being part of the great Lot numbered six which was drawn to my right in the Society land, so called, but now in Antrim in the county of Hillsborough in said state, which large lot was surveyed and laid out in small lots, most of which in one hundred acre lots or thereabouts, and marked in a plan thereof made by Maurice Lynch, surveyor, and returned to me Nov. 3, 1773 — which said lot hereby conveyed to William Boyd aforesaid is numbered twenty-four, at the four corners of said lot, and is situate between the Lots numbered twenty-three & twenty-five, and the side lines one hundred & seventy rods about north & south, and the head and foot lines ninety-four rods about east and west, as may appear by said plan. . . . . In witness whereof I have hereunto set my hand & seal this twenty-ninth Day of October Ann. Domini 1778.

GEORGE JAFFREY

William Boyd m. 1st, Annis Orr, daughter of William Orr of Derry; 2d, Martha Dickey, sister of the late Capt. Joseph Dickey of Londonderry. She is now living, nearly a hundred years of age. Her husband died Oct. 10, 1825, aged 69. In this town he settled the Dea. Worthley farm, and built the large house now standing on the same. Had five children born here. Sold to the Knights brothers in 1795, and returned at once to the old homestead in Londonderry, the occasion being the untimely death of his brother John, who had inherited the paternal acres. The first wife of William had five children, and d. in 1813. All his children were thus: —

*William, Jr.*, (m. Margaret Holmes, and d. in Derry in 1841, aged 59.)

*Letitia*, (m. Samuel Marsh, d. in Pittsburg, Penn., 1845. Her husband d. Oct. 4, 1825, aged 45.)

*James*, (d. Dec. 9, 1809, aged 18.)

*Robert*, (m. Elizabeth Choat, and d. May 19, 1816, aged 27.)

*Mary*, (d. Aug. 28, 1804, aged 3.)

*Col. Calvin*, (b. March 5, 1818, m. Charlotte W. Shepard, and lives on the old homestead in Londonderry. Commanded a regiment of New Hampshire militia, and was an efficient and fine-appearing officer.)

*Maria*, (b. Aug. 19, 1819, m. Horace P. Watts of Manchester.)

*Mason*, (b. Aug. 28, 1821, m. Mary H. Dodge, and lives in Londonderry.)]

3. ISAAC, [drowned in the Merrimack river April 28, 1800. Said to have occurred while he was trying to get a drove of cattle across. His age was 29. His wife, Mary Thompson, d. Feb. 2, 1817, aged 47. They left three children, thus:—

*Dea. Robert*, (m. 1st, Susan Riddle of Bedford; 2d, Martha B. Dickey of Warren, O. He d. in Ohio April 12, 1871, aged 73.)

*Alice*, (unm.; d. in Londonderry Jan. 9, 1852, aged 55.)

*Isaac*, (graduated at Dartmouth College in 1826; studied medicine, taking his diploma at Bowdoin College in 1829. He settled in the practice of medicine in West Newbury, Mass.; m. Sarah C. Hill of that place: d. there in 1844 aged 44.)]

4. JOHN, [m. Naomi, daughter of Hon. John Duncan of Antrim; lived on the homestead of his father, and d. there in early manhood, greatly lamented, July 12, 1795, aged 29.]

5. ALICE, [m. James Steel, lived and d. on the place now occupied by William Curtis.]

6. JAMES, [b. April 3, 1768; cleared and settled the farm now Dea. James Boyd's, probably beginning as early as 1789. He married Fanny Baldwin of Amherst in 1795. She was a sister of Capt. Isaac Baldwin, came here as a teacher, and taught in several places in town. She taught awhile in a dwelling-house on the top of Patten Hill, up to the summit of which there was at that time a rough public road from the Boyd place. Here she made such good impression, it was judged best to keep her for life. Dr. Whiton says she was a "woman of great excellence of character," which seems to be the sentiment of all who knew her. She d. Dec. 25, 1828, aged 57. He d. Sept. 6, 1835, aged 67. The children of James and Fanny Boyd were:—

*Fanny*, (b. July 15, 1796, m. Josiah W. Christie March 16, 1824, and d. in child-birth near the close of the same year, leaving twin infants: Franklin, who d. in 1828, and Francis, who removed from Antrim to Boston in 1845.)

*Harriet*, (b. Sept. 17, 1798, m. Simeon B. Little of Boscawen Sept. 16, 1824, and d. there Oct. 3, 1850, leaving four children: George, Sherman, Arthur, and Evelyn. One of these is Rev. Arthur Little, a distinguished Congregational cler-

*James Boyd*

gyman of Chicago. His letter will be found among the centennial reports.)

*Lucy*, (b. Oct. 6, 1802, m. Dea. Joseph Kimball of Hancock Oct. 20, 1831, d. Feb. 10, 1879.)

*Dea. James*, (b. May 26, 1804, lived on homestead of his father, m. Evelyn Hall in 1832. She was daughter of Gilbert and Phebe (Perry) Hall of Warren, Me. Her father was named a "*good man*," was a sea-captain with a life of romantic successes and reverses, and d. at sea in 1825. Dea. Boyd was a carpenter by trade; built many houses; was characterized by tireless energy; was a hard worker and a constant worker, and an able and careful manager. The land on which Clinton Village is built once belonged to his estate, and was sold off in small lots from time to time. By years of hard labor and good calculation he accumulated the largest property ever collected in Antrim. Was for a long time a chief supporter of the Presbyterian Church, of which he was chosen elder in 1860. Left no children. Was town treasurer for a long time. He d. April 18, 1880, after long and terrible suffering, leaving one hundred dollars per year to the Presbyterian Church, besides thirty dollars per year to its poor, and all the residue of his estate, after the death of his heirs, to missionary and charitable institutions. The " Congregationalist " thus speaks of him : —

> Dea. Boyd was of the Scotch-Irish race, retaining to a remarkable degree the characteristics of the early settlers. He held opinions of his own, and was one of those who in every place will think and act for themselves. Like the fathers, he held his views strongly, yet always meant to be right. He was a thinking man of clear head, strong natural abilities, and sound judgment ; a depositary of many trusts, and strictly reliable in the care of them. Perhaps no really abler man was ever raised in Antrim. For half a century he was a man of great physical endurance, capable of doing two men's work ; and yet in no rash or careless way, since everything was thought out beforehand and done by method.
>
> He was a strong Presbyterian, but he could give the reason why. If, like the Scotch fathers, he was set in his views, he was first thoroughly-satisfied with the reasons for them. He came into the church in the great revival of 1827. For a long series of years he held the office of deacon. In the course of his life he gave more, probably, for the support of religion and the various charities, than any other man that ever lived in Antrim. His last years were full of bodily suffering, and his last sickness painful in the extreme; but he met it all with fortitude, and passed away in the Christian

faith, with the hope of immortal happiness and in sweet peace with all the world.)

*Isaac*, (b. April 28, 1806; m. Mary Hadley of Goffstown; was a roving. stirring, wide-awake man; carried on business of various kinds in different places; was in the bobbin business at the Branch some years; then moved to Waldoborough. Me., and d. there April 24, 1868, leaving children: Mary F., now Mrs. Samuel N. Morse of Nashua; James P., who lives unm. in Waldoborough, Me.; and Sarah M., who was sometime a teacher in Boston, — more recently a traveler in South America and Europe; was a teacher in Brazil; speaks several languages; a woman of rare scholarship and energy.)

*John M. W.*. (b. April 1, 1810, named for Dr. Whiton, m. Mary A. Hall of Boston, and d. in that city in 1847, leaving children: John G.; Henry M., who m. Elvira Marshall, lived in this town some years, had one child, Ida F.. born here, and moved to Boston some two years since; Abbie F.; and Anna E.)

*Abigail W.*, (twin sister of John M. W., and named for Mrs. Dr. Whiton, d. in 1826.)]

## BRACKETT.

The first known in America by this name was Capt. Richard Brackett, a native of Scotland, born in 1610, who came to this country in 1629 in the "Massachusetts Bay Company," under Gov. Winthrop. With others he signed a covenant to establish the first church in Boston. Nov. 25, 1636, he was "admitted a member of the Ancient and Honorable Artillery Company." In 1637 he was appointed "Keeper of the Prison," which office he long held; was chosen deacon of the church July 21, 1642, being then thirty-two years of age; was "chief military commander in Braintry;" was appointed to "marry and take oaths in civil cases." His life is spoken of as "useful, active, and pious." He died March 5, 1690. One of his eight children was James, born in 1645, — a pious and good man, who died in 1718, leaving seven children. The third of these was Nathan, born Sept. 29, 1677. Nathan married Hannah Veasie, and died in Quincy, Mass., in 1743. He left seven children. James, oldest child of Nathan, was born Nov. 3, 1709; married Abigail Belcher; was a hotel-keeper;·and died in 1781, leaving a large family. His fourth child, Samuel, was born in Braintree, Nov. 30, 1741; married Rebecca Hayward of Braintree Dec. 17, 1765, and went at once to Peterborough. His descendants in that town now occupy the spot where he settled. Samuel Brackett had thirteen children in all, as follows: Sarah, Samuel, Betsey, Dorothy, John, James, Josiah, Isaac, Rebecca, William,

Ebenezer, Joseph, and Benjamin. He died March 16, 1826. His wife died July 7, 1832, aged eighty-six.

JAMES BRACKETT, the sixth of these children, was born in Peterborough May 10, 1777. He married Hannah, daughter of Dea. James Carr of Antrim, in the year 1803, and lived several years in Peterborough, doing business as a drover, though by trade a shoemaker. Came here in 1811, and the next year built the house long occupied by Mrs. Sally Sawyer, but recently bought and repaired by his son, James Brackett. He united with the Presbyterian Church in his old age, and his conversion was so remarkable as to be worthy of notice here. He worked at his trade many years, in a little shop nearly opposite to the house; had worked that day early and late; had been very thoughtful all the afternoon; but got through with his work, put out the light, went into the house and sat down. Soon it occurred to him that he had forgotten something, and he went back to the shop. He found it brilliantly lighted, though from no visible source. He sat down on the bench to consider, and the thought at once struck him that this was a call of God. After looking and wondering for near ten minutes, he went into the house and told his wife what had occurred. They agreed that it was either a call to die or to prepare for death. He did not sleep that night, was under great conviction, but came out into religious peace and confidence on the following day. Though a stranger might feel like doubting this, yet it seems well substantiated; and it is certain that as early as practicable he made public his experience, was received into the church, and seemed a peaceful, humble Christian till his death, which occurred March 16, 1861. Mrs. Hannah Brackett died March 21, 1867. Children: —

1. JONATHAN C., [b. July 2, 1804, d. unm. April 23, 1835.]
2. ANN C., [b. Feb. 4, 1806, m. John Woodburn Wallace, May, 1833.]
3. SARAH W., [b. June 6, 1808; m. 1st, James Smith of Antrim, April 19, 1832; 2d, George Merrill of Cambridgeport, Mass.; d. in 1877, aged 69.]
4. BETSEY H., [b. Sept. 6, 1810, m. Thomas D. Twiss Jan. 30, 1834.]
5. HANNAH J., [b. in Antrim, Jan. 1, 1813. The four preceding were born in Peterborough. She m. John McClure March 26, 1840, and lives in Revere, Mass.]
6. JAMES, [b. June 27, 1815; m. Margaret D. Balch of Nashua; was overseer in Nashua mills, where he lived more than twenty years, but came back to Antrim in 1858. Children:
*Clarence A.*, (b. March 2, 1840, m. Juliette Oliver, and lives in Chelsea.)
*Charles P.*, (b. June 9, 1842.)

*Estelle O.*, (b. Jan. 26, 1851, m. Fred L. Nay June 9, 1874.)]
7. SILAS, [b. Oct. 27, 1817, m. Sophia H. Peacock June 20, 1844, and lives in Nashua.]
8. CLARINDA H., [b. March 20, 1820, m. John Little Dec. 1, 1842, and lives in Cambridgeport, Mass.]
9. MARY A., [b. July 5, 1822, m. Luther Campbell Jan. 30, 1843.]
10. HENRY P., [b. July 30, 1827; m. 1st, Sarah Jane Harris of Canaan, July, 1847, who died. leaving one child, Emma Jane, b. July 10, 1851. She followed her mother at the age of thirteen years. He m. 2d, Helen Wadleigh of Oldtown, Me., July 24, 1856, and they have one child, William W., b. Nov. 7, 1862, in Watertown, Mass. He lived on the Jonathan Carr farm (Luther Campell's) several years, then moved to Cambridgeport, Mass.]

## BRADFORD.

JAMES W. BRADFORD was son of Moses E. and Sarah (Holmes) Bradford. He lived in the Dr. Christie house, and was in trade in the Putney store. Was for a time partner of Charles McKeen, then traded awhile in Bennington, then returned here as clerk for McKeen. He married Fannie B. Dane, daughter of John Dane of Francestown, Nov. 27, 1849, and died July 21, 1858, aged thirty-three. No children.

## BREED.

THOMAS KNOWLES BREED, a native of Sudbury, Mass., came here from Nelson, succeeding John Gilmore in the fulling and carding mill in South Village. This was as early as 1803, as he buried a child on the hill that year. He was son of Dr. Thomas G. Breed, who had been a surgeon in the Revolutionary army, and after the war settled in Nelson in the practice of medicine. The son went with his father as a servant, saw many dangers, and was a witness of many historic characters and scenes. He saw the endurances of our fathers in the cause of liberty. Remembered at one time paying ten dollars for a piece of pie! He married Polly Keyes of Chelmsford, Mass., in 1791.. When he came here he bought, and for a long time occupied, a house then standing where the south school-house in the village was afterwards built. Mr. Breed found a small mill where Luke Hill's blacksmith-shop stands, — "a little, old fulling-mill," it is said; but in 1814 he pulled this down and put up a large shop in which he carried on a large business for years in the line of carding and manufacturing woolen cloth. The clothing-mill was burned March 31, 1850. Mr. Breed died in 1846, aged eighty-six, and his widow died in 1869, aged ninety-nine. Children of Thomas K. and Polly (Keyes) Breed: —

1. POLLY, [d. in 1808.]
2. THOMAS K., [b. in 1794; m. Persis Haselton of Manchester; lived with his father some years; then went to Lowell; took jobs building railroads, and was engaged upon a large contract of this kind in the West, when he was suddenly brought down with a fever, and died in Danville, Ill., Sept. 30, 1838. •His widow survives, and lives in South Village alone, her only child having followed his father to the grave at the age of 14.]
3. HENRY K., [b. in 1796, m. Barbara A. Favor Feb. 6, 1821, moved to Lowell, d. May 14, 1863.]
4. THADDEUS B., [d. in 1816, aged 18.]
5. JEREMIAH, [called "Capt. Breed"; b. 1801; m. June 15, 1830, Achsah Moore, a girl brought up by Dea. Weston at the Branch: moved to Sharon, thence to Danville, Ill., and d. there in 1839, leaving three children: —

    *James C.*, (b. in Antrim; m. in Warner; lost life by the war; lived in Contoocookville.)

    *Mary Frances*, (b. in Antrim, d. young.)

    *Harrison K.*, (b. in the West, m. Mary A. Tolman of Northfield, Mass., and lives in Fitchburg, Mass.)]
6. LUCY L., [b. in 1804; m. Jesse Richardson of Bedford Dec. 25, 1828; moved to Lowell, and died there.]
7. ROXANNA, [b. in 1806, m. Otis Smith.]
8. JAMES C., [b. Oct. 12, 1810; m. Elizabeth Brown of Fitchburg, Mass.; built the house now occupied by Dr. Christie; run the mills of his father several years in company with Ezra Hyde, to whom he sold out in 1847. He d. in Marlborough, September, 1878. Left two children: Mary, unm., and Addie, who m. a Mr. Estey of Marlborough.]
9. MARY, [b. Nov. 30, 1812; m. Isaac Barrett July 19, 1845; now lives in Lowell.]
10. THADDEUS B., [b. in 1816, d. in infancy.]

## BROOKS.

JOSEPH S. BROOKS, born in Maine 1816, son of William and Rebecca Brooks, came here to work in the shop of I. B. Pratt, married Jane Brown of Boston, and lived in the house where Mary Clark now lives. There his wife died, leaving one child, Jane E., now of Manchester. August 10, 1851, Mr. Brooks married Betsey V. Whitcomb of Waldo, Me. Built Brooks house in Clinton 1854, the frame being that of the Buckminster shoe-shop once standing at the Center. Mr. Brooks went into the army, was discharged, and died on his way home, September, 1863. Experienced religion in the army, so it was said of him: "He lost life, but gained heaven." Children by second wife were: —

1. JOSIE E., [b. May 22, 1852, m. G. G. Cilley of Lawrence, Mass., in 1875.]
2. FRANK M., [b. Aug. 28, 1854.]
3. JOSEPH W., [b. Dec. 25, 1855.]
4. CARRIE B., [b. May 25, 1859.]
5. MARY E., [b. Sept. 5, 1860.]
6. SARAH R., [b. Feb. 18, 1862.]

LEVI H. BROOKS, son of Dickerson and Hannah (Kemp) Brooks, born in Ashburnham, Mass., in 1831, married Harriet S. Karr of Lyndeborough in 1867, came here in 1869, and bought the first house out of South Village on the Clinton road. This he has enlarged and improved, built a barn, and greatly bettered the premises. This house was built by Dan Dunlap. Mr. Brooks is a stone-cutter by trade, and has laid the foundations of most buildings recently erected in Antrim. Has one adopted son, George A.

CHARLES S. BROOKS, brother of Levi, was born in Ashburnham, Mass., Feb. 25, 1833; came here in 1855 to work in the Clinton bedstead-shops; went to California in 1857, was there nearly five years, mining most of the time, and was considered very successful; married, Dec. 25, 1862, Lizzie B. Paige of Webster, and moved at once to this town. The next spring, in connection with John W. Foster, he bought what is now the Dodge shop in Clinton, but they soon exchanged with the Dodge brothers, taking the large shop below known as the Johnson chair-factory. Mr. Foster died in the spring of 1868, and Mr. Brooks carried on the business till 1873, when he sold out to Tristram B. Paige. Probably as a business man Mr. Brooks had no superior in Antrim. He was energetic, cool, sharp, popular, and *honest*. Moved to Francestown in 1876; has one child, Charles Willis, born Dec. 2, 1867.

## BROWN.

JOHN BROWN, son of John Brown who came over and settled in Londonderry, but soon after settled in Francestown, came here in 1788 onto the John Nichols place (N. C. Ferry's), and died there in 1808. His wife was Mary McConihe of Merrimack. Children: —

1. THOMAS, [m. Belinda Holmes of Francestown; was a soldier in the Revolutionary army; was very fond of telling how the "boys" were compelled by hunger to steal the Dutchman's sheep when stationed on the Hudson river. He didn't state whether fun and mischief contributed any to this stern necessity. Mr. Brown was stationed at West

Point during Arnold's treachery; was near by when Maj. Andre was executed, but was too noble-hearted to witness the scene. On coming to Antrim he settled the place adjacent to the Blanchard or Whiteley farm on the east, and d. there Nov. 2, 1847, aged 85. All his children d. young except Lucy, who m. her cousin Thomas Brown Feb. 5, 1829, inherited the homestead, moved thence to Hancock in 1866, and d. there in 1875.]

2. JOHN, [m. Marena Austin; had one son born in Antrim in September, 1794. Samuel, who m. Louisa Ayer, and is living very aged in Montpelier, Ind. After the birth of Samuel, the family removed in 1800 to Rochester, Vt., and had a numerous household, of whom one son, Thomas, m. Lucy Brown as above, lived near forty years on the place settled by the first Thomas Brown, and moved to Hancock in 1866. Thomas and Lucy Brown had children: Levi H., b. in 1833; Olivia B., b. in 1836, m. Charles F. Bond Feb. 19, 1857; and Francis C., who m. Mary J. Abbott of Lyndeborough. John Brown d. in 1838 in Goshen, Vt., aged 73.]

3. MARY, [m. James Hewey, moved to Springfield, Vt., and d. there in 1850, aged 88.]

4. BETSEY, [m. Nathan Austin, Jr., moved to Rochester, Vt., and d. there in 1808.]

5. JENNIE, [d. unm., aged 80.]

6. MARGARET, [b. in 1772, m. Dea. John Bell, d. in 1860.]

7. FRANCIS, [b. Feb. 9, 1774; m. Mary McMillen; lived many years on Whiteley place; moved in 1818 to Hubbardton, Vt.; thence to Goshen, Vt., where he lived about a dozen years. In 1831 he moved to Perrysburg, N. Y., where he d. in 1861. His wife d. in December, 1853. The children, all b. in Antrim, were as follows: —

*John*, (b. April 27, 1801, m. Mercy Mason, and lives in Fond du Lac, Wis.)

*Margaret*, (b. May 14, 1803, m. William Alden, and d. in Leicester, Vt., 1853.)

*Mary*, (b. Nov. 8, 1805, m. her cousin Francis Brown of Goshen, Vt.)

*Nancy*, (b. Nov. 8, 1807, m. Eli Knapp of Perrysburg, N. Y.)

*Andrew*, (b. Dec. 2, 1810, m. Catherine N. Noyes, and lives in Jamestown, N. Y.)

*Betsey*, (b. March 21, 1813, m. Dan Bryant, d. June 2, 1845.)
*Harriet*, (b. March 11, 1816, became 2d wife of William Alden of Leicester, Vt.)]

WILLIAM BROWN, no doubt son of Samuel and Susannah Brown, which Samuel bore the name "Doctor," lived in Bradford, Mass., 1734, and died in Chester, 1794, came here from Chester in 1786, and settled the Dea. Woods farm. His house stood on the opposite side of the road from the present house. Was selectman in 1791. His first wife, Anna ——, died of spotted fever Feb. 25, 1812. His second wife was Mrs. Sally Hooker of Danvers, Mass. He died in 1830, aged eighty-four. Children : —

1. SAMUEL, [b. in Chester, July 28, 1782 ; m. Betsey Atwood; lived on homestead ; afterwards several years east of Campbell's pond. The house there never had a public road to it, and has been gone for a long period. Samuel Brown d. in 1853. Children : —

*Susannah*, (b. Jan. 4, 1806, d. 1823.)
*Lucinda*, (b. in 1807 ; m. 1st, John McClintock in 1827 ; 2d, Jerome Strickland in 1837 ; 3d, Amasa Fairbanks, and now lives in Washington.)
*Amanda*, (b. in 1808, m. Jotham Moore in 1829, d. Feb. 17, 1857.)
*Daniel N.*, (b. in 1810, m. Jane Morrison in 1836, and lives in Drewsville.)
*William*, (b. in 1812, m. Mary Atwood in 1834, d. in Hillsborough Lower Village Oct. 23, 1859.)
*Eliza A.*, (b. in 1815, was 2d wife of Jotham Moore, and d. Oct. 21, 1860.)
*Samuel, Jr.*, (d. in infancy.)
*Almira*, (b. in 1819, m. Rev. Amon S. Tenney in 1840, and d. in Hillsborough Nov. 17, 1860.)
*Samuel, Jr., 2d.*, (d. in infancy.)
*John S.*, (b. in 1823, m. Maria Strickland in 1849, and lives in Hillsborough.)
*Stephen A.*, (b. Jan. 8, 1826 ; m. 1st, Hannah Strickland in 1850 ; 2d, Mrs. Louisa F. (Winship) Hall Oct. 9, 1876 ; has been extensively engaged in the tannery business at Hillsborough Lower Village for many years.)
*Harriet*, (d. in infancy.)
*Orren C.*, (b. Sept. 3, 1830, m. Rebecca A. Temple, and lives in Enfield.)]

2. JOHN, [all that is known of him is that he m. and d. in Salem, Mass.]
3. POLLY, [b. June 16, 1785, m. Andrew Taylor, son of Dea. John Taylor, Oct. 11, 1815, and d. May 28, 1828.]
4. WILLIAM, Jr., [went to Salem, Mass., in early life, m. and d. there.]
5. JAMES. [b. in Antrim Sept. 22, 1788, m. Lydia Flint in 1816, and had a son, James, b. here March 27, 1817. He seems to have moved soon after to Wales, N. Y. He d. about 1835.]
6. BETSEY, [b. Nov. 25, 1792; m. 1st, Samuel Dunlap, April 19, 1814; 2d, Ammi Buck, Nov. 12, 1822.]
7. DANIEL. [b. May 6, 1796; m. Nancy Appleton of Deering; built the Dea. Woods house, but moved to Hillsborough in 1833.]
8. LUCY ANNA, [daughter of 2d wife, b. April 30, 1816.]

WILLIAM BROWN, brother of the first John Brown of Antrim, named above, came here from Deering several years later than John, and lived in a house in the deep valley at the foot of Coolidge hill on the west. He seems to have been the first on that spot, and lived there till 1802, when he moved to Rochester, Vt. William Brown married Mary Lampson, had twelve children, and died in Hancock, Vt., June 10, 1828, aged sixty-seven. His wife died July, 1861, aged one hundred and two years and six months. The record in their family Bible runs back one hundred and twenty-two years. Children, of whom we can learn little more than their names, were : —

1. JOSEPH.
2. SAMUEL.
3. DAVID.
4. WILLIAM
5. JOHN.
6. DANIEL.
7. SARAH.
8. HANNAH.
9. BETSEY.
10. POLLY.
11. NANCY.
12. MEHITABLE.

ISAAC BROWN, son of Stephen and Eunice (Proctor) Brown of Sudbury, Mass., was born in Mason in 1794. Isaac married Sarah Flagg, came here in the fall of 1819 and located at the end of the road in what is known as "The City," moved to Temple in 1849, and is now living there in vigorous old age. His oldest child was born in Temple. The others were born in this town : —

1. HARRIET, [b. June 20, 1819, m. Rev. Joseph B. Hill Aug. 26, 1845. Mr. Hill was graduated at Harvard College in 1821. His father, Rev. Ebenezer Hill, was pastor of the Congrega-

tional Church in Mason sixty-four years, and d. in 1854, aged 89. Rev. Joseph Hill was some years a teacher, studied law, and was admitted to the bar; afterwards became a Christian, abandoned the law, was ordained to preach, and in August, 1840, became colleague with his aged father in the pastorate at Mason. In 1847 he went to Colebrook and was pastor there ten years, then at West Stewartstown five years, for two of which he was also school commissioner for Coos county, then moving his family to Temple he went at once to the army in the service of the Christian commission. Was accidentally killed by the cars as he was trying to jump onto a moving train at Chattanooga, Tenn., June 16, 1864.]

2. MARY ANN, [b. Oct. 27, 1822, m. James H. Walton in 1852, and lives in Temple. George B., a twin brother, d. in infancy.]

4. ISAAC P., [b. Dec. 12, 1825, and died in infancy.]

5. ADNA, [b. Dec. 11, 1826, m. Mary Newton Sept. 10, 1850, lives in Springfield, Vt., and is a manufacturer of woolen-machinery.]

6. ADDISON, [twin brother of Adna; carpenter by trade; m. Kate Hale of New York city; after a time moved to Macon, Mo., but returned to Temple in poor health and d. there in 1870.]

7. NATHAN A., [b. in 1833; m. Sarah Brown, his cousin, Sept. 19, 1857, and is now a farmer in Temple.]

8. SARAH A., [twin sister of Nathan, m. Charles A. Bales in 1874, and lives in Wilton.]

ARTEMAS BROWN, brother of Isaac, born in Sudbury, Mass., in 1802, came here from Temple in 1823 to work at cooper's trade, onto the James Nesmith place west of the pond. Afterwards bought the Ebenezer Goodhue place (settled by Wiley), but in the course of a few years settled on the Puffer place, where he spent more than half his life. Was found dead in his yard May 31, 1875. Mr. Brown acquired a large property, was the most extensive land-owner in Antrim, hospitable, popular, eccentric, full of jokes, hard-working, old-fashioned in tastes and habits, and HONEST. He once offered the writer all the berries he might ever want, but added: "I don't want you to come berrying on the Sabbath day!" Mr. Brown married, first, Rhoda Robinson Oct. 30, 1827, who died in 1843; second, Almira Goodhue of Hancock in 1844. Children:—

1. SARAH, [child of 1st wife, b. in 1836, m. Nathan A. Brown Sept. 19, 1857.]

2. GEORGE, [child of 2d wife; b. in 1846; m. Sophia L. Barney of Hancock; inherits the land estate of his father; lived some years on Isaac Brown place, but moved the house of his father onto the stand of the Dea. Fletcher house, and with enlargements and valuable improvements now occupies the same. His excellent wife d. Sept. 29, 1877, leaving two children, one Charles Artemas, b. in 1873, the other a new-born babe. The new road cut across the meadow direct from Clinton to his new house, was used almost for the first time at the funeral of his wife.]

3. ALVIN, [b. in 1849; m. Josie M. Dustin Aug. 29, 1872; lived in Nashua some years, but returned and built on the Isaac Brown place.]

## BRYANT.

ELIAS P. BRYANT, son of Elias and Elizabeth (Ingalls) Bryant, born in Stoneham, Mass., July 17, 1806, married Susannah B. Wilson of Francestown, came here and bought the Dea. Barachias Holt farm, April, 1834. The house stood a few rods south of Capt. James Wilson's, and very near the East brick church. Mr. B. moved back to Francestown in 1836, where he now resides. Children:—

1. SUSAN M., [b. in Antrim Nov. 22, 1835, d. aged 30.]
2. MARY J., [now Mrs. Benj. R. Rowe, of Stoneham, Mass.]
3. ELIAS A., [b. in Washington in 1840, m. Leander E. French of Reed's Ferry; lives in Francestown.]
4. SARAH A., [b. in 1844.]
5. CHARLES P., [b. in Francestown in 1849.]
6. SAMUEL E., [b. in 1851.]
7. JOSEPH W., [b. Nov. 11, 1854.]
8. JESSE E., [d. aged 6.]

SAMUEL I. BRYANT, brother of above, born Aug. 27, 1808, married Hannah F. Butterfield of Francestown in 1828; came here in April, 1834, and opened a store in part of his brother's house (Barachias Holt place), where he continued in trade about three years, then moved to Francestown, thence to Stoneham, Mass., where he now resides. Children:—

1. ELIZABETH, [b. in Stoneham, Mass., Sept. 7, 1829, d. aged 14.]
2. SARAH F., [b. in Francestown in 1832; now Mrs. C. S. Nash, Stoneham, Mass.]
3. HANNAH M., [b. in Antrim Feb. 17, 1835, d. aged 20.]
4. SAMUEL I., JR., [b. in Francestown in 1839, m. Mary J. Duncklee; lives in Stoneham, Mass.]

ELIHU BRYANT, known in Antrim as John E. Bryant, also brother of above, was manufacturer of shoes, and was also in company with Samuel I. in trade at East Antrim. Married Mary Steele May 1, 1838. Soon after, he moved to Stoneham, Mass., thence to Geneseo, Ill. Was an able and excellent man, and was deacon in the Congregational Church. He closed his business on account of failing health, and moved to Brooklyn, N. Y., but continued to decline, and died there Feb. 18, 1869, aged fifty-six. Only one child survives him, Robert A. Bryant, born March 19, 1842; married Emma North of Meriden, Conn., in 1868, and is now of Wenonah, N. J.

## BRYER.

JOHN A. BRYER, son of Jonathan K. and Maria (Annis) Bryer of Groton, was born in Gilford, Sept. 1, 1846. He married Deemie E. Bailey of Rumney, June 13, 1869, and came to Antrim in 1870, buying the house and shop formerly owned by Dimond Twiss, in Clinton Village, where he carries on the blacksmith business. Mr. Bryer served in the army, being a volunteer in the Fourth N. H. Regiment. He passed through nine battles uninjured, but was slightly wounded by a sharpshooter's bullet while in camp before Petersburg.

D. PARKER BRYER, brother of John A., was born in Groton, Dec. 29, 1850. He came to Antrim in the fall of 1870; married Mary F. Sawyer, daughter of Edmond Sawyer, June 20, 1872, and succeeded Mr. Sawyer as blacksmith at North Branch. Their children are:—

1. MYRTA MAY, [b. Dec. 5, 1874.]
2. WALTER A., [b. Oct. 20, 1877.]

## BUCK.

STICKNEY BUCK, son of Simeon and Mary (Goss) Buck, was born in Windsor, in 1803; married Maria Wood, and came here in 1838; lived on the George McIlvaine place and other places in town, but left Antrim in 1849. He is said to have moved thirty-three times; now lives in Eyota, Minn. Children:—

1. EMILY M., [b. Feb. 19, 1830, d. unm. in 1852.]
2. WILLIS S., [b. May 31, 1831, m. Alzora C. Richardson, and lives in Rochester, Minn.]
3. FRANK A., [b. Aug. 27, 1833, m. Nellie M. Bolin, and d. in Eyota in 1869.]
4. ELMINA S., [b. Oct. 11, 1835, m. O. B. Cutler, and d. in Minneapolis, Minn., in 1872.]
5. ELVINA M., [twin sister of Elmina S., m. George M. House, and lives in Minneapolis.]
6. CLARK S., [b. May 16, 1837; is a mechanic; m..Almie I. Clark of Hancock, and lives in Minneapolis.]

7. DAVID W., [b. March 5, 1839, m. Emma L. Farmer, and lives in Eyota.]
8. GEORGE G., [b. Feb. 16, 1841, m. Addie A. Glidden, and lives in Eyota.]
9. ALBERT C., [b. June 12, 1843, lives unm. in White City, Kan.]

## BUCKMINSTER.

BENJAMIN M. BUCKMINSTER, son of Solomon and Hannah (Rice) Buckminster, came here from Marlborough in 1834, and bought the place now owned by Capt. Leander Smith. He was a shoemaker by trade. His first wife, Hannah Hardy of Nelson, to whom he was married in 1819, died in 1848, and was the mother of all his children. For his second wife he married Mrs. Lucy (Rice) Osgood in 1854. He moved to Peterborough in 1860, and died there in 1873, at the age of eighty-one years. His children that lived to maturity were: —

1. SOLOMON R., [b. in 1820, m. Betsey K. Boutelle of Hancock in 1844. He lived in the house now owned by Rev. W. R. Cochrane, and was leader of the Center choir (Presbyterian Church) several years. In 1854 he moved to Reading, Mass., from thence to Bear Valley, Minn., in 1858, where he died in 1861, leaving but one child: —

    *Charles E.*, (b. in 1845, m. Emma J. Ambler in 1866, and now lives in Chester, Minn.)

    *Joseph*, (b. May 2, 1853, d. at the age of four months, and was buried in the cemetery at Antrim Center.)]

2. HANNAH M., [b. in 1821, d. at the age of 20 years.]
3. ELISABETH H., [b. in 1825, m. Baker Pratt, and d. Sept. 13, 1860.]
4. SARAH L., [b. in 1827, m. Charles Boutelle of Hancock in 1850, who then came to Antrim, from whence he moved to Bear Valley, Minn.]
5. HARRIET W., [b. in 1837, m. Dr. Geo. S. Nelson of Boston, and resides in that city.]

BENNETT S. BUCKMINSTER, son of Peter D. and Abigail (White) Buckminster, was born in Roxbury, Sept. 4, 1824, came to Antrim in 1850 as a clerk in Woodbury's store, married Nancy J. McKean in 1857, who died in 1866. In 1869 he married Mrs. Fannie B. Bradford (daughter of John Dane of Francestown), and now lives at South Village. Was many years clerk at Woodbury's store, and is now partner in the same.

## BULLARD.

CALVIN BULLARD was born July 28, 1813. His father, Benjamin, was son of Benjamin of Oakham, Mass., married Ruth W. Woodace, and settled in Society Land, now Bennington, where now George Colby lives.

Calvin came here in 1849, occupied the Gibson house, South Village, which he still owns, and moved to Peterborough in November, 1870. He married, first, Mary Jane Dunlap, Nov. 27, 1834; second, Mrs. Jane (Morrison) Dresser, Nov. 6, 1852; third, Mrs. Laura E. Wilson, June 16, 1870.

Calvin Bullard's only child, Mary Frank, was born March 5, 1836, and married Eben Woods of Bennington in 1855. I have learned since this writing, that Benjamin Bullard of Oakham was the son of Capt. Silas, who was the son of Capt. Jonathan, both men of high character and ability. The family was first known in Weston Mass. Edward Everett, on his mother's side, was of this stock.

ADIN B. BULLARD, son of Benjamin and Rosanna (Wilkins) Bullard, and grandson of Benjamin who married Ruth Woodace, was born in Bennington in 1845, and married Augusta Slie of Truro, Mass. He came to South Antrim in 1874. His children are : —

1. AUGUSTA, [b. in 1868.]
2. JOHN I., [b. in 1873.]

JOHN L. BULLARD, brother of Adin, was brought up by Dea. James Boyd, and married Ruth H. Hackett Feb. 28, 1878.

## BURNHAM.

Walter Le Ventre went to England as a friend and follower of William of Normandy in 1066. In 1080, when England was surveyed and divided, this Walter was made a lord, and granted the Saxon village of Burnham in Norfolk county, taking the name of Walter de Burnham. This property remained in the family and name until about 1700. Many of the records and dates are lost, but the descendants have been traced thus : The first generation of which we have any positive knowledge commences with, —

ROBERT BURNHAM, born in Norwich, Norfolk county, Eng., in 1581. In 1608 he married Mary Andrews, and had seven children, three of whom came to America : Dea. John of Essex, Mass., Robert of Dover, and Thomas, mentioned below. Benjamin, the youngest son, born in 1621, went to the East Indies where he amassed a large fortune, purchased one hundred and fifty acres of land, now in the heart of London, which he willed to the three brothers in America. This property is now valued at seventy millions and has never been distributed. Of the second generation, —

Thomas Burnham, son of Robert and Mary (Andrews) Burnham, was born in England in 1623, and came to America in 1635, with his brothers John and Robert, in ship "Angel Gabriel," which was wrecked on the coast of Maine. He settled in Chebacco, now Essex, Mass., and was out in the Pequot expedition. In 1645 he married Mary Tuttle, was selectman in 1647, and deputy to general court from 1683 to 1685 inclusive. He had twelve children, and died in 1694. Of the third generation, —

John Burnham, son of Thomas and Mary (Tuttle) Burnham, was born in 1648, and settled on part of his father's estate. He married Elizabeth Wells, had nine children, and died in 1704. Of the fourth generation, —

Thomas Burnham, son of John and Elizabeth (Wells) Burnham, was born in 1673, and settled on his father's land, which is still in possession of his descendants in Essex, Mass. He had six children, and died in 1748. Of the fifth generation, —

Stephen Burnham, son of Thomas, mentioned above, married Mary Andrews, and settled in Gloucester, Mass. The date of his death is unknown. He had thirteen children, one son, Nathaniel, being the father of Dea. Epps and Dr. Israel Burnham of this town. Another son of the sixth generation, —

Joshua Burnham, son of Stephen and Mary (Andrews) Burnham, was born in Gloucester, Mass., in 1754. He had ten children, none of whom are living. One of them was the late Abel Burnham of Mont Vernon. Another of the seventh generation is identified with Antrim, coming here some years later than his cousins, Dea. Epps and Dr. Israel Burnham, as will be seen by the following record : —

THOMAS BURNHAM, son of Joshua, was born in Milford in 1783, married Rachel Conant in 1807, and came to Antrim in 1821, occupying the Madison Tuttle farm until 1837, when he moved to Hillsborough, where he died in 1856. His wife died in Nashua in 1871, at the age of eighty-seven. Their children are : —

1. ALBERT G., [b. in 1808. He learned the tanner's trade with Dea. Little ; m. Fannie Simonds, and now lives at Hillsborough Upper Village.]
2. SELINA D., [b. in 1810, and m. Phinehas Reed of Litchfield.]
3. DR. ABEL C., [b. in 1812 ; m. Caroline Dascomb, and has been for many years a trusted and successful physician at Hillsborough Bridge.]
4. ORNA B., [b. in 1814, and lived with Hon. Jacob Tuttle for many years. He m. Melinda Gould of Lyndeborough. and lived awhile on the Dr. Cleaves place, then on the James Boutwell place, and is now living in Acworth. He had one child : —

    *Henry F.*, (b. in Antrim, m. Jennie A. Kennedy, and lives in Acworth.)]
5. HENRIETTA B., [b. in 1816, m. Bradley Hall of Chesterfield, and d. in 1872.]

6. G. ERICKSON, [b. in 1819 ; m. 1st, Abby Baldwin of Hillsborough ; 2d, Martha J. McClintock of Hillsborough, and now resides in that town on Bible Hill.]
7. E. HATCH, [b. in this town in 1823 ; m. Maria Keyes of Washington : was for many years a noted stage-driver, and now lives at Hillsborough Bridge.]
8. ORAMUS W., [b. in Antrim in 1827, and m. Ellen M. Hartshorn of Amherst.] .

Of the seventh generation, the first identified with this town is : —

EPPS BURNHAM, son of Nathaniel and Mary (Burnham) Burnham, who both came from Essex, Mass., was born in Greenfield Aug. 17, 1781, married Sarah Cavender of Greenfield in 1806, and came to Antrim the same year. He bought and moved onto the Dea. Aiken farm in South Village, now owned by Mr. Whittum. In 1816 he was chosen elder in the Presbyterian Church, being elected before his union with the church, though no doubt in expectation of it. He served in this capacity until his removal to Concord in 1838, when he was immediately elected to the same office in the South Congregational Church in that city, which place he retained until his death in 1847. He was a good man, a valuable citizen and church-member. A contemporary says of him : "Dea. Burnham was a strong and efficient man." The children are : —

1. CHARLES C.. [b. Sept. 23, 1807, and d. July 10, 1813.]
2. FRANKLIN W., [b. July 2. 1810, and m. Mary Keysar of Canterbury in 1833, who d. in 1839. In 1840 he m. Fidelia Cross of Northfield, and now resides in Concord. He has one daughter married and living with her parents.]
3. SARAH A.. [b. March 28, 1812. In 1836 she m. James Peverly of Canterbury, who was for many years a prominent merchant in Concord, where his wife now lives. In 1873 he went to Europe with their only child, Helen Peverly, and d. in Edinburgh, Scotland, the same year. At that time the daughter became acquainted with Peter Carr of Liverpool, England, whom she afterwards m., and now resides in Liverpool, having two children.]
4. CHARLES C., [b. Feb. 26, 1815. m. Elizabeth Ham of Canterbury, and now resides in Hopkinton, where he holds the office of deacon in the Congregational Church. He has four children living, one of whom, Frederick Burnham, is a physician in Orford.]
5. EPPS, [b. Aug. 15, 1817, and d. at the age of twenty years.]
6. NATHANIEL, [b. Nov. 12, 1819, m. Harriet Youngman of Wilmot, and now resides in Dorchester.]

7. MARY E., [b. Jan. 15, 1823, and d. at the age of three years.]
8. EMILY JANE, [b. Sept. 25, 1824, m. Walter Abbott of Lowell, Mass., in 1849. and resided in Concord, where Mr. Abbott was a prominent citizen. He d. in that city in 1868, and his widow now resides with her nephew, Dr. Fred Burnham, in Orford.]

DR. ISRAEL BURNHAM, brother of Dea. Epps Burnham, studied medicine at Hartford, Conn., and came to this town about the first of 1817, as the successor of Dr. Adams. He moved into the Dea. Aiken house, then just vacated. and planted with his own hand in 1817 the noted poplar-tree now standing at the door. Dec. 11, 1817, he m. Fanny Baldwin, and in 1820 bought the place and built where Elijah Kimball now lives. He was a valuable citizen and highly esteemed, continuing the practice of medicine until 1848, when he gave up to Dr. Hubbard, and died the following year, July 9, 1849, at the age of fifty-seven. At his death he left a small fund to the Presbyterian Church, of which he was a member. He had three children : —

1. FANNY W., [b. June 2, 1819, m. Dr. M. W. Atwood Oct. 10, 1843, and settled at New Hudson, N. Y., where he d. after some years, and she came back to her father's and d. Feb. 22, 1849.]
2. ISRAEL S., [b. June 21, 1824, m. Harriet Leggett of Canada, went to Norwalk, Conn., and d. there in 1865.]
3. GEORGE W. N., [b. May 30, 1828, m. Elizabeth Coburn of Deering Oct. 9, 1849, and d. at his father's homestead May 29, 1864, leaving children : —
 *George F.*, (b. Aug. 14, 1850, m. Florence A. Brooks of Acton Aug. 21, 1873, and now lives in Revere, Mass.)
 *Mary P.*, (b. July 7, 1852, m. William H. Derby of Revere, Mass., Nov. 17, 1874, and they now reside in that place.)
 *Fred I.*, (b. Aug. 5, 1857.)
 *Arthur M.*, (b. Feb. 19, 1860.)
 *John M.*, (b. Aug. 17, 1862, and now lives in Deering.)]

## BURNS.

JOHN BURNS came here from New Boston in 1774, and began the second place west of Reed Carr's on the old road. His only neighbors were on the William Stacey place and at the Branch. Maurice Lynch on the former place was in sight, but there was no road to either of them, nor even a path. He stayed here one year, then sold to his brother Robert, and returned to New Boston. These brothers, John and Robert, seem to have been sons of John Burns of New Boston. This first John was among the early settlers of that town, and signed the call to Rev. Solomon Moor in that town Aug. 25, 1767. He settled in the south part, and built a saw-mill near the foot of Joe English Hill, afterwards known in that vicinity as the Orne mills. The writer remembers the old mill when it was falling to pieces in age and neglect, as it was near his birthplace. In his riper years John Burns, Sen., moved to Francestown and died there quite aged, but no stone marks his grave, and no record can be found.

There was a John Burns in Bedford at the same time that John, Sen., resided in New Boston. These Johns were probably cousins, and their sons married sisters in New Boston. John of Bedford once went to Pennacook (Concord) for corn for his family, and on return was fired upon by the Indians in ambush at Suncook. He escaped by running, but seven bullet-holes in his shirt gave evidence of his danger!

MAJ. JOHN BURNS of Antrim was born in New Boston, Aug. 17, 1755, and died in Whitefield May 6, 1852. His wife, Mrs. Sarah (Smith) McMarston, daughter of Dea. John Smith of New Boston, was born Dec. 26, 1752, and died June 4, 1826. Maj. Burns was out in the Revolutionary army, was in the battle of Bunker Hill, was also out in the war of 1812, and his military record was highly creditable. In 1843 he visited Boston and went out to Bunker Hill, where sixty-eight years before he had marched in the ranks and faced the foe in deadly conflict. At the age of ninety he visited the White Mountains, — walked four miles to the top of Mt. Washington, and returned the same day. He represented New Boston in the legislature, lived on the Luther Colburn farm in that town, was an energetic and live man, and held in the highest esteem. He and his family moved from New Boston in the spring of 1802. Leaving his wife in Lisbon, he and his boys pressed on to Whitefield, and made their clearing and put up their log house. The next spring (1803) they all moved there, making the first settlement in that now flourishing town. Maj. Burns was a cool, fearless man, loving adventure to the last. It is related of him here that he and Moses Steele of Hillsborough went hunting up North Branch river, then an absolute wilderness, Steele on the north bank, Burns on the south. Far up the stream Steele found himself pursued by a bear, and he fled across the stream towards Burns. Bruin entered the water after him. Steele turned to fire on him, but in the motion dropped his flint into the water. He then cried to Burns to climb a tree! But the latter coolly answered that he guessed he could take care of himself, and fired and brought the bear down! It was a dangerous fellow, and had almost reached Steele. In 1843, at the age of eighty-eight, Maj. Burns represented Whitefield in the legislature, and was treated with great deference as the father of the House. In 1848 he made his last visit to Antrim and New Boston, making the journey of nearly one hundred and fifty miles in a wagon alone, being ninety-three years old! Though none of his children were born here, yet we have thought best to give them: —

1. DAVID, [b. in New Boston July 31, 1782; m. Susannah Knights of Bethlehem; inherited the homestead of his

father; d. April 30, 1864. His son, John Burns, Esq., now occupies the original settlement in Whitefield. David was several times in the New Hampshire legislature.]
2. WILLIAM, [b. May 18, 1784, and d. in infancy.]
3. HANNAH, [b. in 1786, m. Enoch Kenney of Whitefield, and d. there in 1815.]
4. POLLY, [b. in 1788, m. Calvin White, and d. in 1813.]
5. SALLY, [b. June 28, 1790, m. Asa King, and d. in 1876.]
6. JANE, [b. March 4, 1793, m. James Burns, and d. April 10, 1876.]

ROBERT BURNS, brother of John, came here in 1775, having bought his brother's farm, on which he lived till 1829, — fifty-four years, — when he died at the age of eighty-nine. He married Janet McNiel of New Boston, from which town he came. It is related of him that he once lost his cows in the woods, hunted for them till dark, got lost himself, and when he began to hear the bears growl near at hand he crept into a hollow log for safety, and, defending the entrance, lay there till morning. His anxious wife sat up all night for him, and felt disposed to know his whereabouts on that particular occasion, but all she could ever get out of him was, in broad Scotch. "Haala laag! Haala laag!" The children of Robert were : —

1. WILLIAM T., [b. March 26, 1780; went below and m. and had several children, but returned to Antrim, and was on the town farm some years before his death.]
2. RACHEL, [m. Joseph Simonds Sept. 3, 1812, and d. in Wilton in 1868.]
3. ROBERT, [b. in 1783; m. Mary Simonds Sept. 1, 1812; lived with his father till 1818, when he bought, cleared, and built where B. F. McIlvaine now lives. The same year, or a little later, he began what was long known as the Burns mill, where he sawed lumber for many years. On this place he d. Sept. 5, 1849, aged 66. His wife d. in 1861, aged 71. Children : —

*Lucy*, (d. Sept. 5, 1833, aged 19.)
*John*, (d. Aug. 16, 1841, aged 26.)
*Luke*, (b. Feb. 22, 1815, m. Lina Hill, and now resides in Hudson.)
*Sabrina*, (b. Nov. 18, 1817; m. B. F. McIlvaine March 20, 1845; received the homestead, but d. Jan. 19, 1860.)
*Mary J.*, (b. May 24, 1820, and m. William P. Little Nov. 12, 1844.)
*Esther*, (d. July 21, 1842, aged 20.)

*Eliza J.*, (b. May 9, 1826, m. Thomas Burtt, and now resides at Hillsborough Bridge.)]

## BUSWELL.

DANIEL BUSWELL came here from Bradford, Mass., in 1791, having been previously married to Ede Bodwell of Methuen, who was born Jan. 13, 1770. Mr. Buswell first occupied the Zadoc Dodge place, and afterwards lived in several different places in town, until the year 1826, when he settled on the Gregg place near the pond, where he died in 1859, at the age of ninety-six years. He was a Revolutionary soldier, and received a serious wound in the eye in a battle near Fort Washington. One part of a bullet, which was cut in two by striking his bayonet as he was reloading, struck his eye, while the larger part was turned aside, thus probably saving his life. His wife died at the age of ninety-nine years, two months, and one day. Their children are: —

1. ABIGAIL, [b. Aug. 22, 1789, d. unm. in Bradford, Mass., in 1871.]
2. SALLY, [b. May 31, 1791, m. Sewall Spalding, and moved to New York.]
3. CHARLOTTE, [b. March 17, 1794, m. and went to Canaan.]
4. THOMAS, [b. Feb. 16, 1796. He bought the Gregg mills in 1826, and d. unm., leaving the property to his father.]
5. PRISCILLA, [b. Oct. 18, 1798, and m. Aaron Parker of Boxford, Mass.]
6. ZELINDA, [b. April 8, 1803, and is supposed to have died in infancy.]
7. ANN, [b. Aug. 13, 1805. She m. John Robinson, went to Alstead, and d. in 1856.]
8. WILLIAM, [b. July 20, 1809, and m. Betsey A. McMaster. He moved to the Gregg place to see his parents through life, but died before either of them, Aug. 9, 1852, leaving three children: —

    *Thomas*, (who d. in the army.)
    *Albert*, (who d. in the army of yellow fever.)
    *Sarah E.*, (m. George F. Mitchell of Clinton, Mass., Nov. 17, 1858.)]
9. ELISABETH, [twin sister of William, is supposed to have died in infancy.]
10. ELIZA M., [b. July 15, 1812, m. Dea. Thomas Thompson.]
11. ISAAC, [b. June 29, 1814. He m. Margaret Hodgman of Ithaca, N. Y.; from that place entered the army as a musician and d. in service.]

## BUTLER.

TOBIAS BUTLER, one of the noted characters in the early settlement of this town, was a fine penman. He it was who wrote on the title page of the town book, in large and elegant hand, —

"The Records of Antrim in the year Of our Lord GOD 1788.
"T. BUTLER
"T. C.
"By commendable deportment you will Rise to preferment &c."

It was natural that the writing-master should "set a copy" in the town book; and it is to be hoped that many who read this will be enabled in this way to "Rise to preferment &c."

Tobias Butler was born in Ireland in 1746, and educated for a Roman Catholic priest, but, becoming a Protestant, he emigrated to America (probably on that account), at the age of twenty-five years. He first owned a place in New Boston, and from that town entered the army of the Revolution, passing through most of the conflicts in New York. He married Mary Hogg, sister of Abner Hogg of New Boston, who was a marked man in his day, and a Revolutionary pensioner within the memory of the writer, bowed and white and nearly one hundred years old, respected by all, and venerated by the young. When his son had his name changed, the old man said, "I've always lived a Hogg and I'll die a Hogg." Mr. Butler came to this town in 1786 and lived on the Eben Bass place. Everybody called him "Master Butler," from the fact that for many years he was a teacher. In 1788 he held the office of town clerk. He moved to Hillsborough in 1804, where he resided for a time, when he came back and lived on the Nat. Herrick place, but died, in 1829, at the age of eighty-three years, on the then-called Weston place. The buildings, now gone, stood northeast of J. G. Flint's. He had a brother John, who lived for a few years in a log house in Eben Bass's pasture, when he returned to Ireland, not regarding rocky Antrim equal to his fatherland. Master Butler was an honest and pious man. His children were: —

1. JAMES, [m. Fanny Stevens, Oct. 15, 1812. lived in many places in town, and d. on the Sam. Wilson place west of Reed Carr's.]
2. ROBERT, [m. Betsey Wilkins of Deering. In 1800 he built a small store at the corner opposite the town-house, where he traded for some years, and then moved to Salem, N. Y., where he died. Robert had children here named Samuel M., Gracie O., and Milton. The last was killed by the falling of an iron bar upon him in Salem, N. Y., aged 12.]
3. SUSAN, [d. young of spotted fever.]
4. MARGARET, [m. Dr. Oliver Brown and went to Vermont, and thence to Salem, N. Y.]
5. NANCY, [was never m., and d. recently on the county farm.]

6. JOHN, [lived with his parents and d. unm. in Hillsborough.]
7. JOSEPH, [went to Canada in 1825.]
8. SAMUEL, [was a victim of spotted fever, d. in 1812 at the age of 19 years.]
9. THOMAS, [b. in 1799 on the Eben Bass place, is the last of the family now living. He m. Abigail Keyes of Hillsborough, and occupied buildings, now gone, situated between widow Levi Curtis's and the Keene road. Having been blind for twenty-five years, and in feeble health, he now lives with his daughter and is supported by pension. His children are : —

*Susan*, (m. Stephen Clement and d. soon afterwards.)
*Betsey A.*, (m. 1st, Alden Hill of New Boston ; 2d, Charles A. Barrett of this town.)
*John*, (entered the army and d. at New Orleans.)
*Harriet M.*, (m. Miles Swinington, and lives in Francestown.)]

## BUTMAN.

JOHN BUTMAN, an excellent man, came here from Topsfield, Mass., in 1794, and settled on the place still called by his name, south of Gregg pond. He died in 1824, aged eighty-seven years. His wife, Hannah Andrews of Boxford, Mass., died aged ninety-four years. Their children, none of them born in this town, were as follows : Ebenezer, Nancy, John, Asa, Thomas, Joshua, Oliver, Eliphalet. Of these, the only one of whom we have any record is Ebenezer Butman, born in Boxford, Mass., in 1767. He came here with his father at the age of twenty-seven, married Mehitable Andrews of Bradford, Dec. 24, 1805, and lived with his parents till 1822, when he moved to Bradford, where he died in 1857. His children are: —

1. HANNAH, [b. Nov. 1, 1806, and is still living unm. in Bradford.]
2. LYDIA B., [b. Sept. 1, 1808, m. Joseph Corser of Webster.]
3. JOSHUA, [b. Oct. 14, 1810, m. Hannah Fulton, and lives in Bradford.]
4. PHEBE, [b. in 1814, m. Dr. Marshall Merriam of Merrimack, and moved to Derry, where she died in 1873.]
5. NANCY, [b. in 1817, became the 2d wife of Dr. Merriam, and lives in Derry.]
6. SUSAN, [b. in 1820, d. unm. at Bradford in 1862.]
7. RUTH K., [b. at Bradford in 1823, d. in 1841.]
8. ABBIE A., [b. in 1826, d. unm. in 1865.]
9. JACOB O., [b. in 1828, m. Mary Palmer of Manchester in 1855, and now resides in Manchester.]

## BUTTERFIELD.

ISAAC BUTTERFIELD, as associated with our fathers, and first captain of the militia of Society Land, deserves a brief notice here, though never living in Antrim. In 1713, or soon after, Samuel Butterfield with other soldiers was stationed at Groton, Mass., to guard and assist the reapers of a large lot of grain. The Indians attacked them, and Mr. Butterfield, after killing one and disabling two others, was overpowered, bound, and marched off to Canada. The Indians intended him for torture and death, and left it to the wife of the Indian he had killed to say in what form he should be tortured. She decided to keep him for a servant. After many months he was redeemed. His son William settled some years afterward in Londonderry, and subsequently in Francestown. Capt. Isaac Butterfield was son of William, and settled in Society Land, now Greenfield, in 1770, near the present school-house in Nahum Russell's district, on the spot where there is now a large stone in the wall inscribed "I. B. 1770." When, on news of the battle of Lexington, the men of Society Land (Antrim, Hancock, and Greenfield) met together and marched toward the scene of conflict, they chose Isaac Butterfield their captain. This was done at the house of Dea. Aiken. Of Capt. Butterfield we know but little further. After the war he lived awhile in Francestown and in Acworth. Thence he went to Homer, N. Y. His old age was spent in Le Roy, that State, where he died at the age of ninety-five. His wife was a Webster. Most of his family went to New York. His oldest son, John, was a noted merchant, went to China for cargoes of tea, was in trade more than half a century, and died in Le Roy, N. Y., aged ninety.

BENJAMIN BUTTERFIELD came here in 1785, and lived a few years in a log house south of Dea. Vose's and west of the pond, when he moved away. Nothing further is known of him.

CHARLES BUTTERFIELD came here in 1795, and lived on the south slope of the mountain north of the Artemas Brown place. About 1800 his buildings were burned, when he left town and nothing more is known of him.

CHANDLER BUTTERFIELD, son of William and Lavinia (Case) Butterfield of Washington, was born in 1812. His father came to Antrim that year to nurse those sick with spotted fever. He lived in several places in town, then went to Massachusetts, and died there. His son, Chandler Butterfield, grew up to manhood in town, married Naomi D. Robinson July 16, 1835, and lived for many years west of the pond. He now occupies the Robert Gregg or David Hill place. His children are : —

1. WILLIAM F., [b. Dec. 22, 1836, m. Carrie Holt July 14, 1863, was for many years a clerk in Boston, and now resides in Antrim.]
2. JOHN C., [b. Jan. 2, 1838, and m. Almira R. Robb June 3,

1863. He is a mason by trade, residing in South Village in Avery house. His children are: —

*John A.*, (b. May 9, 1866.)
*George W.*, (b. Oct. 4, 1868.)
*Mason C.*, (b. Aug. 10, 1872.)
*Carrie M.*, (b. Feb. 15, 1877.)]

3. MARY E., [b. in 1841, and was killed in Bennington September, 1847, by a cart-body falling on her.]

STEPHEN BUTTERFIELD, born in Goffstown Jan. 11, 1794, and Polly (Clogston) Butterfield, his wife, came to Antrim about the year 1823, and lived on the Grosvenor Wilkins place. (His father was Capt. Peter Butterfield of Revolutionary honor. Capt. Butterfield and his brother John filled a uniform in the Revolutionary army each six months alternately for years, as one of them must be at home, their father having died and left a young and needy family.) In 1853 he left Antrim for Nashua, from whence he removed to Beaver Dam, Wis., where he died in 1859. His children are : —

1. FREDERICK, [b. in Goffstown June 28, 1820, m. Elizabeth Hall of Merrimack, and d. at Nashua in 1847.]
2. FRANKLIN, [twin brother of Frederick, m. Eveline Blanchard of Peacham, Vt., and has for many years held a responsible railroad office in Boston.]
3. ELIZABETH, [b. in Goffstown May 21, 1822, m. John Russell of Hooksett April 5, 1844, and d. at Chester, Wis., in 1876.]
4. MARY, [b. in Antrim Jan. 6, 1824, and m. Nathan Corliss of Hooksett.]
5. MATTHEW, [b. in Antrim Jan. 25, 1826, and m. Sarah A. Eaton of Ludlow. Mass.]
6. LYDIA JANE, [b. Jan. 11, 1828, m. J. B. Moulton of Weare, and d. in 1875.]
7. HARRIET, [b. Jan. 9, 1832, m. Charles Marden of New Boston, and is now living at Farley, Io.]
8. SAMANTHA ANN, [b. April 15, 1834, m. Alexander W. Henghins, and now resides in Boston.]
9. JOHN, [birth not recorded, m. Maria Hubbell, and now resides in Sioux Village, Minn.]

ISAAC W. BUTTERFIELD was son of Willard and Betsey (Orcutt) Butterfield, and grandson of Gen. Butterfield of Keene. The last named was a native of Westmoreland, and was for a time a judge in the state court of Vermont. Isaac W. married Naomi Shedd. Their children are : —

1. ANN E., [m. Marcus M. Smith, and lives in Keene.]

2. BILL C., [b. in Reading, Vt., March 29, 1845, m. Abbie L. Parmenter of Antrim in 1866, and resides here. Their children are : —
   *Eva M.*, (b. March 15, 1867.)
   *Charles F.*, (b. Sept. 5, 1868.)
   *George P.*, (b. April 7, 1870.)
   *Fred L.*, (b. Jan. 24, 1873, and d. Dec. 1, 1873.)
   *Elmer H.*, (b. Dec. 13, 1874.)]
3. BENJAMIN F., [m. Ella Vose, and lives in Bridgewater, Vt.]
4. BYRON H., [unm., and lives in Boston.]

GEORGE E. BUTTERFIELD came here from Manchester in the spring of 1870, buying the old Thomas Jameson place of Samuel Wilson. He was born in New Boston, May 19, 1844; married Emily J. Marden, a native of Francestown, June 30, 1864. He was son of Daniel and Martha M. (Caldwell) Butterfield, and grandson of Daniel and Sally (Warren) Butterfield. Daniel, Sen., died in West Deering April 22, 1877, aged ninety-two. He was son of Maj. John and Naomi (Stevens) Butterfield. Maj. John was an officer in the Revolution. Children of George E. : —

1. CHARLES A., [b. in New Boston June 9, 1865.]
2. MARTHA M., [b. in Manchester March 19, 1867.]
3. GEORGE H., [b. in Antrim Dec. 22, 1870.]

## BUTTERS.

WARREN BUTTERS, formerly of Wilmington, Mass., came here from Jaffrey in 1818, married Rebecca Stickney of Jaffrey, cousin to Dr. Stickney, and settled on the place now occupied by Mr. Wyman. He died instantly of heart disease on his birthday, April 16, 1856, at the age of seventy-six, leaving two children : —

1. ABIGAIL, [m. Isaac W. Alds July 19, 1836, and d. in Stoddard in 1865, at the age of 54.]
2. REUBEN, [b. in 1817 ; when a young man became incapacitated by brain fever, but retained the ability to read music and play the violin when every other faculty was gone. He now lives on the county farm.]

## CALDWELL.

SAMUEL CALDWELL was born in Newburyport, Mass., in 1756. He served through the whole of the Revolutionary war, during the first part as privateer, and had an unusual number of hair-breadth escapes and slight wounds. In 1788 he came here from Weare, and bought of Benjamin Gregg the Vose place at the Center, but in later years moved to the Dea. Worthley place, and died on the McFarland place in 1835, aged seventy-nine. He revered the memory of Washington, calling him

"That beloved man." He married Elenor Paige, sister of Lemuel Paige, who lived near him at the Center, and their children were : —

1. JOHN, [m. Mary Cleaves of Amherst, now Mont Vernon, sister of Dr. Cleaves. He traded at South Village in company with Jacob Miller, and d. in early life. His wife soon followed, and their two sons, John and Samuel, are both dead. John lost his life in the Mexican war.]
2. SAMUEL, [went South to live, and d. in Baton Rouge, unm. He served through the war of 1812.]
3. BETSEY, [m. Robert Forsaith, and had four children, Rodney, Eliza, Hiram, and Samuel C., all of whom were probably born here. They lived for a time on the Jonas White place, then went to Goffstown, and her descendants are now among the prominent citizens of Manchester.]
4. SARAH, [b. Feb. 15, 1792, m. Dea. James Hopkins April 13, 1815, and d. in 1856, in Milwaukee, Wis.]
5. ELENOR, [b. July 24, 1794, m. Aaron Kimball of Hopkinton in 1820, and died there in 1826. She had two sons: Horatio, for many years editor of the "Cheshire Republican," Keene; Aaron N., long editor of the "Pilot," Jackson, Miss.]
6. HANNAH, [b. March 25, 1796, m. Dr. Ebenezer Stevens in 1822, and lived in Boston until her death in 1824. She left one child, George A. Stevens, now a commander in the U. S. navy.]
7. FRANCES, [b. Sept. 20, 1801, and d. young. An old person says, "Those girls possessed an inherent goodness that attracted the love and respect of all."]

## CAMPBELL.

The Campbells were of Scotch race and characteristics.

JOHN CAMPBELL was the son of Hugh and Margaret (Kelso) Campbell, emigrants through England, whose children were James, John, Robert, William, and Polly. Of these, William settled in New Boston, and John, mentioned above, came to Antrim from New Salem (now Salem) in 1779, cleared the place where James Wood now lives, for several years occupying a log house near a spring east and below the house. There was no house or road between that and the Goodell place (Dea. Joseph Boyd's), and they were guided entirely by marked trees. He married Barbary Aiken, had a large farm, and built the present house in 1802. He died in 1843, at the age of eighty-eight years. Children were : —

1. JAMES, [b. Dec. 26, 1786 ; m. 1st, Rhoda Baldwin, May 28,

1812, who d. Jan. 1, 1830, aged 39; 2d, Martha D. Little, sister of Dea. Little, May 19, 1838. He lived on the old homestead, and d. Nov. 20, 1858. He was a trader in South Village some years, and was the first postmaster in this town. Children: —

*John.* (m. Eliza A. Dustin. Nov. 14, 1842, and went to Northampton, Mass. Their only child, John, has been for some years head clerk in one of the heaviest dry-goods houses in New York City, though but a young man. Has frequently been sent to Europe on business by the firm.)

*James*, (lives unm. in California. Has traveled the world over.)

*Maria,* (b. Jan. 14, 1817, m. A. C. Palmer April 16, 1848, and lives in Charlestown, Mass.)

*Luther*, (b. Nov. 7, 1818, m. Mary A. Brackett of this town Jan. 30, 1845, and now lives on the Jonathan Carr place. He has but one child, Edward P., who was b. March 26, 1850. and m. Fannie, daughter of John Moore Duncan, Dec. 26, 1877, and lives on the homestead with his parents.)]

2. JOSEPH B., [m. Rispah Baldwin, sister of Rhoda, and d. Feb. 3, 1827, aged 34. The widow m. John Huntington, Nov. 25, 1835, and d. at Branch, July 29, 1871, aged 78. The children of Joseph B. and Rispah Campbell were: —

*Robert*, (d. unm. Aug. 18, 1858, aged 41.)

*Caroline,* (d. unm. Aug. 6, 1853, aged 30.)]

3. WILLIAM, [m. Agnes Smith of Antrim, and d. in 1843. His children settled in New Boston, but soon died.]

4. DAVID, [m. Mary J. Cochran Feb. 13, 1834, d. in Charlestown, Mass., in 1866, leaving children, Kate, Fannie, and Clara.]

5. JOHN, JR., [d. in New Boston many years ago, and of him almost nothing is known.]

6. ROBERT, [d. unm. in St. Louis.]

7. NATHAN, [d. unm. in St. Louis.]

HENRY CAMPBELL came here in 1793 and opened a store on the John G. Newman place, in the east part of the town, where he traded eight years. In 1801 he was drowned while bathing in Charles river near Boston, having gone to that city to purchase goods. The building in which he lived and traded is now standing, attached to the rear of George A. Cochran's house. Two children of Henry and Amy Campbell were buried on "Meeting-House Hill" in 1793 and 1796. Nothing further is known of his family. He is supposed to be the Henry Campbell who signed the Association Test in Windham in 1776. His untimely death was a great shock to the town.

## CARR.

Three brothers, James, John, and David Carr, came here from Merrimack. When young they spelled the name Karr, and it so appears on the Association Test. They were sons of John Carr and Isabella Walker of Londonderry. The father's name appears among the signatures to the Association Test in that town in 1776. He is said to have been brought over with the first settlers of Londonderry, though a small boy. He had a brother James who was killed by the Indians in what is now the town of Bow in 1748. His half-murdered dog guarded the dead body of its master till the neighbors found it the next day, and even then fiercely opposed its removal.

DEA. JAMES CARR, the oldest of these brothers, came here in 1778, and cleared and settled where his grandson William R. Carr now lives. Dea. Carr was born in 1748 in Litchfield, though the home of his parents was in Goffstown. He was a genial, cheery, good man, a great worker, an elder in the Presbyterian Church thirty-four years, and died at the age of eighty-six. His wife was Ann Patterson of Goffstown. Their children were: —

1. JESSE. [b. Dec. 11, 1776; m. 1st, Polly Ayer of Francestown; 2d, Fanny C. Twiss, Dec. 3, 1833; d. in Lowell April 15, 1859.]
2. ROBERT, [b. July 11, 1779; m. Annie Stuart, and lived on part of his father's farm, the house built for that purpose being put up just across the road. It was afterwards moved down to the plain, and is known as the Woodburn Wallace house. Robert Carr d. in 1838. Had three children: —

*James*, (b. Nov. 3, 1803, and d. in infancy.)

*Susan S.*, (b. March 9, 1811, m. M. W. Stickney Feb. 25, 1834, and d. in Albany in 1848.)

*Oren*, (b. Aug. 1, 1815, m. Abbie W. Tyrell Nov. 19, 1840, and d. in March, 1877. Had seven children: Susan S., who was b. May 1, 1842, m. James Carter, and lives in Meriden, Conn.; Ann L., who was b. April 24, 1844, and m. John Johnson; Abbie F., who was b. Sept. 8, 1846, m. Henry Lawrence, and lives on the homestead; Orraetta, who d. in childhood; Lucy E., who was b. May 24, 1852, and m. John N. P. Woodbury Feb. 12, 1873; Orra May, who was b. May 6, 1856, and d. very suddenly May 12, 1875; and James Oren, who was b. Oct. 31, 1863.)]

## GENEALOGIES. 403

3. SAMUEL, [b. Feb. 13, 1782, m. Polly B. Reed of Litchfield, lived on the Dea. Bond place, and d. May 4, 1837. His wife d. Nov. 9, 1853, aged 63. Children: —
*Lydia N.*, (m. Robert Day Dec. 4, 1832.)
*Eliza M.*, (d. in infancy.)
*Louisa*, (d. aged 19.)
*Alonzo G.*, (machinist, m. Elizabeth Truell, and lives in Lowell.)
*Francis R.*, (m. 1st, Nancy McClenning; 2d, Almira Barker; lives in Springfield, Mass.; engaged in steam and gas pipe business.)]

4. HANNAH. [b. May 14, 1784, m. James Brackett, and d. March 21, 1867.]

5. JAMES, JR., [b. Sept. 28, 1786, m. Hannah Carr Feb. 14, 1811, lived some years on the Chessmore place, moved to Burlington, Vt., in 1839, and d. there in 1867.]

6. THOMAS. [b. April 12, 1789, m. Lucy M. Sawyer April 11, 1815, and d. in 1845. Succeeded his father on the old settlement. Children: —
*Susan*, (b. Dec. 26, 1816, m. Calvin C. Gould Sept. 8, 1842, and moved to Ohio, where she d. in 1873.)
*Alice*, (b. in 1818, became 2d wife of Alvah Dodge Sept. 20, 1855.)
*James M.*, (d. in infancy.)
*Lucinda S.*, (b. in 1822, and m. Samuel G. Dodge of Bennington Sept. 21, 1843.)
*William Reed*, (called "Reed Carr," b. March 1, 1825, m. Helen A. Coburn of Deering Oct. 14, 1848, and succeeded his father on the homestead settled by Dea. James Carr. His children are: Celia F., who was b. Dec. 18, 1850, and m. J. F. Brigham of Boston Feb. 17, 1876; Thomas A., who was b. Dec. 8, 1852; Sina M., who was b. Nov. 19, 1854, and m. Frank L. Parkhurst June 17, 1879; William M., who was b. July 1, 1856; Minnie S., who was b. April 27, 1858; Lucy A., who was b. Sept. 24, 1860, and m. Edward A. Cummings March 5, 1879; Walter H., who was b. July 16, 1866; Mary H., who was b. Sept. 1, 1868; George R., b. July 8, 1870; and Levi S., b. Dec. 3, 1877.)
*Thomas M.*, (d. unm. in Manchester in 1854, aged 27.)
*Sarah M.*, (b. in 1833; an invalid and great sufferer many years, almost helpless, though in girlhood one of the spright-

liest; yet her disabled fingers do wonders of fine needlework, and her sweet, cheerful, Christian spirit makes her everywhere a welcome guest.)

*Ellen A.*, (b. in 1837, and m. Benjamin D. Felch of Bennington Nov. 29, 1860.)]

7. ALEXANDER M., [b. Dec. 15, 1791, m. Hannah McIlvaine April 18, 1817, and went onto the old Robert Burns place near the former High Range school-house. Moved about in town somewhat, and then in 1839 went to Bedford, thence to Amherst, where he d. in 1869. Children : —

*Sabra G.*, (b. in 1818. m. Abram J. Twiss, and located in Manchester.)

*Lorenzo C.*, (m. Caroline Hastings of Amherst.)

*Elizabeth M.*, (unm., and lives in Bedford.)

*Mark M.*, (m. 1st, Emma Ferson of Goffstown ; 2d, Mary A. Clement of Hillsborough ; and d. in Manchester in 1872.)

*Hannah J.*, (m. Timothy Jones of Amherst.)

*Alexander M., Jr.*, (d. unm., aged 25.)]

8. SILAS, [b. July 17, 1794, m. Nancy Stuart, and went to Canada.]

9. JONATHAN, [b. April 21, 1797, and d. aged 3 years.]

JOHN CARR, familiarly called "Old John," the second of the Carr brothers in town, came here about 1780, and began the Oren Carr farm. He married Sarah Shackford of Newburyport, Mass., who died young, leaving three children. Her age was twenty-seven, and the year of her death, 1786. Married, second, Chloe Hickson of Sharon, Mass., and died in 1822, aged sixty-three. His widow, a woman of clear mind and accurate memory, survived him long, dying in 1856, aged eighty-eight. Children : —

1. HANNAH, [b. in 1784, m. Otis Howe of Hillsborough, and lived and d. in that town. One daughter, Hannah B., became wife of Cyrus Saltmarsh of Antrim.]

2. JOHN, JR., [b. in 1785 ; m. Polly Holt June 18, 1811 : began the Emery place in the west part of the town ; left that place in 1820 ; lived in several places, West Deering among them, but went to Elmwood, Ill., in 1855, where he d. in 1867. They were members of the East church, — "faithful unto death." Their large family was as follows : —

*Sarah S.*, (b. Sept. 4, 1811, and m. Daniel Willard of Harvard, Mass. He d. in 1854, aged 48.)

*Mary B.*, (b. May 10, 1813, m. Samuel Baker and went to

Lowell. He d. in 1855. Two sons, Samuel R. and George W., were officers, the former colonel, the latter captain, in the late war. She lives with them in Peoria, Ill.)

*Hepsibeth H.*, (b. Feb. 21, 1815, m. Joseph Closson, lives in Elba, Ill.)

*Hannah H.*, (b. June 17, 1816, m. Jonas M. Damon, went to Lancaster, Mass., and d. there in 1864.)

*Sapphira*, (b. March 18, 1818, d. unm. 1836.)

*Jeremiah S.*, (b. in 1820, m. Martha W. Merrill of Bromfield, Me., in 1847, d. at Elba, Ill., 1875.)

*Ottora*, (d. unm. in Lancaster, Mass., in 1848, aged 27.)

*Dorothy H.*, (d unm. in 1847, aged 23.)

*John*, (b. in Deering, in 1826; m. 1st, Fannie A. Wood of Merrimack; 2d, Cynthia Jones of Peacham, Vt. Was drowned in Lake Erie, Oct. 26, 1856.)]

3. SARAH. [b. in 1786, m. Ezekiel Flanders, went to Boscawen, and d. in 1810.]

4. ISABELLA, [town record has it "*Habilla*," m. Enoch Roby Jan. 10, 1811, and went to Warner.]

5. NAOMI, [m. Ezekiel Roby, Aug. 3, 1817; went to Boscawen.]

6. JANE, [m. William B. Walker, Dec. 2, 1819, and went to Warner where she died in 1830.]

7. JONATHAN, [m. 1st, Annis Dinsmore, Feb. 27, 1828, who d. in 1844; 2d, Jane M. Gregg, in 1846. Inherited the homestead, but after some years sold and bought the Twiss place, now Luther Campbell's. Moved to Hancock in 1852, and d. there May, 1858, aged nearly 58. His children were all by his first wife. One son, John Carr, m. Augusta Eaton of Boston, and is cashier of the First National Bank of that city. By the cruel fatality of consumption all the other children were swept away in early life. They were characterized by sweetness and promise, and were greatly mourned. Their names were as follows: Samuel D., who d. in 1853, aged 21; Mary A., who d. 1853, aged 17; Adeline, who d. in 1854, aged 15; and Caroline, twin sister of the last, who d. in 1856, aged 17.]

8. TRISTRAM, [d. unm. in 1834.]

9. MARGARET, [b. in 1807, m. Emmons Burditt of Lancaster, Mass., Nov. 5, 1833, lives in Litchfield, Ill.]

10. SHACKFORD, [went into U. S. navy, d. in Lowell, in 1837, unm.]

DAVID CARR, the third of the Carr brothers in town, considerably younger than the others, followed them here about 1788. He built a log house on the road south of the Oren Carr place, then occupied by his brother John. The farms of the three brothers thus joined each other. A big rock formed one side of his log house, against which he built his fire; and as there was no cellar, this rock is now the only mark of the settler's rude but happy home. After a dozen years, Mr. Carr built in the field near the river, and north of Dea. James. This house has been gone many years, but the Keene road was built past it, and the cellar may be seen now on the north side of said road east of Mr. Atwood's. From this place, he moved to Holderness in 1811, and died there in 1848, aged seventy-eight. The youngest son settled with his father in that town, the other four cleared and settled on either side of their father, all in a row; and hence the neighborhood was called Carrborough. His wife was Sarah Gardiner of New Bedford, Mass. Their children, all born in Antrim, were: —

1. THOMAS, [b. in 1790, m. Mariam Blanchard of Tewksbury, Mass., and d. in 1873.]
2. AMOS, [b. in 1798, m. Lucy Woodbury of Campton, and d. 1876.]
3. DAVID, [b. in 1801; m. 1st, Sally Bethel of Plymouth; 2d, Deborah Bedee of Holderness; d. in 1873.]
4. JACOB, [b. 1802, m. Harriet Bedee of Holderness, d. in 1845.]
5. SAMUEL, [b. in 1808; m. 1st, Sarah Smith of Holderness; 2d, Mary A. Hodgdon of Porter, Me.; 3d, Eliza Shaw of Holderness, and d. in 1874.]

WILLIAM CARR, cousin of Dea. James Carr, came here from Goffstown in 1787, and began the farm now David White's; built the house now on the place; married Ann Boyce of Bedford, and died March 18, 1840, aged eighty-three. His wife died in 1849, aged 93. Children: —

1. PEGGY, [m. Chandler B. Boutwell June 4, 1811, d. October, 1873, aged 89. An excellent woman, smart and vigorous to the last.]
2. THOMAS, [m. Elisabeth Gregg, daughter of Alexander Gregg, Jan. 30, 1817; lived in a house built for the purpose on the farm of his father, a few rods west of David White's; d. Oct. 15, 1837, aged 50. Children: —
*William*, (b. June 21, 1818, m. Mary L. Mitchell, lives at Hillsborough Bridge. His wife was from Lowell, and they were married June 14, 1840.)
*Sarah A.*, (b. Feb. 29, 1820, m. Willard Eaton of Francestown in 1842, and d. March 6, 1857.)
*Alexander G.*, (b. Oct. 7, 1821, lives in Boston.)

*Clark H.*, (b. Jan. 25, 1828, m. Caroline A. Gould of Stoddard, Dec. 1, 1853, served in the army, d. May 3, 1869, in Roxbury.)

*Nancy J.*, (d. in early life.)]

3. MARY, [m. Dan Dunlap Oct. 21, 1813, d. Jan. 9, 1819.]
4. WILLIAM, [b. in 1791: m. 1st, Mary Hosley of Hancock; 2d, Mrs. Martha (Parker) Gregg: 3d, Mrs. Mary (Wilson) Jenkins of Stoddard, May 24, 1842; d. Sept. 12, 1850. Was a capable and honest man, often entrusted with town business. Inherited the homestead of his father. Children: —

*Mary Ann*, (b. March 31, 1817, m. David O. White Dec. 13, 1838, lives on homestead of her father.)

*Benjamin*, (b. April 24, 1822; m. 1st, Ann Jenkins of Stoddard, Sept. 10, 1844; 2d, Angelia S. Moses of Portsmouth. Was photograph artist in Concord. Leaning out the window after some work, he lost his balance and fell to the pavement and was killed, June 9, 1877.)

*William P.*, (b. Oct. 6, 1831, only surviving child of second wife, is a man of note in Nebraska.)]

5. BENJAMIN, [d. young and was buried on the hill.]
6. SAMUEL, [d. young and was buried on the hill.]
7. ANN, [d. young and was buried on the hill.]

## CARTER.

CHARLES H. CARTER, son of Henry and Augusta (Marshall) Carter, was born in Amherst in 1825, married Maria N. Keenan of Rome, N. Y., and came to Antrim in 1860, engaging in the manufacture of the "People's Pump." To enlarge the business he went to Peterborough in 1870, but sold out, and returned to this town in 1876, when he enlarged and extensively improved the George Duncan place in South Village, making the public house known as the "Carter House." He has three children: —

1. CHARLES E., [b. in 1850, m. Julia Taylor of Lowell, and is now a druggist in that city.]
2. EDWARD A., [b. in 1853. Has been for several years a salesman for a Chicago firm.]
3. MARY W., [b. in 1870.]

## CASE.

DAVID CASE, son of John and Elisabeth (Curtis) Case, was born in Lyndeborough. His parents came here when he was eight years old. His father, John Case, was a native of Middleton, Mass., and a Revolutionary soldier, serving during the whole seven years of the war. He had a large family, was very poor, and his wife drove the cattle into the woods daily in winter to browse, this being the only means she had of keeping them alive. He came here from Mont Vernon in 1796, and died at a good old age in 1828. David Case married Huldah Curtis, who died July 28, 1879, aged ninety-three. He lived in various places in town and died in 1867, having two children : —

1. BENJAMIN, [who d. in 1856 at the age of 28.]
2. JOHN, [who m. Maria F. Coburn of Deering, lived on the Moses Duncan place, and d. there Feb. 22, 1858, aged 28, leaving three children : —
  Laura J., (b. June 22, 1854, m. William Ruffle, June 6, 1876.)
  Mary F., (b. March 10, 1856.)
  John B., (b. Feb. 2, 1858, m. Ella F. Ordway of Francestown, May 13, 1875, and now resides in that town.)]

HORACE CASE, son of Amos, and cousin of David, named above, married Almira Twiss of West Deering. He lived in several places in the east part of the town. Had two sons, George and John. Mr. Case was drowned at Hillsborough Bridge in the fall of 1858. He drove into the river by mistake, at a time of high water, and was carried down by the current. The road was fenced up, as it was not considered safe. But he *thought* he could go through. Was found half a mile below the Bridge the next day with his horse, in deep water, both dead.

## CAVENDER.

CHARLES CAVENDER lived here some years in the Jonas Wilson house burned in 1868. His first wife was a Nahor of Hancock. He married, second, Hannah Hopkins of Antrim July 6, 1822, who died in 1834, aged forty-two. Afterwards Mr. Cavender went to Bunker Hill, Ill., and died there in 1878, aged eighty-two. His son, David Cavender, is now living in that place.

## CHAMPNEY.

CHARLES C. CHAMPNEY, son of John and Sybil (Chamberlain) Champney, was born in New Ipswich Aug. 10, 1801; married Jane McIlvaine of Antrim Dec. 26, 1833, and moved from Amherst to this town in 1860, and died at North Branch Aug. 10, 1876. Was long a hotel-keeper in Amherst, and was a genial and friendly man. They had four children : —

1. MARTHA JANE, [b. Sept. 9, 1839, and d. Nov. 28, 1859.]
2. CAPT. CHARLES H., [b. Aug. 9, 1841 ; was a soldier in the Union army ; is now captain of the Granite State Cadets.]
3. JOHN S., [b. June 20, 1847.]
4. HANNAH M., [b. Oct. 4, 1851, and m. Charles Griffin of North Branch Nov. 2, 1869. They buried two little girls in one casket Jan. 6, 1877.]

## CHANDLER.

The Chandlers of America are descended from William and Annis (Alcock) Chandler, who came over from England in 1637, and settled in Roxbury, Mass., and afterwards in Andover, Mass. With other children they had a son William, who married Mary Dane of Andover, Mass. One of the sons of William and Mary (Dane) Chandler was named William, and married Sarah Buckminster of said Andover. These last had a son Philemon, who married Elizabeth Rogers of Andover. Philemon's son William married Mary Ballard of Andover, and their son Philemon came here with his large family from Albany, Me., in the fall of 1816.

PHILEMON CHANDLER was born in Andover, Mass., Dec. 14, 1783, and married Asenath Case of Albany, Me., in 1801, who died in this town in 1817. He afterwards married Mary Whiting of Merrimack, who became the mother of his four youngest children. He was a master-builder and first-class mechanic, and died in Boston July 14, 1847. His children were : —

1. Esther A., [d. in childhood.]
2. Philemon, [b. Aug. 31, 1803, m. Susan C. Patch Feb. 26, 1824, and lived in Bennington. He served in the Mexican war, and d. on his way home, at Philadelphia, in 1847.]
3. Jacob, [b. Aug. 31, 1804; m. 1st, Sarah Beetle ; 2d, Lovina Corner, and lives in Peterborough.]
4. Syrena, [b. in 1806 ; m. 1st, B. Allen Nay of Peterborough ; 2d, William Puffer of the same town.]
5. Thomas J., [b. in 1807, m. Elvira Wilkins of Reading, Vt., in 1838, and lives in Canaan. They have two sons, Rev. Frederick D. Chandler, pastor of the Congregational Church in Kensington, and Dr. M. H. Chandler of Woodstock, Vt.]
6. Vinson G., [b. in 1809. He was a sailor by profession, and d. in Boston in 1853.]
7. Martin L., [known in this town as Luther, was b. July 10, 1810, m. Mary Ann Bean in 1844, and was in trade at the Center for four years, part of the time in company with E. L. Vose. He d. at Caledonia Station, Mich., in 1874.]
8. William, [b. March 26, 1812, m. Ann Straw of Hopkinton, and lives in Henniker. He is a blacksmith, having followed that trade nearly half a century.]
9. John C., [was a plane-maker by trade, and d. in Cambridge, Mass., in 1836, aged 21.]
10. Isaac N., [b. in 1821, and d. in infancy.]
11. Mary E., [b. in 1823, and m. Lewis C. Wheeler in 1838.]

12. SUSAN E., [d. in infancy in 1826.]
13. LYDIA S., [b. in 1827, and is now a teacher in one of the public schools of Boston.]

## CHAPIN.

OBADIAH CHAPIN, grandson of Obadiah, and son of Obadiah and Lois (Rose) Chapin, was born in Granby, Conn., in 1795, married Mary G. McColley of Hillsborough in 1817, and came to Antrim in 1842. The next year he moved onto the place long occupied by the Chapin family, now Daniel Swett's. He died April 24, 1863, leaving children : —

1. HARRIET J., [b. Dec. 1, 1821, m. Isaac Manning, and moved to Nashua. The noted elocutionist, Mrs. Emma (Manning) Huntley, is her daughter.]
2. HENRY D., [b. Dec. 17, 1828, and m. Maria L. Hardy May 4, 1853, who soon d. He m. Thirza A. Davis of Nelson Sept. 4, 1854, who d. in 1859, leaving one son : —

   *Charles H.*, (b. April 2, 1857.)

   For his third wife Mr. Chapin m. Margaret J. Pitney of Sparta, N. J., June 28, 1860, who d. in 1869, leaving two sons : —

   *George A.*, (b. March 1, 1866.)
   *Earnest P.*, (b. Oct. 31, 1868.)

   His fourth wife, now living, was Martha J. Newman of Wantage, N. J., whom he m. Oct. 27, 1870, and they have one child : —

   *Maggie E.*, (b. in 1872.)

   Mr. H. D. Chapin has been quite distinguished as a school-teacher in New Jersey and New York, as well as in this town, where he now resides. Is confessedly a man of very scholarly attainments. Recently fitted up the poor-farm house in excellent shape, and occupies the same.]
3. MARIA L., [b. April 10, 1833. For many years she has been an invalid, and quiet sufferer, living with her brother, H. D. Chapin.]
4. MARY E., [b. May 12, 1835, m. Jacob B. Upham of Amherst Aug. 31, 1871, and d. in that place in 1874. She was a very superior woman.]
5. GEORGE C., [b. June 18, 1837, and d. Nov. 24, 1860. He was a fine scholar and devoted Christian.]

## CHARON.

LEWIS CHARON was born in Canada in 1822. His parents were Roman Catholics, but having been converted to Protestantism when Lewis was a lad, they were constantly annoyed by the Catholics. Their stock was injured, their buildings burned, and the old father persecuted and worried into his grave. Young Lewis obtained most of his education after he was put out to his trade. He was fourteen when he first saw the word of God. He was in college awhile, and was afterward a colporteur and licensed preacher among the French for some years. He married Sarah La Point of Sherbrooke, Canada, in 1865, and came to Antrim from Haverhill, Mass., in 1871, purchasing the old tannery at North Branch with the house adjoining, where he carried on the tannery business, making many improvements and repairs. He moved to Lawrence, Mass., in 1877; more recently to Stoddard. His children are: —

1. SARAH E.
2. JULIA A.
3. GEORGE E.
4. MARY L.

## CHENEY.

DEA. TRISTRAM CHENEY located on the old road from the Jacob Whittemore place to the Gould place, and only a few rods from Hillsborough line. Very likely he supposed his settlement was in that town, in which, alone or in connection with his sons, he also had another settlement. His house was small and low, and has been gone and forgotten long since. Tradition says the barn was moved over the line onto the White place in Hillsborough. Dea. Tristram probably moved to his settlement in Antrim as early as the spring of 1769, or earlier, as he was chosen deacon at the organization of the church in Hillsborough, Oct. 12 of that year. He always went there to church. Dea. Tristram is believed to have been the son of William and Abigail Cheney of Dedham, Mass., and was born in 1720, their home being near Roxbury line. He had four sons, Elias, John, William, and Tristram, Jr., and perhaps daughters. Some of these were grown up on his arrival here. It is not known how many of them were born in Antrim. Dea. Cheney seems to have had a residence part of the time somewhere near Hillsborough Center, though he resided here and was moderator of a town meeting, April 21, 1778. Elias will be noticed below. William went to Acworth and died there. John went to Ohio. Tristram, Jr., unknown. Dea. Tristram moved from Hillsborough to St. Johnsbury, Vt., in 1804, and died in Danville, Vt., December, 1816, aged ninety-six. His wife was a Miss Clapp of Dorchester, Mass. They first resided in Sudbury, that State, and came from that place here. Their descendants are very numerous, and in the highest walks of life. She was daughter of Noah Clapp, who willed her half his real estate, under date of June 20, 1751.

ELIAS CHENEY, son of Dea. Tristram named above, was the first settler of the Dimon Dodge place, near Cork bridge. He served three years in the Revolutionary army from Antrim, one year for himself, one for his father, and one for his brother John. He located on the above-named farm in 1778. He married, first, Miss Blanchard, who lived in West Deering; second, Deborah Winchester of Hillsborough. She was born in 1777, and died in 1853. Her father, Samuel Winchester, fought at Bunker Hill, and died at Danvers, Mass., at the age of one hundred and one years. The six youngest children were by her. Elias Cheney moved from Antrim to Cabot, Vt., in 1804, and died in Concord, Vt., in 1816, aged sixty-two. When he was in the army, Nov. 25, 1782, the town "Voted that Elias Chaney be allowed Twenty Dollars It to be paid in his Reats till hiss Reats Amounts to the S$^d$ Twenty Dollars." All his large family of thirteen children were born in Antrim. Have but limited information concerning them, and that after long search. Part has been furnished by B. P. Cheney, Esq., of Boston. The names are given in order below.

1. WILLIAM, [b. Dec. 31, 1787, m. Mehitable Carr, was out in the war of 1812 from some town in Vermont; d. in Stowe, Vt., 1874, aged 86.]
2. ELIAS, JR., [was probably twin brother of William; m. Nancy Carr; d. at Albany, Vt., December, 1845, aged 58.]
3. JESSE, [b. Oct. 3, 1788, m. Alice Steel Nov. 25, 1813; was a blacksmith by trade, having served an apprenticeship with Isaac Baldwin. He d. in Manchester, June 23, 1863. His wife was b. Aug. 12, 1791, and d. July 28, 1849. She was a sweet singer and leader of her part in the choir. Jesse Cheney lived quite a number of years at the Branch. Had eight children besides one buried in infancy. Most of them were born in Hillsborough or Francestown. He built and occupied the Henry Pierce house, Lower Village.

*Benjamin Pierce*, (b. Aug. 12, 1815; named for Gov. Pierce, who gave the boy three sheep for the name. They doubled the next spring; but as it was the year of almost famine in this section, they had to be killed and the boy lost his flock. B. P. Cheney now resides in Boston; has been remarkably successful in the express business. Has long been at the head of " Cheney & Co.'s Boston and Montreal Express." His boyhood was chiefly spent in this town, and he gives a clear account of the actors then on the stage here. B. P. Cheney married Elisabeth Stickney Clapp of Dorchester, Mass., June 6, 1865. They have children: Benjamin P., Jr., Alice S., Charles P., Mary, and Elisabeth. Mr. Cheney received the degree of A. M. from Dartmouth College. He has just honored himself by giving fifty thousand dollars to that institution. The view of the Steel place appears in this book by his gift. Has quietly been used to doing these

generous things. It has been said of him that he finished his education in the district school under Clark Hopkins; that he never aspired to political life; and that in religion, " he never got beyond the foundation, namely, that of being a sober, energetic, industrious, honest, humble, God-fearing man.")

*James S.*, (b. July 1, 1817; m. 1st, Augusta M. Osgood; 2d, Emma Knowles. He d. Feb. 16, 1873. Left two sons, Frank P., and Benjamin P.)

*Jesse*, (b. Nov. 19, 1819; is a farmer in Goffstown.)

*Gilman*, (b. Jan. 25, 1822, m. Mary A. Riddle. Is general manager of Canadian Express Co. Lives in Montreal. Has one son, William G.)

*Lucy A.*, (b. Jan. 11, 1824; m. John Plumer of Manchester.)

*Alice Maria*, (b. May 26, 1827, in Francestown.)

*Charlotte*, (b. July 3, 1829, in Francestown; m. William H. Plumer of Manchester.)

*John*, (b. May 21, 1833, d. Aug. 28, 1863.)]

4. JOHN, [m. Betsey Newton.]
5. JOEL, [m. Olivia Hills, d. in 1848.]
6. SARAH, [m. 1st, Rev. Benjamin Wells of Concord, Vt.; 2d, Rev. Mr. Capron of Hardwick, Vt.; d. in 1878.]
7. LUCY, [m. Jesse Wells.]
8. BETSEY, [m. John Hunter.]
9. CLARA, [m. Samuel Stiles.]
10. LEMUEL.
11. HANNAH, [m. Samuel Hill.]
12. ROXANNA, [m. Rev. Calvin Stiles.]
13. FRANKLIN, [m. Sarah Abrahams, lives in Lowell, Mass.]

## CHESSMORE.

RANSOM S. CHESSMORE, son of Daniel and Mary (Gibson) Chessmore of Troy, Vt., was born in that town, Sept. 27, 1812. He married Eliza L. Plummer of Rindge in 1847, and moved to Antrim in 1855. Mrs. Chessmore died in 1861, and Mr. C. afterwards married Mrs. Caroline (True) Wilson of Francestown, sister of the late Mark True of this town.

## CHRISTIE.

SAMUEL CHRISTIE, born Feb. 20, 1764, was son of Dea. Jesse and Mary (Gregg) Christie of New Boston. His mother was a sister of Samuel Gregg who settled at the Center in 1777 or earlier. She was a noted woman in New Boston, had a family of twelve children, several of whom settled in New Brunswick; was one remembered by the old people as a noble and devoted Christian of great kindness and full of good works; and was often spoken of on account of her great size. The writer remembers hearing it said in his boyhood that she weighed upwards of three hundred and fifty pounds, and that when she died the narrow doors of her house had to be widened to make a passage for her coffin! Samuel was the third child; was born in New Boston in 1764, and followed his uncle Samuel Gregg to Antrim in 1788. He purchased a large tract of land next east of the cemetery at the old Center, and built there a small, low house in the fall of that year. His father, Dea. Jesse Christie, was a mill-owner and carpenter, well off in the world, and no doubt aided the youthful pioneer on the top of Meeting-House Hill. Near the close of 1788, he received a companion in his new home, in the person of Miss Zibiah Warren of New Boston. She also was very "young and fair," as traditions say. She was the third child of Josiah and Jane (Livingston) Warren and was born in New Boston, 1771. After a few years Mr. Christie put up the large, old-fashioned tavern so long known on the line. It stood some forty rods north of the cemetery, on the opposite side, and a little off from the road. It had the large square rooms, enormous fire-places, and long dancing-hall usual in such buildings. Here he "kept tavern" for many years. There was then, before the day of railroads, considerable travel through the town. Mr. Christie also did a large business on the frequent training-days, and at town meetings; and traditions assure us that on cold Sabbaths many of Mr. Whiton's hearers from the church near by were able better to warm up with the subject by visiting the bar of said tavern! Here for some years the older persons had a Bible-class on the Sabbath under charge of Mr. Whiton. The tavern was amazingly handy. Here Mrs. Zibiah Christie died in 1813. The second wife was Elizabeth Campbell of New Boston, who on the death of her husband returned to that town, and survived him more than forty years. Mr. Christie and his wife joined the church in 1800. He died in the prime of manhood, Oct. 25, 1818. His children were all by first wife and were as follows: —

1. DANIEL M., [known in Antrim as "Miltimore," b. Oct. 15, 1790; worked on the farm and picked up his knowledge as best he could, having few advantages in preparing for his course of higher study. But he entered Dartmouth College in 1811, and was graduated in 1815 at the head of his class, of which he was the last surviving member. Studied law three years in the office of James Walker of Peterborough, began practice in York, Me., in 1818, but soon moved to South Berwick and thence to Dover in 1823, where he pursued his profession over fifty-three years! He died Dec. 8, 1876, having almost no sickness or loss of mental power till the day of his death. He was a remarkable man, of great intellectual power, and spotless integrity. Was one

of the few who were pursued by offices and honors, yet having no relish for them. Every office in the gift of the State is said to have been offered him, and twice the chief-justiceship of the New Hampshire supreme court was urged upon him. The degree of LL. D. was conferred upon him by his Alma Mater in 1857. He was considered the leader of the New Hampshire bar for a generation, and was one of the very ablest men ever produced in this State. The estimate in which he was universally held, is well expressed in the resolutions entered on the records of the court: —

*Resolved*, That we have heard with profound sensibility of the death of the Hon. Daniel M. Christie, the oldest and most distinguished member of this bar, who has by a long life of arduous labor, fidelity to duty, and spotless integrity in every relation of life, adorned and elevated the profession of the law, and imparted dignity and luster to the jurisprudence of our State.

*Resolved*, That in the long, honorable, and conspicuous career of Mr. Christie, — chiefly as a counselor and advocate at this bar, — distinguished by great learning, sound judgment, unwearied industry, and unsurpassed fidelity to every personal and professional obligation, we recognize those qualities which entitled him to the respect and veneration which were universally entertained for him; and that, by his wisdom, prudence, and conscientious attention to all the duties of good citizenship, he exerted a great and salutary influence upon the community in which he lived.

*Resolved*, That we take pride in recording our high estimate of his extraordinary intellectual endowments, his exalted principles, and elevated standard of private and professional morality, and commend his virtues and excellencies of character to the imitation of the members of the profession which he pursued with such assiduity and such remarkable honor and success.

*Resolved*, That we deeply sympathize with the family of Mr. Christie in the bereavement which has deprived them of an indulgent father and faithful friend, and respectfully offer them such consolation as may be found in the heart-felt condolence of the bar, whose leader and exemplar he was for nearly fifty years, and whose affection and veneration he had gained by his pre-eminent abilities and blameless life.

*Resolved*, That the secretary communicate a copy of these resolutions to the family of Mr. Christie, and that the committee present them to the court now in session in this county, with the request of the bar that they be entered upon its records.

These resolutions were put on record in these courts with unanimous approval. They were moved by Hon. Daniel Hall, who paid a beautiful tribute to his old teacher and friend. And so, covered with praise and veneration, he has passed away. Mr. Christie m. a daughter of Dr. Wheeler of Dover, and had six daughters, but no sons.]

2. JOSIAH W., [b. Nov. 6, 1793, lived some years on the hill, but settled afterward in the east part of the town ; was a carpenter, a man of boundless work, and great energy and strength of character ; amassed a large property, and was for many years one of Antrim's most prominent and influential men. He d. April 30, 1862, and was one of the first buried in Maplewood cemetery. He m. 1st, Fanny Boyd, March 16, 1824 ; 2d, Mary Bell, May 11, 1830. Each wife had two children, thus : —

*Francis B.*, (b. Oct. 10, 1824; m. Susan H. Emerson of Boston; was a teacher there; disappeared from that city in 1850, and has not been heard from since.)

*Franklin W.*, (twin brother of above, d. in childhood.)

*Dr. Morris*, (b. Aug. 29, 1832, studied medicine with Dr. Sanborn of Newport two years, then studied three years in New York City. Began the practice of medicine in his native town, May, 1860, and has continued with gratifying success till the present time, having a large practice reaching into many of the adjoining towns, and having fairly won a leading position in his profession. He m. Susan S. Hill of Johnson, Vt., July 22, 1863. They have one child, George W., b. Aug. 5, 1868. Dr. Christie is one having honor in his " own country," a liberal giver, and a worker in every good cause.)

*Mary A.*, (b. April 7, 1834, m. Thomas B. Bradford of Francestown, in 1861, and lives in that town. They have one daughter, Emma A.)]

3. MARY, [b. Oct. 24, 1795, joined the church in 1815, m. Rev. Levi Spalding Dec. 10, 1818, and sailed as missionary June 8, 1819; d. in 1874, after a service of fifty-five years, being the last survivor of the first company of missionaries to Ceylon. She was called by that people, " Our Beloved Mother." Mr. Spalding was born in Jaffrey, in 1791. He graduated at Dartmouth College in 1815, at Andover Seminary in 1818, and entered the service of the American Board at once. On their passage out there was a revival aboard ship and every sailor was converted. Mr. S. wrote a host of tracts in the Tamil language ; was author of

Morris Christie.

many of their best hymns, translated "Pilgrim's Progress" for them, wrote most of their school-books, and was of incalculable service to that people. For forty-five years he did not fail to preach a single Sabbath! He lived to see great success follow his efforts, and great numbers of that people in the fold of Christ. Yet he was a very unassuming and quiet man, making no bluster in all his work. There was something romantic and beautiful in their long life together among the heathen! They came to love that strange people; and though here on a visit in ripe years, they chose to go back and die with the charge God gave them. They deserve great credit as pioneer missionaries, and accomplished a blessed work, for which ages to come will honor them. His service was fifty-four years in length in Ceylon. He d. at the age of 82. Only one of their children survives them.]

4. JANE W., [b. July 19, 1797, m. Matthew A. Fisher of Francestown, Jan. 14, 1817. He died in 1853, aged 68. She is now living in honored old age with her daughter, Mrs. James H. Hall of Brookline.]
5. JESSE, [b. May 17, 1799, m. Zibiah Warren of New Boston, and they are both living in that town, having celebrated their golden wedding April 7, 1875.]
6. SALLY W., [b. May 13, 1801, m. Gilman Clark of Hancock. They have resided many years in Foxcroft, Me. He was for some time a teacher and missionary among the Indians.]
7. HIRAM, [b. April 11, 1803, d. in childhood.]
8. IRA, [m. Anna Collier, an English lady, lived in Dover, and d. there, 1869, aged 62.]

## CLARK.

JOSEPH CLARK lived in Antrim several years and was a soldier in the Revolution from this town. For some charge, probably for debt, he was arrested and thrown into Amherst jail; but the case was of so much interest that under date of July 9, 1782, Capt. Frye brings the matter before the committee of the legislature. By some adjustment he was discharged from jail and went to the front, and his land seems to have been taxed to his creditors, as the town " Voted (Aug. 19, 1782) Richard McAllister pay the Reats of Clark's Lot as it was Invoised to him." Joseph Clark's land was on the Contoocook north of Dimon Dodge place, or Cheney's, as shown by a transcript of a road, July 9, 1783, running " Between Chaney's and Jo$^s$ Clarkes Land to Nathan Austin's Land." He was probably the first settler on the tract afterwards Thomas Jameson's and David Parker's.

CALEB CLARK, son of Daniel and Mary (Bancroft) Clark of Temple, and grandson of Samuel and Sarah (Taylor) Clark of Townsend, Mass., was born April 6. 1798. His father died in middle life, and with his mother (who died in 1852, aged eighty-eight) and young sisters he moved to Antrim, in April, 1824, on to the place previous to that date occupied first by Samuel Sawyer, afterwards by Zadok Reed, and now occupied by L. T. Lovewell. He married Jane Sweetser of Deering (now Bennington), Oct. 31, 1837. They had but one child, a daughter, who died in infancy. Mrs. Clark died May 29, 1861. He died Aug. 31, 1870, leaving a fund of $1,000 to the Center Church, besides various other gifts to charitable purposes. He was a Christian man, highly respected by every one. His four sisters who came to this town with him are as follows: —

Mary Clark was born Aug. 18, 1799, and is the only survivor of the family.

Nancy Clark was born March 1, 1801, and died Nov. 22, 1869.

Hannah Clark was born Oct. 26, 1803, and died Nov. 14. 1869.

Azubah Clark was born June 27, 1804, and died Sept. 5, 1870.

These sisters all lived unmarried, most of the time together, in great quiet, peace, and love, being examplary Christians, very saving, yet liberal givers to all benevolent purposes. Each acquired property, and those who are dead each left money for the preaching fund of the Center Church. Mary Clark lives on the place opposite Eben Bass's (house built by Dr. Whiton), which her brother, Caleb Clark, bought a few months before his death, and where he and his sister, Azubah Clark, died within one week of each other. Mary Clark was one of the heaviest givers to the Center vestry, and has been a silent and constant giver to charitable objects. She has lived to see all her family committed to the grave, is now nearly blind, but bearing all her afflictions with fortitude and Christian resignation, and is still a constant attendant on divine worship, the last of a noble, devoted, Christian family.

WARNER CLARK came here as early as 1834, and soon after commenced the manufacture of bobbins at the Branch. That he was here thus early is shown by the fact that he was chosen hog-reeve at the March meeting in 1835. He stayed here only a short time, when he moved to Francestown, and was there a prominent man for many years, and filled various offices. He had a partner here by the name of Buss, of whom I have no information.

PRENTISS W. CLARK was born in Brandon, Vt., in 1828, and married Maria White of this town. He is a carpenter by trade, and under the firm-name of Clark and Duncan has had a share in most of the building in town for many years. He built his house on Bennington street in 1869. Now occupies the Dea. Baldwin farm. His children are: —

1. HARRY E., [b. in Greenfield in 1853, and m. Mary A. Day of Salem, Mass., in 1876.]
2. JULIA A., [b. May 31, 1860, d. May 27, 1879.]

3. HARVEY P., [b. April 4, 1863.]
4. MINNIE M., [b. June 7, 1865.]
5. EVA MAY, [b. June 19, 1870.]

## CLEAVES.

DR. NATHAN W. CLEAVES was son of Nathan Cleaves, who died in 1812, aged sixty-four. Little is known of his early life, or of where or when he studied for his profession, except that he was for a time under the tutorship of Dr. Jones of Lyndeborough. He came here in 1793 as the successor of Dr. William Ward, being at that time hardly twenty years of age. Soon after he married Jennie Hopkins, a cousin of Esq. James Hopkins and niece of Mrs. Dea. Isaac Cochran. He settled down where Dustin Barrett now lives. Built the large house now standing there. He was smitten down with a fever and died at the early age of thirty-three, leaving six children. Old people have spoken of him as a noble specimen of manhood and virtue; and of his wife as an excellent woman. Was a man of good talents, successful as a physician, and held in high esteem by the people, as one growing up with them, and meeting with them the struggles of the new settlement. Indeed, he got his death by a walk on snow-shoes across lots to see a sick woman in a log house that stood on the mountain northwest of the Artemas Brown farm. At his funeral, April 19, 1807, the snow was four to five feet deep everywhere, covering walls out of sight, and so hard as to carry horses anywhere in the morning of that day. It was an immense funeral, people coming from far and wide to mark the sad event. The long procession, on horseback and on foot, wended their way slowly up the old road from Daniel McIlvaine's to the cemetery on the hill, and there with great labor the body was laid away. But by this time the sun was so warm that water ran deep in the roads, and it was exceedingly difficult to return. The water ran into and filled the sleigh of Judge Tuttle. He was the manager, and his was the only sleigh, the widow and children like others being on horseback. The freshet was so sudden and so great as almost to prevent the return of those from the south part of the town and from Hancock. This part alone made a long procession. When they got down to the Saltmarsh bridge they found it was just swept away. Making a path with great difficulty down-stream across to the other road, they found the Miller bridge frozen firm, but the water was running two feet deep over the top of it. But the men, by wading across and leading the horses, got the women over, and they all arrived home wet and worn! As further showing this remarkable day, it is said the horses that drew the corpse gave out, and had to be left behind, while for the last mile the bearers and mourners themselves actually dragged the dead man to his grave! The widow married James Hopkins, Esq., in 1823. The children were : —

1. DORCAS W., [m. James Jameson, June 18, 1812, and died May 18, 1848.]
2. ROBERT HOPKINS, [b. March 2, 1795, m. Ann Jameson Sept.

24, 1818, and lived on the place where his father died. He was killed by a fall Dec. 2, 1843. Left five children: —

*Thomas J.*, (b. March 17, 1820, m. Annis Barnes. Lived in Antrim, afterwards in Stoddard. Was a helpless sufferer several years, moved to Hillsborough Bridge, and died there.)

*Calvin H.*, (b. Dec. 22, 1822; m. Ruth A. Kennea of Reading, Mass., and died in that place, Feb. 13, 1860.)

*Charlotte M.*, (b. Sept. 28, 1823, unm.; d. at the Bridge, May 19, 1879.)

*Abbie S.*, (d. Aug. 28, 1849, aged 18.)

*Gilman H.*, (b. April 8, 1836, m. Susan M. Preston of this town, is a carpenter by trade, now lives on the Zenas Temple farm, and has one child. Fred. J., b. Jan. 28, 1868.)]

3. SOLOMON, [b. 1800, m. Clarissa Bell of Bennington, Feb. 2, 1831, now lives in Keeseville, N. Y. Business was that of tanner. A most excellent and devoted man.]

4. JOHN, [b. Oct. 10, 1802; m. 1st, Marcia Ellsworth of Willsborough, N. Y., in 1835; 2d, Mary Ann White of Peru, N. Y., 1842, in which last place he lived many years, and had several children. He came back to Antrim to spend his last years, and d. May 1, 1875.]

5. LUTHER, [b. 1804, m. Sarah Cook, went West, and d. in Flint, Mich., in 1868.]

6. CALVIN, [b. 1806, d. in childhood.]

## CLEMENT.

STEPHEN G. CLEMENT, son of Jesse and Eliza (Glidden) Clement of Unity, was born in Lowell, Mass, in 1833. His father died in 1858, and in 1865 he moved to Windsor with his widowed mother and sister Nellie. The last died here Sept. 30, 1870, at the age of nineteen. She had rare accomplishments of mind and heart. Mr. Clement married Susan M. Butler, who lived but a short time. He moved to North Branch in 1868, and bought the Fox place. In 1869 he married Josephine E. Averill of Mont Vernon, and they moved to that town, much to our regret, in the fall of 1877. They have one child: —

1. GERTRUDE, [b. November, 1872.]

JONATHAN D. CLEMENT, known as "Dow" Clement, was son of Jonathan D. and Lucretia (Merrill) Clement of Deering, and grandson of Carleton and Kesiah (Dow) Clement, also of Deering. He married Vienna P. Dickey of that town. Moved here onto the John Shedd farm in 1870. Mr. Clement was out in the late war in the service of his country, and had some thrilling and terrible experiences. He was detailed to run a locomotive from New Orleans eighty miles, into Texas, and back, daily. At one time, to accommodate another engineer who wished to bury his dead child, he took a second train and stayed over night in Texas. That very night the rebels broke the connection and tore up the track. Clement and his associates were captured. They had lost several engines by "burning them too hard," and accused him of being the "d—d Yankee" who had spoiled the engines, and ordered him to be hanged to the nearest tree. While preparations were being made, he asked permission to say a few words. He was answered that he "might say a VERY few words,— couldn't stop to hear much." He then told the facts in the case, assured them he had never destroyed the engines, but was specially sent there to preserve them. His statement seemed so reasonable, that they granted a reprieve, and ordered him off, under guard, fifty or sixty miles to have his case investigated. He was ultimately acquitted of the charge, but detained as a prisoner of war for a long time. Was at last exchanged, and after various services and perils reached home in safety. His children are :—

1. FRANK O., [b. in Cambridge, Mass., May 5, 1854, m. Alma F., daughter of the late Dea. Shattuck, April 22, 1876. Was in business awhile in Manchester, now resides in South Village.]
2. MARY A., [b. in Weare, Jan. 13, 1869.]
3. JONATHAN D., [b. in Weare, Aug. 22, 1870.]
4. CHARLOTTE M., [b. in Antrim, Sept. 27, 1872.]
5. WILLIAM D., [b. in Antrim, July 4, 1874.]

FRANK CLEMENT, son of Jonathan and Betsey (Aiken) Clement of Warren, was born in that place in 1854, married Emily B. Walch of Merrimack in 1875, and came to Clinton Village, this town, in the spring of 1876. After a residence of three years, they moved to Hollis.

## COCHLAN.

MICHAEL COCHLAN lived in the east part of the town many years. He married a daughter of the first settler, Philip Raleigh. Cochlan had a long dispute about maintaining his father-in-law. Year after year by public vote the town "freed him of Reats" on account of his supporting the old gentleman. And even after Philip's death, the town "Voted (March 12, 1793), to free m<sup>r</sup> Cochlan of his poll tax in future."

## COCHRAN.

JOHN COCHRAN, a Scotch patriot and sturdy Protestant, son of John and Elizabeth (Arwin) Cochran of Londonderry, Ireland, was born in that city in 1704. His father seems to have shared in the memorable defense of the city against the Catholics in 1689. It is supposed that this John and his son, only fifteen years old, were the two John Cochrans that signed in 1718 the memorial to Gov. Shute for land in " New England that excellent and renowned plantation." But this is by no means certain, because there was another John Cochran, probably cousin of the son above, and somewhat older, who was one of the elders at the formation of the original church in Londonderry, N. H. This one, known as "DEACON JOHN," may have been one of those that signed the memorial. For some reason, the father did not come over; but the son came over, arriving here in the autumn of 1720, and settled in Londonderry (part now Windham), on a beautiful slope, at the base of which the cars of the Manchester and Lawrence Railroad now run. This ground has always been in possession of the family, and is now owned and occupied by William Davidson Cochran, Esq. At that time the forest was almost unbroken; and the family are justly proud of the courage and fortitude of that young man of eighteen years, and cherish the spot where he first pitched his cabin. His uncle, James McKeen (who married Janet Cochran, sister of his father), had previously settled a few miles to the north; and Peter Cochran, John Cochran, William Cochran, and Andrew Cochran, all near of kin, had made their clearings, though remote from the young settler of whom we speak. Neighbors were far and few. His life must have been hard and lonely. But occasional visits at his uncle's seem to have suggested some improvement, for in the course of time he married his cousin Jenny McKeen. They had a long life together, accumulated property, and did much for the good of the community. Mr. John Cochran, known as "Capt. John," was captain of the military company of Windham, was a man of integrity,— marked by force of character, and held in general respect. He died at the age of eighty-four, and his ashes lie in the old cemetery on the hill, in Windham. He left children: John, Isaac, James, Elizabeth, and Mary.

John, the oldest, married Annis Dinsmore and went to Belfast, Me.

Isaac, the second child, will be noticed below.

James, the third child, was born in 1748, married Elizabeth Nesmith (sister of Dea. Jonathan Nesmith, daughter of James and Elizabeth [McKeen] Nesmith, and granddaughter of James and Janet [Cochran] McKeen), lived on the old homestead, was a leader in town affairs, and died in 1822. His grandson, William D. Cochran, Esq., inherits the homestead. Another grandson, Isaac P. Cochran, Esq., married Martha J. Nesmith of Antrim, and lives in Windham. The last surviving child of James Cochran is Dea. Jonathan Cochran, now living very aged in Melrose, Mass.; but numerous descendants appear among the conspicuous business men of Boston, Melrose, and other places.

Elizabeth, the fourth child, married William Dinsmore, and was the mother of Samuel Dinsmore, governor of New Hampshire in 1831, 1832, and 1833, and grandmother of Samuel Dinsmore who was governor of New Hampshire in 1849, 1850, and 1851. She was also mother of Dea. Robert Dinsmore, the "Rustic Bard," and her descendants are very numerous and respectable.

The fifth and youngest child, Mary, married Andrew Park in 1774, and lived and died in Windham; has a large posterity, among them Hon. John C. Parke, a prominent lawyer in Boston.

It appears that there was a "Mrs. Cochran" in Londonderry who was a sort of doctress, but whether the wife of John Cochran, first named above, probably cannot now be determined, though her character and circumstances would seem to favor it. Matthew Patten of Bedford kept a diary from 1754 to 1789, a curious and rich thing, and in it occurs the following entry: "July 26, 1754, sent Benj$^n$ Linkfield to L. Derry to Fetch my Grindstone and to Mrs. Cochran to get something for Suses toe and Got a Poltice and some salve and brought home the Grindstone." As nothing more is said about "Suses toe," it is concluded that that humble member was in due time healed.

DEA. ISAAC COCHRAN, second child of John Cochran that grew up, was born in Londonderry, now Windham, April 23, 1742. The records speak of Isaac Cochran as "Constable" at the early age of eighteen. He married Ruth Hopkins, Oct. 28, 1765; moved into Antrim March 10, 1784, and was moderator of a town meeting Aug. 29 of that year. He had been an officer in the Revolutionary army, saw the surrender of Burgoyne, Oct. 17, 1777, and followed the flag till the war was over. Coming here he bought of Matthew Templeton the place now belonging to his great-grandson, George A. Cochran, Esq. There was a little barn on it, and the log cabin stood in front, near the site now covered with toolhouse and shed. Mr. Cochran built the first two-story house in town, in 1785, which stood till 1864, when it was replaced by the present structure. In 1786 he built the saw and grist mill which was long a place of considerable business in that part of the town. The magnificent elms he planted with his own hands the year his new house was finished, 1785. Is said to have brought the first wagon to town in 1815. Dea. Isaac Cochran was a man of strong and constant piety, of unusual Christian grace and knowledge, was chosen one of the elders of the church at its formation, was much in office, was one of the ablest and most trusted of the pioneers of the town, and was a man of warm feelings and genuine ability, which is abundantly proved by writings left behind. And there was in him, as in his nephew, the "Rustic Bard," a vein of poetic genius, which, under more favorable discipline, might have given him a distinguished name. Two pieces, not as being the best, but the briefest, are here given. The first seems to have been written after he had passed his eightieth year, at the request of one who sought a memento in rhyme.

"Forbear, my friend, nor once pretend
 To ask from me a song;
My muse is mute, my harp and lute —
 Alas! — are all unstrung!

"Like morning flowers, my mental powers
 Do wither and decay;
Though small at best, what I possessed
 Is flying fast away.

"Nor would I strive these to revive,
 Nor urge them to return;

>    My locks are white, and dim my sight;
>      This body seeks the urn.
>
> "This house of clay must soon decay,
>    And moulder in the dust;
>  This soul must fly to God on high
>    In whom is all my trust.
>
> "Farewell, my friend, my views extend
>    To those bright scenes above,
>  Where pain shall cease and joys increase
>    In rounds of endless love!"

At one time a friend of the deacon had the Western fever, — went out, got sick of it, and was glad to get back. The deacon goes over the several steps in humorous rhyme, at some length, and closes thus: —

> "Whatever place or case we're in,
>    Much ill may be prevented,
>  If we would learn like Paul of old
>    Therewith to be contented.
>
> "Contentment is a noble gift,
>    And happy the receiver;
>  It is the surest antidote
>    Against the Ohio fever.
>
> "That epidemic seized my brain
>    And set my thoughts a-roving;
>  My business overmuch curtailed,
>    Besides the expense of moving!
>
> "A rolling stone ne'er gathers moss,
>    But often wounds the roller; —
>  Now I'm resolved to live content
>    And be no more a stroller."

Dea. Cochran always signed his poems "I. C." He died in good old age, Aug. 21, 1825. His wife died April 11, 1816, aged seventy-three. Their children, all born in Windham, were: —

1. NAOMI, [b. Oct. 29, 1766, d. in Windham Dec. 17, 1783, aged 17. On the slate-stone at her head in the old yard in that town, is engraved an empty hour-glass; and under it a couplet in which the engraver curiously left out the letter "l" in glass, making it read, —

    > "My gass is run
    >   And so will yours."]

2. ANDREW, [b. in Windham May 13, 1769, was two years at Dartmouth College, but did not graduate. Settled on the

south part of his father's large farm. He built and lived in the house now owned and occupied by his grandson, Andrew Cochran ; m. Jennett Wilson of Windham ; d. Oct. 16, 1820 ; wife d. Oct. 10, 1851, aged 83. Had ten children : —

*Naomie*, (b. Dec. 3, 1793, m. James Wallace of Antrim, moved to Manchester, and d. there.)

*Nancy*, (b. Jan. 15, 1795, m. Thomas Jameson of Antrim, moved to Lowell, Mass., d. Nov. 23, 1846. Their son Andrew was ten years in the naval service and was a Union soldier in the late war.)

*Rev. Sylvester*, (b. May 8, 1796, m. 1824 to Hannah Symonds of Hancock, had four children, two dying in infancy. He d. March 14, 1860 ; wife d. Feb. 23, 1863. Both d. in Northville, Mich., where they had resided since 1844. Had two children that survived him. Lyman, b. in Antrim, at the Branch, Aug. 6, 1825, known as Judge Cochrane, was the older of these ; and the other, Miss Sarah A. Cochrane of Detroit, Mich., is the only survivor of the family at the present time. Rev. Sylvester was a graduate of Dartmouth College in the class of 1835. Studied divinity under Dr. Whiton, and entered somewhat late in life into the ministry, settling in East Poultney, Vt., where he continued pastor ten years. In 1837, he went to Vermontville, Mich., where he gathered a church and was five years pastor. Afterwards in several places, he was in the service till near his death. A writer from Vermontville, after forty years, says of him : " His memory is cherished here by many hearts." Another speaks of him as " loyal to his creeds without bigotry, and liberal without laxity," and as one " eminently useful and universally beloved." Evidently he was among the worthiest of the sons of Antrim. In his last years he was a teacher as well as preacher, and acquired considerable prominence as the founder of Northville Academy. Judge Lyman Cochrane, a native of this town, went when a boy with his father to Vermont, and thence to the West. Was graduated at the University of Michigan, in the class of 1849 ; and from Ballston, N. Y., Law School, in 1852. Settled as a lawyer in Detroit. Was early chosen to the legislature of that State. In 1873 he was appointed judge of the superior court, which office he held at his sudden death Feb. 5, 1879. He was a rare scholar, retiring, conscientious, and thoughtful. He was specially successful as a judge, being dignified, courteous, patient, industrious in the management and dispatch of business, and studiously upright. Judge Cochrane was m. Aug. 3, 1876, but left no children.)

*John,* (b. April 24, 1798. Was in trade several years in Boston and Roxbury, Mass. Went to New York City about 1825; was heard from only a few times after.)

*Isaac,* (twin-brother of John, traded in company with his brother John, in Boston and Roxbury; m. Mary A. Lynch of Roxbury. Inherited the homestead. He was a stonemason and mover of buildings; d. Nov. 8, 1869. Had children, Mary Ann and Andrew, both now residing on the old homestead with their aged mother. Andrew served three years in the rebellion of 1861, in the Thirteenth N. H. Regiment.)

*Clarissa,* (b. April 18, 1800, m. Aug. 30, 1827, Alfred Fairbanks. a merchant in Francestown. After his death, went to St. Augustine, Fla.; m. Dr. Andrew Anderson of that place; he d. leaving one son, Andrew, who followed the occupation of his father, and is a physician in St. Augustine. He inherited the homestead. on which he and his mother reside. which is an extensive orangery. From a letter to the " Boston Journal " in February, 1879, we clip the following: " Dr. Anderson's grove is one of the most famous in the South, and is exceedingly profitable. His residence fronts on a street charmingly embowered in orange, lemon, and magnolia trees.)

*Ann,* (b. March 2, 1802, m. David Holt of Lyndeborough, Jan. 18, 1838, d. in that town May 13, 1870. Had four children: Alfred, Andy, Frances, and Ellen. Alfred was a surgeon in the army of the rebellion of 1861, and is now a physician in Cambridge, Mass. Andy served in the rebellion, and is now captain of the Lafayette Artillery Company of Lyndeborough, and a farmer. Frances m. K. Curtis, and lives in Lyndeborough. Ellen is a teacher in Ohio.)

*Joanna,* (b. July 11, 1805, d. of spotted fever, April, 1812.)

*Mary J.*, (b. Sept. 25, 1807, m. David Campbell of Antrim, in 1834.)

*Lorenzo,* (b. Aug. 24, 1809. Went South in early life; when last heard from was boating on the Mississippi river. Supposed to have d. of cholera.)]

## GENEALOGIES.                                      427

3. JAMES, [b. in Windham, Sept. 5, 1771 ; m. 1st, Joanna Creesy of Francestown in 1796 ; she d. March 23, 1829, aged 54 ; 2d, Mrs. Hannah Gibson of Amherst, January, 1830. She d. Nov. 1, 1858, aged nearly 79. He inherited the homestead, except that portion given to his brother Andrew. Was a live man, one of great energy and force ; run the saw and grist mill in connection with his farm. Was noted for accidents and broken bones. By a fall from an apple-tree in the autumn of 1844, he being then seventy-two years of age, one leg was so badly fractured that it had to be amputated. After this he broke his ribs, thigh, and wrist, all by different accidents, yet he survived it all, and d. June 1, 1851, nearly eighty years of age. Children six, all born in Antrim.

*Andrew C.*, (b. April 20, 1797 ; m. 1st, Louisa, daughter of the Hon. Jacob Tuttle, Dec. 11, 1828. She d. Jan. 11, 1849 ; 2d, Mrs. Augusta Kinsley of Peterborough, Oct. 25, 1863. Was in trade in Boston and Medford, Mass., and afterwards in Hancock, where he spent most of his life. He moved to Peterborough in 1863. Was president of the Peterborough Bank from the time of its organization to the time of his death, and owner in a woolen mill in that town, known as the firm of Noone and Cochran. For more than half a century his reputation for integrity and honesty was unsullied. Was a pious, generous, efficient man, a friend to all. He d. May 30, 1865. He left but one child, Lizzie T., born May 5, 1830. She m. L. T. Minor, Oct. 15, 1857. Mr. Minor d. August, 1865, and his wife d. Dec. 31, 1865.)

*Ira*, (b. July 1, 1799, m. Clarissa Taylor of Hillsborough, March 4, 1830. She d. May 27, 1868, aged 60. In early life lived several years in Boston. Kept a tavern at the brick house near the East cemetery in 1826. Inherited the homestead where he and all his children were born ; run the saw and grist mill as his father and grandfather had done before him, until the mill was taken down in 1855. Was an officer in the troop, or cavalry, in the old militia days. It is said that the first and only bowling-alley in town was kept at the brick house by him and his partner, Hiram Bell, while they run the house as a hotel in 1826. A kind, genial, intelligent man, having the efficiency of his fathers, but laid aside in a great measure for years, by deafness. Had six children : Mary Eliza, b. Jan. 13, 1831, d. Nov. 29, 1832 ;

Mary, b. April 3, 1833; George A., b. Dec. 8, 1835, m. Etta
A. Chapman of Windsor, Nov. 26, 1872, occupies the homestead of his fathers, has been much honored by his townsmen with the highest offices they could give, year after year;
Clara R., b. April 24, 1839, m. John R. Whittemore, merchant of Bennington, May 30, 1866, who d. Nov. 20, 1875;
Caroline C., b. July 31, 1841, m. Benjamin P. Baldwin of
Clinton, Io., Feb. 3, 1869; and Ann M., b. Jan. 4, 1849,
m. Charles E. Eaton of Bennington, Feb. 18, 1875.)

*Mary W.*, (b. Jan. 10, 1802, d. of spotted fever, April 2,
1812.)

*Rodney*, (b. Jan. 8, 1806, m. Mrs. Ellen Dodge of New Jersey.
In early life lived several years in Boston. Went to New
York City, kept a hotel there many years; d. July 22, 1876.
Had children, James and Joanna. James served in the
rebellion of 1861, in a New York Zouave Regiment, was
badly wounded in the thigh; lives in New York City. Joanna
m. Gabriel Aguier, a captain of police in New York City.)

*Eliza*, (b. Dec. 24, 1809, m. Dr. Jacob P. Whittemore of Antrim.)

*James*, (b. Nov. 19, 1813, m. Kate Crosby of Milford, Nov. 23,
1853. Traded in Hancock, Marblehead, Mass., Dublin, and
several years in Milford. His health being poor, he went
South to recuperate, where he remained only a few months,
and on his return home d. at Baltimore, March 28, 1854.)]

JOHN COCHRANE of New Boston, nephew of Dea. Isaac, was the
oldest child of James Cochran of Windham, and half-brother to his other
children. His mother died very young, and he was taken in infancy by
a kinsman, Robert Boyd of New Boston, and brought up. He married
Jemima Davis (daughter of Benjamin Davis, a captain in the Revolutionary army, formerly of Goffstown); lived most of his life on the slope of
Joe English Hill, New Boston; was a cripple many years from rheuma-
tism, and died in Chester, Feb. 10, 1845, aged seventy-five. Several of his
large family have come to honor, though pinched and poor in early life.
Their mother was one of the most blessed of women. She died Oct. 7,
1868, aged ninety-four. Their children were nine, as follows: —

Hon. Robert B., who was born in New Boston, Oct. 24, 1794; married
Elizabeth Warren, daughter of Capt. Robert and Prudence (Butterfield)
Warren; was for fifty years a leading man in New Boston; was several
times state senator; several times representative of his town; for a long
series of years selectman; for half a century, justice of the peace; for
nearly half a century a school-teacher winters; was largely in probate
business; was a land surveyor far and near; was most of his life a Chris-

tian; long an officer in the Sabbath-school; and died May 7, 1878. Was a man of marked intellectual ability; self-made, having had very scanty opportunities in early life.

Polly, who married Moses Hall of Chester, was a most devoted Christian, left a large family, died recently at the age of eighty.

Mercy, who married William Haselton, a merchant of Chester, has two sons members of Congress from Wisconsin, and is now living with her children in that State.

Sophia, unmarried, half a century a school-teacher, now of Albert Lea, Minn.

Marinda, a teacher all her life, a woman of marked talent, a Christian whose influence was great, died unmarried in Methuen, Mass., in 1871.

Hon. Gerry W., long a merchant in Boston; on executive council of Massachusetts during the war. Married, first, Mary J., daughter of Rev. Mr. Batchelder of Haverhill, Mass.; second, Helen F. French, a magazine writer of note; lives in Chester; was a donor of Center vestry; one son, Rev. Harry Cochrane, is a pastor in New York.

Abigail, who married Jonathan Pressey and lives in Chester.

Hon. Clark B. Cochrane, born May 31, 1815. Studied at Francestown under B. F. Wallace of Antrim; graduated at Union College, 1839; married Rebecca Wheeler of Galway, N. Y.; was admitted to the bar in 1841; was chosen same year to represent his county in the State Assembly, and was constantly in office till the day of his death. Was in Congress several terms, but died in the prime of life, March 5, 1867. He was among the best speakers and ablest men that ever went out from our State.

Susan, who married David Mallory in January, 1843, and died in March of the same year, aged twenty-four.

REV. WARREN R. COCHRANE was the eighth child of Hon. Robert B. Cochrane, named above, and was born in New Boston, Aug. 25, 1835. Doing his best in a very humble district school, and at the fireside, afterwards by "boarding himself" at select schools here and there, he went to Francestown to finish fitting for college, and was graduated at Dartmouth College in 1859, and was twice elected tutor in said college, in which capacity he served till prevented by failing health. Mr. Cochrane was some time a teacher, and was licensed to preach by the Derry and Manchester Association, April 10, 1866. Was invited at once to Harrisville, where he preached, as health would allow, two summers. He began service for the Presbyterian Church in Antrim, Jan. 1, 1868, and, continuing in the same, was ordained March 18, 1869, as pastor, which office he now holds. He married Lilla C. Cochran of New Boston, daughter of William C. and Harriet (Crombie) Cochran, and granddaughter of Dea. Thomas and Margaret (Ramsay) Cochran, June 14, 1864. Has two children: —

1. HAYWARD, [b. in New Boston, Nov. 27, 1865.]
2. SUSIE E., [b. in Antrim, Nov. 18, 1872.]

CLARK B. COCHRANE, brother of Rev. Warren R. and youngest of the family, was born in New Boston, Feb. 9, 1843. Studied at Francestown and Meriden, graduated at Albany Law School in 1865, and at once settled in the practice of law in Gloversville, that State. Compelled to surrender everything by failing health, he returned to New Boston in 1869. The same year he published a volume of poems. He came here in 1873, into the house in Clinton built by Horace B. Tuttle, and at once opened a store on the premises, — the first store in Clinton. He was superintending school committee in 1875. He married Mary E. Andrews of New London, and has children : —

1. MABEL, [b. in New Boston, May 15, 1871.]
2. ROBERT B., [b. in New Boston, Oct. 5, 1872.]
3. BENJAMIN R., [b. in Antrim, June 21, 1875.]
4. WINIFRED, [b. in Antrim, Dec. 31, 1876.]
5. JULIAN M., [b. Oct. 8, 1879.]

REV. THOMAS COCHRAN, born in New Boston in 1771, was son of John and Elisabeth (Boyce) Cochran, and grandson of Dea. Thomas and Jennett (Adams) Cochran. The father of this Dea. Thomas was James Cochran, and his mother was Letitia Patten, both of whom took part in the defense of Londonderry in the great "Papal siege." This Dea. Thomas was born in that city in 1703, and came over at the age of seventeen. Came to New Boston in 1748, and was chosen elder at the formation of the Presbyterian Church in that town. Rev. Thomas Cochran was graduated at Brown University in 1799, and came here in the earliest weeks of 1805. He was so much loved by the people, that they gave him a call to settle in May of that year. He declined, however, probably for the reason that he was offered a larger salary in Camden, Me. He seems to have thought that God's call was in the line of fair pay. At any rate he was ordained in the latter place, September, 1805. The day of ordination was made, in that place, a day of horse-racing and carousing : one man at the public table was choked to death eating, and many were overloaded with drink ! The character of the people, as thus shown, is further indicated by the fact that at the close of his pastorate, in 1818, he sued the town of Camden for non-payment of dues and recovered $1,400. His wife was Mary Barstow of Hanover, Mass. He died of cholera, in Baltimore, in 1838.

NINIAN COCHRAN, a Scotch-Irish Presbyterian of excellent faith and character, highly recommended by his pastor on the other side of the sea, came to America in 1828. In the fall of that year he came to Antrim to live in the family of Alexander Parker, and remained with them, good and faithful, until 1867, when he went with some of the family to their home in the West, and died at Baxter Springs, Kan., Dec. 25 of the same year, at the age of seventy years. He was smart and respected, was unmarried, and about his retired life there lingers a mystery, which can only be revealed in another world !

## COFFIN.

PHILIP COFFIN came here in the early part of the Revolutionary war, and lived near the Gould place. After some years he moved away and nothing further is known of him. The house he occupied while here was no doubt a small house built by Tristram Cheney on the *old* road from the Gould place to the Whittemore place. The road was thrown up and the house taken down so long ago as to be forgotten by the oldest neighbors. They used to call their name Cofran. Philip was a savage kind of man. When he was dog-pelter, he made a spear with a hook on one side of the blade, so as to spear and pull up dogs as one would throw up fish with a hook, and actually put it in operation ! He had children, Philip, Mary, James, and perhaps others. We know not the mother's name. Some of the children remained a few years in Hillsborough ; but all are now gone and forgotten.

## COLE.

NATHAN COLE, probably son of John and Eunice (Spofford) Cole, was born in 1750. He married Molly Flint and came to Antrim, from Boxford, Mass., in 1792, living on the Jeremiah Hill farm, next west of the pound. He lived awhile on the John Gilmore farm (Whitney's), and a road was laid out from the Nesmith place to his house, Jan. 19, 1793. He moved to Hill, then New Chester, in 1802. He was a soldier at the battle of Bennington, and had a brother John who was killed at the battle of Bunker Hill. He died at Danbury in 1834, aged eighty-four years. He had five sons and four daughters. His first wife, Nabby Brown, had no children. His sons were : —

1. JOHN, [b. 1777 ; m. 1st, Jenny Gregg of Antrim, who d. in 1804 ; 2d, Sally Smith, April 5, 1810 ; lived awhile on Meeting-House Hill, then moved to Hill, where he d. aged 89.]
2. NATHAN, [m. Polly Nichols of Antrim, in 1805 ; lived near Linn Parker's a few years, and moved in the autumn of 1808 to Cattaraugus, N. Y., forty miles west of Buffalo. Thence, in the fall of 1817, they moved to Ohio, finally locating in Columbus, that State. Here he d. Oct. 21, 1856, aged 77. Was an honest and good man ; and left six children, the two oldest being born in Antrim : —

*Frederick*, (b. Nov. 27, 1805, is land surveyor, has been county surveyor, and many years county auditor, and lives in Columbus, Ohio. He m. Rebecca Jane Graham, a native of Virginia. She d. in 1857.)

*Alonzo*, (b. July 29, 1807, has six children, lives in Putnam Co., Ohio, and m. Sarah Caldwell of Ohio.)

*Hannah E.*, (b. Dec. 2, 1808, m. Washington Moore, and lives in Vermillion Co., Ind.)

*Thomas*, (b. Dec. 9, 1810, d. in childhood.)

*Nathan, Jr.*, (b. Sept. 22, 1815, has been register of deeds, or county recorder, at Columbus, Ohio, for thirty-two years, and is a man held in the highest esteem. He m. Mary Sayles of Rhode Island.)

*George N.*, (b. July 9, 1820, d. in infancy.)]

3. LEVI, [m. Polly Philbrick of Andover, Mass. He d. in Danbury about 1850, aged 74.]
4. MILES, [m. Sally Bixby of Hillsborough. Went to Illinois in 1840, and d. at English Prairie, that State, in 1860. His son Nathan was colonel of cavalry in the Union army.]
5. JEDEDIAH, [m. Parmelia Chase of Franklin, and d. in Hill June 25, 1860, aged 72. His son, Charles B. Cole, Esq., of Hill, has furnished most of this information concerning the Cole family.]

The daughters of Nathan and Molly (Flint) Cole were : —

1. POLLY, [m. 1st, James Smith of Hudson, Dec. 19, 1793 ; 2d, James Barrett of Hudson, and d. in that town about 1864.]
2. BETSEY, [b. Aug. 3, 1780, m. John Wadleigh of Hill, where she d. Sept. 14, 1867, aged 87.]
3. SUSAN, [m. William Winter of Danbury, where she d. about 1834.]
4. LUCY, [b. Oct. 26, 1791 ; m. 1st, Samuel Pillsbury ; 2d, C. Roach, and lived in Parkman, Me., being the last surviving child of Nathan and Molly (Flint) Cole. She d. Oct. 12, 1879.]

## COLLINS.

JOHN M. COLLINS, son of James and Sarah (Thayer) Collins, born in Boston in 1768, married Elisabeth Brackett of Peterborough, in 1799. Came here immediately, having bought the saw and grist mill at the Branch. This he occupied till 1806, when he moved to Hancock where he died in 1856. The four oldest children were born in Antrim. He had children : —

1. SARAH, [b. Jan. 4, 1800, m. John Tenney and settled in Hancock.]
2. JOHN M., [b. Oct. 4, 1801 ; m. 1st, Elisabeth Bradford of Francestown ; 2d, Abbie S. Dean of Dover ; lives in Peterborough.]
3. SAMUEL B., [m. Frances M. Wilson and settled in Lempster.]
4. ELISABETH, [m. Alonzo Hall of Hancock.]

5. LYDIA E., [m. Lewis Partridge of Dalton.]
6. REBECCA B., [m. Cyrus Partridge of Peterborough.]
7. JAMES H., [m. Harriet Way, is deacon of Congregational Church, Peterborough.]
8. LOIS H., [d. unm. in 1840.]

## COMBS.

WILLIAM COMBS, son of John and Margaret (Aulds) Combs, was born in Merrimack April 18, 1758, married Thankful Fletcher of Hollis, lived in Landsgrove, now Andover, Vt. There his wife died in 1800, aged thirty-four. Soon after he came to Antrim. He married Mrs. Margaret (Moor) Holmes, widow of William Holmes, about the first of January, 1801, and spent the rest of his days on the Holmes place, dying in 1840 at the age of eighty-two. The two youngest children were by his second wife, and were born in this town : —

1. WILLIAM. [m. Mary Jane Nutt of Manchester; had fourteen children; lived and d. in that city.]
2. JOHN, [m. Jennie Platt of Marcellus, N. Y., and lived and d. in that place; one son, Dr. Henry Combs, is a physician, in Adrian, Mich.]
3. SARAH A., [m. Thomas Stuart of Antrim, May 31, 1814, and was mother of Robert Carr Stuart. She d. in Boston.]
4. ABIGAIL F., [m. Dan Dunlap, being his 2d wife. She is now living with a son in Lynn, Mass., at the age of 84.]
5. BETSEY F., [b. Feb. 16, 1797; m. Gilman Swain, 1825; d. here at the age of 82.]
6. JAMES, [b. in 1800; went to Kentucky, and was a wealthy planter there before the war. Three of his children were educated at Oberlin College, Ohio.]
7. JESSE, [b. in 1801; m. Achsah Cram Sept. 3, 1829. After living here and there in town for many years, he bought the place now Lewis Green's, and lived there till his family was broken up by death. His own death occurred Aug. 8, 1875. Children : —

*Hiram*, (b. Jan. 16, 1831. m. Clara Dunlap, and lives on the Capt. Thomas Dunlap place. He has children, Iza Frances, b. Dec. 17, 1870, and Mary Eloise, b. Nov. 26, 1873.)

*James M.*, (accidentally shot dead by his father while taking a charge from a gun, in 1843, aged 7.)

*Mary J.*, (b. April 22, 1837; m. Edward Roach, but lived only four days after marriage.)

*Charles*, (b. Feb. 16, 1852; m. Mary J. Lyford of Lowell, Mass. They have one child, Warren W., b. Oct. 9, 1875.)
*Etta*, (an adopted daughter; b. in 1844; m. Lewis Simonds.)]
8. ELIZA J., [d. unm. in Cambridgeport, Mass., 1873.]

## CONANT.

JONATHAN CONANT came here from Mont Vernon in 1811, bringing a large family. He lived on the Dea. Shattuck place, and moved back to Mont Vernon in 1816, and died there Oct. 28, 1829, aged seventy. This was a very respectable family. We have but few facts concerning them. One of the sons was Israel Conant, who lived with his father, married Elizabeth Holt of Antrim, in 1815, and had two sons born here. He moved to New Haven, Vt., about the end of the year 1816, and died in Vergennes, Vt., 1857, aged sixty-nine. His two sons born here were: —

1. ALBERT, [b. Oct. 3, 1815.]
2. WILLIAM, [b. Nov. 25, 1816.]

JOSHUA CONANT of Antrim was born in Londonderry March 11, 1798. He was the son of Joshua, and grandson of Joshua who came from England. He married Rebecca Preston of Stoddard in 1824. She was the daughter of Samuel Preston, and was born Feb. 18, 1799, and died June 28, 1848. He married, second, Eliza A. Read of Stoddard, July 25, 1852. He came to Antrim in 1860. His children were: —

1. RUEL K., [b. Sept. 2, 1825; m. Julia A. Curtis, daughter of Levi Curtis, Oct. 6, 1851, and went to Springfield, Mass., where he has since resided with the exception of a brief sojourn in Boston. Has three children, Ella R., George W., and Mary L. Is passenger conductor on the railroad between Springfield, Mass., and New Haven, Conn., and has been for many years; has been in constant service traveling on the rail for upwards of thirty years, commencing Dec. 29, 1848.]
2. HIRAM P., [b. Sept. 18, 1830; went West in 1853, finally locating in Pittsburg, Penn., where he m. —— Kelley, and now lives.]
3. FREEMAN C., [b. Aug. 3, 1837; went to Vermont, and was currier by trade. At the breaking-out of the rebellion he went into the army, and served through the entire war, after which he settled in Wilton, Io., where he now lives. He m. Alice C. Stryker.]
4. ABILENE, [by 2d wife; b. Stoddard, April 17, 1855; m. Willard A. Paige of Munsonville, Oct. 1, 1873.]
5. AUGUSTA, [d. in childhood.]

SAMUEL A. CONANT, of whom I can learn nothing more, came here and built the last house on the canal, at the top of the hill in South Village. The large basement was for a wheelwright-shop. Conant lived but a short time after the building was up, dying with consumption, brought on, it was said, by exposure in trying to build in winter.

## CONN.

The ancestor of the Conn family in New England was George Conn, who came from the north of Ireland and settled in Harvard, Mass., that part called Stillwater, where he spent and ended his days. He had a large family, and among them a son George, who married Martha Kelso of Derry, settled in Harvard, and raised up a family of nine children. The oldest of this large household was John. John Conn married Lucy Sawyer of Boxborough, Mass., and lived in Harvard, Mass., Charlestown, Mass., Goshen and Bethlehem. He died in Milford in 1820, aged forty-nine. His wife died the preceding year in Bethlehem, aged forty-two. Their seven children we will now name : John, who married Philo Fairbanks, and died in 1869, aged seventy-two; Emery, who married Edith Davenport of Ashby, Mass.; Lucy, who married David Baker of Goffstown, and died in 1820; Jefferson, who will be noticed below; Thomas, who married Malinda Sampson of Hanson, Mass., and died in 1846, aged forty-three ; Almira, who died in 1852, aged forty-five, unmarried ; and Abigail, who married Morris Kelly of Charlestown, Mass., and now lives in that place.

JEFFERSON CONN, cousin of Dea. Charles Conn of Hillsborough, and Dr. Granville P. Conn of Concord, son of John and Lucy (Sawyer) Conn, was born in Charlestown, Mass., in 1802. He married Mary Ann McClintock of Hillsborough. Her father, John McClintock, died in that town in 1803. Jefferson came here from Stoddard to the Eber Curtis place in 1854, where he lived till his death, which occurred Aug. 20, 1858. His wife died there June 1, 1869, aged seventy-four. Their children were as follows : —

1. NANCY J., [b. Oct. 14. 1825 ; became 2d wife of Solomon H. Griffin, and d. Nov. 30, 1855.]
2. WILLIAM M., [b. May 9, 1827 ; m. 1st, Margaret A. Boutwell, April 9, 1854, an excellent woman, who died very suddenly of diphtheria Feb. 16, 1876 ; m. 2d, Mrs. Augusta (Smith) Carr, July 26, 1877. He occupies the Chandler B. Boutwell place. Has children : —
    *Clara A.*, (b. Oct. 23, 1855.)
    *Mary E.*, (b. March 24, 1860.)
    *Martha E.*, (twin-sister of Mary ; d. very suddenly of diphtheria, Feb. 24, 1876. A pious and amiable girl, whose early death was mourned by the whole community.)]

3. ANGELINE, [b. Windsor, Oct. 21, 1833; m. Hiram McIlvaine, Nov. 10, 1853.]
4. CHESTER A., [b. Windsor, July 7, 1835; m. Harriet McIlvaine, daughter of B. F. McIlvaine, 1867; inherits the homestead of his father; has children: —
*Nora May*, (b. Feb. 20, 1870.)
*Effie I.*, (b. July 11, 1873.)]
5. FREEMAN, [b. Windsor, Nov. 12, 1837; m. Etta Stevens of Stoddard; now lives in Keene; is blacksmith by trade.]

## COOLEDGE.

The Cooledge family were located in Cambridgeshire, England, probably as early as six hundred years ago. The name in the several centuries has been variously spelled, as Coolyng. Coolidg, Colynge, Cooladge, etc. Walter and Ralph *Coolyng* were assessed on the subsidy rolls for land in Wimpole, Cambridgeshire, in 1327. In the reign of Henry VIII. (1509-1547) the family was located in Arrington, and was a family of distinction and respectability. The records of Cottenham, Cambridgeshire, show that Simon Cooledge married Agnes Kingston. The will of this Simon, dated 1591, mentions three children: William, John. and Thomas.

William, the eldest, died in 1620, having had six children: Richard, William, Simon, John, Elisabeth, and Margaret. The fourth of these, John, was baptized Sept. 16, 1604, came to America and settled in Watertown, Mass. Was admitted a freeman there, May 25, 1636; was among the early proprietors of that place. Was very often selectman from 1636 to 1677. Was representative of the town in 1658. His will, which was proved June 16, 1691, mentions his wife, *Mary*, and four sons, John, Stephen, Nathaniel, and Jonathan. Nathaniel, the third son, married Mary Bright, Oct. 15, 1657, and died in 1711 leaving twelve children. The second of these was Nathaniel, who was born May 9, 1660. and married Lydia Jones, Jan. 2, 1687. He settled in Watertown Farms, now Weston, Mass., and his name is the first on the roll of the original members of the Weston church. He had six children. Josiah, the third of these children, married Deliverance Warren, June 11, 1719. She died Feb. 25, 1764, and he married, second, Mrs. Sarah Muzzey in 1766, and died leaving seven children. Nathaniel, the oldest child of Josiah, was born Oct. 20, 1724, and married Sarah Parker of Sudbury, Mass., April 16, 1749. They had children: Susanna, Paul (born Oct. 20, 1751), Lucy, Silas (born Nov. 14, 1755, was out in the Revolutionary army), Anna, Eunice, Uriah, and Nathaniel. The last named is the one that lived some years in the east part of Antrim, and will be further noticed below. He was born in Weston, Mass., Nov. 19, 1768, and died in Norwich, Vt., at the age of seventy-nine.

DANIEL COOLEDGE, son of Paul and Martha (Jones) Cooledge, and grandson of Nathaniel and Sarah (Parker) Cooledge, was born March 10, 1788. His parents were married April 19, 1784. He married Polly

Spalding Sept. 20, 1808. In 1809 he moved to North Branch and commenced blacksmithing on the stand now owned by D. P. Bryer, where he worked twenty years. He then bought, of Charles Barker, the place the Cooledge family now occupy, and built a second house on the same in 1849. He died Feb. 25. 1869, leaving a large family, all of them characterized by piety and usefulness.

1. MARY. [b. in 1809, m. William S. Foster Nov. 28, 1858.]
2. ABIGAIL, [b. in 1811, and lives unm. on the old place.]
3. CHARLES, [b. in 1813, m. Mary P. Covill, and d. Aug. 2, 1872, leaving two children : —
    *Abby*, (who m. James Richardson in 1871; d. May 28, 1880.)
    *Albert W.*, (who m. Alma J. Severance in 1875, and lives in Washington.)]
4. CLARISSA, [b. in 1816, m. Benjamin Spalding April 3, 1840, and lives in Chelmsford, Mass.]
5. DANIEL, [b. in 1818, m. Lucy W. Ray of Hopkinton, lived in Chicopee, Mass., and d. in 1869.]
6. SARAH, [b. in 1821, and d. unm., after years of sickness and suffering, in 1868.]
7. ISAAC, [d. in infancy.]
8. FRANKLIN S., [b. in 1826, m. Amanda Burrill of China, Me., and now lives in Lowell, Mass.]
9. JACOB S., [b. in 1829, m. Mary W. Raymond of Nashua, and now lives in Lowell.]
10. MARTHA J., [b. in 1831, and was for many years an invalid. She now lives with her sister on the old homestead, spending life in faithful care of their aged mother.]

NATHANIEL COOLEDGE came here from Hillsborough in 1803, and lived in the old McCoy house on the Gould place. He was an uncle of Daniel Cooledge of Antrim, and brother of Paul Cooledge. The father of Nathaniel and Paul, was Nathaniel; and their mother was Sarah Parker; and they were among the early settlers of Hillsborough. The Nathaniel who came to Antrim in 1803, married Rachel Andrews of Hillsborough, moved back to Hillsborough in 1807, and died Jan. 16, 1847. They had thirteen children, nine of whom grew up, as follows : —

1. NATHANIEL, JR., [b. Aug. 14, 1796, was police officer and jailer most of his long life ; was some years U. S. detective, traveling far and wide. His home was in Boston. He d. Aug. 3, 1864.]
2. ISAAC, [most of his life a jailer, or on the police force of Boston.]

3. PERKINS, [b. in 1800, lives unm. in Deering.]
4. HENRY, [no information.]
5. LUCY. [b. in Antrim July 30, 1805, m. Walter B. Lewis, and they now live in Ayer, Mass.]
6. JULIANNA, [m. Samuel K. Martin of Hillsborough.]
7. BETSEY, [m. Amos Jones, and d. in Wilmot.]
8. GEORGE, [U. S. constable and detective, d. in Boston in 1877.]
9. RACHEL, [m. Hiram Morgan of Rutland, Vt.]

## COOPER.

STEPHEN COOPER, an old sailor, came here from Salem, Mass., about 1810, and lived on the mountain west of the Capt. Worthley place. After several years he moved to Francestown. He buried two wives here before his removal. At the funeral of the second wife the horse ran away with the coffin and threw it out over the fence, breaking it in pieces. It was a steady old horse, never known to run before, and the good women asked: "Isn't this a judgment for her cruelty to the first wife's children?" Nothing is now known of his family. His children, as given on the town record, were:—

1. STEPHEN, [b. in Salem, Mass., Jan. 15, 1803, came back here and d. on the poor-farm.]
2. MARY, [b. in Salem, Mass., March 5, 1806.]
3. SAMUEL B., [b. Oct. 1, 1811.]
4. BETSEY H., [b. Jan. 29, 1814.]
5. EDAH, [b. Nov. 6, 1817.]
6. JACOB WILLIAM, [b. June 30, 1819.]

## COREY.

AMOS COREY, son of Amos and Achsah (Townsend) Corey, was born in Washington in 1802; married Roxanna Wright of Sullivan, and moved to Antrim in 1857, where he died in 1872, leaving children:—

1. ACHSAH L., [b. in Washington in 1828, and m. Peter Shuttleworth of Southborough, Mass.]
2. OLIVE W., [d. in 1872 at the age of 42, unm.]
3. MELINDA A., [d. in 1861 at the age of 30.]
4. GEORGE F., [b. in Washington in 1836; m. Clara R. Hill of this town in 1860, and resided several years in Waltham, Mass., working in the watch-factory. Having inherited the old homestead at South Antrim, in 1876 he returned to this town, and engaged in business as a jeweler in that village.]

## COSTELLO.

THOMAS COSTELLO, an Irish emigrant, came here about 1820. Had been in the English army, and was twice wounded at the battle of Waterloo. He married Mrs. Ann (Nichols) Emerson Sept. 21, 1826; lived in several places in town; had two children; cannot learn the time or place of his death. His children were: —

1. ELVIRA. [m. James Foote of Francestown.]
2. MARY, [m. James Preston of Concord.]

## CRAM.

ASAHEL CRAM, son of Dyer Cram of Weare, came here from Francestown in 1795; married Lydia Lewis of Weare, and moved into a house now gone. between Frank Robinson's and S. A. Holt's; afterwards lived on the Prescott Parmenter place (next above the pound), and died in 1835 at the age of sixty-nine. His children were: —

1. ROXANNA. [b. Dec. 12. 1799, and d. unm. in Natick, Mass., in 1863.]
2. ABNER, [b. Nov. 22, 1801; m. Nancy Jones of Windsor, and lived on the Ambrose Story place awhile, when he moved on to the place now George F. McIlvaine's, where he d. in 1830, leaving five children: —
   *Charles B.*, (b. Oct. 4, 1822; m. Elizabeth S. Simonds, and lived in Nashua several years, where the three eldest children were born. He afterwards came to Antrim and built near Lovering's mills. He is a blacksmith by trade, and has five children: Charles E.; Ina S.; Ira S.; Ida J., who was b. Sept. 26, 1859, and m. James A. Salesbury of Greenville, R. I., in 1876; and Reed S.)
   *Abner G.*, (b. June 28, 1824; when last heard from lived in Orange.)
   *Philura S.*, (b. in 1826; m. William Baker of Andover, Mass., and now lives in that place.)
   *Ira D.*, (b. April 27, 1827, and went to sea in early life. After his return he m. Angeline Morse; lived a few years at South Village, and had two children born here: George F. and Madison. In 1860 he moved to Johnson, R. I.)
   *John A.*, (b. Feb. 16, 1829; m. Lydia Thornton of Johnson, R. I., and now lives in that place.)]
3. ABIGAIL H., [b. April 7, 1807, and d. unm. in Natick, Mass., in 1867.]

4. ACHSAH L., [b. Aug. 12, 1809; m. Jesse Combs Sept. 3, 1829, and d. in 1867.]
5. DANIEL, [b. in 1814; m. Mary Blackman, and moved to Elktown, Ohio.]

## CRANE.

JAMES CRANE (the eighth and youngest child of Joseph and Deliverance (Mills) Crane, who came from Milton, Mass.) was born in Washington, June 21, 1799; married Fanny D. Sayward of Gloucester, Mass., March 6, 1828; and came here from Washington January, 1849, into the brick house known as the Cummings place. He died here July 20, 1851, and his wife died in Boston recently. They left two children:—

1. ELIZABETH S., [b. in Washington May 11, 1829; m. Henry McCoy of Sharon, Jan. 8, 1850, and resides in South Boston.]
2. HENRIETTA M., [b. in Washington March 8, 1831; m. Samuel A. Fletcher of Antrim, April 29, 1851, and now resides in Bunker Hill, Ill.]

ALFRED CRANE, son of Joseph and Hannah (Mills) Crane, was born in East Washington July 1, 1821; married, first, Almira Nichols; married, second, Roxanna, her sister. Resides in Merrimac, Mass. Has two children, Frederick and Clarence, neither of whom were born here. He came to Antrim in the year 1858 and lived on the Benjamin Nichols place, but remained but little more than two years.

## CROSS.

NATHAN CROSS came here about 1790 and settled on what is now known as the Steel place, west of the pond. He had lived before in the town of Hudson, which belonged to Massachusetts till 1741. At this last date, or a little later, his name appears on a petition to Gov. Wentworth for a new township, which was incorporated as Nottingham West July 5, 1746. Mr. Cross sold about 1798 and moved to Amherst. But little is known of him. The house in which he lived here stood a few rods north of the present house and on the opposite side of the road at the end of the lane leading down to the James Nesmith place.

## CUMMINGS.

EBENEZER CUMMINGS, son of Dea. Ebenezer and Sarah (Stevens) Cummings of Hudson, was born in that town in 1768. He came here at the age of twenty-three and began the farm west of the pond, long occupied by John R. Hill. He married Lettice Andrews, who died July 1, 1858, at the age of ninety-five, and whose mother, fleeing from the Indians as they attacked her house, was caught by the hair, dragged to a block and her head chopped off. Mr. Cummings died in 1815, at the age of forty-seven. His children were:—

1. ENOCH, [b. Feb. 5, 1796, and killed by the fall of a tree in 1801.]
2. HANNAH, [b. April 2, 1798, and d. very young.]
3. ELISABETH C., [b. Dec. 29, 1799, m. Charles Gates June 9, 1818, and d. Dec. 18, 1861.]
4. ASENATH, [b. Oct. 2, 1801. m. David Hills, Jr., March 28, 1828, and d. Feb. 16, 1873.]
5. HANNAH, [b. in 1803, and probably d. in infancy.]
6. EBENEZER, [b. Jan. 5, 1804, and d. of cancer covering the whole crown of the head, and terrible in the extreme, at the age of 22.]
7. ABNER, [b. March 21, 1806, and is supposed to have d. in infancy.]

SAMUEL CUMMINGS, brother of first Ebenezer of Antrim, was born in Hudson in 1781, married Joanna Wyman, and came here in 1807. He bought the Gregg mills, lived awhile in the Rogers house, then bought an old house just north of Dea. Worthley's, and built the brick house now David Bass's. He also built the mill now owned by Abbott F. True. He died in Hollis in 1864, leaving children, of whom the last four were born here: —

1. SAMUEL, [b. in Hudson July 7, 1805, was a wheelwright by trade. m. Hannah Giddings, and lived awhile in Francestown, then moved to Lawrence and died there in 1875. Two children survive him: Josie, a teacher in Lawrence, and James F., now mayor of Bunker Hill, Ill. This last named went through the mill gate of True's shop, in 1837, at the age of five years, when the current tossed him over the wheel; but he, smart boy, picked himself up and walked off!]
2. JOANNA, [b. in Hudson Nov. 26, 1806, and m. Cyrus Burge of Hollis, Dec. 15, 1835.]
3. SARAH S., [b. Feb. 5, 1813, and m. James Ball of Hollis, Dec. 29, 1847.]
4. JONATHAN W., [b. Nov. 21, 1814, went to Bunker Hill, Ill., m. Frances Hutchinson, was sutler in the army, and was drowned in the Mississippi river in 1864.]
5. REV. SENECA, [b. May 16, 1817, m. Abigail M. Stearns, Oct. 4, 1847, and went to China that year as missionary in the service of the A. B. C. F. M. On account of her failing health they returned in 1855, and he d. in New Ipswich in the course of the following year. His age was thirty-nine. He was a graduate of Dartmouth College, in the class of 1844.

Was ordained as a missionary at the Center, in the church to which he belonged, Sept. 30, 1847. The sermon was by Rev. Dr. Silas Aiken, then of Boston. Rev. Seneca Cummings was a most worthy and devoted man. His early death was greatly mourned, but the record of his sacrifice and the success of his short life may not be measured in this world or by any standards men can apply.]

6. PHEBE A., [b. 1819. m. Dr. Jonathan C. Shattuck of Brookline, and moved to Zumbrota, Minn., where he d. in 1869. He was a graduate of Dartmouth College in the class of 1842. Their daughter, Nellie V., m. Dr. D. O. Brainard of Zumbrota.]

MOODY CUMMINGS, brother of Ebenezer and Samuel Cummings, was born in Hudson. He succeeded Caleb Blanchard as blacksmith, sometime between the years 1814 and 1820. He lived on the Jonas White place, having a blacksmith-shop just south of the present barn. He moved to New York as early as 1824, and died there. He had two sons:—

1. CHARLES, [who was a blacksmith, went to Boston and acquired wealth by his trade.]
2. ROBERT, [a successful merchant in Boston and an estimable man.]

CHARLES E. CUMMINGS, son of Enoch and Dolly W. (Pillsbury) Cummings of Sutton, was born Aug. 5, 1843; came here in 1866, and began trade in the McKeen store in company with E. D. Putney. Sold out to his partner in the spring of the next year, and went into the retail grocery business with the Marshall Brothers in Nashua; married Sophia Cheney of Warner; was sergeant-at-arms of the New Hampshire Senate last year, and has held the same office several years in the House. Is now in the marble and gravestone business, in Nashua.

## CURTIS.

Two brothers, Lemuel and Stephen, sons of Jacob and Mary (Stiles) Curtis of Amherst, previously of Boxford, Mass., came here in 1784, soon after the close of the Revolutionary war, during the whole of which they served, and began to clear on Windsor mountain, near Antrim north line.

LEMUEL CURTIS built a house so near the town line that people said he lived on the fence, and could avoid taxes by dodging into one town or the other as circumstances required. Probably there was no foundation for this report. He married Mary Smith and had children:—

1. ANNA, [m. Levi Curtis April 1, 1816.]

GENEALOGIES.                                        443

2. MARY, [m. John A. Lyon, Dec. 30, 1824, and lived awhile at
   North Branch. After his death she moved to Windsor and
   d. there.]
3. HANNAH, [now living alone in Windsor at advanced age.]
4. DAVID, [m. Betsey Swett, whose children all d. young. His
   second wife was Sally Swett, and they now live in Windsor.]
5. LEMUEL, [m. Pamelia Webster, Feb. 28, 1822, and lived on
   the old homestead where he d. His children are : —
   *Joel*, (m. Abigail Dodge, and went to Connecticut.)
   *Luther S.*, (m. 1st, Sarah C. Smith of Hillsborough ; 2d, Mrs.
   Sarah H. Burnham of Hillsborough, Nov. 28, 1876. Has
   one daughter, Mary, b. May 29, 1856.)
   *Luke*, (m. Lydia E. Drew, and is supposed to have gone
   West.)
   *Washington*, (supposed to be now in Kansas.)
   *Nathan*, (m. Hannah Twiss and lives in Stoddard,)
   *Harlan*, (now resides in Kansas.)]
6. SARAH. [m. James Walker, June 22, 1813, lived and d. in
   Windsor.]

STEPHEN CURTIS, brother of first Lemuel, built on the hill above
Daniel Swett's, but the house has long been gone. He married, first, Abigail Small. For his second wife he married Bridget Smith, and moved
into a house then west of B. F. McIlvaine's, where he died in 1832, at the
age of seventy-seven. His children were as follows, the first three being
by his first wife : —

1. STEPHEN, [m. Lydia McClintock and moved to Danbury.]
2. SARAH, [m. Jonathan Buck, April 13, 1819, and moved to
   Danbury.]
3. ABIGAIL, [d. at the age of 20.]
4. LEVI, [m. Anna Curtis, April 7, 1816. He had several
   children, but buried them all, and ran away many years
   ago.]
5. BENJAMIN, [went away when a young man and has never been
   heard from.]
6. NANCY, [m. James Prince, lived and d. in Amherst.]
7. LETTICE, [m. William Miller of Hillsborough, April 25, 1815.
   She was the grandmother of Arthur Miller of this town.]

EBER CURTIS, son of Jacob Curtis, and grandson of Jacob and
Mary (Stiles) Curtis of Amherst, came here from Mont Vernon in 1819,
and bought of David Gregg the place at the junction of the Stoddard

roads (now Chester Conn's). He married Lucy Bradford of Goshen, who was the daughter of Major William Bradford of Mont Vernon, who, though an old man, commanded under Gen. Miller when the latter was requested to take the fort at Lundy's Lane, and said "I'll try, sir." His second wife was Mrs. Mary (Cox) Herrick, whom he married March 29, 1836. He died Feb. 17, 1858, aged seventy-four. His children were : —

1. GRAFTON, [b. in Mont Vernon, Nov. 16, 1815, m. Mrs. Sabrina (Dresser) Holt of Windsor, June 5, 1850, who d. in 1876. He has no children, and lives on the place next below the Branch, on the old road.]
2. GRANVILLE, [twin-brother of Grafton, fell into a tub of hot water and was burned to death Nov. 20, 1816.]
3. WILLIAM B., [b. in 1818, m. Melinda F. Wilkins and moved into the house by the Steele mills. He subsequently spent four years in California, and now lives on the James Steele place near the mill. He has but one child, Mrs. E. W. Esty.]
4. ANGELINE, [m. John W. Herrick, April 18, 1847.]
5. ELBRIDGE, [m. Laura Shipley of Nashua, and now lives in Deering.]
6. LEONARD B., [m. Emily Holt of Washington. They had several children who all d. and were soon followed by their mother. For 2d wife he m. Addie M. Town of Sullivan, who d. of typhoid fever three weeks after marriage. He now lives on the Moulton place.]

LEVI CURTIS, son of Benjamin and Lydia (Earl) Curtis, was born in 1792; married Lydia Kinson of Mont Vernon (who was born in Acworth in 1794), and came here Feb. 22, 1825, and settled on the place still occupied by his widow. The house was built in 1820 by Stephen Curtis and his son Levi of Windsor. He died in 1861, leaving a large family : —

1. LYDIA, [b. in 1819, m. Jesse Parker of Merrimack, who d. in 1861, and she now resides in Manchester.]
2. JOHN, [b. in 1822, m. Susan Greeley of Litchfield, and now resides in Plaistow.]
3. JULIANN A., [b. in 1824, m. Ruel K. Conant of Springfield, Mass.]
4. SALLY, [b. in 1826, m. William P. Gage, Nov. 12, 1850, and lives in Manchester.]
5. OLIVE, [unm.]
6. GEORGE M., [d. unm. in 1863 at the age of 33.]

GENEALOGIES. 445

7. ANDREW J., [b. in 1833 ; m. Lucy N. Barrett of Hadley, N. Y., May 4, 1856, and lived in a small house on his father's farm, where his children were born. He was sick for many years, and his family endured much hardship and were scattered in childhood. Their names are: —
*Myra*, (m. Sanford Tinker of Alstead, Dec. 28, 1877.)
*Lydia J.*, (b. Feb. 22, 1858; m. Chester A. Holt Nov. 15, 1878.)
*Helen L.*, (b. April 19, 1860 ; m. William Osborne of Lyndeborough, May 25, 1879.)
*Mary Ida*, (b. May 16, 1861.)
*John M.*, (b. Sept. 23, 1864.)
*Stillman E.*, (b. Oct. 22, 1866.)
*Clara M.*, (b. Sept. 11, 1868.)
*Rosa M.*, (b. April 15, 1871.)]
8. LEVI, [b. 1835 ; m. Laura A. Shattuck, daughter of the late Dea. Shattuck, in 1864, and bought the Charles Wood place where he still lives. His children are Anna B., b. in 1866, and Arthur F., b. in 1871.]

## DANE.

JOHN B. DANE, quite prominent in town for awhile, was son of John Dane; married Almira P., daughter of William Whittemore of Greenfield, and lived in a house next south of Putney's store. He was engaged in staging, and moved to Greenfield in 1859. He is now living in Hancock. One son, William F., was born in Antrim.

## DANFORTH.

DAVID DANFORTH, son of David and Elizabeth (Pierce) Danforth, was born in Chelmsford, Mass., in 1784; married Mary Walker of that place Nov. 12, 1812, and came immediately here on to the place next north of the Gould tavern, where he lived till the close of 1837, when he went to Brighton, Me., and died there in 1870. He was deputy-sheriff twenty-eight years. Children : —

1. GEORGE, [b. in 1815 and d. in childhood.]
2. MARY, [b. in 1817 ; m. John Small in 1835, and settled in Hillsborough.]
3. CATHERINE, [lives unm. in Cambridgeport, Mass.]
4. DAVID, [b. in 1821 ; m. Zilpha Danforth of Nashua, and settled in Philadelphia.]
5. REBECCA, [m. Alvah Weeks of Brighton, Me.]

6. BENJAMIN P., [b. in 1831; m. Pleena Weeks, and lives in Brighton, Me.]
7. ANDREW J., [m. Abby Davis of Boston, and moved to California.]

## DASCOMB.

"FARRINGTON" DASCOMB, or Philip F. Dascomb, son of Dea. George and Sally (Lufkin) Dascomb of Hillsborough, came here in 1822; built the Grafton Curtis house; married Elisabeth Peters of Henniker the same year; built a large, two-story wheelwright-shop on the first dam above his house, and carried on the business nearly sixteen years; failed up and left town in 1838; went to Chelsea, Mass., and died there in 1854. Had two children, both born here:—

1. ELISABETH, [m. Austin Dalrymple of Newton, Mass., now lives a widow in Revere, Mass.]
2. ELLEN, [m. John G. Latta, and lives in Newton, Mass.]

## DAVIS.

JOSEPH DAVIS, called "Joseph Davis, 1st," a Spaniard who had come over the water and settled in Atkinson and married Peggy, sister of Charles Wood of Antrim, came here from that town in 1819; lived on High Range near the old school-house awhile, then a short time near the town line on the road to Stoddard Center, and in 1825 moved into a small house now unused between Henry and Alvin Barker's, and lived there till 1859, when he went to the county farm, on which he died the following year, aged about ninety. He left no children. His second wife was Lamira Greenwood, married Dec. 16, 1857, from Nova Scotia.

REV. JOSEPH DAVIS, called on town record "Joseph Davis, 2d," son of James and Meribah (Morse) Davis of Methuen, Mass., was born in that town in 1792. His parents were married March 18, 1781. Left an orphan in infancy, on growing up he worked his way, went through Andover Academy and the seminary, and entered at once upon the life of the ministry. He settled first in Nottingham, next in New London, next in Weare, and next in Antrim, coming here in 1832 and remaining till 1852. He came as pastor of the Baptist Church in the old brick house over east, but did not preach there continuously, being for considerable part of the time in service elsewhere or disabled by sickness. After leaving this town Mr. Davis preached in Manchester a short time, likewise in Rochester, whence he went to Hebron, Ohio, and was pastor of the Baptist Church there at the time of his death, Oct. 4, 1854, at the age of sixty-two. Mr. Davis was held in high esteem in this town; was at one time town clerk; was occasionally on school committee of the town, and represented Antrim in the legislature in 1841, 1842, and 1844. Mr. Davis married, in 1823, Miss Aphia Goldsmith, daughter of Jeremiah and Sarah Goldsmith of Andover, Mass. Her daughter writes of her:

"She was one of a family of eleven children, seven girls and four boys, all strong in the Presbyterian faith." She was the mother of all his children, and died in this town Aug. 14, 1850, aged forty-nine. Her last words were: "They are calling me — oh! 'tis sweet to die!" He married, second, Susan B. Eaton of Weare, in the autumn of 1853. His children were: —

1. JOSEPH C., [b. Nottingham July 2, 1824; m. Emily Barber of Bradford, Vt.; is a broker and trader in Boston.]
2. BENJAMIN F., [b. New London July 4, 1826; m. Caroline S. Averill of Mont Vernon; has been trader in fancy goods, and resides in that town.]
3. SARAH A., [b. in Weare March 24, 1829; unm.; lives in Manchester.]
4. JAMES G., [b. in Antrim May 17, 1833; m. 1st, Frances Stevens, 1851; 2d, Sarah C. Farnsworth of Harvard, Mass.; is agent of Ripha Cotton Mills, Philadelphia, Penn.; is a Christian, very active in temperance and evangelistic work.]
5. GUSTAVUS J., [b. here Nov. 16, 1837; m. Emily Hunter of Salem, Mass.; lived in Lowell, but went into the Union army, and died in the service.]

HIRAM DAVIS, son of Thomas M., and grandson of Jonathan Davis of New Ipswich, married Jane Whittier of Warner; was deputy sheriff; came here from Henniker in 1866, and took the mill, now Parkhurst's, at the Branch, living in the "Mill House;" moved to South Village in 1871, died there June 25, 1873, aged sixty-five. Had six children:

1. GEORGE R., [b. 1834; killed by the "bursting of a swivel," July 4, 1852.]
2. SARAH J., [m. Lewis P. Hanson, 1856; lives in Henniker.]
3. JULIA, [b. Warner 1838; m. Cyrus Goodwin of New Boston, 1869.]
4. THOMAS M., [b. in Henniker, 1842; assistant in insane asylum, Washington, D. C.]
5. MELISSA M., [b. in 1845; m. Harris P. Lewis in 1872; lives in Hillsborough Upper Village.]
6. HIRAM F., [started to go out hunting, laid down the gun in a neighbor's door-yard as he called for a hired man there to go with him; then coming out and drawing his gun toward him, it was accidentally discharged into his bowels, making a terrible wound, from which he died in two or three hours. This occurred Sabbath morning, Oct. 10, 1869. His age was 21.]

## DAY.

THOMAS DAY, a Revolutionary soldier, came here from New Salem, Mass., in 1783, immediately after the close of the war. He built a log house southeast of the Dinsmore place, where he lived many years. He afterwards lived in a house (gone many years) between the Orren Carr and Combs places. He went back to New Salem, Mass., in his old age, and died there in 1824, aged seventy-five. His wife was Hannah Davis of Danvers, Mass., who died in 1821, aged seventy-five. Their children were : —

1. BETSEY, [b. April 9, 1784; m. John Thompson July 25, 1811, and d. in 1868.]
2. HANNAH, [b. July 15, 1787. Nothing can be learned of her except that she went to Cleveland, Ohio, with her brother James, and d. there at a good old age.]
3. JAMES M., [b. March 10, 1791. He was in the war of 1812, and molded bullets in the chimney-corner all the day before he started. January, 1816, he moved to Cleveland, Ohio, and m. there.]

ROBERT DAY, son of Joseph and Esther (Truel) Day of Greenfield, and grandson of Robert Day of Andover, Mass., was born Nov. 23, 1807; is cabinet-maker by trade: married Lydia N. Carr, Dec. 4, 1832, and moved here from Peterborough, April, 1874, into the Dimond house at North Branch (built by John Dunlap in 1806). Their children are : —

1. GORMAN, [b. April 17, 1834; m. Hannah C. Forbush Oct. 9, 1861, and is now living in Peterborough.]
2. EDWIN, [b. in Peterborough July 5, 1836 ; m. Binnie Barton of Windsor, Me., Aug. 15, 1872; he was a photographer in Waltham, Mass., afterwards in Exeter, and came here from the latter place in 1876. He has one child : —
*Harry B.*, (b. here in October, 1876.)]
3. MARY, [b. Sept. 8, 1838, and m. S. S. Sawyer of this town May 18, 1861.]
4. LOUISA, [b. Feb. 9, 1841 ; now Mrs. Horace Gowing of Wakefield, Mass.]
5. HARRY, [b. Jan. 21, 1845; d. Aug. 17, 1865.]

## DERUSH.

JOSEPH DERUSH, a Frenchman, came here in 1825, as a farm laborer. He married Hannah Stuart Aug. 7, 1826. Married, second, Mrs. Lucinda (Bowen) Walker. Lived in various places in town, and died in May, 1859, aged sixty-five. Children : —

1. NANCY J., [m. John S. Hadley July 6, 1842.]
2. JAMES M., [entered the army in the Mexican war and was killed. Enlisted at the age of eighteen.]
3. ANDREW J., [served in Union army in the late war, m. Mary A. Cilley of Orange, and now lives in Canaan.]
4. FRANK L., [by second wife; m. Diantha Atwood, went to California, and, it is supposed, d. in the general hospital there, March, 1877.]

## DICKEY.

There were several families of this name in the State, all Scotch, and, no doubt, all of one stock. There were three James Dickeys in the Revolutionary army from this State; one from Londonderry, one from Raby (Brookline), and one from Antrim. In these several branches we find Williams and Johns and Adams and Samuels, etc., over and over, so as to render it difficult to keep them distinct. Two of these families, as being connected with Antrim people, I will briefly notice.

WILLIAM DICKEY and his wife Elisabeth came over in 1725, and settled in Londonderry, on one of the best and most attractive farms in that town, — a farm still in possession of the family. He died Oct. 9, 1743, aged sixty, and his wife, Oct. 20, 1748, aged seventy. They left children: Samuel, Elisabeth, and Elias. The last settled in New Boston, where several descendants now reside. Elisabeth married John Hall, and her descendants reside in Manchester. Samuel, the oldest, remained on the homestead, married Martha Taylor, who died Oct. 15, 1775, aged seventy-two, and married, second, a Mrs. Parker of Society Land (Greenfield). Samuel Dickey left the homestead to his youngest son, and moved with his second wife to Greenfield, where he died about 1780. He left seven children as follows: Adam, who was born April 17, 1740, married Jane Nahor, and after a few years went to Vermont; Betsey, who married James Betton, and was mother of Hon. Silas Betton, member of Congress from this State in 1803–1807; Nancy, who was the mother of David Parker of Antrim; Mary, who married Robert Boyd of New Boston; Martha, who married John Cochran of New Boston; and Robert, who married Hannah Woodburn, June 10, 1776, and received the homestead. This Robert was remarkable for physical strength; and in a trial of strength, common in those days, he unintentionally killed his antagonist. Robert was a peaceful and excellent man. He died in middle age and left a large family, most of whom have attained to great age. Their names were: Samuel, John, Martha, Mary, Joseph, Robert, Susan, Janette, David W., Adam, and Roxanna. Of these eleven children, I will only add, that Samuel settled in Warren, Ohio; John married Margaret Woodman, and lived and died in Londonderry; Martha, who was born Aug. 11, 1780, became second wife of William Boyd of Antrim, and died recently at the age of ninety-nine; Mary married Edward Ela; Robert married Jenny Morrison and died in Londonderry at the age of eighty; Susan married John

White of Litchfield; Janette married, first, Samuel Gregg, and second, David Dickey, and died aged eighty-eight, mother of Mrs. Samuel Baldwin of Bennington; David W. settled in Salem; Adam went to Claremont; and Roxanna married Robert Stevens of Manchester.

Capt. Joseph Dickey, fifth of those named above, was born May 5, 1784, married Fannie D. Montgomery, April 7, 1813, and died Aug. 30, 1878. He inherited the homestead of his fathers, and left the same to his children. Was a quiet, peaceful, industrious, Christian man, of the old school, hospitable, and honest to the core. His clear memory, reaching back more than ninety years, has been of substantial value in the preparation of these papers.

JOHN DICKEY and his wife Margaret came over in 1729 and settled in Londonderry. This Margaret was probably a sister of Gen. George Reid. They had seven children. The oldest was Margaret, who married Thomas Jameson of Dunbarton, and was mother of all the Jamesons of Antrim. The second child was Adam. He was born in 1722. The third was Matthew, grandfather of Hon. George W. Patterson of Westfield, N. Y., and of Mrs. Abraham Smith of Antrim. John, the fourth child, was killed in battle with the French, about 1750. Three daughters died unmarried.

Adam, named above, married Jane Strahan, and had thirteen children. He was out in the French war and also in the war of the Revolution. Of his children we can only say, that Margaret, the oldest, married Col. John Duncan of Acworth; John died unmarried; James, known as "Capt. James," married Mary Pinkerton and settled in Acworth in 1790; Adam, the fourth child, settled in Acworth; Benjamin married Isabel Marsh, went to Acworth, thence to Holland, Vt.; Sally married Robert Dinsmore of Francestown; Eleanor, the seventh child, married Dea. Jonathan Nesmith of Antrim, and died in 1818; Mary married James Dinsmore of Antrim; Isabel married Thomas McCluer of Acworth; Matthew married Elisabeth Marsh, and settled in Walpole; Joseph, the eleventh child, married Barbara Nelson of Ryegate, Vt., lived in that place and in Burke, Vt. The two youngest children died unmarried. From this large family have descended some of the ablest and best men of the State and country.

James Dickey of Antrim was connected with the family of John and Margaret Dickey, as the old people always said, and names indicate; and also, more remotely, with that of the first William Dickey named above. But I have not been able to give the connection. Nor can I determine who were the parents of this man. There is a tradition that he lived awhile in Francestown before coming here, which probably is incorrect. A *John* Dickey was selectman in that town in 1775.

JAMES DICKEY came here from Londonderry in the fall of 1773, and began the Reuben Boutwell place in the east part of the town. He brought his wife, Mary Brown, and three children, and soon became greatly endeared to the few inhabitants of Antrim. Was ensign in the first military company formed here, probably in the fall of 1775. The next year he went into the army; was posted as sentry in September, 1776, just before the battle of White Plains; and as he was never after heard of, it is supposed he was carried off by the British or Indians, and murdered. He was a patriot of the truest stamp, young, ardent, and fearless. He was most worthy and valuable as a citizen, and was greatly lamented. His widow, called " Miss. Dickey " in the old records, and described as a rare and blessed woman, remained on the farm and trained up her five children. The town exempted her from taxes many years by unanimous vote. They moved to Columbus, N. Y., in 1801, and she died there very aged, in 1831. The children of James Dickey and Mary Brown were : —

1. ADAM, [b. in Londonderry, Dec. 18, 1767, m. Nancy Simpson as early as 1788, since he and his wife were among the original members of the church formed that year. Was a most respectable and devoted man. To the great grief of the people, he moved to New York, as above, in 1801. He d. Sept. 1, 1847. He left eight children : —

*James*, (b. Feb. 24, 1791, d. unm. at great age, in the State of Kentucky.)

*John*, (b. Nov. 14, 1793, m. Catherine Chamberlain, d. in Syracuse, N. Y., June, 1843.)

*Mary*, (b. Sept. 7, 1795, m. Jonas Greenwood in 1820. d. in Baldwinsville. N. Y., Sept. 15, 1846.)

*Betsey A.*, (b. April 2, 1797, m. Bulkley Waters Feb. 1, 1821, lives in Loughborough, Canada.)

*Nancy*, (b. Nov. 25, 1800, m. John James Aug .29, 1831, d. in Rockvale. Ill., May 31, 1876.)

*Rev. David*, (b. after parents left Antrim, at Columbus, N. Y., Sept. 12, 1802, m. Minerva Wilcox, 1825; missionary of Seamen's Friends' Society, Rochester, N. Y., thirty-five years; a most excellent record. Is an able and devoted minister.)

*Adam, Jr.*, (d. unm. in Utica, N. Y., in 1832, aged 28.)

*Harry*, (m. Mary A. Wilcox in 1833. d. at Mount Morris, N. Y., April 1, 1852, aged 46.)]

2. BETSEY, [b. in Londonderry, Feb. 24, 1770, m. Thomas Aiken, a teacher and land surveyor, son of Ninian and Margaret (McLaughlin) Aiken of Deering, 1789. They moved to Edmiston, Otsego Co., N. Y., in 1791. There she d. in 1803. The father, with his family, moved to Emerson, Io., in 1819, and d. there the following year. Several of their children have come to honor. David D. Aiken, their third child, was several years judge in the state court of Ohio,

and d. in that office a few years ago. Mary D. Aiken m. Samuel Morse, a relative of him of telegraphic fame, and is now living, about ninety years of age, in Emerson, Io. James Aiken, Esq., youngest of the family, resides unm. in Lewisburg, Penn. He evinced great interest in the history of these families. A brief poem from his pen will be found among the centennial papers.]

3. JAMES, [b. in 1772, d. young.]
4. DAVID, [known among the kindred as "Dea. David," was b. in Antrim March 27, 1774, being the third child born in this town. His own words are worthy of a place here : —

> The place being new and settlements effected slowly, there were no schools. When eight years old, I attended a school kept in a private family one month, and at ten years of age, another month, and at twelve, another month. When I was fourteen, a district school was commenced in the place (1788), which I attended for three months. Then I continued to improve what little school there was till 1790, when I taught three months in the winter and three months in the summer, being then sixteen years old. March 1, 1791, I started for New York with my sister and family. The next July I commenced chopping on a piece of land I intended to live on, and had worked but a few hours when my leg was broken by the fall of a tree. We sent the man who was with us four miles through the woods for a man to go for a doctor eleven miles farther. My brother-in-law, Aiken, carried me half a mile through the woods to a spring of water, leaned me against a tree, and brought me water in my hat! That water tasted sweet! Then Mr. Aiken carried me to the cabin of logs in which we lived, just ten feet square!
>
> I ought to tell you about my first going to mill. We had to go to Cherry Valley — more than forty miles! I walked seventeen miles to hire a horse ; bought three and a half bushels of grain, had it ground, brought it home on the horse's back, took the horse home, and then walked home myself, having spent just one week's hard work going to mill once!

Mr. Dickey came back to his native town and m. Peggy McMaster Feb. 17, 1794, a brave and worthy woman, who d. Jan. 15, 1840. He was deacon in the Congregational Church, Columbus, N. Y., thirty years. In 1845 he went with his daughter to Belvidere, Ill., and was at once appointed elder in the Presbyterian Church there. In that place he d. Dec. 31, 1850. He was a man singularly lovable and pure. He lived to follow all his thirteen children to the grave save one, Mrs. Sidney Avery, now living in Belvidere. With them his wife's mother died and also an adopted daughter aged sixteen, so that when he went, an old man, with his only living child to the West. he left a row of fifteen graves, many of them fresh and new! His life, so full of adventure, affliction, honor, and "joy and peace in believing," constitutes a record more wonderful than romance.]

5. ANNA, [b. after her father's death, April 19, 1777, m. Elijah Holt, d. Columbus. N. Y., March 20, 1854.]

## DIMOND.

EPHRAIM DIMOND was born in Vershire, Vt., Aug. 19, 1797; married Sophia Wells of Goffstown, April 19, 1824, and came here from Goffstown the same year. In 1825 he built a shop under the bank, above Moor's mill (all now gone), had a trip-hammer, and was a smart blacksmith, having excellent skill in making edge-tools. He bought what is now the Day house (built by John Dunlap in 1806), where he lived much of his later years alone until shortly before his death, which occurred at Windsor, May 26, 1872. His wife died at Wentworth, Oct. 10, 1861, aged sixty-four. They had five children, all born in Antrim: —

1. ALONZO F., [b. Sept. 8, 1825; m. Roansa Swain of Antrim, Nov. 13, 1851, who d. here in 1854; m. 2d, Sarah M. Atwell. He d. in Wentworth June 10, 1868, where the widow still resides.]
2. ALANSON, [b. Jan. 6, 1828; d. unm. in this town, Jan. 12, 1860.]
3. SYLVIA I., [b. Oct. 30, 1832; d. here unm. Aug. 3, 1858.]
4. CELIA B., [b. Jan. 15, 1834; m. Albert S. Hammond of Wentworth, Nov. 12, 1856, and lived there till 1871, when they moved to Concord, where he is now a prominent merchant, and deacon in the South Congregational Church. They have one son, the only grandchild of Ephraim Dimond: —

    *Harry D. Hammond*, (b. at Wentworth, Jan. 4, 1862.)]
5. ABBY S., [b. July 11, 1840.]

## DINSMORE.

JOHN DINSMORE of Achenmead, Scotland, near the river Tweed, emigrated to Bellywattick, in the county of Antrim, Ireland, and there died. All the Dinsmores in Ireland and America sprung from this man. His oldest son, John, came to this country about the same time with the first company of settlers at Londonderry. For some reason he was landed at a place called Georges, in what was known as the "District of Maine." In this place was an English fort. Here he built a house; and the Indians (Penobscots) soon became very familiar with him, calling him and themselves, "all one brother." But soon the French stirred up the Indians to hostility, and one day when Mr. Dinsmore was shingling his house, suddenly the war-whoop was sounded; he was ordered to come down, and they said: "No longer one brother — you go Canada." He was a captive three months, and gained great favor with the chief. In the absence of the latter he was accused on one occasion of parleying with the English, and having some plot in view. At once they decided that he should be burned. They bound him to a tree, built up a pile of wood and dry brush around him, and were just ready to apply the torch when the chief returned. He commanded the execution to be delayed, and soon proved the charge false. Mr. Dinsmore after this was the servant and companion of the chief. When they crossed a river it was his business, as soon as the chief got in and got seated, to push off the canoe and then jump in. On one occasion the chief refused to let him in. He begged not to be left, but the chief said: "No; you much honest man, John — you walk Boston." Then he told the captive how to avoid the Indians, where to hide, and what course to take. Following his directions, he found the hiding-place just in season, and lay there three days and three nights; saw the savages pass by tribe after tribe, then almost starved he pressed on his way, supporting life by a few cranberries found on the banks of a stream, till after about a week he reached an English fort on the shore. He did not attempt to reach his house, but took passage for Boston, and thence came at once on a visit to his old friends in Nutfield, now Londonderry. They had all known him in Ireland. At once they called him "Daddy Dinsmore." It was a term of reverence and respect. Afterwards he always went by this name, unless sometimes a few called him the "Indian captive." For old friendship's sake and on account of his losses and sufferings, the proprietors of Londonderry gave him a hundred acres of land. This land is in possession of the family to the present time. He settled upon it immediately; being a mason by trade he built on it a stone house, and when everything was ready he sent over to Ireland for his wife and the two children. They all arrived safe in 1730. In the many years of his absence both his children had matured and married. The son, Robert, married in Ireland Margaret Orr, and brought over with him four children. The daughter married John Hopkins, and they brought over two children with them. She afterwards had children: John, Robert, Nancy, and Ruth, the last, born in 1743, and becoming the wife of Dea. Isaac Cochran. "Daddy Dinsmore" divided his farm between his two children, and died in 1741. He was held in respect by all who knew him. With his son Robert, who was also a mason, he built most of the old stone garrison-houses in Londonderry, the remains of which may be seen at the present day. Robert's children were John, Mary, Elisabeth, Robert, and William. The last was born this side of the water in 1731; married Elisabeth Cochran in 1755 (sister of Dea. Isaac Cochran); was a leading man in the town of Windham; was a military officer; was father of Gov. Samuel Dinsmore, and of Dea. Robert Dinsmore, the "Rustic Bard," and died in 1801. Robert's oldest child, John, was born in Ireland; married Martha McKeen. (This Martha was daughter of Justice

McKeen by his second wife, Annis Cargil; was sister of John McKeen, the father of Robert McKeen of Antrim; and was half-sister of Jenny McKeen, Dea. Isaac Cochran's mother.) John and Martha Dinsmore lived in Windham, and raised a large family,—five of whom we will mention below.

The first child of John and Martha we will notice was Hon. Silas Dinsmore, who was in Antrim considerably in early life, and was thirty years in public employ as government agent to the Cherokee Indians, and other places of honor and trust. He married Mary Gordon of Hampstead, in 1806, and died at Bellevue, Boone Co., Ky., 1847, aged eighty-four. He graduated at Dartmouth College, 1791. For a time Mr. Dinsmore lost his office by a joke, as is shown by the following correspondence: —

" *Dear Sir*, — Please inform this department, by return mail, how far the Tombigbee river runs up.
"Respectfully,
"J. K. PAULDING,
"*Secretary of the Navy.*"

"MOBILE.
"HON. J. K. PAULDING.
"*Dear Sir*, — In reply to your letter just at hand, I have the honor to say that the Tombigbee river don't run up at all.
"SILAS DINSMORE,
"*Agent.*"

The next mail brought Mr. Dinsmore a dismission from office. But in this the secretary exhibited his own weakness, besides showing inaccuracy in the use of language not very creditable to his high position. Dinsmore was a man of wit and learning. Gen. Jackson threatened to "tear him up by the roots" because he would not allow him to carry slaves through the station without the permit required by law. (See "Parton's Life of Jackson.")

The second child of John and Martha coming under our notice was Dea. Robert Dinsmore; was representative and held various town offices. He married Sarah Dickey, sister of Dea. Jonathan Nesmith's wife; lived in west part of Francestown (now Bennington). He died Dec. 17, 1830, aged seventy-four; his wife died Nov. 12, 1832, aged eighty. Had eleven children, one of whom, Betsey, married John Dodge, Esq., of Bennington; was mother of John C. Dodge, Esq., Mrs. N. W. C. Jameson, Mrs. Reed P. Whittemore, and others. Robert Dinsmore's family were very intimate with Antrim people, and came here to church. One daughter, Martha, aged six years, lies buried on Meeting-House Hill. She died Nov. 30, 1789.

The third child of John and Martha, we speak of, was William Dinsmore, who married Katherine Brown of Boston, was a merchant in that city, and was father of Hon. William B. Dinsmore of New York, who was one of the donors of the Center vestry, and has made many liberal gifts in this town and Bennington. Hon. William B. was one of the founders of the express business in this country, has amassed great wealth, and is a man greatly respected and loved. He married Miss Augusta M. Snow of Boston; and has two children, William B. and Clarence G.

JAMES DINSMORE was the fourth son of John and Martha, that we shall name. He was a carpenter by trade, and came here in 1778. Began soon after the Zadok Dodge place. Married Rachel Dickey. Was one of the committee of three to build the first meeting-house in 1785. He was killed by a fall from the roof of said house, June 3, 1786. He and his brother Samuel were shingling, when the staging broke and they both went to the ground. Samuel was not much hurt, but James fell across a rock and broke his back. He lived to be carried home, but never spoke. His age was thirty-two. Was a smart and good man. His death was a heavy loss to the town, and filled the settlement with universal sadness. James Dinsmore left two children. The older of them died in childhood, and its name cannot be ascertained. The other bore the name "Rachel," like her mother. She was born June 15, 1786, only twelve days after her father's death. In her many changes of fortune she was said to have "been three times without a home, — never without friends." She married James Dunlap, and died in childbirth, Aug. 13, 1811. The babe did not survive but was buried with her on the hill. A flattering notice of Mrs. Dunlap may be found in the "Amherst Cabinet" of Aug. 20, 1811.

SAMUEL DINSMORE was the fifth and last child of John and Martha, falling under our notice. These five sons were cousins of Samuel Dinsmore who was governor of New Hampshire in 1831-1833; and of the "Rustic Bard." Samuel Dinsmore of Antrim was born in 1756; was out nearly three years in the Revolutionary war, and came here near the close of 1778. Several times while he was in the service, the town voted to clear and burn pieces of his "chopped land." One such tract was where the Dinsmore house now stands, which would lead us to conclude he had been here and located his tract of land before entering the army. He was a carpenter by trade and at once prepared his cabin. It was then on the extreme west of the town. His nearest neighbor on the east was Robert Burns, near the old High-Range school-house; while on the north and west there were no neighbors for many miles, nothing but an unbroken forest. There was no road near him. For years he had to watch the bears nights in the fall of the year to prevent their destroying his corn. Built the saw and grist mills where now Loveren's mills stand, in the year 1805. Was one of the committee of three to build the town's meeting-house in 1785. Was often selectman. Though one of the wealthy men in town, he never had a wagon. He married, first, Sarah Dunlap of Antrim; second, Mary Parke of Windham. His first wife died very young and left no children. He died in 1822. Children: —

1. SARAH, [b. May 3, 1795, m. Thomas S. Holmes, March 2, 1820.]
2. JOHN, [b. Feb. 6, 1797, d. in childhood.]

3. ALEXANDER, [b. Dec. 7, 1798, d. in childhood.]
4. ANNIS. [b. in 1800, m. Jonathan Carr Feb. 27, 1828, d. in 1844.]
5. SILAS, [b. in 1802; widely known as " Col. Dinsmore;" was long prominent as a military man; rose through all the steps till he commanded the regiment in which Antrim was located: was one of the marshals at the centennial celebration. His response on the military of Antrim will be found in another place. He m. Clarissa Copeland of Stoddard, lived some years on the homestead of his father, then moved to Stoddard where he now resides. He has been trusted with responsible positions by the people of that town. His children were all born in Antrim, and were as follows: —
    *Jacob C.*, (b. Nov. 13, 1832, m. Lucinda Hoar, lives in Keene.)
    *Clarissa M.*, (b. Dec. 26, 1833, m. Virgil A. Wright, lives in Keene.)
    *Dr. Silas M.*, (b. June 22, 1836, studied medicine, began practice at North Branch, m. Georgianna Carey of Alstead, soon moved to East Washington, thence in 1874 to Francestown, where he pursues the profession he has chosen with ability and honor.)]
6. MARGARET, [d. unm. in 1857.]
7. BARSABAS, [b. Sept. 17, 1806, m. Ann Bowen of Newbury, Vt., and lives in that place.]
8. SAMUEL, [b. July 7, 1808, followed the sea many years, never married, owns and occupies the Dinsmore homestead; selectman in 1851. A kind and upright man.]
9. MARY, [b. Sept. 22, 1810, m. Jonas W. Tuttle Feb. 20, 1834, lives in Newbury Vt.]
10. ALICE, [b. in 1812, became 3d wife of Solomon H. Griffin, Oct. 19, 1856.]

### DODGE.

DIMON DODGE, son of Nehemiah and Ruth (Woodbury) Dodge of New Boston, was born in that town in 1778; married Ann Wilson of Francestown in 1811, and moved at once to the Cheney farm, next to Cork bridge (house now gone), and lived there until 1838, when he moved to New Boston, and died there in 1840. He was deacon in the East Church, and had a large family, but all died in childhood except the following: —

1. JAMES M., [b. in 1818; m. Lucy J. Philbrick of New Boston, and lived in that town. In 1850 he sailed for California,

via Panama, and d. on the voyage. He left one child, Clarence M. Dodge, M. D., of Nashua.]
2. WILLARD, [b. in 1828, and was unm. He started with his brother for California, and both d. the same day, July 28, 1850, and were buried together at sea.]
3. CLARISSA, [b. in 1831 ; m. Benjamin F. Kendrick of Nashua, who is general ticket-agent of the Boston and Lowell Railroad, and they reside in Nashua.]

AMOS DODGE, son of Amos and Lydia (Batchelder) Dodge of Wenham, Mass., was born in 1784, and came to Antrim about 1814. He married, Patty White of Wenham, and in 1816 bought the Capt. Morse place in the west part of the town, where they spent the remainder of life, he dying in 1862, she in 1874, leaving two sons: —

1. JOHN, [b. March, 1816 ; m. Sarah J. McVennan of Berkshire, Vt., in 1842, and lived about 20 years in Antrim, then moved to Marlow, where he d. in 1874, much respected and lamented by all. His children are : —
*Mary M.*, (m. F. A. Warner, and lives in the West.)
*Sarah J.*, (m. M. F. Jones, and lives in Marlow.)
*George H.*, (lives in Marlow.)]
2. AMOS, [b. Nov. 6, 1819 ; m. Mehitable B. Weston, April 18, 1844, and lives on the old homestead, having four children : —
*George W.*, (b. Nov. 17, 1845 ; m. Emelia Bradford, and lives in Antrim, Minn.)
*John W.*, (d. in 1868, at the age of 20.)
*Delia J.*, (b. May 18, 1851; m. C. W. Flanders, April, 1869, and lives in Lawrence, Mass.)
*Flora S.*, (b. Oct. 30, 1863.)]

ZADOK DODGE, brother of Amos, was born in 1780. The two brothers came here together to purchase farms. After some delay, he bought the place next west of South Village, begun by James Dinsmore in 1779. This was in 1814, and he moved there in the spring of 1815. He married Lydia Hadley of Andover, Mass., early in 1806. After her death, Aug. 8, 1820, at the age of fifty-two, he married Sally Lowe of Greenfield, and died June 9, 1860, leaving two children, both by his first wife. His second wife died Nov. 10, 1867, aged seventy-six. His children were: —

1. HEPSIBAH, [b. Nov. 27, 1806 ; m. George R. Johnson, and lives in Nashua.]

2. ALVAH, [b. Feb. 8, 1811 ; m. Lydia Elliot of Mason, in 1836, who d. in 1852, aged 35, leaving six children : —

*Jennie M.*, (b. Oct. 5, 1836 ; m. Orville J. Coburn of Lowell, Mass., Dec. 31, 1862. He is now a trader in Nashua.)

*Anna S.*, (b. Sept. 16, 1838 ; m. E. A. Colburn, M. D., of Nashua, June 24, 1861.)

*Hattie M.*, (b. Feb. 13, 1841 ; m. William H. Flinn of Nashua, Sept. 2, 1866.)

*Charles H.*, (b. March 18, 1844. He was killed in the army Oct. 21, 1862.)

*Hiram D.*, (b. July 14, 1846 ; m. Mary E. Philbrick of Washington, Feb. 3, 1867, and lives at South Village, having one child, Herbert E.)

*Fossie M.*, (b. Nov. 17, 1851 ; m. Henry H. Barker of Nashua, Nov. 5, 1873. He is now a dry-goods merchant in Milford.)

For his second wife, Mr. Dodge m. Alice W. Carr of this town, Sept. 20, 1855. They have one daughter : —

*Katie A.*, (b. July 12, 1857.)

He is a carpenter by trade, and lived on the old homestead until 1850, when he moved to South Village, where he now resides.]

ROBERT S. DODGE, son of Robert and Phebe (Ditson) Dodge of New Boston, was born in 1807; married Mary A. Kimball of Fisherville, Nov. 15, 1835, and came here in 1857, engaging in the manufacture of wash-boards in the old peg-shop at North Branch, where he remained until 1875; then moved to South Village, where he now resides. His children are : —

1. WILLIAM S., [went to California when young ; m. Lizzie A. Messer of Dixon, Ill., in May, 1864 ; now lives in Sitka, Alaska.]
2. LYDIA A., [m. Charles N. Foster Dec. 11, 1865, and lives in Williamsport, Penn.]
3. GEORGE F., [m. Emma J. Hall of Ellenburg, N. Y., June, 1873 ; lived in Wheelock, Vt., now lives in Antrim.]
4. LOUISE M., [m. Harrison C. Ferry May 1, 1876, and lives in Deering.]
5. FRANCES J., [m. Edward L. Eaton Oct. 28, 1875, and lives in this town.]

"GILMAN" DODGE, or Samuel G. Dodge, was born in Bennington, Nov. 27, 1821, and was killed at the battle of Fredericksburg, Dec. 13,

1862. His grandfather, Capt. Gideon Dodge, married Charity Cole of Beverly, Mass., March 10, 1785, and brought her to his home in Society Land, which he had settled two years before. Capt. Gideon was son of James Dodge of New Boston, and his mother was an Ober from Beverly. He died April 16, 1822. The children of Capt. Gideon and Charity Cole were four sons and four daughters. The sons were Gideon, Jr., John, Samuel, and Solomon. Gideon, Jr., married Mary Bowers of Hancock, and was killed in Antrim by the fall of a tree, June 12, 1815, aged twenty-six. His young wife survived him less than six months, but left one child, who married Phillips T. Gile and was mother of Rev. Orrison Gile. Young Dodge was killed west of the pond on a tract of land known as the Woodbury pasture. It was the plan sometimes to have what was called a "jam;" that is, they would cut all the trees on a tract about three-fourths off, or a little more, and then, when all was ready, start the whole by falling a big tree against one side, and then the whole piece of forest would go down at once, with a terrible crash, filling the air with broken limbs and shaking the ground by the shock. This was supposed to save labor and make cleaner work, besides affording the grand and startling scene of a falling forest. With those giants of the first growth it was a great sight. On this occasion the wind started the "jam" a little too soon, and all ran for life, and Gideon, Jr., almost escaped with the rest, but was struck dead by a limb of the last tree that fell. John, the next son of Gideon, settled on the homestead, and died there Sept. 23, 1865, aged seventy-two. Was known as "Squire Dodge;" was much in public business, and was called a "live man." He married Betsey Dinsmore, and among their children were John C. Dodge, Esq., of Bennington, and Mrs. N. W. C. Jameson and Mrs. R. P. Whittemore of Antrim. Samuel, third son of Gideon, married Jane Dodge, and was father of Samuel Gilman. Solomon, the other son of Gideon, married Susan Felch; lived in Franklin; was father of John F. Dodge, Esq., of Bennington.

"Gilman" Dodge, as he was called, lived three or four years in Antrim, in all. He married Lucinda S. Carr, sister of Reed Carr. Their children were all born in Bennington except two: —

1. CHARLES A., [b. in Antrim, Oct. 19, 1843; agent for the Reaper and Mower Co. of Chicago.]
2. FRANCIS G., [b. Sept. 1, 1846.]
3. SAMUEL ARTHUR, [b. in Antrim, Oct. 4, 1848; m. Fannie A. Lane of Manchester, July 4, 1878; is overseer of a hosiery mill at Hillsborough Bridge.]
4. GEORGE W., [b. Aug. 20, 1853.]
5. MARIA A., [b. March 12, 1858.]
6. NELLIE H., [b. Jan. 7, 1861.]
7. JENNIE G., [b. Nov. 13, 1862.]

WILLIAM B. DODGE was born in New Boston, Dec. 24, 1800, and came here from New Boston in 1865. His father, having the same name, and known in New Boston as *Lieut.* William B. Dodge, was a prominent man in that town in his day; was quite a musician, and was chairman of the committee on music at the installation of Mr. Bradford, Feb. 26, 1806. Lieut. Dodge married Margaret Willson, daughter of James of New Boston, and granddaughter of Robert Willson of Londonderry. He (Lieut. Dodge) was born May 6, 1777, and died Sept. 20, 1807, in the prime of his days. Of his ancestry but little is known. The first Dodge of whom we have any knowledge, came into England with William the Conqueror, in 1066, and subsequently settled in Cheshire, where the descendants became quite numerous. Two of them emigrated to this country, and settled in Beverly, Mass.; and it is believed that all the Dodges in the United States sprung from these two. They came in 1629. Their names were Richard and William. Jacob Dodge, of the third generation from this William, was born in Beverly, in 1717, and married Abigail Edwards of Ipswich, Mass. One of the children of Jacob and Abigail Dodge was Jacob, Jr., who was born in 1752, and in 1772 married Anna Batchelder of Wenham, Mass. This last couple moved to New Boston three or four years after marriage, taking his father with them. Jacob, Sen., died in New Boston, 1801. Jacob, Jr., was in the Revolutionary army, and fought at Bennington under Stark. In later life he went back to Beverly, Mass., and died there Oct. 25, 1810, leaving eight children, of whom the oldest son was Lieut. William B. Dodge, named above. The others were Polly, Ezra, Abner, Reuben, Betsey E., Hannah B., and Nancy.

William B. Dodge of Antrim married Sophia Friend of Beverly, in 1823. He died Nov. 26, 1867. Was found dead in the stream close to his mill in Clinton, having fallen in and been drowned. His children are: —

1. WILLIAM B., [b. March 31, 1825, and m. Mary A. Morgan of Peabody, Mass., Jan. 20, 1847. Their only child, Freddie W., d. Sept. 4, 1849.]
2. CHARLES B., [b. April 10, 1829; m. Grace Hall of New Boston, July 29, 1857; has been town clerk of Antrim several years; has children: —

    *L. Fannie*, (b. Oct. 19, 1858; m. Frank L. Eastman of Weare, Feb. 27, 1879.)

    *Sophia F.*, (b. May 30, 1868.)]
3. ELISABETH F., [m. David T. Burley, and lives in Manchester.]
4. AUGUSTA P., [m. William Hood, and lives in Danvers, Mass.]
5. FRANCES, [d. in New Boston, April 7, 1856.]
6. CALEB F., [was a Union soldier, and d. of starvation in Andersonville prison, aged 23, July 20, 1864.]
7. SOPHIA, [b. in 1844; m. Capt. Horace S. Taylor, Oct. 11, 1866. He died Dec. 10, 1869.]

## DOW.

PERCY DOW came here from Methuen, Mass., about 1780, and lived on Meeting-House Hill. Dr. Whiton says that he "became an inhabitant in 1785," which probably means that he purchased land and became a "freeholder," as they called it at that time. He seems at that time to have succeeded John McAllister, and the house stood on the west side of the old road, about one-fourth of a mile north of the old cemetery. There he lived about fifteen years, and most of his children were born in this town. His wife was Zeborah Barker, sister of Capt. Peter Barker. Percy Dow died in 1824. His wife died February, 1844, aged ninety-three. They moved from Antrim to Newport about 1795. Their children were: —

1. REBEKAH, [b. Sept. 26, 1776; d. Jan. 24, 1805.]
2. HANNAH PEASLEE, [b. Feb. 7, 1778; probably d. in infancy.]
3. DANIEL, [b. June 11, 1779; d. in 1812.]
4. ZEBEDIAH B., [b. in Antrim, March 10, 1781; m. Asenath Smart of Croydon; had children: Hiram, Rebecca, Addina, Hial, Asenath, Edward, Caleb, Adalia, Lucy, Caroline, Lucinda, and Alphonso. These are all very respectable people. Hial Dow and Son are among the heaviest manufacturers of woodenware in the State. Are extensive builders and dealers in lumber. Zebediah B. Dow d. in 1863, aged 82.]
5. DEBORAH, [b. here Jan. 2, 1783; m. John Webster of Newport; had eleven children; d. February, 1833.]
6. ZILLAH, [b. here March 12, 1785.]
7. HANNAH PEASLEE, [b. here Feb. 8, 1787.]
8. POLLY BOYD, [b. May 26, 1789, in Antrim; m. Thomas Whittier of Newport; had eight children, most of whom d. young.]
9. ELISABETH, [b. in Antrim, April 27, 1791.]
10. ANNA B., [b. in Antrim, April 30, 1793; m. Abram Henderson, and moved to Salisbury, Vt.]
11. CAROLINE M., [b. in Newport, Feb. 10, 1796.]

LYMAN DOW, son of Joseph and Mary (Wells) Dow of Deering, was born in 1809; married Elisa Wood of Antrim, Feb. 11, 1836. In 1840 he came here and bought the Esquire James Hopkins farm, now A. A. Miller's. His wife died July 16, 1843, aged thirty-eight. He married, second, Esther Hadley of Hancock. He moved to Hillsborough Bridge in 1861. Children were: —

1. MARY JEANETTE, [b. Feb. 8, 1837; m. George Eaton, Nov. 4, 1860; resides in Woonsocket, R. I.]

2. SYLVANUS, [b. April 7, 1844; unm.]
3. CHARLES L., [b. April 21, 1846; m. Lizzie Sawyer of Pembroke, where they now reside.]
4. ESTHER A., [b. March 21, 1849; married Arthur A. Miller, Nov. 2, 1868.]

## DOWNING.

The history of the Downing family, as narrated below, was collected by the writer at great pains, and after long correspondence. Much help was given by descendants in Marlow, and Edinburg, N. Y.; tombstones and records were consulted; and after all had been thus put together, I heard of a very rare book, entitled "The Last Men of the Revolution," and through the kindness of Hon. Charles Adams, Jr., this book was hunted up and put into my hands. I found it contained a history of Samuel Downing, and confirmed in every particular, so far as it went, my own laborious conclusions. It was published by Rev. E. B. Hillard, Hartford, 1864.

Daniel and Samuel Downing were sons of David and Susannah (Beechem) Downing of Newburyport, Mass.

DAVID DOWNING, the father, was a ship-carpenter; was born in Portsmouth in 1738; was in the British service; was sent out by them in the last French war; went into the ranks as a soldier, and was wounded; afterwards went into the Revolutionary army; and came here in 1781. He settled what is known as the William Wilkins place, at the foot of the sand-hill, and lived there thirteen years, moving with his son to Marlow in 1794, and dying in that town in 1798. His widow survived till 1831, and reached the age of nearly one hundred and one years. Of the two sons, Daniel came here to live with his father in 1783, having entered the army of the Revolution at an early stage of the war, and serving till its close. He married Betsey Blanchard; lived here till 1794, when, taking his parents with him, and his only surviving child, he moved to Marlow, and began a farm in the wilderness; but had barely got it into comfortable condition when he died, the same year with his father, in 1798, aged thirty-five. James, the only child that survived him, was born in Antrim in 1790, being four years old when he moved away; yet on return remembering after many years every mark of the place of his birth. On growing up, he received the farm his father had cleared, and on which he had died in his prime. He married Lydia, daughter of Christopher and Lois (Huntley) Ayers of Acworth, and died in 1868. He left a numerous family, of whom James, the second son, married Electa F. Foster of Stoddard, and now lives in Marlow, near the place where he was born. James Downing, now living, is a man of wealth; holds with special care, for the sake of the past, the homestead where his grandfather Daniel, and father James settled, and is among the most respectable men of his town.

SAMUEL DOWNING, the other son of David, was born in Newburyport, Mass., Nov. 30, 1761. When a small boy, about nine years old, he was playing with other children in the streets, when a passing stranger asked if there was any boy there who would like to go home with him and learn to make spinning-wheels. Sam volunteered to go. His parents were gone for the day, but he told the man "that wouldn't make no odds." So they met at Greenleaf's tavern, a little past noon, and started on the journey. They came to Haverhill, Mass., that day, and the next day to Londonderry. There they stayed over Sabbath. It was in October, and young Downing went out and picked the fruit on the ground, and was as happy as a boy need be. On Monday they came to Antrim. The man who thus brought the boy here was Thomas Aiken, cousin of James of Antrim. He was a manufacturer of spinning-wheels, then used in every house, and supplied the whole vicinity with them. The shop was in the south part of Deering, near Francestown, but the whole section was then called "Antrim" by many settlers. As the country then was for the most part covered with woods, and neighbors and playmates scarce, the boy soon became homesick, and went off in the woods many a time to cry. But there was no help for him. Sam was put at the work of making spokes for spinning-wheels. He split out spokes in the evening, and shaved them the following day. This did very well for a few days, but grew exceedingly monotonous and hateful by and by, especially in contrast with the fact that in Portsmouth he had had all the time to play and a plenty of associates. Yet it could not be helped, for there was no public conveyance whatever, and there was no road, and return was out of the question. Sam used to threaten to run away, but he remained nearly seven years. He liked the Aikens, yet thought Mr. Aiken's good wife (Mary Anderson, daughter of James Anderson of Londonderry) was superior to her husband as a disciplinarian, and he said she never failed in her noble solicitude to keep him always at his work!

Meanwhile, Sam's parents mourned for him as dead. They supposed he must have fallen off the dock and been drowned, and never expected to see him again. But after a year or more, Mr. Aiken wrote to them, telling them Sam was alive and well, and promising to send him to school if he might remain. Whether this was prompted by the kind heart of Mr. Aiken, or the solicitude of the boy, does not appear. The parents, however, as they had a large family and were very poor, as Sam was well situated and learning a trade, and as the journey was at that time so long and difficult, consented to let him stay. But the promise of schooling in this vicinity at that day was easier made than kept. No doubt Mr. Aiken intended to give him all the chance there was. But Sam didn't get a day of schooling. He was getting tired and restive when the war broke out. Mr. Aiken was an officer of the militia, and they met in little squads in his shop to talk things over. Sam's heart was fired with enthusiasm, and he made up his mind to run away and enlist. So, one day in June, 1777, when the family was away to take dinner, he slipped off and walked down the river eighteen miles to Hopkinton where there was a recruiting station. Sam was only fifteen years old and small at that, and was refused at Hopkinton. But he got a kind letter of introduction to Col. Fifield of Charlestown, and walked the whole distance to that place alone. There, as men were scarce, and Sam was terribly in earnest, he was accepted, and he served till the close of the war. He was a stirring, agile, fearless soldier, ready for any adventure; was in many of the hardest battles of the war, was firm in its darkest hour; was an exceedingly useful man, always on "peril's brink," yet never received a scratch! His memory of Arnold, Gates, Burgoyne, Washington, Lafayette, of men on both sides, and Revolutionary battles and scenes, was clear and full. Mr. Downing was intensely wrought up against the rebels in the last war, stirred up all he could to go to the front, and declared, though nearly blind and past his hundred years, if the rebels came North he should himself "sartingly take his gun and meet them!" He said he "longed to live to see Jeff Davis hung." Mr. Downing's veneration for Washington was very great to the last, and he declared that if the "Old General" were living he would "hang every rebel to the nearest tree."

Sometime in the course of a year the father, David Downing, met his son in the army — their first meeting since the boy ran off from Newburyport. The father was now forty, the son sixteen, shoulder to shoulder against the oppressor. No report of that first meeting is given, but it must have been impressive. The boy mourned as dead was a noble soldier in a noble cause.

At the close of the war Mr. Downing returned to Antrim and visited his old friends, the Aikens, "too big to be punished for running away." He had been acquainted in the army with the Georges of Antrim, six of whom, the father and five sons, were in the service. Perhaps they were relatives, as the mother of these five sons was Susan Downing, and the Georges, like the Downings, came from Newburyport. At any rate he married Eunice George very soon after his return from the war, and at once began the Stephen Butterfield farm, adjoining his brother's on the north, now occupied by Grosvenor Wilkins. She was eighteen years old at marriage, had thirteen children, and died in 1846, aged eighty-one. Mr. Whiton speaks of Samuel as living subsequently in a log house on the Bond place, but the history of the family makes it certain that it was *David*, father of Samuel, that occupied the log house a few years. After Mr. Downing's settlement on the farm as above, he learned to read, being twenty-two years old, and became an energetic and good citizen. Here he had six children and resided eleven years. He and his wife were very pious people, were members of the Center Church, had their six children baptized in the old edifice on the hill, and were heartily recommended on departure "to any church where Providence is pleased to fix them." Their letter of dismission bears date Feb. 25, 1794, and has the signature of "Isaac Cochran, Session clerk." In their New York home they united with the Methodist Church, the only one near them, and lived in that faith very happily till death.

In the year 1793 there was much talk in this vicinity of the fertility of lands in "York State," which, at that time, was "out West;" how people could live there by working three days in a week, and so on; and a company of twenty men was formed to leave Antrim and form a settlement there. But Samuel Downing was the only one that went, and he afterwards bitterly regretted the step himself. "But," said he, "I have sold my farm for a trifle and have nothing to buy another with: here I have got to stay." So he bought at a very low rate a tract of land in what is now Edinburg, Saratoga County, N. Y., worked his way through many privations, and lived on that spot for nearly seventy-three years! There was no settlement, not even as much as a marked tree in the vicinity, when he began in 1794, at the age of thirty-two, with four little children dependent on him, and put up his rude cabin in the forest. It was an incorporated town, rich and full of people, when he died in 1867. The valleys where he had hunted were crowded with villages, and the locomotive whistled on its way where once he had met the savage in deadly conflict. Mr. Downing celebrated his one-hundredth birthday Nov. 30, 1861. As he was known far and wide, being a man greatly loved, and among the last of the pensioners of the Revolution, considerable preparation was made by the people generally for his centennial, and the advertisement of it was in the papers several weeks beforehand. His nephew, Mr. James Downing of Marlow, happened to take up a paper containing this notice, and, as his eye fell upon the name, the thought flashed into his mind that this might be his uncle whom he supposed was dead, and whom he remembered well, though he was only four years old when they all moved away from Antrim in the spring of 1794 — sixty-seven years before! At once the nephew started for Edinburg, and found the long-lost uncle was indeed alive. The centennial birthday celebration was very gratifying and noteworthy in every respect; but the most romantic and remarkable thing about it was this meeting of kindred. It was stranger than fiction. On this birthday a thousand persons from the surrounding country visited the venerable man; one hundred guns were fired; and an address was delivered by George S. Batcheller of Saratoga. On this anniversary Mr. Downing was hale and hearty, seeming young as a man of seventy. To show his vigor he cut down in the presence of the company a hemlock-tree five feet in circumference. This tree was sold on the spot, and was cut up into canes and keepsakes, and carried off by the multitude. The ax he used was sold for seven dollars and a half! Mr. Downing lived years after this in good health and in full use of all his faculties except that of sight, which gradually failed him so that he was nearly blind at the last. He died Feb. 19, 1867, aged 105 years, 2 months, and 21 days! He had been a professor of religion seventy-nine years! He was the last survivor of the Revolutionary army! What emotions he must have had in joining the full ranks on the other side! I count it an honor to write the biography of this quiet, useful, Christian man, venerable in years, loved by all who knew him, and the last of the noblest army that ever battled for liberty or stood for human rights!

It may interest the reader to know that at the publication of the volume referred to in 1864, there were only seven Revolutionary soldiers living: Samuel Downing, Daniel Waldo, Lemuel Cook, Alexander Millener, William Hutchins, Adam Link, and James Barham. Cook and Millener were older than Mr. Downing, but they dropped away soon after the above date; but he, lingering about two years after all the rest, followed on, and millions lamented that the last warrior of 1776 was gone! This event was conspicuously noted by the press throughout the land, and the pay-roll of Revolutionary pensioners was folded up to be called for no more!

Of Mr. Downing's large family, two children rest in unmarked graves on Meeting-House Hill. Four others were born here, as follows:—

1. SUSANNAH, [b. Dec. 14, 1784; m. Zephaniah Cornell of Bridgewater, Penn., and d. March 31, 1823.]
2. ANNA. [b Nov. 12, 1786; m. William Cornell of Edinburg, N. Y.; went to Michigan in 1822; d. there Aug. 7, 1838.]
3. MARGARET, [b. Aug. 5, 1788; m. James Barker of Edinburg, N. Y., and d. in that place March 27, 1851.]
4. HANNAH, [b. Jan. 20, 1794: m. Perris Fuller; settled in Greenfield, N. Y., and d. Aug. 18, 1865. This child was carried at the age of four months in a cart and on horseback the whole distance from Antrim to the forests of Saratoga.]

After arriving in New York seven children were born to them, two of whom died in infancy. The others were as follows:—

5. THOMAS J., [b. Edinburg, Sept. 1, 1800; d. unm. Jan. 1863.]
6. MARY, [b. Nov. 3, 1802; m. a Cornell and d. July 2. 1830.]
7. ELISABETH, [b. July 25, 1805; m. a Mr. Hunt and d. Feb. 20, 1827.]
8. GEORGE W., [b. Dec. 9, 1807.]
9. JAMES M., [b. Aug. 15, 1811.]

## DRAKE.

REUBEN DRAKE, son of Reuben and Olive (Chessman) Drake of Brockton, Mass., was born in 1826; married Ann E. Thayer of Braintree, Mass., and came here on to the Ambrose Story place in 1864, but returned to Brockton in 1868, having three children, none of whom were born here:—

1. CHARLES R.
2. FRANCIS E.
3. SARAH A.

## DRAPER.

TIMOTHY W. DRAPER was son of William and Sarah (Merriam) Draper of Lexington, Mass. His mother watched the red-coats when they first fired upon the American farmers, and saw their disastrous retreat later in the day. At their marriage, or soon after, William Draper and wife moved to Francestown, and there Timothy W. and other children were born. He married Mary Flanders of Lancaster, Mass., April 6, 1824. Came here from Charlestown in 1849. He lived a year on the Reuben Boutwell farm (east), and a year on the William N. Tuttle farm, but in 1851 bought of George F. Parmenter the place opposite the Center Church, where he lived till death. This last event occurred on the morning of April 10, 1874. He was a very lame man and a great sufferer, but he had no sickness, so called, and died in his chair while the family were about their preparations for breakfast. He remained in position in the chair as though there had not been the least motion or even a shock of pain. They had seven children: —

1. GEORGE A., [d. 1847, aged 22.]
2. CHARLES G., [see Gibson.]
3. MARIA M., [d. 1856, aged 28.]
4. AUSTIN R., [d. in Francestown, 1837, aged 7.]
5. LUCY A., [b. June 8, 1833; m. Alvin D. Charters of Lowell, Mass., Dec. 14, 1852. He was killed by a fall in that city, May 11, 1859. Only one of their children survives. Alvia A., who was born in Antrim, May 4, 1859.]
6. RICHARDS, [b. July. 24, 1837; left Antrim in the spring of 1857; when last heard from, years ago, was in Kansas.]
7. WILLIAM H., [d. March 20, 1860, aged nearly 20 years.]

## DUNCAN.

GEORGE DUNCAN, the first Duncan in New Hampshire, was the son of George Duncan who was born, lived, and died in Ireland. His father, George, was born in Scotland. He brought over his second wife, Margaret Cross, and seven children: John, George, William, Robert, Abraham, Esther, and James. Of these, as only the first two are connected with our history, we will only say in regard to the others, that William married Naomi Bell, lived in Londonderry, had a large family several of whom settled in Acworth, and died in 1798 aged eighty-two; that Robert married Isabella Caldwell, moved to Boston, and prominent residents of that city descended from him; that Abraham went in early life to North Carolina, married, and raised a family there, of which almost nothing is known; that Esther married John Cassan and went to Connecticut; and that James, the youngest, married Elisabeth Bell, settled as a merchant in Haverhill, Mass., acquired large property, raised an excellent family, and died in 1818, aged ninety-two. Of the other two, first named above, John, the oldest of the family, only child of the first wife, and therefore half-brother of the rest, married Rachel Todd in Ireland. He brought with him five children, and had five in this country, thus: John, George, Abraham, Margaret, William (born on passage over), James, Naomi, Polly, Rachel, and Rosanna. He lived all his days in Londonderry, was an elder in the church, enjoyed the confidence of all, and died in good old age. John, the first child of John Duncan and Rachel Todd, married Hannah Henry. Though hardly more than a boy, he was engaged to marry her before the voyage to this country. He came over, prepared a place to live, and then sent for her. Her brother there paid her passage, and agreed with the captain to land her in Boston. But he took her to Nova Scotia and sold her to pay her passage, and left her among strangers. But after a time John heard of her sad fate, hunted her up, and married her. The false captain was eventually punished for his crime. All the circumstances of this case, — her courage, her forlorn condition in slavery for debt among strangers, her rescue by her lover, their beginning in the wilderness, and their long and happy life, their early betrothal, and their old age together, — would form a story more marvelous than many a fiction. They had a large family, one of whom, John, remained on the homestead in Londonderry; another was a merchant in Candia, and became father of Hon. William H. Duncan of Hanover; and a third, Robert, came to this town. John Duncan and his wife, Hannah Henry, were both noted for personal beauty. This John kept the first store in the present town of Londonderry. Many of the race were merchants.

ROBERT DUNCAN, son of John and Hannah (Henry) Duncan, and nephew of James of Antrim, was born in 1763, and came here in 1787, and located where his son John has always lived. When he came, Dea. Daniel Nichols was on the Turner place; Adam Nichols on the McCoy place; John Nichols on the Ferry place, and Thomas Nichols on the Shattuck place. Mr. Duncan bought in the valley between them. There was a cleared spot, and a small log house a few rods north of the present dwelling, though it seems it had never been occupied. He bought of Daniel McFarland, but was sued by parties from Weare who claimed the land, and he had to pay for it a second time. After all was settled, he married Grizzy Wilson of Londonderry; lived a quiet and industrious life, and died on the spot he had settled, Sept. 26, 1837, at the age of seventy-three. His children were: —

1. THOMAS W., [b. in 1791; was graduated at Dartmouth College in the class of 1817; studied divinity, after the method of those days, with Dr. Whiton and Rev. E. P. Bradford of New Boston; was settled in various places, and was a sound and faithful minister till disabled by old age. Though shaken by infirmities he continued to preach occasionally till near his end; he died in Nelson, in 1877; his wife was Lucy North; they left no children.]
2. HANNAH, [d. unm. in 1859, aged 66.]
3. SARAH, [d. in childhood.]
4. JOHN, [b. Sept. 7, 1796; inherited the homestead; built the present house in 1811; m. 1st, Jenny Carter of Hillsborough, in 1823, who d. in 1829; m. 2d, Mary Farrington of Greenfield, in 1831. Has children : —
  *Mary C.*, (child of 1st wife, b. Oct. 14, 1825; m. George G. Hutchinson, May 12, 1853.)
  *Lucy J.*, (b. Oct. 2, 1833; m. N. C. Ferry, Dec. 29, 1853.)
  *Lynda F.*, (b. April 27, 1836.)]

5. GRIZZY, [m. Willard Rice of Henniker, Nov. 9, 1826.]
6. SARAH, [m. Jonathan Paige, Oct. 18, 1821; lived and d. in Bradford.]
7. JANE, [m. Daniel Rice of Henniker, Feb. 3, 1831.]
8. WILLIAM, [b. Oct. 30, 1806; built in 1830 on the east part of his father's farm; cleared most of the land, and has resided there till the present time; m. Betsey W. Rice of Henniker, Feb. 3, 1831. She was an excellent woman, and died in a Christian hope Aug. 26, 1870, aged 61. They had children as follows: —

*George*, (d. in infancy, December, 1831.)

*William H.*, (b. Dec. 10, 1834; d. unm. March 20, 1861.)

*John E.*, (b. March 25, 1836; m. Sarah J. Blanchard of Washington: she d. in 1870, aged 31, leaving one child, Emma J., b. in 1863.)

*Caroline E.*, (b. Nov. 7, 1838; m. George Turner, Jan. 1, 1863.)

*Moses G.*, (known as "Granville," b. July 20, 1841; lives on the old homestead; m. Augusta C. Spalding of Francestown, Oct. 3, 1872, and has children: Edith A., b. 1873; Anna E., b. Dec. 13, 1875; and Harry S., b. June 22, 1878:)]

George, the second child of John Duncan and Rachel Todd, married Mary Bell, and settled in Peterborough. Of their third child, Abraham, nothing is ascertained. The fourth child was Margaret, not mentioned by Parker. She married William Smith of Antrim, and died in 1790, aged sixty-seven. William, the fifth child (born on the voyage over), married Jane Alexander, and lived in Londonderry. His family were all daughters.

JAMES DUNCAN, the sixth child of John Duncan and Rachel Todd, the first born to them in this country, came to Antrim and began the Saltmarsh place in 1774. He was the first constable of the town, and long held that office, which was of much more importance then than now. His name appears very often in the early records. He married Jane Adams of Londonderry (sister of Mrs. Alexander Gregg and Mrs. Adam Dunlap), and died in 1825, aged seventy-nine. Children were: —

1. JOHN, [disappeared from town when a young man, and was never heard of more; was mourned as dead.]
2. MOSES, [built first on the spot now occupied by Elijah Kimball; m. Kate Dwinnells, and had two daughters, Kate and Betsey; Kate died in childhood, and Betsey m. a Mr. Felt and lived in Manchester, but all this family of Duncans and

descendants are believed to be dead. Moses Duncan d. on the Daniel Farrington place.]

3. ROBERT, [m. Katherine Fairbanks; lived some years on his father's farm, but d. in the prime of life ; left two sons : —
John G., (b. July 22, 1811 ; long an overseer in Lowell mills ; m. 1st, Grace Sanborn ; m. 2d, Phebe Morrison.)
Samuel, (b. July 23, 1813, left town young and nothing is known of his fate.)]
4. MARY. [d unm.]
5. PEGGY, [d. of spotted fever in 1812.]
6. JANE. [m. Stevens Paige Feb. 8, 1838, had no children, lived many years a widow and alone in the house where her husband died, and passed away after great suffering in the summer of 1869, aged 75.]

Naomi, the seventh child of John Duncan and Rachel Todd, left no record of which we know. Polly, their eighth child, married her cousin, Hon. John Duncan of Antrim. Rachel, their ninth child, married Samuel Archibald of Nova Scotia, and was mother of Hon. Samuel W. Archibald, long attorney-general of that province. Of Rosanna, their tenth child, the writer has no information.

Having now followed out the family of John, the oldest son of George the first settler, and having briefly noticed the other children of said settler, save one, we now return to him, viz., *George*, oldest child of George and Margaret (Cross) Duncan. He was the second son of his father, but the first by the second wife. This George was the third George Duncan in succession; was an elder in the Londonderry church; was highly esteemed by all; married Letitia Bell; settled in Londonderry at the same time with his father, having grown to manhood in Ireland; and is believed to have died in 1780, aged seventy. He left seven children: John, Robert, George, James, Josiah, Elisabeth, and Letitia. Of these seven, John will be noticed below. Robert married a daughter of Col. Andrew Todd of Londonderry, as is claimed by descendants, though it may have been a *granddaughter*. Robert Duncan settled in Hancock, was deacon of the church there, and died Jan. 25, 1793, aged forty-three. He was father of Dea. Josiah and Dea. Robert of Antrim, and of Margaret who married Andrew Todd. George, third child of Dea. George and Letitia (Bell) Duncan, settled in the West. James, the next child, born Nov. 11, 1749, known as Dea. James, settled in Hancock; was deacon there till death; married Jane Christie; was a man of unusual local influence and note; and was father of George Duncan of Antrim. He died May 3, 1805. Josiah, the fifth child, we have no information of. Perhaps this may be the Josiah Duncan whom the old people used to call "Jabbering Si," and who died in this town Jan. 23, 1811, unmarried, aged sixty-nine. If so, he must have been the second or third instead of fifth in the family. Elisabeth, the sixth child, married James Cunningham of Pembroke. And Letitia, the youngest, married Capt. Alexander Todd and lived in Hooksett.

JOHN DUNCAN, son of George and Letitia (Bell) Duncan, named above, called in Antrim "Capt. John," "Dea. John," and specially known as "Hon. John," was born in Londonderry March 3, 1734. He was cousin of Gov. John Bell and Senator Samuel Bell of Chester. He was a captain in Col. Moore's regiment in the Revolution, and was considered the leading man in this section for many years. He seems to have come here a part of the seasons in 1770-71-72, clearing the land and preparing for his future home. He moved his family here Sept. 20, 1773. They came in an ox-cart, with five little children, the first cart ever in Antrim. Hon. John Bell, his uncle, drove the team. There was nothing that could be called a road. But they picked their way along, and forded the river at a shallow place near the mouth of the Clinton Brook (for many years called Great Brook), and arrived safely at the log cabin ! What a long, hard, painful journey it must have been ! The spot where he settled is still in the possession of the family, the house of his great-grandson, John M. Duncan, Esq., standing almost on the site of the log cabin of 1773. It is one of the most desirable locations in town. Here the "Hon. John" lived and died. He was not an educated man, but one of good judgment and strong common sense. He was at the head of the militia; was the leading man in getting the town incorporated; was almost constantly in town office for many years; represented this town, with Deering, Hancock, and Windsor, in the state legislature; was the first representative "Antrim district" had; was some time state senator; was one of the committee to ask the presbytery to organize a church here; was an elder in that church; and was a stirring, earnest, wide-awake man, honest, and eminently a peacemaker. He was of great service to the early settlers as a justice of the peace, doing their writing, settling their disputes, and giving them advice. In his long service in the House of Representatives, he was occasionally speaker *pro tem.* Was very Scotchy in his brogue, and quick at repartee and full of fun. It is related that on one occasion, when something was said about lawyers in the House, and a Mr. Pickering, a lawyer of eminence, declared that lawyers were the pillars of the State, Mr. Duncan interrupted him with an "explanation." In his broad Scottish accent he said: "There are different kinds of *pallyars;* there is a kind of *pallyars* that support buildings; and there is a kind of *pallyars* called *caterpallyars* that eat all before them and poison all behind them, and it is this latter kind to which the gentleman refers ! "

Hon. John Duncan closed his useful and eventful life Friday, Feb. 14, 1823, aged eighty-nine. He married first his cousin, Mary Duncan, Dec. 10, 1762, who died of dysentery Sept. 20, 1800. A very happy notice of her may be found in the "Amherst Cabinet" of the week following. She was a Christian woman, full of good works, especially by the sick-bed and in the house of trouble. She went everywhere to succor the distressed, and it is probable that her continual watching over sick children in that awful summer was the cause of her own death. The second wife of Mr. Duncan was Ann Seaton of Amherst. She died Oct. 4, 1834, aged seventy-five. Was daughter of Dea. John Seaton and also had a brother Dea. John. The first Dea. John was a man of remarkable musical capacity, and was also endowed with a nose of tremendous dimensions. On one occasion, he was seated at a hotel table when a stranger sitting opposite sharply suggested that the application of a handkerchief to the conspicuous member would improve its appearance. Always very pleasant and obliging, the deacon, with his usual politeness, handed him the handkerchief across the table, and requested him to use it, as he was nearer the offending member than he was himself!

The house of Hon. John Duncan was burned in open day, Jan. 31, 1812, and, as he was aged and alone, it was with difficulty that he escaped the flames by means of a window. His children, all by his first wife, were as follows:—

1. ABIGAIL, [m. John Moor; was forty years a widow; had no children; d. 1848, aged over 80. She was the last survivor of the original members of the Presbyterian Church, having been a member a little more than sixty years.]
2. LETTIE, [m. James Cochran of Pembroke, and lived and d. in that town.]
3. WILLIAM, [m. Esther, daughter of Capt. Josiah Warren of New Boston; inherited the homestead; had four children; and d. June 16, 1847, aged 82.

   *John*, (b. Feb. 21, 1795; a distinguished school-teacher; disappeared from Boston 1834, and never after heard from.)

   *Josiah*, (b. March 17, 1797; m. Lucinda Fairbanks Dec. 28, 1826; inherited the homestead of his father, and d. 1867. His widow yet survives. They buried six little ones side by side within a few years, and only two children are now living. The first is John Moor, who was b. Oct. 18, 1827; inherits the homestead occupied by the family for a hundred years; was representative in 1874; a carpenter doing a large business in building for a country town; m Eliza A. Parmenter Dec. 16, 1851. They have two children: Fannie E., who m. Edward P. Campbell Dec. 26, 1877, and John W., who was b. Oct. 13, 1861, and is now in trade in Fitchburg, Mass. The second is William W., who was b. Nov. 12, 1831; m. 1864 Mary Hart, cousin of the then pastor, Rev. J. H. Bates; is a druggist in Lowell; was one of the donors of the organ to the Center Church, 1864, and of the vestry, 1875. Has children: Winthrop H.; William W.; and Hart.)

*Abigail M.*, (twin-sister to Josiah; d. unm. Jan. 15, 1860, aged nearly 63.)

*Mary*, (b. April 13, 1801; for years her services were sought as a school-teacher in this and neighboring towns; m. Eben Towne of Hillsborough in 1857, and resides at the Bridge; one of the amiable and blessed of the earth.)]

4. NAOMI, [b. Dec. 9, 1769; m. 1st, John Boyd of Londonderry; m. 2d, Giles Newton of Francestown, and was mother of Giles Newton of Antrim; m. 3d, Dea. Robert Duncan, and d. Sept. 25, 1858, aged 88.]

5. MARY, [m. Dea. Arthur Nesmith May 30, 1793; d. in Wadsworth, Ohio, Nov. 23, 1841.]

6. RACHEL, [b. in Antrim Jan. 7, 1776; m. James Taylor; d. in Herkimer, N. Y., 1852.]

7. MARGARET, [m. William Stow of Hillsborough Dec. 13, 1808; lived in that town, and d. 1856, aged 74.]

DEA. JOSIAH DUNCAN, born Feb. 29, 1772, son of Dea. Robert and —— (Todd) Duncan, and therefore nephew of "Hon. John," came here from Hancock about 1792, and married Mary, daughter of Samuel Gregg, in 1792. On his first coming here he bought and cleared the farm now Mr. Greeley's (next east of the Bootman place), which he occupied till his death. The first wife died in 1809, and he married, second, Sally Morrison of Peterborough. He died Nov. 3, 1833. Was a thoroughly true and good man; was an elder in the Center Church; and it used to be said of him that "he served two worlds well," true to earth and heaven. An old associate spoke of him as a living example of Rom. xii. 11: "Not slothful in business; fervent in spirit; serving the Lord." His children were six daughters and one son, thus: —

1. MARGARET G., [d. Jan. 27, 1815, aged 18.]
2. SARAH, [m. Daniel Waldron; parents and children all now dead. Mr. Waldron lived some years in town, chiefly west of the pond.]
3. ELISABETH P., [b. Feb. 9, 1801; m. John Muzzey Nov. 27, 1821; d. Manchester, January, 1852.]
4. MARY, [m. John Town Dec. 28, 1824; lived some years on her father's place; went to Western New York about 1835, where they prospered, and had a large family.]
5. ROBERT, [d. Feb. 10, 1820, aged 16.]
6. ADELINE, [b. Nov. 26, 1806; m. Robert L. Livingston May 24, 1827; d. Dec. 27, 1866.]
7. SOPHRONIA, [m. Tristram B. Paige Sept. 21, 1826. She d. June, 1848, aged 40.]

DEA. ROBERT DUNCAN, brother of Dea. Josiah, born Sept. 11, 1783, came here in the fall of 1806 and bought the Zaccheus Perkins place, now the home of J. W. Perkins; married his cousin, Mrs. Naomi (Duncan) Newton, daughter of "Hon. John;" was chosen elder in the Center Church 1825, and old people say he was one of the most efficient ever appointed to that office. Was captain in the first artillery company in the Twenty-sixth Regiment. Was a man of great natural ability and strong will; unlearned; was left an orphan when quite young; had the credit of doing much good, and died Dec. 2, 1859. Left no children. He left a small legacy to the church in which he was so long an officer.

GEORGE DUNCAN of Antrim was born in Hancock, Sept. 28, 1789; was son of James Duncan, Esq., of that town. This James, Esq., or "Dea. James," was brother of "Hon. John," of Antrim, and his wife was Jane Christie, one of the smartest women of her day. She could reap more grain than any man in Londonderry, and on one occasion she won forty dollars on a wager from the smartest male reaper in that town. Her endurance and strength can be judged from this. She died July 1, 1834, aged eighty-two. George Duncan married Isabel Hopkins of Antrim, Dec. 20, 1814. Before this he had been here at work for Frederick Poor in the old Starrett tannery at the foot of the hill in South Village, and soon afterwards he bought this stand, and here carried on business till his death, Jan. 9, 1840. Mr. Duncan also had a store some years in the old low house then on the site of the present Carter House. The chief part of the latter was built by Mr. Duncan in 1820. His name often occurs in town records as moderator, selectman, or town clerk. His wife died June 26, 1864, aged seventy-seven. His children were: —

1. JAMES M., [b. Sept. 27, 1815; went to Boston in company with N. W. C. Jameson, but soon d. aged 23, and unm.]
2. GEORGE C., [b. April 26, 1818; tanner by trade; m. Mary E. Whiton, Nov. 3, 1841; built the Levi Woodbury house in 1850; succeeded his father in the old tannery, which was burned in 1841; he rebuilt the same, and it was again burned in 1852, but not again rebuilt. He d. Sept. 24, 1855, leaving two daughters: Kate A., who m. Edward S. Paine of Boston, Sept. 11, 1877, and Mary, who has won success as a teacher in the city schools of Boston.]
3. CATHERINE J., [b. Sept. 2, 1825; m. Albert Allen, and settled in Jamestown, N. Y., but now lives in Lawrence, Kan.]
4. DR. EDWARD A., [b. June 22, 1830; studied medicine with Dr. Hedges of Jamestown, N. Y., and settled in practice in that place; he m. Jennie Hedges; has held for many years an important position in the general land office, Washington, D. C.]

## DUNCKLEE.

HENRY DUNCKLEE came here, it is said, from Milford, and began the silk business at the Branch; sold out to Kelsea, and went to Nashua. Was here but a short time.

## DUNLAP.

THOMAS DUNLAP, son of James Dunlap of Windham, was a soldier in the last French and Indian war: was in Fort William Henry when it was surrendered to the French under pledge of protection from their savage allies. But as soon as the English had surrendered their arms and marched out of the fort, the Indians fell upon them, and murdered several hundred in cold blood. One New Hampshire regiment of two hundred men had nearly half its whole number butchered in this way. An armed savage seized Mr. Dunlap by the hair and was in the act of splitting his head with a tomahawk when he sprung away, leaving half his hair in the monster's bloody hand, and flying back to the fort the French protected him. He came here in 1785, but became a freeholder in 1788; clearing and settling in the east part of the town on a beautiful spot, now overlooking Hillsborough Bridge and South Village. This spot is still in possession of the family, being owned by his great-granddaughter, Mrs. Hiram Combs. Thomas Dunlap married Elisabeth ——, and died March 7, 1815, aged seventy-five: was a respected and pious man. His wife died Aug. 1, 1807, aged sixty-six. His children were:—

1. SARAH, [m. Samuel Dinsmore; d. Sept. 3, 1790, aged 26.]
2. HANNAH, [d. on county farm very aged.]
3. POLLY, [m. Daniel Griffin of Hillsborough, March 25, 1817; d. in Nelson, aged 89.]
4. ALEXANDER, [m. Jane Gregg; lived in Deering, but went in old age to Bennington. and d. with his daughter, Mrs. William Roach.]
5. JAMES, [b. in 1766; m. Jane McNeil of Hillsborough, in 1802; had four sons, Thomas, Daniel, James, and Robert; inherited his father's homestead; was several times selectman; was feeble many years, but reached his fourscore, dying July 8, 1846. Of his four sons we add:—
    *Thomas,* (b. Feb. 23, 1803; m. Mary B. Averill of Mont Vernon, Aug. 30, 1821, and d. Aug. 17, 1865; was many times selectman. His widow d. June 18, 1874, aged 70. They had thirteen children, as follows: John, who was b. in 1822, and lives in California; Hiram W., who was b. in 1825, and lives in California, and is judge of the probate court there; Edwin, who d. of small-pox in Boston, May 19, 1846, aged 17; James S., who was out through the last war, passed through many fierce battles unhurt, but was

murdered in Missouri in 1871 ; Jane, who was b. in 1831, and m. Asa B. Lyford of Lowell; Cummings, who d. of cholera in Illinois in 1854 : Helen. who was b. in 1834, and m. James L. Howard of California; Chillis. who was b. in 1836, and d. aged 19 ; Frances, who was twin-sister of the last, m. Henry August. and d. in California in 1875 ; Perley, a merchant, recently murdered in California ; Clara C., who was b. in 1840. m. Hiram Combs, and inherits the homestead ; Martin R.. who now lives in California ; and Frank, who was b. in 1844, m. Nettie S. Little, Oct. 14, 1869, and lives in California.)

*Daniel,* (b. July 19, 1804 ; d. in Boston, in 1830, unm.)

*James,* (b. Dec. 20. 1806 ; went to Missouri and d. there. Little is known of him.)

*Robert,* (b. Aug. 18, 1809 ; moved to Illinois ; had a large family, and d. in 1855.)]

ADAM DUNLAP, half-brother of the first Thomas mentioned above, cleared and settled the place next west of William M. Conn's, in 1784. Had been a soldier in the Revolutionary war, and at its close married Elisabeth, daughter of Hon. William Adams of Londonderry, and came at once to Antrim. He and his wife were among the original members of the church. He was a small man, always went stooping, and was a shoemaker by trade. He died in 1823, aged seventy-three. His wife lived to extreme old age. Saw all her children dead. Afterwards it is said that her eyes actually dropped out of their sockets, and that without pain! Children: —

1. SARAH, [b. Nov. 16, 1784; m. John W. Moore of Bedford, Feb. 7, 1809; had two or three children, and soon d. with consumption.]
2. JAMES, [b. March 24, 1787 ; supposed to have d. in childhood.]
3. SAMUEL, [b. Nov. 16, 1789; m. Betsey Brown of Antrim, April 19, 1814 ; lived awhile at the *old* Reuben Boutwell place ; afterwards went to live with his wife's parents, and d. Sept. 15, 1839. Had children : —

*William,* (m. Millie Howe of Henniker ; was killed by bursting of a grindstone in a shop in Springfield, Mass., June 19, 1866.)

*Lizzie,* (m. Floraman Howe, brother of Millie Howe, and d. in childbirth in Henniker.)

*Ira,* (b. Aug. 2, 1822; m. Sarah Parker of Stoddard ; lives in Lowell.)

*Mary*, (d. aged 19.)

*Mark*, (went West ; m. Mary L. Davis ; now lives in Texas.)]

4. MARY, [b. March 10, 1794 ; m. Samuel Weston of Stoddard ; was mother of Mrs. Amos Dodge, and d. September, 1833.]
5. THOMAS, [known as " Capt. Dunlap;" b. April 19, 1797 ; m. Feb. 22, 1825, Polly W. Wallace of Windsor, a girl brought up by Stephen Wyman of that town. The old lady Dunlap used to say she had two sons: " Samuel and Tomuel." Capt. Thomas kept the Box tavern in Stoddard awhile. He had a daughter, Olive, who died young. Also a son, Whitney Dunlap, who married Abby F. Hills, and died at the house of Reuben Hills, Manchester, in early manhood. Capt. Thomas died in town, but I have not the date. He was captain of the Antrim Grenadiers: lived in various places in town. and left but one child living, Lydia, brought up by John Barker, now Mrs. Nathaniel Morrill of Lawrence, Mass.]
6. JENNETT, [b. Oct. 23, 1799 ; d. in infancy.]
7. JENNETT, [b. Oct. 23, 1801 ; m. Nov. 12, 1822, Ammi Buck of Windsor, and moved to Alexandria.]

JOHN DUNLAP of Antrim, only remotely connected with the Dunlaps who came here before him. was born in Bedford 1784. He was the son of Maj. John Dunlap, of Revolutionary honor, and Martha Gilmore, his wife, and grandson of Archibald Dunlap, who was an officer in the Scotch army, and settled in Chester in 1740 or a little earlier. Maj. John was a famous military man in his day. One of the earliest old-fashioned New Hampshire musters was at his house, and he entertained the whole regiment. Was a farmer on a large scale, and also a manufacturer of furniture, and acquired a large property for that time. He first settled on what is now called Shirley Hill in Goffstown, on a beautiful slope at the present time commanding a view of the city of Manchester, and there built a large, square, two-story house, which he occupied till 1779. He then bought another tract of land a mile below in the northern part of Bedford. The great house was taken down, each piece marked, carried to the new location, and put up with such care that there was only part of one clapboard missing. Maj. John Dunlap was found dead in his bed in the forty-seventh year of his age, in 1792. His son John came here soon after becoming of age, and married, June 26, 1807, Jennie Nesmith. He built the house at the Branch now occupied by Robert Day, in 1806. There he lived and carried on the cabinet-making business for a long time. He had also looms to weave gentlemen's underclothes, considered a great novelty in those days. Afterwards he moved to the Collins Whittemore place, and there his wife died March 29, 1835. Soon after this event, he moved to South Village and put up the first-built part of the factory now used in the manufacture of silk. March 16, 1837, he married Abigail Spalding of Hillsborough, and in 1844 moved to Zanesville, Ohio, where he lived twenty years, then came back to Nashua and died there Dec. 15, 1869, in good old age. His body was brought here and laid beside his companion, under the shadow of the church where they had worshiped together. His children were:—

1. JONATHAN N., [d. of spotted fever in 1812.]
2. JOHN. [d. of spotted fever within a few days of his older brother.]
3. ROBERT N., [was in company with his father in building the old part of the silk-mill in South Village. He m. Martha Gillespie; went in early manhood to Zanesville, Ohio, and d. there in 1861, aged 48.]
4. RACHEL E. D., [m. S. A. Lasley, Esq., and lives in Springfield, Ohio.]
5. HON. ARCHIBALD H., [called "Harris" by the old people. He was b. in North Branch village, Sept. 2, 1817; m. Lucy J. Fogg of Exeter, Aug. 12, 1841; has lived for many years in Nashua. Mr. Dunlap has had the confidence of the people of Nashua, as shown by the fact that he has several times been called to important offices in the city government. He was a representative from Nashua in the legislature of the State two years. In 1858 he was elected railroad commissioner for three years. In 1864 he was chosen one of the presidential electors for New Hampshire, and when they met in Concord to discharge the duties of their office, another son of Antrim, Hon. Daniel M. Christie of Dover, was also a member of the electoral college. Thus two of the five were born in this little town of Antrim. The meeting of these two gentlemen under such circumstances must have been exceedingly happy and interesting; and they united in casting their votes for Lincoln, whom all men unite in praising now. In 1855 Mr. Dunlap was chosen deacon in the Olive-street Congregational Church, and continued in the discharge of said official duties more than twenty-two years. And after the subsequent union of his own with the Pearl-street Church he was chosen deacon in the united, or "Pilgrim Church,"—all which, as indicative of confidence after a trial of years, is highly creditable. Mr. Dunlap has been known in the business world as the proprietor of " Dunlap's Garden Seeds." He may fairly be classed among the most successful sons of Antrim. His able response on Centen-

nial Day may be found on another page, among the addresses of that interesting occasion. His children are James H., Georgie A., John F., Abbie J., and Charles H. I must not omit to add that Dea. Dunlap gives a hundred dollars toward putting the steel engravings of Dr. and Mrs. Whiton into this book, " as a testimony of the high appreciation in which he held their memory and worth; and also as an expression of the great regard he has for the church and society over which Dr. Whiton presided as pastor for so many years." He spoke also of the " blessed impression Dr. Whiton left on the minds of the young in his visits for many years among the schools of the town." I take the liberty to put this on record and tender the thanks of myself and a multitude of others.]

6. DAVID R., [went to Zanesville, Ohio, in 1842; m. Harriet Wilkins of that place, and d. there in 1872, aged 52.]
7. MARGARET ISABEL, [m. Hanson Blaisdell, Esq., of Lowell, Mass.]
8. JONATHAN D., [unm.; has resided in California since 1849; resides in Los Angeles; is assistant U. S. marshal for Southern California.]
9. MARY JANE, [m. William Andrews of Gallipolis, Ohio. Since his death in 1866, she resides in Nashua.]

JAMES DUNLAP, brother of John, came here somewhat later. He married Rachel Dinsmore, daughter of James, in 1811; was painter by trade, and first settled in Henniker, but came here on to the farm inherited by his wife. After her death, as they had no children, he could not hold the estate; but to the great credit of her heirs, they generously gave up their portions to him in his affliction. Soon after he went into the army and went through the war of 1812. At the close of the war in 1815, he located in Missouri; married again and had several children, among them two sons who lost their lives in the Union army in the late war. James Dunlap died in 1862, aged eighty.

DAN DUNLAP, cousin of John and James, who came from Bedford, was born in that town Jan. 15, 1792; came here about 1812; married, first, Mary Carr, Oct. 21, 1813; second, Abigail Combs, May 18, 1820. The first wife had three children. Having lived in various places, Mr. Dunlap built the house next east of John Moor Duncan's in 1838. He died in 1866. He had ten children in all, thus:—

1. EDWARD, [b. Sept. 10, 1814; m. Sarah Richardson; d. April 23, 1839; no children.]
2. MARY, [b. Aug. 1, 1816; d. in 1836, unm.]

3. BENJAMIN, [b. Oct. 12, 1818; m. Charlotte Harvey of Manchester, and d. in Goffstown, date not given.]
4. GILMAN, [b. May 20, 1821; m. Lucinda Temple of Stoddard, and d. in that town, date not given.]
5. ALFRED, [b. Aug. 28, 1822; m. Sarah Goldsmith of Manchester; has a large family; lives in Lynn, Mass.]
6. HARRIET, [b. Sept. 6, 1825; d. in infancy.]
7. JOHN, [b. March 5, 1827; date of death not given.]
8. SARAH, [b. July 26, 1829; m. John H. Dadman; d. in Lynn, Mass., March 13, 1876.]
9. JAMES, [b. Sept. 20, 1831; m. Anthana Wilson, and lives in Nashua.]
10. ABIGAIL, [b. May 19, 1836; m. Horace Walter; d. in Lynn, Mass., Feb. 15, 1872.]

## DUSTIN.

ZACCHEUS DUSTIN, a great-great-grandson of Hannah Dustin of Indian fame, — some of Hannah Dustin's wearing apparel being still in possession of some of this branch of the descendants, — was the son of Eliphalet and Jennet (McCollum) Dustin of Francestown. He married Mary A. Dustin (his cousin), and came here in 1812 on to the Burns place, near Reed Carr's. After some twenty years he moved to the Weston place at North Branch, where he died in 1845, at the age of sixty-six years. His children were: —

1. LUKE LINCOLN, [b. March 21, 1806, and d. Feb. 27, 1818.]
2. JANE M., [b. April 8, 1808; m. John G. Proctor of Francestown, and moved there, where she d. in 1859, leaving one son: —
   *George A.*, (who entered the Union army, and was killed at the battle of Port Hudson.)]
3. BENJAMIN F., [b. Sept. 10, 1810; m. Roxanna Robb, Oct. 14, 1845, and lived at North Branch until after his father's death. In 1854 he moved on to the Swain place; thence in 1878 on to the Sylvester Preston farm. His children are: —
   *Washington F.*, (b. June 5, 1846; m. Alfaretta Batchelder of Hudson in 1876, and settled on the Foster place, having one child, Mark W., b. in January, 1877.)
   *Josie M.*, (b. March 31, 1848; m. Alvin Brown, Aug. 29, 1872.)
   *Charles H.*, (b. March 3, 1850; m. Eliza A. White of Keene, and is now a blacksmith at Marlborough Harbor.)
   *Mason E.*, (b. March 5, 1854.)

*John E.*, (b. Jan. 21, 1856.)
*Stella A.*, (b. Dec. 20, 1860.)
*Elmer A.*, (b. July 12, 1863.)
*Herbert W.*, (b. Feb. 3, 1865.)
*Marietta R.*, (b. May 29, 1872.)]

4. BETSEY A., [b. Jan. 15, 1813; m. John Campbell of this town, Nov. 14, 1842, and now resides in New York City.]
5. CALISTA, [b. July 15, 1815; m. Stephen Holmes, June 11, 1857, and d. in Greenfield, June 18, 1877, aged 62.]
6. MARIETTA, [b. July 6, 1819; m. Alexander W. Thayer, and lives in Brookline, Mass.]
7. LUCETTA M., [b. Jan. 8, 1823; m. Daniel A. Parsons, and lives in Worcester, Mass.]

## DUTTON.

HOSEA E. DUTTON, son of Reuben and Arthusa (Evans) Dutton, was born in Greenfield in 1835, and married Eliza A. Burton of Wilton in 1860. He came to Antrim in 1869, and bought the old Reuben Robinson place, where he was chiefly engaged in the lumber business, about nine years. Has recently moved to Francestown. He has one child:—

1. ANNIE E., [b. in 1871.]

MOSES DUTTON lived awhile on the Hiram Eaton farm. He united with the church in 1817. Little is known of him.

## EATON.

HIRAM EATON, son of James and Sarah (George) Eaton, was born in Deering, Dec. 11, 1817; came to Antrim in 1841, and built, in company with Jonathan White, the old shovel-shop on the street in South Village. There they carried on blacksmithing and the manufacture of hoes, and later the celebrated "Antrim shovel" was made by them. It is claimed that this patent originated in the mind of Mr. Eaton, while it was put in execution by the skillful hand of Mr. White. They were laughed at for thinking they could weld sheet-steel; but they succeeded, and now the best shovel in the world is thus made. Mr. Eaton married Edna C. Sweetser of Deering, March 28, 1844; moved on to the John McNiel place in 1856, which he has since occupied. Children:—

1. CHARLES H., [b. May 22, 1845; m. Addie L. Ellms of Scituate, Mass., March 11, 1871; has been several years in business in Boston. Is now one of the leading officers of the Knights of Honor in New England.]
2. LUVIA A., [d. in 1853, aged 6 years.]
3. WALTER S., [b. Feb. 22, 1855.]

JAMES EATON came here from Bethlehem in 1854, into the house east of Maplewood cemetery, and died in 1860. His father, James Eaton of Deering, married, first, Martha McClure; second, Mrs. Sarah (George) White. He was the son of Martha McClure, and half-brother to Hiram Eaton named above. His wife was Olive Wilson, and his children as follows: —

1. REBECCA, [b. in 1812; m. Amos Hemphill of Medford, Mass., and d. in 1872.]
2. HIRAM, [d. unm. in 1853, aged 40.]
3. LUCINDA, [m. Clinton French of Lyndeborough, and d. there in 1848.]
4. ROXANNA, [m. Sewall Skinner of Laconia, and d. there in 1840.]
5. JAMES, JR., [b. in 1823; came here in 1841 to help build Poor's reservoir; thence to Boston; served awhile getting out oak ship-timber in Louisiana; m. Mary C., daughter of Alexander Caldwell of Medford, Mass., in 1845; resided here till 1878, when he built in Bennington near the Antrim depot. Has three children living, as follows: —
*Francelia A.*, (m. Amos Wyman of Hillsborough Bridge.)
*Martha J.*, (m. Albert Baldwin, and lives in Brattleborough, Vt.)
*Edwin L.*, (b. in 1853; m. Fannie J. Dodge in 1875.)]
6. JOSEPH, [d. in South Village. unm., in 1853, the same day his brother Hiram was buried; he d. just while the funeral procession of his brother was on the way to the grave; aged 33.]
7. MELISSA, [m. John Sampson of Charlestown, Mass., and d. in that place childless; in 1876.]
8. LUCETTA, [m. Henry Delano of Duxbury, Mass., and d. in 1871.]

GEORGE W. EATON, son of Isaac and Betsey (Atwood) Eaton, was born in Francestown Nov. 30, 1840, and came to Antrim when quite young to work for Mrs. Alice Woodbury. He married Mary Jeanette Dow of Antrim Nov. 4, 1860, and succeeded Lyman Dow on the Esq. Hopkins place, from which he moved to Suncook in 1868, thence to Woonsocket, R. I. All their children but the youngest were born here.

1. ANNIE J., [b. Feb. 20, 1862.]
2. HATTIE W., [b. March 17, 1864.]
3. JENNIS S., [b. July 29, 1865.]
4. CHARLES L., [b. Oct. 1, 1867.]
5. NELLIE M., [b. Sept. 30, 1870.]

## EDES.

SAMUEL EDES came here from Needham, Mass., 1791, and settled a short distance southeast of the Dinsmore place, on High Range. His father was Nathan Edes. His mother was Mrs. Sarah (Smith) Hawes. This Nathan was a direct descendant of John Edes, who was born in Lawford, England, in 1651, and who came over and married Mary Tufts of Charlestown, Mass., in 1674. The family in England was of high character and position. Samuel Edes married, first, Elisabeth Baker, who was mother of all his children, and who died in Antrim Jan. 22, 1793, aged forty-five; married, second, Sarah Hutchinson, who died in Peterborough 1816, aged sixty-four; married, third, Mrs. Mary Eaton, who survived him and died in 1864, aged eighty-nine. Samuel Edes died July 10, 1845, aged ninety-two. He took an earnest part in the Revolutionary struggle. At the battle of Lexington he was in the Needham company of minute-men, out of which seven were killed. He had several narrow escapes that day. The night before the battle of Bunker Hill he was engaged driving oxen, getting ready for the morrow. He followed this all night, and there was no speaking above a whisper as the determined work of the patriots went on. The next year he became quartermaster and continued in that capacity for three years. Then retiring from the war, he lived for a time in Stoddard, but we cannot learn much more of him until his coming here, as mentioned above. His children were:—

1. SAMUEL, [b. March 15, 1775; m. Mary Waite of Londonderry; killed by fall of a timber in raising a barn in Peterborough, June 15, 1816. His widow became second wife of Robert Carr, named below. He left eight children. The youngest, left fatherless in infancy, after many hardships and struggles, is now an eminent physician in Cedar Rapids, Io.]
2. CATHERINE, [b. Feb. 16, 1777; m. Robert Carr of Hillsborough; d. 1819.]
3. ELISABETH, [b. July 15, 1779; m. Michael Walker, and moved to Maine.]
4. SARAH, [b. Sept. 6, 1781; m. John Howe, and settled in Temple, Me.]
5. JOSEPH, [b. Sept. 10, 1783; was killed by one of his neighbors in Temple, Me., 1863.]
6. JEREMIAH, [b. Aug. 24, 1785; m. Rebecca Whitney of Dedham, Mass.; went to Elizabeth City, N. J., and d. there 1865.]
7. REBECCA, [b. Sept. 17, 1787; m. Asahel Smith, and lives in Dedham, Mass.]
8. PATIENCE, [twin-sister of Rebecca; d. at the age of 3.]
9. DANIEL, [b. Jan. 2, 1790; m. Feb. 12, 1817, Jane Craige; d. in Peterborough, June 22, 1860.]

10. AMASA, [b. in Antrim March 21, 1792; was graduated at Dartmouth College, 1817; studied law in Belfast, Me., and then in Keene, under James Wilson, Sen. Was admitted to the bar in October, 1822. Between 1817 and 1822, while studying law, he taught a large part of the time in the academies of New Ipswich, Hancock, and Newport. In this last town he settled in the practice of law, and there he now resides in honorable and quiet old age. Is the oldest lawyer in practice in the State, and is president of the Sullivan County Bar. The reader is referred to his letter among the centennial papers. His wife, Sarah Hart of Keene, d. Oct. 8, 1869, aged 74. Their only surviving child, Samuel H. Edes, Esq. (Dartmouth College, 1844), is a lawyer of some note, and has been solicitor of Sullivan County.]

11. ISAAC, [b. in Antrim March 31, 1795; m. Elisabeth Mitchell; occupied the homestead of his father in Peterborough; was for many years a teacher, and had a local distinction as such that was just and well-deserved; was one of the selectmen of Peterborough in 1835, 1836, 1837, and 1838; was killed instantly by fall from a tree while picking apples, Oct. 26, 1859.]

12. POLLY, [b. in Antrim Dec. 6, 1797; m. Andrew Templeton, and went to New York.]

## ELLIOT.

ANDREW W. ELLIOT, son of Barnard C. and Deborah Elliot, was born in Concord in 1824, married Mary J. Gregg of Antrim, came here in 1850, and went to North Easton, Mass., in 1866 to continue there the manufacture of shovels in which he had been engaged here. They had one child born in Antrim: —

1. EDWIN L., [b. April 16, 1852; m. Martha A. Underwood of Orange, Mass., June 28, 1874.]

## EMERY.

JOHN EMERY, son of Daniel and Elizabeth (Straw) Emery, was born in Henniker, Nov. 24, 1799, and married Jane Sweetser of Bennington in 1820. He moved here the same year into a house then standing north of the now Keene road, in the extreme western part of the town, unto which there was no road of any kind above Chester Conn's corner. The Keene road was built in 1834. In 1835, Mr. Emery moved his buildings from their old location down to the Keene road, where he now lives.

He was a man of great endurance, as well as of courage and energy, for a long series of years. In 1862, Mrs. Jane (Sweetser) Emery died, and in 1863 he married Betsey Colby of Sutton. His children are: —

1. AURILLA, [m. Samuel Robb of Stoddard, July 3, 1851.]
2. MARTHA J., [m. B. F. McIlvaine Sept. 12, 1860.]

## ENGLISH.

THOMAS ENGLISH came here in 1779, probably from Hancock, and settled on the old road from the Madison Tuttle place to the Branch. The house stood on the north side of the road on the highest knoll in the field now James M. Tuttle's, but the cellar is filled up, and fifty harvests have grown upon the spot. He married Nancy Moore, daughter of Dea. William Moore of Bedford; was constable and tax-collector; was fifer in the Revolutionary army; was trusted and respected, but absconded with a portion of the town's money in 1782. The town attached his land, and friends settled it up; but he came here no more to live. He had a family of six children, but all have been dead many years, and nothing is known of their descendants.

It appears from the records of Bedford, that Nancy Moore, named above, who was a sister to Mrs. Alexander Jameson, was a second wife, inasmuch as it speaks of children of "Thomas English and *Agnes* his wife" and then speaks of the two youngest as "born in Antrim." The names of his children, so far as known, were these: —

1. JENNY, [b. in Bedford, April 12, 1771.]
2. JAMES, [b. Sept. 16, 1773.]
3. WILLIAM, [b. in Bedford, Jan. 23, 1776.]
4. ELIZABETH, [b. in Hancock, June 6, 1778.]
5. SARAH, [b. in Antrim 1781.]
6. ANDREW JACK, [b. in Antrim, April 21, 1783.]

## ESTEY.

EDGAR W. ESTEY was born in Hillsborough, Oct. 6, 1841. He came here at the age of twelve years to live with James Wood, where he remained until he entered the army in 1861. He was in the Ninth N. H. Regiment, and passed through many conflicts, and now carries in his body a bullet received in the battle of Spottsylvania Court-House. He was son of Joshua C. and Paulina (Emerson) Estey, and grandson of Joshua Estey, who was born in Hillsborough, July 2, 1776. The "Annals of Hillsborough" speak of "Joshua Easty," who was head of a family there in 1767. This Easty, or Estey, was from Middleton, Mass., and is no doubt the one who died Oct. 2, 1807, aged seventy-two. The father of Edgar W. was born Saturday, Oct. 17, 1812. Edgar W. Estey married Helen B. Curtis of Antrim, March 18, 1869; lived awhile at Staatsburg, N. Y., but now occupies the house at the Steele mills. Children: —

1. DANA W., [b. Nov. 28, 1870; d. March 19, 1872.]

2. Eva B., [b. Feb. 27, 1875.]

JOSHUA B. ESTEY, brother of the above, was born July 1, 1846; lived many years with Rev. Mr. Bates. He is now one of the leading dry-goods merchants in Manchester. He married Florence M. Burnham of Hartland, Vt.

## FAIRBANKS.

ZACCHEUS FAIRBANKS lived here nearly fifty years. His mother and the house she occupied were swept away by a hurricane. The house was carried forty rods. Portions of her clothing were torn off and carried five miles. Yet she survived and lived to be nearly one hundred years old. He came here from Framingham, Mass., and bought of Samuel Caldwell the Luke Vose place, as now known, in 1798. He was several years licensed to keep a hotel and sell liquor, which was not a disreputable business at that day. In 1835, being then an old man, he moved into a house built for the purpose by his son Woodbury, between Caleb Roach's and Thomas Flint's, where he died Jan. 6, 1845, aged eighty-six. He married, first, Mary Brinley, March 3, 1779, who lived but a few years; married, second, Martha Gates. The latter died May 21, 1853, aged eighty-six. There were fourteen children, two of them by the first wife; the five last being born in Antrim, the others in Framingham: —

1. Nancy, [m. 1st, a Mr. Bannister of Framingham; 2d, a Mr. Easty.]
2. Thomas, [b. June 17, 1783; m. Mary Laws of Acton, Mass., lived in Natick, Mass.; had a large family; d. about 1870.]
3. Mary, [known as "Polly," b. April 23, 1787; m. Solomon Rhodes, Oct. 22, 1807; d. Aug. 23, 1867. No children.]
4. Katherine, [b. March 20, 1789; m. Robert, son of James Duncan, Aug. 29, 1811; d. about 1847.]
5. Capt. Dexter, [b. Dec. 19, 1790; went into the war of 1812; after his return sunk into consumption and d. at age of 27.]
6. Samuel, [b. Jan. 11, 1793; d. unm., aged 32.]
7. Clarissa, [b. Oct. 4, 1794; m. Nathaniel Nichols of Haverhill, Mass., Oct. 20, 1814; d. in 1842.]
8. Charles, [b. Sept. 15, 1796; was out two years in the war of 1812; afterwards m. Maria Parker of Bradford, Mass.; was long in business in that place; has sons in trade in Haverhill, Mass., and there he is now living.]
9. Curtis, [b. Nov. 13, 1798; d. of spotted fever in 1812.]
10. Peter Woodbury, [always called simply "Woodbury," b. in Antrim, Oct. 31, 1800; m. Miriam Wilcox, Aug. 23, 1825; built the Caleb Roach house, where he lived many years, but in later life he moved to Lowell, Mass., and d. there in 1870. Children: —

*Mary*, (b. Jan. 20, 1827; d. March 4, 1834.)

*Kate*, (b. Feb. 20, 1830; m. Harrison Flint of Danbury, Conn.)

*Frances*, (b. April 20, 1833; m. John M. Godown of Fort Wayne, Ind.)

*Clark*, (b. July 31, 1834; unm.; has long been editor of the " Free Press," Fort Wayne, Ind.)

*George D.*, (b. Feb. 13, 1840; m. 1st, Lucy Putnam of Lowell, Mass.; m. 2d, Nannie Miner of Alexandria, Va. Is a merchant in Springfield, Mass.)]

11. SUSAN, [b. June 25, 1802; d. in childhood.]

12. LUCINDA, [b. March 30, 1804; m. Josiah Duncan, Dec. 28, 1826.]

13. WILLIAM E., [b. April 17, 1806; m. Hannah Coburn of Dracut, Mass.; moved to Cranston, R. I., and d. there.]

14. ABIGAIL MORRIS, [b. June 16, 1808; m. W. W. Coburn of Deering; lived and d. in that town. Her death occurred in March, 1853.]

## FAIRFIELD.

ALMUS FAIRFIELD, son of Joseph and Ruth (Campbell) Fairfield of New Boston, was born in that town Sept. 12, 1821. Ruth Campbell was a daughter of William and Ann (Christie) Campbell, and niece of John Campbell who settled in Antrim. Joseph Fairfield was son of Joseph and Elisabeth (Sweetser) Fairfield of Wenham, Mass. The last was son of Benjamin Fairfield, the leading man in Wenham in Revolutionary times. Benjamin's father was Hon. William Fairfield, who was for a long time the most prominent man in that section, was speaker of Massachusetts House of Representatives, and held every office *then* within the gift of the State. While he was speaker, all traveling then being on horseback, he started one morning to catch the animal and ride in for the usual session, as was his custom; but being absent-minded and much absorbed in the expected business of the day, he walked into Boston, seven or eight miles, bridle in hand, and mounted the speaker's desk before he noticed that he *hadn't got the horse!* The Hon. William was born in 1661, died 1742; was son of Walter, and grandson of John Fairfield, who was the first of the family this side the water, and died at a very great age in 1646. Almus Fairfield came to Antrim in 1841 as clerk for Hiram Griffin at the Branch. Bought out Mr. Griffin in 1849, and has been doing business there up to the present date. Has been postmaster since 1850, — longer probably than any other man in the county. Has been ten times elected town clerk. Has been much employed by his townsmen in probate business and making conveyances of real estate as justice of the peace. Married Lydia A. Gregg of Deering, Jan. 8, 1852. Their only child, Ruth Antoinette, born Nov. 12, 1853, married Charles E. Averill of Mont Vernon, Sept. 1, 1875, and now lives in Nashua. Almus Fairfield carried on an extensive business as a printer for many years in connection with his store, but relinquished it about 1875.

## FARRINGTON.

BARNARD FARRINGTON came here from Greenfield 1819, lived on the Dea. Shattuck farm, built the present house in 1829; was son of Ebenezer and Mary (Cudworth) Farrington; married Elenor Brewster of Francestown; lived here till 1830, when he sold to J. W. Christie, and moved to Deering, and died in that town 1848. His leg was badly broken and lacerated by the fall of a tree; he lingered several months in great distress, and passed away at the age of fifty-eight. Left three children besides two sons that died in childhood: —

1. EBEN, [b. here Nov. 27, 1820; m. Laura Sherborne, and now lives in Lowell.]
2. JAMES B., [b. Sept. 12, 1825; m. Sarah Taylor of Atkinson; has been many years a trader in Holyoke, Mass.]
3. MARY, [b. May 30, 1827; m. Caleb W. Roach, March 14, 1850.]

DANIEL FARRINGTON came here from Deering in 1823, and built the same year what was known as the Moses Duncan house. This house stood next west of Thomas Flint's, and was taken down in 1870. He was a brickmaker by trade; though an old man he superintended making brick for the Center Church, 1826. Died at great age, Feb. 25, 1842. He married, first, Barrodil Bucknam; second, Mrs. Elenor (——) Rhodes. They moved to Alexandria, and he died in that town. Had children (all we know of): —

1. DANIEL, JR., [b. in Medford, Mass., May 22, 1789; m. 1st, Nancy Green of Francestown, who d. 1817, aged 27; m. 2d, Elisabeth Gibson of Francestown in January, 1822; went from Antrim to Great Valley, N. Y., 1815; was town clerk in that place twenty years, postmaster fourteen years; held many other important trusts; left a large family, and d. there Sept. 25, 1863.]
2. FANNY, [m. Charles Houghton; d. De Oota, Io., Oct. 17, 1857.]
3. NANCY, [d. 1822 unm., aged about 25.]

## FERRY.

NOAH C. FERRY, son of Daniel and Elenor (Clark) Ferry, was born in Granby, Mass.; married Mary Smith of Deering; lived some years in Vermont; came here on the Alexander Parker place in 1838, but after a few years moved to West Deering, where he died in 1876, aged eighty-five years. His children are : —

1. LUCINDA, [m. Henry Holton and lives in Deering. Their only child, Edwin C. Holton, was editor of the "Hillsborough Messenger," and is now on the "Boston Globe."]
2. NOAH C., [b. in Vermont in 1825; m. Lucy J. Duncan of this town, Dec. 29, 1853, and now lives in the first house east of the East school-house, having children : —

    *Jennie M.*, (b. May 1, 1855; m. John C. Holt of New Boston, Jan. 2, 1878.)

    *Horace C.*, (b. Aug. 9, 1857; m. Annie George of Weare, March 5, 1880.)

    *Morris C.*, (twin-brother of Horace C., d. in 1865.)

    *Francis H.*, (d. in 1868, aged nearly 2 years.)

    *Nettie C.*, (d. in 1872, aged 3 years.)

    *Nellie F.*, (b. in 1875.)]
3. ALVIN, [m. Diana Marshall and lives in Hillsborough Upper Village.]
4. SARAH, [m. John A. White of Deering; d. Aug. 16, 1878.]
5. JAMES P., [b. in Johnson, Vt., in 1835; m. Nancy W. McClure of New Boston, and lives in West Deering.]
6. HARRISON C., [b. in Antrim in 1838; m. 1st, Clintina Colby of Bennington; m. 2d, Louise M. Dodge of Antrim, and lives in West Deering. Is editor and proprietor of the "Hillsborough Messenger."]

## FERSON.

JOHN FERSON, son of James and Margaret (Starrett) Ferson, came here from Francestown in 1819 and lived on the James Nesmith place, on the northwest slope of Meeting-House Hill. He married Lucy F. Wood of Francestown in 1819; moved to Nashua, where he died in 1872, aged eighty-two. His children were : —

1. LUCY M., [b. in 1820; m. Granville Rideout, and d. at Nashua in 1860.]
2. MARY S., [b. in 1822, and d. in Francestown in 1840.]
3. JOHN L., [b. in 1823; m. Mary Branch, and is now living in Oshkosh, Wis.]
4. CLARA A., [b. in 1826, m. Amos Fletcher, and now lives in Nashua.]
5. JAMES S., [b. in 1827; m. Augusta Willard, and lives in Pine City, Minn.]

GENEALOGIES.  491

MOSES B. FERSON, brother of above, married Sally Colby, Oct. 21, 1823. He owned and lived on the place where N. C. Ferry now resides, and died in 1857. His children are : —

1. LEVI C., [b. Dec. 13, 1824; m. Lizzie R. Fields of Northfield, and now resides at Andover.]
2. HARRIS DANE, [b. June 30, 1826; m. Lucy Codman of Deering, and now lives in California.]
3. SARAH M. C., [b. June 27, 1829; m. George Holt, and lives in Chelmsford, Mass.]
4. JOHN J., [b. Dec. 8, 1831, and now lives in Hanover.]
5. VERONA E., [b. Dec. 16, 1833; m. Stillman Willard, and lives in Methuen, Mass.]
6. MARY A., [m. John N. Webster; lives in Fitchburg, Mass.]
7. GEORGE L., [now living in Lowell, unm.]

## FIELD.

OTIS FIELD, son of John and Ruth (Thayer) Field of Peterborough, was born in that town Jan. 12, 1794; married Lydia Dodge; came here and lived a few years at the Center of the town. Here his wife died Nov. 10, 1839, aged forty-seven. He died in 1863. They had six children, but we have no knowledge of them further. Otis was a brother of Dea. John Field of Peterborough. The family came from Braintree, Mass.

## FISHER.

DEA. SAMUEL FISHER came from Ireland at the age of eighteen, in " the starved ship," in 1740. A table-spoonful of oat-meal moistened with salt water was the daily allowance for fourteen days. This failing at last, they lived on the bodies of the dead. When these were consumed they drew lots to determine which should die to preserve the rest, and the lot fell on Mr. Fisher. But as the sad preparations were nearly completed, a ship came in sight, signals of distress were made, the work of death was delayed, and all were soon rescued. In all his long life Dea. Fisher could never after " see, without pain, the least morsel of food wasted, or a pail of water thrown carelessly on the ground." His first wife was Sarah Taylor of Londonderry. In that town he settled, and died there April 10, 1806, aged eighty-three. Dea. Fisher was tall, grave, commanding, and able both in body and mind. He had twelve children. One of them was Dea. James Fisher, who married Sarah Steele of Antrim, aunt of Dea. Robert Steele. This James Fisher seems to have been here for a time, and probably his oldest child may have been born here. He then settled in Francestown, and was a leading man in that place. He was a very devoted man. Some of the first meetings in Francestown were held in his barn. He is said to have given the ground on which the church of Francestown stands. He was a vigorous and consistent Presbyterian. Himself and wife in the early days came to Antrim to communion, and brought their children here to be baptized. The mother was a fleshy woman and had to have a horse by herself. Sometimes they came with the cart and oxen.

There was a Samuel Fisher in this town two or three years, running the first little fulling-mill in South Village. He advertised in the Amherst paper May 12. 1798, for payment by "all indebted for dressing cloth as he should leave town in three weeks." He was probably a son of Dea. Samuel of Londonderry, and brother of Dea. James named above. I have found no further information concerning him.

Matthew A. Fisher, born in 1785, was son of Dea. James Fisher and Sarah Steele; married Jane Warren Christie of Antrim; settled in Hancock, where his two oldest children were born, and subsequently located on the homestead of his father in Francestown. Their five children are all living as follows: Zibiah Ann, who married Roswell N. Temple of Reading, Mass.; Mary Jane, who married James H. Hall of Brookline; Samuel C., who married, first, Mary E. Barnes, and second, Sarah Jane Christie, and lives in Dover; Charles W., who married Elisabeth Nott, and lives in Chelsea, Mass.; and Gilman C., who married Hattie W. Stevens, and lives in Dover.

CHRISTOPHER C. FISHER was son of Jonathan and Rebecca (Adams) Fisher, and grandson of Jonathan and Phebe (Thurston) Fisher of Alstead, and was born in Dalton, Sept. 8, 1809; came here in May, 1847; married Mary A. Hills, July 29, 1839; had charge of town farm from 1859 to 1865; moved to Antrim, Minn., in 1865, where he yet lives. They had but one child: —

1. LIZZIE A., [b. May 1, 1847; m. Jason K. Webster, Jan. 1, 1867. (See Webster.)]

## FLANDERS.

JONATHAN FLANDERS lived here five or six years, say from 1790 to 1795; but I have not found where, nor learned much concerning him. Jonathan and Sarah Flanders had two children born here: —

1. BETTY, [b. Aug. 18, 1790.]
2. THOMAS, [b. March 29, 1792.]

## FLETCHER.

ROBERT FLETCHER, the ancestor of the American Fletchers, came from Yorkshire, England, to Concord, Mass., and settled there in 1630. His fourth son, Francis Fletcher, was born in Concord, Mass., in 1636. *His* son Joseph was born in 1661, and *his* son Francis in 1698. This second Francis had a son Francis, who was born in Concord, Mass., in 1733; served through the Revolutionary war; married Sarah Parker of Westford, Mass., and moved to New Ipswich in 1760, where he died in 1797, leaving a large family, one of whom was Samuel, who came to Antrim.

DEA. SAMUEL FLETCHER was born in New Ipswich, April 19, 1789. At the death of his father he was but eight years of age, and he then went to live with Dr. James Crombie of Temple. He came to Antrim in 1813; April 20, 1814, he married Annie Bodwell of Antrim, and settled on the farm near the late Artemas Brown's, in the west part of the town, where he died in 1845. His mother, Mrs. Sarah (Parker) Fletcher, died in this town in 1825. His widow now lives in Bunker Hill, Ill. Dea. Fletcher was for many years an elder in the Presbyterian Church, and prominent in various public affairs. He represented Antrim in the legislature six years, and was one of the selectmen twelve years, being most of the time chairman of the board. He was justice of the peace, and for a time town clerk. He was highly and universally esteemed, and his death in the prime of his years was an event of public sorrow. He died suddenly of malignant erysipelas. Being called to assist in preparing for burial the body of his near neighbor, Joseph S. Atherton, who died of that disease, he is supposed to have been inoculated with it, as it soon after came upon him in terrible form. His children, all of whom are gone from Antrim, are as follows: —

1. LYDIA, [b. June 8, 1815 ; m. Reuben Hill, Nov. 4, 1834, and d. April 25, 1852.]
2. LOUISA, [b. June 26, 1816 ; m. George W. Winship of Nashua, Feb. 1, 1841, and d. at Brighton, Mass., Aug. 31, 1845, having children : —

*Georgianna*, (b. Dec. 17, 1841.)

*Louisa F.*, (b. Aug. 19, 1845 ; m. 1st, John A. Hall of Hillsborough ; m. 2d, Stephen A. Brown of that place, Lower Village.)]

3. HANNAH K., [b. March 17, 1818 ; m. Milton Hill of Hancock, Oct. 23, 1838. They removed to the West in 1859 and now live in California. Three children grew up, as follows : —

*Lorenzo M.*, (b. Jan. 2, 1840 ; m. Annie Sheppard ; lives in Macon, Ill.)

*Elisabeth*, (b. June 10, 1842 ; m. 1st, Reuben Bates, who was killed in the capture of Fort Blakely, Mobile, in 1864 ; m. 2d, A. D. Kieth, and lives in Geyserville, Cal.)

*Ellen E.*, (b. Oct. 16, 1846 ; m. Henry Judd, Aug. 10, 1876, and lives in Cottonwood Falls, Kan.)]

4. JOANNA C., [b. Jan. 24, 1820 ; m. J. H. Muzzey, Sept. 27, 1846 ; d. at Bunker Hill, Ill., in 1864.]
5. RACHEL, [b. Sept. 23, 1822 ; m. Samuel Fletcher of East Washington, and has but one child living, Ida Florence, b. June 26, 1859.]
6. SAMUEL A., [b. Sept. 26, 1824 ; m. Henrietta M. Crane in

1851; moved to Bunker Hill, Ill., in 1857; has been mayor of that city. Has children: —

*James A.*, (b. in Antrim, Feb. 29, 1852.)
*William F.*, (b. in Bunker Hill, Ill., June 7, 1860.)
*Fannie May*, (b. Dec. 2, 1868.)]

7. SARAH E., [b. Dec. 27, 1827; m. John R. Gregg of Peterborough, May 20, 1847; he d. April 16, 1873, aged 55; she has recently followed him; was a most devoted woman. They had three children: —

*Annie J.*, (b. March 23, 1848; m. Wiley J. Macy of Munfordville, Ky, and lives in that place.)
*Sarah E.*, (b. April 24, 1851, m. Frank Wright, and lives in Harrisville.)
*Harriet L.*, (b. Nov. 21, 1860, d. aged 17.)]

8. FRANCIS, [b. May 3, 1830, and d. April 4, 1831.]

9. MARTHA J., [b. in 1832; m. John Johnson, Dec. 21, 1852, a mechanic, who d. in 1857. She removed to Bunker Hill, Ill., m. Henry Wise in 1864, and d. Aug. 18, 1867, leaving two children: —

*Nellie Johnson*, (b. in Antrim March 26, 1855, m. John Hill, and lives in Bunker Hill, Ill.)
*Henry H. Wise*, (b. Feb. 20, 1865.)]

GEORGE H. FLETCHER, known as "Howard Fletcher," moved here in October, 1866, and from here to Mont Vernon, April, 1873. The family for several generations lived in East Washington, where George H. was born March 6, 1844. He married Luthera C. Barney of Washington, July 4, 1866. Lived in the Charon house, North Branch. He was the son of Samuel and Rebecca Fletcher, and grandson of Jeremiah and Lucy Fletcher. This Jeremiah was brother of Dea. Samuel Fletcher of Antrim.

ISAAC FLETCHER, son of Samuel and Beulah (Hathorn) Fletcher of Chelmsford, Mass., was born in Temple in 1805, married Roxanna Blanchard of Washington in 1827, lived in Unity, Lempster, Milford, and other places, and came here in 1860, on to the Starrett place in South Village. His children are: —

1. SILAS, (m. Mary J. Fifield of Nashua, and d. in Antrim in 1860, leaving two children: —

    *Annie.*

    *Charles*, (b. here a few weeks after his father's death.)]

2. CHARLES S., [b. in 1831, m. Sarah A. Allds March 25, 1874, and now lives in South Village.]

3. JANE, [m. George Smith of Mont Vernon; d. there in 1869.]

4. NANCY, [d. unm. at the age of 20.]
5. ALMIRA, [m. John H. Smith of this town, in 1862.]

## FLINT.

Four men by the name of Flint came over and settled in Massachusetts as early as 1640. Thomas and William, brothers, came from Wales, and settled in Salem, Mass. This Thomas was ancestor of Hutchinson Flint of Antrim. William owned nearly all the land on which the city of Salem now stands, was a prosperous man, and died in 1673, aged seventy. His daughter Alice was arraigned before the Essex County Court in 1652, for " wearing a silk hood;" but on proving she was worth two hundred pounds (and therefore could afford to dress better than other girls), she was discharged. Two other brothers, probably akin to those named above, came from Matlock, Derbyshire, England, and settled in Concord, Mass., in 1638. The older of these, Rev. Henry Flint, married Margery Hoar (sister of President Hoar of Harvard College), and was settled in Braintree, now Quincy, in 1640, and died at his post in 1668, leaving five children. Thomas, brother of Rev. Henry, was a man of wealth and Christian excellence, and died in 1653, aged fifty. His descendants are very numerous and respectable; among them the Flints of Rutland, Mass., from whom came the family of John G. Flint, Esq., of Antrim. This Thomas settled and died in Concord, Mass. His wife, Abigail, died Dec. 18, 1689. Thomas and Abigail had a son, Col. John Flint, who married Mrs. Mary Oakes, Nov. 12, 1667. Col. John was representative of Concord, Mass., in 1678, 1680, and 1682; was town clerk from 1680 to 1686; and died Dec. 5, 1686. Col. John had a son Thomas, born Jan. 16, 1682, who married Mary Brown, and had a large family, among them a son, Thomas, Jr., who settled in Rutland, Mass. Thomas of Rutland was thus a great-grandson of the Thomas who settled in Concord, Mass., in 1638. Thomas Flint of Rutland married Eunice How, Jan. 22, 1745. He died May 6, 1802. She died Sept. 10, 1796, aged seventy-nine. She was daughter of Moses How, Esq., formerly of Brookfield, Mass. Her brother, Samuel How, born Sept. 23, 1719, was the first white male child born in Rutland, for which his father received one hundred acres of land.

Thomas, of *Salem*, first mentioned above, was in that place as early as 1640. He purchased tracts of land in 1654, and again in 1662, which are in possession of the family to this day. Giles Cary, who witnessed these deeds, became a victim to the witchcraft delusion in 1692, being very aged, and was executed by being "pressed to death." Thomas of Salem, by his first wife, Ann, left six children. Capt. Thomas, the oldest of them, was a brave military man, was in King Philip's war, was badly wounded, but lived to good old age and left a large family. Ebenezer, his son by his second wife, Mary Dounton, was born in 1683, married Gertrude Pope, and died in 1767. Nathan, son of Ebenezer Flint and Gertrude Pope, was born May 8, 1716, and moved with his family from North Reading, Mass., to Amherst, in 1774. His wife was Lydia Hutchinson, and the youngest of his six children was Hutchinson Flint, who came to Antrim, and whose record is given below.

HUTCHINSON FLINT was born in North Reading, Mass., June 10, 1764; married Lucy Cole, and came here from Amherst (now Mont Vernon) in 1795. He succeeded Robert Holmes on the place long known as the town farm, where now is the new and desirable residence of H. D. Chapin. His first residence here was in a log house a little west of the Bond place. Afterwards he built a better log house about sixty rods north of the first one, and after a few years built the framed house on the present site. Mr. Flint was many years a sufferer from paralysis, — became almost helpless, — and passed away with the sympathy and respect of his fellow-men. His death was in June, 1817. His children were: —

1. LYDIA, [b. March 5, 1788; m. James Brown, Dec. 5, 1816; lived awhile where Mrs. Joy now lives; had two children, James and Lucy, b. here; went to Wales, N. Y., about 1830; d. in 1859.]
2. LUCY, [b. Feb. 1, 1790; m. Benjamin Pollard; went to Wales, N. Y., and d. there in 1858. She left only two children, Hopkins and Seymour.]
3. LOIS, [b. March 9, 1792; m. Benjamin Pike, April 5, 1814; lived in Montpelier, Vt., but d. in Lexington, Mass., in 1840; no children.]
4. LYNDA, [b. Aug. 28, 1793; was a tailoress; lived alone awhile on the place now Mrs. Joy's; went to Wales, N. Y.; m. —— Holman; afterwards joined the Mormons, and d. in Salt Lake City, in 1855.]
5. ADAM, [b. March 7, 1796; m. Mrs. Lydia (Eaton) George of Deering, Dec. 11, 1834; lived on homestead till he sold it to the town in 1833; then lived quite a number of years in Deering, but came back and put up the frame of a large house on the site of Dea. Putney's present residence. Before the house was finished outside or inside, he d. Jan. 9, 1854. It was never inhabited, and, after standing in a dilapidated condition some time, was taken down and removed. Adam Flint left no children; was a respectable and good man, and his sudden death was greatly lamented.]
6. CYNTHIA, [b. Feb. 3, 1798; went to New York in 1828; joined the Mormons; was one of the large number disaffected by polygamy who left Salt Lake and settled seven hundred miles west of that place, in a town called San Bernardino. She m. a man by the name of Meesic.]
7. DEA JOHN, [b. May 28, 1800; m. Sally Atwood, Jan. 31, 1822; put up the Dea. Bond farm-buildings; there lived some years and had children: Thomas, Joshua, and Claor-

rie; moved to Wales, N. Y., about 1830; thence to Albany, Wis., where his large family are settled close about him, and where he d. Nov. 18, 1878; was deacon of the Congregational Church; a man of thought, and of sincere piety.]
8. EUNICE, [twin-sister of John; m. Amos Blanchard, April 6, 1820; went to Wales, N. Y., and d. there Jan. 20, 1874.]
9. ANSTISS, [b. Sept. 28, 1803; d. Jan. 12, 1852; m. in Aurora, N. Y., to Palmer Bowen and d. there. Left seven children. The oldest, Byron, was a lawyer in Buffalo; the others were Webster, Jane, Charles M., Kate, Frances, and Clark B.]
10. NATHANIEL, [b. April 3, 1805; m. Hannah Nabor of Hancock; went to Lexington, Mass., and d. there, March, 1874. Left several daughters, and two sons, George and William W., now both of Lexington. Nathaniel was in shoe business in that place most of his life.]
11. JAMES M., [b. Oct. 1, 1807; d. of spotted fever in 1812.]
12. THOMAS, [b. Nov. 9, 1809; was several years in the West; in 1837 bought the John Smith place, which he now occupies; is unm.; a peculiar man, but one of much reading, intelligent mind, and honest piety. When he was two years old he was very sick and they sent for Dr. Adams. He came, prepared a cup of medicine, a powerful dose after the custom of those days, and set it down before the old-fashioned fire to warm it a little. Just then Tommy slipped out of his mother's arms, waddled along to the fire, and kicked the cup under the back-log. The doctor only remarked: " D——n him, he'll live!" and he lived.]

THOMAS FLINT and Eunice How, referred to above as having settled in Rutland, Mass., had ten children, all born in that town, as follows: Sarah, who married James King; Thomas, who married Anne (or Nancy) Lilly, and settled in Rutland; John, of whom nothing is known by the writer; Eunice, who married Daniel Nitt of Paxton, Mass.; Dorothy, who married Daniel Snow of Paxton, Mass.; Lucy, who married John Hayden of Oakham; Tilly, born March 17, 1759, who married Ruth Forsdick, settled in Rutland, was many years deacon in Congregational Church, and was a most efficient and estimable man; Dr. Jonas, who will be further noticed below; Moses How, born Feb. 6, 1763, who died in infancy; and Caroline, who married Elisha Allen of Petersham, Mass., Aug. 30, 1787.

Dr. Jonas Flint, with twelve others, enlisted in the Revolutionary army from their native town, Rutland, Aug. 29, 1777. Dr. Jonas's name appears several times on the pay-rolls now in the state-house, Boston. On return from the army he pursued his studies with such poor advantages as were at hand, then after a time went to study medicine with Dr. Frink of Westmoreland. He married Eunice Gardner of that town, and settled down there in the practice of his profession, in which he was very successful. But after a time, at the importunity of relatives there, he was induced to move to St. Johnsbury, Vt., where most of his children were born. There he had an extensive practice, though he used to say " there was no money in it, because the settlers in that then new country were poor." There, except a short sojourn in Stoddard, and another in Windsor in old age, Dr. Flint remained, dying July 20, 1849, aged eighty-nine. He had children: Alvin, Henry, Austin, John G., William, Jonas, Jr., Shubel, Laura, and George, — eight sons and one daughter. John G. Flint, Esq., of this town, is the only one of them living. He was born in St. Johnsbury, Vt., Feb. 12, 1797. In 1802, though only five years old, he was apprenticed to Stephen Wyman of Windsor. There he remained some thirty-five years, and in due time inherited the Wyman farm. He married Sarah Gregg of Antrim. All his children were born on the farm in Windsor. Mr. and Mrs. F. celebrated their golden wedding Nov. 22, 1871. He was often representative of Windsor; was a prominent military man in his day, of soldierly address and bearing; enjoyed the respect and confidence of the community in his old age; a man of fine natural abilities, and Christian faith and character. He died Feb. 6, 1880. His children are: —

1. STEPHEN W., [b. July 11, 1824 ; m. Almira, daughter of Dr. Stickney, July 17, 1848; lives in Bellows Falls, Vt.; was one of the givers of the organ to the Center Church ; is engaged in trade and manufacture; a very efficient business man; has children : Sarah L., b. Nov. 22, 1851 ; Anna L., b. July 11, 1855 ; Frank G.; Mary G.; and John W. The two first were born in Antrim.]
2. ELISA, [d. in childhood.]
3. JOHN G., JR., [b. Feb. 16, 1829, m. Frances Kneeland of Milwaukee, Wis., and lives in that city. Is engaged in the spice trade. Is a wide-awake and able man, and has been very successful in business. A self-made and fearless man. Was one of the donors of organ and of vestry to the Center Church, and one of the heaviest givers to the chapel at the Branch. The two brothers, John G. and Stephen W., were in the business of wooden manufactures at the Branch awhile on their first starting in the world. John G. has but one child, Wyman Kneeland, b. March 4, 1869.]
4. LOUISA A., [b. Nov. 17, 1831, m. Rev. Henry Dorr, d. Aug. 9, 1877.]
5. SARAH O., [b. March 1, 1835, m. Rev. Jesse Wagner, now of Boston.]

6. LAURA, [b. Nov. 8, 1839, m. George W. Kittredge of Mont Vernon. They lived with her parents at the Branch, and he d. there, Nov. 7, 1869, aged 33, leaving one child, John G., b. Nov. 2, 1864.]

JOHN .FLINT, son of Bateman and Polly (Emerson) Flint, married Susan Barker of Hancock, Jan. 30, 1821; came here in 1837, buying of James Styles the farm set off to Hancock in 1847; lived there till 1865, when he moved to Hancock village, and died there in 1872, aged seventy-nine. His children that grew up were : —

1. AARON B., [b. in 1824, m. Loisa Healy of Washington, lives in Ancoria, N. J.]
2. ELIZABETH A., [b. in 1827, m. J. H. Wood of Hancock.]
3. CHARLES M., [b. in 1829, m. Mary R. Richardson of this town ; lives in Fitchburg, Mass. : is a machinist, and an inventor and manufacturer of valuable saw-mill machinery.]

## FORSAITH.

SQUIRES FORSAITH, son of David and Nancy (Mills) Forsaith, was born in Deering in 1840, and married Abbie H. Colby of Hillsborough Bridge. He learned the tinman's trade at that place, came here in 1872, and bought out the shop of Luke Thompson. He built his house in 1875. Is leader of Antrim Cornet Band, and has a high musical reputation. He has three children : —

1. STELLA F., [b. Dec. 11, 1866.]
2. MARY E., [b. April 26, 1875.]
3. EDITH B., [b. Oct. 24, 1877.]

## FOSTER.

WILLIAM S. FOSTER, born in Essex, Mass., March 19, 1801, was son of Zebulon and Polly (Story) Foster, and grandson of Aaron and Ruth (Lowe) Foster. Aaron was a soldier at the capture of Louisburg, and was out in most of the Revolution. Two of his sons, Moses and Thomas, were soldiers in the Revolution. This family descended from Reginald Foster, who came from England with a large family and settled in Essex, formerly Chebacco, in 1638, and died in 1680. His son, Reginald, Jr., was two years old when brought to this country, and died Dec. 28, 1707, leaving a large family, among whom was John, who died Dec. 9, 1736, aged seventy-two. Moses Foster, son of this John, was father of Aaron named above, and died September, 1785, aged eighty-five. Zebulon Foster was born Aug. 2, 1766; moved to Henniker in 1814, after the birth of all his children, and died in the last-named place, Dec. 16, 1849. His wife survived him and died Aug. 3, 1851, aged eighty-one. Her father, William Story, was a captain in the Revolution.

William S. Foster was a carpenter by trade and came to Antrim in the spring of 1826 to help build the Center Church. He boarded with Stevens Paige, and thus became acquainted with his daughter, Harriet, whom he married Dec. 27, 1827, after which he continued to reside in this town. In 1829 he moved on to the William McDole place, where he lived forty-six years. He married, second, Mary Cooledge, Nov. 28, 1850. Mr. Foster was one of our best and most conspicuous men for many years; was representative of the town; was chairman of the selectmen during the war; and was called to fill many positions of trust and honor. In old age he made profession of his faith in Christ, and, after a long and painful sickness, he passed away in Christian confidence and peace, July 10, 1875. His children were: —

1. STEVENS P., [b. in 1828. He left Antrim in early manhood, and was last heard of in London, in 1851.]
2. WILLIAM S., [b. in 1830, m. Margaret Shaw of Massachusetts, and has lived many years in Mobile, Ala.]
3. AARON W., [b. in 1832, and went South. He entered the rebel army, lost an arm at Malvern Hill, and d. from effects thereof in 1872.]
4. JENNETTE A., [b. in 1834, and d. April 6, 1858.]
5. JOHN W., [b. in 1837, m. Hannah E. Hunt of Newton, N. J., in 1862, and settled in Clinton Village, where he was engaged in the manufacture of bedsteads. He was a young man of excellent character and unusual promise. He d. April 13, 1868, in the prime of life and deeply mourned, leaving children: —

    *Harriet A.*, (b. Feb. 27, 1863.)
    *Emma J.*, (b. Aug. 2, 1866.)
    *William S.*, (b. March 20, 1868.)]
6. HENRY H., [b. in 1841. He entered the Union army, the Sevehth N. H. Regiment, and died in the service, in Florida, in 1862.]
7. LEONARD M., [b. in 1846, and d. in 1853.]
8. HARRIET A., [twin-sister of Leonard M., d. in 1849.]

CHARLES H. FOSTER, son of Isaiah and Patty (Hartwell) Foster, was born in Hillsborough in 1819, married Martha A. Sargent, and came here in 1855, into a house moved from Stoddard for that purpose, and put up opposite the old Burns mill, on Stoddard road. He came here to run the mill, but moved away in two years. He had two sons, Charles N. and Leona W., the latter of whom was born in this town.

## FOX.

ELIPHALET FOX, son of Samuel and Sarah (Duncan) Fox, was born in Hancock in 1802, and came here when a small boy to learn the tanner's trade with his uncle George Duncan. He married Mary Barker in 1837, and went to Stoddard, where he died Oct. 11, 1862. The same year his widow and children moved to North Branch, and went thence to Pittston, Me., in 1869. The children were: —

1. SARAH J., [b. in 1840, m. Joseph Moulton in 1865, and now lives in Cushing, Me.]
2. GEORGE DUNCAN, [b. in 1843, and was killed at the battle of Antietam Sept. 17, 1862.]
3. SAMUEL B., [b. in 1846, m. Louise Gray in 1869, and lives in Westfield, Mass.]
4. MARIANNA, [b. in 1852.]

JEDEDIAH FOX came here from Hancock with his friend George Duncan, and worked apparently at the tanning business for Frederick Poor, a part of several years. He was born in New Ipswich in 1781, and was somewhat older than Duncan. After his marriage Fox seems to have boarded here with his wife, part of the time for two years or more. Duncan bought the tannery here, and Fox that in Hancock; to which town the latter with his young child soon moved. He died there, Sept. 21, 1858, aged seventy-seven. He was the oddest and strangest of men, and his sayings are still common in the community where he spent most of his life. Was a genial, good man, rigidly honest, and of marked ability, highly and universally respected, and mourned at his death by all. He was son of Timothy Fox. His mother's name was Dudley. The family came from Woburn, Mass. I find the name conspicuous in that ancient place, among the officials both of church and town. Jedediah Fox married Sarah Wheeler, a native of Mont Vernon, being daughter of John and Mary (Butterfield) Wheeler, who afterwards settled in Hancock. John Wheeler is said to have kept the tavern at Hancock till his death; and Fox, marrying his daughter, left the tanning business in later years, and kept the same hotel till death. Jedediah's brother Samuel was father of Eliphalet Fox, named above. The only child of Jedediah and Sarah (Wheeler) Fox was Charles James, born in Antrim, Oct. 28, 1811. He was one of the ablest and best men New Hampshire ever produced.

There has been some questioning as to the birthplace of Charles James Fox. I have given the matter the most painstaking search for a long time, with the object of determining the truth, and I cannot avoid the conclusion that Mr. Fox was born here. And this with not the remotest wish to rob Hancock. That town has sent forth a multitude of noble men into the world, and has a plenty of good stock left. I cherish the highest regard for Hancock and its people, and the honor of its good name, and noble record. But the facts convince me that in this case the honor of a great man's birthplace belongs to Antrim. The traditions and recollections of aged people are so vague and contradictory, now after seventy years, as to seem to about balance each other, and be of small value as evidence. The birth is on the Hancock town record, but was entered there many years subsequent to the event, as an examination of the page will show. It does not mention the *place* of birth, but was probably put there at the father's request to preserve the date and parentage. Many such entrances are found in Antrim and other town records, which I have found to have value only as determining dates. On the other hand, the records and various biographies in connection with Dartmouth College, which must have *originated with Mr. Fox himself*, give his residence Hancock, but his birthplace Antrim. This is on record also as the impression of some of his college mates *at the time*. I know of no way to avoid this evidence. As one of the oldest and most distinguished professors wrote me about it, "It must have come from some one who knew the facts." And these "facts," to my certain knowledge, are taken if possible from each member of college *himself*. The "History of Dunstable," published by Mr. Fox, the same year of his death, gives his birthplace as *Antrim*. This was not written by Mr. Fox himself, but by his pastor and most intimate friend after the author became too feeble to write, and appears in an introductory biographical notice, dictated without doubt by Mr. Fox, in those weeks when his head was clear but he was too feeble to write. As his childhood and youth were spent in Hancock, and his parents, quite noted, were then living in Hancock, there does not seem to be any reason for mentioning Antrim, except the *fact* that he was born here. I can't see any chance to call it a mistake. Also in " Drake's American Biography," with early and careful pains to get at the facts, it is said that " Charles James Fox, lawyer and author, was born in Antrim." I have not room to say more, but this seems to me conclusive concerning this modern Homer; at least sufficient to warrant the following notice. This also explains why this great and honored man was not mentioned in any of the exercises at Hancock centennial.

 Charles James Fox fitted for college at Francestown Academy, and under the private tuition of Rev. Archibald Burgess of Hancock. He was graduated at Dartmouth College with high honors, in the class of 1831. He studied law with Hon. Isaac O. Barnes, then of Francestown, and completed his legal studies at the New Haven Law School. He then entered the office of Hon. Daniel Abbott of Nashua, with whom he soon became a partner in the practice of law. Was treasurer of Nashua and Lowell Railroad; county solicitor in 1835–44; commissioner of bankruptcy; was appointed one of a committee of three to revise the " Statutes of New Hampshire " in 1841–42, the other members being Judges Bell and Parker (a remarkable compliment to his learning and knowledge of law, as he was not quite thirty years old when appointed); was member of the legislature in 1837; published " The Town Officer," a most valuable book, in 1843; compiled, in connection with Rev. Samuel Osgood, D.D., " The New Hampshire Book of Prose and Poetry;" traveled in West Indies and Egypt in 1844–45, of which he published an interesting sketch; and, last, published the " History of Dunstable " (Nashua) in 1846. Mr. Fox also wrote many poems which went the round of the magazines and brought him much praise. These have never been collected in a volume. He died after long sickness in Nashua, Feb. 17, 1846, aged thirty-four. With all the honors of his life, he was a Christian. Very few men so young have left so glorious a record. What he accomplished in about nine years of active life, is truly marvelous! (See sketch by Dr. Samuel Osgood, D. D., "Christian Examiner," 1846.) Mr. Fox married in June, 1840, Catherine Pickman Abbott of Nashua, daughter of Judge Abbott. Their only child, Charles William Fox, was born March 9, 1843; graduated at Harvard College in 1864; after study in New York, and in foreign lands, he settled as a physician in Philadelphia, in 1870. Mrs. Catherine P. Fox married Ex-Gov. Samuel Dinsmore in May, 1853. I have heard her spoken of as a woman of remarkable grace of manner, and excellence of life. Ex-Gov. Dinsmore died Feb. 27, 1869.

## FRYE.

A DR. FRYE was the first physician in Antrim. He seems to have come here about 1786, and to have stayed about two years, when, thinking he could do better elsewhere, he moved away. He was probably a young man without a family. It is not known whence he came or whither he went; and his principal distinction is that he was the first of the medical art among us, leading the van of the little army dealing out pills and potions, and having a line of most worthy successors, whatever he might have been himself.

## FULLER.

JOSEPH FULLER, a shoemaker, came here from Massachusetts about 1806. He lived in the Henry Hill house, built by B. Ballard, and had a shop in it for many years. He married Nancy George, and had one son born in Antrim. The family all moved to the State of Maine long since, and I have not been able to learn more about them.

1. AUSTIN GEORGE, [b. Jan. 13, 1807.]

## GATES.

STEPHEN GATES, son of Thomas, of Norwich, England, came over in 1642 and settled in Hingham, Mass., and had four children: Stephen, Simon, Thomas, and Mary. Simon, the second of these, also had four children: Simon, Jr., who settled in Marlborough, Mass.; Amos, who settled in Framingham, Mass.; Samuel, and Jonathan. Capt. Amos Gates of Framingham had children: Amos, Molly, Anna, George, Charles, Henry, Oakham, Trowbridge, Martha R., Ruth, Susanna, and John. Of these, George, Henry, Oakham, and John were out in the Revolutionary army.

GEORGE GATES came here from Framingham in 1800. His wife was Hannah Barrett. They settled on the south side of Holt's Hill, where they lived several years in a log house. Afterwards a more substantial dwelling was erected. Here Mrs. Gates died March 28, 1834, aged eighty-four. He died Dec. 13, 1845, aged nearly ninety-three. Was a man remarkable for health, contentment, and Christian peace. Had a remarkable memory. He recollected many things he heard at the age of ten years from Capt. Clark who died in Framingham in 1762, at the age of one hundred and five, and who had in his youth personal acquaintance with several of the Pilgrim fathers, and most of the first settlers of New England. Mr. Gates took great pleasure during his long life in narrating well-remembered incidents and struggles in the war of the Revolution. He and his three brothers were distinguished for bravery and hardihood, and were out during most of the war. None of them were killed, but at the battle of Bunker Hill Henry was shot through the neck and terribly wounded. The bullet entered the right cheek and went downward and passed nearly through the neck, lodging at the skin on the opposite side. George carried him off the field. Beyond all expectation he survived and attained to perfect health. This was considered very remarkable in that day, and on account of it Henry attained some notoriety. He was present when the corner-stone of the Bunker-hill monument was laid, being then an old man, and attracting much attention. The brothers were also present, and all lived to advanced age. The children of George and Hannah (Barrett) Gates were: —

1. POLLY, [b. in 1789; m. John Hutchinson of Washington, March 23, 1815; was a most excellent woman, a Christian of rare faith, and d. in this town March 28, 1873.]
2. PATTY, [b. in 1791; m. Timothy Hills Feb. 25, 1813; lived in various places for some years, then moved to Penfield, N. Y., where she d. Dec. 14, 1829.]
3. CHARLES, [b. in 1793; m. Elisabeth C. Cummings June 9, 1818, and lived in many places in town. He was out in the war of 1812; was a hard-working, driving man, having a hand in every business. He was a farmer, carpenter, storekeeper at the Center in 1836, and once fitted up the Rogers mills for the manufacture of starch; he was a good singer and leader of the Center choir .for many years, and for nearly half a century a member of that church. He d. June 12, 1862. He had done a hard day's work, and went over at sunset to chat with his neighbor, John S. Parmenter, as he frequently did. He was leaning against the barn, talking, as Mr. Parmenter was milking, when he sunk down and d. instantly. The heart ceased beating without a word or a groan. His wife d. Dec. 18, 1861. They had no children but an adopted daughter: —

*Harriet Cordielia Hills*, (called Cordelia H. Gates, who m. E. W. R. Huntley in 1849, and d. Aug. 10, 1851, aged 23.)]

## GEORGE.

SIMEON GEORGE married Susan Downing, and came here from Newburyport in 1781 with four grown-up sons. He built a log house a few rods west of the Dea. Nichols or Jonas White place. He and his five sons were all out in the Revolutionary army, and the one who never lived here was killed in battle. He died blind at an advanced age. All the family moved to New York before 1794. Of his children:—

1. DAVID, [lived in a house then standing in the corner of the pasture below Eben Bass's on the old road; m. Frances ————, and had a son:—

    *Josiah*, (b. July 20, 1781.)

    He moved to Sackett's Harbor, N. Y., and d. there at an advanced age.]

2. MICHAEL, [began the Dea. Wilkins farm, sold to James Wilkins in 1799, and went to Fairfax, Canada, and d. there. His first wife's name was Hannah ————.]

3. SIMEON, [lived at first in a log house on the Dea. Parmenter place, on the old road west and near the orchard. After some years he built on the spot now occupied by the Jonas White brick house. He m. Jean White, March 18, 1790, and had two daughters b. in Antrim:—

    *Mary*, (d. unm.)

    *Sarah*, (m. Silas White of New York, and afterwards James Eaton of Deering. She is the mother of Hiram Eaton, and now lives in ripe old age in South Antrim.)

    In 1794 Mr. George moved to Salem, N. Y., where a numerous family were born to them. He d. there of spotted fever in 1812.]

4. MOSES, [went West about the year 1800, and was never heard from.]

5. SALLY, [m. Moses Flanders, and went to Rochester, N. Y.]

6. EUNICE, [m. Samuel Downing, and lived and d. near Saratoga Springs.]

## GIBSON.

CHARLES GIBSON (formerly Charles G. Draper) married Elisabeth S. Jones of Milford, in 1855, and now lives in South Village. He has one child:—

1. GEORGE C., [b. March 25, 1864, in Bennington.]

JOHN P. GIBSON lived in Antrim nearly six years, moving back to Hillsborough in January, 1873. He owned and occupied the Austin, or

Danforth place in the northeast part of this town. He was son of Rodney and Minerva (Hosley) Gibson, and grandson of Samuel and Mary (Miller) Gibson. The family were from Merrimack. He was born in Hillsborough, Sept. 6, 1835. He married, first, Almira S. Brown of Hillsborough, who died Oct. 1, 1877; married, second, Eva A. Gilman of Goshen, Dec. 13, 1878. He is now a merchant in Hillsborough Lower Village. Is chairman of the board of selectmen of that town. Children : —

1. JOSETTA A., [b. July 15, 1861, in Hillsborough ; d. in Antrim Aug. 24, 1872.]
2. HARRY S., [b. in Hillsborough June 15, 1863 ; d. in Antrim Jan. 31, 1871.]
3. J. FRED, [b. in Hillsborough June 28, 1865.]
4. WALTER S., [b. in Hillsborough April 8, 1877.]

## GILLIS.

JOHN GILLIS, son of Thomas and Nancy (McCowan) Gillis of Merrimack, settled in Deering. He married Hannah, daughter of Dea. William Aiken of that town. She was a most noble woman, one of the old order, vigorous, generous, fearless, and devoted. She died in Bennington Dec. 16, 1859, in good old age. They raised a large and noteworthy family, all born in Deering, but so connected with Antrim as to justify a brief notice here. They were nine in number, as follows : —

1. WILLIAM, [b. Jan. 3, 1803, m. Dorcas Pattee of Methuen, Mass. Has lived in Bennington since 1831.]
2. COL. MARK, [m. Elvira Wilson of Stoddard ; was deputy-sheriff many years ; was landlord of the noted Indian Head House, Nashua ; was a man of considerable note in New Hampshire ; d. in Nashua Jan. 26, 1862, aged 57 ; left no children.]
3. HON. THOMAS W., [m. 1st, Rhoda Fuller of Milford ; 2d, Elisabeth French of Bedford. Was twenty years agent of the Nashua Manufacturing Co. ; was trustee of the State Reform School, and mayor of Nashua ; now lives in Milford. His son John F. was graduated at Dartmouth College in 1854, but soon after died.]
4. JOHN, [settled in Hudson, and there resides ; m. Jenny Fulton of Deering.]
5. HON. DAVID, [m. Susan Merriam of Shirley, Mass. Was seventeen years agent of the Amoskeag Co., Manchester. Was presidential elector in 1860. Is trustee of the State Reform School, and also of the New Hampshire Insane Asylum. Resides in Nashua.]

6. JAMES M., [m. Martha Woods of Hollis ; d. in Nashua Sept. 19, 1830.]
7. CHARLES G., [m. Deborah Knowlton of Lancaster, Mass. ; d. in Milford May 1, 1856, aged 35.]
8. HORACE, [b. Aug. 9, 1817, m. Elisabeth Tuttle of Antrim; was for many years clerk of the Indian Head House, Nashua. Has lived in this town perhaps twelve years in all. Occupied the Cram place from 1854 to 1856. Lived a few years on the E. L. Vose farm. Their only child, Lizzie M., was b. in Manchester, Dec. 25, 1846, and m. Samuel G. Newton, April 27, 1871, residing now in Ashburnham, Mass.]
9. HANNAH G., [m. Reuben Boutwell of this town ; now lives a widow in South Village.]

## GILMORE.

JOHN GILMORE came here from Bedford as early as 1778 and began the Weston place, now Cyrus J. Whitney's. He was the son of Dea. Robert Gilmore of Bedford, who came directly to that town from over the water, and was not very closely connected with the Gilmores of Londonderry. Some of Dea. Robert's children seem to have been born in the old country, and were as follows : Robert, Jr., who settled in Goffstown, went into the Revolutionary army and lost his life in the service; John of Antrim; James, who settled in Acworth; Peggy, who married a Gilmore and remained in Bedford ; and Martha, who married Maj. John Dunlap of Bedford. Dea. Robert, father of all these, died in Bedford April 14, 1778, aged sixty-eight. John, who came here, married Hannah ——; remained on the farm he cleared until 1795, when he sold; run the clothing-mill in South Village a short time, and then moved to some place in New York. Thence after some years he moved, it is thought, to Ohio. But little can be learned of him at the present time. One child, William, was born here, Aug. 1, 1781. The following occurs in the Bedford records : —

"Robert Gilmore and Elisabeth Gilmore, son and daughter to John and Hannah Gilmore, were born the fifth day of July, 1772."

These children, Robert and Elisabeth, were probably brought here, and perhaps others were; William, born in Antrim, appearing to be the youngest of the family. There is a family of Gilmores in Cambridge, Washington Co., N. Y., who I think are descendants of John of Antrim. This has at least been claimed. But I have no evidence rendering it certain. All the parties are people of worth and high standing.

## GOODELL.

DAVID GOODELL, son of David and Elisabeth (Hutchinson) Goodell, and grandson of David Goodell of Amherst (now Milford), was born in Amherst, Sept. 15, 1774; married Mary Raymond of Mont Vernon; lived most of his life in Hillsborough, where all his children were born; moved to this town to live with his son in 1844, and died here in 1848. His wife died May 17, 1864, aged eighty-five. Children: —

1. GEORGE D., [b. in 1799; m. Rebecca Andrews of Windsor; lived in Hillsborough, and d. in that town in 1867. He was the father of Dr. John Goodell.]
2. JOHN, [d. in 1816, aged 13.]
3. DEA. JESSE R., [b. Feb. 12, 1807; m. Olive A. Wright of Sullivan; came here in 1841 and bought of James M. Wilder the Dea. Joseph Boyd farm. Has extensively improved the buildings and surroundings, making the situation now one of the most desirable in the county. Has been for many years a deacon in the Baptist Church. His wife, younger than himself by only sixteen days, d. June 13, 1877. He m. 2d, Mrs. Ruth (Wilkins) Bennett. Dea. Goodell has but one child: —

*David H.*, (b. in Hillsborough, May 6, 1834; m. Hannah J. Plummer of Goffstown, Sept. 1, 1857; remained on the homestead with his father, and was chosen treasurer of the Shovel Company at the early age of 22. He has been for recent years largely engaged in manufacturing apple-parers, cutlery, etc. Is at the head of the Goodell Company; was inventor of the "lightning apple-parer," patented in 1864. Some more particular information concerning his inventions and enterprises will be found in the chapter on manufactures. A writer in the Manchester "Mirror" thus speaks: —

> David H. Goodell, the head of the company, and the owner of more than five-sixths of its stock, happened to be brought up in Antrim, where his father owned a large farm, and, as he was an only child, his father naturally wanted him to stay at home. At that time South Antrim, where the farm was located, was not much of a place. It had a store, a church, a post-office, and a few houses. It was seven or eight miles from any railroad, and a considerable distance from the main road to anywhere. A brook ran through the village, making a descent of several hundred feet on the way, and furnishing a reliable though small water-power. On this brook there were a saw-mill or two and a shovel-factory. Goodell wanted to stay at home, but did not want to confine himself to the farm; so, as there wasn't much else to take to, he took to the water; in other words, he connected himself with the shovel-factory. In process of time the parties who owned the factory were bankrupted by speculations elsewhere, and the concern passed into Mr. Goodell's hands. Then he abandoned the shovel business, and turned his attention

to the manufacture of apple-parers and other labor-saving machines, and went on adding to the list of his productions and the capacity of his shops until to-day he gives employment to one hundred and twenty operatives, to whom he pays about four thousand dollars per month. Among the articles for which the factory is noted are several varieties of apple parers, slicers and corers, peach-parers, cherry-stoners, and the Cahoon seed-sower; but the leading production is table-cutlery of all descriptions, which is known and commands a ready sale all over the country. We need more such men as David H. Goodell, and more such industries as the one of which he is the master-spirit, in our State.

Mr. Goodell is an extensive and successful farmer, is prominent as an agriculturist, and was several years president of the Oak Park Association, an institution started to promote mechanics and agriculture ; has done much to enlarge and improve the village. He has been school committee, town clerk, moderator, and representative. Is a liberal giver to religious and educational objects ; is president of Antrim Temperance Association. Has two children : Dura Dana, who was b. Sept. 6, 1858 ; and Richard C., who was b. Aug. 10, 1868.)]

ASA GOODELL, son of Asa and Ruth (Butterfield) Goodell, and grandson of David and Elisabeth (Hutchinson) Goodell, was born in Wilton, Me., Aug. 7. 1808; was brought up in Hillsborough with his cousin Jesse R. Goodell, now of Antrim, and married Sarah Smith of Mont Vernon, daughter of Dea. William Smith. He came here from Windsor on to the William Stacey place in 1844, where he lived five years. Then he sold the Stacey place and bought the Steele place (William Curtis's), and lived on this last five years. Thence he moved to Hillsborough, and thence to Windsor, where he now resides. Is a man of wealth and a very extensive land-owner. Children: —

1. GEORGE, [b. May, 1845 ; d. at the age of 5.]
2. ELMIRA, [d. same time with her brother, at the age of 3.]
3. OLIVE JANE, [m. Melvin Temple, and they now live near her parents in Windsor.]

## GOODHUE.

EBENEZER GOODHUE, born in ' Littleton, Mass., married Sarah Potter, lived some five years on the Zadok Dodge place, and moved to Hancock in 1790. He died in 1853, aged ninety-nine years, nine months, and nine days.' He had no children born here, but Ebenezer, his eldest son, quite a lad when his father came here, married Mehitable Knights, daughter of Benjamin Knights, and lived many years on the old Wiley place, next south of the Capt. Worthley place, west of the pond. He moved to Hancock in 1827, and died in 1869, aged ninety. His children, all born in this town, were: —

1. LYDIA, [b. Dec. 1, 1803, m. Samuel Knights Nov. 26, 1822, and lives in Hancock.]
2. SALLY, [b. Sept. 18, 1805, m. Warren Clark, and lives in Hancock.]
3. MEHITABLE, [b. June 27, 1807, m. Avery Clark, went to Hancock and d. there.]
4. PRISCILLA, [b. May 10, 1809, m. Asa Simonds, lived in Hancock, and d. in 1839.]
5. EBENEZER, [b. May 17, 1811; m. Almira Dane, daughter of Dea. Samuel Dane of New Boston, in 1844. He was a carpenter by trade, and was killed by falling from a roof in Nashua, in 1862.]
6. RODNEY, [b. Aug. 26, 1813, m. Susan Davis, and for some years owned the Willey mills in Hancock, from whence he moved to Peterborough.]
7. GARDINER, [b. July 30, 1816, supposed to have d. in infancy.]
8. BENJAMIN, [b. in 1818, m. Caroline Andrews of New Boston in 1841, and now lives on her father's place in that town. Is there held in high esteem by all, and is often elected to office by the town.]
9. REV. DANIEL, [b. in 1820; was ordained over the church in Bradford, in 1846; m. Mary P. Morrill of Gilford in 1848; was settled subsequently in Danbury, and was afterwards acting pastor in Greenfield, and in Troy. He now supplies in Burlington, Vt.]
10. LUCY, [m. Orren Nelson and went to Sutton, and afterwards to Stoddard, but is now living in Hancock.]
11. FANNY, [b. in 1827, m. John Bullard of Peterborough, and both are now dead.]

## GORDON.

JOHN GORDON and his brother Daniel, when nearly grown up, being on their way to school one morning among the Highlands of the county of Inverness, Scotland, were seized by a band of troopers, and with others impressed into the British service. Anxious parents waited in vain for their return, and they never met again. This being at the opening of the French war, they were sent over to fight in this country. Daniel died on the passage. John served through the whole war, closing in 1763. In the service he became acquainted with some soldiers from Londonderry, and when discharged he came directly there. Thence he came to Antrim in 1769, but made no permanent location till 1772, having spent a year or more of this time in New Boston. He married Mary Boyce of Londonderry, and established his log house on the Dea. Weston place at the Branch, now Oliver Swett's, making the fifth family in town. The first summer a bear killed his cow. His nearest neighbor was Maurice Lynch on the William Stacey farm; the next was James Aiken on a place now in South Village, — four miles; and no roads anywhere. The usual frontier hardships and perils were met and overcome. When the Revolutionary war broke out and the men of Antrim all marched toward the scene of conflict except Mr. Gordon, it is supposed that he hesitated on account of having so recently fought for the king, since he had been under Gen. Wolfe at Quebec, and had done good service as a loyal subject. But he soon after enlisted in the American army and served most of the time till the close of the war. Was in most of the important battles and many skirmishes, and was never seriously hurt. After the war he remained on his farm at the Branch till 1786, when he moved to Windsor. A few years later, in order to get possession of a tract of land awarded him for service in the French war, he moved his family to Chelsea, Vt., and leaving his family there went to Canada to claim his land. While on this service he was taken sick, and died at Quebec. This was in 1798. His son John seems to have obtained the land in question. John Gordon was a tailor by trade. He seems to have owned land in New Boston, and to have lived there part of the time, probably working at his trade some part of each year there, for some time. He signed the call to Rev. Solomon Moor in that town, Aug. 25, 1767; and also, April, 1778, he signed a protest against the "Town's meddling with a dispute between Rev. Solomon Moor & his Dissatifyed hearors." Gordon's second wife was no doubt Esther Snow. Some of the family say *Margaret*, but she signed a deed as *Esther* Gordon, Dec. 1, 1788. It appears that the first wife had five children and the second three, as follows: —

1. MARGARET, [who was b. early in the year 1765. Was not quite seven years old at her mother's death, which event probably occurred in New Boston. Margaret was taken into the family of Gen. John McNiel of Hillsborough to live, where she made her home till her marriage to James Dodge, when she went to Goffstown. They settled on the west slope of the Uncanoonucks in that town, where she lived to good old age and d. Sept. 5, 1849, aged 84. She raised a large family, among them the late Daniel Dodge of Windsor, and John G. Dodge, now one of the wealthiest citizens of Goffstown.]

2. DANIEL A., [m. 1st, Sally Temple; 2d, Azubah Munroe of Carlyle, Mass. Had a son James who m. Belinda Tubbs, and settled in Goshen, where both d. I have no knowledge of other children. Daniel A. Gordon lived chiefly in Windsor, but somewhat in neighboring towns; and after many

changes and reverses, came back alone to Antrim to end his days. He lived but a few weeks after his arrival here, dying Nov. 17, 1850, aged 84. A modest stone marks his grave in the southeast corner of the Center yard.]

3. JOHN, JR., [went to Canada with his father, and resided there most of his days. He m. Jerusha Barnard; had children: John, Charles, Alexander B., Mary, Sarah, Daniel, Electa, Margaret, and Ann. A. B. Gordon, Esq., of Otsego, Canada, the third son, has kindly given much information concerning the family. John, the father, d. in 1844, aged 76.]

4. JAMES, [killed near Branch village at a chopping-bee, by the fall of a tree. He was a lad of considerable age. The precise place or time cannot now be ascertained.]

5. ALEXANDER, [nothing definite known. The marriage records of New Boston have the following, referring no doubt to this man: "Feb. 15, 1796, Alexander Gordon & Mary *Hosston* both of New Boston." The latter name was no doubt *Houston*. It may be added that a *Mary Gordon* m. Phinehas K. Dow of Goffstown, Nov. 16, 1796. Possibly there was this sister whose name we had not received, as the names of all John Gordon's children are given from memory of aged persons, with no records to lean upon. The marriage referred to occurred in New Boston.]

6. SAMUEL, [by second wife; m. 1st, ——— ———; 2d, Mary Wells, and lived in Ogdensburg, N. Y.]

7. WILLIAM, [settled in Stanbridge, Canada. His son William was sheriff of Broome county.]

8. HANNAH, [b. Feb. 11, 1786; m. Ethan Allen, nephew and namesake of the Vermont general, in August, 1805. She d. in 1862. Her husband was from Washington, Vt.]

## GOULD.

ELIJAH GOULD, son of Stephen Gould, was born in Boxford, Mass., in 1780. He came to Antrim in 1800, on to the Maj. Riley farm, now owned by E. F. Gould. In 1804 he married Hannah Bradford of Hillsborough, and moved into the McCoy house, some rods nearer the mountain than the present brick house, which he built in 1822, having a year or two before moved up the Jameson store for the wooden part. Mrs. Gould died April 24, 1814. He married for his second wife, Mrs. Hannah (Spalding) Chapman of Windsor, Sept. 18, 1823, and in 1840 bought the Smith tavern to which he moved the next year, and died there in 1863. His children are as follows, the first three being by his first wife: —

1. FRANKLIN, [b. Oct. 5, 1805, and d. unm. at the age of 70.]
2. DAVID B., [b. Sept. 3, 1807; m. Hannah C. Chandler, Oct. 12, 1837, and d. in Tilton, in 1874.]
3. NANCY, [b. March, 1810; m. Luke McClintock of Hillsborough, May 12, 1835. and d. in 1861.]
4. HANNAH L., [b. Nov. 27, 1825; m. Reuben Colburn of New Boston, and now lives in Hillsborough.]
5. ELIJAH F., [b. Oct. 17, 1827; m. Elisabeth Dunklee of Danvers, Mass., and lives on the Maj. Riley place, formerly owned by his father. His children are:—
    *Addie E.*, (b. Sept. 5, 1855.)
    *Henry F.*, (b. Sept. 16, 1857.)
    *Walter P.*, (b. June 19, 1859.)
    *Alice A.*, (b. March 8, 1861.)
    *Herbert A.*, (b. Sept. 5. 1867.)]
6. LEONARD P., [b. April 15, 1829; m. Sarah E. Cooledge of Hillsborough, and lives in New London.]
7. LUTHER A., [b. April 16, 1832; m. Josephine E. Tuttle of Hillsborough, and now lives in Woburn, Mass.]
8. EMILY L., [b. July 21, 1835; m. Dexter O. Lincoln of Hillsborough in 1861, who d. the next year, and she came to live with her mother in this town. The mother d. Sept. 15, 1878, aged 85.]

## GOVE.

SAMUEL GOVE, son of Samuel and Abigail (Newman) Gove, and grandson of Abraham and Mary (Nudd) Gove of Kensington, was born in Henniker, July 24, 1813; married Harriet N. Newman of Washington, Dec. 15, 1842, who is a sister of Dea. Newman. Mr. Gove moved from Washington to Antrim in 1876, on to the Aiken or McKeen place in South Village. In 1878 he sold to George E. Whittum, and bought the E. L. Vose place at the Center. He has two sons, both residing in Antrim:—

1. JAMES M., [b. in Deering, Jan. 1, 1844; m. Abbie S. Wilson of this town, Oct. 11, 1877.]
2. GEORGE F., [b. in Deering, April 22, 1854; m. Delia B. Merrill, April 17, 1876.]

## GRAHAM.

DR. WILLIAM GRAHAM came here about 1847 from Templeton, Mass. Nothing is known of his family, but they lived where Caleb Roach now lives. He was a "Thomsonian" doctor, made something of a breeze here, was said to be "successful in fevers," but his stay here was short for some reason. He went to Ludlow, Vt., about 1851.

## GREELEY.

ALFRED H. GREELEY, son of Seneca and Priscilla (Fields) Greeley, was born in Hudson in 1820; married Laura F. Woods of Hillsborough in 1847, and came here in 1852, into the east house on the William Stacey farm. After five years he moved to Nashua, but came back to Antrim in 1863, and bought the McKeen place (now Mr. Whittum's) in South Antrim, but soon sold to Isaac Barrett, and after several other changes bought, in 1868, the Dea. Josiah Duncan place, where he now resides. They have no children but one son, Morris Burnham Greeley, adopted in 1870.

## GREEN.

LEWIS GREEN, a native of Massachusetts, was born Sept. 5, 1807, and carried to Stoddard when a child. He married Asenath Butterfield of Bennington, March 24, 1836, and had a large family, none of whom now living were born in Antrim. He came here in 1865, buying the Caleb Clark place, which he exchanged for the Jesse Combs place in 1875. His son, Reuben S. Green, was a member of the Sixteenth N. H. Regiment, and died in the service.

## GREGG.

BENJAMIN GREGG, eighth son of John and Agnes (Rankin) Gregg, and grandson of Capt. James and Janet (Cargil) Gregg of Londonderry, came here in 1776 and began the Vose place at the Center. He was brother of Col. William Gregg, who commanded the advance guard in the battle of Bennington, and who built the old church on the hill, and died in 1815, aged eighty-five years. He moved his family, then consisting of wife and two children, on to said place in the spring of 1779, having in previous summers cleared his land and prepared his log house for occupation. His wife was Lettice Aiken, sister of Dea. James Aiken of Antrim. He was a mechanic of rare ingenuity; was said to be one who could plan well, and do for others, but had small force to do for himself, and hence was poor all his life. He was a man of unsullied reputation. In 1791 he sold to Samuel Caldwell and returned to Londonderry, where he died in 1816, aged sixty-eight. He had four children: —

1. JOHN, [b. in Londonderry; wheelwright of limited means; m. Mary Hobbs, and d. in Derry, Jan. 17, 1836, aged 65.]
2. DEA. JAMES, [b. in Londonderry. He was a wheelwright of much skill, and made the first horse-wagon in Londonderry in 1814. He was a long time elder of the Presbyterian Church in his native town; was a great hand to write poetry, some of which was creditable; was a man of more than ordinary ability, but, having small tact in accumulating the

GENEALOGIES.   515

things of this world, he was very poor in his old age. He m. 1st, his cousin Anna Gregg of Derry ; 2d, Betsey Ann Hopkins of Windham, who became the mother of Prof. Jarvis Gregg, a most brilliant young man, who graduated at Dartmouth College in 1838 ; 3d, Mary Glazier of Warsaw, N. Y. Dea. Gregg d. Feb. 27, 1856, aged 82.]
3. LETTICE, [b. March 4, 1780, in Antrim ; m. Thomas Caldwell ; lived in Derry.]
4. JANE, ["Jinett" on town record, and "Jeany" on gravestone, b. here July 12, 1784, and d. March 8, 1787 ; buried on the hill.]

SAMUEL GREGG, cousin of Benjamin, came here about a year later, beginning the farm now in part Mrs. H. B. Newman's, in 1777 or earlier, as he was on the spot and had a house built in which they had a town meeting in 1778. He was a son of Samuel Gregg and Mary Moor, his wife. His grandfather, Capt. James Gregg. married Janet Cargil in Ireland, but was old enough before leaving Ayrshire, Scotland, where he was born, to learn business as tailor and linen-draper, at which he accumulated quite a fortune for the times, and was able to render valuable pecuniary assistance to the early settlers of Londonderry. He was one of the sixteen that originally settled that town, having embarked in 1718, and being one of the number that wintered under so many privations and sufferings at Cape Elizabeth, Me. At this time it is said of Mr. Gregg that he had " both the means and the disposition " to aid the suffering families in their search for a place to settle. Not long after the settlement he received a captain's commission, and commanded the first company of soldiers ever raised in Londonderry. Samuel Gregg of Antrim married Margaret Wallace, and moved his wife and six children here in the spring of 1778, having previously cleared and built. He was a man of courage, energy, and great labor. The family relate of him, that, coming home on a certain occasion just after sunset from Mr. George's (Jonas White place) with a jug of milk, he was attacked by a bear. Not being the man to run, he struck him a terrible blow on the head with the jug, breaking it in pieces, stunning the bear, and giving him a face for once perfectly white! As bruin did not understand this kind of warfare he left as soon as possible, and Mr. Gregg quietly walked home. Samuel Gregg was wealthy before the Revolution, but in the course of the war large amounts of continental paper came into his hands, by the depreciation of which he lost the bulk of his property. Years afterward this paper was redeemed as far as possible, but Mr. Gregg had *buried* his ; and it was never known where or how much. These pecuniary reverses are said to have shortened his life. At one time he owned the Newman place, the Eben Bass place, all the places now known as the Center, and his premises extended north to the old common, which was a gift from him to the town. He sold to Lemuel Paige in 1793 and bought the place at the outlet of the pond, now known as the Rogers place.

There he started new; built the house and the mill; and from that day the beautiful sheet of water adjacent has been called "Gregg's Pond." He died in 1809, aged sixty-nine; and his wife followed him but a day or two later, dying at the age of sixty-six. They were both, as well as their cousin Benjamin Gregg and wife, among the original members of the Center Church. They had children: —

1. EBEN, [b. March 25, 1768; m. Annie Arnold of Benson, Vt., Dec. 29, 1799, where he lived till 1827, and d. in Malone, N. Y., Nov. 4, 1847. A son, Samuel A. Gregg, Esq., lives in Brushton, N. Y.]

2. ROBERT, [b. Nov. 6, 1769; m. Margaret, daughter of Robert and Jane (McAdams) McIlvaine, Dec. 25, 1798; began the David Hills farm above Clinton, in 1797, where he resided till his removal to Ontario, N. Y. Robert Gregg was for a time town clerk, and was at different times selectman for fifteen years, always having the confidence and respect of his townsmen. His removal to New York was an occasion of general regret in Antrim. He d. Jan. 11, 1847. His children were all born here: —

   *Salerina*, (b. Nov. 16, 1799; went out to Webster, N. Y., as a teacher, and m. Asa D. Twitchell, a substantial farmer of that place, where she yet lives with a large and respectable family.)

   *Sarah*, ("Sally" on records, b. Aug. 9, 1802; m. in 1832 George W. Lambert, tanner and currier; went to Newark, Wis., and d. there Sept. 20, 1856.)

   *Achsah*, (b. Nov. 16, 1804; m. Rev. Philo Forbes, a Baptist clergyman, in 1835; d. in Sturgis, Mich., Sept. 10, 1851.)

   *Jennette*, (b. Nov. 2, 1806; d. unm. in Quincy, Mich., Aug. 6, 1859.)

   *Alfred*, (b. Nov. 3, 1808; d. in infancy.)

   *Sabra*, (b. Sept. 25, 1811; d. aged 6.)

   *Zibiah*, (b. Feb. 9, 1816; m. William S. Morris in 1837; he is a carriage-maker, and they reside in Beatrice, Neb.)]

3. DAVID, [b. Aug. 13, 1771; m. Mary McIlvaine in December, 1799, and soon after settled the Chester Conn place (on Stoddard road), where he lived till 1819, when he sold to Eber Curtis, and built on the old road west of his brother Robert's farm, and near by. These buildings have recently been taken down. He d. July 1, 1859, being 88 years of age. His wife survived to enter her 94th year, a venerable and devoted woman. They had children: —

GENEALOGIES.                                517

*Jane,* (b. Nov. 26, 1801; became 2d wife of Jonathan Carr in 1846.)

*Minda,* (b. Oct. 25, 1803; m. Hervey Holt, Feb. 4, 1834; d. of apoplexy July 24. 1877; was a woman of remarkable vigor; her life was devoted and without reproach, and she d. without sickness or struggle.)

*John.* (b. Sept. 18. 1805; m. Phebe Edwards of Elizabeth, N. J.; settled in Newark, that State; is a house-builder; has four children: Anna, Charles V., Mary F., and Florence.)

*Betsey,* (b. Aug. 8, 1807; m. Lewis Fletcher of Alstead, July 7, 1832. He was a paper-maker by trade, and settled in Bennington; built and occupied where the paper-mill now stands in that town, but the mill he erected was burned. He built in 1840. In later years he went West, and d. in Wisconsin Aug. 10, 1856. He left but one child, Frank A., b. in Bennington, Feb. 23, 1838; now a paper-maker in Watertown, N. Y., and with him his mother resides.)

*Hannah,* (b. July 14, 1809; became 2d wife of Daniel Story Sept. 10, 1847.)

*Alfred,* (b. Dec. 5, 1811; d. in infancy.)

*Samuel,* (b. May 27, 1814; d. aged 22.)

*Mary,* (d. Oct. 23, 1848, aged 28.)

*Margaret,* (b. Aug. 14, 1821; m. A. R. C. Pike in 1844.)]

4. SAMUEL, [but little known of him.]
5. MARGARET, [m. William McNiel, and went to Marietta, Ohio.]
6. MARY, [m. Dea. Josiah Duncan; d. Jan. 19, 1809, aged 35.]
7. JENNIE, [called "Jinet" on town book, b. here Nov. 14, 1778. The other children named above were b. in Londonderry. Jennie m. John Cole, and a few years subsequently they moved to Hill, where she d. in 1804.]
8. JOHN W., [b. Nov. 3, 1780; m. Abigail Arnold of Benson, Vt.; settled in that town, and d. there in 1810, aged 30 years. His son, Eben Gregg, lives in Mount Victory, Ohio.]
9. CAPT. DANIEL, [b. Jan. 12, 1783; m. Phebe Maxfield of Claremont; moved a house from the Hutchinson Flint farm (H. D. Chapin's) on to a spot between Mr. Greeley's and the Butman place, where he lived for several years. This house is said to have been moved again, on to the Mansfield place, so called, near the north end of the pond, from which place it was again moved, this time by James Hill, to the Center, and now in part constitutes the large and attractive

dwelling of Mrs. Joy. On the breaking-out of the war of 1812, Daniel Gregg enlisted for one year, and at the expiration of that term went into the regular service; was promoted to be captain and was an excellent soldier. After the war he lived several years near the old High-Range schoolhouse, but moved to Cleveland, Ohio, about 1827, and died there. His children were all born here, and their names were Thomas, Lizzie, Mary, Caroline, and David. This is all known of them.]

10. ELISABETH, [b. July 30, 1785, usually called " Betsey ; " m. 1st, Gilbert Smith, Feb. 11, 1806, and moved to Rockingham, Vt., thence to Nunda, N. Y., where he died. She m. 2d, —— Ferris, and died in the last-named place.]

11. LETTICE, [b. May 10, 1788; lost her eye-sight by sickness at the age of 14, lived among her brothers and sisters in that condition more than half a century, faithfully and kindly cared for till the last, and d. Nov. 28, 1857.]

ALEXANDER GREGG, son of William and Elisabeth (Kyle) Gregg, was born in Londonderry, Feb. 9, 1755. This William was born in Londonderry, Ireland, 1714, and was son of David and Mary (Evans) Gregg, who came over and settled in the south part of Londonderry, now Windham, in 1722. David was son of John and was born in 1685, being a mere child of only four years as he passed through the terrible siege of his native city in 1689. Alexander Gregg had a brother who lost his life in the war against the French and Indians in 1755. Others of his numerous brothers and sisters settled in Acworth, Francestown, Londonderry, and Boston. Alexander was a soldier in the Revolution, and also enlisted subsequently as a privateer, and served through the war, chiefly in the northern seas, to the great detriment of British whalers and traders. He made several of these voyages before peace was declared, and escaped out of all risks unhurt. Soon after the close of the war, he married Sarah, daughter of James and Mary (Montgomery) Adams of Londonderry. He came here in 1785, beginning the second farm east of William M. Conn's, and, having made ready, was married Dec. 28, 1786. He died April 1, 1830. His wife died March 9, 1839, aged seventy-nine. They were both among the original members of the old church. Mr. Gregg was a strong, athletic, and fearless, but peaceable man. He had a neighbor, whose name we will not give, who was not able-bodied, and who, under stimulants, was full of noise and fight. On most occasions of merry-making, as drink was plenty, the latter would indulge too freely, would soon provoke a fight, would invariably get worsted, and then call for " Alec," who would walk in and rescue him. This state of things not being agreeable to the said " Alec," and faithful advice being disregarded time after time, he gave his tippling and pugnacious friend'solemn assurance that under such circumstances he should never help him again, and appeal would be useless. But his friend had not grace to change his habitual course. On the next training-day, the weak brother excited by liquor got into a fight, in the midst of which he yelled "Alec! Alec!" with all his might. But the latter, true to his declaration, did not respond; and the poor fellow was unmercifully beaten, sneaked off home across lots, and went into retirement for ten or twelve days. But he couldn't forgive "Alec" for leaving him to his fate. So after due time he sought his friend for redress. They were both members of the Presbyterian Church, and the season of communion was drawing near. Hence, not apparently troubled with his own sin in drinking and fighting, he accosted his neighbor thus: "Alec, I have somewhat agin ye." — "Tut, tut, mon! and what have ye agin me?" asked Alec. — "Ye let me be whipped, Alec!" — "But didn't I tell ye I would, if ye were at it agin? Did ye think I would lie to ye, mon? Ye should ha' behaved yoursel'!" — "Alec," said he, "I cannot sit doon at the table of the Laird with ye!" — "What, mon?" exclaimed Alec in tones of astonishment. — "I say. Alec, I cannot sit doon at the table of the Laird with ye, unless ye make me redress!" — "Ye can't; well, then stand up, ye puppy, for I shall sit doon!" History does not inform us how this matter was adjusted, or whether there were any more fights, or whether the aforesaid complainant "stood up;" but certain it is that "Alec" did "sit doon," and continued to do so very consistently as long as he lived.

Mrs. Alexander Gregg was remarkable for her knowledge of the catechism, and her interest in it, having been trained in it like all the children of those times. In her last sickness, the only way she could be quieted was by repeating the catechism. Her children would purposely make a mistake, when she would smartly chide them and ask if they were "heathen children:" and then commencing, "What is the chief end of man?" she would go on with questions and answers till soothed to sleep by the sound of her own voice! In later years her daughter Mrs. Flint lived in Windsor, about two miles off by a lonely road over the mountain, and the old lady would walk over alone and cheer her way by repeating said catechism. Her explanation shows how it was done. "I would begin at my own door with the first question of the single catechism, and questions and answers, single and double, would take me from my own door to Sally's; and *I'd ne'er mind the way!*" The children of Alexander and Sarah (Adams) Gregg were as follows:—

1. WILLIAM, [b. Oct. 12, 1787, m. Sophia Weston Feb. 7, 1814; was known as "Capt. William;" was a pious and valuable citizen, was a devoted member of the church, and a long time leader in the church music; d. in the prime of life and universally lamented, June 11, 1829. Had children:—

*Caroline E.*, (b. near close of 1814, m. Charles Flint and lived in Bedford.)

*Sophia*, (b. in 1817, d. few days before her father.)

*Sarah A.*, (b. in 1820, m. Moses French of Nashua, d. in Milford in 1861.)

*Frances M.*, (b. in 1823, m. Hiram Forsaith of Manchester, and d. in 1856.)

*William A.*, (b. in 1825 ; m. 1st, Nancy J. Foster of Nashua ; 2d, Harriet Henline ; lives in Bradner, Wood Co., Ohio.)

*Mary J.*, (m. Andrew W. Elliot.)

*Sophia R.*, (d. in Nashua, 1841, aged 12.)]

2. MARY, [b. June 26, 1789, m. Stephen Danforth April 23, 1818, d. Oct. 6, 1852.]

3. JAMES A., [b. Jan. 1, 1791, m. Sarah W. Wallace of Antrim, Sept. 27, 1810, and settled on the James Wallace place. There his young wife d. with spotted fever in 1812. She did up her washing, finishing it at three P. M., and was perfectly well, but suddenly sickened and was laid out in death before the next morning. Their only child soon followed from the same fearful disease. After this, left alone, he commenced the study of medicine with Dr. Stickney; taught school and taught writing to help himself along; began practice in Brattleborough, Vt., then awhile at Henniker, this State, then went West as a teacher, but returned and settled in practice of medicine in Unity; m. 2d, Priscilla Glidden of that place, Dec. 31, 1818 ; practiced there twenty years ; represented that town in the legislature several years ; removed to Hopkinton, where he remained till he was unable to continue riding, when he went to Manchester and associated himself with his son, Dr. J. A. D. Gregg. The latter graduated at Dartmouth College, class of 1841, subsequently at New York Medical College, and d. in early life while on a visit with his father at California. Was a young man of thorough education and much promise. The father returned in great sadness, and retired to Newport to spend his old age. He d. on a visit to his daughter, Mrs. F. S. Canfield, at Arlington, Vt., Oct. 26, 1866.]

4. ELISABETH M., [b. July 15, 1792, m. Thomas Carr Jan. 30, 1817, d. Jan. 23, 1844.]

5. THOMAS, [b. Jan. 18, 1795, m. Martha Parker Dec. 24, 1822. Settled in Unity and d. there Dec. 31, 1824.]

6. SARAH, [b. Feb. 7, 1797, m. John G. Flint Nov. 22, 1821.]

7. JANE, [b. Aug. 28, 1800, m. Jeremiah Hills Dec. 24, 1846.]

## GRIFFIN.

NATHANIEL GRIFFIN, son of Nathaniel and Sarah (Ranals) Griffin, came here from Milford when a boy, and lived with Hon. John

Duncan. He married, first, Patty Hopkins, daughter of Boyd, and lived on the Tenney place. After a time he sold and went to Temple, but returned and bought the Daniel Nichols place (now George Turner's), but died in the west part of the town, Feb. 3, 1852, aged seventy-two years. His first wife died in 1827, and was the mother of all his children. He married, second, Annie Ross, April 14, 1840, who died in 1868. The children of Nathaniel and Patty (Hopkins) Griffin were : —

1. SOLOMON H., [b. in 1807 ; m. 1st, Elisabeth McCoy, May 8, 1838, and lived on the place now owned and occupied by Dustin Barrett. They had three children : —

    *Henry H.*, (m. Emily C. McCalley, and now lives in Templeton, Mass.)

    *Mary J.*, (now Mrs. John Muzzey of Somerville, Mass.)

    *Laura J.*, (now Mrs. Mark C. Felch of Somerville, Mass.)

    For 2d wife, Mr. Griffin m. Nancy J. Conn, who d. Dec. 1, 1855, leaving one child : —

    *Nancy*, (b. Oct. 13, 1855, m. Frank E. Kenion of Keene in 1876.)

    Oct. 19, 1856, Mr. Griffin m. Alice Dinsmore. He d. Jan. 2, 1857.]

2. HIRAM, [b. Jan. 9, 1809 ; m. Lydia S. Tuttle, daughter of Hon. Jacob Tuttle, Oct. 27, 1835, and has but one child : — .

    *Charles H.*, (b. Oct. 25, 1840, m. Hannah Champney Nov. 2, 1869. Their two children, Bertha aged five, and Anna aged three, d. of diphtheria, and were both buried in one casket, Jan. 6, 1877. On the morning of Centennial Day, June 27, 1877, another child was born to them, Carrie Lena by name. May she live to attend the centennial of 1977!)

    Mr. Griffin became a clerk in the store of Hon. Jacob Tuttle in 1827. With Hiram Bell he bought out said store in 1833. In three years Mr. Bell left, and Mr. Griffin carried on the business until 1849, when he sold to Fairfield and Shedd. He was town clerk many years, representative four years, and was delegate from Antrim to the constitutional convention of 1850.]

3. SARAH, [b. in 1811, and d. in 1825.]

4. BETSEY, [b. in 1813, m. Charles Perkins of Nashua, and d. leaving two sons : —

    *George H.*, (m. Ella Little and lives in this town.)

    *Charles.*]

5. NANCY, [b. in 1815, m. E. S. Dickerman of Manchester.]

6. MARY, [b. in 1817, and was for many years insane. Was

a pious girl, handsome, attractive, and smart. She d. Dec. 17, 1879.]

7. ELENOR, [b. in 1819, m. Warren Kendrick, and is now living in West Lebanon.]

## HACKETT.

MICHAEL C. HACKETT, son of John H. and Mary (Horr) Hackett, was born in Futhard, Ireland, in 1844; married Mary A. Murphy of Albany, N. Y., and came here from Bennington to the Henry Hill house in 1875, where he remained about three years. He was out through the war in the Fourteenth Mass. Battery, was three times wounded, and now carries a bullet in his body. He has children: John H., Mary A., Josie, Annie, Cathline, Alice, and Jennie. The first was born in 1867, the last in Antrim, Nov. 24, 1876.

## HADLEY.

ABIJAH HADLEY, son of Eliphalet and Elizabeth (Davis) Hadley of Hudson, was born in 1762. He was out in the Revolutionary army, and came here to work for Dea. Aiken in 1781. He remained here six years, and after working awhile in Hancock he married Abigail Johnson of Hollis in 1793, and immediately settled on the Butman farm in this town. After about two years, he moved to Hudson; from thence, soon after, to Hancock, where he died in 1837. He was a prominent man in that town. His children are: —

1. ABIJAH, [b. in Antrim in 1794, m. Mary P. Whittemore of Hancock, March 31, 1818, and d. June 18, 1879, in that town, leaving children: Dewitt C. and Edward J.]
2. ABIGAIL, [b. in 1804, m. David Bonner and lived in Hancock, where she d. in 1853.]

JOHN S. HADLEY, son of Benjamin and Esther (Lawton) Hadley, was born in Hancock in 1810, and came here to work in 1833; married Nancy J. Derush, July 6, 1842, and has always lived in or near the South Village. He died Aug. 14, 1879. His children are: —

1. MARY E., [now living in Peterborough.]
2. SARAH R., [m. Frank A. Smith, and lives in Peterborough.]

JOHN HADLEY, son of John and Submit Hadley of Sterling, Mass., was born Aug. 22, 1796; married Ruthy S. Ames of Peterborough in 1820. He was a clothier by trade, came here from Peterborough in 1847, and carried on business awhile in South Antrim, where he died Aug. 8, 1850, leaving children: —

1. JOHN A., [b. Feb. 22, 1822, m. Hannah B. Taggart of Sharon, Nov. 3, 1845, and lives in that town.]

## GENEALOGIES.

2. TIMOTHY R., [d. in 1841 at the age of 17.]
3. ALVAH A., [b. Dec. 5, 1824, m. Sarah J. Smith of Antrim, Nov. 9, 1849, and settled in Cambridge, Mass.]
4. HARVEY C., [b. Aug. 3, 1826, m. Henrietta D. Richardson of Antrim, Jan. 26, 1851, and settled in Temple.]
5. CYNTHIA M., [b. Aug. 10, 1828, m. Samuel Aiken of Fisherville, Aug. 9, 1853, and d. in Nashua, June 25, 1858.]
6. HEPZIBETH A., [b. Oct. 28, 1830, m. Ephraim K. Slade of Alstead, Oct. 16, 1851, and went to Charlestown, Mass.]
7. ABBY R., [b. March 30, 1834, m. Manly Colburn of Newbury, Vt., and lives in Fitchburg, Mass.]
8. MARY E., [b. July 8, 1837, and d. aged 6 years.]
9. ELIZA M., [b. April 3, 1844; has been for years an invalid, and lives unm. in Fitchburg, Mass.]
10. GRANVILLE H., [b. March 29, 1847, and d. in infancy.]

## HALL.

SAMUEL HALL, son of Ebenezer and Deborah Hall of Dracut, Mass., came here from Windham as early as 1790, and the following year married Mary McAdams (sister of Mrs. Robert McIlvaine) and settled on the Grosvenor Wilkins place. After some years he moved into the Robert McIlvaine house, and subsequently put up the house now Nahum Swett's, at the foot of the sand-hill. From this last place, he followed his children to Washington in 1824, and died there in 1829, aged sixty-two. Children : —

1. BETSEY, [b. Sept. 27, 1792, m. William Stuart April 18, 1811, went to Washington and d. there, August, 1828.]
2. JOHN, [b. Aug. 1, 1794, d. in infancy.]
3. MARY, [b. July 17, 1795, m. Joseph Snow of Washington, and d. in that town in 1875.]
4. SALLY, [b. Sept. 15, 1797, m. Samuel Clyde of Hillsborough in 1823. Mr. C. was killed by the fall of a tree July 14, 1826. She subsequently m. Ward Ware of Lempster, and is yet living in the town of Unity.]
5. SAMUEL, [b. Feb. 11, 1800, m. Mary Brooks of Deering, d. at Washington in 1828.]
6. EBENEZER, [b. April 7, 1802, m. Abigail D. Pitcher of Stoddard, lived chiefly in Washington, but moved to Unity in 1875.]
7. DANIEL, [b. March 23, 1804, d. unm. in Lowell in 1826.]
8. SUSAN, [b. Nov. 24, 1807, d. unm. aged 20.]
9. JANE, [b. Dec. 30, 1809, d. unm. in Washington in 1830.]

10. SABRINA, [b. May 12, 1812, m. Daniel McAdams, and lives in Washington.]

WILLIAM HALL, brother of Samuel, came here a little later; is supposed to have lived here and there till 1794, when he succeeded Daniel Downing on the place now Nathaniel Swett's, on west side of road at foot of the sand-hill. Sold this to William Wilkins in 1798, and not long after moved to Malden, Mass. Nothing more is known of him.

ENOCH HALL, another brother, married Mary Atwood of Cornish, and lived awhile in that town, his children being all born there. He lived in this town eighteen years, chiefly at the Branch, moving away (to Hillsborough) the last time in 1826. He died May 30, 1863, aged ninety-three. Children: —

1. DAVID, [b. Sept. 16, 1803, m. Elisabeth Field of Weymouth, Mass., where they still live.]
2. JOHN, [b. March 30, 1806, m. Martha S. Smith of Hillsborough, in which place he yet resides.]
3. SUSAN, [d. unm. July 13, 1859, aged 50.]

JAMES HALL, born Aug. 20, 1773, brother to Mrs. Jesse Wilson and son of Ephraim and Lydia (Russell) Hall, came here from Dracut, Mass., in 1790: was blacksmith by trade. Began the farm now James Wilson's. The house in which he lived was south of the present house, and near the site of the East Church. He soon sold and moved to Hillsborough, and thence to Alstead. He died Aug. 5, 1810. He married, first, Sally Stone of New Boston, June 25, 1795, who died May 17, 1804; married, second, Relief Small, who died June 26, 1828. Four of the children were born in this town: —

1. JAMES, [b. Nov. 15, 1796, m. in Alstead.]
2. BETSEY, [b. Aug. 26, 1799, d. unm. in Alstead, aged about 20.]
3. WILLIAM, [b. Dec. 22, 1800, went to Dracut, Mass., afterward unknown.]
4. JOHN, [b. July 31, 1802.]
5. SALLY, [b. March 13, 1804, m. and located in Pembroke.]
6. HIRAM, [by 2d wife, b. Oct. 5, 1806, d. unm.]
7. CAROLINE, [b May 25, 1809, d. of spotted fever.]

EPHRAIM HALL, born Jan. 5, 1776, brother of James, whose father, Ephraim, died Feb. 6, 1793, aged seventy-five, came here soon after James, and after a short sojourn on the same place, sold to Dea. Barachias Holt, and went to Unadilla, N. Y. Was a shoemaker by trade. His wife was Mary Ann Nichols of Antrim. Three children were born here, and others subsequently.

1. NANCY, [b. June 19, 1802, d. young.]
2. BETSEY. [b. Aug. 22. 1804.]
3. REV. SOLON, [b. June 13, 1806, was a clergyman in the Methodist Church.]
4. REV. WILLIAM. [Congregational pastor, and afterwards a missionary to the Indians.]
5. EPHRAIM C., [d. when his studies for the ministry were nearly completed.]

STEPHEN HALL, another brother of James, came here about 1794, and located on the Jonathan Ladd place, being that part of James Wilson's farm west of the road, from which the old buildings are gone. His wife was Patty Wilson, sister of the first Jesse Wilson of Antrim. He moved to Unadilla, N. Y. Three children were born here, others there : —

1. RUSSELL, [b. Nov. 20, 1788, fine man, well situated at Unadilla.]
2. RUTH, [b. March 4, 1791.]
3. HANNAH, [b. Oct. 20, 1792, d. young.]
4. MERRILL, [b. March 10, 1795, d. young.]
5. LYDIA, [b. Dec. 24, 1797.]
6. EPHRAIM, [b. Sept. 7, 1799.]
7. PHINEHAS, [b. Oct. 31, 1801.]
8. LOUISA. [b. March, 1804.]
9. SAMANTHA, [b. July, 1807.]
10. JESSE, [b. April 18, 1810.]

RUFUS HALL, son of Timothy and Polly (Chapman) Hall, of the State of Maine, was born in Nobleborough, Me., in 1811; came here from Natick, Mass., in 1850; bought and refitted the house east of the schoolhouse in No. 6. He was a painter by trade. His wife was Eunice R., daughter of David Marrow of Jefferson, Me.,'a colonel in the Revolutionary army, to whom he was married in 1830. Had children as follows : —

1. MARY J., [b. in Jefferson, Me., in 1832, m. Alfred Rogers of Natick, Mass., in 1856.]
2. WILLIAM R., [b. in Salem, Mass., in 1837, m. Sara Hackett of Bedford in 1859, and d. in 1861.]
3. LOUISA A., [b. in Damariscotta, Me., July 14, 1840 ; m. Dustin Barrett of this town, July 10, 1858.]
4. EMELINE C., [b. in Bath, Me., in 1844, m. Albert Haselton of Manchester in 1871.]
5. GEORGE, [b. in Holliston, Mass., in 1847, and d. in 1871.]

6. ORRIN B., [b. in Natick, Mass., in 1849, m. Frances Hardy of Manchester in 1869, and d. in 1877.]
7. CHARLES M., [b. in Antrim in 1851, m. Lucie Allen of Concord in 1871.]

MARTIN HALL, son of Martin and Nancy (Dunklee) Hall, married Susan Ober of Amherst; came here in 1845, and carried on manufacture of bedsteads on E. Z. Hastings stand in firm of Hall and Putnam; sold his half to Isaac B. Pratt, sometime in 1846; went to Milford, and thence to San Francisco, Cal.

## HARDY.

DEA. NOAH HARDY went from Hollis to Nelson, and came here in his old age to live with his daughter, Mrs. Buckminster, and died Dec. 21. 1835, aged seventy-seven. His wife was Sarah Spofford, and she died May 9. 1850, aged eighty-five. He was in the army at Rhode Island, in 1777. A good man. But little is known of his history. He was a Revolutionary soldier, as were his father and three brothers. He seems to have been son of Phinehas and Abigail Hardy, who came to Hollis from Bradford Mass., in 1751. The children of Noah and Sarah (Spofford) Hardy were : —

1. NOAH, [lived in Nelson. His descendants are still in that town.]
2. BETSEY, [m. Ezra Prescott, who was long a register of deeds in Amherst.]
3. SALLY, [m. David Ames of Hancock, and went to Charlotte, N. Y.]
4. DAVID, [m. Sally Farwell of Hancock, and came from Westminster, Vt., to North Branch, in 1833, on to the John G. Flint place. In 1837 he moved to Hancock, thence to New York, and now lives in Homer, that State. His children were : —

   *Nancy.*
   *Leonard*, (now a high-school teacher.)
   *David*, (who was a professor in a college in Kentucky. He d. in early manhood, and a volume of his poems was published after his death.)
   *Wealthy*, (no information of her.)
   *Angeline*, (b. here in 1834; m. in New York, and soon d.)]
5. HANNAH H., [m. Benjamin M. Buckminster in 1819 ; d. June 19, 1848.]
6. SILAS, [b. in Nelson, Nov. 20, 1799; m. Abigail Farley of Hollis in 1826 ; came to Antrim from Westminster, Vt., in

1835, on to the Dr. Whiton farm, where he remained until 1853, when he sold to Eben Bass, and moved to New Ipswich. He d. March 5, 1855, leaving two children: —

*Sarah A.*, (b. June 25, 1827, in Westminster, Vt.; m. Dr. A. J. French, Nov. 11, 1852, and lives in Lawrence, Mass.)

*Ann Eliza*, (b. in Westminster, Vt., May 18, 1834; m. Robert F., son of Dea. Robert Steele of this town, in April, 1857, and they now reside in Genesco, Ill.)]

7. Lois, [m. Henry Kelsey.]

JOHN HARDY, son of David Hardy, was born in Wilmington, Mass., June 23, 1791. His father was born September, 1746; moved from Massachusetts to Lyndeborough in 1790, and died June 8, 1821. John Hardy married Mary Morrill, Jan. 11, 1820. They lived some years in Francestown, from which town they came here on to the Munhall place in 1834. There he died Jan. 23, 1850. Was shoemaker by trade. Children were: —

1. William, [b. Feb. 7, 1821; d. Nov. 28, 1870; enlisted in the Fourteenth N. H. Regiment, and served till close of the war; m. 1st, Mary Ann Senter of Hudson, May 12, 1846; 2d, Lucinda Spalding, Oct. 21, 1854.]
2. Mary, [b. June 30, 1824; m. Peter C. Gregg, Oct. 28, 1854; lives in Bradford.]
3. Gideon, [b. June 21, 1827; m. Ursula Lovejoy of Nashua, July 3, 1854; resides in Nashua, and is foreman of a bobbin-factory in that city.]
4. Charles, [b. June 19, 1829; m. L. Jane Blood of Goshen, June 19, 1852; resides in Nashua; is foreman of a bobbin-factory, and a man of some prominence in that city.]

## HARTWELL.

WILLARD HARTWELL, a cooper by trade, was born in 1781, and came here from Temple about 1799. He married Betsey Spofford of Temple in 1803, and lived on the Fletcher place now owned and occupied by George Brown. He moved to Keene, N. Y., in 1813, thence to Westport, N. Y., where he died in 1867. His wife died in the same place in the year 1875, aged ninety-two. Their children were: —

1. Isaac S., [b. in 1803, and d. unm. in 1852.]
2. Imla, [b. in 1806; m. Avis Storrs, and lives in Westport, N. Y., having ten children.]
3. Betsey, [b. in 1809; m. Alanson Denton, and d. at Lewis, N. Y., in 1876.]

4. NANCY, [b. in 1811: m. Richard Brown of Westport, N. Y., and has a large and respectable family.]
5. ARTEMAS S., [b. in 1813; m. Lucy Gibbs of Westport, N. Y., and d. in that place in 1874.]
6. MARY, [b. in 1817; m. Alanson Byam of Orwell, Vt., and d. there in 1851.]
7. LUCY M., [b. in 1819; m. J. C. Barnes of Westport, N. Y.]
8. WILLARD, [d. in 1825, aged 4.]
9. JESSE S., [b. in 1823, and lives in Westport, N. Y., unm.]
10. PHINEHAS N., [b. in 1825; m. Elmina Jackson of Panton, Vt.]
11. HELEN M., [b. in 1827; m. Stephen Gibbs, and lives at Fort Ann, N. Y.]

## HASTINGS.

DEA. EDWARD Z. HASTINGS, son of Zadok P. and Hannah (Dutton) Hastings of Deering, was born in Westford, Mass., in 1831, and came to Antrim in early life to work in a shop at Clinton. He went into the door and blind business in company with Chapin Kendall, in the shop now owned by Abbott F. True, but sold out in about three years, and worked for J. R. Abbott till 1865, when he bought the Danforth place. In 1867 he sold that to John Gibson, and soon after bought of Enoch Paige the old factory stand in Clinton, built the two-story part of his shop in 1870, and put the upper story on his house in 1873. Mr. Hastings was appointed deacon in the Baptist Church in 1875. He married, first, Nancy Jackson of Tamworth, Nov. 5, 1853, who died of consumption the next year; second, Sarah J. Tuttle, Nov. 8, 1855, who died in 1860. He afterwards married, Aug. 21, 1860, Mary J. Tuttle, niece of Sarah J. Tuttle, his second wife. His children are as follows, the oldest being the child of his second wife: —

1. GEORGE E., [b. June 25, 1858.]
2. JULIA A., [b. Jan. 7, 1864.]
3. MINNIE A., [b. March 3, 1867.]

DEA. JOHN E. HASTINGS, brother of Dea. Edward Z., was born Aug. 5, 1836; came to Antrim to live with Dea. Boyd in 1851, where he remained three years, and has since worked in the shop at Clinton. For the last twelve years he has been foreman in the shop of J. R. Abbott and Company. He was appointed elder in the Presbyterian Church in 1870. In 1863 he married Mary E. Tarbell of Hancock (born Sept. 19, 1839), and their children are: —

1. GERTRUDE A., [b. June 25, 1867.]
2. MABEL S., [b. May 4, 1870.]
3. JOHN R., [b. April 4, 1872.]

4. Harriet J., [b. June 1, 1875.]
5. Frank P., [b. Feb. 1, 1877.]
6. Luther W., [b. May 5, 1879.]

## HATCH.

WARREN D. HATCH, son of Sanford and Annie (Keith) Hatch, was born in Oakham, Mass., April 9, 1821; married Eunice L. Peabody of Dorset, Vt., Jan. 15, 1852, and came here from Jaffrey the same year. He lived near Willard Pond fourteen years; engaged in various manufactures in the shop there; then moved to South Village. Built his residence on Pleasant street in 1879. His children are: —

1. Sarah A., [b. Nov. 3, 1852, m. Charles E. Wilkins Aug. 18, 1872, and lives in Boston.]
2. Sanford K., [b. March 1, 1856, d. April 9, 1857.]
3. Clara E., [b. April 13, 1858, m. Hiram A. Curtis April 24, 1879.]
4. Viola G., [b. April 17, 1859.]
5. Cora A., [b. Oct. 3, 1860. m. Josiah P. Curtis, Jr., Jan. 15, 1879.]
6. Warren D., Jr., [b. Nov. 27, 1865.]
7. Ellen M., [b. Nov. 26, 1868.]

Mr. Hatch is a man of many inventions, some of which have been patented and are as follows: —
 1. A "self-acting car-coupler," patented in 1869; a good thing but not remunerative.
 2. A machine for making slate-pencils, patented in 1867; afterward applied for working wood and proved a very valuable machine.
 3. A "peach-stoner." Patent sold to D. H. Goodell.
 4. "Sewing-machine caster," patented in 1871, and held in high estimation.
 5. The "adjustable spring-bed," patented in 1875, and now manufactured for him, on small royalty, by Dea. E. Z. Hastings. This is considered by many the best spring-bed in existence.

## HAWES.

NATHAN HAWES came here from Goffstown soon after the close of the Revolutionary war; was the first settler on the Butman farm, on which he built a house in 1788. He sold to John Butman in 1794, and moved back to Goffstown. In great old age he found a home with friends on Hackett Hill in Hooksett, where he died in 1853. Was out in the Revolutionary war; was sixteen years old at the battle of Bennington; lay down in a hollow while the Hessian bullets cut the grass down above him; then he sprung up and got behind a large tree, and there, in connection with Capt. Richards of Goffstown, he kept shooting away at the enemy till the battle was over.

## HAYWARD.

JOSIAH HAYWARD was born in Braintree, Mass., in 1766. In 1772 his mother died, and he went the next year to live with his uncle Moses Burge of Westford. There he married, first, Rebecca Reed in 1786, and came here with two children in 1790. He lived in various places in town, and moved from here to the Benjamin Tuttle place in Hillsborough, but in 1804 changed that with Tobias Butler for the Eben Bass place, on which he was soon succeeded by Dr. Whiton. He moved to Alexandria in 1838, from thence to Bristol in 1842, where he died in 1845, aged seventy-nine. His wife and three children died within nine days, of spotted fever, in March, 1812. Married, second, Abigail Sawyer, Nov. 11, 1813. His children were all by first wife, and were: —

1. SAMUEL B., [b. in 1787, m. Nabby Killam of Hancock, and had one child b. in Antrim. He went to Rutland, Vt., in 1805, and died in 1840.]
2. SARAH, [b. in 1789, and d. unm.]
3. REBECCA, [b. in Antrim in 1791, m. Silas Rhodes Nov. 26, 1815, lived some years on the Thomas Flint place, then moved to Alexandria, and d. there in 1857.]
4. JOSIAH, [b. in 1793, and went to Connecticut.]
5. JONATHAN, [b. in 1794. He enlisted in the war of 1812, and served in the army five years; was discharged, but was never heard from after.]
6. THOMAS P., [b. in 1797, and d. aged 18.]
7. BETSEY, [d. in 1812.]
8. CHARLES P., [b. April 6, 1801; m. 1st, Lucinda Rhodes of Antrim; 2d, Loisa Whittemore of Pembroke, and lives in that place.]
9. WALTER, [b. March 27, 1803; m. 1st, Ann Sales of Boston; 2d, Mrs. Peter Bullock of Alexandria.]
10. JONAS R., [b. April 25, 1805; m. 1st, Maria Sleeper of Alexandria; 2d, Mrs. Mary (Webster) Bodwell of Pembroke, and d. in that town in 1873.]
11. HANNAH, [b. April 26, 1807, d. in 1812.]
12. MARY, [b. Aug. 17, 1809, d. in 1812.]

## HAZELTON.

DR. DANIEL W. HAZELTON, son of Daniel and Mary (Walker) Hazelton, was born in Hebron in 1824. He studied with Dr. Gilman Kimball of Lowell, and took the degree of M. D. from the Vermont Medical College in 1848. He came to North Branch early in 1849, and in 1850 married Laurette Hammond of Hebron. He was highly esteemed in Antrim, but removed to Cavendish, Vt., in 1853, where he has sustained a large practice to the present time.

# GENEALOGIES.

## HEATH.

RICHARD HEATH came here from Hampstead in 1795 or before, and bought a tract of land, "eighty acres more or less," on the west side of the road from Clinton to Dea. Boyd's. He sold to James Boyd, Sen., in September, 1800, and moved from town; but I have not been able to discover where he went or to find any further traces of him. The house stood a few rods west of the present road.

## HERRICK.

JOSIAH HERRICK, son of Josiah and Mary (Low) Herrick of Boxford, Mass., was born in 1762; married, first, Esther Tarbell of Hudson; came here in 1807, and bought, of the elder Samuel Dinsmore, the saw and grist mill, and homestead at the mill. He was a cooper by trade, and a large manufacturer of pails and barrels, for that day. He was also a Revolutionary soldier. His children all died in childhood. For his second wife, he married Fanny Howard, March 16, 1841. He died April 8, 1853.

JOSEPH HERRICK, brother of Josiah, was born in 1783; married Mary Cox of Beverly, and came here in 1821 into the old mill-house at Loveren's mill. He was in company with Josiah, and died in 1833; having children: —

1. JOSEPH, [b. in 1807; m. Julia Willoughby of Milford, and had a large family, one son being George L., who m. Lucy A. Tuttle, and resided in Clinton several years. His wife d. there leaving one child, Walter L., b. June 7, 1868. Joseph Herrick d. in 1847, aged 40, being killed by a cow, in Wilton.]
2. WILLIAM C., [m. Sarah Russell, and lives in Nashua.]
3. SARAH B., [b. in 1810; m. Ira A. Fuller, April 2, 1835; lived for some years in Stoddard, then moved to Bristol Station, Ill., and d. there in 1864.]
4. NATHANIEL B., [b. in Beverly, April 22, 1813; m. Elvira Simonds, Oct. 6, 1835, and carried on the town farm for many years. In 1856 he moved on to the John Simonds place, on which he lived until the spring of 1877, when he bought the Draper place opposite the Center Church, where he d. Sept. 1 of that year, after a long and wearisome sickness, in the peace and assurance of a Christian hope. He was a man singularly good and pure. They had children: —

*Timothy*, (b. Oct. 19, 1836; m. Elisabeth Muldoon of Staatsburg, N. Y., Oct. 2, 1858, where he now resides.)

*Almena*, (d. in 1847, aged 9.)

 *Clementine*, (b. July 18, 1840; m. H. D. Robb of Stoddard, Jan. 1, 1860, and lives in Staatsburg, N. Y., having two children : Edward H., b. here March 5, 1862, and Grace A., b. in Staatsburg, June 20, 1873.)

 *Luella L.*, (b. in Windsor. Dec. 22, 1850; m. James D. Cutter, Oct. 11, 1868, and lives in Stoddard, having, besides other children, one child, Emma N., b. in this town June 23, 1873.)]

5. SAMUEL D., [b. in 1815; m. Mary E. Abbott, and was long a trader in Beverly, Mass., but now lives in Amherst.]
6. JOSIAH, [d. in April. 1871. unm.. in Londonderry, aged 50.]
7. JOHN W., [b. here April 17, 1822; m. Angeline Curtis in April, 1847; lived in various places. mostly in Peterborough, but came back to Antrim in 1875. Has children : —

 *Laura E.*, (b. in 1848 ; m. Calvin Bullard, and lives in Peterborough.)

 *Frank C.*, (residence unknown.)

 *Alphonso S.*, (d. in 1872, aged 18.)

 *Fannie F.*, (m. Charles A. Preston ; lives in Peterborough.)

 *Emily.* (d. in 1875, aged 16.)]

8. CHARLES, [m. Mary Dodge, and lives in Londonderry.]
9. HARRIET E., [b. Aug. 24, 1828 ; m. William H. Gilmore in 1848, and lives in Hillsborough.]

 ELIJAH HERRICK came here in 1832 as the successor of Benjamin Rollins in the old grist and saw mill at South Village. But little is known of him. He lived here several years. Had four sons and some daughters.

## HILDRETH.

 WILLIAM A. HILDRETH, son of George and Lucy (Winslow) Hildreth (she was a descendant of the Plymouth Winslow), and grandson of George Hildreth of Westford, Mass., was born in Quincy, Mass. ; married Helen J. Smith of Lunenburg, Mass., in 1869; moved here in 1871, and built the Hildreth mill the same year. His children are: —

1. WILLIAM A., [b. in Lunenburg, July 13, 1870.]
2. ROSA MAY, [b. in Antrim, April 28, 1873.]
3. ELVIRA R., [b. in Antrim, Nov. 29, 1874.]

## HILLS.

 DAVID HILLS, born in 1770, was son of Jeremiah and Hannah (Dow) Hills of Hudson. This Jeremiah was son of James Hills, and was

GENEALOGIES.    533

born in 1726 in Newburyport, where his father settled in 1716; was out in the French war and Revolutionary war, and was married in 1776. David came to Antrim in 1802 and bought the Nathan Cole place, now owned and occupied by Franklin Robinson, just west of the pound; married Mehitable Robinson, and lived there over half a century. In old age he lived with his oldest son at the Branch, and died there in 1861 aged ninety-one. Children: —

1. JEREMIAH, [b. Nov. 23, 1798: m. Jane Gregg Dec. 24, 1846; no children; d. at Branch, July 1, 1868.]
2. DAVID, [b. March 1, 1801: m. Asenath Cummings March 28, 1828, and succeeded Robert Gregg on the place now Chandler Butterfield's, but sold this and moved to Clinton in 1869, and d. Dec. 2, 1879. Has children: —
    *Cummings E.*, (b. May 25, 1835; m. Lizzie Rogers of Concord, Aug. 24, 1865; has two children: William C., b. Jan. 17, 1868, and Oscar E., b. Feb. 13, 1877; lives in Clinton.)
    *John M. W.*, (b. in 1843; m. Sarah Whitmore, Aug. 21, 1871; has one son, Morris D., b. Dec. 11, 1873; lives in Clinton.)]
3. JOHN R., [b. Aug. 20, 1803; m. Mary Worthley April 6, 1830; moved on to the Cummings place west of the pond, and lived there twenty-nine years, but d. in South Village in the summer of 1869; a social, cheerful, live man, with hosts of friends, and his sudden death was lamented by all. Had but two children: —
    *Elisabeth*, (d. aged 17.)
    *Phebe*, (b. in 1839; m. Ezra Pettingill Nov. 21, 1870; d. Oct. 26, 1874; was librarian of the library association till her death; a most faultless and amiable woman.)]
4. SARAH, [b. April 6, 1805; m. Rodney Sawyer Oct. 29, 1835; d. Feb. 11, 1853, without a moment's warning and in the prime of life.]
5. REUBEN, [b. July 4, 1807; m. 1st, Lydia Fletcher Nov. 4, 1834; built the house in Clinton occupied by his brother David; there his wife d. April 25, 1852. He m. 2d, Emily S. Worthen of Montpelier, Vt., and now lives in South Weare. Children: —
    *Abby Frances*, (m. Whitney Dunlap; d. in 1861, in Keene.)
    *Samuel F.*, (d. in California, unm., in 1865.)
    *James Austin*, (m. Ellen Blood of Manchester, and d. in that city in 1877.)
    *Helen M.*, (b. in Nashua; is school-teacher in Boston.)
    *Emma H.*, (adopted child; d. in 1870, aged 11.)]

6. SOPHIA, [b. Aug. 9, 1813; m. Smith Campbell June 5, 1848; they settled in Litchfield; he d. March 25, 1864. Had children: Matthew, Alfred H., Clara S., and Arthur S. Alfred H. Campbell graduated at Dartmouth College, and is in preparation for the ministry.]
7. MEHITABLE, [b. Oct. 12, 1815; became 2d wife of Dimon Twiss June 10, 1845; d. in Mont Vernon, June, 1874.]
8. LOUISA, [b. July 22, 1821; m. John W. Tenney April 18, 1844; d. Nov. 2, 1870, aged 49; a most amiable and pious woman, — beautiful in sickness, and happy in death.]

WILLIAM HILL came here from Hudson, where there were many by the name of Hill, or Hills. In a petition to Gov. Wentworth about 1743, of the people in that place to be incorporated as a town, fully one-third of the names are Hill. James, grandfather of David, Sen., is among them, and probably the "Henry Hill, Jr.," of that paper was father of William who came to Antrim. This William came here in 1810, on to the Dea. Worthley farm; came in the prime of life, bringing five sons, the oldest twenty-six, the youngest sixteen. Their mother was Sarah Smith. After a few years Mr. Hill moved to Newport, and thence in 1818 to Penfield, N. Y., where he died in 1830. His sons were as follows: —

1. TIMOTHY S., [b. May 5, 1784; m. Patty Gates of Antrim, Feb. 25, 1813; lived with his father a short time; moved then to Penfield, N. Y. He d. in Rochester, N. Y., Sept. 13, 1837. Children: —

   *Timothy S., Jr.*, (b. Aug. 11, 1814; d. Sept. 5, 1853; was called "Smith Hills;" m. 1st, Elisabeth Coldren in 1844; 2d, her sister, Cornelia Coldren, in 1847.)

   *Luther B.*, (b. Sept. 1, 1815; lives in Irving, Mich.; m. his brother's widow, Cornelia, in 1854.)

   *Sarah J.*, (b. April 12, 1816, in Antrim, as the preceding, but the following were b. in Penfield, N. Y.; m. H. Bovee of Utica, Mich., in 1834; now lives in Big Rapids, Mich.)

   *Mary A.*, (b. Nov. 20, 1818; m. Christopher C. Fisher July 29, 1839, now of Antrim, Minn.)

   *George W. P. G.*, (b. Aug. 12, 1820; d. aged 2.)

   *Martha A.*, (b. May 19, 1822; m. William Marvin of Green Bay, Wis.)

   *Charles G.*, (b. April 21, 1824; d. aged 18.)

   *Alta M.*, (b. March 29, 1826; m. Buel Bradley in 1853; lives in Wayland, Mich.)

   *Harriet Cordelia*, (b. Nov. 15, 1828; d. Aug. 10, 1851; was adopted by Charles Gates; m. E. W. R. Huntley March 15, 1849.)]

2. WILLIAM, [b. 1786; m. Anstiss Smith, his cousin; had but one child, Sarah, who m. a Van Deiburg, and whose sons live in Hillsdale, Mich. William Hill d. in that place in 1845.]

3. HENRY, [b. in 1789; m. Rebecca Kelso Dec. 9, 1824. Her father, Ananias Kelso, son of Daniel and Mary (McAllister) Kelso of New Boston, d. in this town May 27, 1872, aged 93. Mr. Hill the same year of his marriage settled as a blacksmith on the Jonas White place, where he worked at his trade till 1832, when he bought the Ballard house in South Village, which he occupied till his death in 1871. Thus he was nearly thirty-nine years in service as a blacksmith in that village, and plied the hammer in all more than half a century. Children: —

*Mary E.*, (d. in 1837, aged 12.)

*William H.*, (b. in 1833; m. Judith N. Kelsea; built the double house in South Village in 1864, and the one he now occupies in 1877; has been some years a member of the Silk Manufacturing Company; has children: Annie E., b. Sept. 1, 1860, and Grace M.)

*John G.*, (d. in infancy.)

*Luke W.*, (b. Sept. 20, 1837; now owns and occupies the Gilman Cleaves house in South Village; is one of our best men; is a blacksmith, honoring the trade of his father; m. 1st, Jennie Roach of Bennington, Dec. 22, 1863, who d. Feb. 16, 1872; m. 2d. Jan. 19, 1875, Hannah B. Duston of Henniker, a direct descendant of Hannah Duston the famous captive, who slew the savages and escaped.)

*Clara R.*, (b. in 1841; m. George F. Corey, Nov. 29, 1860.)

*Annie R.*, (d. in 1859, aged 16.)]

4. JAMES, [b. in 1792; m. Hannah Sprague of Bedford. He moved the Ambrose Story house from west of the pond to its present location, and lived in it several succeeding years; subsequently he moved to Bedford, but early in 1837 he went to his brother's in New Boston, where he d. of consumption April 16, 1837. He had Children: Gates, Sabra, Ursula, and Alden, as they were called. The latter m. Betsey A. Butler of Antrim, and soon d. leaving one son. The daughters both lived and d. in Bedford. Of Gates, or prob-

ably Charles G., I have but little information. He went to sea in early life, and the family had no definite tidings of him after that.]

5. JOHN, [b. in 1794; m. Mrs. Hannah (Twiss) Livingston July 17, 1836, and settled in New Boston, where he d. Sept. 10, 1873. He was a tanner by trade; was a man of taste and skill in music, and, as playing the violin, was long held as an essential part of the old choir in New Boston. The writer remembers him as being, always in a pleasant way, a skillful and most amusing tantalizer of the young folks, always having a shrewd, sharp hit at each one he met. He left no children.]

## HOLMAN.

REV. MORRIS HOLMAN came here from Deering on to the John S. Parmenter place in the spring of 1875. Was son of Jeremiah and Sarah (McIntire) Holman of Charlton, Mass., and grandson of Thomas Holman of Union, Conn. Was born in Union, Conn., Feb. 11, 1811, graduated at Amherst College in 1837, and at Andover Seminary in 1840. Was ordained at York, Me., Jan. 15, 1845, where he remained fifteen years; was then pastor at Kennebunkport, Me., five years; and soon after became stated supply of the Congregational Church, Deering, this State, where he continued in service nearly twelve years. Has been known as a clear writer and a man of sound scholarship. He married Mary A. Lunt of York, Me., Feb. 18, 1845, and has children : —

1. ALFRED MORRIS, [b. Nov. 18, 1845, m. Lilla Haskell of Lowell, Mass., and lives in Lowell; was a seaman and traveled the world over in his boyhood.]
2. WILLIAM A., [b. Nov. 27, 1849; was graduated with first honors at Dartmouth College, in 1872; is now a lawyer in Pittsburg, Penn.]
3. SAMUEL W., [b. June 5, 1855; is a lawyer, of firm Pierce and Holman, Hillsborough Bridge.]
4. SADIE M., [b. Oct. 24, 1857.]

## HOLMES.

WILLIAM HOLMES, a wheelwright by trade, came here in 1785 and settled on the place known as the James Baldwin place. About 1793 he moved to Peterborough. Nothing further can be learned of him.

WILLIAM HOLMES was son of John and Mary (McCauley) Holmes of Dunbarton. His mother was born in Ireland and came over when a little girl. It was a vigorous Scotch family. William came here from Dunbarton in 1786, and began the farm now in the possession of his grandson, Ira Holmes. He married Margaret Moore of Bedford. Built a few rods north of the present buildings. Was a large land-owner and an upright man; but died in the prime of his years in 1798, aged thirty-eight. His widow afterwards married William Combs. William Holmes's children were : —

1. JOHN, [b. 1789; went to Canada in early life, thence to Buffalo, N. Y., where he d. in 1835. In 1815 his brother Thomas went out to visit him and walked every step of the way! John m. Hannah Douglass of Toronto, Canada; was a carpenter; left three children : William, Robert, and John.]
2. ROBERT M., [never m.; was b. in 1792; was out through the war of 1812, was wounded and pensioned, but on return gradually failed in health and d. in 1818.]
3. THOMAS S., [b. March 14, 1793; m. Sarah Dinsmore, March 2, 1820; inherited the homestead of his father; built the present house in 1812; was a carpenter by trade, and a hard-working, diligent, and honest man. He built the Levi Curtis house (on the mountain) in 1815, that being the first building ever framed in Antrim by " square rule." The neighbors laughed at the innovation and said he could never get the frame together. But it went up like a charm, and that was the end of the old way in this vicinity. Previously, the timbers had to be laid together, marked and fitted separately, and then numbered and " scribed " before they were taken apart. Mr. Holmes was quite a reader, and in his old age could quote Pope's " Essay on Man," and other old writers, with ease and accuracy. His widow yet survives in active and smart old age. After fifty-six years of life together, he dropped away April 8, 1876. They had children : —

*Ira*, (b. March 6, 1821; was ten years in California; was familiar with all our Western country; m. Mary W. Williams of Clear Lake, Io., May 30, 1864; inherits the paternal homestead; has greatly improved the buildings and farm; is among our most substantial men. Has two children : Minnie V., b. Aug. 4, 1866, and Mabel F., b. Aug. 14, 1879.)

*John*, (b. Feb. 20, 1823, d. Oct. 17, 1841.)

*Samuel D.*, (b. Dec. 24, 1824, d. Oct. 3, 1828.)

*Mary E.*, (b. Feb. 4, 1828, m. Hiram Fifield of Andover, April 20, 1867.)

*Vienna*, (b. June 23, 1830, d. of consumption in 1860.)

*Eliza*, (b. Jan. 27, 1833, d. aged 16.)

*Hiram L.*, (b. March 25, 1835; m. Mary Boquith of Elgin, Ill., in 1870 ; now lives in Chicago.)]

4. MARY, [b. 1794; never m.; lived in Boston; a woman of piety and good works; brought to Antrim for burial Jan. 24, 1880.]

ROBERT HOLMES, brother of the last-named William, was born in Dunbarton, March 5, 1766. He came here at the same time with his brother, and began the place known as the poor-farm. Here he resided a number of years, and then he moved back to Dunbarton. He married Susannah Chandler of Hopkinton. Was often in town office in Dunbarton. Was colonel of the Ninth N. H. Regiment in 1811, and subsequently, and is spoken of as a "good officer." He died Feb. 28, 1850. It is worthy of note that Anna Holmes, sister of William and Col. Robert, is now living in Webster, smart and well at the age of ninety-nine years. She married Perley P. Ray, a native of Amherst, Oct. 11, 1807; and after a married life of forty years she has now been a widow more than thirty years ! The children of Col. Robert were as follows : —

1. MARY, [m. Dea. Thomas Giles of Gloucester, Mass.]
2. BETSEY, [d. young.]
3. CHARLES, [m. Louisa Pope, lived and d. in Dunbarton.]
4. CHARLOTTE, [d. unm. at New Bedford, Mass., August, 1853.]
5. JOHN, [d. young.]
6. ELIZABETH, [m. Jonathan Wheeler; now lives a widow in Boston; her daughter m. Charles Hutchins, manager of the "Missionary Herald."]
7. ROBERT C., [m. Julia Bosworth of Springfield, Mass.; now lives in Tiskilwa, Ill.]

AUGUSTINE HOLMES came here from Stoddard, and lived in the James Eaton house in South Village about a dozen years. Was tithing-man in 1829. Subsequently lived in East Sullivan. Was a shoemaker. Remembered as an eccentric and fun-loving man. One dark evening a company of neighbors were in, and Holmes, talking of his sobriety and prudence, said, among other things, that he disapproved of frightening children, and *his* boy was never afraid in the night. To prove this, he called the boy, who had fallen asleep on the trundle-bed at one side of the room, and ordered him to go up to the store and get a pint of rum. The little fellow got half up, rubbing his eyes, and blurted out, " Why, father, have you drinked the rest of that two quarts I got for you last night ? " The boy was excused. He was, however, pretty thoroughly waked up by the shouts of laughter which followed. Holmes used to enjoy telling this story, though the joke lay rather heavy on himself.

## HOLT.

ENOCH HOLT, and his brothers Elijah and Barachias, sons of Jeremiah and Hannah Holt, were born in Andover, Mass., and came here from Wilton, in 1794. Enoch lived in several places in town; for several years in a house (now gone) near the school-house at the foot of Perry's Hill. He died in 1805, and nothing is known of his family.

ELIJAH HOLT, who was born July 31, 1768, cleared and built near the river, southwest of the East burial-ground, but sold in a few years and went to Columbus, N. Y., in 1802. These buildings have long been gone, and there never was any road to them. Mr. Holt married Anna Dickey in Antrim, March, 1794, and died Sept. 2, 1850, aged eighty-two, in Columbus, N. Y. Their children were: —

1. JAMES D., [m. 1st, Temperance Denison; 2d, Gertrude M. Gritman, and settled in Columbus, N. Y.]
2. JEREMIAH, [b. June 9, 1797; m. 1st, Eliza Allen of Oswego, N. Y.; 2d, Anna Williams of Columbus, N. Y.; 3d, Jane Williamson of Chenango, N. Y., where he settled, and d. Sept. 22, 1858. He is spoken of as a "plain, industrious, upright, Christian man."]
3. DAVID D., [m. Griselda Miller and settled in Chenango, N. Y. He d. in Painesville, Ohio, Nov. 28, 1876.]
4. DANIEL N., [m. Prudence Tinker; soon ran away and was never heard from.]
5. MARY A., [b. after her parents moved to New York; m. Anthony Olney, and lives in Columbus, N. Y.]
6. HANNAH, [d. unm. June 23, 1843.]
7. BETSEY, [d. in infancy.]
8. JOHN, [m. Ann M. Foster, and lives in Berlin, Wis.]
9. ADAM, [m. Frances M. Sheldon, and lives in Clinton, N. Y.]

DEA. BARACHIAS HOLT built near Elijah's, by the river, but afterwards bought part of the farm now James Wilson's and lived in a house now gone, a few rods south of Wilson's. He was appointed deacon in the Presbyterian Church, in 1800, and his piety was of the kind never questioned by anybody. His wife died Oct. 4, 1821, aged sixty-five. In 1845, Dea. Holt asked the town for a small donation to help him along, which request was most cheerfully granted. He died in 1846, aged eighty-nine. His children were: —

1. ELIZABETH, [m. Israel E. Conant of this town, Aug. 31, 1815.]
2. AMOS, [b. in 1789; m. 1st, Rhoda Messer, and kept tavern on the old place. He moved to Hillsborough in 1828. His first wife d. March 3, 1839, and he m. her sister, Lucretia Messer, March 12, 1840. He d. in Hillsborough, Jan. 11, 1846, aged 57.]
3. DOLLY.

4. ZEBEDIAH S., [b. May 11, 1797 ; moved to Maine about 1820.]
5. PHŒBE, [b. April 17, 1800 ; she was long a singer and leader in the Center choir, and noted for her beauty.]

DANIEL HOLT, son of Daniel and Dorcas (Abbott) Holt, was born in Wilton, Feb. 13, 1796; married Hannah Green of Brookline in 1822, and came to Antrim the next year. He bought the Dea. Alexander place (now "Holt's Hill"), afterwards occupied by Samuel McAdams, then by Isaac Barrett, and lived there forty-five years. Mr. Holt was a great worker, made many improvements on the farm, and built the massive stone walls that attract the notice of the passer-by. His house was burned, Sept. 2. 1833. but the people turned out nobly to help him, and in just four weeks from the day of the fire he moved into the present house. In 1868 he moved to Hillsborough Bridge, where he died Aug. 31, 1876. His children are : —

1. SARAH W., [b. May 19, 1824 ; m. Luther M. Parker Nov. 2, 1843, who went into the army from Keene, and d. in service. Their eldest son was killed at the battle of Gettysburg.]
2. SAMUEL A., [b. April 27, 1827. and d. at the age of 7.]
3. DORCAS A., [b. March 29, 1829.]
4. ELISABETH, [b. March 11, 1830, m. Thomas S. Preston of Hillsborough. After his death she m. Orrell Abbott, and lives at Hillsborough Bridge.]
5. SAMUEL A., [b. Jan. 28, 1836, m. Mary M. Whitney Aug. 15, 1861, and lives on the homestead, "Holt's Hill." Their children are : —
    *Emma E.*, (b. May 29, 1862.)
    *Cora E.*, (b. Sept. 12, 1863.)
    *Frank A.*, (b. Jan. 13, 1865.)]
6. ABBOTT D., [b. July 10, 1839 ; went into the army at the age of twenty-three, passed bravely and safely through some of the hardest battles of the war, and then d. of fever, Oct. 4, 1862.]

HERVEY HOLT, brother of Daniel, was born in Wilton, April 30, 1803; married Minda Gregg of Antrim, Feb. 4, 1834, and came here that year. He bought of Dea. Parmenter about four acres of land, right in the pasture and woods, and built the house and mill now the property of his son. He was a man of hard work and great endurance, sustaining numberless bruises and broken bones. He was peaceable and respected, and died July 20, 1873, leaving children : —

1. MARY G., [b. Nov. 9, 1834, and lives unm. on the homestead.

She has, for many years, been a faithful and efficient helper in every kind of sickness.]

2. CAROLINE, [b. Sept. 3, 1836, m. William Butterfield in 1863; d. April 6, 1869, having had but one child, who d. before her.]
3. CHARLES F., [familiarly called "Free," was b. July 27, 1841. He was a fearless and determined soldier in the army; was terribly wounded and left for dead on the field, in the second battle of Bull Run, his upper jaw being shot away. He was twice wounded before this. After his return he m. Emeline Smith in 1863, and lives on the old homestead, having greatly enlarged and improved the mill. Is deputy-sheriff of Hillsborough county. His children are: —

*Charles L.*, (b. Feb. 2, 1866.)
*Nellie J.*, (b. Jan. 3, 1869.)
*William A.*, (b. Nov. 6, 1870.)
*Carrie M.*, (b. Oct. 21, 1873.)
*Arthur*, (b. Nov. 1, 1875.)
*Alfred*, (b. April 12, 1880.)]

4. MARGARET J., [b. May 14, 1843; m. Charles H. Story in 1862, who died in the army. Mrs. Story afterwards m. Lorenzo Grace, and now lives in Lowell.]
5. SARAH JOSEPHINE, [b. May 30, 1847, and d. at the age of 14.]

FRANK E. HOLT, son of Horace E. and Maria (Stewart) Holt, was born in Greenfield in 1856; married Jennie S. Hall of Hancock; came here in 1876, and lives in the old Woodbury house at South Antrim. They have one child: —

1. GRACE EVA, [b. in Hancock in 1876.]

## HOLTON.

HENRY HOLTON came to Antrim from Boston in 1862, and lived in the house next east of William Duncan's a few years, when he moved to his present residence at Holton's Crossing in West Deering. He was born in Windsor Aug. 10, 1825, but was brought up by James White on the spot which afterwards came into his own hands, and is now his home. He married Lucinda Ferry, Aug. 15, 1847. Went to Boston in 1842; was a mason by trade, and accumulated property by building and selling houses on the "Back Bay;" was in this last business about ten years; is now one of the most extensive farmers in the State. Children: —

1. GEORGE HENRY, [b. May 24, 1848; d. May 20, 1849.]
2. EDWIN CLARK, [b. in Boston, July 6, 1852; was for a time editor of the "Hillsborough Messenger;" is now on the "Boston Globe."]

## HOPKINS.

JAMES HOPKINS, Esq., was son of John Hopkins and Isabella Reed, and grandson of John Hopkins and Elisabeth Dinsmore, and was born in Windham, Aug. 14. 1761. He came here from that town in 1783. It seems from the old records that four brothers came over from Scotland together. One of them, whose name I cannot obtain, settled in the eastern part of Maine, among those of Scotch origin who had located there, and left a numerous race. Those who came to Londonderry were John, James, and Robert. John, the oldest, married Elisabeth Dinsmore as indicated above. James married Mary ———, settled in Londonderry, and there had children: John, born July 18, 1747; James, Jr., born May 31, 1749; and Robert, born Nov. 1, 1750. He may have had other children, but this is all we find record of. Robert, the youngest of the emigrants, married Elenor Wilson; settled in Londonderry (part now Windham), but afterwards moved to Francestown, being among the early inhabitants of that town. He cleared and settled the well-known "Gibson place" there. It was in his barn that Rev. Mr. McGregor of Londonderry preached, and many early children of Antrim were carried for baptism. Robert, or "Dea. Robert," as he was known, was a devout man, and long held the office of deacon. One old record speaks of his wife as "Martha," and it is possible he had a second wife. The children born before his removal to Francestown were Elenor, born March 5, 1738, Elisabeth, Sarah, James, Robert, and Boyd. As the last was born in 1755, it is concluded that he moved to Francestown among the first settlers there. This is all that can be learned at present writing about these brothers. Capt. Joseph Dickey, who died in Londonderry in 1878 aged ninety-five, gave me many items from personal memory in regard to these men, and in regard to others of the old stock, having remarkable recollection and reaching back as far as 1789 in some cases. John, who married Isabella Reed, is undoubtedly the one he used to speak of as called "Woods John," because he lived in the woods; while another John, probably son of James and Mary, was called "Baptist John," because of his belief. The latter he remembered as a "very knowing man and always ready to impart information, and very pompous in manner." These two "Johns" lived and died in Londonderry. The first brothers and their sons internamed their children so much that one gets fearfully tangled in the Roberts and Johns and Jameses. The first John, and Elisabeth Dinsmore, left on record the birth of only one child; but it is certain they had others, one of whom, James, was father of William, Ebenezer, and David, who settled in Francestown.

James Hopkins, always called "Esquire Hopkins," on coming here in 1783 at once commenced the Whiton farm, now occupied by Eben Bass, but soon exchanged for the place by the river, now Arthur Miller's, where he lived till his death, Jan. 2, 1843. Before coming here, though quite young, Mr. Hopkins was out in the Revolutionary army. In this town he was a prominent man for more than half a century. Was a large land-holder; was frequently in town office, and held in general respect. He married, first, Katherine Aiken in 1788. Mr. Whiton says "she was a woman of more than ordinary benevolence and excellence of character." In papers left behind, Mrs. Whiton says she was "a lovely woman, and might well be considered one of the salt of the earth." She died Sept. 6, 1820. He married, second, Mrs. Jennett, or Jennie, Cleaves, May 4, 1823. she being his cousin. The children were:—

1. JAMES, JR., [known as " Dea. James," b. March 7, 1789; m. Sally Caldwell April 13, 1815; lived with his father; was chosen elder in the Presbyterian Church in 1835; but d. in 1838 in wonderful triumph and peace. He was in the prime of his years with his young family about him; but he gave up all, and with faithful admonitions to every one, in the very expressions of dying joy, his lips stopped, and he was gone. He had six children, two of whom died young, and the others were as follows:—

    *Luther A.*, (went South for his health in 1838; was assistant quartermaster in regular army in the Seminole war and had many narrow escapes. After the war he settled in Florida, and d. at Key West in 1848, aged 30. He picked out the spot, and had his grave cut in the solid limestone, as a surety against the washing of the waves in the occasional inroads of the sea at that place.)

    *Fanny J.*, (m. John F. Marshall, Sept. 5, 1839; d. in Nashua in 1846. Her only child, James Hopkins Marshall, served with distinction in the late war, and now lives in Webster, Mass.)

    *Kate L.*, (m. Parker H. Pearson, and went to Milwaukee, Wis., where he d. in 1869.)

    *Mary E.*, (went to visit her sister in Milwaukee, in 1857, and there m. Michael H. Dousman in 1861. She has one child, James Hopkins, and is prominent in benevolent and missionary enterprises in that section.)]

2. JANE, [b. Sept. 6, 1790; m. Jacob Miller Dec. 16, 1813; d July 30, 1815. He d. seven years later in Arkansas. Jacob was brother of Gen. James Miller, who, having been surrendered by Gen. Hull at Detroit, and being released on parole, was present here at the wedding of his brother.]

3. ISABEL, [b. July 28, 1792; m. George Duncan Dec. 20, 1814; d. June 26, 1864.]

4. JOHN, [b. Oct. 30, 1794; m. Abby Pratt of Antrim; moved to Jamestown, N. Y. He and his wife d. only a few days apart in 1873. One son, Henry Reed, is a physician in

Buffalo. John Hopkins built an addition to the Corey house for a store, and was in trade there from 1817 to 1820; then was in trade awhile in Roxbury, Mass.; was noted as a teacher, and went to New York for that purpose.]

5. WILLIAM CLARK, [b. July 1, 1799; d. Sept. 3, 1800.]
6. CLARK, [b. Jan. 14, 1801; was a man of large size and great physical power. At the annual "Cork Musters" he used to break up the gamblers and drive them by scores off the field. He would rush in among them, knock them down, smash their furniture, break their bones, till they scattered like wild birds, in sheer terror at the presence of one man. Clark Hopkins had a reputation far and wide as a school-teacher,— able, scholarly, and fearless, and a terror to evil-doers. If there was a school anywhere that nobody else could keep they sent for him. Was by natural endowment one of the ablest men ever raised in Antrim; was some years deputy-sheriff. His careful memory has been of great service in the preparation of this book. In his old age Mr. Hopkins gave his heart to Christ; after an adventurous, changeful, and oft afflicted life, he was moved to seek the Savior by the memory of the prayers of his mother, who had been dead fifty-four years. In relating his experience he said that for many weeks "her loving face confronted him at every turn." And may not our best answers to prayer come after we are gone? Clark Hopkins m. Lucy P. Lawrence of Tyngsborough, Mass., March 26, 1845; bought the McFarland place (N. W. C. Jameson's), and lived there many years. His wife d. Oct. 23, 1852, aged 39. Their children were:—

*Amorett*, (b. Jan. 26, 1846; m. George B. Williams of Williamsville, Vt., Nov. 3, 1869, and has children, John and Luella.)

*Luella*, (b. Feb. 27, 1848; d. April, 1860.)

*James C.*, (b. Oct. 10, 1852.)]

7. BETSEY ANN, [b. Feb. 29, 1804; m. Amasa Kimball; lived in Lowell, Mass.; had one son, John Kimball, now a prominent railroad man in the West.]
8. MILTON W., [b. Dec. 20, 1807; m. Rachel Newhall of Boston; lived some years in Boston, then went to St. Louis, thence to Upper Alton, Ill., and d. there, but we have no dates.]

Perhaps it should be added of the parents of James Hopkins, Esq., that his father, John Hopkins, was a jolly, easy, good-natured, happy man,

a shoemaker by trade as well as a farmer. His grandson says of him that he would sit at work on his shoemaker's bench and sing Scotch songs from morning till night, without a word of repetition. He had a great memory, and took the world easy. On the contrary, his wife, Isabella Reed, was a woman tremendously nervous and active. She had strong convictions and great energy, no patience with idleness, was fearless and ready for anything; could do two days' work in one and not feel injured by it. She came to this town to spend her old age, was greatly venerated and loved, and died here with her son, June 7, 1823, aged eighty-three, and was buried on the hill. Her daughter, Mary Ann, sister of James Hopkins, Esq., married Nathaniel Morrison of Peterborough, and was mother of John H. Morrison, D. D., of Milton, Mass., and Prof. Nathaniel H. Morrison, LL. D., of Baltimore, Md., and also Prof. Horace Morrison, president of the University of Maryland. John Hopkins, named above as marrying Isabella Reed, was born in Londonderry, March 10, 1731, and was son of John and Elisabeth (Dinsmore) Hopkins. (See Dinsmore family.) Isabella Reed was daughter of Matthew Reed and Mary Ann Holmes. John and Isabella Hopkins had another daughter, Betsey Ann, twin-sister of Mrs. Mary Ann Morrison, who married James Gregg of Antrim, afterwards Dea. James of Londonderry, and was mother of Prof. Jarvis Gregg, one of the most precocious and remarkable young speakers and scholars ever produced in New Hampshire. He married a daughter of Ezekiel Webster, but died very suddenly but a week or two after marriage.

BOYD HOPKINS, a relative of "Esq. James," and son of Dea. Robert and Elenor (Wilson) Hopkins, was born in Windham, Aug. 17, 1755; married Jane Burns of New Boston; came here in 1794 and bought the John McIlvaine place. The buildings, now gone, stood a few rods west of the school-house in No. 6. Boyd Hopkins remained on said place nearly forty years, till his death, which occurred Sept. 26, 1833. Children, of whom half the number were born in Francestown, were as follows:—

1. PATTY, [*Martha* on town record, b. Dec. 27, 1783, m. Nathaniel Griffin, d. 1827.]
2. SOLOMON, [b. Sept. 8, 1785; m. Dec. 26, 1811, Sarah, sister of Zenas Temple. His father gave him the east half of his farm, on which he built what is known as the James Baldwin house in 1811, but afterwards moved to Alstead, and d. there in 1852.]
3. ELISABETH, [b. Aug. 25, 1787; m. William Wilkins Feb. 3, 1856.]
4. JANE, [b. Aug. 12, 1789, d. unm. 1820.]
5. HANNAH, [b. May 28, 1791; m. Charles Cavender of Greenfield, July 6, 1822; lived awhile in Keyes house in Antrim, and d. there, Sept. 29, 1834.]
6. POLLY, [b. May 4, 1793, d. in childhood.]

7. SALLY, [b. in Antrim. May 14, 1795; m. Joshua Foster of Hancock, Oct. 8, 1816, and d. in that town in 1823.]
8. ELENOR W., [b. April 19, 1797; m. William Cavender, and moved to Fairfield, Mich., and d. there in 1839.]
9. NANCY, [b. May 11, 1799, d. aged 20.]
10. ROBERT B., [b. June 16, 1803; m. Dec. 23, 1834, Caroline Rugg of Rindge. She was daughter of William and Sarah (Buswell) Rugg, and was b. May 30, 1808. Mr. Hopkins occupied the homestead of his father till 1858, when he sold and moved to the Branch where he now lives. Has but two children: —

*Caroline E.*, (b. Sept. 10, 1835; m. Harvey A. Chamberlain in 1866, and moved to Thetford, Vt.)

*Harvey B.*, (b. Nov. 10, 1836; m. Alice B. Putnam of Thetford, Vt., Feb. 16, 1876.)]
11. POLLY, [b. Dec. 11, 1805; m. John Peabody of Antrim, Dec. 31, 1829.]
12. FANNY, [b. Feb. 12, 1809; m. Jan. 29, 1833, Benjamin Tuttle of Hillsborough, and d. in that town in 1840.]

DAVID HOPKINS, a relative of James, Esq., and of Boyd, and brother of William and Ebenezer of Francestown, came here from Francestown in 1794, and lived in a small house opposite the Christie tavern, till the spring of 1800, when he went to Plainfield, Vt. His wife was Polly Fellows. He went into the army in the war of 1812, and died in the hospital at French Mills, Canada, in 1814, aged forty-seven. His wife died Feb. 15, 1853, aged eighty-six. They had two sons in the army of 1812, and eleven grandsons in the Union army in the late war. Left children: —

1. DAVID, JR., [b. in Francestown, Sept. 25, 1792; m. Barbary Low; was out in the war of 1812; settled in Freedom, N. Y., and d. 1839. Children all dead.]
2. LOIS, [b. 1794; m. Joseph Gunney; settled in St. Johnsbury, Vt.]
3. MARY, [twin-sister of Lois; m. John Hopkins of Francestown; d. in Vineland, N. J., in 1875.]
4. BETSEY, [b. in Antrim, Oct. 17, 1796; d. of spotted fever in 1812.]
5. ABNER F., [b. in Antrim, May 14, 1798; was a soldier throughout the war of 1812; m. 1st, Almeda Rand; 2d, Mrs. Sarah Clay; d. in Charlestown, Mass., in 1867.]
6. LATTA, [b. in Plainfield, Vt., in 1800; m. 1st, Simeon

Fletcher of Greenfield ; 2d, Benjamin Bailey of Greenfield; d. at Waukon, Io., in 1867.]
7. LAWSON, [m. Eliza Smith of Boston; d. in that city, February, 1834, aged 32.]
8. LUCY, [d. in infancy.]
9. JAMES, [b. June 18, 1806, in Montpelier, Vt. ; m. Harriet Watson of Northwood; celebrated their golden wedding March 25, 1877 ; he was twenty-six years a machinist in employ of Dover and Lowell companies, was twenty-one years a sheriff in Lowell ; has lived in Lowell since 1832. Through all his long life has been honored with numerous and important trusts.]
10. JOHN, [twin-brother of James ; m. 1st, Lydia A. Spear of Freedom, N. Y. ; 2d, Parthenia Humphrey of Charlestown, Mass. ; 3d, Lucy Bryant of same place. He d. in that city in 1874.]
11. PHILANDER, [b. 1808 ; m. 1st, Mariam R. Gipson of Hampden, Me. ; 2d, Caroline E. Rand of Chichester, and d. in Chichester in 1875.]
12. ELIHU H., [b. 1811 ; m. Susan Watkins of Portsmouth; was killed by railroad accident in Sonoma, Ohio, in 1858.]
13. ELIZA, [b. in Francestown in 1813 ; m. Phinehas Davis; lives in Charlestown, Mass.]

## HOUGHTON.

CHARLES HOUGHTON, son of Euclid and Elisabeth (Pettingill) Houghton, was born in Attleborough, Mass., in 1790 ; married Fanny Farrington, and came here in 1816. They lived in a house (gone for many years) east of the corner below the Dea. Shattuck place. This house was several years the parsonage of the East Church; was built in 1812, and taken down by J. W. Christie. Mr. Houghton was a little, nervous, fidgety man, a carpenter by trade, and lived awhile in the Ambrose Story house. He was a devoted and good man. In 1833 he moved to Alexandria, and from thence to Boston, where he died in 1861. His children were : —

1. EUCLID B., [b. in Boston in 1816, m. Catherine B. Blaney in 1839, and d. in a hospital at St Louis in 1862, whither he had gone to take care of sick and wounded soldiers.]
2. CALISTA A., [b. in Antrim Dec. 18, 1818, m. Nathan Tilden, and is now living in Worcester, Mass.]
3. NANCY F., [b. in Antrim Dec. 31, 1821, and d. unm. in Gardiner, Me., in 1846.]

4. DANIEL F., [b. in Antrim July 27, 1824, m. Caroline E. Drew, and resides in Worcester, Mass.]
5. FANNY E., [b. in Antrim Jan. 7, 1827, m. Reuben C. Mayo in 1846, and now resides in Boston.]
6. MARY E., [b. in Antrim May 19, 1830, m. E. Welton Roach in 1851, and lives in Boston.]
7. ABBY W., [b. in Alexandria in 1834, m. J. Franklin Tobey, and d. in Boston in 1876.]

## HOUSTON.

WILLIAM HOUSTON was born in Bedford in 1755, and came here from that place in 1790. He was a mason by trade, and for many of his later years a maker of basket-bottom chairs; lived at first on the Isaac Patterson farm, and afterwards settled the place now M. B. Tuttle's, and died in 1830, aged seventy-five. His first wife was Betsey Miller of Hillsborough, who was the mother of all his children. His second wife was Isabel Campbell. The children were:—

1. JOHN, [b. in 1782; m. Rachel Lowe, June 9, 1809, and went to Nashua, where he d. in 1858.]
2. THOMAS, [d. at the age of 19. "Tom," as he was called, was a mason by trade. When finishing the top of the chimney of the three-story house at the Branch, he slipped from the staging and fell to the ground. It was a terrible fall, but he was not seriously hurt. It might, however, have hastened his early death.]
3. KATHERINE, [m. Silas Marshall, and lived and d. in Hillsborough.]
4. POLLY, [m. David Bell, Jan. 24, 1809.]
5. BETSEY, [m. John Tennent of Antrim, and d. April 18, 1833, aged 31.]

## HOWARD.

PITMAN HOWARD, a Revolutionary pensioner, came here about 1800, and lived awhile in a house southwest of Samuel Dinsmore's, but afterwards went to live in the Ring house on the east side of the road from Chester Conn's to Nathaniel Herrick's (taken down in 1837). The name of his first wife and the mother of his children, who were all born before he came here, I cannot learn. She died suddenly while out in the pasture, and he married for a second wife Fanny Stevens of Mont Vernon, and brought her here on an ox-sled. He died Aug. 29, 1830, aged eighty-three. The children were:—

1. WILLIAM, [b. March 5, 1795; m. Betsey F. Fay of Walpole, Sept. 14, 1819; d. in Keene at the age of 79. Had six

children, one of whom, Rebecca Frances, is the wife of Dr. Gardiner C. Hill of Keene.]
2. FANNY, [m. Josiah Herrick of Antrim, March 16, 1841; d. May 13, 1871, aged 83.]
3. REBECCA, [d. unm. in Stoddard.]
4. BETSEY, [d. unm.]
5. SAMUEL, [went West, and nothing more can be learned of him.]

## HUBBARD.

JONAS HUBBARD came here from Hollis, it is thought in 1794, and the following year built a small house a little north of the road from the north end of the pond to the Steele place. This house has been gone more than half a century, the cellar and apple-trees now alone marking the spot. Here he lived till 1801, when he moved back to Hollis; but he probably soon after moved again, as no trace of him can subsequently be discovered in that town. An old record there reads: "Betty, born July 28, 1771, daughter of Jonas Hubbard and Betty, his wife."

DR. GEORGE H. HUBBARD came here from Washington in 1848 to take Dr. Burnham's place; married Sarah Jones. He lived in the McFarland house, but remained only two years, when he moved to East Washington; thence to Manchester, from which place on the breaking-out of the war he went as a surgeon into the army. After the war he had charge of a hospital in New York, and died there in 1876. He was on the superintending school committee both years of his residence here.

## HUDSON.

JOHN G. HUDSON, son of Robert and Betsey (Tyrrell) Hudson of Keene, was born July 7, 1832; married Kate Bishop of Ellenville, N. Y., Sept. 25, 1861, and settled in Stoddard. He came to Antrim on to the Zadok Dodge place in 1874. His children, all born in Stoddard, are: —

1. JOHN E., [b. Aug. 7, 1862.]
2. JAMES R., [b. Aug. 20, 1863.]
3. WILLIAM H., [b. Feb. 22, 1865.]
4. OSCAR U., [b. Oct. 22, 1866.]
5. IDA F., [b. June 6, 1868.]

## HUNT.

DAVID F. HUNT, son of David and Lucinda (Matthews) Hunt, was born in Hancock in 1836; married Hattie W. Burbank of Worcester, Mass., in 1864, and came here first in 1868, and again, after two years' absence, in 1873. Their children are: —

1. NETTIE A., [b. in Worcester in 1865.]
2. FLORENCE C., [b. in North Chelmsford, Mass., in 1871.]

## HUNTLEY.

ERASTUS W. R. HUNTLEY, son of Rufus and Betsey (Morrison) Huntley, and grandson of Gen. Elisha Huntley, was born in 1825, in Marlow, and came here in 1849. He was a cabinet-maker; married, first, Cordelia Hills Gates, March 15, 1849, who died Aug. 10, 1851. In 1852 he married, second, Emeline Wilson of Temple. He died Dec. 15, 1856. His children are as follows, the eldest being the child of his first wife: —

1. HELEN CORDELIA, [called "Ella," b. Feb. 28, 1850; m. George Folsom, and lives in Antrim, Minn.]
2. EDWINA E., [d. in 1867, aged 14.]
3. NETTIE A., [d. July 19, 1872, aged 18.]
4. L. JENNIE, [b. May 4, 1856.]

## HURLIN.

REV. WILLIAM HURLIN, son of William and Elisabeth (Evens) Hurlin, and grandson of Martin and Sarah (Marchand) Hurlin, was born in London, England, July 31, 1814, and married Harriet Brown of London, Dec. 25, 1836. He preached his first sermon in April, 1835; served gratuitously as a lay preacher in and around London for five years; and in 1840 received an appointment as missionary of the "London City Mission," where he served nine years. In 1849, with broken health, he resigned, and started with his family for America. In January, 1850, he was ordained pastor of the Free-will Baptist Church in North Danville, Vt. Subsequently he served the churches of that order in Alton, Acton, Me., and Amesbury, Mass. In 1855 Mr. Hurlin transferred his ecclesiastical relation to the Baptist denomination; then, successively, he became pastor of the Baptist churches in Acton, East Sumner, Damariscotta Mills, and China, all in Maine. In 1866 he received a call to the Baptist Church in South Antrim, and was its pastor for seven years. He settled in 1873 in Plaistow; then in Goshen, and then returned without charge to Antrim. His family were originally French Huguenots, and the estate of his fathers was confiscated for heresy. Since his resignation at Goshen, Mr. Hurlin has been secretary of the New Hampshire Baptist Convention. Also for many years he has been an extensive and honored writer for the periodicals of his denomination. Children: —

1. HARRIET, [b. Sept. 25, 1837; m. Ira Palmer of East Sumner, Me., June 13, 1863.]
2. ELISABETH, [b. June 10, 1840; m. Lucius M. Robinson, April 14, 1864. He d. in the army in August of that year.]
3. ROBERT, [b. Feb. 10, 1842; d. in infancy.]
4. WILLIAM, [b. May 7, 1843; d. Oct. 8, 1861.]
5. EDWARD, [b. June 12, 1845; d. in infancy.]
6. SARAH, [b. Oct. 12, 1846; m. Orlando J. Lincoln, Sept. 27, 1872; residence, Santa Cruz, Cal.]

7. JOHN M., [b. March 19, 1848; m. Mary J. Brown, Nov. 19, 1874; resides in Boston.]
8. SOPHIA E., [b. Sept. 27, 1850; m. Samuel R. Robinson, Dec. 24, 1870.]
9. MARTHA A., [b. Jan. 27, 1853; d. Sept. 30, 1861.]
10. HENRY A., [b. Nov. 6, 1856; is clerk of Goodell Co.]
11. CHARLES S., [b. Aug. 6, 1858; d. Oct. 9, 1861.]
12. CLARA M., [b. July 22, 1859.]

## HUTCHINSON.

JAMES HUTCHINSON was son of George and Elisabeth (Bickford) Hutchinson, and grandson of Ambrose Hutchinson. Ambrose was born in Salem, Mass., in 1684, was son of Joseph, and grandson of Richard who was born in England in 1602, and who was descended from Barnard Hutchinson, which last was known to be living in 1282. James came here in the spring of 1774 to live, and there is little room to doubt that he had worked somewhat clearing his land the preceding season. He settled on the place at the foot of the hill next west of Daniel Swett's, and his farm was afterwards occupied for many years by Reuben Boutwell, Sen. He married, in 1771, Sarah Averill of Amherst (now Mont Vernon) and lived awhile in that part of Amherst now Milford. He was one of those who started at once for the scene of conflict on the breaking-out of war, April 19, 1775, and he did not return; for he enlisted at once in the company under Capt. Josiah Crosby, and was in the battle of Bunker Hill, June 17 following. The next day, venturing to go to a house on Charlestown Neck in range of the British men-of-war, he was struck in the neck by a fragment of cannon-ball, and, though the wound was not very severe, it was of such a nature that they could not stop its bleeding. He was helped back to the American lines and everything possible done for him; but he died the next morning from loss of blood. His age was twenty-six. His going there at that time was a piece of daring characteristic of the New Hampshire men. It is said, that, when the British were marching up in front, Gen. Stark stepped forward of his regiment thirty-five paces and deliberately drove a stake into the ground; and then turning to his men and raising his hand he said: "There, don't a man of you fire till the redcoats get up to that stake! If he does, I'll knock him down!" Gen. Washington used to speak of these things as bits of New Hampshire courage! James Hutchinson's widow, born 1751, married Ebenezer Chandler in 1779, and died in Wilton in 1803. The first husband left one child, James Hutchinson, Jr., who was born 1772; married, first, Ruth Styles, 1797; second, Anna Spalding, in 1824: settled in Wilton; was a very genial, interesting, and good man; and died in that town in 1856, leaving a large and honorable family.

REV. AARON HUTCHINSON was born in Hebron, Conn., in 1724; was graduated at Yale, 1747; married Margaret Carter of his native town; was a long time pastor in Grafton, Mass.; came here in 1786 and preached a part of two years. He was a man of remarkable memory. His friends claimed that he could write out the whole Bible again from memory, if it were lost, and even the New Testament in Greek as well as English. Often he went into the pulpit, read his chapter, gave the hymns, delivered his sermon, and finished up the whole service without opening a book or referring to a paper of any kind! He was a stout defender of the faith of the fathers, and, though an old man, was very pleasing to the people of Antrim. He died in the fiftieth year of his ministry. His son, Rev. Aaron Hutchinson, Jr., was the first candidate for the ministry ever in Antrim. He came here in 1778, and preached several Sabbaths: but, for some reason, went into the practice of the law, locating at Lebanon. Was a lawyer of good standing, and died July 27, 1843, aged upwards of eighty years. He married Eunice Bailey of Lebanon, October, 1784. His two sons, Henry B. and James B., were graduates of Dartmouth College (1804 and 1806), and both adopted the profession of law.

GEORGE G. HUTCHINSON was son of John and Polly (Gates) Hutchinson. John was born March 21, 1784, and died Jan. 19, 1825. His first wife was Phebe Hovey, who left a son Daniel, who was a merchant in Lowell, Mass., and died there. George G., oldest of Polly Gates's children, was born in Washington, Feb. 9, 1816; his father died leaving five small children. The widow returned at once to her father's in Antrim, but moved with her father and her children on to the Dea. Sawyer place in 1833. George G. came here in 1825 to live with Stevens Paige. He remained four years, then lived with William S. Foster eight years; married Mary C. Duncan, May 12, 1853, and moved into the Dea. Sawyer house, which had been moved down whole over the rocks from the top of Meeting-house Hill. His barn was burned with all his hay, Aug. 17, 1866, and the house was barely saved by the desperate efforts of his neighbors, under lead of Eben Bass. Mr. Hutchinson has worked his way most worthily through many hardships and losses, and has made many laborious improvements in his rocky but excellent farm. Has children: —

1. WILLIAM. [b. April 1, 1854.]
2. JOHN D., [b. April 25, 1856; now of Middlebury College, Vt., class of 1882.]
3. CHARLES I., [b. March 14, 1858.]
4. GEORGE H., [b. Nov. 1, 1859.]
5. LYNDA E., [b. Oct. 1, 1861.]
6. LINCOLN H., [b. June 27, 1863.]
7. IRA P., [b. April 8, 1865.]
8. ALDEN C., [b. Nov. 1, 1867.]

JOHN HUTCHINSON, the second child of John and Polly (Gates) Hutchinson, was born Sept. 1, 1817. He married Ann M. Boutelle; lived in several places in town, chiefly in Clinton; has been in Chetopah, Kan., several years. Was out in the war in the Seventh N. H. Regiment. Children, besides two that died in childhood: —

1. GEORGE EDWARD, [b. June 4, 1845 ; was out through the war, chiefly in the N. H. Seventh ; m. Emma C. Ashe of Lowell. Is wood-dealer in that city.]
2. MARTHA JANE, [b. Aug. 8, 1847 ; d. Sept. 24, 1867.]
3. JOHN M., [b. Feb. 27, 1851. Has been in the regular U. S. army seven years in the Indian country.]
4. FRANK H., [b. Sept. 26, 1856 ; m. Helen Ashe, sister of above ; lives in Lowell ; assistant of his brother in the wood business.]

The third child of John and Polly (Gates) Hutchinson was Phebe J., who married Stephen Sylvester of New Ipswich, and died in that town Sept. 8, 1864, leaving two children, William H. and Mary E.

The fourth child was Charles Gates Hutchinson, who was born Feb. 22, 1821; married Susan Hoyt of Lowell. They went to Nevada, and after a time to Los Angeles, Cal., arriving in the latter place about 1855. His wife died July 25, 1859. No children. He is an extensive farmer and fruit-grower, having 250,000 oranges as one item of his last crop.

The fifth child of John and Polly (Gates) Hutchinson was William, who was born Nov. 27, 1822, married Adeline Sherman of New Castle, Me., and was a broker in Boston. On account of failing health, he moved to Antrim into the David Hills house, Clinton, where after about a year he died, his death occurring July 24, 1854.

## HYDE.

EZRA HYDE, son of Ezra, and grandson of Ezra, came here from Winchendon, Mass., in 1840, and engaged in the manufacture of woolen cloth, under the firm name of Hyde and Breed. They carried on business in the Breed mill. He enlarged the Dunlap mills, now Kelsea's, for the same purpose in 1846; also built Union Hall for a woolen mill, but failed, and in 1849 moved to Lawrence, Mass. While here he built the Edward Adams house, and lived in it some years; the back part of it had been previously used for a tailor's shop. Mr. Hyde had no children here. After a short sojourn in Lawrence he moved back to Winchendon, his native town, where, in the lumber business, and in the manufacture of various wooden wares, he was engaged till his recent retirement from business. Was a stirring, enterprising man, and his business here was prosperous until the "hard times" of that day compelled him to stop. His mother was Betsey Perley. His father was an old mate of Dr. Whiton in Winchendon, often came here, and thus the son was led to this town. The grandfather of Ezra of Antrim came from Newton, Mass. His wife was a Whiting. They came on the day of their marriage on horseback into the woods of Winchendon, and built them a log cabin. Subsequently he went into the Revolutionary army, and she would take her baby, lay it down between the rows, and dig fifteen bushels of potatoes per day, and put them in the cellar alone! Ezra Hyde, father of Ezra of Antrim, published a history of Winchendon many years ago, being a man of quite a literary turn. Ezra of Antrim was born Aug. 17, 1807; married, first, Adeline Everett of New Ipswich, who died here and was buried in Bennington; married, second, Mrs. Nancy J. (Whitney) Young of Gardner, Mass. Had three children, born in Winchendon: —

1. EZRA WARREN, [b. June 18, 1854.]
2. MARY J., [m. William D. Beman of Winchendon.]
3. EMMA E.

JAMES RAYMOND HYDE, son of Ezra and Polly (Raymond) Hyde, was a half-brother of Ezra of Antrim, and came here in 1843 to work for him in the manufacture of woolen goods. He was born in Winchendon, Mass., Feb. 23, 1816. He married Emma Mellish, daughter of Stephen and Roxcelana (Eaton) Mellish of Walpole, July 5, 1843. He lived here in the Widow Breed house, and also on the Kelsea place in South Village. He left Antrim in 1849, going to Lawrence, Mass. Resided some years in Hartford, Conn.; now lives in Hyde Park, Mass. Had two children, both born in Antrim. These two were the eighth generation from Jonathan Hyde, who was born in England in 1626, and settled in Newton, Mass., in 1647. James R. Hyde's children were: —

1. WILLIAM E., [b. July 29, 1844; d. here Sept. 9, 1844.]
2. GEORGE MELLISH, [b. Feb. 19, 1846; m. Sara V. Mitchell of Watertown, N. Y.; was till recently a book-publisher in Hartford, Conn.; now resides in Hyde Park, Mass.; is preparing a history of the Hyde family in America.]

## JACKSON.

CHARLES E. JACKSON, son of Charles A. and Elisabeth (Dean) Jackson of Tamworth, was born in 1827, married Pamelia J. Kittredge of Mont Vernon, and came here to manufacture doors in 1853. He occupied the shop now A. F. True's, and went into company with Stephen C. Kendall. He died in 1862, leaving children: —

1. MARY F., [b. Jan. 19, 1856.]
2. NELLIE M., [b. May 15, 1858.]
3. CHARLES H., [b. May 8, 1860.]

## JAMESON.

HUGH JAMESON, and his brother Thomas, came over and settled in Londonderry, though some years later than the pioneers of that town. They were sons of William Jameson, a vigorous Scotchman of Belfast, Antrim county, Ireland. At one time he is said to have been in business in Londonderry, Ireland. It has been a tradition among their descendants that they fled to this country to avoid impressment into the British service; but such traditions are too common for all to be true, and may be

taken with some allowance. Hugh was a widower and brought five children with him. He had married Christine Whitehead of the Isle of Man, who died leaving seven children, two sons and five daughters. One of the boys died early in the passage, and the other soon after died from grief at his loss; and their two little bodies were buried in the sea. The five daughters were: Jane, of whom we know nothing; Molly, who married, first, William Todd, and second, Dea. Robert Moore of Goffstown; Rosina, of whom we can learn nothing; Esther, who married Jonas Hastings of Dunbarton; Martha, who married a Mr. Hersey of New London. Hugh married, in this country, Jane Barr, and by this second marriage had children: Peggy, of whom I find no information; Alexander, grandfather of Judge John A. Jameson of Chicago; Elisabeth, who married John Taggart of Goffstown; Daniel, grandfather of Rev. E. O. Jameson of East Medway, Mass.; Hugh, afterwards of Canandaigua, N. Y.; and Thomas, who graduated at Dartmouth College in 1797, a lawyer in Goffstown, died in 1813 at the early age of forty-two. The descendants of Hugh are smart people wherever we find them.

THOMAS JAMESON, brother of Hugh, was born in Belfast, Ireland, in 1710, and died in Dunbarton, Aug. 23, 1764. He married Margaret Dickey. She was born in 1718, and died June 21, 1800, and was daughter of John and Phebe (McIntyre) Dickey of Londonderry. These two brothers moved from Londonderry to Dunbarton soon after their marriage, and were among the most efficient of the early settlers of that town. They were wide-awake people, and thorough-going Presbyterians. The three sons who came to Antrim, and their wives, were all members of the old church on the hill. The descendants of Hugh and Thomas are now very numerous, spread over the whole country, in the highest ranks of society and learning, and are, almost without exception, virtuous and intelligent people. Thomas Jameson and Margaret Dickey had seven children. The first was Mary, who died in childhood; the second was Alexander of Antrim, noticed below; the third was John, who was born in Dunbarton, March 8, 1075, and died Feb. 14, 1806. He married, first, Sally Mills, the first white child born in Dunbarton; second, Mrs. Elisabeth (Ely) Fulton. He lived in Dunbarton, and among his children were Rev. Thomas Jameson, a graduate of Dartmouth in class of 1818, and John Jameson, who was a graduate of the same college in 1821. The fourth child of Thomas and Margaret was Margaret, who married John McMillen of Fryeburg, Me., and was the mother of Mrs. Francis Brown of Antrim. The fifth child was Hugh of Antrim, noticed below. The sixth was Isabel, who was born Aug. 15, 1755; married James McCauley of Dunbarton, and died Dec. 20, 1843. She left many descendants, prominent among them Prof. William McCauley of Roanoke College, Virginia. The seventh and youngest child was Capt. Thomas Jameson of Antrim, noticed below. He was a soldier of the Revolution, and had a pension. He entered the service very young, was acquainted with all its hardships, and was once reduced to the extremity of eating horseflesh to support life. Capt. Thomas was a very apt man at work, being tailor, blacksmith, and farmer. On one occasion he went over to

Society Land (Bennington) to cut a pair of pants for a man. He went on a raft up the river; coming back, the water being very high, he lost his shears through a crack in the raft. At once he marked a tree near the spot, and then the next summer went to the place and found his shears! It is said that when the land was new they cut two tons of hay to the acre without manure. Mr. Jameson had to go *six miles* to grind his scythe. This explains somewhat the willingness of Randall Alexander to borrow a grindstone, as related elsewhere, and the willingness of the neighbors to use that " borrowed " stone !

ALEXANDER JAMESON, second child of Thomas and Margaret (Dickey) Jameson, was born in Londonderry, in 1743. He came to Antrim first in 1775, and the following year located on what is now known as the Temple place. He was prominent among the early settlers, and he and his wife were among the original members of the church (1788). Having erected his log house and got enough cleared for a beginning, he brought his young wife here for a home. She was Jenny Moore, daughter of Dea. William Moore of Bedford. Here they lived till 1798, when he went to Cherry Valley, N. Y., to which place many emigrated from Antrim in the early part of this century. He died in that place, Sept. 1, 1807, aged sixty-four. His wife died in Hamburg, N. Y., July 22, 1830, aged eighty-nine. She was called a very smart woman; used to raise flax, spin her linen thread, and then walk to New Boston, sixteen miles, and sell it, and back home the same day ! Their children were all born here, and were as follows : —

1. THOMAS, [b. May 13, 1778 ; settled in Hamburg, N. Y.; cooper by trade; was justice of the peace ; moved to Boston, Erie Co., N. Y., and d. there March 27, 1859. His wife was Rebecca Taggart of Antrim.]
2. MARY, [b. Nov. 22, 1779; reputation of being very handsome.]
3. WILLIAM, [b. March 20, 1781 ; lived in Rochester, N. Y. Was an officer in the war of 1812; d. at Gates, N. Y., Jan. 16, 1836. His wife was Hannah Reed of Bloomfield, N. Y.]
4. MARGARET, [b. May 1, 1782; m. Israel Ferris, 1800. Lived at Cherry Valley. She d. July 25, 1853, at Madison, Ind. Her husband went West on speculation and was murdered for his money.]
5. NANCY, [b. July 7, 1784, m. Elisha Clark, and lived at Hamburg, N. Y. ; d. Dec. 22, 1868.]
6. HUGH, [b. Oct. 1, 1786 ; m. 1st, Aug. 6, 1809, Susanna Moore ; 2d, Mrs. Mahala (Hall) Clark. Had ten children; lived in Brant and Hamburg, N. Y., and d. in the former place, Aug. 19, 1870.]

GENEALOGIES. 557

HUGH JAMESON, fifth child of Thomas and Margaret, settled in 1777 on land now Elijah F. Gould's. His house stood on the turnpike a few rods north of the present school-house, though some things lead us to think that his first home was nearer the mountain. He had a house burned, but we are unable to find out the date of the fire. He died Aug. 17, 1795, aged thirty-seven. He was a soldier in the Revolution, drew a pension, and finally died from the effect of disease contracted in the war. His widow, Margaret Steele before marriage, followed her son to New Hudson, N. Y., many years after her husband's death, and died June, 1848, aged ninety-five. Their children were all born in Antrim, and were thus: —

1. THOMAS, [b. in Antrim Aug. 28, 1781; went to New Hudson, N. Y., and d. in Howard, Ill., unm., Jan. 7, 1864.]
2. HUGH, [b. Nov. 5, 1793; familiarly called "White Hugh;" m. Harriet Pierce, sister of Pres. Pierce, and was a long time in Boston custom-house; had been a shoemaker by trade, and about 1818 carried on quite a business in that line in the old McFarland house, South Village. Hugh d. in Boston, April 23, 1854. His wife d. at the age of thirty-seven. Two children survive, Charlotte Josett, who m. Joseph C. Bond of Boston, and Jane F., who m. Henry P. Henshaw and now resides in Independence, Io.]
3. PEGGY, [d. 1788, aged 2.]
4. JAMES, [b. June 4, 1790; m. 1st, Martha Dinsmore, 1813, who d. Jan. 10, 1815, at the age of 24; 2d, Indiana E. Kendall, Dec. 4, 1817; had a store a few years at Hillsborough Upper Village. Moved to New Hudson, N. Y., in 1824, and d. March 16, 1837, in that place.]
5. BETSEY, [b. Nov. 4, 1788; m. James Dinsmore of Society Land, Dec. 6, 1814, and went to New Hudson, N. Y., with the family in an ox-wagon covered with leather and containing all their furniture and effects. She was a woman of great memory, smart and good, and left a worthy family. She d. June 10, 1877, in Hastings, Minn. Two sons, Solyman and J. H. G. Dinsmore, are extensive manufacturers of agricultural implements in the West. The family have taken some pride in that ox-wagon journey of three hundred miles. It was more romantic than ten thousand miles by rail. It was both conveyance and inheritance, since they took with them all they had. The covering of tanned leather was for the manufacture of boots and shoes on arrival. Tools and all the et cæteras of the expected little home were

stowed away in that ox-wagon. And so the young couple started out in life! Such brave, strong hearts are sure to win success.]

CAPT. THOMAS JAMESON, youngest child of Thomas and Margaret (Dickey) Jameson, came here in 1783 and cleared on the banks of the Contoocook, and built on the spot now the home of George E. Butterfield. He was known in all the region as "Capt. Jameson," and his name is only that on the town records, for the most part. He obtained his title by having command of a local company of militia. He was a first-rate officer, and the company insisted that he should retain command some three years after his time of service expired. He agreed to do this on condition that the company should pay the bills, as the captain was supposed to "treat" the company in those days! He was a pronounced Democrat, and once gave his brother-in-law, who was opposed to him in politics, a thrashing for saying that he hoped the time would come when men would have to work for a sheep's head and pluck a day, and sleep under the cart-body at night. He was an energetic, capable, and useful citizen. He married, first, Mary Steele, who was the mother of all his children; second, Mrs. Mary (Baldwin) Kendall, June 28, 1832. She married, first, James Stickney; second, Joshua Kendall; third, Thomas Jameson, and outlived him! The first wife was a remarkably robust and strong woman, — of the olden kind, — brave, smart, and quick. When they were clearing land she split a hollow log and took one half of it for a cradle; laid her baby down in it in the field, and reaped daily more grain than any man on the lot! They paid for the land with the rye they raised on it. It is said that her half-brother once offended her in politics, when she seized him by the collar and slammed him against the cellar-door over and over till he begged for release. Women had some rights then! He didn't talk politics with Mrs. Jameson any more. She died June 5, 1831, aged seventy-one. Capt. Jameson died June 12, 1837, aged seventy-eight. Children : —

1. JOHN, [b. July 6, 1785; went to Salem, Mass., when a young man; m. Mary Pierce of that place in 1811. He d. June 15, 1849. She d. Sept. 4, 1868. They had children : —

   *Mary*, (Mrs. William A. Symonds of Salem, Mass.)

   *Ann*, (Mrs. Lucius B. Martyn, Salem, Mass.)

   *Harriet*, (Mrs. Thomas Beddoe, Charlestown, Mass.)

   *John*, (m. Rachel Stedman; d. in Hartford, Conn., Oct. 4, 1849. Prof. Henry W. Jameson of St. Louis is his son. Another son is Edward S. Jameson, a prominent newspaper man of the same city. Another son was John S. Jameson, who died in Andersonville prison; a rare and noble young man, whose life was published by his regiment. Though young, he was distinguished as an artist and musi-

GENEALOGIES. 559

cian ; and his face may be seen in the " Arts and Artists of Connecticut.")

*Caroline.* (Mrs. John W. Stedman of Norwich, Conn. Mr. S. has been bank commissioner, postmaster, etc. Is insurance commissioner of the State of Connecticut.)

*Ellen*, (Mrs. James D. McMurphy of Salem, Mass.)

*Laura*, (unm.)

*Delina*, (unm., Norwich, Conn.)]

2. MARGARET, [b. Wednesday, May 16, 1787 ; m. Zenas Temple Dec. 23, 1813 ; d. Aug. 4, 1870.]

3. THOMAS, [b. Tuesday, March 17, 1789 ; m. Nancy Cochran, Sept. 27, 1814 ; lived in the Hugh Jameson house on the turnpike : in 1816 built a store on the opposite side of the road from the house, and was there in trade till 1819, when, not meeting with satisfactory success here, he moved to Medford, Mass.; afterwards he moved to Lowell, and d. there Oct. 10, 1852. Children : —

*Thomas C.*, (b. June 2, 1815 ; d. in Cincinnati, some years ago, which is all known of him.)

*John C.*, (lost at sea in the autumn of 1842, aged 23 ; only two on the vessel saved.)

*Maria F.*, (b. in 1830 ; d. young.)

*Isaac*, (unm. : was a young man greatly devoted to study ; was very early a school-teacher ; began to study for the ministry, but lost his health, and going to Florida to regain the same in the year 1842, he sunk away on the passage, and was buried at sea, aged 20.)

*Andrew*, (b. Oct. 19, 1818, in this town ; m. 1st, Lucinda Hobbs of Malone, N. Y.; 2d, Mrs. Jennie (Palmer) Richards of Taunton, Mass. ; is now a respectable and worthy citizen of Littleton, Mass.)

*Nancy*, (b. in 1816 ; d. in Lowell, Mass., in 1846.)

*Clarissa A.*, (b. in 1825 ; m. Vespasian Danforth of Lowell, Mass.; d. in 1858.)

*Caroline*, (b. in 1834 ; d. in infancy.)

*Carrie M.*, (b. in 1838 ; became 2d wife of V. Danforth ; d. in Amherst, in 1864.)]

4. JAMES, [b. Friday, March 25, 1791 ; m. Dorcas W. Cleaves, June 18, 1812 ; d. March 27, 1825, and left children : —

*Harriet*, (b. Feb. 26, 1813 ; m. Michael Mongan, and lives in Philadelphia, Penn.)

*Isabel*, (b. Aug. 6, 1815 ; m. Charles F. Hirsch, and lives in Keene.)

*Nathan W. C.*, (b. on Dustin Barrett, or Cleaves place, July 19, 1818 ; went to Boston at the age of sixteen, with only $1.50 in his pocket, and all the world before him ; went into a store as clerk, and after a few years had a store of his own in that city, remaining there till 1851, when he moved back to Antrim. He bought the McFarland house in South Village, and repaired and adorned that ancient building, built barns, etc., making a beautiful residence. These all were destroyed by fire Aug. 9, 1861, in the evening. The present capacious buildings were at once erected on the site of the old ones, being nearly completed before the close of that year. Mr. Jameson, since returning to Antrim, has been deputy-assessor of United States revenue, postmaster, representative, Sabbath-school superintendent, auctioneer, and farmer, leading a life of constant and great activity. He m. 1st, Mary A. Mixer of Cambridge, Mass., Aug. 6, 1839, who d. in about eight weeks ; 2d, Caroline E. Mixer, sister of the above, Aug. 10, 1841, who d. July 11, 1856, aged 34 ; 3d, Mary J. Dodge of Bennington, May 14, 1857. His children are nine in number, thus : First, Mary Caroline, b. Jan. 11, 1845 ; d. in infancy. Second, Nathan C., who was b. May 4, 1849. He m. Idabel, daughter of John D. and Mary (Burnham) Butler of Bennington, March 15, 1871. Resides in the Mark B. Woodbury house ; has children : John Butler, b. Aug. 2, 1873 ; Robert Willis, b. July 23, 1875 ; and James Walker, b. May 28, 1878. N. C. Jameson was representative in 1875 and 1876, and delegate to the constitutional convention of 1876. Third, Charles R., who was b. April 20, 1856 ; now in trade at Hillsborough Bridge. Fourth, Anna Belle, who was b. June 10, 1858, and d. June 4, 1877, being a fine scholar, an excellent organist and pianist, a sweet singer, and a most humble and devoted Christian. Adding to this, that she was beautiful in features, most attractive in manners, and the same to all, it is not strange that she was spoken of as " too fair for this world." Her death was a glorious triumph of grace. She d. exactly six years from the day she united with the church, and lacked six days of being nineteen years old. Her face finds a welcome place in this book. Fifth, Caroline E., b. Aug.

*Anne Belle Jameson*

23, 1860, and m. Herbert H. Whittle, Jan. 1, 1879; sixth, Ada Grace, a loved and beautiful child who d. Oct. 8, 1871, aged 8 years; seventh, Walter D., b. July 10, 1865; eighth, Jennie May, b. Sept. 1, 1868; and ninth, Gertrude D., b. Aug. 1, 1872.)

*Jane S.*, (b. Jan. 6, 1824, m. Charles Rice Oct. 11, 1848, and lives in New York City.)]

5. ANDREW, [b. Wednesday, Feb. 6, 1793; m. Louisa Phippen of Salem, Mass. He was hotel-keeper at Hillsborough Bridge in 1826, and went to Cincinnati, Ohio, where he d. March 20, 1839. No children.]

6. ANN, [b. Thursday, Oct. 30, 1794, m. Robert H. Cleaves Sept. 24, 1818, and d. Oct. 8, 1868.]

7. HUGH, [b. Thursday, Aug. 18, 1796, m. Sophia Cummings of Tyngsborough, Mass., May 30, 1822, and d. in Boston Feb. 26, 1861. Gen. Horatio Jenkins, of Yale College and Cambridge Law School, now of Jacksonville, Fla., m. a daughter of this Hugh. This Hugh was in trade in Nashua many years.]

8. MARY, [b. Monday, Aug. 16, 1798; m. 1st, John Hosley, Aug. 14, 1817; 2d, Dr. Thomas Preston of Hillsborough, and d. Aug. 20, 1831, aged 33. Her son, John Jameson Hosley, was last known as a tanner doing business in Green, N. Y.]

9. ALEXANDER, [b. Wednesday, Jan. 15, 1800; lived and d. on the old homestead. He m. 1st, Lucinda Averill of Mont Vernon, Nov. 16, 1829, who d. Nov. 6, 1843, aged 34. He m. 2d. Nancy J. Bell, daughter of Hugh and Nancy (Wilson) Bell of Bennington, April 3, 1845. He d. Tuesday, July 26, 1864. Soon after this the old homestead was sold, having been occupied by the family eighty-two years. The widow and children moved to South Village. Alexander Jameson was one of the most worthy and upright men ever resident here; unassuming and universally respected. His children were: —

*Mary R.*, (b. Sept. 9, 1831; m. D. F. French of Washington, Jan. 24, 1855, but lived only four weeks after marriage.)

*Anne W.*, (b. Aug. 31, 1837, m. Harris E. Cutler Aug. 12, 1855, and lives in Chicago.)

*Emily S.*, (d. May 3, 1869, aged 27.)

*Edwin D.*, (b. Dec. 27, 1846 ; is engineer from Decatur, Ill., to St. Louis; resides at the former place.)

*Frederick W.*, (b. April 19, 1850; is music-teacher in New York City. Is solo tenor in one of the most fashionable churches in that city.)

*Mary A.*, (b. Dec. 28, 1854.)]

## JOHNSON.

VOLNEY HILL JOHNSON, son of Jesse and Betsey (Fay) Johnson, was born in Hancock. Feb. 1, 1806. He came to Antrim in 1834 to work for Thomas Poor at South Village, and soon after bought of Elijah Herrick the old mill in the village next below the bridge on the Bennington road. The same year he built the house now the Widow Eaton's, under the hill. The next year (1835) he tore down the old mill, and at once built a new saw, grist, and shingle mill. This he kept running till 1841. These mills were burned in 1842. Mr. Johnson married, first, Ede Gould of Greenfield, Feb. 9, 1830, who died Sept. 29, 1853; married, second, Nancy M. Richardson of Washington, Dec. 20. 1854. He moved from Antrim to Washington in 1845, whence he returned after fifteen years. Has been living recent years with his son in Washington, D. C. Of his large family of ten children, all except the oldest and four youngest were born in Antrim.

1. JESSE ORVILLE, [b. in Greenfield July 18, 1833, m. Emma A. Austin Nov. 6, 1864, and lives in Washington, D. C.]
2. FRANCIS R., [b. July 26, 1836 ; unm., and lives in Washington, D. C.]
3. ALFRED OTIS, [b. June 14, 1837 ; was in Arkansas when the war broke out, was pressed into the rebel army, and killed in battle.]
4. JULIA S., [b. April 26, 1840 ; m. George A. Guild of Nashua April 22, 1864, and now lives in that city.] .
5. AULDIN S., [b. June 16, 1842 ; m. Clara E. Gray of Reading, Mass., Nov. 3, 1869, and now lives in that city.]
6. IRA STRAW, [b. June 28, 1844 ; was killed at the battle of Fredericksburg, Dec. 13, 1862.]
7. CHARLES SHERMAN, [b. in Washington, Dec. 28, 1846, and d. March 1, 1864.]
8. JAMES HOWE, [b. in Washington, Jan. 17, 1850, and d. in infancy.]
9. WALDO M., [d. in infancy.]
10. GEORGE VOLNEY, [b. in Washington, Sept. 11, 1856 ; d. in Antrim, March 8, 1862.]

CURTIS JOHNSON, brother of Volney, came here from Hancock, and fitted up for a dwelling the house now Mr. Balch's at South Village, in 1836. He married Jane Matthews, and after two or three years removed to Jaffrey.

CALEB JOHNSON succeeded John Ball, who moved from town in 1835. He lived in the Ball house until his death in 1845. The buildings are now all gone. Nothing further known of him or his family.

A SAMUEL JOHNSON entered his protest against the settlement of Mr. Whiton, on the town book, Sept. 4, 1808. He lived a short time somewhere on the mountain in the west part of the town; but his property was not such as to justify a great deal of worry about his tax for Mr. Whiton's support.

JOHN JOHNSON, son of John and Betsey (Mead) Johnson of Society Land, now Bennington, was born in November, 1829. In June, 1836, he was taken by James M. Wilson from the poor-farm of Hillsborough, and was brought up by him. He turned out to be a smart and good young man. Was a carpenter and house-builder; built the meeting-house in Windsor. Accumulating some property, he went into manufacturing in Clinton, in company with Samuel A. Fletcher. In this he was unfortunate, and failed; and he soon sickened and died. Married Martha J., daughter of Dea. Samuel Fletcher, Dec. 21, 1852. He died Jan. 29, 1857. His daughter Nellie was born March 26, 1855, married John Hill, and lives in Bunker Hill, Ill. The widow married, second, Henry Wise, in 1864, and died in 1867.

JOHN JOHNSON, son of Alfred and Lucy (Lawrence) Johnson, was born in Meriden, Conn., in 1833; married Ann L. Carr, and moved here in 1875. He is a tool and die maker, and has one child:—

1. ELMER OREN, [b. Feb. 22, 1870, in Meriden, Conn.]

## JONES.

JOEL JONES came here from Hillsborough in 1807, and put up the Langdon Swett house at the Branch. He was a blacksmith, and built the first shop on the Sawyer stand. In 1809 he sold out to Daniel Coolidge, and moved back to Hillsborough. His wife was an Abbott, daughter of "King Abbott," so called. As his stay here was so short, no special efforts have been made to enlarge this notice of him.

## JOSLIN.

TAYLOR JOSLIN, son of Nathaniel and Katherine (Joslin) Joslin probably of Stow, Mass., and afterwards of Henniker, was out in the Revolutionary army several years; was wounded in battle, causing him to be lame for life. He enlisted at one time for Deering, but was paid by John Duncan, July 15, 1786, as shown by old state records. He was once taken prisoner by the Indians and compelled to "run the gauntlet" between two lines of savages, one line being of men and the other of women, each striking a blow with the fist and hitting him if they could. He always declared that the squaws hit him the hardest and most! Why not? Mr. Joslin spoke often of his hardships in the army. Soon after peace was concluded he came back to Antrim (ten years earlier than Mr. Whiton's date), working here and there at the shoemaker's trade. He worked some years for Lemuel Paige at the Center. Oct. 20, 1796, he married Sally Heath of Pelham; built a small house in the corner of the field about four rods north of George Parmenter's barn, where he lived and worked at his trade and on his small farm till 1802, when he moved to Orange; thence to Hill in 1809, where he died in 1817. His widow died in Randolph, Vt., in 1832. They had six children; the youngest, a son, died in infancy, but the five daughters are all now living and in prosperous circumstances.

1. REBECCA, [b. in 1797; m. 1st, William Stevens: 2d, —— Jackson; 3d, another William Stevens; survived them all and now lives in Franklin, having had no children.]
2. KATHERINE, [m. Simeon Fuller, and lived in Brookfield, Vt.]
3. ABIGAIL, [m. John Wells of Franklin, and lives a widow in that place.]
4. SABRINA GREGG, [m. John Bean, and is now living in Wisconsin.]
5. ROXANNA, [m. Joseph French, and lives in Randolph, Vt.]

## JOY.

MRS. MARY B. JOY (Gould of Newfane, Vt., before marriage), widow of Daniel Joy of Putney, Vt., came here in 1875, and in the spring of 1876 bought the Ambrose Story place. She and her daughter, Mrs. Perry, built the present house mostly new in the spring of 1876, and tastefully furnished the same for the purpose of keeping summer boarders. Daniel Joy was son of Jedediah and Patience Joy. He died Jan. 20, 1866, aged seventy-three. Only two children grew to maturity:—

1. SARA E. D., [b. Nov. 27, 1838; m. Newton Perry, April 18, 1858.]
2. TYLER H., [killed in the second battle of Fredericksburg; had been skirmishing all day, and just at night received the wound from which he soon d. His death was Dec. 13, 1862, aged 20.]

## KEESER.

SAMUEL P. KEESER came here from Bennington, and lived in one of Thomas Poor's houses. He was a lame man, a shoemaker by trade, and after living here about a dozen years he moved back to Bennington in 1865, and died there Nov. 9, 1869, aged forty-five; was buried in Antrim. His wife was Mary Burtt, and their children were all born here : —

1. MARY J.
2. CHARLES.
3. JUDSON.

## KELSEA.

HAROLD KELSEA, son of William and Phœbe (Ladd) Kelsea, was born in Landaff in 1807, and married Harriet Noyes of Landaff. At the age of twenty-one he was licensed as a Methodist preacher. He invented a trebling machine for silk threads, which was held to be of great value and which he set in operation at North Branch in 1856, buying the mill of Henry Dunklee, but moved from the Branch to South Antrim in 1857, exchanging mills with Mark Woodbury, who then owned the upper mill in South Village. This mill, the machinery of which he has enlarged and increased from time to time, putting in steam-works in 1871, is now run by a company. They manufacture raw silk into all the various kinds of thread, making more than one hundred different shades, and nothing superior to theirs is made in the world. Mr. Kelsea built his house in 1863. His children are: —

1. ABEL M., [b. in Lisbon July 16, 1829, and now lives in Waterbury, Conn.]
2. PHŒBE A., [b. in Lisbon, May 2, 1831 ; m. Ephraim Simonds, Dec. 24, 1857, and lived awhile in South Village.]
3. JUDITH M., [b. May 1, 1833 ; is now Mrs. William Hill.]
4. JOSEPH N., [b. June 12, 1837 ; was in the drug business for some years in Tilton ; m. Maria L. Noyes of Montreal, Canada, formerly of Lowell, Jan. 9, 1877, and resides at the South Village, occupying a large and handsome house built by him in 1877.]
5. CHARLES W., [b. in Littleton, Sept. 29, 1844, and is now of the Silk Company at South Antrim ; was several years selectman of the town.]

## KENDALL.

CAPT. NATHAN KENDALL was born in Litchfield in 1726, and died in Amherst in 1791. He married Rebecca Converse of Merrimack in 1753. She died in Antrim in 1818, aged eighty-eight. They had children: Nathan, Joshua, Rebecca, Jesse, Timothy, Thaddeus, and John C. These all lived to good old age, the first death among them being that of Joshua, who died in 1823, aged sixty-five. They were all born in Amherst.

TIMOTHY KENDALL, son of Capt. Nathan and Rebecca, born Aug. 1, 1770, came here on to the place vacated by Nathan Austin, now called the Gibson place, near the turnpike. He married Mrs. Esther (Pierce)

Walker in 1793. She was a sister of Gov. Benjamin Pierce, and died in Antrim, Nov. 15, 1826, aged sixty-four. They settled in Amherst, whence they moved here. Lived on above-named place till 1812, then in several other places in town: but died in Bennington, April 14, 1827. Children are: —

1. INDIANA EMERSON, [b. Dec. 21, 1795, in Amherst; m. James Jameson, Dec. 4, 1817; d. in Lowell, Dec. 14, 1847; her six children are all dead.]
2. TIMOTHY CONVERSE, [b. June 1, 1797; went to Boston in early life, and d. there in December, 1860; m. 1st, Sarah Fenner of Providence; 2d, Sarah Eveleth of Stow. Mass.; 3d, Mrs. Mary Bartlett of Boston. His children, all by the first wife, were: George, Thomas, Josiah, Esther Pierce, and Sarah. He was in the hide and leather business; was often councilman and alderman of Boston, and many years on board of directors of public institutions.]
3. CONVERSE, [d. in infancy.]
4. REBECCA S., [b. in September, 1801, and d. Sept. 9, 1868; she m. John Banks Warren, a cousin of Gen. Banks, and left but one child, George K. Warren, Esq., a noted photographer and artist of Boston.]
5. ELISABETH PIERCE, [b. in June, 1803; d. January, 1837; m. Gen. Israel Hunt of Nashua, in 1832.]

STEPHEN C. KENDALL, son of Josiah and Mary (Lovett) Kendall, was born in 1825. He came here in 1849 from Mont Vernon, and was engaged in the manufacture of doors in the shop now .A. F. True's, in company with his brother John, and afterwards with Charles E. Jackson. He built the part of the shop now standing. He married Alfreda Jackson of Tamworth; built the house now Lewis Bass's; left Antrim in 1859, and now lives in Fitchburg, Mass.

JOHN L. KENDALL, brother of Stephen C., married Christiana Lovejoy in 1851, and lived in the Cummings house. He entered the army and was lost overboard on the Potomac. The children are all dead.

ADONIRAM J. KENDALL, another brother, lived here awhile, and moved to Nashua in 1851. His parents came here and lived in the Simon Story house some years, which house was built for them. Adoniram had an arm sawed off in that shop above the elbow, and he did not know it was off till he saw it on the floor, it was done so quick! He married Amanda Abbott, and had one child: —

1. FRANK E., [b. here in 1851.]

## KEYES.

VERANUS KEYES came here from Nashua in the spring of 1857 to take charge of the town farm, which he managed for two or three years. He then bought the William Wilkins farm at the foot of the sand-hill, which he occupied some years. He then bought the place next east of school-house No. 6, where he lived till the house was burned, when he went to Ashland. He is now living in Weston, Mass. Veranus was the fourth child of Abner and Susannah (Barton) Keyes, and was born in Hancock, Sept. 22, 1813. Abner Keyes was the fourth generation of exactly the same name. Veranus married Mary G. Lewis of Pittsfield, Mass., Nov. 6, 1831. His father had a large family; and it is said every one in the whole race able to bear arms was in the Union army in the late war. Veranus had three children : --

1. FRANKLIN L., [b. in Lee, Mass., Aug 31, 1833 ; m. Eliza Hay of Nashua, Oct. 30, 1854. She d. April 9, 1860. Their two children d. before the mother. He was in a good position at Concord on the breaking-out of the war, but was one of the first in the State to enlist. Was in the company of sharp-shooters attached to the Second N. H. Regiment. Was one of eight men picked out of his division by Gen. Joe Hooker for the signal corps. Was afterwards messenger between Washington and Gen. McClellan on the field. Subsequently, Signal-Officer Keyes was on duty in the Peninsula, was always at headquarters, and was entrusted with many perilous and important undertakings. On the last day of the seven days' fight before Richmond, McClellan ordered a council of war; and Keyes and other officers were sent to the several commanders for reports of their condition. Keyes had accomplished his errand, and was on his return, when a shell burst near his horse's feet, knocking over both horse and rider and stunning both. He was found senseless partly under the horse, was carried to Harrison Landing, and there lay in a field of wheat two days in the rain. There friends found him, and did what they could for him. Thence, in a terrible condition of wounds and bruises, he was taken to a hospital in Philadelphia. There he remained six months, in great suffering. Everything possible was done for him; but his case was given up as hopeless. It was then decided to send him North, and by easy stages he arrived at Antrim in the summer of 1863. Here, though very slowly, his condition improved, and in the course of a year he was taken to Concord. There he was m. Aug. 1,

1866, to Miss Almena P. Quimby, sister of Prof. Quimby of Dartmouth College. This most estimable lady had been engaged to him before the war; and in his weak, wounded, suffering condition she refused to be set free. But soon after marriage he had a shock of a paralytic nature, on account of which he was confined to the bed nine years, always in a sitting posture night and day. He is now living in Newcastle, a helpless cripple, but a worthy and much-respected man. Letters written by him on the bed show considerable mental character, and a patient spirit in sufferings. He gave all but life to his country. Few lives can be found of such distress and affliction as his. He has shown a nobleness and courage worthy of note. His noble wife ministers to him with heroic devotion. Though deprived of many blessings, yet they are so happy in life that the complainer visiting them goes away and murmurs no more. It is proper to say, in short, that the facts here narrated are a continual honor to "Signal-Officer Keyes."]

2. SUSAN E., [b. Aug. 26, 1835, m. Andrew J. Varnum, and now lives in Ashland.]
3. FLORA M., [b in Nashua Sept. 21, 1846. Is m. and lives in North Adams, Mass. Her husband's name is Arthur Porter.]

## KIDDER.

EBENEZER KIDDER, son of David and Esther (Corey) Kidder of Chelmsford, Mass., and a descendant of James Kidder who arrived in New England before the year 1650, came to Antrim from Chelmsford in 1785, having been married to Esther Wilson in 1784. He bought of Frank Stuart, who had begun the present Kidder place. Stuart had cleared about two acres, and had a log house on the site where the Kidder family have since lived. Mr. Kidder died in 1816, leaving children:—

1. REUBEN, [b. May 2, 1788; m. Sally Bickford of Hillsborough in 1817; moved to Goshen and d. there in 1862.]
2. JOHN, [b. April 8, 1793; m. Sarah Chandler of Hillsborough; lived with his father, and d. in 1828. One child survives him:—

    *Warren R.*, (who lives in Hillsborough, was b. June 30, 1822, and m. Hannah J. Hoyt of Gilford.)]
3. LYDIA, [b. Dec. 4, 1795; m. Jonas Wilson Dec. 31, 1818, and lived some time in this town, then went below, thence to Hillsborough, where she still survives.]
4. BENJAMIN, [b. Oct. 19, 1801; m. Sarah A. Wilson of Chelms-

ford June 3, 1829, and occupies the old farm. He built his present house in 1866. His children are : —

*Lucy A.*, (d. in 1841, at the age of 10.)

*Benjamin F.*, (b. April 3, 1834 ; lives with his father.)]

5. PATTY, [d. in 1828 at the age of 24.]
6. AMOS, [b. Jan. 16, 1807 ; m. Lucinda Barton of Croydon, where he learned the clothier's trade. Thence he moved to Newport, where he still resides.]
7. SALOME, [d. in 1828, aged 19.]

## KIMBALL.

EBENEZER KIMBALL, son of Ebenezer and Ruth (Waldron) Kimball, came here about 1787; married Polly Aiken, the first American child born in Antrim; where the George Duncan, or Carter House now stands, he had a long, low house, with the gable end standing square up to the road. In the back part he opened a store in 1788, or a little earlier, where he traded five or six years, then sold to Andrew Seaton. It was at Ebenezer Kimball's that town meetings were held for several years, when Hancock was classed with Antrim, to choose a representative. Mr. Kimball moved to Hill in 1797, and was for a long time a merchant in that place. He was representative, justice of the peace, and postmaster, and died in 1835 aged seventy-two. His children that lived to adult age were : —

1. RUTH W., [b. in Antrim in 1793 ; m. George W. Crockett, a prominent merchant of Boston, and state senator, who d: in 1859, aged 79. She still lives in Boston.]
2. TIRZAH, [b. in 1800; m. A. W. Burnham, D. D., of Rindge, in 1822, who was pastor there forty-seven years, and she his faithful helper. Samuel Burnham, once editor of the "Congregationalist," was her son. She now resides in Keene.]
3. DR. GILMAN, [b. in 1804 ; m. 1st, Mary Dewar of Edinburg, Scotland ; 2d, Isabel De Fries of Nantucket, Mass. He has been for many years a very distinguished physician and surgeon in Lowell. After fitting for college, failing health prevented his pursuing the course, and after a time he determined to enter at once on the study of medicine. This he accomplished chiefly at Dartmouth College, and he took his medical degree in 1827. He then studied three years abroad, leaving Paris to return to America on the very day of the famous Revolution, July, 1830. He located in Lowell, Dec. 2, 1831, where he has continued in extensive practice till the present time. He was chosen professor of surgery in the Vermont Medical College in 1840 ; was surgeon and

superintendent of Lowell Hospital twenty-seven years; and is justly famed for surgical skill and success both in this country and England.]

4. MARY, [b. July 5, 1807; m. Dr. John S. Sanborn, and settled in Elyton, Ala. Dr. Sanborn soon d. and she m. a planter by name of Carroll, who d. after a few years. She then came back and was matron of Mt. Holyoke Seminary fourteen years, and is now living in Mattapoisett, Mass.]

5. CAROLINE, [b. Aug. 1, 1809; m. George E. Sherman, a merchant of Hill, who afterwards settled in Newton County, Miss.; some years ago he d., and she came North, and now resides with her sister at Mattapoisett.]

REV. WILLARD KIMBALL came here from Brandon, Vt., early in 1856, and soon after became pastor of the Baptist Church. He remained here six years in all; lived most of the time in the Charles D. Sawyer house in Clinton. Went back to Brandon. Went about 1870 to Newton. Mass., in midsummer on a visit, was taken with dysentery, and suddenly died. His wife was Amanda True. They had two children, George and Mary. The former was last known in Boston. The latter was noted as a teacher, and was very successful as such, having place in the higher female institutions. She married Job Clement, Esq., of Brandon, Vt.

DR. J. R. KIMBALL, son of Jonathan and Pamelia (Holt) Kimball, and grandson of Edward and Elisabeth (McAllister) Kimball, was born in Pembroke in 1844; went to Maine in 1854, and studied at Hebron Academy in that State. He studied medicine with Dr. Phillips of Pembroke, attended lectures awhile in Portland, Me., and graduated at Bowdoin Medical College in 1869. He came to Antrim the same year as successor of Dr. William M. Parsons; married Clara A. Phillips, daughter of Dr. Phillips of Pembroke, in 1872. After getting well established in practice, and in the confidence and regard of the community, to the general surprise and regret he removed to Suncook in 1873, where he now resides and has an extensive practice.

DEA. JOSEPH KIMBALL, son of Dea. Daniel and Abiah (Holt) Kimball of Ipswich, Mass., was born in Hancock, June 21, 1801, and died in September, 1864. Was long a deacon in the Hancock church. The family was of English descent. The father, Dea. Daniel, was one of the first settlers of Hancock, and when making his clearings he worked alone by day, and slept nights in a hollow log. Dea. Joseph Kimball married Lucy Boyd of Antrim, Oct. 20, 1831. The widow and daughters moved to South Antrim in 1867. The children were:—

1. JAMES B., [d. in childhood.]
2. JOSEPH M., [d. in 1862, aged 28.]
3. MARY F.
4. L. HELEN.

ELIJAH KIMBALL, son of Benjamin and Susanna (Gerry) Kimball, and grandson of Benjamin and Mehitable (Parker) Kimball, was born in Hillsborough, Oct. 25, 1814. The father was born in Hillsborough in 1780, but the grandfather moved there from Topsfield, Mass., and was among the early settlers. Elijah Kimball married Caroline Stratton of Bradford, April 21, 1842. She was a daughter of Lemuel and Philippa (Jackman) Stratton, who were near relatives of Daniel Webster. He came to Antrim on to the Dr. Burnham place in 1873. His children, all born in Hillsborough, were: —

1. HENRY P., [b. Nov. 15, 1843; carpenter by trade; resides on Dr. Burnham place, having greatly enlarged and improved the buildings; m. Susan E. Towne of Peabody, Mass., April 8, 1869.]
2. JOHN C., [b. Jan. 3, 1848; has been a successful teacher in the West; m. Mary Newman, and settled in Hamel, Ill., where she d. March 9, 1877.]
3. ELIZA A., [b. March 26, 1851.]

## KNIGHTS.

JONATHAN KNIGHTS came here from Middleton, Mass., with six children, in 1795, and bought the Dea. Worthley place (Mr. French's) of William Boyd. He died west of the pond, in 1814, aged ninety-four. His wife's name was Mary Perkins, and their children were: —

1. JONATHAN, [lived here and there in town; m. Mehitable Andrews of Boxford, Mass.; went to Boxford, and d. there in 1845, aged 92, leaving a large and respectable family.]
2. NEHEMIAH, [m. 1st, Mrs. White; 2d, Phebe, the widow of Lemuel Paige, Feb. 12, 1809, from whom he separated, and in 1816 went with the Robbs to New York, and d. there about 1830, aged 70, having no children. He was a very eccentric man, and gave his iron bar for digging his grave.]
3. PHŒBE, [was killed by the fall of a tree in 1799, as she was picking up wood where her brothers were chopping, near the house, aged about 25 years.]
4. RUTH, [m. Solomon Balch of New Boston; went to Johnson, Vt., and d. there in 1832, aged 56.]
5. ROBERT, [m. Priscilla Hutchinson of Middleton, Mass., and was killed by the fall of a tree as they were clearing land, in 1800. He was fearfully lacerated, his ax being driven through his shoulder. His widow m. Thomas Andrews of Hudson, Nov. 8, 1804, and d. there in 1818. Robert left three children, born here: —

*Polly*, (b. June 20, 1796; m. Dea. James Hartshorn, and

lives in Nashua, aged 82. Her husband has recently d. aged 92.)

*Lydia*, (b. April 28, 1798, and d. in infancy.)

*Jonathan*, (b. Dec. 4, 1799; m. 1st, Lucy A. Putnam ; 2d, Ann M. Patten of Bedford ; 3d, Mary A. Dodge of Amherst; 4th, Mrs. Mary J. Davis of Amherst, where he now resides.)]

6. BENJAMIN, [b. in 1785 ; m. Lucy Barden; lived here and there in town, and d. in Peterborough in 1849. They had one son who d. in infancy, and seven daughters as follows: —

*Phœbe V.*, (b. June 19, 1807 ; m. Josiah S. Morrison of Peterborough, in 1831, and lives in Alstead. He has been engaged in building machinery, and has held several important public offices.)

*Lydia*, (b. March 26, 1809, m. Luther Darling of Dublin, March 24, 1831. and d. at Fitchburg, Mass., in 1874.)

*Lucinda*, (b. March 13, 1811, m. Walter W. Blake Oct. 11, 1838, and d. in Hollis in 1874.)

*Esther*, (b. March 7, 1813, m. Samuel W. Billings Dec. 24, 1835, and d. in Hancock in 1876.)

*Mary*, (b. Oct. 18, 1815 ; m. Nathaniel Morrison of Peterborough ; lived in Lowell for many years, and now resides in Greenfield.)

*Mehitable*, (b. March 28, 1818, m. James Mitchell of Manchester, and d. in 1846.)

*Achsa*, (b. Aug. 12, 1820 ; m. Thomas Colby of San Francisco, Cal.)]

## LADD.

JONATHAN LADD was the first settler on the farm now Capt. James Wilson's. His house stood on the ridge west of the present house, near the southeast corner of the field. He seems to have commenced there about 1785. He lived there nearly ten years. It is not known whence he came. He moved to a small town in Vermont, then called Tunbridge, about twenty miles from the Connecticut River, and opposite Orford. I have not been able to learn anything of his descendants.

## LAWRENCE.

WILLIAM LAWRENCE, son of Jonathan and Esther (Shedd) Lawrence, was born in Groton, Mass., in 1762; married Sarah F. Farwell of that place, and came here from Washington in 1812. He kept a hotel several years on the Gould place. He was a very respectable man, and had meetings at his house two Sundays in the year, at which Mr. Whiton preached. In 1818 he moved back to Washington, where he died in

1830, aged sixty-eight. His wife died in 1850, aged eighty-two. Their children were: —

1. SARAH, [b. in Groton, Mass., in 1787, m. Sylvester Hubbard of Washington, and d. in Hillsborough in 1824.]
2. EDMUND, [b. in Groton, Mass., in 1793; m. Harriet M., daughter of Dea. Brainard of Washington, and d. at West Dennis, Mass., in 1854.]
3. MARY, [b. in Washington in 1795; m. Dea. Samuel Burbank of that place; moved to Hillsborough, where she d. in 1876.]
4. WILLIAM F., [b. in 1803; m. Mary L. Churchill of Nashua; kept a hotel in Washington, and was afterwards for several years a stage-driver; was highly esteemed. He finally moved to Nashua, and there d. in 1856.]

HENRY S. LAWRENCE, son of Sherman B. and Theresa (Clark) Lawrence, and grandson of Silas B. and Azubah (Curtis) Lawrence, was born in Meriden, Conn., Jan. 30, 1837. The family was from Troy, N. Y. He married Abbie F. Carr June 26, 1867; came here in 1875; occupies the Oren Carr homestead; is a mason by trade.

EDWIN LAWRENCE lived a short time in South Village, and died here Dec. 20, 1862, aged forty-six. Nothing more known of him.

## LAWS.

AUGUSTUS LAWS, son of Joseph Laws and Abigail Pike, was born in Brookline in 1820; married, first, Mary E. Burke, and came here to work at making hoes and shovels in 1846. He married, second, Nancy C. Robbins in 1847, and after a residence of about nine years went to Peterborough, where she died in 1871. He now lives in Marlow; had no children born here.

## LITTLE.

The first family of Littles of which we have any knowledge in America descended from George Little who came from London to Newbury, Mass., in 1640. This family is large and very respectable. Some of them remain on the spot originally settled, and others are settled near by; among them Dea. Joseph Little of Newbury, and William Little, Esq., town clerk of the above place. Alfred Little, Esq., the distinguished singer and player on the melodeon, now residing in Webster, is of this stock. Also Rev. Geo. A. Little, pastor of the Presbyterian Church at Plymouth, Ind.; Rev. Arthur Little, D. D., of Chicago; Rev. Joseph B. Little, Rev. Henry S. Little, Rev. George O. Little, and Rev. Charles H. Little, pastors in the West. Many others of this family are found in professional and cultivated ranks. The Littles of Antrim and Peterborough, as indicated by personal appearance and tradition and favorite names, are probably related to the foregoing family. They are of Scotch descent, it appears; and the ancestor, Thomas Little, with his wife Jean and several children, came over from the north of Ireland, county of Antrim, in 1737, and settled in Shirley, Mass. His son, Thomas, Jr., was ten years old on arrival in this country. It seems to have been in his twenty-seventh year that he married Susanna Wallace, herself born in the north of Ireland in 1734. The old records speak of them as being married in Peterborough, and living there a short time several years previous to their permanent settlement in that town. They had eight children : Dr. William, born in Peterborough, Oct. 20, 1753; Esther, born in Lunenburg, Mass., in 1755; Elisabeth, born in Shirley, Mass., in 1756, in which town the family continued to reside till 1764; Susaunah, born in 1759; Joseph, born in 1760; Thomas, born May 11, 1763, married Relief White, and died in 1847; John, born in Peterborough in 1764, married Lucinda Longley, and died Sept. 19, 1850; and Rev. Walter, born in 1766, and noticed below. The father of these eight children died in Shirley, Mass., while on a visit there, June 6, 1808, aged eighty-one. His widow, daughter of William and Elisabeth (Clayland) Wallace, died in Peterborough March 6, 1822, aged eighty-eight.

Dr. WILLIAM LITTLE, oldest child of Thomas and Susanna, was born in Peterborough, Oct. 20, 1753, during a temporary sojourn of the parents in that place. He studied medicine with Dr. John Young, the first physician of Peterborough, and established himself as a physician in Hillsborough in 1782. He married Betsey Fletcher of Westford, Mass. She soon died, and it is believed she left but one child, Betsey F., born Sept. 27, 1775, who married Samson Keyes, went to Wilton, Me., and died there Aug. 26, 1810. Her husband was a native of Westford, Mass., born Nov. 22, 1777; died April 24, 1861. Hon. Alvah Keyes, of Claremont, is her son. Dr. Little married, second, Ruth, daughter of Dea. Joseph Symonds of Hillsborough, May 12, 1787, and had children : Dea. William, named below; Martha D., who married James Campbell, May 19, 1836, and died Dec. 29, 1852, aged sixty-three; Ruth S., who died in Antrim, Nov. 28, 1838, aged thirty-nine; Lucy R., who married Bartlett Wallace and died July 11, 1855, aged fifty-five; and Hiram, who died young. Dr. Little had a large practice, was a social, wide-awake man, of hearty friendships and much influence, but in the midst of his usefulness he came to a sudden death, being drowned Nov. 7, 1807, aged fifty-four. He had been that day to an auction on the Whittemore place near by in Antrim; the evening came on early, and very dark and cold; he started alone to walk back to the Bridge, and seems to have walked over the bank into the river at the bend close by the road. Great search was made for him, the whole town turning out for that purpose. But he could not be found; people considered his disappearance a great mystery, and his body lay in the river all winter. When the ice broke up in the spring, it floated down, and was first discovered in the north edge of the stream just above the new factory at the Bridge. On the following day, which was the Sabbath, no minister could be found in this section. Dea. John Duncan went over and offered prayer at the funeral, and the body, fresh as life, was carried to its rest in the grave.

## GENEALOGIES.

Dea. WILLIAM LITTLE was born in Hillsborough March 10, 1788; married, first, Abigail Wells of Goffstown in 1814; second, Mrs. Lydia S. Dow. Came to Antrim in 1815, and built the tannery at the Branch, in which he did business more than forty years; was a leading man in town; was chosen elder in the Presbyterian Church in 1831; died Dec. 18, 1869. His second wife is yet living. The first wife died Feb. 1, 1846, aged sixty-eight; and she was the mother of his children named below: —

1. Hiram, [b. Aug. 8, 1815; d. in early life: buried on Bible Hill, Hillsborough.]
2. William P., [known as "Plummer Little." b. May 24, 1817; m. Mary J. Burns, Nov. 12, 1844; opened a public house at the Branch in 1841, which he continued to keep till death. The building, originally the Dea. James Nesmith house on the northeastward slope of Meeting-House Hill, had been moved and put up by Jacob Tuttle about 1838. Plummer Little d. very suddenly, Sept. 1, 1869, aged 52. His children were three: —

   *George P.*, (b. Oct. 4, 1845; m. Media M. McIlvaine, March 30, 1870; is trader at the Branch.)
   *Nettie M.*, (b. April 24, 1847; m. Frank Dunlap, Oct. 14, 1869.)
   *Ella E.*, (b. June 14, 1858; m. George H. Perkins, April 1., 1875.)]
3. John, [b. May 24, 1819, m. Clarinda Brackett, and lives in Cambridgeport, Mass.]
4. Jane W., [b. Dec. 15, 1821, m. John McIlvaine April 23, 1846, and d. April 28, 1849.]
5. Willis, [b. Feb. 9, 1824; d Jan. 12, 1861, aged 36.]
6. Frederick S., [b. July 20, 1825; m. Julia Keyes of Goshen; has been noted as teacher of vocal music; now lives in Newport; spent several years as school-teacher in New Jersey. Has been one of the town officers of Newport several years.]
7. Isaac W., [b. March 14, 1829, d. aged 9.]
8. Abby. [b. March 24, 1831; m. Randolph Gilman of Unity, Jan. 12, 1871.]
9. Sylvester, [b. May 28, 1833; m. March 26, 1860, Mary E. Vose, daughter of Dr. Samuel Vose, formerly of Antrim; was a very efficient and successful teacher of sacred music for many years, and was a long time leader of the Center choir; is the traveling agent of the Goodell Company. He greatly modernized and improved the house built by his father in 1824 at the Branch; built and removed to South Village in 1879. Has children: —

*Helen L.*, (b. Jan. 27, 1864.)
*Harry H.*, (b. Oct. 27, 1867.)
*Ruth Evangeline*, (b. July 3, 1872.)]

10. BETSEY K., [b. April 4, 1836; m. J. M. Brigham of Cambridgeport. Mass., and d. there Oct. 8, 1874. Was a sweet singer in the house of the Lord.]

REV. WALTER LITTLE, youngest child of Thomas and Susanna (Wallace) Little, and brother of Dr. William of Hillsborough, was born in Peterborough in 1766; was a graduate of Dartmouth College in 1796; was the first minister of Antrim, being settled here in 1800. He was a tall, slim, dark-complexioned, fine-looking man, a smart preacher, and the church greatly prospered under his care. But his manners were disliked; he was considered proud and authoritative and unsympathetic, and the people got so generally against him that he resigned at the end of four years. This was his first parish and his last. Soon after his dismission he went into the State of New York; preached here and there, but, failing of a satisfactory settlement, he fell into a wandering habit, roamed over the country, was considered partially insane, and on one of these tramps he died in the State of Maryland, sometime in 1815, far from acquaintances and friends. He was never married. Before leaving New Hampshire he had his name changed to Fullerton, but nobody ever knew a reason why. Probably it should be added that his talents commanded respect, notwithstanding all opposition and dislike. Decidedly, he was an able man. After Mr. Little was dismissed, he had his farewell meeting at Dea. Aiken's house. It was a week-day evening. The meeting was crowded and solemn. Mr. Little was making his closing prayer when Isaac Baldwin, a boy of eight years (afterwards Dea. Baldwin), climbed up on the high chair-back, and tipped over, chair and all, falling with such force against the minister's back as to throw him forward against the pantry-door, which opened at touch, and he fell flat on his face on the pantry-floor! It is not reported whether he said his "amen" in that position or not. But there was great consternation in other parts of the house, and the meeting closed rather curiously for a farewell occasion. Mr. Little demanded that the boy be whipped on the spot; but, as it was entirely unintentional, the mother declined, whereupon he took the future deacon into another room and whipped him himself!

## LIVINGSTON.

ROBERT L. LIVINGSTON, son of Robert and Mary (Leslie) Livingston, and grandson of Robert and Zebiah (Sargent) Livingston, who were among the first settlers of New Boston, was born in New Boston, Sept. 12, 1797; married, first, Adeline Duncan, daughter of Dea. Josiah Duncan of Antrim, May 24, 1827. He came here in the year 1825; lived some years in the McFarland house (Jameson's), and built the house now John Butterfield's in 1834. He left town in 1850. His wife died in 1866, and he married, second, Mrs. Lucinda Mills, and is now living in Goffstown. His children, all by the first wife, and born here, were: —

1. LUTHER, [b. April 27, 1828; his name was changed to Frederick L., because there were so many of the same name; m. Libbie Ward of Norwich, Conn.; now lives in Philadelphia.]
2. JOSIAH D., [broke through the ice on the brook near the Butterfield place, and was drowned, March 10, 1836. He was a beautiful boy, six years of age.]
3. HIRAM L., [b. June 16, 1832; is a mute; m. Mary Pressey of Canaan, and lives in North Salem.]
4. MARY G., [d. in infancy.]
5. JOSIAH EDWIN, [b. March 13, 1836; m. 1st, Nancy, daughter of Hon. Abel Haley of Wolfeborough; 2d, Maria A. Ingraham of Springfield, Mass., and lives in North Salem. He is the inventor of a " nutmeg-grater " of great convenience and value, also inventor of a " mitring machine " which promises much.]
6. ADDIE M., [b. Oct. 17, 1839; m. Benton W. Cutting of Thetford, Vt., and lives in Manchester.]
7. SARAH E., [b. March 23, 1844; her name was changed to Libbie E.; m. Matthew B. White, and lives in Manchester.]
8. ROBERT DUNCAN, [b. May 24, 1847; is a mute; now living unm. in Boston.]

## LOVEJOY.

REV. WILLIAM W. LOVEJOY, son of William and Dorothy (Johnson) Lovejoy, was born Aug. 27, 1810. He studied for the ministry at New Hampton, and was ordained at Littleton in the summer of 1840. After preaching in several places, he came here from Bennington about 1850 as pastor of the Baptist Church. It is said of him that he was " a faithful, earnest preacher, and one of the kindest and most loving of men, happy, and lived near to God." He married, first, Hannah T. Lovejoy, who died in Antrim, May 6, 1855; second, Eliza J. White of this town, July 31, 1855. He died at Pottersville while pastor of the Baptist Church in that place, April 4, 1862, aged fifty-two. Children: —

1. RUTHVEN M., [b. Jan. 13, 1832; d. May 14, same year.]
2. EMILY J., [b. Aug. 14, 1834, m. Eben P. Knight of Marlow, Jan. 1, 1856, and d. Sept. 29, 1859.]
3. ANTOINETTE E., [b. in Marlow, Aug. 30, 1856.]
4. ALFARATA J., [b. in Dublin, Oct. 17, 1859.]
5. FLORA I., [b. Sept. 9, 1861, in Dublin.]

## LOVEREN.

JOSIAH LOVEREN, son of John and Clarissa (Richardson) Loveren, and grandson of Ebenezer and Eunice (Hadlock) Loveren, was born in Deering, Dec. 4, 1817. The family came from Kensington, and were among the very first settlers of Deering. He married, first, Asenath Gregg of Deering, who died in 1855, aged forty; second, Nancy J. Peabody of Antrim, Dec. 18, 1856; moved here in 1864, and bought the Peabody mills, which he has very much enlarged, and filled with improved machinery. This is now a large establishment of its kind, and is extensively known as "Loveren's Mills." Has children: —

1. SAMUEL S., [b. in Deering, May 19, 1846.]
2. JAMES G., [b. in Deering, May 3, 1850.]
3. FRANK P., [b. in Deering, Nov. 28, 1851; m. Sarah J. Ogden, May 1, 1878; settled at once in Deering, but d. of fever Oct. 18, 1878. Was an excellent and amiable young man, having many friends, and his early death saddened the whole community.]
4. JOHN E., [b. Feb. 2, 1858.]
5. GEORGE M., [b. Aug. 14, 1866.]

## LOVEWELL.

LYMAN T. LOVEWELL, son of Isaac and Eliza (Moulton) Lovewell of Gardner, Mass., grandson of Joseph and Sally (Wilkinson) Lovewell of Weston, and great-grandson of Joseph Lovewell (who was taken prisoner in the French and Indian war, but with three others escaped in so nearly a starving condition that they divided a snake between them for food), was born in Gardner, Mass., Oct. 17, 1842; married Sarah L. Stowell in 1867, and came here from Gardner in 1875, buying one-half of the Caleb Clark place, where he resides, having since purchased the other part of the farm. Mr. Lovewell was out in the Fourth Mass. Heavy Artillery, and remained till the close of the war. Has no children.

## LOWE.

DANIEL LOWE came from Greenfield to Antrim, about 1817. He bought of Samuel Caldwell the Dea. Worthley place (cleared by William Boyd). He married Hannah Kidder of Lyndeborough, and lived on the Dea. Worthley place many years, being there as late as 1848. He afterwards sold to David Starrett and moved to North Branch, where he built the Sylvester Preston house, and there died Dec. 14, 1857, aged seventy. A young girl, Mary Woodward, was brought up by them. She came here from Lyndeborough in 1819, and married Prof. Leonard Marshall of Boston, Sept. 17, 1835. Mr. Lowe left but one child: —

1. LOISA JANE, [m. Isaac C. Tuttle, Nov. 11, 1846.]

## LYNCH.

MAURICE LYNCH was born in Ireland in 1738. He was educated for a Catholic priest; came to Newfoundland, renounced the papacy, and married Catherine Sheehan. Became a land-surveyor. After a residence of about two years in Newfoundland, he came to New England and settled in New Boston. From that town he came here in 1772, and began the James Wallace farm, now William Stacey's. Was the first town clerk of Antrim. Was a man of wit and many jokes, some of which have survived one hundred years in the town where he died. He sold his farm and went back to New Boston, probably in the fall of 1777, where he died Jan. 7, 1779, aged forty. His wife died March 3, 1803, aged sixty. Only three children are known of: —

1. JOHN, [b. in Newfoundland in 1766; came with his father to New Boston; m. Alice McMillen of that town in 1789, and had a family of eight children. The descendants of Maurice Lynch by his son John are very numerous, and some of them remain in New Boston.]
2. Child of unknown name, [d. here it is believed in the autumn of 1772, being three or four years old. All the father could do was to cover up the little body in a trough, carry it in his arms three or four miles through the woods, and bury it alone as near as possible to the spot which would be the future Center of the town. Now neither name nor grave is known. But God has not forgotten the little face laid so sadly away.

    " These ashes, too, this little dust, —
    Our Father's care shall keep."]
3. MARY ANN, [grew up in New Boston; m. a sea-captain from Boston, Mass., about 1793, and nothing more can be learned concerning her. An old bear and nine cubs once drove Mary Ann home; and her mother, greatly frightened and somewhat mixed from excitement, ran over to Dea. Christie's and shouted: " Deacon, Deacon, catch your dog and call your gun; for nine she-bears and one old cub chased my Mary Ann clear from Lyndeborough woods to my own door!"]

## MANAHAN.

DR. VALENTINE MANAHAN was son of John and Zurintha (Felch) Manahan of Deering. He was a student of New London and Dartmouth, and a graduate of Jefferson Medical College in 1850. He came here the same year, got well started in practice, but suddenly left the next year and went to Springfield. In 1851 he married Abby E. Porter of Sutton, and is now living in Enfield, engaged in large practice.

## MANSFIELD.

JAMES A. MANSFIELD lived here for a time in the Jonas Hubbard house northwest of the pond, in connection with Bezaleel Wheeler, moving away about 1824. Little is known of him, but it is believed that he went to Boston and died there.

## MARSH.

EBENEZER MARSH came here from Hudson, about 1798, and located on the mountain west of the Capt. Worthley place, beyond the pond. After about ten years he moved back to that town, where he died. The name "Marsh" occurs now and then in the old papers and records of that vicinity, but of this one nothing further has been learned.

## MARSHALL.

SAMUEL MARSHALL came here from Hudson and succeeded Nathan Cross on the Asa Robinson or Steel place. The house stood near the end of the lane on the opposite side of the road from the present house. On the "Cold Friday," Jan. 19, 1810, the wind took the roof off his house, and the whole family barely escaped perishing with the cold. He had five children born here. Four were by his first wife, Hannah, daughter of Jacob Paige of Litchfield; and one by his second wife, Abigail Robb, whom he married March 18. 1817.

1. SAMUEL, [b. March 8, 1809.]
2. ELIZA, [b. Feb. 7, 1811.]
3. ENOCH, [b. Jan. 1, 1813.]
4. JOHN, [b. Oct. 24, 1814.]
5. HANNAH, [b. Nov. 30, 1817.]

## MATTHEWS.

ROBERT MATTHEWS and his wife (Gibson) came to Hancock among the first settlers of the town. He came from Londonderry, bringing his son James, then a very small boy. The latter married Abigail Kieth of Sullivan, in 1810. She was a native of Uxbridge, Mass. In 1815 James Matthews moved to Antrim, and lived in this town fifteen years, when he moved back to Hancock. All the children except the two first were born in Antrim. He died Nov. 13, 1852, aged seventy-one; and his wife died Dec. 30, 1872, aged eighty-three. He lived in the southwest part of Antrim, near Hancock line, and was chiefly identified with the latter town. The farm was chiefly in Antrim, but the town line ran through the room in which the children were born. Children were : —

1. ELVIRA, [b. March 29, 1811 ; m. Franklin Robinson of Greenfield, in 1838 ; d. in California, Dec. 2, 1878.]
2. ABIGAIL, [b. Feb. 15, 1813 ; m. Lewis W. Alcock of Hancock, Aug. 31, 1837, and is now living in that town.]
3. HANNAH, [b. April 15, 1815 ; m. A. R. W. Burt of Bennington, Oct. 28, 1845 ; d. April 2, 1876.]
4. MELVIN, [b. Feb. 19, 1817 ; m. 1st, Sarah Richardson of Ashby, Mass.; 2d, Hannah Watson of Charlestown, Mass.; d. March 28, 1861.]

5. ARVILLA, [b. Dec. 26, 1819 ; m. David Seward of Sullivan, Oct. 1, 1840. She was mother of Rev. F. L. Seward of Lowell (Harvard College, 1868).]
6. ADELINE, [b. Jan. 2, 1821 ; d. Oct. 20, 1847.]
7. NORMANDA, [b. Aug. 6, 1822 ; d. Jan. 25, 1844.]
8. EMILY, [b. Sept. 15, 1824 ; m. Gardner Town of Sullivan, Jan. 4, 1870.]
9. DAVID, [b. May 20, 1826; unm.; lives in Hancock.]
10. ELMINA, [b. July 7, 1828, d. in infancy.]

## McADAMS.

SAMUEL McADAMS and his brother William, cousins of Mrs. Robert McIlvaine, came here in 1795 from Hudson, where they had lived but a short time, as they were from Londonderry, in which town they signed the Association Test in April, 1776, and they also signed a petition there as late as 1778, and may have lived there some years after that. A Samuel McAdams was one of many protesting against the formation of a new parish in Londonderry, Feb. 9, 1740. These brothers were Scotchmen. They located on the "tops of the mountains" in Antrim. Samuel McAdams succeeded Dea. Alexander on what is now the S. A. Holt farm on Holt Hill, while his brother William located on Patten Hill, not far from Samuel Patten's. But little is known concerning these two brothers. They moved together to Tunbridge, Vt., in 1808.

## McALLISTER.

The McAllisters came from Argyleshire in Scotland. The name is very common in many parishes of that country to the present day. In the Scotch colony in the north of Ireland, there were also many McAllisters; and from the last-named locality there were three families that came to New Hampshire, though from names and association in the early days we conclude they were near of kin. These have been traced back through the sojourn in Ireland to Scotland, but it is impossible at present to give ancestral names prior to the emigration from the latter country. A later branch of McAllisters is represented by Judge W. K. McAllister of Chicago, Ill., who was son of William, who was son of Hamilton, who came from Edinburg, Scotland, and bought his farm in Salem, Mass., April 26, 1776. This farm remained in the family more than a hundred years, and from it went out many to New York and the West.

The ancestor of the Londonderry family was Angus (sometimes called Ananias) McAllister, who married Margaret Boyle, and came to this country with eight children in the year 1718, and settled in Lancaster, Mass. The old people say he was near of kin to Richard who settled in Bedford, and John who settled in New Boston. In 1731 Angus moved to Londonderry, and settled the farm now in possession of his descendant, Jonathan McAllister, Esq. He had been a soldier in the wars of Ireland,— had an ear shot off in an engagement of Pennyburn Mill,— and was exempted from taxes on account of his military services. At his death, his body was carried six miles for burial on a bier on the top of men's shoulders, as was always the custom in that day. On the way they met Thomas Wilson, an old companion in arms, who took off his hat and shouted: "Auld Ireland forever! Weel, Angus, they're na taking the lug [ear] aff you head at Pennyburn Mill the day, mon!" William, son of Angus, married Jennette Cameron, and died in 1755, aged fifty-five. His descendants removed to Jaffrey, and thence William, Jr., one of his sons, went to Berlin, Vt., and his descendants are numerous in that State. David, second son of Angus, married Elenor Wilson; died in Londonderry in 1750, aged forty-six, and left children: Alexander, John, Archibald, George, Margaret, and Jennette. Of these six children of David, we have only room to say, that Alexander married Abigail White of Goffstown, and his descendants remain in that town. John married Mrs. Rebekah (Henderson) White of Bedford in 1770, and died in 1780, aged thirty-six. His widow died in 1839, aged ninety-six. She was the girl that went with Hon. John Orr after the cows, in the early history of Bedford. He was about fifteen, and she some younger. They came across a bear, and she picked up stones for Johnny to throw at him. Bruin stood it awhile, and then went for them. He treed Johnny, and Beccie ran; and while bruin looked after the more offensive party, she escaped and got help! Isaac McAllister, son of John and Rebekah, was born Jan. 19, 1776; married Sarah Harriman of Londonderry in 1814, and was father of Jonathan McAllister, who now occupies the original homestead settled by Angus in 1731, and is one of the leading citizens of Londonderry. He married Caroline Choate of Derry, Nov. 11, 1852, and has a son, George I., who graduated at Dartmouth College in the class of 1877. It may be added that John, the other son of Angus, returned to Ireland, and that his five daughters were: Mary Ann, who married David Morrison; ———, who married John Taggart of Coleraine, Mass.; ———, who married Thomas Knox of Pembroke; ———, who married James White of Pembroke; and ———, who married John White of Pembroke. The descendants of Angus are very many, and stand well in the world. It seems probable that Randall McAllister of Peterborough, a Revolutionary soldier terribly wounded at the battle of Bunker Hill, was of the same stock. The latter died in 1819, aged seventy-five. Dr. Thomas S. McAllister of Amesbury, Mass., was son of Benjamin, and grandson of Isaac and Sarah named above.

RICHARD McALLISTER, ancestor of one branch of the Antrim McAllisters, and of that which was earliest here, married Ann Miller in Ireland, about 1735; came over in the winter of 1738–39, and found his way at once to Londonderry, as we conclude from the fact that he was a citizen in full standing there in 1741. But soon after there was quite a migration from Londonderry to the promising settlement of Narragansett No. 5 (now Bedford), and Richard McAllister seems to have been among the number. He settled on a farm now a few rods west of Bedford village, and four miles from the present city of Manchester. He went to Bedford probably in the spring of 1743, and was one of the leading land-holders at the organization of the town in 1750. His name appears among the petitioners of Bedford, then called "Souhegan East," to the governor and assembly for protection against the Indians, June 12, 1744. His wife died March 12, 1776, in the sixty-seventh year of her age. The children of Richard and Ann (Miller) McAllister were nine in number, thus: First, "Archy," who was born in Ireland. He settled in Wiscasset, Me., and lived to great age. George C. McAllister, Esq., of Milltown, New Brunswick, is his great-grandson. The second child of Richard and Ann McAllister was John, who was born on the ocean Jan. 18, 1739. The fact that he is recorded as born in "Chelsie, Mass.," arises from their making the registry of birth at the first place where they stopped on arrival in this country. The tradition in all branches of the family as to the birth on the water is so strong as to leave no reasonable doubt of its truth. John McAllister enlisted as a soldier in the French war, April 17, 1758, and served six months. He also enlisted a second time in the spring of 1760. He was also out for a time in the Revolutionary army. Was a stirring, wide-awake man. He was a blacksmith by trade; came here about 1776, and located on the north side of Meeting-house Hill, building his log cabin on the west side of the road near where a branch turns eastward towards the old McIlvaine place. He was the only blacksmith in town for many years. His shop on the hill stood in the corner of the roads opposite his house. He did not, however, remain long on the hill, but cleared and settled what is now the Pelsey farm. His humble dwelling stood nearly opposite the Sally Sawyer house, and the old shop he worked in stood on the same side of the road a little east of his dwelling. He raised a large family, who all left town in early life. In his old age he followed his children. In the year 1814, and at the age of seventy-five, he moved to Rochester, Vt., and died there in 1828. His wife was Anna Steel, who lived some twenty years longer, and died very aged in the same town. His children, of whom we know but little, were as follows, most of them being born here: —

1. JOHN W., [b. in 1784; m. Vina Jones of Hillsborough, and d. in Rochester, Vt., aged 64. His death was early in the year 1849. His wife, while walking out, dropped dead in the road, in September, 1858, aged 72. His children were: —

    *William*, (b. in Antrim, m. Orlena Brown, and d. in Champaign, Ill., in 1863. His first wife d. Nov. 3, 1839. His house was burned in 1827, and three of his children perished in the flames. His eldest son, Stillman McAllister, when on a deer-hunt with his father-in-law in New York, was shot dead by the latter. His age was 44. They put on deer-skin coats so as to deceive the animals, and separated in the forest. The shooting was at long range with the rifle, and was done on the supposition that a deer was aimed at.)

584 GENEALOGIES.

*Julia Ann,* (b. in Antrim. She m. a shoemaker by name of Kidder, of Hancock, Vt., and is now living in Leicester, Vt.)

*Vianna,* (b. in Antrim; m. Alvah Russ of Stockbridge, Vt.; he d. there; she lives in Manchester, with Dr. Alvah A. Russ, her son, as is thought.)

*Paulina,* (m. Manning Finney, and they live in Stockbridge, Vt.)

*Pamelia,* (m. Horace Brink, and d. in Rochester, Vt.)

*Orrilla,* (m. Ithiel Austin. They live in Pulaski, N. Y.)

*Hiram,* (b. in Hancock, Vt., m. Olive Brown, and d. in Elgin, Ill., July 7, 1870.)

*Sophronia,* (m. Samuel Parsons of Manchester.)

*Adeline,* (d. in Whiting, Vt., unm.)

*Sylvester,* (b. in Hancock, Vt., in 1820; m. Mary Munger of Whiting, Vt.; has lived in Elgin, Ill., since 1861, and is a man of high standing.)

*Milo,* (m. Abbe Goodrich, and lives in Whiting, Vt.)

*Lovica,* (d. in Rochester, Vt., unm.)

*Philena,* (m. George Piper. They live in Manchester.)]

2. DANIEL, [nothing known.]
3. JESSE, [m. Deborah Paige April 20, 1815; can't trace further.]
4. ISAAC, [reported to me as "a Methodist exhorter and an old man;" was last known in Pulaski, N. Y. He m. a Miss Benson of Benson, Vt. Nothing known of his family.]
5. DAVID, [m. Susan Nason of Rochester, Vt., moved to Pennsylvania in 1836, and nothing more is known of him.]
6. WILLIAM, [b. in Antrim, m. Diadamia Washburne, and d. at age of sixty-four in Rochester, Vt. What is on a preceding page about *Stillman McAllister*, killed on a deer-hunt, another authority would put here, making him son of *this* William, which was probably the case.]
7. BETSEY, [nothing known.]
8. ANNA, [m. Dudley Reed, April 1, 1813. A large family were born to them here, but am unable to find one of them.]
9. FANNIE, [b. in Rochester, Vt. She is known to have m. a Mr. Austin of Rochester, Vt., who was killed in moving a building in that place, when a young man. She afterwards m. a Smith, and d. recently in that place.]
10. NANCY, [nothing known.]

The third child of Richard McAllister and Ann Miller was William, who was born in Londonderry, July 14, 1741. He married Jerusha Spofford of Rowley, Mass.; remained in Bedford; was out in the French war; and died Feb. 11, 1787. He had children: Sally (b. Dec. 25, 1766), Ann, William, John, Martha, Polly, James, Benjamin, and Apphia. The descendants are very numerous. John, the fourth child, remained in Bedford; married Jane, daughter of Capt. James and Margaret (Waugh) Aiken, and died July 25, 1853, aged seventy-seven. Their son, William McAllister, Esq., now owns and occupies the homestead. Commodore Belknap, of the U. S. navy, is said to be a great-grandson of William and Jerusha McAllister.

The fourth child of Richard and Ann was Mary, who was born in Bedford, Aug. 10, 1743. Have no further positive knowledge concerning her.

The fifth child was Ann, who was born in Bedford, Nov. 6, 1745, and died in her native town, Oct. 31, 1760.

The sixth child of Richard and Ann (Miller) McAllister was Susannah, born Aug. 20, 1747. A Susannah McAllister married Hugh Moore in Bedford, March 21, 1792. They settled in Amherst and lived to good old age. Circumstances indicate that the first Susannah died in infancy, and that the wife of Moore was a second daughter to whom the same name was given, and who was born about 1756. She died June 8, 1842.

RICHARD McALLISTER, JR., the seventh child of Richard and Ann, was born Oct. 20, 1749. He was last taxed in Bedford, his native town, in 1772. He seems to have been here part of the two following years preparing his clearing on the northward slope of Meeting-House Hill. He moved here in 1775. His house stood first north of the fork of roads, and is known as the Abraham Smith place. He was prominent among the first settlers, and was a member of the first board of selectmen. His wife was Susannah. He moved to Alstead, giving place to Abraham Smith in 1795. Subsequently, for a time, he lived in Springfield, Vt., beyond which we cannot trace them. They had children, several in number, it is believed, when they came to this town. Have made great effort to hunt up this family. Two children were born to them after arrival here, of whom we can give only the date of birth.

1. RICHARD, [b. Dec. 25, 1779.]
2. ANN, [b. March 8, 1782.]

JAMES McALLISTER, the eighth child of Richard and Ann (Miller) McAllister, was born in Bedford, Feb. 29, 1752. He was last taxed in Bedford in 1773; came here the same year, and pitched upon a tract of land now the farm of Isaac M. Tuttle, Esq. After working two summers or more, and building, he moved his family here. The house stood on the old road five or six rods north of the present dwelling, and the cellar still marks the spot. James McAllister married Sally McClary, daughter of David McClary of Bedford, October, 1773. He died Aug. 27, 1823. The widow survived till July 2, 1841. She was a rare and excellent woman, her long life was one of energy and consistent piety, and she was one referred to as being ready for any emergency. It is related, that, when they raised their barn, she saved the men from a serious accident. The population being very sparse for many miles, only a handful of men could be found. These got a band part way up — they couldn't raise it an inch farther — it was so situated that they dare not let it down. Their shouts alarmed Mrs. McAllister, and she ran out with her lady visitors to their help. Instead of shrieking and crying " Murder ! " she snatched up a pole and put her shoulder to the lift. By the addition of this help of the women, with great difficulty the timbers were raised to their place. The children of James and Sally McAllister were : —

1. RICHARD, [b. in Bedford ; m. Peggy Aiken, daughter of Dea. James Aiken. She d. March 1, 1813, at the age of thirty-five, and leaving four children. Sometime in the following year he m. Mrs. Betsey Grant, who soon d. leaving a son Richard. For a third wife he m. Hannah Taylor, March 26, 1818. He built and lived and d. in a house recently taken down, which stood on the opposite side of the river from Miles Tuttle's on the road leading to James Wood's. He d. Nov. 19, 1845, and was buried on the hill. The children were as follows : —

   *Nancy*, (d. unm. in Manchester in 1856, aged 49.)
   *Sophronia*, (m. Jonas Harvey, Jr., of Manchester, and d. in that city Nov. 25, 1873, aged 62.)
   *Nathan W. C.*, (d. unm., in Weare, Aug. 9, 1835, aged 30.)
   *Mary*, (b. in 1813 ; was brought up in Hillsborough by a Mr. Newman ; then all went to Vermont.)
   *Richard, Jr.*, (b. Nov. 19, 1815, m. Susan Ordway April 4, 1841, and lives at Hillsborough Bridge.)
   *James B.*, (b. Nov. 25, 1818 ; m. Fidelia Champlin of Sutton, in 1842, and lives in the south village in that town. Is a trader and postmaster there.)
   *Leonard*, (at seven years of age a fork was thrust into his eye, destroying his mind. He d. unm., in 1867, aged 47.)
   *Benjamin*, (b. Sept. 22, 1821, m. Mary A. Bryant Dec. 23, 1841, and now lives in Stoneham, Mass.)
   *David*, (b. Dec. 19, 1824, m. Harriet White Dec. 14, 1853, and lives in Deering.)
   *Louisa*, (b. Sept. 22, 1826 ; m. Everett Cowdry of Stoneham, Mass.)
   *Stickney*, (b. in 1827 ; d. at age of 4.)]

2. DAVID, [d. when one year old.]
3. THOMAS, [b. in 1775 ; m. in Boston, 1803, to Nancy Smith ; lived here and there in this town about a dozen years after marriage, and all his children save the last two were born in

## GENEALOGIES. 587

Antrim; moved to Windsor about 1820, and d. there April 2, 1840, aged 65. After his death the widow and several children lived some years at the Branch in a small house in Parkhurst's mill-yard. His children were: —

*James*, (b. Sept. 17, 1804, m. Charlotte Moulton of Shirley, Mass., in 1827, and d. in Boston March 29, 1860.)

*William*, (b. Feb. 1, 1806; m. Harriet Moulton of Shirley, Mass.)

*Sylvanus*, (b. Jan. 6, 1808; m. 1st, Susan Long of Harwich, Mass.; 2d, Jane Wetherell of Pocasset, Mass., where he now lives.)

*Sally*, (b. Jan. 26, 1810, m. Daniel Dresser of Windsor Oct. 31, 1833, and now lives in Grafton, Vt.)

*Nancy*, (b. Sept. 26, 1811; unm.; is an invalid in Londonderry, Vt.; is a beneficiary of the society of Cincinnati, on account of her grandfather, Capt. Sylvanus Smith of Shirley, Mass., a captain in the Revolutionary army.)

*Katherine*, (b. Sept. 21, 1813; m. Merrick Woods of Londonderry, Vt., Sept. 19, 1854, and they now live in that town.)

*Thomas*, (b. Oct. 6, 1816; m. Anna Gibbs of Pocasset, Mass., June 27, 1841, and lives in that place.)

*Benjamin*, (b. in Windsor, April 3, 1821, and d. September, 1868. He m. Charlotte Sargent of Lawrence, Mass., in 1850.)

*Mary Ann*, (b. Feb. 3, 1823, m. Barnet S. Waite June 17, 1849, and lives in Londonderry, Vt.)]

4. JAMES, JR., [lost overboard in Chesapeake bay.]
5. WILLIAM. [b. May 3, 1781; m. Rachel Kendall of Hillsborough; lived awhile in this town, and had four children here; moved to Deering, thence to Wilmot, and d. March 23, 1862, in that place. The children were: —

*Orrin*, (d. aged 13, in the year 1831.)

*Joshua H.*, (b. March 27, 1820; m. Margaret Spear of Stoneham, Mass.; went into the war, was disabled, and d. in a Soldiers' Home at Togus, Me., Oct. 18, 1874, aged 54.)

*George S.*, (b. Feb. 5, 1822; m. Martha A. Ferson of Lebanon, June 9, 1850, and lives in Lyndeborough. Is a tanner by trade. He m. 2d, Ellen L. Pollard of Nashua, Jan. 28, 1869.)

*Sarah Olivia*, (b. June 11, 1827; m. John L. Farwell July 10, 1853, and d in Hillsborough, Aug. 11, 1858, childless.)

*Clara S.*, (b. in Deering Feb. 14, 1831 ; m. Eldridge Fisher of North Weare July 1, 1855, and d. there Feb. 6, 1865.)]

6. ANNE, [b. Aug. 12, 1783; m. Benjamin Tuttle, April 17, 1804; lived in Hillsborough, near her father's residence in Antrim, and d. April 20, 1855. She was the mother of Isaac M. Tuttle, Esq., of this town, and Benjamin Tuttle, Esq., of Newport.]

7. BENJAMIN, [b. July 3, 1785; went to Canada in early life, and nothing more is known of him.]

8. RACHEL, [m. Jonas Harvey of Manchester, February, 1827, and d. in that city Nov. 19, 1860; left no children.]

9. SALLY, [b. June 20, 1789, m. Dr. Charles Adams Feb. 13, 1809, and d. in Oakham, Mass., Dec. 5, 1868. She was mother of a noble family, including Hon. Charles Adams, Jr., who has done a great deal to help in the preparation of this book. She is spoken of as a rare and blessed woman, with charity for everybody, and never knowing one that wished her ill.]

10. POLLY, [b. Feb. 21, 1792; m. Sampson Tuttle, Jr., of Hancock, May 30, 1820, and d. in that town Nov. 10, 1857. Her husband d. Feb. 19, 1857, aged 67.]

The ninth child of Richard McAllister and Ann Miller was Benjamin, who was the youngest of the family, and was born in Bedford, May 31, 1754.

JOHN McALLISTER of New Boston was the ancestor of the third family of McAllisters in New Hampshire. He came over from the north of Ireland and settled in that town in 1748. He owned a large tract of land near Joe English Hill; was an energetic, live man, was strongly religious, was on the first board of selectmen in 1763, and died in a good old age. The writer remembers hearing much said about the McAllisters of New Boston by old people now gone. This John had three sons and one daughter, as follows: Archibald, who was born in Ireland, and married Maria McKeen; lived awhile on the homestead, but after many years moved to Francestown, and thence came here about 1790, and died here in good old age. He and his wife were among the early members of the church on the hill, and were most worthy and devout people. The second child of John was Agnus, who settled near the south line of New Boston on a beautiful farm, but afterwards moved to Fryeburg, Me., and died there quite aged. The third son of John of New Boston was Daniel, who settled on what is called the Lamson farm in that town; was selectman of New Boston; moved in mature life to New Brunswick, and died there. Mary, the daughter of John of New Boston, married Daniel Kelso, and was the mother of Ananias Kelso, who recently died in South Village at great age. Thus this Mary was grandmother of Mrs. Henry Hill of this town. She was born during the passage across the ocean; was a praiseworthy woman, and was up to jokes, — like many of her descendants. The writer remembers hearing it said that when Rev. Solomon Moor, the first minister of New Boston, made his first call upon her, about 1769, he asked her if she were born in Ireland. " Na, indade, I was not," said she. — " Were you born in England ? " again he asked. — " Na, sir, indade I was not."—" Then you must have been born in America." — " Na, na, I was not born in America, sir." — " Then where upon 'arth *were* you born ? " — " Indade, sir, I was not born upon the 'arth at all, sir ! " The minister, who was a jolly, witty man, soon saw through the matter, and long laughed over the joke.

ROBERT McALLISTER, son of Archibald and Maria (McKeen) McAllister, and grandson of John of New Boston, came here from that, his native town, about 1793, and lived in a house at the foot of Perry's Hill, near the brick school-house, and raised up a large family. He was a carpenter, school-teacher, and farmer. In 1805 he moved to Newbury, Vt., and died there March 7, 1862, aged eighty-eight. His wife was Sarah Stewart of Amherst. His children are highly respectable. All but the two youngest were born here.

1. WILLIAM, (b. in 1795; was a cabinet-maker; m. Jane Delano of Acworth : settled in Norway, N. Y., and d. there in 1846.]
2. FRANCIS G., [b. in 1797 ; m. Betsey Chamberlain in 1819, and lives in Newbury, Vt.]
3. JONATHAN, [m. Charity Chatman of Haverhill, and d. in Willsborough, N. Y.. in 1862, aged 62. His grandson, Rev. W. C. McAllister, is pastor of the Baptist Church in Morrisonville, N. Y.]
4. DAVID. [m. Betsey Tucker of Newbury, Vt., in 1822, and now lives in that town.]
5. SARAH, [m. Nehemiah L. Clark, and lives in Manchester.]
6. MARY, [m. Archibald Dow, and lived and d. in Hillsborough.]
7. HARRIET, [m. Jeremiah Tewksbury, and lives in Newbury, Vt.]
8. ARCHIBALD, [m. Susan S. Clark, and lives in Newbury, Vt.]

## McCAULEY.

ROBERT McCAULEY came here very early in the history of the town, certainly as early as 1777, and built on the west side of the road between William and Grafton Curtis's, east of the Branch village, and near the river, as it bends to the south. Was the first tailor in town, and followed that business here nearly twenty years. Was out in the Revolutionary army. Was a cripple in old age. His father was Alexander Mc-

Cauley, brother of James, the first settler in Hillsborough, in 1741. Alexander seems to have lived in Hillsborough for a time, and Robert came here undoubtedly from that place. James and Alexander were born in the Province of Ulster in Ireland; were genuine Scotchmen; located awhile in the vicinity of Boston after arrival in this country, and then came to Hillsborough. Alexander was born in 1707. His wife, Mary Pinkerton, born in Ireland in 1712, was cousin of the first John Pinkerton of Londonderry. She died in Merrimack, Jan. 20, 1791. He died in the same place Oct. 11, 1788. They were parents of James McCauley, who married Isabel Jameson, and of Robert McCauley of this town, and of Sarah McCauley who married Thomas Stuart of this town. Robert married Abigail Smith of Dunbarton, July 11, 1774. She was called "Nabby," and our records call her "Neaby." He was credited with a second wife, whose name I have not been able to find, and whose existence I doubt. He is believed to have left Antrim about 1794. The house he lived in has been gone many years. She called herself (Nabby Smith) a niece of Gen. John Stark, and was his adopted daughter. Robert McCauley died in Crown Point, N. Y., 1826, aged ninety-three. He kept his payments of continental money till the day of his death. The children, as far as known, were thus given on the town record, though an older one may have been brought here on removal to this town.

1. JOHN, [b. Feb. 12, 1778; settled in Potsdam, N. Y.; m. Dolly Moody.]
2. ALEXANDER, [b. Aug. 25, 1780, and d. young.]
3. JAMES, [b. May 2, 1783; went to Ashtabula, Ohio; m. Charlotte Hancock.]
4. ISABEL PINKERTON, [b. Jan. 28, 1785; m. 1st, Isaac Everett, who d. in Minerva, N. Y., 1833; 2d, a Mr. Rose. She d. at Mendon, Mich., October, 1846.]
5. THOMAS, [b. March 1, 1787; went to Ashtabula, Ohio, and d. there. He m. Mary Town.]
6. SMITH, [b. April 9, 1789; d. in Crown Point, Ind., in 1862. His wife was Dorcas Dowley of Mount Holly, Vt. His son, Randall S. McCauley, Esq., is now living in Crown Point Center, N. Y., and has furnished items for these pages. A. O. McCauley of Crown Point, Ind., is a son of a 2d wife whose name was Loisa Rossey, of Athol, N. Y.]
7. MOODY, [b. Nov. 15, 1792; moved in 1836 to Ashtabula, Ohio. His wife was Hannah Hill of Walpole, this State. In later life he went to Wisconsin and d. there.]
8. CHARLES, [m. Rachel Barrett and went to the West. His name is not on the Antrim records, and there are some indications that he was the oldest instead of the youngest child.]

GENEALOGIES. 591

CAPT. DAVID McCAULEY, nephew of Robert, and of Mrs. Thomas Stuart, came here from Merrimack, as heir of Capt. Thomas Stuart's property, and received the farm now that of John G. Flint, Esq., at the Branch. He probably came not long subsequent to his uncle's death in 1803. He was a smart young man, and took a prominent place in town. Was much in town business. Had a store at the Branch in the Swain house, under firm name of " McCoy and McCauley." At the time of his death he had a store in the basement of the three-story house at the Branch. He took a wager to reap an acre of rye in Hiram Griffin's field east of the Branch for $2.50, to be done before noon or no pay. Won the pay, being done a half-hour before noon, but it cost him his life. He lived several months after, but was never well. His death occurred April 16, 1818, aged thirty-five. Never married. Was greatly mourned. Soon after his death, his father, Alexander McCauley of Merrimack, moved on to his farm at the Branch; but in three years he moved back to his own town. Capt. David McCauley was captain of the grenadiers. He had two sisters in Antrim, Mrs. Thomas McCoy and Mrs. Sutheric Weston.

## McCLARY.

JOHN McCLARY of Antrim was son of David and Rachel (Strathearn) McClary of Bedford. The parents were married in the north of Ireland, and five of their children were born there. The two youngest were born in Boston. The family came over to Boston in 1751 and resided there about eight years. They removed and settled in Bedford in 1759. David was constable of that town in 1771, — an office then of considerable importance. Various circumstances indicate a relation, perhaps cousinship, between David McClary of Bedford and Lieut. David McClary of Londonderry, who was killed at the battle of Bennington. David McClary of Bedford had children: David, Jr., Thomas, John, Molly, Sally (who married James McAllister of Antrim), Betty, and William. David, Jr., and Thomas were out in the Revolutionary army, probably from Bedford. Some of these lived in Merrimack. Some were officers in the " Training-Band and Alarm-List " of these two towns. Chiefly, however, we have to do with John, who came here. He was born in Ireland about 1735. Whom he married we cannot learn, nor aught of his early history. He came here with his family in 1775, though he had no doubt been here a summer or two previous in making preparation. The opening he made was adjoining that of his brother-in-law, James McAllister, and was the place known now as the " Madison Tuttle farm." There was a John McClary in the battle of Bennington, in the Londonderry company, — perhaps this man. John McClary was a linen-weaver by trade, — a trade then frequently followed by men as well as women, and notably so among the settlers of Londonderry and Bedford. These Scotch weavers were known far and near; and they did very superior work. The death of John McClary occurred in 1796, at a good age. His children were: —

1. JOHN, JR., [date of birth unknown. He m. a McNiel of Hillsborough, and settled in that town; but afterwards

moved to some town in Vermont, after which we lose track of him. He had a son, David, who remained here and made his home with the Woodburys at South Village, and d. there in 1850, unm. This David was, at times in his life, greatly troubled with witches. He thought that on certain nights he was bridled and ridden by a witch. On one occasion, therefore, having borne with said witch as long as he felt disposed to, and having got a trunk ready beside his bed, at the critical moment he grabbed the bridle and threw it into the trunk. Then he put that trunk within another trunk and that within another, till there were seven trunks, and then he hid the keys. This summary and desperate process broke up the riding business of that witch! It was a wise step! The only improvement that could be suggested at this remote day would be to have put in the witch instead of the bridle! That trunk was promised as a legacy to a certain doctor in town, and would have been very valuab'e in those days; but it never appeared!]

2. THOMAS, [frozen to death in 1790. He went to Hillsborough in the evening, and on his return home lost his way and perished. This Thomas was probably in the army, as the town "Voted that Thomas McClearys Reats be freed," April, 1782.]

3. WILLIAM, [possibly oldest child. Don't know whom he married. He was the first settler on the Lawson White place; had a large family; was frozen to death on the turnpike Dec. 25, 1811. Have no means of knowing his age, but can judge somewhat by the fact that he was highway-surveyor in 1783. An old person remembers him as "sixty years old or a little more," though probably this is a high estimate. Nothing can be learned of his children. Since writing the above, I find, that, in noticing his death, the "Cabinet" of Jan. 20, 1812, speaks of him as "aged about 61."]

## McCLURE.

DAVID McCLURE came from Scotland to Boston in 1720. In that city he married Martha Glenn, and had a large family. He moved to Candia, where he died, and David, his eldest son, married a Dinsmore, and settled in Goffstown, but in mature years moved to Deering and died there. *His* son, Col. David McClure of Antrim, grandson of the first David, came here in 1784, married Martha Wilson of Londonderry, and began the farm at the corner next east of the Jonathan Nesmith place.

After some years he exchanged his farm for the one now known as the McClure place, on the old road east of Samuel Dinsmore's, where he died May 25, 1835, aged seventy-seven. His wife died Jan. 18, 1847, aged eighty-six. He was a worthy and respectable citizen; was greatly interested in the militia, held many military offices, and was, a long time, commander of the noted Twenty-sixth Regiment. His family are all gone from town, and most of them from earth, but were as follows: —

1. JAMES, [b. March 23, 1788; m. Mary Wilson of Hillsborough, lived in that town and in Antrim, and d. here Feb. 15, 1855. Their only child, —
*Newell J.*, (b. in Hillsborough in 1819, m. Hannah W. Chase, and lived in New York City, where he d. in 1856.)]
2. POLLY, [b. Jan. 9, 1790, and d. unm. in 1849.]
3. DAVID, [b. March 2, 1791, m. Rebecca Yewer, and lived in Boston, where he d. April 25, 1828, leaving one child: —
*Mary J.*, (who came here to live with her grandfather after her father's death, and was counted as one of the family. She m. John Barker of Henniker, Nov. 21, 1839, and lived some years in that town, and her children were born there. They subsequently moved to Boston, where he d. in 1873, and she still survives.)]
4. ELENOR, [d. in childhood.]
5. ROBERT, [b. April 14, 1794; m. Esther L. Weston in 1828; lived on the old homestead in Antrim, where all his children but Esther were born, then lived in Boston awhile, but eventually moved to Stoddard. where he d. June 6, 1872, aged 78. His wife d. in 1835, aged 27 years. Their children were: —
*Elenor W.*, (m. Joel Starkey Dec. 11, 1851; d. June 17, 1852, aged 25.)
*Robert C.*, (b. in 1830, m. Carrie Cragin of Greenville, and d. in that place in 1858.)
*Grosvenor*, (b. in 1832; m. 1st, Lucy E. Townes of Roxbury; 2d, Maria E. Roberts of Peterborough, and now lives in Stoddard.)
*Esther A.*, (b. in 1834, m. George W. George of Amherst, and now lives in Washington, D. C.)]
6. SAMUEL W., [b. July 1, 1796, and d. unm. at the age of 32.]
7. BOYD H., [b. March 18, 1798; m. Roxy Peltz of Stoddard; lived awhile with his parents in Antrim, and d. in 1869. His children are: —

*Manly*, (b. in Stoddard in 1827, m. Experience Hastings, and lives in Greenfield.)
*John*, (b. in Antrim in 1829, m. Hannah Upton, and lives in Stoddard.)
*Lucinda*, (b. in Antrim in 1831, m. Samuel Dutton, and lives in Pensaukie, Wis.)
*Martha J.*, (b. in Antrim in 1833, became 2d wife of Joel Starkey, and lives in' Staffordshire, Conn.)
*Boyd J.*, (b. in Antrim in 1836, and d. unm. in 1870.)
*Caroline*, (b. in Antrim in 1838, m. Dr. M. V. B. Morse, and lives in Marblehead, Mass.)
*George A.*, (b. in Antrim in 1841, m. Sarah E. Barden, and lives in Stoddard.)
*Emeline S.*, (b. in Antrim in 1843, m. Charles Kimball of Hillsborough, and d. in 1866.)
*Augusta M.*, (b. in Antrim in 1845, m. Henry Bidwell, and lives in Swanzey.)]

8. CYRUS, [b. March 4, 1800, m. Nancy Davison of Framingham, Mass., and d. in 1847.]
9. MARK F., [b. April 4, 1802, m. Mary Vinton, and d. in 1836.]
10. JOHN, [b. Feb. 22, 1804, m. Jane H. Brackett March 26, 1840, and lives in Revere, Mass.]
11. MANLY, [b. in 1806, m. Martha Page, and d. in Mason in 1855, aged 49.]

## McCOY.

THOMAS McCOY lived, in the early years of the town, near Dustin Barrett's, but nothing is known of whence he came or whither he went. The last record of him here was in 1783, when a road was laid out by his house.

ENSIGN JOHN McCOY, son of Dea. Alexander McCoy, whose ancestors went from Argyleshire, Scotland, to Ireland, thence to Londonderry (now Windham), was born in the last-named town in 1750. He served five years in the Revolutionary war; was a privateersman, and helped capture thirteen merchant-ships, — one, he said, for every State in the Union; marched in a company from Londonderry to join the army at Saratoga against Burgoyne; returned from the army in 1780, and the same year married Margaret Boyd, and moved to Hillsborough, but soon came to Antrim and began the Elijah Gould place, which, in subsequent years, was long occupied as a tavern stand. There his children were born; but in his later years he bought, of Adam Nichols, the place on the hill in the east part of the town next south of George Turner's (buildings now gone). He died Jan. 9, 1823, aged seventy-two. His wife, Margaret, died April 4, 1817, aged sixty-three; married, second, Mrs. Mary (Hutchins) Hartwell of Hillsborough, and after his death she married Obadiah Hadley of Bradford, and died in Peterborough in 1848, aged eighty-one. The children were: —

1. THOMAS, [b. March 10, 1782, m. Betsey McCalley of Merrimack, and lived on the paternal estate. He was a man of executive ability, and was kept by his townsmen in positions of trust for many years, having been chosen selectman eighteen times. He was one of the committee to build the Center Church. He d. May 22, 1851. His wife d. Oct. 24, 1871, aged 87. Children : —

*David*, (b. in 1811, and d. in infancy.)

*Mary*, (b. in 1813, m. David W. Bell of Bennington, Jan. 28, 1836, and is now living a widow in Francestown.)

*Eliza A.*, (b. in 1816, m. Solomon H. Griffin May 8, 1838, and d. in 1853.)

*Caroline*, (b. in 1818, m. James M. Appleton in 1839, and now lives in Deering.)

*James Madison*, (d. Dec. 31, 1826, at the age of six.)

*Milton*, (b. in 1824, m. Elisabeth Appleton, and lives in Deering.)]

2. JOHN, [b. June 14, 1784 ; m. Hannah Taylor April 13, 1813; settled on the Samuel Weeks place, where the large brick house by the East cemetery now stands, and which he built in 1822. After some years he sold and moved to Bennington, where he d. Dec. 7, 1861, at the age of 77. His children were : —

*Louisa*, (d. in childhood.)

*Mary*, (b. July 18, 1815 ; m. David Tapley, a merchant in Lowell.)

*Prof. James M.*, (b. June 15, 1817 ; m. 1st, Alma L. Mooar of Francestown ; 2d, Annie M. Dennis of Lowell. Has been for thirty years a teacher in that city, having begun there in 1842. He entered Amherst College in 1841, but was soon compelled by ill health to leave. In 1859 he established a commercial college in Lowell, which was very successful, and of which he remains the leading officer. Has one child, Louise J. McCoy, and she is the only great-grandchild of the early settler and soldier, John, that bears the name of McCoy ; she is a student of Wellesley College, class of 1879.)

*Hannah W.*, (b. March 15, 1819; m. George Young of Dubuque, Io.)

*John, Jr.*, (b. Jan. 21, 1822; was formerly a teacher in Georgia, but went to California in 1849, where he d. the next year, May 30, aged 28.)

*Louisa J.*, (d. Sept. 29, 1845, aged 20.)]

3. ALEXANDER, [b. July 21, 1786; m. Katherine Gibson; built the Widow Newman's house and there kept store, but afterwards engaged in trade at Hillsborough Upper Village. He lived to old age, and d. without children.]

4. ROBERT, [was a trader in company with his brother Alexander, at Hillsborough, and, like him, d. there in old age, childless, June 19, 1866.]

## McDOLE.

WILLIAM McDOLE came here from Bedford in the year 1779, and built his cabin on the William S. Foster place. He bought the land for twenty-five cents per acre. Here he lived till 1808, when he moved to Landgrove, Vt. Two sons, David and William, were born here, and had been at school here several winters before they moved away.

Alexander McDole, supposed to be a brother of William, Sen., and living in the same house with him, bought one of the first pews in the old meeting-house. This is all now known of this respectable family that lived here about thirty years. The town voted to have a road to "William McDoals," March 14, 1780.

## McFARLAND.

DANIEL McFARLAND was born in Goffstown. He came here in 1774, and settled where N. W. C. Jameson now lives. He married Martha Steele, and died in 1829, at the great age of ninety-six. His wife died April 25, 1831, aged seventy-nine. Mr. McFarland was a man of many oddities and air-castles. He imagined himself to be heir of great honor and wealth in Scotland, and planned his mansion accordingly; but he never finished it, and never got the title, and never got the money. Part of the enormous building was taken down after his death, and out of the remaining part Mr. Jameson made the beautiful residence burned in 1862. But, though he never received either the title or the treasure he dreamed of, he was generous as a prince; his great house was never fastened against anybody by night or day, and the class called "tramps," then less numerous, always found with him a fire to warm by, and a sheltering roof. In his latter days he was a great reader, and the Bible came to be the only book he read. He was a sturdy Presbyterian, and his name is signed to a petition from Goffstown in 1771 to Gov. Wentworth, to have a Presbyterian parish formed in that town. Mr. McFarland was a man of genuine Scotch wit and cunning, always turning jokes on the young folks. Some of the boys remember his giving them apples when he would always have an old potato or a stone in his hand to slip into the boy's pocket. On one occasion he went to Dea. Baldwin's on an errand, at an hour a little later than the usual mealtime, and as they were just sitting down to breakfast they asked him to sit down with them. But he replied, "Na, na, I have my breakfast in the marnin'!" But little is known of Mr. McFarland's family. He had four sons and one daughter, but all have been long since dead, or gone from town. All known of them is as follows : —

1. JAMES, [the eldest son, m. Rena Stewart, had a son and a daughter here, and then moved to New York. The daughter, Betsey, remained here, m. Oliver Dickey, and then moved to New York. The son, Henry, was the only descendant of Daniel bearing the name of McFarland.]
2. DANIEL, [the second son, m. Katy Miller of Peterborough, sister of Gen. Miller, but she soon d. (April 4, 1810), aged 26 ; and he went West and never returned. The "Cabinet" of April, 1810, paid her the highest possible praise].
3. JOHN, [the third son, became a lawyer, being admitted to the bar February, 1815. He practiced at Hillsborough Upper Village, and d. there unm. in 1819, aged 31.]
4. THOMAS, [d. in Antrim about 1824, aged 30.]
5. PEGGY, [m. Isaac Reess, and went to Maine.]

## McGEE.

SOLOMON McGEE came here from Lempster about 1836, and lived some years with Clark Hopkins in the McFarland house. Subsequently, he bought the Calvin Bullard house (Gibson's) in South Village, which he occupied up to the time of his death. His wife was a Wellman. He had three children: Ann, ———, and Sydney. The widow and children went to New York. The following notice in the "Amherst Cabinet" about April 6, 1845, is spoken of by an aged person as "every word true " : —

"At the Washington House, Nashua, March 27, 1845, after a short but severe illness, Mr. Solomon McGee of Antrim, aged thirty-seven. Mr. McGee has for several years driven the stage between Antrim and Nashua, in which vocation he shared the utmost confidence of the community. A true and ardent advocate of the cause of temperance, and an honest man, he lived and died universally beloved and respected. Some two years since, he united with the church in Bennington, and lived and died rejoicing in the Lord."

## McILVAINE.

An old record of the McIlvaine family states that Robert McIlvaine and his wife, who were Scotch emigrants to the north of Ireland, and stanch Protestants, were murdered in their bed by the Catholics in Ireland. Their son, Daniel McIlvaine, then a small babe, escaped in bed by avoiding notice of the murderers, was brought up by friends, and in early manhood came over to America, and settled in Windham about 1740, where he married Mary Smith and had children, three of whom — John, William, and Robert — came to Antrim. Mrs. Mary (Smith) McIlvaine died in Antrim at advanced age, Feb. 16, 1803.

The name of this family is variously written, — MacIl'Vaine, McAlvin, McIlvin, and McIlvaine. The name was undoubtedly MacIlvaine, written in full, with double accent, — on first syllable and last. It would seem that good taste, and respect for the Scotch fathers, would combine to retain the form here placed at the head of the family. The form "McIlvin" is of recent date, unpronounced, and never seen outside of this town.

JOHN McILVAINE, son of Daniel and Mary (Smith) McIlvaine of Windham, came here first, and settled the Boyd Hopkins place (house now gone; stood about ten rods west of school-house No. 6) in 1782. He married Mary A. Quigley of Francestown, and moved back to that town in 1794. He had no children, and died in good old age. He was selectman in this town in 1793.

WILLIAM McILVAINE, brother of John, came here the same year (1782), and settled the John Barker place. He married Jane Quigley of Francestown (sister of Mary A. who married John), buried all their children here, and went back to Francestown in 1790, where they had other children, but all are now dead.

ROBERT McILVAINE, another brother. was born Sept. 19, 1748. He married Jane McAdams Dec. 30, 1773; came here in 1785, and built a house on the old road leading at that time from the present Daniel McIlvaine's to the top of Meeting-house Hill, on the same farm, and some fifty rods west of the present house, where he died March 27, 1833, one month later than his wife, who died Feb. 17, 1833, aged eighty-two. In those days, when there were almost no books, Robert McIlvaine got up a written arithmetic for his own family, and taught them. This book, in manuscript, is still in existence, and exhibits much mathematical knowledge and skill. The children were: —

1. ELIZABETH, [b. in Windham Dec. 29, 1774; d. Dec. 26, 1776.]
2. MARY, [b. in Windham Dec. 8, 1776, m. David Gregg in December, 1799, and d. April 11, 1870. She was a woman of great piety and kindness.]
3. MARGARET, [b. in Windham Aug. 26, 1779, m. Robert Gregg, and moved to New York, where she d. June 14, 1854.]
4. JANE, [b. in Windham, Aug. 17, 1781; d. Nov. 4, 1796.]
5. SARAH, [b. in Windham Sept. 26, 1783, m. Henry Todd in first part of 1802, and d. Nov. 2 of the same year, on the day of the birth of her only child.]

GENEALOGIES. 599

6. LIEUT. DANIEL, [b. in Windham, Oct. 24, 1785; m. Hannah Barker Jan. 28, 1808, and lived on the old homestead, being the only son of a large family who lived to adult age. His descendants are numerous, and nearly all of them have settled in Antrim. He d. Feb. 25, 1833, in the prime of life, and highly respected. His widow d. June 15, 1867, aged 80. Their children are as follows: —

*Sarah*, (b. Oct. 30, 1808; m. Henry B. Swett, Oct. 23, 1834.)

*Daniel, Jr.*, (b. April 6, 1810; m. Mary A. Marshall of Bradford, March, 1854, and they live on the old homestead, having children: Myra E., who was b. Feb. 2, 1855; Ida L., who was b. March 18, 1857, and d. April 8, 1877, — a young lady attractive in person, devoted in religion, and resigned to her early death; Mary Abbie, who was b. March 23, 1859; and Abi L., who was b. May 2, 1863.)

*Moody B.*, (b. July 12, 1812; m. Mary W. Stickney, daughter of Dr. Stickney of Antrim, Oct. 29, 1835. He carried on the wheelwright business at the Steele mills, built the Esty house in 1835 where he lived some years, and then moved to the old Stickney place at Branch Village. He was engaged in trade several years, and built the George P. Little stand for that purpose in 1852. He d. Dec. 16, 1877, after a long and most distressing sickness, which he bore with great patience. Was chief-marshal Centennial Day; a good presiding officer; and was one of the pleasantest and kindest of men. His children are: Augusta S., who was b. July 3, 1837, m. Andrew J. Bennett of New Boston July 3, 1859, and lives in that town; Louisa H., who was b. Oct. 23, 1840, m. Abner B. Crombie Nov. 29, 1860, and they live on the Stickney place at the Branch; Almeda M., who was b. Aug. 4, 1844, and m. George P. Little of Antrim March 30, 1870; and Myra F., who d. Sept. 24, 1851, aged 2 years.)

*Jane*, (b. June 23, 1814, m. Charles C. Champney Dec. 26, 1833, and d. Aug. 18, 1879.)

*Harriet*, (b. Aug. 19, 1816, m. Sewall Preston of Windsor, May 15, 1854, and now lives, a widow, at North Branch.)

*Benjamin Franklin*, (b. May 4, 1818; m. 1st, Sabrina S. Burns, March 20, 1845, and lives on the Burns place, where she d. Jan. 19, 1860, aged 42, leaving children thus: Esther M., who was b. Jan. 11, 1846, m. Charles E. McColley of Hillsborough Dec. 25, 1865, and lives in that town; Harriet

600 GENEALOGIES.

P., who was b. Nov. 25, 1848, m. Chester A. Conn July 4, 1867, and lives in this town ; George F., who was b. Aug. 8, 1851, m. Sarah A. Boutelle Dec. 3, 1875, and lives on the Abner Cram place in this town; and Henry, b. April 14, 1858, who d. in childhood. Mr. McIlvaine m. 2d, Martha J. Emery, Sept. 12. 1860, and their children are: Nellie S., b. Sept. 27, 1862 ; Madison P., b. Jan. 24, 1865 ; and Lillie B., b. Nov. 30, 1867.)

*John*, (b. April 28, 1820 ; m. 1st, Jane Little, daughter of Dea. William Little, April 23, 1846, who d. April 28, 1849, aged 27, leaving one son, John S., who was b. in Antrim April 18, 1849, m. Abbie H. Cram of Stoddard, and lives in Washington. In 1850, Mr. McIlvaine m. 2d, Elmina Sweet of Washington, and has since resided in that town.)

*Hannah*, (b. Nov. 18, 1822, m. John Twiss of Amherst, Sept. 5, 1846, and d. Sept. 4, 1856.)

*Robert*, (b. June 25, 1824, m. Rosina Richardson of Stoddard, and now lives in Stedman, N. Y.)

*Peter*, (b. June 2, 1826 ; d. Oct. 15, 1828.)

*Hiram B.*, (b. April 28, 1828 ; m. Angeline Conn, Nov. 10, 1853; lived where Mary Clark now lives, but soon moved to Windsor. He returned in 1862, and the following year built where he now lives, just east of the Branch. He is a wheelwright by trade, and has carried on business for several years in the old Steele shop. They have two children: Willie B., b. June 16, 1867 ; and Herbert C., b. Oct. 11, 1870.)

*Emeline D.*, (b. June 30, 1832 ; m. 1st, Willard Preston of Windsor, Oct. 4, 1853, who d. in 1863. She m. 2d, William H. Hopkins of Francestown, March 6, 1873, and lives in that town.)]

7. ELIZABETH, [b. in Antrim Jan. 14, 1788; became the 2d wife of Asa Robinson, May 19, 1832, and is now living at advanced age in Clinton.]

8. SAMUEL, [b. in Antrim May 23, 1790 ; d. June 27, 1792.]

9. HANNAH, [b. in Antrim Oct. 7, 1792 ; m. Alexander Carr of Antrim, and moved to Mont Vernon about 1845. She d. at the age of 86. An amiable and noble woman.]

10. JANE, [b. Oct. 27, 1796 ; m. Abijah Barker Aug. 8, 1817, and has always lived in Antrim. She was one of those who spun flax on Centennial Day, after the example of the olden time.]

## McKEEN.

JAMES McKEEN of Londonderry, Ireland, was a stout Protestant, and was one of the bravest defenders of that city during the Papal siege. He had three sons: James, who came to this country in 1718, and who was called "Justice McKeen," because he held the first commission of magistrate in the new settlement of Londonderry in this country; John, who was intending to come over, but died a few days prior to the time of departure, but whose widow and children came over, and from whom are descended the McKeens of Deering, of Amherst, David McKeen of Antrim, the McKeens of Nashua, and Robert McKeen of Cherry Valley, N. Y., which last was grandfather of Dea. Robert Steel, Mrs. Edmond Sawyer, and others of this town; and William, who was born in 1704, was left behind in 1718, but came over in 1727 and settled in Pennsylvania, and was grandfather of Thomas McKeen, who was a signer of the Declaration of Independence, and many years governor of that State.

James McKeen, or "Justice McKeen," the eldest of these brothers, had two wives. His first wife was Janet Cochran, who was buried in the old country. By her he had two daughters: Janet, who married her cousin, John Cochran of Windham, and was mother of all the Antrim Cochrans; and Elisabeth, who, before coming over, married James Nesmith, and was mother of the Nesmiths of Antrim. His second wife was Annis Cargil, sister of Marion Cargil, wife of Rev. James McGregor. Justice McKeen died Nov. 9, 1756, aged eighty-nine. The second wife died Aug. 8, 1782, aged ninety-three. They had children: John, Mary, David, James, Janet, Martha, Margaret, Annis, and Samuel. Of these children, we will only speak here of Martha, who married John Dinsmore, and was mother of the Dinsmores of Antrim; of Mary, who married Robert Boyd, afterwards moved to New Boston, — was the good old "Molly Boyd," — had no children, but brought up her half-sister's grandchild, John Cochrane (see page 428); and of John, afterwards known as "Dea. John," who was elder in the Presbyterian Church, married his cousin, Mary McKeen, and was father of a numerous and honorable family, among them Robert of this town, Judge Levi McKeen of New York, and Joseph McKeen, the first president of Bowdoin College.

ROBERT McKEEN, son of Dea. John and Mary (McKeen) McKeen, came here in 1778 and began the McClure place, east of Samuel Dinsmore's. He was cousin of Dea. Isaac Cochran and of Samuel Dinsmore, was near relative of the Nesmiths, and these kindred seem to have been much bound up with each other, and almost one in heart in the hardships of their settlement here. He married Mary McPherson of Raymond. After a few years he exchanged farms with Col. David McClure, who had begun the farm east of Jonathan Nesmith, now known as the Raymond or Taylor farm. Here Mr. McKeen lived till 1800, when he moved to Corinth, Vt. He took with him only two children, having buried three upon the hill. In Corinth he purchased a farm adjoining that of his cousin, David McKeen, their wives being sisters. Thus situated, they lived very happily two or three years. In February, 1804, the daughter, Mary, died suddenly of fever. She was born in Antrim April 10, 1787.

Then in the following September her mother died with the same disease, aged fifty-one; her sister, Mrs. David McKeen, having died Sept. 17, — just a week previous! After this the two broken families lived together till 1810, when the small-pox was brought upon them by certain persons from Canada. Robert McKeen, on taking the disease, was hurried off to a remote camp in the woods; and with only one attendant, — poorly but most kindly cared for, — after great suffering he died, in frightful disfigurement, Oct. 27, 1810, aged sixty-one. The remaining child, Joseph, then in his twenty-third year, having been born in Antrim Aug. 29, 1788, was ambitious of learning, and was eager at his books every spare minute; and having obtained a good academic education at Haverhill (N. H.) Academy, and under the help of President McKeen at Bowdoin, he went to New York City and served an apprenticeship in a printing-office. But preferring to teach, and an opportunity occurring, he commenced that occupation, rose rapidly, and was soon appointed one of the superintendents of the city schools, — which honorable and important trust he held till death. He died April 12, 1856. On the day of his funeral all the public schools in the city were closed, as a mark of respect, — an honor conferred on very few! He was a most efficient and distinguished educator. The degree of LL. D. was conferred upon him. He was among the foremost of the sons of Antrim. Starting in orphanage, and with small means, and compelled to work his way slowly and enter upon his profession late in life, his marked success ought to stimulate the sons of his native town to follow his persevering and praiseworthy example! He married Jane McLeod of Claverack, N. Y., and had three sons, all of whom died before their father. The mother, left alone, and discouraged, soon followed, dying May 11, 1860; and now all sleep together in Greenwood cemetery!

DAVID McKEEN — son of Dea. William McKeen, who married Ann Graham and was one of the first settlers of Deering, grandson of Samuel and Agnes McKeen of Amherst, and great-grandson of John McKeen, who was getting ready to come over with his brother in the emigration of 1718, but suddenly died in the prime of life — was born in Deering in 1784. In 1805 he went to Boston on foot, with a pack on his back, to find work; married Nancy Ferson of Deering in 1810, and went to Salem, Mass., to live, but moved back to Deering in 1815, and came here in 1840, buying the Aiken or Dea. Burnham place, where he died in 1862. He was a useful citizen and several times selectman. His children were: —

1. DRUSILLA, [b. in 1811, m. Fisher Silsby in 1835, and lives in Troy.]
2. EVELINE L., [b. in 1812, m. Benjamin L. Willoughby, and d. in Lowell, Mass., in 1864.]
3. CHARLES, [b. in 1816; m. Maria Bradford of Francestown in 1841, and was a trader in that town until 1845, when he came here and opened a store (now Putney's). He was a

smart and agreeable man, was town clerk and representative, and d. in 1862 in the prime of life. The only living children are : —

*Charles A.*, (b. here in 1844, m. Franc Ambler, and is now living in Chester, Minn.)

*William*, (b. in 1854 ; is now a teacher in California.)]

4. MARY ANN, [b. in 1819, and d. in 1833.]
5. WILLIAM H., [b. in 1822, and d. in 1836.]
6. NANCY JANE, [b. in 1828, m. Bennett S. Buckminster Dec. 22, 1857, and d. in 1866, without children.]

## McMASTER.

THOMAS McMASTER, son of John and Betsey (Brown) McMaster of Windham, married Lydia, daughter of Dea. David Badger of Lyndeborough. Mr. McMaster cleared the ground and built his log house on the Hiram Whittemore place, just over the line in Hancock, which he left in 1799. He died in Antrim in 1841, aged eighty. His wife died in 1853, aged eighty-seven. Their children were: —

1. LYDIA, [b. in 1787; m. Archiless Tay of Woburn, Mass.]
2. DAVID, [drowned in 1790 by falling into a well on the Whittemore place, aged one year and six months.]
3. HANNAH W., [b. in 1789; d. unm. in Lowell, Mass., Sept. 23, 1846.]
4. MARGARET D., [b. Jan. 29, 1793, m. Abraham McNeil of New Boston, Nov. 11, 1813, and d. in Lowell, Mass., Nov. 7, 1849.]
5. THOMAS, [b. in Hancock, Jan. 22, 1795 ; m. Lydia C. Thompson of Stoddard, Dec. 29, 1829. He lived some years at the South Village, and in 1830 built the house long occupied by Mark Woodbury (now N. C. Jameson's) ; was in trade a short time in Woodbury's store ; was much in town office ; moved to Hancock in 1838, and d. in Southborough, Mass., Dec. 21, 1875, aged nearly 81. His wife is still living in Southborough, Mass. Their children were : —

*DeWitt C.*, (b. Oct. 20, 1830; is a painter in Southborough, Mass., living, unm., with his aged mother.)

*Miranda A.*, (b. May 29, 1832, and d. Oct. 23, 1832.)

*Thomas Allen*, (b. Aug. 27, 1833 ; m. Sarah A. Hadley of Lowell, Mass., June 12, 1872, and is now engaged in the boot and shoe business in that city.)

*Lucas Irving*, (b. Sept. 8, 1835, m. Nancy P. Davis of Waterville, Me., June 4, 1860, and now resides in Apopka, Fla.)

*Lydia A.*, (b. in Hancock May 1, 1838; m. Milo A. Crouch of Southborough, Mass., Jan. 25, 1865, where they now live.)
*Angeline E.*, (b. in Hancock Sept. 12, 1840; d. Feb. 16, 1841.)
*Louisa*, (b. in Hancock Jan. 21, 1842; m. Charles B. Sawin of Southborough, Mass., where she d. March 11, 1869.)
*Henry Austin*, (b. in Hancock June 24, 1844; m. Mary C. Rymes of Boston, May 1, 1869, and is now engaged in market business in Boston.)
*Anna M.*, (b. in Dublin Oct. 7, 1847; d. in Southborough, Mass., June 3, 1867.)]

6. SETH H., [b. July 29, 1797; was a machinist; d. unm. in Pelham.]
7. RACHEL B., [b. Sept. 6, 1800; m. Dea. Imla Wright of Antrim, July 7, 1823.]
8. BETSEY, [b. in 1802, and d. aged 3 months.]
9. ANN M., [b. July 31, 1803; m. Asa McClure of Amherst.]
10. SARAH B., [b. March 29, 1806; m. Peter Andrews of Shirley, Mass., April 20, 1831.]
11. STEPHEN, [b. in 1808, and d. in infancy.]
12. BETSEY A., [b. Sept. 16, 1810; m. William Buswell May 20, 1834, and lived on the Gregg place near the pond. He d. in 1853, leaving three children, and Mrs. Buswell afterwards m. Hugh Rogers, and still lives on the same place.]

SAMUEL McMASTER, younger brother of Thomas, Sen., came here from Windham as early as 1790. He was here only a few years, and lived a part of the time in the old house between Frank Robinson's and Samuel A. Holt's, known as the Joel Reed house. He married Jennie Smith of New Boston. She was a daughter of Dea. John Smith by his second wife, Ann Brown of Francestown, and was sister of Dea. Thomas Smith, long prominent in that town. She was probably born in 1763, as she was older than Dea. Thomas, and he was born May 7, 1765. Samuel McMaster lived here until about 1795, when he moved West, and soon died with consumption. He is supposed to have left six children, but nothing is known of them. Two who were born in Antrim were as follows:—

1. ANNE SMITH, [b. March 5, 1791.]
2. JOHN SMITH, [b. Oct. 4, 1792.]

## McNIEL.

There was a tradition among the early settlers, that the first McNiel came to America in flight from the revenge of injured nobility, like some others whose blood flows in our sons. Having visited a friend who gave him a stick well shaped to make a scythe-snath, he was met by the lord of that district, who charged him with stealing it from his forest. On his denial, the lord flew into a passion, called him a liar, and lashed him with his whip; whereupon McNiel struck him probably a fatal blow with the stick, and then fled to this country. Among his descendants were two brothers, Abraham and John McNiel, who came to this town. They were sons of Dea. William (who was born March 28, 1746) and Rachel (Patterson) McNiel of New Boston, and grandsons of Abraham and Jane McNiel of Ballymoony, county of Antrim, Ireland. Abraham was born in New Boston July 24, 1782, and came here about 1800. Feb. 3, 1807, he married his cousin, Mary Patterson of Londonderry, sister of Hon. George W. Patterson of Westfield, N. Y. He was here considerably in his childhood; has grown to opulence and honor, and has been in Congress many years, being now (1877) the oldest member of that body. He was one of the donors of the Center vestry. Mr. Patterson has great regard for the hills of New Hampshire, and often speaks of the spot where his sister was buried in the lofty cemetery of Antrim. She was noted for her great beauty, in that day. Mr. McNiel lived nearly half a mile north of the first meeting-house, and boarded the ministers a long time, among them Mr. Whiton. After a time the family moved to the South Village, where they remained awhile. He was deputy-sheriff in 1833, and moved to Lowell in 1840, where he died June 20, 1846. Mrs. Mary McNiel died of spotted fever, Feb. 22, 1812, greatly loved and lamented. She was taken with pain in the little finger and lived but a few hours. It is said, that, under the fearful and mistaken applications of heat, she was nearly roasted to death. She was every way a noble woman, and her early death was one of the saddest of that awful winter. In 1813, Mr. McNiel married Margaret McMaster. The children of Abraham McNiel were as follows, the three eldest being the children of his first wife : —

1. ELISABETH P., [b. Dec. 26, 1807 ; m. Samuel Ladd of Warsaw, N. Y.; now lives in Utica, Mich., having a family of ten children.]
2. SALLY JANE, [b. April 9, 1809, and d. unm. in Lowell in 1846.]
3. RACHEL, [b. March 31, 1811, m. Hon. Ira H. Butterfield of Greigsville, N. Y., in 1839, and d. at Utica, Mich., Oct. 26, 1846.]
4. MARY P., [b. July 15, 1814, and lives unm. in La Pier, Mich.]
5. ALICE WOODBURY, [b. Oct. 2, 1816; became the 2d wife of Hon. Ira H. Butterfield of La Pier, Mich., in 1847.]
6. LYDIA TAY, [b. June 29, 1818, and d. in 1836.]
7. GRISSY MARGARET, [b. Nov. 9, 1820 ; has never married, and has her home with Hon. G. W. Patterson in Westfield, N. Y.]

8. SABRINA W., [b. July 1, 1823; lives in La Pier, Mich., unm.]
9. WILLIAM T., [b. Oct. 8, 1825, m. Jane Stiles Feb. 10, 1848, and lives in Worcester, Mass.]
10. JOHN A., [b. July 19, 1828, m. Mary Tozer of New York City, and lives in Sacramento, Cal.; is a leading man in that city, widely known, trusted, and wealthy. Himself and wife are prominent musicians there.]

JOHN McNIEL, a younger brother of Abraham, was born Nov. 14, 1788, and came here some years later. Dec. 26, 1815, he married Susan Warner (a girl brought up by her mother's sister, Mrs. John (Wilson) Smith, on the Thomas Flint place), and lived on the farm now occupied by Hiram Eaton, where he built the south house as a factory for making winnowing-mills; but after his death it was no longer used for that purpose, and was finished up into a dwelling-house by Bartlett Wallace, for his aged father. Mr. McNiel was found dead in the field, on that place, July, 1825, at the early age of thirty-seven. His wife died two years before him at the age of twenty-eight. They left two children: —

1. JOHN S., [b. Sept. 27, 1818, m. Lucretia Robb of Stoddard in 1841, and d. in Bedford Jan. 25, 1877. His two daughters were Martha Jane, who m. John A. Robb of Waterman, Wis., and Frances Maria, who m. Edmund Kendall of Bedford.]
2. MARTHA J., [b. Sept. 28, 1823; m. David Crowell of Goffstown; lived awhile on the Flint place, and moved to Manchester, where she d. Jan. 11, 1857. He d. in Newton in 1872.]

## MILLER.

JACOB MILLER, brother of Gen. Miller, son of James and Catherine (Gregg) Miller of Peterborough, and grandson of Samuel Miller of Londonderry, was born about 1783. About 1808 he came here and went into trade under the firm name of "Miller and Caldwell," in the Whittemore store at South Village (now Gibson house). This firm also largely manufactured potash in Aiken's upper mill. Near the close of 1812, he sold out and went into business in Peterborough, but came back to Antrim, and married Jane Hopkins, Dec. 16, 1813. After several years he went to Arkansas, where he died in 1822, leaving no children.

ALFRED ARTHUR MILLER, son of Alfred and Mary (Munroe) Miller, was born in Hillsborough Oct. 15, 1842; married Esther A. Dow, Nov. 2, 1868; has since lived on the James Hopkins farm; was one of the selectmen in 1875 and 1876. His grandparents, William Miller and Lettice Curtis, were married in Antrim, April 25, 1815. Farran Miller, father of this William, was a Revolutionary soldier and associate of Gov.

Pierce. Mr. Miller has now, in good preservation, the powder-horn carried through many battles by his great-grandfather. Has but one child : —

1. ETTA MAY, [b. March 18, 1872.]

## MILTIMORE.

COL. DANIEL MILTIMORE, son of James and Elisabeth (Aiken) Miltimore of Londonderry, was born in that place in 1752. His father was the first one of the name in this section, being a Scotchman from the north of Ireland. His mother was a sister of Dea. James Aiken. He came here from Londonderry in 1777; married Agnes Hunter in 1778, and began the Whitely place. He was among the ablest of the early settlers, was much in town office, and moved back to Londonderry near the close of the century, where he was known as "Col. Miltimore." He was a Revolutionary soldier, being a lieutenant in the battle of Bennington, and was efficient in the war. His name occurs in the military history of Antrim. His children, besides four that died in infancy and were buried on the hill. were : —

1. JAMES, [b. Oct. 13, 1780, and d. at the age of 6.]
2. JOHN HUNTER, [b. Jan. 8, 1783, and d. unm. in Londonderry.]
3. ELISABETH, [b. July 30, 1789, m. Leonard Hale of Hollis, and is now living in Derry.]

REV. JAMES MILTIMORE, brother of Daniel, was born in Londonderry in 1755, graduated at Dartmouth College in 1774, and was licensed by the Londonderry Presbytery in 1776. He preached here a part of five years; was called in 1780 and declined; declined three other calls, but settled in Stratford in 1786, where he married Dolly Wiggin the same year. He was dismissed in the fall of 1807, and the next spring was settled in Newburyport, Mass. In 1831 he gave up that charge, and died in 1836, aged eighty-one. He was an able and good man, much loved here and always tenderly remembered.

## MOORE.

JAMES MOORE (formerly spelled Moor), a Scotchman, came originally from Ireland, probably to Londonderry, as one of the proprietors, and from there to Antrim with his nephew, Samuel, who was also his son-in-law, about 1776, and settled on the Wallace place at the Branch. They had the first grist-mill in town at North Branch. James Moore was known as "Miller Moore." He died here, about 1788, well advanced in years. The most diligent search has failed to ascertain anything with regard to his family, save that his daughter Hannah married his nephew, Samuel Moore, mentioned below.

SAMUEL MOORE, nephew of James, married Hannah Moore, daughter of James, mentioned above, and lived at the Branch. It is supposed

608 GENEALOGIES.

that he lived some years in Londonderry before coming here. Dr. Whiton says he had twelve children, and moved to Walpole with his family in 1790. A sister Betty remained here and was for some years a town charge. The births of seven of his children are on the town record as follows : —

1. MARTHA, [b. April 27, 1774.]
2. DANIEL, [b. Feb. 1, 1778. He seems to have m. and lived in town, as his name occurs on the records after his father moved away.]
3. SAMUEL, [b. May 20, 1780.]
4. CALDWELL, [b. Oct. 15, 1782.]
5. SARAH, [b. Dec. 3, 1784.]
6. SARAH, [b. Dec. 3, 1785.]
7. REBECCA, [b. Dec. 5, 1787.]

JOHN MOORE was shot dead in his yard in the infamous and devilish massacre of Glencoe, Scotland, Feb. 12, 1692. He had two little daughters, which a servant took care of and safely removed to Ireland. Mrs. Moore, after covering up her dead husband, fled to a malt-kiln for safety, and that same night was delivered there of a son. This child was the John Moore who came over to Londonderry in 1718 or 1719. One of the daughters was Beatrix Moore, who married Col. Andrew Todd. This John Moore married Janet Cochran, and had the following children: Robert, Samuel, William, John, Agnes, Mary, and Ann. Samuel and William settled in Peterborough, and their descendants have remained permanently in that town.

JOHN MOORE of Antrim, son of John and Janet (Cochran) Moore, and grandson of John, the victim of Glencoe, came here about 1785 and began the place now Hiram Eaton's. He married Abigail, daughter of Hon. John Duncan; was fatally wounded by the limb of a tree falling on his head in the woods, but lived over six days in an unconscious state, and died Jan. 3, 1809. aged forty-nine. Left no children.

JOSEPH MOORE came here from Washington when a young man, and married Esther Wier of this town; lived in Antrim about forty years, chiefly on the Lawson White place, afterwards on various places, and died in Wilton July 6, 1880, aged ninety-one. Had but three children: —

1. ELISABETH, [b. in Antrim Nov. 2, 1820; m. Jeremiah S. Atwood.]
2. NANCY A., [d. at age of 5.]
3. MARY R., [m. Nathaniel Philbrick. They lived some years at Butler's Crossing, and then moved to Harrisville where she d. in 1869.]

GENEALOGIES. 609

## MORRISON.

BENJAMIN F. MORRISON, son of Samuel and Betsey (Hosley) Morrison, grandson of Moses Morrison of Hancock, and great-grandson of John Morrison of Londonderry who was born in Ireland in 1679, was born in Alstead in 1813, married Sophia K. Dodge of Hartland, Vt., and came here from Marlow in 1844. He lived at the South Village, but remained in town only five years, and is now living in Central City, Io. His children were: —

1. JAMES H., [b. in Marlow Aug. 11, 1840; m. Silvia M. Corey of Washington, July 4, 1864; is a currier by trade, and lives in his native town.]
2. FRANCES A., [b. in Antrim July 9, 1845, and d. in Alstead in 1853.]

## MORSE.

ANTHONY MORSE was born in Wiltshire, England, May 9, 1606; came to America and settled in Newbury, Mass., in 1635. His grandson, Dea. Benjamin Morse, was born there in 1676; and this Benjamin had a son, Capt. Abel Morse, who married Grace Parker of Bradford, Mass., in 1714. Their son, Josiah Morse, married Mary Chase, and settled in Chester. Dea. Parker Morse, son of Josiah and Mary, was born in that town in 1751, married Love Knowles, and went to Deering, where he died in 1805.

CAPT. PARKER MORSE, son of Dea. Parker and Love (Knowles) Morse, was born in Chester July 12, 1774, and came here from Deering on to the Amos Dodge farm in 1798. In 1799 he married Jane Langdon of Beverly, Mass., and moved to Rochester, Vt., in 1815; thence to Metamora, Ill., where he died in 1862. His wife died in 1853, aged seventy-four. He was a most worthy and desirable citizen, and had a large family. Some of his children were buried on the hill. Three sons in the West are now deacons. Children are as follows: —

1. ELISABETH T., [b. March 22, 1800, m. Joel Ramsey of Stockbridge, Vt., and d. in 1858.]
2. DEA. MARK, [b. Sept. 18, 1801; m. Mehitable Jones of Alstead; is now deacon of a Congregational Church in Galesburg, Ill.]
3. DEA. PARKER, [b. Jan. 6, 1803; m. Roxanna Child of Sharon, Vt.; is now deacon of a Congregational Church in Metamora, Ill.]
4. LOVE K., [b. June 20, 1804; m. John Obrien, Esq.; lived in Groveland, Ill., and d. there in 1871.]
5. JANE L., [b. Dec. 21, 1805, m. Harry Waters of Lebanon, and d. in Groveland, Ill., in 1838.]

6. DELIVERANCE, [b. Dec. 5, 1807 ; probably d. in infancy.]
7. WILLIAM L. S., [b. July 29, 1809, and d. Sept. 20, 1810.]
8. JOSEPH T., [b. April 29. 1811, m. Phœbe Morse of Boscawen, and d. at Pleasant Hill, Mo., in 1870.]
9. JOHN M. W.. [m. Mellissa Barton of Manchester, Vt., and now lives in Chester, Vt.]
10. DEA. LEVI P., [m. Mary A. Parmenter from England ; is now deacon of a Congregational Church in Cazenovia, Ill.]

SUMNER MORSE. son of Zelotus and Lydia (Clark) Morse, was born in Thetford, Vt., in 1821 ; married Susan Springer of Colebrook, and came here from Hillsborough in 1870. He built his house near the south end of Main street, South Village, in 1876. The children are : —

1. CHARLES S., [d. in 1873, aged 19.]
2. ALFARETTA, [b. Aug. 30, 1855.]
3. JAMES N., [b. July 21, 1858.]

## MOULTON.

JOSEPH MOULTON, son of Cutting and Judith (Emery) Moulton, was born in Parsonfield, Me., in 1791. His father was born in Newbury, Mass., in 1748. He came here in 1826 and built the house now occupied by James Wilson. He married Ruth Messer of Newport in 1815, who died in 1841, aged forty-four. Shortly before her death he moved to Hillsborough, but came back to Antrim and married Polly Barker, April 13, 1843, and bought the Adam Dunlap place, where he died in 1864. His widow died in 1872, aged seventy-five. The adult children of Joseph and Ruth (Messer) Moulton were : —

1. SOLON W., [b. March 5, 1817, in Newport ; m. 1st, Sarah Spears of Waterville, Me., May 5, 1840, 2d, Huldah J. Hinkley of Lewiston, Me., Dec. 17, 1854, and d. in that place Nov. 13, 1877. Was a merchant in that city. His two children, Walter and Ruth, both d. young.]
2. MARTHA J., [b. in Newport Feb. 20, 1821 ; m. 1st, Walter Brooks of Milford, March 31, 1842 ; 2d, James T. Fields of Nashua ; d. Oct. 30, 1879. Was sick three years, and blind two years, yet d. in great resignation and peace.]
3. LUCETTA M., [b. June 20, 1826, in Antrim, and now lives in Lowell.]
4. LUCRETIA M., [b. in Antrim Dec. 4, 1828 ; m. 1st, George O. Lathe in 1844 ; 2d, Oliver Fiske, A. M., of Tewksbury, Mass., in 1859.]
5. REV. JOSEPH, [b. in Antrim Aug. 12, 1834 ; m. Sarah J. Fox in 1865, and succeeded his father on the homestead. He

was colporteur in the service of Bible and missionary societies fourteen years; moved to Cushing, Me., in 1873, and is now pastor of Methodist churches in Cushing and South Waldoborough, Me. His children are:—

*Arthur S.*, (b. in Antrim in 1867.)
*Ruthie Florence*, (b. in Antrim in 1869.)
*Agnes Lucetta*, (b. in Maine in 1874.)]

## MUNHALL.

JOHN MUNHALL came here from Flushing, Long Island, in 1862; married Eliza T. Fitzgerald of Keene, the same year, and moved on to the William Parker place, the house having been moved thither in 1857 from the place east of Thomas Flint's. His children are:—

1. WILLIAM HENRY, [b. March 22, 1863.]
2. MARY ELISABETH, [b. Aug. 5, 1867.]
3. ANNIE JOSEPHINE, [b. Sept. 2, 1874.]

## MUZZEY.

JOHN MUZZEY, son of Dimon and Mary (Waldron) Muzzey, and grandson of John and Priscilla (Johnson) Muzzey, was born in Weare Oct. 23, 1799. His older brother, Johnson Muzzey, was killed going home from church in Weare. The harness broke, and the horse ran, and he was thrown with such violence against the wall, that his skull was broken in, and the bones of his broken arms protruded through his coat-sleeves! John Muzzey married Elisabeth P. Duncan, daughter of Dea. Josiah Duncan, Nov. 27, 1821. He lived in several places in town, and died on the Zadok Dodge place, dropping dead in the field, July 8, 1866. Children:—

1. JAMES H., [b. Jan. 28, 1823; m. Joanna Fletcher in 1846; lived here subsequently a few years, and then moved to Bunker Hill, Ill., where he d. Feb. 19, 1858. Three daughters were b. in Antrim, thus:—
   *Caroline C.*, (b. Sept. 21, 1847; unm.; lives at Bunker Hill, Ill.)
   *Mary A.*, (b. Oct. 23, 1850; m. Abram Turk, a farmer near Bunker Hill, Ill., June 1, 1876.)
   *Eva J.*, (b. Oct. 26, 1853; m. Dr. William Furgerson May 2, 1876, and lives in Swanwick, Ill.)]
2. SABRA A., [b. Feb. 17, 1825; m. Luke Thompson, April 18, 1844.]
3. HIRAM, [d. in childhood.]
4. ELECTA, [b. Jan. 31, 1831; m. Samuel Maynard of Peter-

borough; was m. on her death-bed. and lived just one week, dying Dec. 1, 1852.]
5. HIRAM W., [b. Oct. 13, 1833; m. Emma M. Holdaway of Stanton, Ill.; lives in South Village; no children ]
6. FRANKLIN J., [b. in Hillsborough. Nov. 25. 1835; m. Martha J. Holdaway, sister of above, in 1860: is a machinist; has worked at almost everything done in Antrim shops; has generally lived in or near South Village; has children:—

*Eugene*, (b. in Bunker Hill, Ill., March 17, 1861.)
*Nellie B.*, (b. in Antrim. March 7, 1863 )
*Nina Maud*, (b. June 24, 1866.)
*H. Carlton*, (b. Nov. 24, 1867.)]
7. MARIANNE, [b. Feb. 22, 1840; d. in infancy ]
8. LOAMMI, [b. May 4. 1843; d. in infancy.]

## NAHOR.

DAVID NAHOR, son of James and Jane (Nichols) Nahor, was born in Litchfield, April 25, 1766: married Esther Peabody of Hudson; and moved to Hancock from Litchfield in 1800. He lived near Antrim line, on what is called "Nahor Hill." He moved to Antrim March 31, 1834, and lived seven years where Mrs. Joy now lives. Was appointed justice of the peace from this town, as he had been, probably, years before in Hancock. In the spring of 1841, he went to his son's in Peterborough, and in just five weeks from the day he went he died, the event of death occurring May 2. His children were:—

1. DAVID, JR., [b. Dec. 9. 1794. in Litchfield; was clerk in a store in Boston five years; at the age of 27 he went to New Orleans, and that is the last known of him.]
2. MARY, [b. Sept. 29, 1796; m. Charles Cavender March 26, 1818; d. aged 25.]
3. ESTHER, [b. in Litchfield, Sept. 6. 1798; d. in infancy.]
4. SARAH, [b. in Hancock. Oct. 19, 1800; m. Sanford Adams of Westborough, Mass., March 19. 1829; d. Aug. 22, 1876.]
5. JAMES, [b. Aug. 13, 1802; d. March 17, 1829.]
6. ESTHER, [b. April 25, 1804; m. James Robb of Stoddard, March 27, 1834.]
7. LEONARD, [b. Dec. 8, 1806; m. Marinda Tenney of Hancock, April 7, 1837; d. April 23, 1878.]
8. HANNAH B., [b. Dec. 4, 1810; m. Nathaniel Flint of this town, Nov. 24, 1837; d. in Lexington, Mass., July 22, 1852.]

## NAY.

This name was originally spelled "McNee." Dea. William McNee was born in Ireland in 1711; came from Roxbury, Mass., and settled in Peterborough in 1752, and died in 1789. He had a son, Dea. William McNee, Jr., whose son William was the father of Maj. Samuel Nay of Sharon.

SAMUEL NAY, son of Maj. Samuel and Mary (Felt) Nay of Sharon, was born in that town May 19, 1818; married Nancy B. Vose; and came to Antrim in 1849, on to the Thomas Vose place (west of the pond). He moved to Clinton in 1856, and now lives at South Village. His children are : —

1. FRED. L , [b. Sept. 5, 1848; m. Maggie P. Heath, Jan. 13, 1870, who d. in 1873. June 9, 1874, he m. Stella E. Brackett, and lives at South Village. He is a photographer and painter. The drawing of the old church in this book was by his hand. He has one child : —
*Harry E.*, (b. Aug. 6, 1872.)]
2. CHARLES P., [b. Sept. 3, 1853; m. Lizzie A. Crosby of Peterborough, June 30, 1874; is a blacksmith by trade, and lives at South Village, having children : —
*Archie N.*, (b. July 31, 1875.)
*Ethel C.*, (b. March 28, 1878.)]
3. MORRIS E., [b. May 7, 1864.]
4. SAMUEL V., [b. April 6, 1866, and d. Aug. 20, 1872.]

## NESMITH.

JAMES NESMITH, one of the signers of the memorial to Gov. Shute March 26, 1718, and one of the proprietors of Londonderry, was also one of the original sixteen that first struck for settlement on the soil of that ancient town April 22, 1719. He was a strong man, worthy of respect, and honored by his associates. Was appointed elder of the West Parish Presbyterian Church, at its formation in 1739. The date of his death was 1767, and his age seventy-five. He married, in Ireland, in 1714, Elisabeth, daughter of James McKeen and Janet Cochran. This Elisabeth McKeen was sister of Janet McKeen, Dea. Isaac Cochran's mother. She died in 1763, aged sixty-seven. The Nesmiths lived in the valley of the Bann in Ireland, and emigrated to that place from Scotland in 1690. Dea. James Nesmith had two children in Ireland, and seems to have buried the eldest child there. Seven children were born to them in America. The names of all were : Arthur, buried in infancy in Ireland; James, born in Ireland in 1718; Arthur, born in Londonderry April 3, 1721; Jean, born March 12, 1723; Mary, born Jan. 24, 1726; John, born Feb. 11, 1728; Elisabeth, born Jan. 8, 1730; Thomas, born March 26, 1732; Benjamin, born Sept. 14, 1734.

## GENEALOGIES.

James Nesmith, Jr., the son born in Ireland, was born early in 1718, just before embarking for America, and was brought over in his mother's arms. He married Mary Dinsmore and settled in the northern part of Londonderry. Though an old man when the Revolutionary war broke out, he went with all his heart into the struggle against the British; marched among the minute-men at the first call, and was a participant in the battle of Bunker Hill. He had children: James, Jonathan, Robert, Elisabeth, Mary, and Sarah; and died where he settled, July 15, 1793. Of these six children, we will only say as follows: James, the oldest, was born in 1744; married Mary McClure (Parker's History is wrong in saying Martha); was elder in the West Parish Church: left children, — William M., Robert, Isaac, James, Martha, Jane W., and Margaret, — of whom William M., the first named, married Harriet Willis, and was father of Hon. James W. Nesmith, long U. S. Senator from Oregon. Senator Nesmith was born in 1820, married Pauline Goffe in 1846, and now lives in wealth and honor at Dixie, Ore. The second child of James, Jr., was Jonathan of Antrim; Robert, the third child, married Jane Anderson; Elisabeth, the fourth child, married James Cochran of Windham; Mary, the fifth child, married James McClure of Acworth; and Sarah, the sixth, married Daniel Anderson of Londonderry.

Returning now to Arthur, the third child of Dea. James the emigrant, we have to say that he was born April 3, 1721. He married Margaret Hopkins, and settled in the south part of Londonderry; but in later life he moved to the State of Maine. He had two sons in the Revolutionary army, one of whom, John, was a captain noted for valor and strength, but died near the close of the war from effects of excessive exposure and hardship. Of Jean and Mary, daughters of the first Dea. James, I know nothing. But John, the sixth child of the emigrant, married Elisabeth, sister of Gen. George Reed of Londonderry, settled on the first Nesmith homestead with his father, and died there in 1815, aged eighty-seven. His children were: James of Antrim; Arthur of Antrim; John, Jr., who married, first, Susan Hildreth, and second, Lydia Sargent. and died on the homestead in Londonderry in 1844; Ebenezer, who married Jane Trotter; Thomas; Elisabeth, who married Dea. James Pinkerton; Mary, who married John Miltimore, moving to Reading, Penn.; and Jane, who married Hugh Anderson. Of Elisabeth, the emigrant's seventh child, I have no data. Thomas, the eighth child, was born March 26, 1732; married Annis Wilson, and settled in Londonderry (now the north part of Windham), and had three children: John, Elisabeth, and Thomas, Jr. Of Benjamin, the ninth child of the first Dea. James, I have no information of importance in the present undertaking.

JONATHAN NESMITH, second child of James and Mary (Dinsmore) Nesmith, and grandson of the proprietor Dea. James, was born in Londonderry, in August, 1759. He came here in May, 1774, and began to clear the farm that remained in possession of the family until 1865. He made successive clearings each year, and with vigorous hand put up his log cabin, — though only a boy of sixteen years when he began. He permanently moved here in 1778. He subsequently had to pay for the most of his land a second time. Was one of the leading spirits of the town. Was eleven years selectman, and was four times chosen representative of the town. Was always on important committees, and was known and confided in by all. He was chosen one of the elders of the Presbyterian Church at its formation in 1778, though only twenty-nine years of age. For fifty years he only failed of officiating at one communion. Dea. Nesmith was a man of great sociality. — up to jokes, — genial, jolly, and good-natured; was very hospitable and benevolent; anxious for the public welfare; stoutly in earnest to maintain the faith of his fathers; a man of strong ability, good judgment, and irreproachable character. He was an honor to the town he helped to establish. His death occurred Oct. 15, 1845, aged eighty-six. His first wife was Elenor Dickey, whom he married in 1781. She was the daughter of Adam and Jane (Strahan) Dickey of Londonderry, and granddaughter of John and Margaret Dickey of Londonderry, Ireland. She was born Jan. 1, 1761, and died Sept. 17, 1818. He married, second, Mrs. Sarah (Wetherbee) Hamblin of Concord, Mass. She was twelve years of age when she witnessed the battle of Lexington and Concord from her father's door. She saw those brave men fall, remembered everything, and was always fond of telling of those first blows for liberty. She died Jan. 16, 1852, aged eighty-nine. Dea. Nesmith's cabin was burned one day when the family were absent; and he used to remark, in after years, that he never felt so poor as then. Yet, undismayed, he went about building another, being generously aided by neighbors he had himself always been forward to help. After several years he put up a substantial framed house, which was burned March 4, 1841, from a spark catching on the roof. In his old age Dea. Nesmith resigned his office in the church; and it is spoken of as a remarkable scene, when he stood in the public assembly and offered his resignation, and then, with trembling voice and with uplifted and palsied hand, invoked God's blessing on his successors in coming time. His children were: —

1. JAMES. [b. Oct. 5, 1783; m. Polly Taylor April 10, 1810; cleared and settled west of the pond and west of the Steele place, on land now George Brown's, — often called the Boyd place; went thence to Solon, N. Y., in 1822, with six children. There his wife d. in 1846. In 1852 he m. 2d, Mrs. Susan Clark; moved to Waukon, Io., and d. there in 1862. He had children: —

*Mary*, (b in 1811; d. in infancy.)
*Mary E.*, (b. in 1812; m. John Stillman of Cortlandville, N. Y, in 1833; went to Waukon, Io., in 1857, where they now live.)
*Rev. John T. G.*, (b. in 1814; studied at Cazenovia Seminary; m. Harriet N. Taylor; entered the Methodist ministry; was a faithful and able man; d. while pastor, at the age of 36.)
*Hannah E.*, (b. in 1816; m. John Reed; moved to Waukon, Io., in 1857, and d. there in 1877.)

*Abigail S.*, (b. in 1818; became second wife of Isaac Barker in 1847; went to Waukon, Io.. in 1854.)

*Mark W.*, (b. in 1820; d. unm.. at Solon. N. Y., in 1848.)

*James A.*, (b. in 1822; carried to Solon, N. Y., when an infant; went thence to Illinois in 1844; m. Laura Post.)

*George W.*, (b. in Solon, N. Y., in 1825; m. Mary C. Farrar of Fairfield, Vt.; resides at Waukon, Io.)

*Dr. Milton W.*, (b. in 1828; m. Margaret Donoughue in 1852; is now physician and druggist at Waukon, Io.)

*Woodbury T.*, (by second wife; b. in 1852; remains at Solon, N. Y.)]

2. JEAN, [now called " Jane," or " Jenny;" b. May 14. 1787; m. John Dunlap June 26, 1807. and d. March 29, 1835.]

3. THOMAS D., [b. March 22. 1789; m. Martha Weeks March 30, 1813; succeeded his father on the homestead. His first wife d. in 1828 aged 35. and he m. 2d, Nancy Gregg, Feb. 4, 1830. He d. Sept. 10, 1841, aged 52. The second wife d. Feb. 9, 1856, aged 63. He was known in town as " Capt. Nesmith;" was captain of the Antrim Grenadiers, and was often marshal of the day on special occasions. He was a useful man and d. in his prime. His children were : —

*Robert W.*, (b. May 3. 1814; m. Olive Dunlap of Bedford, June 1, 1839; settled in Jefferson. Tex., and d. at Sulphur Springs in that State, Nov. 28, 1866. He left two daughters: Oriette, now in the Metropolitan Railroad office, Boston; and Sally V.. who m. Com. Decatur Morris. and lives in Little Rock, Ark.)

*Jonathan*, (b. Jan. 24, 1816; m. Marietta F. Morrill of Franklin, Nov. 15, 1841; inherited the homestead of his father and grandfather. sold the same in 1865, and two or three years later moved to Hancock where he now resides. He was the last of the name in town. At one time there were three Dea. Nesmiths in town, known as " Dea. James," " Dea. Arthur," and " Dea. Jonathan." and they each had nine children. — making, with sisters and friends, nearly forty by that name in this place. Jonathan's children are: Jennie M., who was b. Sept. 23, 1842. — an excellent teacher; Thomas S., who was b. May 12, 1846. and d. at the age of three years; Fannie H., who was b. Dec. 8, 1848, and m. Frank H. Baldwin June 19, 1876, residing in Keene; Annie M. T., who was b. Sept. 12, 1852; Abbie Isabel, who was b. Nov. 15, 1854, and d. 1856; Miles G., who was b. Sept. 26, 1857; Addie M., who was b. Jan. 27, 1860; and John S., who was b. May 5, 1863.)

*Sarah E.*, (b. Dec. 24, 1818, m. John W. Buttrick, and lives in Lawrence, Mass.)

*Miles*, (b. Feb. 2, 1821; went to California in 1849, and was driver for the California Stage Company; the horses became unmanageable, and the whole team was thrown down a fearful precipice near Virginia City, Nev., by which the driver, all the horses, and most of the passengers were instantly killed. This sad event occurred in December, 1862.)

*Harriet F.*, (b. Feb. 2, 1823, m. Walker Flanders, and lives in Lawrence, Mass.)

*Martha J.*, (b. June 9, 1825; m. Isaac P. Cochran of Windham, Nov. 12, 1846.)

*Melvin*, (b. Dec. 20, 1830; d. in Sacramento, Cal., Dec. 31, 1853.)

*Hiram G.*, (b. Feb. 18, 1833; d. in Jefferson, Tex., in 1857.)

*Nancy R.*, (b. Jan. 24, 1836, m. Josiah Melville, and lives in Nelson.)]

4. ADAM, [b. March 5, 1792; m. Rebecca Dale; settled in Beverly, Mass., and d. Jan. 15, 1865.]

5. MARY D., ["Molly Dinsmore" on town record, b. April 11, 1794; called "Long Mary," being tall in form; a talented, respected, and Christian woman; d. unm. April 6, 1874.]

6. MARGARET, [b. May 4, 1796; d. unm. in 1827.]

7. ISABEL, [b. March 6, 1798; d. unm. March 8, 1862.]

8. HON. GEORGE W., [b. Oct. 23, 1800; was graduated at Dartmouth College in 1820; m. Mary M. Brooks; settled in the practice of law at Franklin; was long judge of the New Hampshire Supreme Court, remaining on the bench until relieved by the constitutional limitation of years. Is now president of the N. H. Orphans' Home, and trustee of Dartmouth College; is a man of noble principles and honored life, enjoying in his old age the highest confidence and esteem of men. The degree of LL. D. was conferred upon him by Dartmouth College. He stands among the best and noblest of the sons of New Hampshire, and is an honor to his native town.]

9. ROBERT, [b. Feb. 20, 1803; first victim of spotted fever, Feb. 9, 1812.]

DEA. JAMES NESMITH of Antrim, son of John and Elisabeth (Reed) Nesmith, grandson of Dea. James and Elisabeth (McKeen) Nesmith, and cousin of Dea. Jonathan, was born in Londonderry in 1758. He came here at the age of twenty, and began the farm which has been so long occupied by Chandler Boutwell. This he sold to John Woodcock about 1790, and began another farm on the northeast slope of Meeting-House Hill. This was a good farm; the house was nearly down at the foot of the hill on the east fork of the old road, and he had Robert McIlvaine for a near neighbor. Here he lived in comparative comfort for about thirty years, when, it is said, his children insisted on his building a finer house, and he erected a very large mansion. But he was unable to finish it, became embarrassed with debt, and eventually had to give up everything and move away. The large house was taken down and moved to the Branch. By help of his old neighbors, a small house was built for him in 1821 at the foot of the hill east of Henry M. Barker's, and on that spot his days were ended in the year 1845, at the age of eighty-seven. He died poor, but universally respected. He was a Revolutionary soldier, and was in many battles. He was chosen elder in the Center Church in 1800, and held the office till death. His pension was his principal reliance for support in his old age. Dea. James was frequently selectman, and was twenty-seven years town clerk; was chosen by unanimous vote, though party excitement was as great as it is now; and it is said they would have continued him in the office if he had not fallen into the legal disqualification of ceasing to hold real estate. He used to say that his fees just about kept him in tobacco. Probably his voice helped to keep him in the office, as it was his duty in those days to publish intentions of marriage by crying them in the meeting-house on three successive Sabbaths. In very pressing cases it was sometimes done twice on the same day! The deacon's voice was not very musical, but was heavy and loud and ringing, — and everybody was sure to hear! At the sound of the "Amen," — high over the din of falling seats, — were thundered the words: "This is the first publishment of intention of marriage between Mr. Jacob A. B. C. and Miss Polly X. Y. Z.!" People stopped and listened in amazement and curiosity; but it is not told us how much of the sermon this peculiar ceremony drove out of their heads! Dea. James Nesmith of Antrim married, first, Elisabeth Brewster of Francestown, in 1781; second, Charlotte Walker, youngest child of James Walker, the first settler of Bedford. His children were : —

1. JOHN, [b. Aug. 19, 1782; was brought up by his uncle, Dea. James Pinkerton of Derry; old people in that town speak of him as a beautiful player on the flute; was some years a peddler; wandered off westward in that business in 1814, and has never since been heard of. Probably was robbed and put out of the way.]
2. ISABELLA REED, [b. Oct. 16, 1784; m. Prof. Joshua Holt, May 11, 1815; d. in 1851. Mr. Holt graduated at Dartmouth

GENEALOGIES. 619

College in 1814 ; was many years a teacher in the West,
and d. in 1848. aged 60.]
3. JAMES, JR., [b. April 2, 1787 ; went when a young man to
Kentucky ; was three times m. there, and d. there at the
age of 52. All his children d. before him.]
4. ELISABETH, [b. Nov. 29, 1789; went as a teacher into the
State of Pennsylvania; there m. Rev. George White, and
they are said to have moved to Nebraska.]
5. POLLY. [b. Jan. 1, 1793 ; was called " Short Mary," to dis-
tinguish from Dea. Jonathan's Mary ; was nearly forty years
a teacher ; was one of the godly and blessed ones of the
earth ; d. unm. at the Branch in 1867.]
6. JEAN, [b. Sept. 23, 1795, and d. in 1800.]
7. DAVID B., [b. March 18, 1798, and d. in infancy.]
8. GEORGE REID, [b. April 18, 1801 ; was a carpenter by trade ;
went to New York when young, and nothing more can be
learned of him.]
9. DEA. ERASTUS, [b. June 28, 1804; was a woolen-manufac-
turer; learned his trade at the Branch under Reed and
Wallace ; was apprenticed to them in 1818, and served
seven years for his trade ; made cloth at Hillsborough and
other places ; lived chiefly in Canaan; was deacon of the
Congregational Church, — a thoroughly good man. He m.
Lucy Wilson of Antrim. Their only child, a promising
young man, d. a few years before his father. Dea. Erastus
d. in Enfield, in 1869, universally lamented.]

DEA. ARTHUR NESMITH, brother of Dea. James of Antrim, came
here somewhat later than his brother, and began the Jonathan Carr place
(now Luther Campbell's) about 1784. He married Polly Duncan (daughter of Hon. John), May 30, 1793: was a man of more than ordinary ability; was a great reader; was frequently selectman; and was elder in the
Presbyterian Church. Dr. Whiton says that " his cheerful and uniform
piety was an ornament to the Christian profession." What higher praise
could be conferred ? His amiable manners and intelligence and goodness gave him great influence, and endeared him to all. The aged remember him with much affection. He was distinguished as a singer,
and led the church music for nearly thirty years, being elected every
March meeting by the town to that then important office. He is said to
have kept his large and scattered choir in good order and good feeling !
What a pity he couldn't have lived two or three hundred years ! It
should be added that his children and grandchildren have been notable
choir-leaders in the West. To the surprise and regret of the whole town,
Dea. Arthur moved to New Portage, Ohio, in 1816, hoping that a different

climate would build up his health. This recuperation was realized to some extent. But on his way to church one bright Sabbath morning in the summer of 1823, while supposed to be in his usual health, he fell down in the road and died in a moment. His age was sixty-three. Through his many years in Antrim he was never known to fly into a passion, and his rebukes were of a persuasive and gentle order. It is said, however, that on one occasion when they were singing in church, and he was annoyed beyond measure by the loud, unmelodious bellowing of his brother at the foot of the choir, he reached over the pew-tops with his cane and gave him a nudge, saying: "Dea. Jamie, Dea. Jamie, I wish you would sing in the spirit; for you do make an awfu' noise in the flesh!" It will be noticed that for sixteen years there were three Dea. Nesmiths in town; and they were known as "Dea. Jonathan," "Dea. James," and "Dea. Arthur," and certainly were noteworthy men. Dea. Arthur's children were:—

1. JOHN, [b. March 6, 1794; fitted for college in company with Hon. George W. Nesmith, but, his father feeling unable to send him, he went to Ohio, and there gained a noble reputation as a teacher; m. Mary A. Hull of Canandaigua, N. Y.; d. at the age of 63; left no children.]
2. MARY D., [b. Feb. 5, 1796, and d. in 1800.]
3. CYRUS, [b. Jan. 1, 1798, and d. in 1800.]
4. ELISABETH PINKERTON, [b. Aug. 3. 1799; m. 1st, Col. Talcot Bales of Norton, Ohio: 2d, Thomas Brown, and settled in Buchanan, Mich.; left large family, and d. at the age of 74.]
5. CYRUS ARTHUR. [b. Oct. 24, 1801; m. Marinda Hurlburt; settled near his brother John in Wadsworth, Ohio, but moved in 1847 to Metamora, Ill., where he now resides. He remembers Antrim with great interest. Has a large family, several of whom live near him. His children have come to honor. As inventors and merchants and stock-raisers, they may be counted successful men. All are musicians.]
6. MARY D., [b. March 31, 1803, m. Hiel Bronson, and lives in Princeville, Ill.]
7. ABIGAIL MOOR, [b. Oct. 5, 1805; d. young.]
8. MILTON WHITON, [b. Feb. 9, 1809; m. 1st, Antonette Bronson; 2d, Mary Sabin; lives in Princeville, Ill.]
9. THOMAS, [b. Oct. 5, 1810, m. Reesa Northe, and lives in Western Star, Ohio.]

## NEWMAN.

DEA. HARRIS B. NEWMAN, son of Joseph and Pamelia (Bingham) Newman of Washington, and grandson of Benjamin and Abigail

(Lewis) Newman of Deering, was born in Washington, Oct. 31, 1814; married Mary B. Gray of Hancock in 1842; came here from Hillsborough in 1855, and bought the Jonathan Carr place, which he sold in 1868 and bought the Gates place (where Rev. Mr. Bates lived), where he died Feb. 28, 1876. The family were from Woburn, Mass. Dea. Newman was representative in 1872 and 1873, and was appointed deacon in the Presbyterian Church in 1870. He was a man of singular purity. Among all the good men of this town, probably no one has ever been superior to him in sweetness and holiness of life. All people held the same exalted opinion of him. Though he was not what the world calls great and learned, he was *good*, and highly honored by all who knew him. His sickness was long and distressing, and death came to him as a friend long sighed for and welcome. His widow and two youngest children live on the homestead. The children are as follows : —

1. HELEN, [b. Aug. 23, 1843, in Hillsborough ; m. John H. Wilkins Nov. 4, 1873, and lives in Boston.]
2. GEORGE, [b. in Hillsborough, Sept. 23, 1845 ; d. aged nearly two years.]
3. GEORGE F., [b. in Fitzwilliam, Sept. 30, 1848 ; m. Ella Bass of Antrim, Nov. 30, 1871, and lives in Somerville, Mass.]
4. JOSEPH W., [b. Jan. 20, 1852, in Hillsborough, and lives on the homestead.]
5. MARY LOUISE, [b. in Antrim, Oct. 23, 1857.]

JOHN G. NEWMAN, shoemaker, son of Benjamin and Sarah (Gordon) Newman of Washington, and cousin of Dea. Harris B. Newman, was born in 1798; married Margaret M. Ring of Hillsborough, and came here in 1824, into the Robert McCoy house (once a store and liquor-shop), which he occupied till his death in 1874. His children are : —

1. ELIZA J., [b. in 1825, m. Frank A. Stone, and lives in Holliston, Mass.]
2. JOHN B., [b. in 1832 ; has been in California since 1853.]

## NEWTON.

GILES NEWTON, son of Giles and Naomi (Duncan) Newton of Francestown (this elder Giles built and occupied the old Dane store, and the hotel, burned in that town in 1854), and grandson of Isaac Newton of Newport, was born Jan. 25, 1799; married Sally Bell, Aug. 25, 1825; bought of Daniel Buswell the farm next east of Mr. Greeley's, now unoccupied, and lived there till his sudden death July 14, 1868. He went into the field to get a load of hay and dropped dead while engaged in loading. Was a good and pious man. His children were : —

1. ELISABETH, [b. June 14, 1827, m. J. C. Loveland of Springfield, Vt., and d. there in 1868.]

2. MARY, [b. May 18, 1829, m. Adna Brown of Springfield, Vt., Sept. 10, 1850, and d. there in 1861.]
3. SARAH N., [b. Feb. 12, 1832, m. Obed Spalding of Stoddard, May 5, 1852, and now lives in Springfield, Vt.]
4. ROBERT D., [b. Jan. 31, 1834, m. Lizzie Albee, and lives in Troy, Penn.]
5. SAMUEL GILES, [b. Dec. 27, 1839; m. Lizzie M. Gillis of Antrim, April 27, 1871; was for a long time clerk in the Treasury Department at Washington, and had an extensive acquaintance with public men. He now lives in Ashburnham, Mass. Has three children: —

*Mary G.*, (b. July 2, 1873.)
*Annie Bell*, (b. Oct. 2, 1875.)
*Helen*, (b. Nov. 8, 1876.)]

## NICHOLS.

Four brothers, Daniel, Adam, John, and Thomas, lived in a row in the east part of the town. Daniel lived on the Turner place, Adam on the McCoy place, John on the Ferry place, and Thomas on the Shattuck place. They were sons of Samuel Nichols, who came from Antrim, Ireland, in 1754, and after living in several other towns came here to spend his old age with his children, and died very aged in 1804. The first to break the continuity of the land of those four brothers was Robert Duncan, who bought and built in between in 1787. Each of these four brothers had a son Samuel, so there were at one time five by the name of Samuel Nichols in town. It has been found very difficult to get information of these families, as they have been all gone from town more than fifty years. All these brothers served more or less in the army of the Revolution.

THOMAS NICHOLS was born in Ireland and was brought over when an infant. He was the first of the four to set foot on the soil of this town. He ran away from a master in Newburyport, and came here to live with Dea. Aiken in the fall of 1767. He began the Dea. Shattuck farm when a mere boy. It is said he hunted the town over for game, and had a chance to pick his farm where he chose. Is spoken of as "an Inholder in Antrim" in 1788. Was a man of much life and energy. Was captain of the militia, which was an office of great honor and importance in those days. It is reported that he had trouble with the Indians. He was a great hunter, and often traded with the natives. They came to the conclusion that he cheated them, and sought to take his life in revenge. His method was to tell them that his fist weighed a pound, and then to use said fist to balance furs, etc., in weighing them! The red men soon thought he got "too much pound," and laid their plans to kill him! But he suspected trouble, and prepared a hiding-place under his house, made by digging a hole out horizontally from one side of the cellar, which he entered by removing a stone and replacing it behind him. Here he slept for a long time, and succeeded in escaping his foe. But he was on the watch for years, till the Indians disappeared forever. He used to go by the name of the "Indian Trader." His wife was Hannah Clark, whom he seems to have found in Francestown, though said to be a Boston woman. In the dysentery of 1800 he buried three children, Betsey, Thomas, and Nancy, in one day, Aug. 21. Capt. Nichols moved to New York in the fall of 1808, and, after living in several places, settled in Cattaraugus, that State, in 1811. He died there the next year, dying in bed beside his wife, so silently that she did not know it till morning. They dug out a huge trough and buried the body in that, as it was all a new country and they had no means of procuring a coffin. The next year the family forsook their settlement and moved to West Bloomfield in the same State. There, soon after, the mother died, aged sixty-six. Capt. Nichols's life was full of romance. He had a roving disposition — was smart and cunning — was an influential, stirring man; and he ended his active life as he began it, — a pioneer in the wilderness. His age was sixty-seven. His children were : —

1. MARY ANN, [b. in Francestown, Dec. 31, 1778 ; m. Ephraim Hall, April 21. 1801 ; went to New York in 1808.]
2. POLLY, [b. in Antrim, July 2, 1781 ; m. Nathan Cole, Jr., Oct. 22, 1805 ; d. in Franklinton, Ohio, in the fall of 1846.]
3. SAMUEL, [b. June 3, 1783 ; m. 1st, Clarissa Lee of West Bloomfield, N. Y. ; second wife unknown ; moved to Munroe, Mich., and d. there.]
4. SALLY, [b. March 23, 1785 ; m. her cousin Samuel Nichols, son of Adam ; lived and d. in Munroe, Mich.]
5. PEGGY, [b. Aug. 23, 1787 ; m. a Mr. Nevins of Cattaraugus, N. Y., and d. there.]
6. NANCY, [b. May 2, 1790 ; d. of dysentery, Aug. 20, 1800 ; a younger sister and brother d. of the same disease the day previous, and they were all buried in one day, and in one grave.]
7. BETSEY, [b. Dec. 15, 1792, and d. Aug. 19, 1800.]
8. GEORGE C., [b. July 25, 1795 ; m. Hester Ball of West Bloomfield, N. Y. ; d. Aug. 4, 1864. Was thrown from a carriage and survived his injury but an hour.]
9. THOMAS, [b. Dec. 21, 1797, and d. Aug. 19, 1800.]

DEA. DANIEL NICHOLS, brother of Thomas, came here in 1774 to make his beginning on the farm now Mr. Turner's. For several years he lived alone, or boarded with neighbors. Was one of the most efficient men in town in his day. Was much in town office. He represented Antrim, Deering, and Hancock in the constitutional convention of 1791-92. Dr. Bouton (Provincial Papers, Vol. X., page 37) represents

Hon. John Duncan of this town as being in said convention. But in this he is mistaken, and he applies the "pallyar" story to the wrong man. Col. John Duncan of Acworth, cousin of "Hon. John" of Antrim, was a member of the convention, and the good Dr. B. confounded the two. Daniel Nichols, often designated "Esquire," was a small man. He being a land-surveyor, this was convenient, as when they came to a brook they were in the habit of picking him up and carrying him over! Was chosen elder in the Presbyterian Church in 1800, which office he held till death. He married Mary Dinsmore, sister of Samuel Dinsmore, Sen., of Antrim, Dec. 29, 1785. Was selectman nine years. He died March 3, 1812, aged fifty-eight. His death was caused by the spotted fever, was very sudden, and was among the most lamented of the many fatalities by that terrible scourge. He was an able and good man. On his now broken tombstone it is written: "The poor will cherish his memory; the widow and the fatherless shall call him blessed." His children were:—

1. MARY ANN, [b. Oct. 29, 1786; m. 1st, John Emerson of Deering; 2d, Thomas Costello, Sept. 21, 1826. She d. in Concord in 1875.]
2. MARTHA, [b. May 30, 1788; m. James Maberry, and went West.]
3. REV. JOHN, [b. June 20, 1790; graduated at Dartmouth College in 1813; m. Elisabeth Shaw of Beverly, Mass., in 1817, and sailed for India as a missionary. He d. on the field in the prime of his usefulness, Dec. 9, 1824, at the early age of 34. He was an able and devoted man, and an honor to his native town. Was much beloved and lamented by the natives generally, and they tenderly cherished his memory, saying to one of his successors, "*He* was a good man." His widow m. an Episcopal missionary in Ceylon.]
4. MARY, [b. Sept. 19, 1793: was finely educated, and became a successful teacher; d. in New York while visiting there in 1823.]
5. SAMUEL, [b. Aug. 17, 1795; went to New York, and thence to Michigan.]
6. SILAS, [b. June 21, 1797; d. in childhood.]

ADAM NICHOLS, another brother, came here with Daniel in 1774, and soon after began the McCoy place (next north of John Duncan's). He married —— Atwood, probably of Francestown; moved to New York, and thence to Kentucky, where he died in 1846, aged ninety. He was several times selectman while living here; was a soldier of the Revolution. Children:—

1. SAMUEL, [m. his cousin Sally Nichols; d. in Munroe, Mich.]

## GENEALOGIES.

2. DANIEL, [m. a Smith, and lived and d. in Western New York.]
3. JAMES, [nothing known.]
4. THOMAS, [nothing known.]
5. DAVID, [nothing known.]
6. DOLLY. [m. Jesse Atwood, and went to Kentucky.]
7. MARY, [m. —— Vanpelt, and went to Kentucky.]

JOHN NICHOLS, brother of the three mentioned above, came here somewhat later than his brothers, and began the Ferry place. He was a soldier under Stark, and participated in the battle of Bennington. He married Sarah Steele; moved to Francestown about 1789, and thence to New York, where he died in 1849, aged ninety. The only children we know of are these:—

1. PEGGY, [taught school in Antrim as early as 1805.]
2. SAMUEL, [m. Betsey Moor in Francestown, Dec. 25, 1809.]

EBENEZER NICHOLS, son of Benjamin Nichols, was born in Reading. Mass., in 1755; married, first, Rebecca Howard, and after her death married Elisabeth Dix of Townsend, Mass. He came here from Hillsborough about 1800 and settled on the north side of Tuttle Mountain, where he lived till 1812, and then moved back to Hillsborough. He afterwards lived some years in Windsor, and died in Wakefield, Mass., in 1840, aged eighty-five. His children, all by the second wife, were:—

1. EBEN, [b. in 1790; m. Susan Avery of Middleton, Mass., and settled in Danvers, where he d. in 1820.]
2. BETSEY, [m. Paron Wheeler of Windsor, April 20, 1814, and is still living there at an advanced age.]
3. REBECCA, [b. in 1796; m. Jonathan Wilson, and went to Danvers, Mass.]
4. SALLY, [m. Henry Wardwell of Lynn, Mass., and lived and d. in that city.]
5. JONATHAN, [b. in 1800; m. Betsey Emerson of Wakefield, Mass., and is one of the heaviest farmers in that place.]
6. NANCY, [d. at the age of 28.]
7. DANIEL, [b. in 1806; m. 1st, Eliza Jones of Windsor; 2d, Mary Green of Wakefield, Mass., where he now lives.]
8. MARY, [b. in 1808, m. Daniel Rowe of Lynn, and d. in 1864.]

DEA. BENJAMIN NICHOLS, son of Phinehas and Polly (Chase) Nichols, was born in Haverhill, Mass., in 1775; married Polly Hardy of Bradford, Mass.; came here in 1825, and bought of Henry Hill what is now known as the Jonas White place. He was appointed deacon in the Baptist Church, March 13, 1806. He died here in 1859, aged eighty-four.

His wife died in 1856, aged eighty. Their children, all born in Bennington, were : —

1. POLLY, [d. in childhood.]
2. ANN, [b. in 1798; m. 1st, Charles Stewart; 2d, Timothy Hardy, March 23, 1826; d. in Cornish.]
3. JOSEPH, [b. in 1801; m. Philo Mellen, and lives in Milford.]
4. CONVERSE, [b. in 1803; m. Sylvia Cummings, and resides in Lowell.]
5. BENJAMIN, [b. in 1806; m. 1st, Nancy Smith; 2d, Mary Smith; 3d, Mrs. E. H. White, and now lives in Keene.]
6. ROXANNA, [b. July 25, 1808; m. 1st, Jonas Ball; 2d, Alfred Crane, and now resides in Amesbury, Mass.]
7. JOHN, [b. in 1810; m. Julia Chase, and resides in Haverhill, Mass.]
8. LUKE, [b. April 4, 1813; m. Lucy E. Tenney, April 21, 1836; lived on the homestead, where he d. Aug. 12, 1856. His children were : —
    *Luke A.*, (b. March 17, 1837; d. on homeward trip from West Indies, May 8, 1860, and buried at sea.)
    *Elvira H.*, (b. Dec. 8, 1838; d. in infancy.)
    *Henry M.*, (b. in Acworth April 12, 1842; m. Ella E. McCoy; is a provision-dealer in Boston.)
    *Alden S.*, (b. March 15, 1844, in Acworth; went to Minnesota in 1865, and has not been heard from since.)
    *Elvira L.*, (b. March 13, 1848, in Antrim; m. William H. Gray of Charlestown, Mass.)
    *Adna L.*, (b. Oct. 16, 1855; is a clerk in Boston.)]
9. ALDEN, [b. Nov. 11, 1814; m. Almira Tilton and lives in Somerville, Mass. Was a teacher in Baltimore and elsewhere in the South, many years.]
10. ABIGAIL, [b. in 1816, m. William H. Drake of Marlow, Jan. 23, 1844, and d. in 1852.]
11. ALMIRA, [b. April 10, 1819, m. Alfred Crane Aug. 14, 1844, and d. in Amesbury, Mass., in 1874.]

## ORDWAY.

ELIEZER ORDWAY came here from Deering on to the Dimon Dodge place in 1825, and moved back to Deering in 1833. He died in Deering in 1846, aged eighty-six. His wife was Susannah Dow, and she died in 1836. Their children were : —

1. JUDITH, [m. John Putney, and lived and d. in Bradford.]

2. LYDIA, [m. William Stanley, and they moved to Canada many years ago.]
3. HANNAH, [m. Nathan White of Deering.]
4. BETSEY, [m. James M. Palmer of Deering, May 1, 1831.]
5. ABIAL, [lived mostly in Deering, but d. in Goffstown in 1858, unm.]
6. BENJAMIN, [m. Sally Temple, Aug. 19, 1827; lived in the Thomas Carr house in the east part of the town, and afterwards in South Village, where he d. We have no record of dates except that a grave was dug at Maplewood cemetery for Mrs. Benjamin Ordway, Aug. 6, 1868; and for her husband, Dec. 18, 1868. I can only learn that they had three children. A daughter m. Selden Miller of Windsor, but soon d. Another daughter m. Lorenzo D. Richardson of Bennington. The only son I can learn of is Eben Ordway, now living at Hillsborough Lower Village.]
7. ABIGAIL, [m. Stephen Barker, July 12, 1835; d. in Lyndeborough, July 15, 1850.]
8. SUSAN, [m. Richard McAllister of Hillsborough, April 4, 1841.]
9. JONATHAN, [b. Nov. 9, 1814; m. Mehitable Gay of Deering, Oct. 4, 1835, and lives in Hillsborough Lower Village.]

## ORR.

HUGH ORR, son of John and Margaret (Kamel) Orr, came over from the north of Ireland with his father in 1726, and settled in Bedford. There his father and mother died within four days of each other in the year 1754. Hugh was the oldest child, and remained on the homestead and took care of the family. He married Sarah Reed of Londonderry. After some years he sold to his brother, Hon. John Orr, and came here. His settlement here was in 1790, or a little earlier. He built near the Temple place,— a little southwest of the same. The house stood on the north side of the road as now made, and, very much to his lament, proved to be just within the limits of Hancock. This fact seems to have been the occasion of his removal. He was a man of intelligence and honesty. People regretted his departure from them. He moved to Rockingham, Vt., in 1795; thence, after a short stay, to Homer, N. Y., where he died. He is said to have had six sons and three daughters. Many of his descendants are supposed to be scattered over the Western States. One daughter married James Aiken of Antrim.

## PAIGE.

JOHN PAIGE, born in Dedham, England, in 1586, came over in the company which, under Gov. Winthrop, founded Boston in 1630. He afterwards settled in Dedham, Mass., and died there in 1676, aged ninety years. His wife's name was Phœbe. This first John Paige had a son Samuel, born in 1633, who lived in Salisbury, Mass.; and *he*, among other children, had a son John Paige, Jr., born in 1696. This second John, grandson of the first, married Mary Winslow, and lived in Salisbury, Mass. He raised a large family, and afterwards moved to South Hampton, where he died. Among the sons of this second John was Samuel, called "Col. Paige" (which commission he held before the Revolution). This Col. Paige married, first, Eleanor Stevens, and settled in South Hampton, but moved to Weare in 1772. Their children were Samuel, Jonathan, Lemuel, John, and Eleanor. Col. Paige married, second, Mrs. Sally (Osgood) Evans, and died in Weare in 1800, quite aged. Of these children of Col. Samuel Paige: —

Samuel, the first son, married Sally Osgood in 1769, and died in Weare in 1815.

Jonathan, the second son, married, first, Miriam Barnard, and had the following children : Jonathan, Jr., Tristram, Enoch, Moses, and John. The elder Jonathan Paige married, second, Hannah French, and died in 1814. This eldest son, Jonathan Paige, Jr., was born in Weare in 1775, married Judith Coburn of Wilton, had a large family, and died in Deering. One son of Jonathan, Jr., was Tristram B. Paige, who married Sophronia Duncan of Antrim, lived here, on the place now owned by Mr. Greeley, and will be noticed below.

Lemuel, the third son of Col. Samuel Paige, had two wives: first, Betsey Brown, and second, Mrs. Phœbe (Sargent) Green. He settled in Antrim and left a large family, which will be further noticed.

John Paige, the fourth son of Col. Samuel Paige, married Hannah Barnard, had three daughters, and died in 1812.

Eleanor, daughter of Col. Samuel Paige, married Samuel Caldwell of Antrim, and is further noticed under the Caldwell family.

**LEMUEL PAIGE**, son of Col. Samuel and Eleanor (Stevens) Paige, and the fifth in descent from John and Phœbe Paige who came from Dedham, England, was born in 1752. He settled in Weare, but came here from that place in 1793, and bought of Samuel Gregg the Dea. Newman place. The present place known by this name was then the center of a large tract of land, now divided into half a dozen small farms. Mr. Paige married, first, Betsey Brown, who died in Weare in 1785, leaving two children. He married, second, Mrs. Phœbe (Sargent) Green, who died in 1833. Lemuel Paige died Nov. 13, 1805, aged fifty-three. All his children were : —

1. ELEANOR, [m. a Mr. Barnard, and went to Barnet, Vt.]
2. BETSEY, [b. July 17, 1780 ; m. Robert Boyd ; went to Providence, Penn., and d. there in 1869, aged nearly 90.]
3. STEVENS, [b. in 1786 ; m. 1st, Jenny McAdams, Nov. 27, 1806, and lived on the old homestead. Mrs. Paige d. Dec. 20, 1836, aged 54. He m. 2d, Jane Duncan, Feb. 8, 1838, and

built the house on the cross-road west of the Dea. Parmenter place, where he d. July 1, 1853, aged 67. He had one child : —

*Harriet*, (b. July 7, 1807, m. William S. Foster Dec. 27, 1827, and d. Feb. 19, 1850.)]

4. REUBEN, [m. Sarah Forsaith of Deering. and d. at Oil Mill Village in Weare at the age of 35. He was a blacksmith by trade, and had a shop for a few years, it is believed, on the spot where the town-house now stands ; seems to have worked awhile subsequently in Deering, and then in Oil Mill Village. He probably d. in the year 1823. I have knowledge of only two children ; others might have d. young.

*Dr. Lemuel W.*, (b. in Antrim Aug. 3, 1807. He studied medicine with Dr. Adams of Goffstown, and began practice at East Weare. Had an extensive business in all that vicinity for twenty-five years. He moved to Chicopee Falls, Mass., in 1853, and had a large practice until his death, which occurred Dec. 31, 1857, in the prime of his usefulness. Dr. Paige m. 1st, Harriet Little, daughter of Thomas Little of New London ; 2d, Hannah J. Abbott of Concord. Had six children, five daughters and one son. The latter is now a druggist in Chicopee Falls, Mass., — Edgar T. Paige, Esq.)

*Lorinda P.*, (b. in Deering; m. Joseph C. Emerson, and is now living in Cleveland, Ohio.)]

5. ADONIRAM, [b. in 1791 ; m. 1st, Eunice Blake, who d. Oct. 20, 1833 ; 2d, Mrs. Abigail (Gilman) Tilton. Went to Pittsfield when a young man, and d. there in 1843. Had but one child, a daughter, Louisa.]

6. JONATHAN, [b in 1793 ; m. Mehitable Dodge of Bennington in 1813 ; was a saddler by trade. He carried on this business in South Village a short time, but built the Draper house at the Center soon after the erection of the church, and here he lived many years. Worked at his trade in the basement of his house for a time. Afterwards he built a small harness-shop a little east of the house and nearer the road. He moved to Bennington in 1850, and d. in that town in 1852. His four children were all b. in Antrim, and all d. in Bennington.

*Gideon D.*, (b. Dec. 18, 1816 ; m. Harriet Alcock of Deering, and lived in Hancock ; d. in Bennington Dec. 18, 1847.

Two children survive him : first, George B., who was b. in Hancock in 1841, lives in Antrim, m. Carrie Howard and has children, Martha A., b. May 28, 1866, and George K., b. Oct. 9, 1870; and second, Mary F., who was b. in Bennington in 1843, and m. Charles H. Edgewell of Tamworth.)

*Adeline A.*, (b. Dec. 22, 1820, m. William Griswold, and d. in 1843.)

*Mary W.*, (b. March 30, 1824, and d. aged 17.)

*Harriet*, (d. unm. Dec. 6, 1860, aged 33.)]

7. SALLY, [b. April 17, 1796, m. John Wallace Feb. 24, 1824, and d. Jan. 22, 1864.]
8. PHŒBE, [b. May 25, 1799, and d. Aug. 24, 1800.]
9. HANNAH, [b. April 11, 1801, and d. unm. in 1843.]

TRISTRAM B. PAIGE, son of Jonathan, Jr., and Judith (Coburn) Paige, grandson of Jonathan and Miriam (Barnard) Paige, and great-grandson of Col. Samuel and Eleanor (Stevens) Paige, was born in 1804. He married Sophronia Duncan, daughter of Dea. Josiah Duncan, Sept. 21, 1826; came here from Deering, and lived on the Josiah Duncan place, now occupied by Mr. Greeley. He died in Amherst in 1855. The children were : —

1. MARY, [d. in 1831, at the age of about three years, and was buried on the hill.]
2. JACOB, [b. in 1834; d. in infancy and was buried on the hill.]
3. SOPHRONIA A., [b. Jan. 26, 1832, and d. in 1851.]
4. TRISTRAM M., [b. April 25, 1836; m. Lizzie M. Whitmore of Salisbury on Thanksgiving Day, 1868. He bought the bedstead-factory in Clinton of Charles S. Brooks, and carried on the business until the factory was burned Feb. 8, 1876. He has no children.]
5. DEA. ENOCH C., [b. Oct. 20, 1839; m. Harriet E. Parmenter, daughter of George F. Parmenter, Feb. 21, 1861. He bought the Dodge mills in 1859, and engaged in the manufacture of bedsteads, cradles, etc. Then sold out, and shortly after, in 1862, he entered the army in the Ninth Regiment. Near the close of the next year he was " sent home to die, but says he isn't dead yet ! " After his recovery he bought the Hastings house and privilege (mill burned before), put up the small part of the mill, and again commenced the manufacture of bedsteads. In about five years he sold to Mr. Hastings, and soon after built the George B. Paige

house, now house of Henry Rogers; then bought the Cummings shop, where he manufactured some fourteen kinds of cribs and cradles. He built the house by the shop in 1870, and occupied the same till 1880, when he sold to Abbott F. True, and bought the brick house known as the Cummings house. Built a new mill in 1880 on the spot where that of his brother had been burned, and continues similar manufactures there. He was appointed deacon in the Presbyterian Church in 1876. Dea. Paige m. 2d, Lizzie C. Fleming of Bennington. His children are : —

*Clara E.*. (b. July 30, 1862.)
*Bertolette*, (b. March 3, 1865.)
*Morton*, (b. July 15, 1867.)]

A family of Paige brothers, not known to be closely connected with the preceding, came to Antrim from Hudson in 1808. There were John, Jacob, Isaac, Seth, Ezekiel, Daniel, and David. John was killed in battle in the Revolution. Jacob settled in Litchfield; Seth in Bedford; Isaac remained in his native town; and the three last came here. Fannie Paige, a daughter of Jacob, was brought up by Samuel Marshall of Antrim, married Moses Robb of Stoddard, and is now living very aged in that town.

EZEKIEL PAIGE, of whom we know almost nothing, succeeded McDole on the Foster place, now Washington Dustin's, in 1808, and moved to some place in Vermont in the fall of 1815, beyond which we cannot trace him. He was collector and also constable of Antrim in 1809. Of his children we learn only this, though probably he had quite a family : —

1. DEBORAH, [m. Jesse McAllister April 20, 1815.]

DANIEL PAIGE, born in Hudson Nov. 14, 1777, came here about the same time as Ezekiel, and lived south of the pond in a pasture afterward Capt. Worthley's. There never was any road to this humble home. It has been gone many years. He married, in 1801, Elisabeth Robinson of this town, who died April 8, 1817, having had eight children and being thirty-seven years old. He married, second, Mrs. Sarah (Hartshorn) Riddle of Merrimack, and by her had four children. He died at Amoskeag, April 21, 1838. He moved from Antrim to Bedford about 1810, and the five oldest of the children were born here. They were : —

1. DANIEL, JR., [d. in infancy in 1803.]
2. REUBEN R., [b. in 1804, m. Mary Smith of Henniker, and d. at Beaver Dam, Wis., in 1873.]
3. SARAH R., [b. in 1806 ; m. Mark Dodge of Henniker; moved to Monticello, Io., and d. there in 1872.]

4. ELIZA, [b. in 1809; m. Simon Jenness of Bedford, and d. in that town in 1868.]
5. JOHN R., [b. in 1810; m. Mariam Elliot of Boscawen, and lives in Manchester.]
6. WARREN, [b. in 1812, m. Martha H. Roby of Merrimack, and d. in Manchester in 1868.]
7. HORACE C., [b. in 1814: m. Sarah W. Davis of Concord, Nov. 7, 1841; lives in Manchester; is surveyor of lumber on the corporations, and is a man worthy and highly esteemed.]
8. MARY H., [b. in 1816; m. Robert Sloan of Maine; went to Monticello, Io., and d. there.]
9. JERUSHA H., [b. in 1818; d. aged 10.]
10. HANNAH M., [b. in 1820; m. Frank Raymond of Hopkinton, and d. in that town.]
11. CLARISSA R., [b. in 1822; m. Benjamin Hartshorn of Manchester, and d. there in 1863.]
12. DANIEL, JR., [b. in 1824; d. in Amoskeag, aged 16.]

DAVID PAIGE came here probably somewhat later than Ezekiel and Daniel, and lived several years on the Isaac Brown place at the end of the road in what was called the "city." Later he lived on the Samuel Weeks place in the east part of the town, and perhaps in other places. He was in Stoddard from 1828 to 1835, in the east part of that town near Antrim line, where there is no house now. He married, first, ———, who died of spotted fever in March, 1812; second, Polly Witherspoon of Antrim, Dec. 11, 1812; third, it seems, a Mrs. Richardson, at one time of Peterborough. The last survived her husband, and died in Henniker. David Paige had a large family, of whom but little is known. The first wife left three children.

1. DAVID, JR., [went from here to Hudson.]
2. WILLIAM, [went to the Mormons and became a preacher among them.]
3. POLLY.
4. ACHSAH, [m. and d. in Nashua.]
5. HARRIET, [m. Joseph Copp.]
6. DUSTIN.
7. LOVISA.
8. HORACE, [lived awhile in Hillsborough.]

## PARKER.

WILLIAM PARKER, son of William Parker, came here in 1787, from Dracut, Mass. His father, then quite aged, came with him, and died here a few years after. He settled the farm now John Munhall's; went to the South Village in 1809, and tended the grist-mill many years. He married a Widow Harvey, had no children, and moved to Anson, Me., about 1820.

CAPT. ALEXANDER PARKER, long a selectman of Society Land and Greenfield, came here in his old age to live with his son David. He died here about 1815, aged about eighty-seven, and was buried, it is said, on the hill, though his wives lay elsewhere.

DAVID PARKER, son of Alexander and Nancy (Dickey) Parker of Litchfield, afterwards of Greenfield, and grandson of Alexander Parker, an emigrant from England to Nashua, was born in 1766; came here in 1792, and began the farm, now unoccupied, next south of the old Thomas Jameson place (George Butterfield's). The old house was burned in 1873. Mr. Parker married Martha Ramsay of Greenfield, and died at the age of eighty-eight, March 19, 1854. Their children were as follows : —

1. ALEXANDER, [b. June 8, 1795; was out in the war of 1812; m. Nancy Smith of Deering, April 13, 1824, and lived some years on the old farm; then lived some thirty years where Charles Appleton now lives, and d. in 1872. His fourteen children were as follows : —

*Harrison*, (b. Jan. 11, 1825, and d. in childhood.)
*Milton*, (b. Aug. 12, 1826, and d. in childhood. Harrison and Milton both d. in one day.)
*Capt. Allen*, (b. Jan. 13, 1828; m. Amorette Preston Nov. 1, 1848; lived on the old place and d. there, Nov. 29, 1857, being fatally injured by blasting rocks under his barn. He was captain of the grenadiers at the time of his death. His widow became second wife of David W. Bowman of Henniker, Nov. 17, 1874. The latter d. Nov. 8, 1877. Capt. Parker left four children, as follows : Ella J., who was b. Oct. 18, 1849, m. Enoch E. Jackson Aug. 29, 1877, but lived only two days; Charles, who was b. March 6, 1852; Lizzie L., who was b. April 17, 1854; and Georgia A., who was b. June 17, 1857.)
*Judson*, (b. March 15, 1829; m. Elizabeth McColley, and lives in St. Paul, Minn., being mail agent between that place and Chicago.)
*Nancy J.*, (b. Oct. 8, 1830; m. Charles Appleton, Dec. 17, 1850.)
*Margaret A.*, (b. Jan. 13, 1833; m. Albert Fisher; moved to Weare, and d. May 30, 1859.)

*Mary S.*, (b. April 24, 1834, and d. Oct. 30, 1860.)

*Sarah M.*, (b. May 29, 1835; m. James H. Favor, and lives in California.)

*Milton*, (b. June 2, 1838; went to California many years ago and is supposed to be dead.)

*Almira*, (b. Dec. 21, 1839; m. William Brandon, and lives in Champlain, Minn.)

*Mindwell*, (d. in childhood.)

*Ruhama*, (b. Feb. 16, 1841; d. at age of 20.)

*Alfred*, (b. June 13, 1844; now lives in the West.)

*Eben*, (b. May 12, 1846; lives in Texas.)]

2. MARTHA, [b. Dec. 1, 1796; m. William Carr.]
3. JANE, [b. June 30, 1802; d. unm. aged 35.]
4. LINN, [twin-brother of Jane; m. Ruth Holden of Orange, Mass., June 23, 1835, and moved on to the Stephen Woodbury place. The children are: —

*Edward E.*, (b. March 26, 1838; m. Mary Ballard of Ware, Mass., and d. there Sept. 17, 1874, aged 36.)

*Helen A.*, (b. Aug. 15, 1841; m. Henry A. Waite, and lives in Greenfield.)

*Abbie J.*, (b. Sept. 2, 1847; d. May 24, 1878.)

*Emma A.*, (b. Dec. 23, 1849, and d. Nov. 5, 1869.)]

5. EBENEZER. [b. July 18, 1804; m. Deborah Robinson, and lives in Charlestown, Mass.]
6. ALMIRA, [b. April 8, 1806; m. Alvah White; went to Francestown, and d. there Dec. 21, 1838.]

NATHANIEL PARKER, the only colored man in town, son of Cæsar and Margaret (Spear) Parker, was born in Weare in 1802, and came here at the age of seven to live with David McCauley. He has lived in Antrim most of the time since; has never married; is a kind, industrious, and smart man, whose memory has been of great service in preparing this book.

JONAS PARKER and his sister Lydia, simple-minded and amiable souls, came here from Methuen, Mass., about 1810, and lived in a small house, opposite the town-house, where a store had formerly been kept by Robert Butler, and both died there very aged. They were cared for by the neighbors with great kindness, being invited here and there in turn, and always having the best of Thanksgiving dinners, — all of which exhibited a most commendable trait of character in the people, which trait is very apt to show itself among them to this day! After their death the house stood empty, and out of repair; and as no one seemed to have any business with it, one moony night the boys quietly took it to pieces and piled it up. Nobody appeared to hear the sound or know anything about it; and if any inquiry was made as to who did it, the answer always was, "Dr. Whiton and Mr. Pratt!" The latter was an aged invalid at the time, and the former the minister of the town!

LUTHER C. PARKER, son of William and Susanna Parker, came here from Groton, Mass., on to the William Parker place (Munhall's); married Relief Bowers of Hancock; died Aug. 21, 1824, aged thirty-eight. His wife died Feb. 12, 1843, aged fifty-one. Had children:—

1. JOHN, [m. Cynthia Bullard, Jan. 13, 1841; lived in many places in town; d. June 11, 1874, aged 60. His wife d. May 21, 1872, aged 70. They had children:—
*Melissa*, (d. March 1, 1873, aged 29.)
*Martha E.*, (d. Nov. 23, 1861, aged 16.)]
2. MARY A., [m. Dexter Symonds; d. in Lowell, March 18, 1855.]
3. LUTHER, [d. unm. in early life.]

OREN D. PARKER, son of Silas and Alvira (Keyes) Parker, came here from Hillsborough; married Elisabeth A. Webster; lived in several places in town, and then moved to Stoddard Box, and died there in 1862, aged thirty-two. His children were all born in this town, and were as follows:—

1. CARRIE E., [b. Oct. 26, 1851; m. G. F. Crowell of Hillsborough, who is now a druggist in Indianapolis, Ind.]
2. LUVA A., [b. Feb. 24, 1853; m. Andrew S. Mack, and lives in Rice county, Kan.]
3. CHARLES C., [b. Jan. 17, 1860; now lives in Windsor.]
4. EDDIE O., [b. June 7, 1861; now lives in Antrim, Minn.]

## PARKHURST.

DANIEL J. PARKHURST, son of Luke and Laurana (Priest) Parkhurst of Troy (part formerly Marlborough), and grandson of Josiah and Nancy (Jones) Parkhurst, was born in 1833. The family came from Framingham, Mass. He was taken to Fitzwilliam to live at the age of fourteen years; married Ellen M. Rugg in 1853, and came here in 1873, and bought the Wallace mills at the Branch. These he has enlarged, repaired, and improved, and filled with new machinery. Is every inch a driving, live man. Employs five or six men, and does a smart business in sawing lumber, manufacturing shingles, staves, pail-handles, etc., etc. His wife died Jan. 23, 1876. She was amiable, smart, and universally loved. He married, second, Margaret J. Wood of Antrim, Feb. 20, 1879. He has one child:—

1. FRANK L., [b. May 12, 1855; m. Sina M. Carr; is in company with his father in manufacturing.]

## PARKINSON.

REV. ROYAL PARKINSON lived on the farm now Franklin Robinson's through most of the year 1855. He was son of Robert and Elizabeth (Kelso) Parkinson, and grandson of Henry and —— (McCurdy) Parkinson, and was born in Columbia Nov. 8, 1815; was brother of Hon. Henry Parkinson, county commissioner, recently killed by the cars in Nashua; was graduated at Dartmouth College in 1842; at Andover Theological Seminary in 1847; ordained over Congregational Church in Cape Elizabeth, Me., Oct. 18, 1848; married Joanna Griffin of Brunswick, Me., Nov. 21, 1848; came here in feeble health, but after partial recovery had a call to West Falmouth, Me., whither he went from Antrim; and was afterwards for years pastor at Randolph, Vt. He had a family of six sons, but buried two from scarlet fever in Falmouth in 1858. The others were : —

1. JOSEPH G., [b. in Cape Elizabeth, Me., Aug. 10, 1849; lost hearing by scarlet fever; graduated at the National Deaf-Mute College, Washington, D. C., in 1869; went into Patent Office and was promoted to a chief-examinership; is now a lawyer in Washington; received degree of A. M. from Dartmouth College in 1873.]
2. ROBERT H., [twin-brother of Joseph; graduated at Dartmouth College in 1870; is law-partner of his brother Joseph in Washington.]
3. GEORGE B., [b. in Nashua, March 5, 1852; graduated at Dartmouth College in 1875; is now a lawyer in Boston.]
4. WILLIAM D., [b. in Falmouth. Me., Aug. 10, 1857; graduated at Dartmouth College in 1878; is law-student in Nashua.]

## PARMENTER.

The name Parmenter signifies "a mountaineer." They were French Huguenots, and fled to England in 1520 to escape massacre. John Parmenter (whose father John came over with him) came from England in 1635, and became one of the first proprietors of Framingham, Mass. He had a son George, who married Hannah Johnson, and died in 1727. Amos, son of this George, married Mary Wood in 1715, and, besides other children, had a son Phinehas, who was born in 1717, married Zebulah Parmenter, and *they* had but one child, Amos, born in 1736, who was the father of Dea. Amos Parmenter of Antrim.

DEA. AMOS PARMENTER, son of Amos and Mary (Berry) Parmenter, was born in Framingham, Mass., in 1769. (The town records of Framingham show that he was four years older than his tombstone indicates.) He married, first, Tryphena Bannister of Framingham in 1798, and came from that place to Antrim in 1800. He had great difficulty in finding the town, then called in common talk " Enterum," a pronunciation not yet dead. He traveled several miles northwest of Antrim, was displeased with the land, and was on his return home; but, on being told again of this township, he turned back and bought twenty-five acres on the spot now owned by his son, George F. Parmenter, on which there was then a small house in the corner of the field northwest of the present house, which seems to have been built and occupied some years by Taylor Joslin. The rest of his large farm he subsequently bought and cleared. His wife died Feb. 2, 1818, aged thirty-six, and he married, second, Mrs. Hannah Heald of Carlyle, Mass., in 1821. In 1827 he built the brick house; was appointed deacon in the Presbyterian Church in 1825. He was a live, wide-awake man, doing business for other people constantly, and filling many important places during his long life. Held all the offices the town could confer. His second wife died Dec. 29, 1859, aged eighty-six, and he survived her, dying Aug. 15, 1865, as easy as a child drops to sleep. Thus he entered on his ninety-seventh year. His children, all by the first wife, were : —

1. NANCY, [b. in Framingham, Sept. 21, 1798 ; m. Isaac Proctor April 22, 1828 ; settled in Bennington, where she d. in June, 1880.]
2. PRESCOTT, [b. April 26, 1800 ; m. Nancy Smith of Providence, R. I., and followed the sea many years, but finally settled on the Cram place, where he d. Nov. 24, 1868. His widow d. Aug. 22, 1872, aged 71. They left but one child : —

*Charles H.*, (m. Jennie E. Haskins ; lives in San Francisco.)]
3. LUKE, [b. March 1, 1802, m. Mary A. Pitcher, and d. at the age of 26, leaving one daughter who is a resident of Rhode Island.]
4. JOHN S., [b. Jan. 18, 1804, and in early life worked as a harness-maker in Canada ; m. 1st, Eliza Muzzey of Weare, June 20, 1829, and moved into the house at the Center where he d., which was the old Paige house, moved and fitted up by him, with harness-shop beneath, about 1829. His wife d. Nov. 29, 1831, aged 22. He m. 2d, Caroline E. Tenney, April 5, 1832. She was found dead in her bed Dec. 31, 1867, and in the fall of 1868 Mr. Parmenter m. 3d, Mrs. Ruth E., widow of Erastus W. R. Huntley. Mr. Parmenter was a very genial, agreeable man, an excellent singer, and member of the Center choir nearly forty years. He was also sexton of the Center church many years, a member of the same, and his smiling face and gentlemanly bearing will long be remembered. He d. May 3, 1874, after a long and distressing illness, in Christian peace and hope. His

children were as follows, the eldest being the child of his first wife, and the others by his second wife: —

*Eliza A.*, (b. June 12, 1831; m. John Moor Duncan of Antrim, Dec. 16, 1851.)

*Amos*, (d. at the age of 7.)

*Martin L.*, (b. October, 1836; m. Edna S. Munroe of Washington; was in the army, and d. in service Jan. 11, 1863, leaving one son, Frank M., b. in East Washington May 20, 1862. The widow m. Lyman Cram and now lives in Marlow.)

*Mary C.*, (b. March 9, 1840, m. Dr. Levi J. Pierce Feb. 19, 1861, and d. very suddenly April 15, 1863.)

*Dr. Amos Irving*, (b. Aug. 17, 1841; was in a drug-store at ———, several years; during the war was steward in a hospital, and soon after commenced the practice of medicine in Winchester, where he remained until failing health compelled him to come home to die. He d. Aug. 17, 1868, aged 27.)

*Edwin A.*, (b. Sept. 7, 1846; m. Mary S. Pierce of Winchester, June 26, 1877; is a merchant in Fitchburg, Mass.)

*Fred C.*, (b. July 4, 1849. Was a merchant-tailor with store in Antrim for a time.)]

5. LAWSON, [b. Dec. 8, 1805: d. in infancy.]
6. CHARLES A., [b. March 10, 1807; m. Mary Barnes of Greenfield, and moved to Bunker Hill, Ill.]
7. HORACE, [b. Dec. 13, 1808; m. Betsey Glover of Leominster, Mass., and resides in Lowell.]
8. GEORGE F., [b. July 4, 1810; m. Lucinda F. Green of Pittsfield, May 15, 1835; lived some years in Dover; moved on to the old homestead in 1844, which he still retains in thrift and vigor. He is a seventh-son doctor, going far and near for many years, and credited with many cures. Their children are all dead save one, and in their repeated afflictions they have the sympathy of the whole community.

*Olive*, (b. Jan. 18, 1836; d. Sept. 10, 1838.)

*Charles F.*, (b. Aug. 23, 1838; d. in the army, at New Orleans, La., Feb. 12, 1863, and brought home for burial.)

*Mary Tryphena*, (b. July 16, 1840; became second wife of Theodore Graves of Boston, Jan. 16, 1866, where she d. Sept. 3, 1868. Katie A. Graves, b. in 1863, a daughter of Mr. Graves by his first wife, has lived with George F. Parmenter since the death of her step-mother, loved and cared for as an own child.)

*Harriet E.*, (b. March 3, 1842, m. Dea. Enoch C. Paige Feb. 21, 1861, and d. Feb. 6, 1879.)

*Abbie L.*, (b. Dec. 7, 1846; m. Bill Butterfield.)

*Ann M.*, (b. June 5, 1850; d. in infancy.)]

9. ALMIRA, [b. April 16, 1812, m. Daniel Story Sept. 24, 1835, and d. July 25, 1846.]
10. GARDINER, [b. Jan. 18, 1814; m. Mary A. Huggins of Newport, and went to Bunker Hill, Ill.; was one of the donors of the Center vestry. Is a furniture-dealer, and is a leading man in that place.]
11. HARRIET, [b. July 24, 1815, m. Dimon Twiss Oct. 30, 1834, and d. Dec. 2, 1844.]
12. TRYPHENA, [b. Feb. 11, 1818; d. Dec. 6, 1818.]

## PARSONS.

DR. WILLIAM M. PARSONS was son of Josiah and Judith (Badger) Parsons of Gilmanton, and grandson of Abraham and Abigail (Burleigh) Parsons of Newmarket, and was born in Gilmanton Dec. 30, 1825. Judith Badger was sister of Gov. Badger of this State. Dr. William, or, as he was known in all this section, "Dr. Bill," studied at Gilmanton Academy, and with his brother, "Dr. Jo," and subsequently attended medical lectures at Dartmouth College, and at Woodstock, Vt., and was graduated at the latter place in 1851. Came to Antrim and established himself in practice in 1855, and continued in the same for about fifteen years, when he went West. Is now in practice in Manchester. Was reputed an excellent and skillful physician, and in difficult cases was called long distances into other towns. Dr. Joseph Parsons, brother of Dr. William, practiced in Bennington and Hillsborough, had a very marked reputation, is spoken of as holding the highest rank in his profession, and died Sept. 2, 1859, aged thirty-nine. Another brother is Hon. Daniel Parsons, a lawyer of Rochester. Another brother, Prof. Chase Parsons, has just died in Evansville, Ind. A sister, Emily Parsons, is the wife of Rev. Dr. Charles Tenney of Chester. Another sister, Elisabeth Parsons, married Rev. E. N. Hidden, formerly of Milford.

## PATCH.

DAVID A. PATCH, son of Asa and Elizabeth (Averill) Patch, was born in Westfield, Mass., in 1783; married Susannah Parker of Groton, Mass., in 1804, and came here in 1815, bringing with him five children. He was a carpenter, and lived a few years in the McFarland house, then in the old Knights house, moved to Deering in 1820, and died in Lowell, Mass., in 1839. His children, of whom little can be ascertained, were as follows: —

1. SUSAN C., [b. in Charlestown, Mass.]
2. DAVID, [b. in Charlestown, Mass.]
3. WILLIAM, [b. in Jaffrey.]
4. ELISABETH, [b. in Jaffrey.]
5. CAROLINE, [b. in Jaffrey.]
6. MARY JANE, [b. in Antrim in 1818, m. James M. Hopkins in 1836, and d. in Mont Vernon in 1863.]
7. ISRAEL B., [b. in Deering, m. Susan H. Whittemore in 1839, went to Milford, and d. in California in 1852.]
8. FANNIE B., [b. in Deering; m. John W. Hutchinson in Milford in 1843, one of the famous Hutchinson singers.]
9. MARTHA A., [b. in Deering, m. Joseph C. Duncklee, and d. in Boston in 1865.]
10. LOUISA M., [b. in Deering, m. Samuel Gould, and d. in Boston in 1869.]

## PATTEE.

HON. LEMUEL N. PATTEE, son of Peter and Polly (Merrill) Pattee of Goffstown, and grandson of John and Hannah (Hadley) Pattee, was born in that town Feb. 5, 1804; married Vashti Little in 1827. They had only one child, Mary F., born May 29, 1828, who graduated at the New Hampton Seminary, and married John B. Woodbury, March 6, 1849, and died Oct. 15, 1858, leaving three children, whose names are given under the Woodbury family. Mr. Pattee was appointed register of probate in 1841 for Hillsborough County, and held the office ten years, residing at this time in Amherst. He then removed to Antrim. Was moderator here for four March meetings; was representative for Antrim in 1855, 1859, and 1860; was secretary of state for New Hampshire in 1853, 1854, and 1855. He moved back to Goffstown in 1861, and died April 1, 1871.

## PATTEN.

SAMUEL PATTEN, son of Samuel and Mary (Bell) Patten, and grandson of John Patten who came from Ireland in 1728, and nephew of Hon. Matthew Patten, who was appointed probate judge of this county in 1776, was born in Bedford in 1752; married Deborah Moore, and came here with two children in 1780. He cleared and settled on the top of the hill that bears his name. Was known as "Capt. Patten." Was occasionally in town office, and moved to the State of Maine in 1800, to the general regret of the community. Every mark of his old home save the cellar and rocks is now gone. Capt. Patten died in Norridgewock, Me., in 1809, and his widow died in 1815. Their children, all born in Antrim except the two oldest, were: —

1. JOHN, [b. Feb. 6, 1778, m. Betsey Hilton of Embden, Me., and d. in 1860.]

2. JENNIE, [b. Nov. 26, 1779 ; d. at the age of 16, and was buried on the hill.]
3. JOSEPH, [b. Nov. 8, 1781 ; m. Joanna Harlow, daughter of Rev. John Harlow of Norridgewock, Me. ; was a merchant, and was a conspicuous and devoted citizen. He d. in 1858 in Skowhegan, Me.]
4. MARGARET, [b. Nov. 9, 1783 ; d. at the age of 16, and was buried on the hill.]
5. DEBORAH, [b. Nov. 19, 1785 ; m. John Dinsmore of Norridgewock, Me., in 1802, who was clerk of county court twenty years. She d. in 1862.]
6. SARAH, [b. May 6, 1788, m. Rev. Moses French of Solon, Me., and d. in 1852.]
7. MARY, [b. April 28, 1790, m. Dr. David Raymond of Skowhegan, Me., and d. in 1842.]
8. OLIVE, [b. April 16, 1792 ; m. Daniel Stewart, a merchant of Anson, Me., and d. in 1868.]
9. ALICE, [b. July 30, 1795 ; m. her cousin Goffe Moor ; d. in Anson, Me., in 1842.]
10. SAMUEL, [b. Dec. 12, 1797 ; m. Betsey Savage of Anson, Me., and went West.]

## PATTERSON.

ISAAC PATTERSON was one of the early settlers of Antrim, of whom we know not whence he came or whither he went. He was a Revolutionary soldier, and the town voted to clear his land in August, 1782. He came here some years before that date. He lived on the west side of the road just below James Wood's in 1783, afterwards in the west part of the town, and moved away near the close of the century. The town records give the following: "Isaac Patterson and Mary Nelson published Aug. 25, 1788." He had a farm of fifty acres, which passed into the hands of William Houston, and is now owned chiefly by James Wood.

## PEABODY.

CAPT. DAVID PEABODY, a connection of George Peabody the banker, was born in Boxford, Mass.; married Phœbe Andrews, and came here in his old age, about 1802, from Hudson, to live with his granddaughter, Mrs. David Hill, on the Frank Robinson place, and died there in 1806, aged seventy-two. His wife followed in 1807, aged seventy-five.

JOHN PEABODY, son of Dea. Isaac and Mary (Dodge) Peabody of New Boston (and grandson of Francis Peabody of New Boston, whose grandfather Francis came to this country from Wales, England, in 1735, and settled in Topsfield, Mass., where he erected mills which are still in possession of his descendants), was born in New Boston in 1803; married Mary Hopkins of Antrim, Dec. 31, 1829; came here in 1838, and lived awhile on the William Wilkins place, then in the Jedediah Tuttle house on the old road near Samuel Dinsmore's, and still later in the old Herrick house. He helped John Robb build the mills in 1839, bought them in 1850, and built the present grist-mill about the same time, on nearly the same spot where an old one built by Herrick once stood. He was a prominent and devoted man, and died in 1865, leaving children: —

1. JOHN D., [b. in 1831; m. Ann Green and went West, but after some years came on to visit in poor health, and d. here in 1869.]
2. NANCY J., [b. May 1, 1833; became second wife of Josiah Loveren, Dec. 18, 1856.]
3. SATIRA, [b. in 1835, m. John Burnham of Contoocook, and d. in 1869.]
4. MARY E., [b. June 14, 1838, in Antrim; m. Alonzo Rand, and lives in Portsmouth.]
5. MILES, [b. July 18, 1840; d in the army in 1864.]
6. GEORGE H., [b. Nov. 3. 1842; d. in 1863.]
7. HIRAM G., [b. May 25, 1845; m. Effie Gardiner of Medybemps, Me., and went to Wisconsin; returned after several years, and now lives near Loveren's mills.]

## PELSEY.

FREEMAN PELSEY, son of Isaiah and Belinda (Curtis) Pelsey, and grandson of Oliver and Betsey (Wright) Pelsey of Chelmsford, Mass., was born in Windsor in 1833; married Laura C. Gilbert of Turner, Me.; came from Windsor to Antrim in 1873, and bought the Brackett place (house built by Woodburn Wallace). His children are: —

1. WILLIS E., [b. Aug. 15, 1870.]
2. ELWIN A., [b. May 20, 1872.]
3. FRED G., [b. Dec. 22, 1873.]
4. LEROY F., [b. April 20, 1876.]

## PERKINS.

ZACCHEUS PERKINS cleared and settled the Dea. Robert Duncan place, not far from 1790. He was here and well established in 1793. But whence he came, or whither he went, we have no means of knowing.

DEA. JAMES WARREN PERKINS was son of James and Hannah (Preston) Perkins, and grandson of David and Mehitable (Swett) Perkins of Epping, and was born in Windsor, Nov. 1, 1821. In early life he followed the sea some years, returning in August, 1840. He married, first, Mary J. Somes of Chelsea, Mass., who died Aug. 25, 1851; second,

Aurilla W. Stacey, Oct. 31, 1852. Came here from Windsor on to the Dea. Robert Duncan place in 1862. Built the new house in 1868. Is deacon of the Presbyterian Church. Has two children: —

1. MARY M., [b. Sept. 16, 1849; m. Charles Banfield of Boston, and now resides in that city.]
2. JAMES ELROE, [b. Sept. 23, 1858.]

GEORGE H. PERKINS, son of Charles and Betsey (Griffin) Perkins, was born in East Wilton, Oct. 15, 1852; m. Ella E. Little; has one child, Carlton W., born Sept. 30, 1875.

JOHN BLAISDELL PERKINS, son of Alvin T. and Eliza A. (Savilles) Perkins of Gardiner, Me., and grandson of Jonathan and Susan (Manwell) Perkins of Wakefield, was born in Lexington, Mass., Aug. 8, 1853. His father was a druggist and chemist, and died June 23, 1862. Came here in the spring of 1872, to live with Moody B. McIlvaine, making his home there some years. Is now a clerk in Boston. Was in trade for a time in Mont Vernon.

## PERRY.

GATES PERRY, son of Joseph and Sarah (Pollard) Perry, was born in Greenfield in 1777. He married Mary Fletcher of that town and resided there for a time; lived awhile in Hancock; came here in the fall of 1805 and bought the Aiken place in South Village. After a residence here of two years he sold and moved to Saxton's River, Vt., where he died in 1858. Most of his large family married and settled around him in the last-named place, and are wealthy and respectable people. His children's names were Mary, Gates, Jr., Clarissa, George, Fletcher, Sophronia, Persis A., and Sarah Jane, none of whom were born here. It may be added that his father, Joseph Perry, had four children: Gates, Eunice, Franklin, and Crucia. Franklin died Oct. 29, 1825, aged forty-one; and his wife, Anna Straw, died here March 1, 1872, aged eighty-one.

FRANKLIN PERRY, nephew of Gates, son of Franklin and Anna (Straw) Perry, and grandson of Joseph and Sarah (Pollard) Perry of Greenfield, was born in that town Nov. 18, 1810. He married Deidamia White of Peterborough, April 24, 1833, and settled in Bedford. Subsequently he lived awhile in Goffstown, and in Saxton's River, Vt. He came here on to the Dea. Steele place in 1862, and still occupies the same. The house, built in 1822, he has enlarged and repaired, has built over the barns, and has made many improvements on that excellent farm. They have had but two children, now both gone from earth. At a later day it is added that Mr. Perry died Sept. 4, 1880.

1. NEWTON, [b. in Bedford, Aug. 2, 1835; m. Sara E. D. Joy of Putney, Vt., April 18, 1858; lived on the farm with his father; was a superior carpenter and builder; was a trust-

worthy and good man ; d. with consumption, Oct. 15, 1871. Left two children : —

*George F.*, (b. March 11, 1860, in Westminster, Vt.)

*Nellie S.*, (b. in Antrim, Feb. 11, 1869 ; d. Jan. 13, 1873.)]

2. SOPHRONIA J., [b. in Goffstown, July 31, 1842 ; d. in Chester, Vt., Oct. 22, 1865. She was a rare and beautiful girl, remembered with great affection by all who knew her, and leaving her parents in almost inconsolable sorrow.]

## PETTINGILL.

JOHN PETTINGILL came here from Methuen, Mass., about 1830; married Sarah, daughter of John and Jean Stuart, and lived in a house opposite George Thompson's till the death of his wife in 1855. The old house, after being occupied by several families, was taken down in 1868. Two sons, named Elbridge and William, both went to sea quite young and never came back to this town. Mr. Pettingill died in 1870. The sons were seen on shipboard in the Pacific ocean by Dea. Perkins in 1840.

EZRA PETTINGILL, son of Herman and Hannah (Frye) Pettingill, was born in Wilton in 1827; came to Antrim in 1868; married Phœbe, daughter of John R. Hills, Nov. 21, 1870, and lives on the old Woodbury stand at South Village. He was a stage-driver most of the time for thirty years. Mrs. Pettingill died Oct. 26, 1874.

## PHILBRICK.

WILLIAM PHILBRICK came here from New London (or near there), built the Atwood house, and married Ann Keyes March 27, 1834. He soon returned to his former abode, but afterwards came here again with a large family, and built the house now Charles Barrett's. He lost two sons in the army, and drew a pension. In 1866 he moved back to the town from which he came, and died in 1875. His children were : —

1. WILLIAM K., [was a member of the Second N. H. Regiment; was severely wounded July 2, 1863 ; was discharged, and re-enlisted. He was promoted to corporal Jan. 1, 1865, and served till the close of the war. He now lives in Sutton.]
2. CYRUS, [d. in the army.]
3. GEORGE, [was killed in the battle of Fair Oaks.]
4. MARY A., [m. Benjamin Fisk of Sutton, and d. in 1870.]
5. ELVIRA, [m. George Sanders, and d. about the same time as her sister.]

CALEB PHILBRICK, a mere sojourner, was here several years; lived in an old house, now gone, at what is called "Butler's Crossing," on the Keene road, and moved to Harrisville in 1865. He had one son who enlisted in the army from this town : —

GENEALOGIES.                                                                 645

1. REUBEN C., [enlisted in the Fifth Regiment.]

NATHANIEL PHILBRICK, brother of Caleb, married Mary R. Moore, and lived in Antrim a short time, and moved to Harrisville. Now lives in Henniker. He had two children born here: —

1. HATCH, [d. aged 17.]
2. LUCY B.

## PIERCE.

JAMES PIERCE (son of Joshua Pierce, who was born in 1722 and died in 1771, and Esther Richardson, who was born in 1727 and died in 1819) was born in 1768; married Molly Stacey; came here from Hudson in 1791 and built a house on the hill west of the Capt. John Worthley place, west of the pond. The house has been gone many years, being occupied by various transient parties after Mr. Pierce left it. He moved to Swanzey in 1796, where he died in 1849. His children were: —

1. ALVAH, [b. in 1795; m. Leafy Miller; settled in Bellows Falls, and d. there in 1869.]
2. AVERY, [d. in infancy.]
3. POLLY, [b. in 1799, m. Solomon Fields of Winchester, and d. in 1837.]
4. DANIEL, [b. in 1801, m. Ursula Caldwell, and d. in Bolton, Mass., in 1874.]
5. ENOCH C., [b. in 1803; d. at the age of 12.]
6. SARAH C., [b. in 1806, m. Charles Green, and d. in Swanzey in 1876.]
7. NANCY, [b. in 1808; d. unm. in 1853.]
8. JAMES, JR., [b. in 1810, m. Chloe Holbrook in 1839, and d. near Sharpsville, Penn., in 1874.]
9. WILLIAM, [b. in 1813; m. Martha M. Whitcomb in 1844, and lives at Empire Prairie, Mo.]

DR. LEVI J. PIERCE, son of Dr. Levi Pierce, took his medical degree in Philadelphia; came here from Francestown in 1859; married Mary C. Parmenter Feb. 19, 1861, and commenced practice in South Village, but sold out to Dr. Christie and went to Keene early in the year 1863, and was planning to move there when he died suddenly of diphtheria April 8, 1863, aged twenty-seven. His wife died of the same disease one week later, aged twenty-three. They were buried together in Maplewood cemetery.

NATHAN PIERCE, a cousin or near kinsman of Gov. Benjamin Pierce, was a native of Hudson, — born near the spot called "Indian Head." He married Phebe Cummings of that town, and moved to Hillsborough, where he lived many years. In 1816 he came here and bought the Dea. Arthur Nesmith place, now Luther Campbell's. He remained here only two years, selling out to Dimon Twiss and moving to Bradford, where he died in 1851, aged eighty-eight. His wife died there in 1860, aged ninety-two. Six children came here with them and moved away with them.

1. NATHAN, JR., [m. Abigail Graves of East Washington; d. in Bradford in 1875, aged 85.]
2. MARY, [d. unm. in Bradford in 1863, aged 77.]
3. SUSAN, [m. Enos Collins of Warner; d. in Warner in 1873, aged 76.]
4. DANIEL, [m. Lucy Wheelock ; d. in Eden, Vt., 1848.]
5. CUMMINGS. [m. Caroline Dowlin ; now living in Bradford.]
6. STEPHEN C., [m. Martha Collins ; lives in Warner.]

## PIKE.

AMMI R. C. PIKE, son of Ebenezer and Catherine (Seward) Pike, of English descent, was born in Portsmouth, Dec. 1, 1820; married Margaret W. Gregg in Boston. Oct. 30, 1844. She was a daughter of David Gregg of this town. He was long engaged in the manufacture of fancy goods; came to Antrim in 1851, built his house in 1854, and in recent years has been in the shop with Daniel Story. His children are:—

1. ELLA M., [b. July 21, 1845.]
2. A. LINCOLN, [b. Sept. 25, 1847.]
3. JOHN L., [b. Aug. 15, 1849.]
4. EMILY M., [b. Feb. 25, 1851.]
5. OTIS, [b. June 22, 1854.]
6. CLARRIE K., [b. Aug. 19, 1856.]
7. CLIFTON, [b. July 3, 1862 ; d. at the age of 3 years.]

## POLAND.

CHARLES H. POLAND, son of Rev. J. W. and Sarah (Ayer) Poland of Goffstown, was born in 1847, and came here in 1872. His father was for a long time pastor of the Baptist Church at Goffstown Center, and has been long known as the inventor of valuable patent medicines. In 1873 Charles H. married Martha M. Morse, from one of the best families of Methuen, Mass. One child, James, was born here March 18, 1875. They moved to Providence, R. I., in 1876. While here he was clerk of the Goodell Company, and afterwards for a time a traveling salesman for the same.

## POOR.

FREDERICK POOR was son of Abraham and Hannah (Parker) Poor, and grandson of Thomas and Mary Poor. The first in the family in America was Daniel Poor, one of the first settlers of Andover, Mass.

Abraham was born Feb. 23, 1742. Frederick came here from Andover, Mass., where he was born. He came about 1800, and after a time bought the old Starrett house and tannery in South Village. He carried on the tannery business at the old stand till about 1816, when he sold to George Duncan. Then he began the establishment now Thomas Poor's. At that time it was a most uninviting collection of underbrush and rocks. Mr. Poor started at great expense, involving him in debt; and the loss and depression in business were too much for him, and under pressure of debt he went off to Canada. He died in Ogdensburg, N. Y., in 1841, aged sixty-one. His wife, Mercy Barber of Peterborough, died Feb. 13, 1875, aged ninety-three. Their eight children were all born here except the oldest, of whose place of birth we are not positive.

1. PRUDENCE, [m. Hezekiah Ober; lived in Bennington till his death, afterwards in Peterborough. She d. in 1877, aged 76.]
2. MARIA, [b. in 1804; became 2d wife of Dea. John Vose in 1832, who d. in Peterborough in 1867, and she now resides, a widow, in that place.]
3. CHARLES, [b. in 1806; m. Hepsibeth Hills in 1832, and lives in Depuyster, N. Y.]
4. LOISY, [probably "Louisa," b. in 1808; d. young.]
5. FREDERICK, JR., [b. in 1815; m. Eliza B. Ingalls in 1841; lives in Preble, N. Y.]
6. FRANCIS, [d. aged 19.]
7. LUCY, [d. in childhood.]
8. ELISABETH, [b. in 1819; m. Edwin Hardy of Nashua; d. in 1848.]

STEPHEN POOR, an older brother of Frederick, was born in Andover, Mass., Feb. 13, 1771; married Ruth Davis of New Ipswich; was a long time a tanner in Hancock; came here in 1823 and bought at auction the tannery his brother had left, standing between the present grist-mill and the house. Stephen built the saw and grist mill in 1825; sold to his son Thomas in 1828, and went West. He died March 16, 1842, in Cuba, N. Y. None of his children were born here. Their names were Stephen B., Mary, Thomas, Franklin, Oliver L., Elaezar M., Elisabeth, Stephen B., and Mary. The two last named were children of a third wife in Cuba, N. Y., the others of the same name having previously died. The second wife was Phebe Parker, who had no children.

THOMAS POOR, son of Stephen and Ruth (Davis) Poor, was born in Hancock, Dec. 16, 1800. He married Roxan Colby of Bennington, Sept. 16, 1830. Bought the saw and grist mill, tannery, and house of his father; built the present house in 1833. Carried on tanning business till March 18, 1858, when the tannery and all the mills were burned. Rebuilt the saw and grist mill the same year. He put up a large building opposite his dwelling-house in 1835 for the manufacture of patent leather, but this was burned March 9 of the next year. He rebuilt this in 1837, and used it for making patent leather several years. It was finished into a tenement-house in 1861. He has but two children living.

1. MELVIN. [b. Jan. 24, 1832; m. Elsie J. Felch of Henniker, Jan. 18, 1878.]
2. FRANKLIN, [b. July 28, 1836; d. Jan. 20, 1856.]
3. LUELLA, [d. in infancy, Jan. 25, 1846.]
4. ALBERT M., [b. April 12, 1847; m. Emma J. Smith, Jan. 19, 1875.]

OLIVER L. POOR, brother of Thomas, was born in Hancock Oct. 12, 1805, and came here with his father in 1823. He went from town in 1830; married, June 5, 1832, Mary Jane Taylor of Bennington, afterwards of Cuba, N. Y., who died Jan. 25, 1865. He now lives in Jefferson, Io. Children: —

1. FRANCES E., [b. Jan. 4, 1834; m. Henry L. Powell; lives in Glidden, Io.]
2. JOHN M., [b. Oct. 11, 1835; m. Josie Morse of Hartford, Conn., in 1867; lives in Centreville, Io.]
3. MARY J., [b. Oct. 18, 1837, in Cuba, N. Y., and d. there in 1841.]
4. LAWRENCE M., [b. Dec. 15, 1839; m. Lottie Bell; lives in Deloit, Io.]
5. MARY JANE, [b. July 4, 1842; m. Francis A. Benjamin of Hamburg, N. Y.; d. Feb. 25, 1868.]
6. JULIA E., [b. Jan. 1, 1849; m. Will Bracken; lives in Tama, Io.]

## POND.

GEORGE M. POND, son of James W. and Electa J. Pond, was born in Bennington, June 13, 1851. Came to Antrim in April, 1872; married Mary C. Miller June 13 of the same year, and died Sept. 14, 1873. Their child, Minnie M., was born Oct. 26, 1873. His widow married Aaron Pearson of Boston, March 7, 1877, and now resides in that city.

## POTTER.

SAMUEL POTTER came from England with two brothers, one of whom was a captain and lost at sea, and the other went South and soon died. In early life he was for several years a ship's mate at sea. He came to Antrim from Goffstown in 1796, and lived with his family on the Stephen Butterfield farm, now Grosvenor Wilkins's. In the dysentery of 1800, he lost all his children, and never had any more. He moved to

Henniker in 1803, where his wife, Mary, died in 1831. He lived alone three years, and then went to Goffstown and died at the house of Mrs. William Sargent; was buried in Goffstown, and the inscription on his tombstone says he was a Revolutionary soldier and died Jan. 22. 1839, aged eighty-eight years. He was highly respected here as a quiet and good man.

## PRATT.

John and Rebecca Pratt of Medfield, Mass., had a son John, who was a blacksmith in that town. This second John was born in 1665; his wife's name was Sarah; and he had a son Timothy, born in 1702, who married Tabitha Boutwell and was father of Isaac Pratt.

WILLIAM PRATT, son of Isaac and Mehitable (Nichols) Pratt of Reading, Mass., was born in 1770; came here on to the E. L. Vose place in 1816; married, first, Betsey Flint of North Reading, Mass., who died in 1818, aged forty-five; married, second, Joanna Holden of Tyngsborough, Mass., who died in 1842, aged sixty-eight. He is remembered for his extreme oddities. He died May 6, 1845, aged seventy-five. His children were as follows: —

1. OLIVE, [m. Enoch Kellogg; went to Michigan and d. there.]
2. DR. GARLAN F., [m. Susan Pratt of Buffalo, N. Y., and was long a physician in that city, where he recently d.]
3. ABBY, [m. John Hopkins and moved to Jamestown, N. Y., where she d.]
4. WILLIAM F., [m. Miss Nancy Nelson of Peterborough, and settled in that town, where she d. in 1868. Buried their only child. He still resides there.]
5. ISAAC B., [b. July 4, 1812 ; m. Elizabeth Buckminster, who d. childless, Sept. 13, 1860 ; m. 2d, Mrs. Mary (Bradford) McKeen. Mr. Pratt was for some years a manufacturer on the E. Z. Hastings stand in Clinton, but went West in 1854, and now lives in Chester, Minn. He has one son : —
*Edward B.*, (b. Oct. 4, 1863.)]

## PRESTON.

SYLVESTER PRESTON, son of Reuben and Nancy (Dresser) Preston of Windsor, was born in 1811; married Achsah, daughter of Chandler B. Boutwell, Dec. 26, 1837, and came to Antrim in 1849; bought the Abraham Smith farm (now occupied by B. F. Dustin), and lived there till 1869, when he sold to Spencer Worthley and moved to North Branch. Two children were born in Antrim, and three in Windsor: —

1. SUSAN M., [b. March 26, 1839 ; m. Dea. Gilman H. Cleaves of Antrim, Sept. 29, 1859.]

2. MARY E., [b. Dec. 1, 1846.]
3. SCOTT, [b. Aug. 22, 1848.]
4. NANCY J., [b. Oct. 11, 1852 ; d. aged 8 years.]
5. KATE J., [b. Sept. 26. 1854 ; m. Dr. I. G. Anthoine, Jan. 2, 1877, and lives at South Antrim.]

SEWALL PRESTON, brother of Sylvester, was born in Windsor in 1813 ; married Harriet McIlvaine of this town, May 15. 1834. Their only child, James M. Preston, grown to manhood, died in Windsor in 1856; and in 1860 the father, greatly discouraged, sold his farm and bought the Theodore Wallace place at North Branch, where he died in 1866. His widow still resides at North Branch, an excellent helper in sickness, and a woman full of Christian grace.

WILLARD PRESTON, another brother, was born in 1829; married Emeline D. McIlvaine, May 15, 1854; moved to Antrim in 1861, and lived where Sylvester Preston now lives, at North Branch. He died there Nov. 6. 1863, aged thirty-three, leaving one child, Clarence A. Preston, who died July 6, 1868, aged twelve. Mrs. Preston became second wife of William H. Hopkins, Esq., of Francestown, March 6, 1873, and now lives in that town.

## PRITCHARD.

This family came from Wales and settled in Rowley, Mass., among the pioneers of that town. Paul Pritchard, a grandson probably of the first settler, was born there in 1721. He married Hannah Perley, and settled in New Ipswich in 1772. His son, Capt. William Pritchard, was born Sept. 19, 1759; was three years in the Revolutionary army; was "Captain of the Troop;" married Didamia Cummings; was killed by being thrown from a chaise in 1835. Five years later his wife was found dead and her room in flames, having accidentally set fire to her clothes on retiring. William Pritchard, son of Capt. William, was born in New Ipswich in 1792, and came here from that place in 1822. He married Elisa Butman, and lived west of the pond, but remained only five years, moving back to his native town sometime in 1827. He died April 19, 1857. His wife was a daughter of John and Betsey (Wheeler) Butman. Their children were : —

1. WILLIAM H., [d. in infancy.]
2. ELISA M., [d. in infancy.]
3. EMILY WHEELER, [b. Oct. 22, 1821 ; m. Sumner Chamberlain in 1847.]
4. WILLIAM BARNARD, [b. in Antrim, July 30, 1823 ; m. Lydia E. Templeton, Dec. 30, 1845.]
5. JOHN WALLACE, [b. Feb. 4, 1829 ; m. Fannie C. Benjamin ; was freight-conductor on the Fitchburg Railroad ; was in-

stantly killed by being knocked off the train by a bridge, Aug. 24, 1854.]
6. GEORGE H., [b. June 17, 1830; lost an arm in the late war; lives at Hillsborough Bridge.]
7. CHARLES H., [b. March 5, 1832; lives at Fitchburg, Mass.]
8. EDWARD M., [b. Jan. 28, 1834; m. Annie E. Rathburn in 1860.]
9. AUGUSTUS DANE, [b. April 11, 1839; son of Mary Dane, second wife of William Pritchard, whom he m. May 18, 1837. The first wife, Elisa, d. Oct. 20, 1835.]

## PUFFER.

JACOB PUFFER settled the Artemas Brown farm about 1788 — perhaps a little later. Dr. Whiton says he came from Weare. No trace or record of him can be found in that town. A Jacob Puffer, son of Jabez and Hannah, was born in Sudbury, Mass., April 10, 1743, from which place several individuals came here. This Jacob settled in *Ashby*, and might subsequently have come here. Jabez was son of James, and grandson of George. The name was then spelled *Poffer*. Jacob had a son Jacob, born in Ashby Nov. 22, 1770; and possibly this last was the one who came here. These are all by this name Jacob that can be found. Puffer of Antrim was a blacksmith by trade. Was certainly a courageous man, to start in where he did, it being a time when all that section of the town was an unbroken forest. Nothing is known of Puffer's family. He is believed to have gone in 1799 to some town on the Hudson River near Albany.

## PUTNAM.

HARVEY PUTNAM, son of Aaron K. and Polly (Shattuck) Putnam, married Lavina Hall of Milford, and came here in 1845 from Milford to manufacture bedsteads, on the E. Z. Hastings stand, in company with his brother-in-law, Martin Hall. In less than three years he sold to I. B. Pratt and moved back to Milford. One son, William K., was born here, of whom I have no further information.

## PUTNEY.

DANIEL PUTNEY, who lived some years in Antrim, was born in Newbury Oct. 30, 1814. He was son of Daniel and Lois Foster Putney, grandson of Henry and Dolly (Jewett) Putney, and great-grandson of Joseph Putney. Joseph, the last named, in company with James Rogers, moved from Londonderry and made the first settlement of the town of Dunbarton in 1749. They were of Scotch race, like the settlers of Antrim. They settled on the eastern border of what is called the "Great Meadow," and called their new settlement "Stark's Town," in honor of their chief proprietor. After having erected their log houses and humble barns, and getting their land so brought into cultivation as to give them a comfortable living, they were driven off by the Indians, and took refuge in the fort at Concord. On subsequent return, they found their buildings all destroyed, and their young orchards cut down. The Indians had ruined everything. But, undismayed, they began again, — this time to abide permanently. "The old Putney Farm" has long been known in that town of excellent farms. Henry Putney, son of Joseph, had three wives, Mary Wells, Dolly Jewett, and Deborah Austin. He died April 13, 1807, aged eighty-six. His descendants have gone out into all the land. His son Daniel was born in Dunbarton, but on maturity settled in Newbury. Daniel of Antrim (Daniel, Jr.) married, first, Lucia Dow of Bedford, who died in 1861, and married, second, Minerva Watson. He came here in 1839 into the old Cummings house, then standing on the old road a few rods north of the Dea. Worthley place (Henry C. French's). Thence he moved to Sutton in 1844, but now lives in Henniker. Children: —

1. DEA. EDWARD D., [b. in Antrim in the old Cummings house, Dec. 9, 1841. Served as a clerk in a store in Bradford six years; then was clerk for a time in Concord. Came here and went into trade in the McKeen store in firm of Putney and Cummings, Sept. 10, 1866. After six months he bought out the latter, and has continued there in trade till the present time, — in later years in company with his brother. Is postmaster at this writing; has been town clerk; was chosen deacon in the Presbyterian Church in 1870. Built his present residence in 1876; m. Angie M. Marshall of Bradford, Nov. 21, 1866. They have only one child: —

    Bertha Angilene. (b. July 3, 1878.)]
2. DEA. CHARLES G., [b. in Sutton, July 22, 1846; m. Izora Chote of Leominster, Mass.; is a cabinet-maker by trade; lives in Orange, Mass.; is an officer of the Congregational Church in that place.]
3. LUCIEN W., [b. in Sutton, June 29, 1852; m. Clara L., daughter of Eben and Clara (Wilkins) Bass, Nov. 25, 1875; the same year went into trade with his brother in South Village as firm of E. D. and L. W. Putney.]
4. EMMA, [b. Aug. 13, 1860.]
5. CARRIE, [child of second wife, b. July 10, 1864. ]

## RALEIGH.

PHILIP RALEIGH, a Scotchman, formerly called Riley, the first settler of Antrim, was born in Ireland in 1719; came to Boston late in 1743, and at once joined the settlers in Hillsborough, and in the spring of 1744 he began his clearing and put up his log cabin on the farm now occupied by Reed P. Whittemore. He married an English woman by the name of Sarah Joiner, but it does not appear that his family came with him at this time. Being driven away from his cabin by Indians in 1746, he went to Sudbury, Mass., where he lived for fifteen years, returning to Antrim in 1761, with his family, and for the next six years his was the only family in Antrim. By some means he became dependent on the town in his old age. This record occurs for March, 1783: " Voted Michael Cochlan be freed of Reats this year, he providing for old Mr. Realy for this year." After Cochlan's failure to do this, Raleigh being a simple, peaceable old man, and pioneer of the town, was kindly boarded round (by public vote) till the close of 1789, when he went to Sudbury, and died there in 1791. He had eight sons and four daughters. One daughter married Michael Cochlan, named above, and another married Philip Coffin and died in Antrim in 1822, aged ninety. It may be added, that, as the families of the settlers were large, and either poor or of limited means, in the course of a few years the expense of boarding the old gentleman became burdensome. Others thought that his relatives were able to take care of him and should be compelled to do it. Something was done, therefore, in this line, under date of June 26, 1788, as appears by the following papers left by Hon. Matthew Patten: —

" State of New Hampshire }
  Hillsborough SS.        }

" To Matthew Patten, Nenian Aiken, David Starret Esqr$^s$,

" A Petition from the Selectmen of Antrim in said county humbly Shows — that Phylip Ralley of said Antrim is now become a publick charge. & Whereas disputs have arisen concerning his Support Whither he ought to be maintained by Major Ralley his natural soon and other Relatives, or the town of Antrim therefore we your petitioners pray your Hou$^s$ would take the Matter under your Consideration and appoint a time and place to Enquire into and determine Said Dispute and we shall ever pray

" THOMAS STUART    }
" SAMUEL DINSMOOR  } *Selectmen.*"
" DAVID M. CLUER   }

" Hillsborough SS.

" On reading and Considering the foregoing Petition ordered That the Petitioners be heard thereon on Wednesday the ninth day of July at nine O Clock in the forenoon at the Dwelling house of Thomas Nichols Inholder in Antrim — And that the Petitioners serve Major Ralley and Mical Cochland with a Copy of the above Petition and order thereon eight days before the Day of hearing that they May appear and shew cause if any they have Why the Town of S$^d$ Antrim should maintain the said Philip.

" MATTHEW PATTEN }  *Justices*
" NENIAN AIKEN    } *of the Peace*
" DAVID STARRET   } *and Quorum.*"

This petition may account for the fact that within a few months Philip went off among his children near Boston, and died there. Nothing is known of his daughters except that one of them married Michael Cochlan, and another married Philip Coffin of Antrim. The "Miels Really" supported by the town in 1778 is supposed to be a son of Philip, the first settler. Money was voted for "Miels Really's Family," but nothing is known of any children. Probably they returned to the vicinity of Sudbury, Mass., whence they came. A "Susey Realy" lived at Dea. Isaac Cochran's in 1789. Also, March 23, 1802, "Boarding of Susannah Raly Struck off to Samuel Christie at three Shillings a week." This girl spent some years at Dea. Joseph Boyd's; was insane at intervals; and an old person says of her, " She made us much sport by her antics." A daughter of Philip Riley may be referred to in the following marriage record: "John Beady and Margrat Raley Sept. 21, 1779."

MAJOR RALEIGH, one of Philip's sons, was a young man living in Concord, Mass., when the Revolutionary war broke out, and participated in the battle of Lexington. He came here in 1779, and began the Elijah Gould farm; after selling to Gould he lived awhile on the Gibson place, but moved to Derry in 1815: married Mary Blanchard, and had two sons and one daughter. He died in Deering in 1838, aged eighty-nine. The bed of the railroad is now laid on the spot where his humble dwelling stood. The daughter of Major Raleigh, whose name has not been ascertained, died at the age of twelve years. His sons were:—

1. MAJOR, JR., [b. March 15, 1785; m. Nancy Ordway of Goffstown; lived several years in Hillsborough, then in Washington a few years, from whence he moved to Pennsylvania, about 1835, where he d. in 1848. His wife d. in Goffstown in 1863. They had five sons:—

    *John*, (b. in 1807; m. 1st. Roxanna Merrill; 2d, Hannah Wheeler, and lives in Hooksett.)

    *James*, (lived in Newport, and d. there in 1872.)

    *Joseph*, (was never heard from after going to Pennsylvania with his father.)

    *David*, (m. Sophia Morrill, and d. in Goffstown in 1873, aged 57.)

    *Daniel*, (went to Pennsylvania; entered the Union army from that State in 1861 and was killed in battle.)]

2. JAMES, [b. March 11, 1790; m. Susan H. McCoy of Pembroke; lived awhile in Goffstown, then in Francestown, and moved back to Antrim about 1827. Among other children b. in Goffstown and Francestown were two sons:—

    *George W.*, (m. 1st, Lucy Hutchinson of Milford; 2d, Mary Jane Wheeler of Warren; now resides in Milford, and is a veterinary surgeon of considerable note.)

    *Alonzo H.*, (is a noted Mormon of Salt Lake City.)

The children of James and Susan Raleigh b. in Antrim were : —

*Mary Jane*, (b. in 1829 ; m. 1st, Homer S. Lathe in 1850, and lived in Claremont; m. 2d, George B. Putnam, and moved to the West.)

*Maria W.*, (b. in 1830.)

*Joshua Blanchard*, (b. in 1833 ; went into the army ; was wounded and had his leg amputated. He soon d. from the operation, and was buried at Hillsborough Lower Village.)

*Hiram B.*, (b. in 1835 ; m. Jenny Murdough of Hillsborough and now lives in Windsor.)

*Jacob P.*, (b. in 1838, and d. in 1840.)]

## RAMSAY.

ABRAM A. RAMSAY, son of Ebenezer and Mary D. (Butler) Ramsay, and grandson of Samuel and Betsey (Wilson) Ramsay, was born in 1836; came to Antrim in April, 1852, at the age of sixteen, to live with Widow Alice Woodbury, working on the farm in summer and attending school in the winter. Went away and remained one year, but in April, 1854, came back to work in the store for L. and J. B. Woodbury, where he remained six years. In 1859 he married Helen P. Baldwin of Bennington, bought the house now owned by Mrs. Nancy Jameson, and also the store owned by the late Charles McKeen, now owned by Putney Brothers, and traded there till the spring of 1864, when he sold to Treadwell and Company of Boston, and moved from Antrim to Bennington in the fall of 1865, where he lived until April, 1867, and then moved to Wilton, where he now resides, being engaged in trade. He was town clerk here several years. He has one child: —

1. ANNE A., [b. in Wilton Aug. 23, 1870.]

## RAND.

DEA. JONATHAN RAND was born in Lyndeborough June 24, 1762. His father was Rev. John Rand, who was graduated at Harvard College in 1747, and settled in Lyndeborough as first Congregational minister of that town about 1761; and his mother was Sarah Goffe, daughter of Col. John Goffe of Derryfield. Rev. John and Sarah (Goffe) Rand had seven children, of whom Dea. Jonathan and his twin-brother John were the eldest. Dea. Jonathan Rand married Sarah Abbott of Mont Vernon, and came here in 1844. He lived in Clinton in part of the house owned by his nephew, John R. Abbott, where he died in 1848. His wife died the same year. He was deacon in the Baptist Church, probably at Goffstown, and was a most excellent man. An acquaintance says of him: " He was a man of prayer and walked with God, and though poor in this world's goods he had treasure laid up in heaven." Children: —

1. MILLE, [b. April 29, 1795 ; m. Robert Parker of Bedford.]

2. ESTHER P., [b. Dec. 30, 1796 ; now Mrs. Tollman of Nelson, and the only one of Dea. Rand's children now living.]
3. JONATHAN, [b. Jan. 11, 1799, and drowned in Merrimack river June 6, 1810.]
4. JOHN, [b. Jan. 27, 1801 ; was quite distinguished as a portrait-painter, which art he practiced some years in England, where he m. ; but he afterwards came to New York, and d.]
5. EPHRAIM, [b. Dec. 17, 1803 ; m. Catherine Gray of Augusta, Me.]
6. SARAH, [b. Feb. 3, 1806 ; d. Feb. 8, 1832.]
7. DOROTHY, [b. May 15, 1809 ; d. May 16, 1811.]
8. PHILANDA P., [b. July 9, 1811; was a fine scholar and teacher at New Hampton, but d. April 6, 1832, at the early age of 21.]

## RANSOM.

MANLY RANSOM, no doubt born a slave, and the only one ever held in Antrim, was the servant of John Moore when the latter was killed, and was given by his widow to Dr. Charles Adams, at the Center, in 1808. He lived with Dr. Adams till his removal to Oakham, Mass., in 1816, when he went to live with Dr. Adams's father in Brookfield, Mass. When the first school-house at the Center was burned in 1811, school being in session at the time, this boy was so frightened that he hid under a seat, was fearfully burned, and would have been burned to death had he not been missed, searched for, and dragged out. After he went to Massachusetts he finally drifted off and married among the people of his own color. He lived in Sturbridge, Charlton, and at last settled in Spencer, Mass. Many years after, in a paroxysm of anger he struck his wife a blow (from the effects of which she died), and then fled to Stoddard, where he remained concealed about two years. He then returned to Massachusetts, and learned for the first time of the fate of his wife, when he again fled to Northampton, Mass., but was soon discovered and arrested, tried, convicted, and sent to prison. Serving out his sentence, he returned to Spencer, paid a visit to Worcester, and while walking on the railroad track in that place he was struck by a locomotive and fatally injured. He died June 29, 1861, aged fifty-nine.

## RAYMOND.

GEORGE RAYMOND, son of George and Mary (Wallace) Raymond, was born in Mont Vernon in 1820; married Eleanor Pollard (who was born in Hudson in 1828), came here on to the Dea. Taylor farm in 1847, and moved to Concord in 1854. His two children were born here:—

1. EDWIN H., [b. in 1849, m. Eva G. Wheeler, and lives in Anna, Ill.]
2. ELSIE A., [b. in 1853.]

## REED.

JOEL REED, son of Eliphaz Reed, was born in Woburn, Mass., in 1757; married Keziah Reed, and came here from Deering in 1790. He built a house between S. A. Holt's and Frank Robinson's, about half-way down the hill, but moved to Washington about 1803, where he died in 1830. His widow died in 1845, aged eighty. Their children were :—

1. KEZIAH, [b. in Francestown; m. John Metcalf of Washington, and d. in 1874, aged 88, leaving five children.]
2. MARY, [b. in Francestown, and d. unm. in 1819.]
3. SALLY, [b. in Deering; m. Silas Fisher, and lived in Washington, where she d. in 1875.]
4. OLIVE, [b. in Antrim; m. Benjamin Jefts; went to Alstead, and d. there in 1848.]
5. ASA, [b. in Antrim; m. Sarah Davis of Stoddard, and d. in 1830, leaving one son, George D. Reed of Washington.]

A SAMUEL REED lived on the Thomas Flint farm, or near there, in 1804. Nothing further known of him.

ZADOK REED, son of William and Lucy (Spaulding) Reed, whose ancestors were of English descent, and came from Westford, Mass., was born in Litchfield in 1752. His father was killed while raising a building only eight feet square, but the son served through the whole seven years of the Revolutionary war without receiving a scratch. He married Lucy McLane of New Boston, and lived in that town some years, but came here in 1795, following his daughter, Mrs. Sawyer, who had settled here the year previous. He lived awhile on the Abraham Smith farm, and moved on to the Clark farm with his son-in-law, Samuel Sawyer, and died in 1827. His children were: —

1. FRANCIS, [was a sailor and d. at sea.]
2. SUSANNAH, [b. in 1774; m. Samuel Sawyer in 1794, and d. June 17, 1815.]
3. SALLY, [m. Samuel Wilson; d. Nov. 4, 1844, aged 68.]
4. DUDLEY, [m. Anna McAllister April 1, 1813; lived awhile on the Clark place; had a large family; moved to New York, in 1825, since which I can find no trace of him.]

NATHANIEL REED, son of Dea. William Reed of Litchfield (which Dea. William was a brother of Zadok), was born in 1784; came to Antrim to work in the store for the elder Mark Woodbury in 1805, and died here in 1808, unmarried, aged twenty-four. He was an excellent man, and his early death was the occasion of general sorrow.

FRANCIS REED, a brother of Nathaniel, was born in 1792; came here in 1814, and learned and afterwards carried on the clothier's business at North Branch. He married Betsey Wallace of this town, Dec. 23, 1817, and moved to Manchester in 1836; thence to Haverhill, Mass., in 1854, where he died in 1866, leaving children : —

1. SAMANTHA R., [b. in 1818 : m. 1st, George Minot of Manchester, and went to New Orleans, where he soon d.; m. 2d, Ezra Kelley, and lives in Haverhill, Mass.]
2. CAROLINE G., [b. in 1820 ; unm.]
3. LAURA F., [b. in 1822; m. Samuel E. Huse, and lives in California.]
4. BETSEY, [d. in 1843. aged 19.]
5. LOUISA L., [b. in 1826 ; m. Eustice P. Bowman of Manchester, in 1852, who is manager of a gold-crushing machine in Black Hills.]
6. GEORGE W., [b. in 1828 ; m. Maria Brigham of Manchester, in 1855, and lives in Montreal, Canada.]

ROBERT REED, another brother, was born in 1790; married Mary Moody of Newburyport in 1820, and in the spring of the same year came here. He opened a store at the Center. in the building next west of the church, in 1826. where he continued in trade until 1834, when he moved to Lowell, where he died in 1879, in piety and general respect. He had six children, all born here : —

1. WILLIAM W., [b. in 1822 ; m. Hannah J. Pusher of Lowell, where he lives.]
2. ENOCH M., [b. in 1824 ; m. Carrie Conant of Newburyport, and lives in Boston.]
3. ROBERT, [d. in 1829, aged 3.]
4. MARY M., [lives unm. in Lowell.]
5. ROBERT L., [b. in 1830 ; m. Maria H. Fox of Dracut, Mass., who d. the same year; lives in Lowell.]
6. JOHN R., [b. in 1832; never m.; is a leading merchant in Charleston, S. C.]

HENRY REED, another brother, was born in 1804; came here in the fall of 1825 and entered into partnership with his brother in trade at the Center; where he remained five years, then went into trade in Pelham; married Rowena, daughter of Dr. Israel Hildreth of that place; went thence to Lowell in 1850, and died in that city in 1878. He was a talkative, jolly boy, always up to jokes. A man once called at the store to borrow a harness, and young Reed sent him up to Lynda Flint, a maiden lady who lived alone, and had the greatest antipathy to horses. She not only never owned one herself, but could not be persuaded to ride with any one else. As may be imagined, on being applied to for the loan of a harness, she made some remarks not of a complimentary nature !

Henry Reed's wife was sister of Gen. Butler's wife, and he followed the General through the war, being post-sutler at Ship Island, New Orleans, Fortress Monroe, and Norfolk. His only surviving children, Philip and Henry, are lieutenants in the regular United States army. He was in trade in various places forty years, and acquired a large property. Was unable to be here Centennial Day, but sent his address in manuscript.

JAMES REED came from Francestown to South Village in 1840, into what is now the Corey house. First wife unknown; second, Ruth Buxton of Weare, who died at West Deering. He afterwards moved into the Samuel Wilson house west of Reed Carr's. He married, third, Mrs. Lucinda (Bowen) Walker, and died Aug. 3, 1865.

## RHODES.

SOLOMON RHODES was born in New Marlborough, Mass., Nov. 30, 1783. His parents, Solomon and Elenor Rhodes, had fifteen children: Reuben, Solomon, Elenor, Rufus, James, Silas, Amos, Levi, Nancy, Patty, Chesterfield, Betsey, Abigail, Lucinda, and Harriet. Solomon of Antrim came here from Deering; married Mary Fairbank of this town in 1807, and lived many years on the John Smith place (now Thomas Flint's). He had no children. Died in 1850.

SILAS RHODES, brother of Solomon of Antrim, born March 8, 1792, married Rebecca Hayward Nov. 26, 1815. He lived many years in the Moses Duncan house, next west of his brother's, but afterwards moved to Alexandria. There he married, second, Laura C. Ballou, had several children, and died in January, 1880. He lived for a time in Stoddard. Four children were born in Antrim, the others after his removal from town, and all were as follows: —

1. THOMAS H., [b. March 8, 1816; m. Jennie C. Taylor; is a farmer in Lexington, Mass.]
2. HARRIET, [m. Hezekiah C. Gale; lives in Cambridge, Mass.]
3. SILAS, [b. Feb. 11, 1820; m. 1st, Luciana Sleeper; 2d, Mary Jane Stickney; 3d, Angie Lyon; lived in Cambridge, Mass.; was a house-builder, very respectable, and filled many places of trust; d. Jan. 3, 1879.]
4. SARAH ELENOR, [b. June 7, 1822.]
5. SOLOMON, [lives in Somerville, Mass.]
6. JAMES, [lives in Winona, Minn.]
7. JOSIAH R., [carpenter in Cambridgeport, Mass.]
8. MARSHA R., [d. in the West, unm.]

## RICHARDSON.

JOHN P. RICHARDSON, familiarly known as "Cap'n P.," came here in 1832, and built a house on the west side of the road, nearly opposite George Thompson's. He was a blacksmith by trade, and his shop stood on the south side of the road, a little east of George A. Cochran's. This shop was afterwards bought and moved away by Dea. Isaac Cochran, and is now used for a store-house. Mr. Richardson married Abigail Manning of Bennington. After remaining here a few years he moved to Hillsborough, thence in 1842 to South Antrim, thence to Deering, thence to Hancock, where he died May 14, 1871. aged sixty-one. His children were : —

1. PUTNAM, [b. in Deering. March 18, 1829; m. Eliza A. Kelley of Deering, and lives in Peterborough.]
2. MARY R., [b. in Deering, July 12, 1831; m. Charles M. Flint of Fitchburg, Mass.]
3. MATILDA M., [b. in Deering, Jan. 14, 1833; m. Russell Martin. and lives in Richmond.]
4. NANCY J.. [b. in Antrim, March 7, 1836 ; m. Israel F. Walker, now of North Weare.]
5. WILLIAM C.. [b. in Hillsborough, July 31, 1838; d. Feb. 25, 1840.]
6. ABIGAIL E., [b. in Hillsborough, Nov. 20, 1840; m. Albert Gay Aug. 24, 1860, and lives at Hillsborough Bridge.]
7. JOHN C , [b. in Antrim, March 6, 1842; m. Anna Scott, and lives in Peterborough.]
8. LOUSTER A., [b. in Antrim, July 26, 1846; d. aged 6.]
9. LORINDA S., [b. in Antrim, Feb. 13, 1849; m. Levi Ring of Deering, and lives at Hillsborough Bridge.]

JOHN RICHARDSON, son of Thomas Richardson, was born in Deering in 1788 ; married Huldah Batchelder of Francestown, in 1815, and moved from there to the McNiel place (Mr. Eaton's) in 1826, where he remained seven years and then moved back to Francestown, where he died in 1864, leaving children as follows : —

1. EMELINE B., [b. in Francestown in 1818; m. David Smiley, and lives in Stoughton, Mass.]
2. HULDAH A., [b. in Francestown in 1821; m. 1st, William Woodbury of Pelham ; 2d, Philip Piper, and lives in Newburyport, Mass.]
3. MARY D., [b. in Antrim in 1827.; m. John E. Parker, and lives in Boston.]
4. DEA. JOHN P.. [b. in Antrim in 1830; m. 1st, Mary A. Hardy of Greenfield ; 2d, Amelia Cutter of Pelham, and lives in Francestown, being deacon of the Congregational Church in that town.]

JAMES C. RICHARDSON, grandson of Phinehas, and son of Phinehas and Mehitable (Clark) Richardson of Lempster, was born June 15, 1834; married Harriet E. Potter, Nov. 24, 1853; came to this town in August, 1854. He was a member of the Thirteenth N. H. Regiment, from this town, — a soldier brave and true. Their infant child died in Hillsborough, April 16, 1864. The other children are: —

1. LOUISA E., [b. Feb. 18, 1859; d. March 15, 1879.]
2. EOLE J., [b. Feb. 24, 1861.]
3. PERLEY ERNEST, [b. Aug. 3, 1880.]

WILLIAM H. RICHARDSON, son of Moses and Esther (Richardson) Richardson, was born in Pelham in 1819; married Lydia Hale of Temple; came here in 1856, took the town farm one year, and then bought the James Baldwin place, which he occupied many years. Subsequently lived in South Village. His children are: —

1. MARY E., [b. in Lowell in 1851; m. Charles W. Thompson, Oct. 7, 1875.]
2. JOHN W., [b. in 1860.]

JAMES RICHARDSON, brother of William H., was born Sept. 1, 1832; married Abbie A. Cooledge Nov. 30, 1871, and bought the Dea. Bond place in 1876, where he now resides.

## RING.

BENJAMIN RING, a man of whom little can be learned, came here from Dunbarton; lived here and there in town awhile, but built in 1792 a small house on the east side of the road between the Nathaniel Herrick place and Chester Conn's. He deserted his family in 1802, and nothing has been heard of him since.

## RITCHIE.

REV. WILLIAM RITCHIE, of Scotch-Irish descent, son of James and Sally (Dunlap) Ritchie of Peterborough, and grandson of William and Mary (Waugh) Ritchie, who were among the first permanent settlers of Peterborough, was born in Peterborough March 25, 1781. He graduated at Dartmouth College in 1804; studied theology with Dr. Lathrop of Springfield, Mass.; preached here awhile in 1806, and received a call from the Presbyterian Church in this place, which he declined, and went to Canton, Mass. He was ordained there July 1, 1807, and dismissed June 18, 1820. Being settled at Canton, as was supposed, for life, and being strongly attached to the place, he felt disposed to stand on his legal rights, and the parish gave him fifty dollars to leave quietly. Wouldn't liberal farewell presents often be a good investment for parishes to make now? After Mr. Ritchie left Canton, he was settled over the First Parish in Needham, Mass., to which he ministered twenty years, and died Feb. 22, 1842. Chapman's "Graduates of Dartmouth College" says that he became a Unitarian. He married Clarissa Kimball of Bradford, Mass., who died at Needham, leaving children: William, James, Sophia, and Kimball.

## ROACH.

CALEB W. ROACH, son of Timothy and Susan (White) Roach of Deering, was born in that town Jan. 19, 1809. He married Mary Farrington March 14, 1850, and moved on to the Woodbury Fairbanks place, which he still occupies. Has but one child, Frank F., born Jan. 12, 1851, who is a tailor by trade and has carried on business in South Village some years; married Emily A. Clapp of Hillsborough, Jan. 31, 1877.

EDWARD B. ROACH, son of Josiah and Hannah (Weeks) Roach, married Mary J. Combs, who lived but a few days. Both are buried at the Branch cemetery. He built the house in South Village now Mr. Sweetzer's. He died July 16, 1864, aged thirty-one. She died Nov. 6, 1863, aged twenty-six.

CHARLES W. ROACH, brother of Edward, inherited the house built by him; married Jennie M. Day, and lived here a few years. Left Antrim about 1872, and now lives in Salem, Mass.

## ROBB.

ANDREW ROBB (son of John Robb, whose wife was a Scott) came here from Peterborough, cleared on the west of Robb Mountain, and settled there in 1796. He owned a vast tract of land, and the mountain still bears his name. He married Betsey Robb, and went to Webster, N. Y., in 1816. The children were:—

1. JAMES, [went to New York; m. there and went into the army in the war of 1812; was captured, and d. a prisoner at Halifax, N. S.]
2. JOHN, [went to New York in 1811, and d. there.]
3. NANCY, [m. John Robinson, March 28, 1816.]
4. PATTY, [m. Reuben Cobb of Nelson, and moved to Webster, N. Y., where all the family went.]
5. DAVID, [went to New York while quite young, and we know nothing more of him, or of the younger children named below.]
6. ANDREW.
7. SAMUEL.
8. POLLY.
9. BETSEY.

MOOR ROBB, cousin of Andrew, lived on Robb Mountain many years, and moved to Webster, N. Y., in 1817, with an ox-team, being eighteen days in making the journey. Now we could go to San Francisco and back in the same time! His wife's name was Mary Evans.

Besides the two Robbs, Andrew and Moor, Nathan Cram, Thomas Aucerton, Daniel Paige, Thomas Carleton, Sampson Reed, Luther Conant, and John Edwards all lived in log houses on Robb Mountain; had large families, embracing in the neighborhood of sixty persons, — well-to-do, as shown by the fact that Andrew Robb carried with him three thousand dollars in silver when he moved away. They had a school-district, but there never was any public highway. Now all are gone, and scarcely any relic of a building can be found. Cattle roam wild where once were thrifty homes. But little can now be learned of these families.

MOOR ROBB, nephew of Moor Robb mentioned above, lived on the Andrew Robb farm several years after his uncle's departure. He married Lucy Barden, and they had one child born here but now dead. He moved to Stoddard, and now lives there in ripe age. Christopher Robb is his son.

SAMUEL ROBB and his brother William, sons of Moses and Fanny (Paige) Robb, and nephews of the last-named Moor Robb, each lived some years in Antrim. Samuel married Aurilla Emery of this town, July 3, 1851, and lived on the Eber Curtis place; moved to Stoddard and died there in 1873, aged fifty-one. William lived in the mill-house at North Branch, where his wife and two children died in 1871. He now lives in Harrisville, and draws a large royalty from Goodell Company for inventions used by them.

JOHN ROBB, son of Samuel and Abigail (Alexander) Robb of Peterborough, was born in 1799; married Roxanna Woodward of Marlborough; came here in 1838, and lived where William Boutelle, Jr., now lives. He built the present house on that place, though a small shelter had been there for years before. He also built the Loveren mills in 1839. He died in Stoddard, Dec. 23, 1855. His children were as follows, the three oldest being born before he came to Antrim: —

1. ROXEY A., [b. Jan. 14, 1824; m. B. F. Dustin of Antrim, Oct. 14, 1845.]
2. JOHN A., [b. Jan. 16, 1833; m. Martha J. McNiel; now lives in Waterman, Io.]
3. ESTHER, [b. Feb. 27, 1827; m. Mark Wilkins, and d. after a year or two.]
4. DAVID C., [d. at the age of 13.]
5. ROANCA A., [b. Feb. 19, 1842; m. John Butterfield.]

## ROBBINS.

JOSIAH ROBBINS, son of Josiah and Anna (Felt) Robbins of Nelson, was born in 1791; married Polly White, and came here from Claremont in 1837, and lived in the South Village. He died in 1865, leaving children: —

1. WELLS, [b. in 1814; m. Emma Youngman, and lived awhile on the Robert Dodge place at South Village, where he had three children; moved to Dorchester, where he d. in 1860. The children were: —
    *Emma F.*, (m. 1st, a Cogswell of Dorchester; 2d, Byron Shackford of Canaan, and is now living a widow in Concord.)
    *Josiah W.*, (d. young.)
    *Walter S.*, (now living in Dorchester.)]
2. LOVELL, [m. Joan Wheeler of Nelson, and lives in Peterborough.]
3. LOIS W., [b. in 1817; m. James T. Balch of this town in 1844.]
4. MARY, [m. Edward Goodrich, and lives in Claremont.]
5. JANE, [m. Silsby Cowles of Claremont, Dec. 21, 1837, and d. in 1865.]
6. LUTHER B., [m. Sarah Clark of Deering, June 1, 1853, and now lives in Warner.]
7. CHARLES G., [m. Margaret Austin, and lives in Oregon, Ill.]
8. NANCY C., [m. Augustus Laws, Oct. 30, 1847; d. in Peterborough, Jan. 5, 1871, aged 42.]
9. ALFRED F., [m. Susan Steenburg, and lives in Auburn, N. Y.]
10. GEORGE E., [m. Sarah Johonnett, and lives in New Boston.]
11. CALVIN C., [m. 1st, Susan Hews; 2d, Charlotte Hutchinson; 3d, Elizabeth Gowing, and lives in Peterborough. He has one son b. here: —
    *Frank J.*, (m. Sarah E. Stanley of Peterborough, and lives in that town.)]
12. HENRY T., [m. 1st, Sarah Merrill of Goffstown; 2d, Clara ———, and now lives at St. Katherine's, Ontario.]
13. LUCY A., [d. at the age of 21.]

CAPT. JOHN G. ROBBINS, a native of Hillsborough and born in that town in 1801, came here and bought the place next eastward of William Duncan's in 1849, and lived there till his death in 1859. In the prime of his earlier days he was captain of the "Troop." Was a friendly, jolly man, and is spoken of as a "good joker!" He married, first, Sybil Taylor, who was the mother of his children; second, Sarah N. Greenwood of Halifax, N. S. Children: —

1. ALMIRA, [m. George Johnson, and lives in Hillsborough.]
2. CAPT. JOHN G., JR., [unm.; was one of the best soldiers New Hampshire sent to the war. Enlisted in the Twenty-sixth Mass. Regiment, Sept. 14, 1861, and was promoted from a

private to first sergeant, first lieutenant, and captain. He was so good a soldier that he was retained in the service after the close of the war, being stationed at Pensacola, Fla. He was mustered out April 10, 1866, on account of ill health brought on by exposure and hardship in the war, and coming home d. in Hillsborough, Sept. 8. 1867, aged 35. Capt. Robbins was entrusted with many perilous duties, was in many battles, and was often called to serve on the court-martial. While stationed at New Orleans, it was reported to Gen. Butler one Sabbath that a certain minister was uttering disloyal language from the pulpit. He ordered Serg. Robbins with a squad of six men to go and arrest the rebel preacher, — which he did, arresting him in the act of service, and leading him out of a large audience straight to Butler's headquarters. On another occasion, with a similar squad of men, he was on duty guarding a levee above New Orleans, when they were suddenly surrounded by thirty or forty cavalrymen under command of a major. The major asked, revolver in hand, " Who has command here ? " — " I have," said Serg. Robbins. — " You are my prisoners," cried the major. — " Not alive," said the sergeant. The major, flourishing his revolver as if to fire, sung out, " Shut up, you " — when a bullet from Robbins sent him to the ground without finishing the sentence. Immediately the rest of the rebels fled, and Robbins " appropriated a pair of *cavalry boots*." Another Antrim soldier speaks of having seen him with them on.]

3. ABBY, [d. aged 9 years.]

## ROBINSON.

But little definite information can be gained concerning the ancestry of Peter Robinson of Antrim. The only person of this name in Hudson who signed any of the various petitions to governor or legislature from 1741 to 1765, was John Robinson. He was a freeholder as early as 1743, and probably was the father of Peter of Antrim. A Peter Robinson, probably the one afterwards of this town, was " Post Rider " for the State during much of the Revolutionary war, — a position of importance and peril, as may be seen in the Journal of the House, 1778-81. The father of Peter of Antrim, whom we suppose to be John Robinson, had two wives, whose names I cannot obtain. The first wife left two sons, Simeon and Douglas, and possibly other children. Simeon married Susannah Tarbox, and was father of Isaac Robinson, D. D., of Stoddard, who was a noted preacher in his day. Douglas Robinson settled in Greenfield in

1773, and was grandfather of Moses Robinson, Esq., now of that town. The *second* wife of John left several children, as follows so far as is known : Peter Robinson of Antrim, named below; Andrew, who settled in Francestown; David, who remained in Hudson; also Samuel and Moses, who, I am told, both settled in Greenfield. There was also at least *one* sister, and she married a Mr. Grimes. Some of these brothers, or their descendants, also subsequently settled in Hancock. This is about all that can be found, as yet, concerning this ancient family. There was a Capt. Samuel Robinson in the Revolutionary army from New Hampshire. Also a John, and an Alexander, signed the Association Test in Londonderry, their being in that town suggesting that they were of Scotch race. A family of Robinsons are found in Salem, Mass., very early, since Daniel, of the *fifth generation*, was born as long ago as 1783, in that town. These were, no doubt, of English origin. The children of the celebrated Rev. John Robinson, pastor of the Pilgrims at Leyden, settled in this country. Altogether the Robinsons are now a host in number, this side the water, and include many famous and widely cherished names.

PETER ROBINSON came here from Hudson in 1799, bringing quite a large family. Married, first, Sarah Peabody, who died March 8, 1802, aged forty-two; married, second, Naomi Darrah, who died Feb. 8, 1842, aged seventy-five. Peter died Aug. 5, 1828, aged seventy-one. He lived and died on the place west of the pond, first settled by William Bodwell, occupied (1877) by Hosea Dutton. Children : —

1. ELISABETH, [m. Daniel Paige in the year 1801 ; d. in Bedford April 8, 1817, leaving a large family.]
2. MEHITABLE, [m. David Hills ; d. Sept. 28, 1850, aged 72.]
3. ASA, [b. Dec. 13, 1781 ; m. Rebekah, sister of Chandler Boutwell, Feb. 23, 1804 ; lived some years in Stoddard ; moved on to the Cross place, now known as the Steele place, west of the pond ; m. 2d, Elisabeth McIlvaine, May 29, 1832. She survives at the age of 92, a pious and worthy woman, being now the oldest person in town. He d. Sept. 29, 1866, aged nearly 85. His children were : —

*John*, (b. Jan. 28, 1805 ; m. Ann S. Buswell, Dec. 31, 1826 ; moved to Alstead, thence to California, and d. there.)

*Reuben*, (b. April 13, 1807 ; m. Mary Sweetser, Nov. 28, 1837 ; lived on the paternal farm, and d. there ; built in Clinton and his family moved there soon after his death. He d. Nov. 19, 1852. His children were : Elisabeth R., who m. Benjamin R. Cree, her husband dying Oct. 18, 1872, and she Feb. 9, 1879 ; Lucretia M., who m. Geo. W. Shaw March 4, 1873 ; and Samuel A., captain of the Granite State Cadets, who m. Sophia, daughter of Rev. William Hurlin, and has one child, Fred William, b. May 3, 1872.)

*Rhoda,* (b. June 8, 1810 ; m. Artemas Brown, Oct. 30, 1827 ; d. Nov. 24, 1843, leaving one child, Sarah, b. 1836, who m. Nathan A. Brown.)]

4. JOHN, [b. Jan. 18, 1784 ; m. 1st, Polly Boutwell, sister of Rebekah, named above, and settled on the Robert Willey place adjacent to his father's, occupied (1877) by James E. Tenney. He m. 2d. Nancy Robb, March 28, 1816, and d. Feb. 25, 1854. aged 70. Mrs. Nancy Robinson d. Dec. 20, 1865. Children : —

*Naomi D.*, (only child of first wife ; b. Jan. 17, 1808 ; m. Chandler Butterfield, July 16, 1835.)

*John,* (b. Dec. 1, 1817 ; m. Hadie Ann Marshall of Charlestown, Mass., May 27, 1845; went to Sparta, Wis.)

*Betsey*, (b. Jan. 8, 1823. m. John A. Sawyer April 1, 1847, and d. July 8, 1866, in Stranger, Kan.)

*Franklin*, (b. Oct. 8, 1824 ; m. Nov. 8, 1853, Mary E. Worthley ; lives on David Hill farm, next west of the pound. Have one adopted daughter, Mary Ella (Worthley) Robinson.)

*Mary K.*, (b. May 12, 1826 ; m. Thomas S. Worthley, Aug. 31, 1847 ; d. June 15, 1857, aged 31.)]

5. REUBEN, [remained with his parents and inherited the old farm from them. He d. unm. Nov. 28, 1864, aged 72.]

## ROGERS.

HUGH A. ROGERS, son of James and Hepsibeth (Tyler) Rogers, was born in Coventry in 1819; married, first, Mary J. Thorning of Peterborough, in 1841, who died in 1860. Mr. Rogers married, second, Mrs. Betsey A. (McMaster) Buswell in 1862, and came here from Bennington to live on the Buswell place. His children, all by his first marriage, are : —

1. LUCY A , [b. Oct. 20, 1842; m. Micajah George of Bennington, and lives in that town.]
2. LORENZO A., [b. Aug. 17, 1845 ; killed in battle at Wagner, S. C., July 22, 1863.]
3. MARY A., [b. July 17, 1847 ; m. Charles Shirley, and lives in Lowell.]
4. SOLON W., [b. July 27, 1849 ; d. at the age of 3.]
5. HENRY A., [b. in Bennington, Jan. 10, 1852; m. Clara E. Whitney, Nov. 27, 1872 ; moved into the stone house built by Charles Gates, and bought the Gregg mills in 1872. Subsequently lived on the E. L. Vose farm. They have two children : —

*Gracie E.*, (b. Nov. 30, 1874.)
*Mary Caroline*, (b. July 21, 1877.)]
6. ALMUS T., [b. in Bennington, May 21, 1854; m. Julia E. Whitney in 1873, and lives at South Village, having one child: —
*George G.*, (b. Sept 12, 1874.)]
7. GEORGE HARVEY, [b. May 13, 1856; m. Josephine N. Whitney, Oct. 18, 1879.]
8. ALBERT C., [b. May 22, 1860; m. Jennie F. Senter in 1879.]

## ROLLINS.

BENJAMIN ROLLINS, son of David and Judith (Leach) Rollins, and grandson of John Rollins of Newburyport, was born in Salem, March, 1784; married Martha Nevins of that town in 1810; went to Tyngsborough, Mass., from which place he came to Antrim in October, 1815, and bought of Isaac Baldwin the old mill in South Village, which was burned Dec. 11, 1817. By the vigorous assistance of the public, a new mill was so far completed that he ground grain again the first day of the following month (New Year's, 1818). Mr. Rollins was conspicuous in building the East meeting-house, and was one of the committee to build the present town-house. He was a carpenter and bridge-builder. He sold to Elijah Herrick in 1832 and went into the provision business in Lowell, from which place he moved to Hopkinton in 1837, where he now lives with his daughter, Mrs. Colby, at great age. His children are: —

1. MARTHA M., [b. in Tyngsborough, Dec. 3, 1811; m. Rufus W. Long (son of Dea. Isaac Long of Hopkinton), who is now a cabinet-manufacturer in Manchester, Mass.]
2. BENJAMIN B., [b. in Tyngsborough, Mass., April 10, 1814; m. Alice Clark of Hopkinton; lives in South Orange, N. J.]
3. LUCIA A. D., [b. in Antrim, April 16, 1816; m. William H. Long (son of Dea. Isaac Long of Hopkinton), a graduate of Yale College, class of 1840, and of Yale Theological Seminary in 1847. Bronchial illness prevented preaching, and he has been for thirty years principal of one of the large schools in Boston.]
4. MARGARET B., [b. in Antrim, June 8, 1818; m. Timothy Colby, a farmer and lumber-dealer of Hopkinton.]
5. ALFRED A., [b. in Antrim, April 18, 1820; m. Mary E. Colby of Hopkinton, and lives in that town, having a large family. He was in the Union army three years, was wounded at Chancellorsville, and now draws a pension.]
6. NANCY W., [b. in Antrim, May 8, 1822, and d. of consumption

in Hopkinton in 1851. She was a devoted Christian and much beloved by every one.]

## ROSS.

JOHN ROSS, son of Hugh and Mary Ross, was born in Woburn, Mass., in 1759. He was a Revolutionary soldier. He married Mary Barr of Bedford, and came here from Goffstown, bringing his family of children with him, and lived on the road east, between Mr. Turner's and the river, in a house put up by Dea. Daniel Nichols before the present century. He moved away in 1824, and died in Deering in 1843. The children were as follows: —

1. HUGH, [m. Abigail Sawtell of Sidney, Me. ; was out through the war of 1812, and d. in 1873.]
2. JAMES, [m. Melinda Grimes of Francestown: was in the army through the war of 1812, and d. in 1853.]
3. ANNA, [m. Nathaniel Griffin, April 14, 1840, and d. in 1868.]
4. MARY, [m. Isaac Templeton of Hillsborough, March 15, 1814, and d. in 1873.]
5. BETSEY, [m. Luther Sumner of Boston, and d. in 1869.]
6. SARAH, [m. Luke Sumner of Deering, and d. in 1862.]
7. JANE B., [m. Moses Codman of Deering, and d. in 1879 in Francestown.]

## SALTMARSH.

ISAAC SALTMARSH, son of Thomas (whose name is prominent in old records in Goffstown) and Betsey (Abbott) Saltmarsh, and grandson of William Saltmarsh of Watertown, Mass., was born in 1779. Betsey Abbott, the mother of Isaac Saltmarsh, was the daughter of Edward Abbott, who was one of the original proprietors of Concord, and grandson of George Abbott who came from Yorkshire, England, and settled in Andover, Mass., in 1643. Isaac Saltmarsh came here from Goffstown in 1793, married Phœbe Stratton of Bradford (whose mother was Abigail Barnes, sister of Rev. Jonathan Barnes), and settled on the Rodney Sawyer place west of the pond. In 1818 he bought the James Duncan place, built the Saltmarsh house in 1820, and died in 1825, aged forty-four. His wife died Sept. 13, 1872, aged eighty-two. Their children were: —

1. CYRUS, [b. May 21, 1809 ; m. Hannah B. Howe of Hillsborough; succeeded his father on the Duncan place, and d. Aug. 5, 1872, leaving one child : —
 Mary J., (b. in 1861.)]
2. STILLMAN, [b. Dec 12, 1811 ; d. in childhood.]
3. BETSEY A., [b. in 1815 ; was many years an invalid, and d. Jan. 11, 1870.]

4. REED P., [b. Dec. 4, 1820; lives unm. on his father's place. His extensive and accurate memory has afforded many items for this work. In his school-district, with a population of more than three hundred, he is the only native now living here whose years go back to 1820.]

## SARGENT.

BENJAMIN SARGENT came here from Mount Vernon about 1786. He was a clothier by trade, and lived on the old Breed stand at South Village some over seven years, when he moved to the State of Maine, and nothing further has been ascertained with regard to him. He seems to have built the first little fulling-mill in Antrim in 1787, and was succeeded by James Taylor in the spring of 1796, the mill falling into the hands of Breed about 1803. Sargent's mill was a very humble affair of the kind, but a decided convenience to the people.

## SAWYER.

ENOCH SAWYER, who came here from Goffstown in 1794, was the son of Edmond Sawyer, who moved from Hampstead (in which town he was selectman in 1758) to Sutton and died about 1805, aged ninety-two. This Edmond had three children: Joseph, whose descendants are very numerous and honorable; Enoch, who married Sarah Little and moved to Antrim; and Abigail, who married a Kimball, lived in Sutton, and has numerous descendants by the names of Martin, Andrews, Eaton, Adams, etc. Enoch Sawyer, who came to Antrim, brought with him four sons and four daughters. In Goffstown he was a leading man and had represented that town in the legislature. He lived in a house, now gone, south of Amos Dodge's, and often picked up deer's horns on his land. He was a vigorous and able man, and died in 1817, aged seventy-six. His four daughters were as follows: Betsey, who married Jonathan Marsh and lived in Hudson; Abigail, who became the second wife of Josiah Hayward Nov. 11, 1813, called "Nabby" on town record; Lucy, who married Richard Chase, and lived in Hillsborough; and Sally, who never married. The four sons will now be noticed separately.

SAMUEL SAWYER, son of Enoch and Sarah (Little) Sawyer, who came here from Goffstown in 1794, was married Dec. 29 of the same year to Susannah Reed, daughter of Zadok Reed who came from Litchfield to Antrim. He (Samuel) began the Caleb Clark farm, joining his father on the south, the following year, where his children by the first wife were all born. She died Jan. 17, 1815. Soon after he moved to Bedford. He married, second, Eleanor Orr of that town, May 16, 1816. She was daughter of Daniel Orr, was cousin of Hugh Orr of Antrim, and was sister of the celebrated teacher, Ann Orr. Samuel Sawyer died in Francestown June 22, 1848, aged seventy-seven, and was buried by his first wife on Meeting-House Hill. His children were:—

1. LUCY M., [b. Nov. 23, 1795; m. Thomas Carr, April 11, 1815; d. April 2, 1867.]

*Reed P. Saltmarsh*

2. SALLY L., [b. Dec. 24, 1797 ; d. Aug. 9, 1800.]
3. ZADOCK R., [b. Oct. 3, 1799 ; d. Aug. 10, 1800.]
4. SALLY L., [b. Sept. 24, 1802 ; m. Samuel Murch of Quincy, Mass. ; d. in Boston. Jan. 2, 1858.]
5. MARIA N., [b. Aug. 25, 1804 ; d. March 5, 1876, unm.]
6. WILLIAM REED, [b. Dec. 22, 1806 ; m. Abby Stevens of Francestown, June 22, 1835 : is one of the leading citizens of that town, and one of its worthiest men. Has but two children: Susie M., wife of Dea. Amasa Downs of Francestown, and William Reed, Jr., who m. Ella F. Camp of Manchester, and lives in that city.]
7. ABIGAIL P., [d. in childhood.]
8. POLLY W., [b. Jan. 8, 1811 ; m. Francis B. Merriam of Boston. She now lives, a widow, in Nashua. Her son, Capt. Francis B. Merriam, was a commander of a gun-boat in the navy during the war, and made a brilliant record.]
9. NATHANIEL N., [b. June 12, 1812 ; was out in the Seminole war three years, and was wounded in the forehead. He m. Sarah Bagley of Windsor in 1842, and d. in that town April 18, 1851, leaving no children. His widow lived alone on the farm eleven years, when she fell and broke her hip. It was in midwinter, and she was alone. She managed to crawl into the house, and lay there several days without help, and must have perished had not a neighbor happened to call. Having survived her terrible sufferings, she sold and came to Antrim, buying the old Brackett house, where she has lived alone. She is old, lame, her large property gone, and her kindred mostly dead ; but she is sustained and comforted by a blessed Christian hope.]
10. GEORGE O., [child of 2d wife, b. in Bedford June 27, 1818 ; m. Elisabeth Beard of Wilmington, Mass. ; has been an extensive furniture-manufacturer in Charlestown, Mass.]
11. JONATHAN M., [b. March 22, 1820 ; m. Rebecca Lund of Boston. He d. in Stirling, Mass., October, 1873.]

ENOCH SAWYER, the second son of Enoch and Sarah (Little) Sawyer, was born in 1777; married Lucy Simonds in 1802, and began the Tenney farm, joining his father on the east, where Rodney was born. He afterwards moved into a house with his brother Tristram on Meeting-House Hill; thence on to the mountain southwest of the Dinsmore place, — a wild tract of land, part of which he cleared, and on which he built a house, which has been gone many years. There his sons Edmond and Enoch were born. Mr. Sawyer died with his son Rodney, March 5,

1840, being a feeble man for more than twenty years. His children were : —

1. RODNEY, [b. March 10, 1804; m. Sarah Hills, Oct. 29, 1835, and moved on to the place west of the pond (begun by Samuel Vose), where he lived till 1855. His wife d. very suddenly, Feb. 11, 1853. He now resides in Clinton, working busily at the cooper's trade, quiet, respected, industrious, and devoted. Rodney Sawyer, though a man of unaffected manners and retiring habits, is possessed of tastes and capacities which favorable circumstances might have made conspicuous in the world. Like many a child of genius, he has lived unknown. Many of his musical compositions are worthy of a high place. The following poem, entitled "To the Friends of My Dear Wife," selected at random out of many, would do credit to many a writer's pen : —

> "Go to the church-yard — there alone
>   I often go and weep,
> For dearly loved ones down below
>   In death's cold prison sleep.
> My aching heart, though bold and brave,
> Melts there, beside the silent grave.
>
> "In that lone place, my dear wife lies;
>   Death came and took her there;
> She was, to me, earth's greatest prize,
>   She shared with me life's care.
> But. oh ! what bitter grief I've known
> Since o'er her breast the clods were thrown !
>
> "And oft I go, with reverent tread,
>   Where sleeps her sacred clay,
> To muse on joys forever fled,
>   Since she has passed away.
> For oh ! 'tis sweet e'en through my tears
> To look back on departed years!
>
> "But while I muse on that dear one
>   Of tried and changeless love, —
> That love, like rays shot from the sun,
>   Doth bear my thoughts above !
> So I'll not grieve that thus she lies,
> Since heaven, I trust, has been her prize.
>
> "So in that church-yard let her sleep;
>   Her rest is still and sweet,
> All undisturbed by storms, that sweep
>   Around our living feet !
> Ere long, I must, like her, repose,
> I trust, oblivious to my woes ! "

The children of Rodney and Sarah (Hills) Sawyer are:—

*Dr. Albert R.*, (b. Dec. 15, 1838. He graduated at a medical school in Cincinnati ; m. Sarah A. Wright, daughter of Dea. Imla Wright of Antrim, in 1856; was a young man of sound mind and great promise, and established as a physician in Bunker Hill, Ill., where he d. June 21, 1868, at thirty years of age. Was a surgeon in the army, and his early death was supposed to be the result of his exposure on the field.)

*Dea. David H.*, (b. Aug. 13, 1840 ; m. Ann R. Wood from Venice, N. Y., and now lives in Bunker Hill, Ill., being engaged, in company with Gardiner Parmenter, in a large furniture business. Is deacon in Congregational Church of that place.)]

2. REUBEN M., [b. August, 1805; m. Mary Preston, and moved to Francestown. Was frequently in office in that town, a faithful and efficient man ; d. July 9, 1878. He left but two children, Henry H., who is a merchant in Boston, and Clara, who m. Garvin D. Sleeper, Esq., of Francestown.]

3. EDMOND, [b. Sept. 17, 1807. He learned the blacksmith's trade by an apprenticeship of four years with Dea. Isaac Baldwin, and began business in Bedford; m. Nancy J., sister of Dea. Robert Steele, Nov. 19, 1835 ; bought out the blacksmith-shop at the Branch, in 1837, where he worked at his trade nearly forty years, hard and constantly, and has accumulated a large estate. He first lived in the Jones house, now Langdon Swett's ; then exchanged with Francis Reed for the locality opposite, where he built the present house in 1846, and the old one, being removed from the spot, was taken across the river, and is now occupied by Robert Hopkins. Mr. Sawyer's children are : —

*Samuel S.*, (b. Nov. 8, 1836 ; m. Mary Day of Peterborough, May 18, 1861; is chairman of the selectmen and representative of the town ; lives at North Branch, on the John Wallace place, having children as follows: Willis H., b. Jan. 6, 1863 ; Eva L., b. Dec. 31, 1865 ; Georgie Anna, b. April 10, 1867 ; Alice B., b. Dec. 12, 1869 ; Harry G., b. May 18, 1873.)

*Mary F.*, (b. June 18, 1846 ; m. D. P. Bryer, June 20, 1872.)]

4. ENOCH, [b. in 1812; m. Jemima Jones of Hillsborough, Dec. 10, 1835 ; moved to that town, and now lives in the Lower

Village, having only one child, Mrs. Sylvester Atwood, who lives with them.]

5. JOHN A., [b. in 1818; m. Betsey Robinson in 1847; learned the blacksmith's trade with his brother at the Branch, and now lives in Kansas.]
6. LUCETTA T., [worked many years in mills at Nashua, and d. at the Branch in 1868, aged 44.]

DEA. TRISTRAM SAWYER, the third son of Enoch and Sally (Little) Sawyer, was born in Goffstown in 1780; came here at the age of fourteen: married Mary Ann Templeton of Hillsborough; bought of Henry White and lived in the first house north of the cemetery at the old Center; built him a new house in 1810, which he moved whole down the hill in 1821. He was chosen deacon in the Presbyterian Church in 1816; moved to Hillsborough in 1831, where he died Aug. 11, 1859, leaving children:—

1. SILAS N., [b. June 19, 1805; m. 1st, Lucy P. Moore, June 4, 1833; 2d, Sarah A. Gunnerson; lived mostly in Hillsborough, but recently moved to Newport, where he d. in 1877.]
2. MARY ANN, [b. Sept. 14, 1806; d. Sept. 4, 1807.]
3. MARY WEBSTER, [b. June 5, 1808; d. July 23, 1810.]
4. ELIZABETH, [b. Sept. 17, 1809; m. Andrew Mack, and settled in Orange. Mass.]
5. SAMUEL, [b. May 8, 1811; d. in infancy.]
6. JANE, [b. Dec. 26, 1812; m. Warren Foster, and lives in Keene.]
7. SAMUEL, [b. July 30, 1813; d. young.]
8. HARRIET N., [b. Aug. 6, 1814; d. unm. in 1864.]
9. JOHN NICHOLS, [b. Sept. 1, 1816; m. 1st, Frances Whitmore; 2d, Susan Newell, and lives in Denison, Tex.]
10. ABBY WHITON, [b. Dec. 28, 1817; m. John S. Burtt, and lives in Fitchburg, Mass.]
11. TRISTRAM, [b. Nov. 3, 1819; m. Sarah J. Morrison; settled in Keene, and d. there, July 24, 1872.]
12. EDMOND, [b. May 11, 1821; m. Louisa Wright, and lives in Charles River Village, Mass.]
13. FRANCES CHRISTIE, [b. Oct. 5, 1825; lives unm. at Keene.]

EDMUND SAWYER, fourth son of Enoch and Sarah (Little) Sawyer, came to Antrim with the rest of the family from Goffstown, being the youngest. He learned the joiner's trade, and worked with his brother Tristram. He married Jane Taggart of Hillsborough; lived in Antrim somewhat over a year, and had one son, named Mark, born here. He then went to Stockbridge, Vt., and began a new farm in that town, where he had a large family. His third son, Levi Parsons, graduated at Dartmouth Medical College in 1854, and was a very successful physician in Nashua. Dr. Sawyer married his second cousin, daughter of Frank and Polly (Sawyer) Merriam, and died at Nashua a few years ago. His widow still resides there. Edmund's youngest son, Reuben M., named for Reuben Mark Sawyer, his cousin, late of Francestown, has lived in Nashua several years, where he is largely engaged in the grocery business.

CHARLES SAWYER, son of Abel and Elisabeth (Goodhue) Sawyer, and grandson of Jonathan and Isabel (Grimes) Sawyer, was born in Hancock, Dec. 19, 1812; married Olivia B. Priest of Dublin, Oct. 4, 1838, and moved here from Stoddard in 1867. He soon after bought the place now Freeman Pelsey's, on which he remained till his death, which occurred May 8, 1872. His children were : —

1. CHARLES D., [b. in Hancock, July 26, 1839; m. Martha A. Swett, daughter of Daniel Swett, Nov. 5, 1863 ; now lives in Clinton, in the Widow Tenney house. Is a carpenter by trade.]
2. MARY A., [b. Feb. 26, 1841; m. Asher S. Burbank, April 4, 1867. They now live in Boston.]
3. ALLEN L., [b. in Hancock, Oct. 6, 1843 ; m. Carrie A. Wilson of Stoddard, Nov. 2, 1865 ; lives in Clinton; has children, as follows : —
*George A.*, (b. in Stoddard, Sept. 6, 1866.)
*Mary L.*, (b. in Antrim, Nov. 11, 1870.)
*Lora*, (b. Dec. 7, 1874.)]
4. GEORGE A., [b. Oct. 26, 1848 ; d. in infancy.]
5. CLARENCE E., [b. in Stoddard, Feb. 22, 1857.]

## SAXBY.

MARK SAXBY came here and bought the Ferry place about 1816. He brought with him his aged father, James, a retired sea-captain. They came from Beverly, Mass. Mark also had followed the sea and commanded a ship. They came here under pressure of "hard times," at the suggestion of Dea. Taylor, a former acquaintance. Were a very respectable family, but poor. Mark worked here at the shoemaker's trade. After a few years they moved on to the McFarland place, but they all went with Dea. Taylor to Newark, N. Y., in 1824. They had several children, of whom old Mr. McFarland, living in the other part of the house, said: "If there's anything in the saying that snotty-nosed boys make respectable men, there's wisdom in them heads!" And these children are reported to have stood well in the world ! So far as known, they were as follows : —

1. JAMES, [became a Methodist minister, and is spoken of as a man of culture and ability.]
2. MARK, [nothing known.]
3. MARIA, [nothing known.]

## SENTER.

JAMES S. SENTER, son of Zaccheus and Dorcas Senter of Charleston, Vt., was born in that town, Dec. 7, 1822. Has lived in town in various places about a dozen years. Came here from Nashua. He married Ann Skinner. Only one child lived to maturity, Ada A., who was born in Morgan, Vt., June 25, 1855, and married Charles D. Whiting in 1876, and now lives in Nashua.

## SHADDOCK.

JOHN SHADDOCK came here from Hillsborough, and built in 1812 what was subsequently known as the "Minister-Davis house," on the north side of the cross-road a few rods east of the Shattuck corner. He married Hannah, daughter of Dea. Barachias Holt. Was a shoemaker. Had two children here. Then went to Charlestown, Mass., where he buried his wife. He came back to Antrim, but soon went to New York, the time being about 1821, since which but little can be learned of him.

## SHATTUCK.

DEA. FRANCIS M. SHATTUCK, of English descent, son of Abial and Sarah (King) Shattuck, and grandson of Abial and Phebe (Shattuck) Shattuck, cousins, of Andover, Mass., was born in Merrimack, Feb. 17, 1819. He spent most of his early years with Dr. Spalding in Amherst, where he received his religious impressions, and united with the church at the age of twenty-one. He married Almira Blanchard of Greenfield, Oct. 15, 1840, and lived in various places till 1855, when he bought the Dea. Steele farm and moved to Antrim in the spring of 1856. Having sold the Steele place, he bought the Warren Christie place in 1862, where he died Jan. 16, 1876. He was appointed deacon in the Center Church in 1866. Dea. Shattuck was an iron-molder by trade, and was a master-workman at that business many years. Was a man of remarkable energy and perseverance; a great worker; always the man sent for, for hard or dangerous jobs. He was a hearty, earnest Christian, always at his post, and greatly endeared to his church and all believers that knew him. On the whole, he was one of the most efficient men ever living in Antrim. His children are: —

1. MARY E., [b. in Amherst, July 11, 1841; m. Alvin R. Barker, June 1, 1859.]
2. LAURA, [b. Oct. 31, 1845, in Lyndeborough; m. Levi M. Curtis, March 19, 1864.]
3. MARTHA J., [b. Feb. 20, 1849, in Greenfield; m. Horace Brown Tuttle, Oct. 27, 1870.]

4. ALMA F., [b. May 19, 1855, in Nashua; m. Frank O. Clement, April 22, 1876, and now lives in Manchester.]

FRED H. SHATTUCK, who was a nephew of the deacon, and had his home here with him several years, was supposed to have been lost in the railroad calamity at Ashtabula, Ohio, as one item among the "killed" was "Fred Shattuck,— place unknown," and nothing was heard from him for a long time. But recently it is believed he has been heard from as a lumberman in the forests of Maine, and there disabled by an accident.

MRS. PHEBE SHATTUCK, the deacon's grandmother, lived to a great age, only lacking a few months of one hundred years. Her first home after marriage was in Hillsborough, where they remained but a short time. They then moved to Plainfield, Vt., and there raised a large family of children. When her son Abial last visited her, though upwards of ninety years of age, she walked with him some two miles when he left, and then with her blessing gave him ten dollars as her parting gift.

## SHAW.

REV. E. M. SHAW, son of Jacob, Jr., and Hannah (Bartlett) Shaw of Rockland, Me., and grandson of Jacob and Sybil (Ward) Shaw, was born Oct. 14, 1842. His mother was a daughter of Rev. Daniel Bartlett of China, Me. Mr. Shaw fitted for college at Waterville, and was graduated at Colby University in 1871. He studied theology at Newton, Mass., and was ordained as pastor of the Baptist Church in Antrim Sept. 30, 1873. He was a man of culture and grace, and held in the highest esteem by all. He married Carrie M. Burpee of Rockland, Me., Oct. 7, 1873, and they have one child:—

1. MINNIE M., [b. May 3, 1875.]

GEORGE W. SHAW, son of Joseph and Martha (Farrar) Shaw, was born in Meredith in 1847; came here to work for Mark True in 1872; married Lucretia M. Robinson March 4, 1873, and lives in Clinton Village. Their children are:—

1. HATTIE ALICE, [b. Jan. 22, 1874.]
2. LILLIAN EMMA, [b. Aug. 10, 1875.]
3. WARREN COCHRANE, [b. Dec. 9, 1876.]

## SHEDD.

JOHN S. SHEDD, son of John Shedd, Jr., and Betsey White, was born in Hillsborough, Oct. 15, 1819. John, Jr., was born Sept. 5, 1784, and married May 3, 1807. His wife Betsey died in Antrim, 1870, aged ninety. John, Jr., was son of John, who was born in Billerica, Mass., Aug. 7, 1756, and married Sarah Sprague Dec. 24, 1778. John moved to Hillsborough, and lived to great age. Was a witty man and always ready with a story, and was not in the habit of being outdone in that line. Coming down to John McNiel's store one afternoon in the "Grasshopper Year," they were telling what monstrous creatures of the kind had been found in the village. McNiel declared that one weighed two and one-half pounds. Shedd said that was nothing to what they had out on the farms; for that morning he went out a little before it was light to catch his horse, put his bridle on to the head of a grasshopper, and did not discover his mistake till he tried to get on and ride down to the house! Another story which is believed to belong to him is this: That he " went out one night to shoot skunks, and before nine o'clock he shot twenty on one log, — and it wasn't much of a log for skunks either!" John S. Shedd married Mary E. Tuttle of Antrim, May 20, 1846. Began life in New Bedford, but moved here in 1849 and went into trade with Almus Fairfield at the Branch. Soon sold out, and bought the south part of the Jacob Tuttle, or McClary farm, and put up the buildings there in 1850. In 1868 he moved into the Jonathan White house, South Village, which he still occupies. Children: —

1. MARY JOSEPHINE, [b. April 20, 1854; d. Aug. 17, 1856.]
2. NETTIE E., [b. July 5, 1857; m. Ruthven Childs, Jan. 1, 1879.]

## SIMONDS.

BENJAMIN SIMONDS of Antrim probably descended from William Simonds, who married Mrs. Judith (Phippen) Hayward and settled in Woburn, Mass., about 1643. William had a son, grandson, and great-grandson by name of Benjamin. A very numerous posterity branched out into Eastern Massachusetts and New Hampshire. Benjamin Simonds came here from Mont Vernon in 1793, on to the place next north of Loveren's mills (begun by the first Reuben Boutwell in 1783); married Polly Avery; and died in 1826, aged sixty-five, leaving children as follows: —

1. LUCY, [b. in Amherst, Jan. 30, 1784; m. Enoch Sawyer, in 1802; d. June 7, 1853.]
2. POLLY, [b. in Amherst, May 21, 1787; m. Robert Burns, Sept. 1, 1812; d. Oct. 3, 1857.]
3. JOHN, [b. in Amherst, May 3, 1790; m. Sally B. Preston, Feb. 3, 1814; after living in various places, cleared and settled the Nathaniel Herrick place in 1816, where he d. in 1858, leaving children : —

  *Mark*, (b. Aug. 23, 1815; m. Abney McClintock, and went to Windsor.)
  *Elvira*, (b. Oct. 19, 1816; m. Nathaniel B. Herrick, Oct. 6, 1835.)
  *Charles*, (b. Oct. 3, 1818; m. Harriet Buck of Windsor, and now lives in Providence, R. I.)
  *Lowell*, (b. June 30, 1820; m. 1st, Nancy Barrett of Stoddard,

GENEALOGIES. 679

and went to Goffstown, where she d.; m. 2d, Marina Brown, and afterward lived at North Branch, owning the saw and grist mill there. He now lives in Northumberland.)

*Achsah*, (b. April 1, 1822; m. John Pitman, and lives in Nashua. Her husband d. January, 1875.)

*Franklin B.*, (b. Feb. 20, 1825; m. Nancy Steele, and lives in Greenfield. Is conductor on the railroad.)

*Almina*, (d. in childhood.)

*Mary P.*, (b. July 14, 1829; m. Alvah Copeland, and lives in Hancock.)

*John R.*, (was drowned in the river near the house, April 29, 1838, aged 6.)

*Reuben S.*, (b. Sept. 19, 1833; m. Sarah M. Pike of Windsor in 1860, and lives at South Village, in a house built by himself in 1864. His children are Harvey C., b. March 9, 1862, and Ned M., b. July 16, 1866.)

*Henry*, (b. May 11, 1836; m. Rebecca Blood, and lives in Marlow.)]

4. SALLY, [b. in Amherst, March 8, 1792; m. William D. Atwood, May 7, 1812; moved to Hartland, Vt., and d. in 1836.]

5. BENJAMIN, [b. in Antrim, June 5, 1796; m. Betsey Preston of Windsor; lived on his father's farm, and d. Oct. 27, 1850, leaving children: —

*Daniel*, (b. Dec. 5, 1822; lives unm. on the old place.)

*Belinda M.*, (b. July 11, 1824; m. David Marden, and lives in New Boston.)

*Cyrus H.*, (b. Sept. 28, 1826; went to Antrim, Minn., and was in the army.)

*Elizabeth S.*, (b. July 14, 1830; m. Charles B. Cram.)

*Ephraim*, (b. July 27, 1832; m. Phœbe Kelsea, Dec. 24, 1857; built the Baker house, and lived some years at South Village. He now lives in Lowell, and has two children: Luella H., b. Jan. 16, 1859, and Fannie E., b. May 14, 1866.)

*Lewis*, (b. June 15, 1834; m. Etta Combs, Sept. 18, 1871, and they have two children: Willie H., b. in Antrim, Minn., July 22, 1873, and Mary, b. here Jan. 12, 1877. Mr. Simonds lost his right hand in the gearing of a threshing-machine in 1870. As he was oiling the machine his foot slipped and he fell forward, striking his hand into it. He now lives on the Conant place in the east part of the town.)]

6. NANCY, [b. in Antrim, Feb. 24, 1798; became second wife of Simeon Buck. Dec. 29, 1818, and d. in Windsor.]
7. SABRINA, [b. in Antrim, Feb. 25, 1803; became the third wife of Simeon Buck; d. in Windsor about 1860.]
8. MARK, [b. May 24, 1807; d. Nov. 1, 1807.]

JOSEPH SIMONDS, JR., was son of Joseph and ——— (Phelps) Simonds of Townsend, Mass., but afterwards of Wilton, this State. Joseph, Sen., married, second and third, two wives by name of Spalding, — not sisters. Joseph, Jr., married Rachel Burns, Sept. 3, 1812. He lived in several places in town, longest on the Whitney place, then belonging to Dr. Whiton. He died in Wilton in 1874, aged eighty-two. Children:—

1. WILLIAM, [m. Mary Ann Gale: lives in Stoddard.]
2. JAMES, [m. Mary A. Gerry: lived thirty-eight years in Boston; in recent years has been a trader in Stoddard; was b. Oct. 5, 1822.]
3. JOHN, [m. Mary A. Burrill; lives in Charlestown, Mass.]
4. ROBERT B., [was in Sandwich Islands when last heard of, many years ago.]
5. ABBY J., [b. in Townsend, Mass.; m. Curtis Bellows; lives in Wilton.]

JOHN SYMONDS, son of Charles and Sally Symonds of Hancock, married Caroline E. Robbins, Nov. 3, 1841; lived here in 1840–42; has no children; went to Keene, where he yet lives, and has been a leading business man in that place.

DEXTER SYMONDS, brother of the last, was born in Hancock, April 17, 1818. He married, first, Mary A. Parker of Antrim; second, Arabella H. Closson of Lyme. Came here in March, 1847, working at tanning business in South Village about five years. Has one son, Hartwell Dexter, born in Marlow, May 29, 1844. Went from Antrim to Lowell, and is now in business on Middlesex street in that city.

## SMITH.

WILLIAM SMITH, a Scotchman, and intimate friend of Dea. Aiken, was born in Ireland, Feb. 9, 1715; was son of James and Jean Smith, and came here from Londonderry in the spring of 1771. He was the second settler in South Antrim, and the third in town. Coming here at the age of fifty-six, his children were all born in Londonderry. He settled south of South Village, a few rods west of the road to Bennington, and not far from the south line of the town. The house was taken down in 1841, and the barn subsequently was moved up to the village, being the barn on the Chessmore farm. Smith was a peaceable, excellent, and pious man, — of a simple and practical religion worthy of notice. When his son John was designated to muster among the quota from Antrim in the company at New Boston, July 23, 1777, the father, though sixty-two years old, decided to take his son's place, "giving as his reason, that should he himself fall in battle he trusted he was prepared to meet his Judge in peace; while should his son go and be killed, he could cherish in relation to him no such hope!" So the old man went into the ranks and marched to join the forces under Stark, went through the battles against Burgoyne, and was present at his surrender, Oct. 17, 1777. Returning safe, he survived twenty-three years, was held in great love, and died in peace in 1800, aged eighty-five. His wife was Margaret Duncan, who died in 1790, aged sixty-seven. She was a sister of James, and cousin of Hon. John Duncan. Their children were: —

1. WILLIAM. [b. in 1749; d. in 1813, aged 64; unm.]
2. JOHN. [b. in 1757; m. Jane Wilson; cleared and settled where Thomas Flint now lives. He had no children. His death occurred in 1826. His widow survived till 1856, and d. aged 88. There being no room either side, they opened her husband's grave and laid the coffin upon his bones, — all there was left of him! He was a Revolutionary soldier.]
3. JEMIMA. [b. in 1753; m. William Ramsay of Greenfield, in 1785. Mr. and Mrs. Ramsay joined the Center Church at its formation in 1788. She d. in 1825, aged 72. He d. in 1833, aged 82.]
4. ROBERT. [b. in 1761; m. Hannah Moore, and lived a little southwest of S. S. Sawyer's at North Branch. He moved to Anson, Me., in 1816, and d. there in 1830, aged 69. His children have been prospered, and several of them live near one another in honored old age in North Anson, Me. They were as follows, all but the youngest b. here: —

*Samuel*, (b. June 7, 1796; m. Betsey Getshell of Madison, Me., and now lives in Anson, that State.)

*John*, (b. Oct. 6, 1797; d. in infancy.)

*Peggy*, (b. April 7, 1799; d. in infancy.)

*Mary Duncan*, (b. Aug. 28, 1800; m. Lemuel Rogers of Anson, Me., and d. there in 1869.)

*John*, (b. Aug. 31, 1802; d. of spotted fever in 1812.)

*William*, (b. May 5, 1804; m. Almeda Savage of Anson, Me., and d. there at the age of 33.)

*Sutheric Weston*, (b. Jan. 29, 1806; m. Allema Sawyer of New Portland, Me., and occupies the farm where his father settled in 1816.)

*Jemima Ramsay*, (b. Jan. 31, 1808; d. unm. at the age of 33.)

*Peggy Jane*, (b. Sept. 9, 1809; m. James Young of Madison, Me., and lives at a place called "The Forks," in Maine.)

*Hannah*, (b. May 30, 1811; m. John Caswell of New Portland, Me.; d. in 1840.)

*Betsey Tuttle*, (b. May 24, 1814; m. David B. Rogers of Anson, Me.)

*Joseph M.*, (b. in Anson, Me., in 1818; m. Sarah E. Walker of that place, and now resides there, having eight children, all daughters.)]

5. JAMES, [went to Ohio, and nothing further is known of him.]

ABRAHAM SMITH, son of Alexander Smith of Londonderry, was born Jan. 23, 1768; came here from Hudson in 1795, and lived on the north side of Meeting-House Hill, on the farm now in part Benjamin F. Dustin's. The buildings were on the old road. He married Jane, daughter of Dea. William McNiel of New Boston, had a large family, and died in 1816. She died Sept. 26, 1842, aged sixty-four. Their children were: —

1. SARAH, [b. June 18, 1796; d. in infancy.]
2. JAMES, [b. July 27, 1798; m. Sarah W. Brackett, April 19, 1832, and lived on the old place. He d. in 1841, leaving no children. His widow m. George Merrill. She d. Aug. 12, 1877.]
3. JOHN, [b. May 2, 1800; m. Clementine Hamblin of Tewksbury, Mass., in 1830. He was a carpenter by trade; built the George McIlvaine house (now B. F. Dustin's) in 1829, and lived there, while his brother James lived on the east part of the old farm. He moved to Andover, Mass., in 1840, and d. July 10, 1842. His only child d. in infancy.]
4. WILLIAM, [b. April 13, 1802; d. in infancy.]
5. RACHEL, [b. Dec. 12, 1803; m. 1st, Prescott Melvin of Londonderry; 2d, Samuel Corning. The first marriage took place Feb. 14, 1826. Moved to Londonderry and d. there. Her son, Horace Corning, was killed in the Union army in the late war.]
6. BETSEY, [b. Aug. 22, 1805; m. Samuel Gilchrist, March 24, 1829; went to Andover, Mass., where she now resides.]
7. JANE, [b. Oct. 5, 1808; m. David Boynton of Lowell, Mass., and is now living, a widow, in Milford.]
8. WILLIAM McNIEL, [b. Nov. 12, 1810; was disabled, having lost a leg by fever-sore when five years of age. He m. Lucinda Fowler of Hudson; went to Merrimack, where he d. Dec. 10, 1872, leaving no children; was a shoemaker by trade, and once had a shop on Meeting-House Hill.]
9. SAMUEL, [b. Sept. 4, 1812; d. in 1837, aged 25.]

10. GRISEL M., [b. Nov. 7, 1814; m. Reuben Melvin, Nov. 15, 1836; went to Londonderry, and d. there April 12, 1846.]

CAPT. ISAAC SMITH, son of Ichabod and Mary Smith, was born in Deering in 1766; married Nancy Codman, daughter of Dr. William Codman of Deering, and came here from that town in 1818. He bought the farm now the Widow Gould place, on which the three-story tavern (built by William Barnes of Hillsborough) had been burned Feb. 1 of that year, at once built the present house, and kept tavern there many years. He finally went back to Deering, where he died in 1834. His widow died in 1837. Their children were: —

1. ISAAC, [b. in 1791; m. Pamelia Stevens of Hillsborough, June 10, 1817, and settled in Deering on the old farm, now occupied by his son, Isaac Smith, now one of the chief men in that town. Thus three Isaac Smiths were b. on that spot.]
2. CATHERINE, [b. in 1793; m. Joseph Merrill of Deering.]
3. RHEMY, [b. in 1794; m. a Mr. Jones, and went to Western New York.]
4. AGNES, [b. in 1796; m. William Campbell of Antrim, and d. here in 1828.]
5. HENRY C., [b. in 1798; went to Cambridge, Mass., in early life; m. Mary Tuten of that place: after some years came to Antrim to live with his father, but, on removal of the latter to Deering, moved to Nashua, where he d. Had children, all of whom but the two oldest were b. in this town: —

    *Mary Jane*, (b. in Cambridge, Mass.; d. aged 20.)
    *Ann Maria*, (b. in Cambridge, Mass.; m. John Robinson of Nashua, now of California.)
    *Sarah*, (lives in Nashua; m. 1st, John Wright of Brookline; 2d, George McIntosh.)
    *Charles H.*, (went quite young to South America; m. a Chilian lady; after her death he came back to the United States; was awhile an orange-planter in Florida; subsequently in the meat business, firm of Smith and Leighton, in Nashua, but has now fixed his home in Florida. He m. 1st, the lady referred to above, who never came to the United States; 2d, Albertine Ball, daughter of Dr. Ball, a dentist of Nashua and vicinity for many years.)
    *Robert*, (at age of 17 went to Texas; was drafted into the rebel army and served till the close of the war; is now a stock-raiser in the Lone Star State.)

*Rebecca*, (m. George McKeen of Nashua, where they now reside.)]

6. TURNER, [b. in 1800; went West in early life, and this is all that is known of him.]
7. LAURAIN, [b. in 1802; m. Samuel Gibson of Hillsborough, after whose death she went to Milford and d. there.]
8. JAIL, [d. at age of 11.]
9. ACHASA, [m. Charles W. Spalding, Sept. 17, 1832; went to Albany. N. Y., thence to Zanesville, Ohio.]
10. PRINCESS, [b. in 1806; m. a Mr. Fletcher; went to Albany, N. Y., thence to Zanesville, Ohio. Fletcher and Spalding, named above, were merchant-tailors, in company in both these places.]
11. LARNERD, [b. in 1809; went to Buffalo, N. Y., in 1830, thence to St. Clair City, Mich., where he amassed a large fortune, and d. in 1874, the last of the family.]

OTIS SMITH, son of Uriah and Susan (Cram) Smith, was born Nov. 2, 1807; came here from Wilton in 1837, and built the house he now occupies the next year. He married Roxanna Breed March 10, 1827. Their children are: —

1. SUSAN B., [b. Aug. 5, 1828; m. Cyrus P. Tenney of Hancock in 1849.]
2. SARAH, [b. Aug. 29, 1830; m. Alvah Hadley of Peterborough. and lives in Cambridge, Mass.]
3. GEORGE, [d. in 1841, aged 9.]
4. JENNIE. [b. March 16, 1835; m. Lewis Worcester of Rochester, and lives in Dubuque, Io.]
5. MARY, [b. April 9, 1837; d. in infancy.]
6. LIZZIE, [b. July 19, 1839; m. John May, and lives in Fitchburg, Mass.]
7. ALBERT O., [d. in infancy.]
8. WILLIE O., [b. Sept. 5, 1849; m. Delia Pettee of Francestown; now lives in Boston.]

DAVID O. SMITH, son of David and Mary (Averill) Smith, married Mary Stone, and came here from Mont Vernon in 1846. He moved to Concord in 1852, where he still abides. He had two children: —

1. DAVID A., [m. Lydia A. Gray of Hancock; lived in Concord; was killed on the railroad at Canaan Nov. 25, 1868, aged 34.]
2. HELEN L., [with her father at Concord; unm.]

CAPT. LEANDER SMITH, son of James and Sarah (Hildreth) Smith of Mont Vernon, and grandson of Cooley Smith of Middleton, Mass., was born in Mont Vernon, Aug. 22, 1808; married Sophronia Wilkins, Nov. 29, 1833 ; came to Antrim from Mont Vernon in 1860, and bought the Buckminster place, where he now lives. He represented Mont Vernon in the legislature five years, and has been many years selectman, both in Mont Vernon and Antrim. His children are:—

1. GEORGE W., [b. April 19, 1835 ; d. in the service of his country, Oct. 15, 1863, being a member of the Sixteenth N. H. Regiment.]
2. AUGUSTA. [b. June 5, 1837 ; m. 1st, Moses Carr of Newport, Nov. 15, 1861, who d. in 1864 ; m. 2d, William N. Conn, July 26, 1877. She has one child : —
   *George M.*, (b. Nov. 5, 1864.)]
3. ELBRIDGE F., [b. Dec. 14, 1839 ; d. in the army at New Orleans (Eighth N. H. Regiment), Dec. 25, 1862.]
4. JAMES M., [b. Sept. 19, 1842 ; d. from disease contracted in the army (Ninth N. H. Regiment), July 15, 1865.]
5. EMELINE W., [b. Jan. 19, 1844 ; m. C. F. Holt of Antrim, Nov. 26, 1863, and lives in Clinton Village.]
6. EMILY W., [twin-sister of Emeline W. ; m. Francis White, Nov. 7, 1865, and lives in Cambridge, Mass.]
7. ARTHUR L., [b. July 29, 1855 ; lives with his father.]

JOHN H. SMITH, son of John and Cynthia (Smith) Smith, was born in Mont Vernon in 1835; married Almira Fletcher in 1862, and came here to work in Clinton in 1867. He bought the north school-house in South Village in 1870, and fitted it up for a dwelling, which he has since occupied. He was out in the army as a member of the Thirteenth N. H. Regiment.

FRANK G. SMITH was born in Francestown in 1827; married Harriet N. Damuth of Calais, Me., and came to Antrim from Bennington on to the Jonathan Nesmith place in 1872, but moved back to Bennington in 1876. Their children are: —

1. CHESTER R., [b. in 1864.]
2. FRANK U., [b. in 1866.]
3. CHARLES W., [b. in 1867.]
4. HATTIE K., [b. in 1869.]

CHARLES H. SMITH, son of Prosper and Monica Smith, was born in Woodstock, Vt., Dec. 21, 1823; married Nancy M. Mumford of Eastford, Conn. He entered the N. H. Conference of the Methodist Church in the spring of 1853. Was stationed first in Derry one year; then in Gilmanton two years; then came here in the spring of 1856 and was stationed at the Branch two years. After four years elsewhere, was again appointed to Antrim, 1863-64. Now lives in Sandown. Was looked upon while in Antrim as a man good and faithful. Children: —

1. GEORGE A., [b. in Antrim, May 6, 1857.]
2. LIZZIE, [m. Forrest E. Cate in 1877. and they live in Epping.]
3. JENNIE S.

## STACEY.

HARVEY STACEY, son of David and Rhoda (Curtis) Stacey of Windsor, was born in June, 1821; married Caroline E. Woods of Hancock in 1845, and moved to Antrim in 1849, on to the James Wallace place, now occupied by William Stacey. He now lives at South Village, having no children.

WILLIAM STACEY, brother of Harvey, was born in Stoddard in 1823. He moved to this town, on to the James Wallace place, with his father; and after the death of the latter in 1851, he bought out the other heirs, and still occupies the farm. In 1852 he married Mary A. Taylor, daughter of Dea. John Taylor of Danbury, and their children are : —

1. LIZZIE J., [b. Nov. 6, 1860.]
2. CHARLES E., [b. Oct. 31, 1865.]

DAVID M. STACEY, half-brother of Harvey and William (his mother being Louisa, sister of Rhoda Curtis), was born in Windsor in 1838. He came to Antrim with his father; married Mary E. Swett of Antrim, Nov. 27, 1862, and lives at North Branch. They have one child : —

1. MABEL, [b. April 24, 1867.]

NATHAN STACEY, cousin of Harvey, William, and David, named above, was born in Stoddard April 5, 1816. He was son of Samuel and Mary (Hardy) Stacey, and grandson of Ebenezer and Rebecca (Sawtelle) Stacey of Groton, Mass. Ebenezer had been many years a sailor, and was among the earliest settlers of Stoddard. Nathan Stacey came to Antrim in 1865, and moved back to Stoddard in 1870. He married Huldah Copeland of Stoddard. Children, all born in Stoddard, were : —

1. NETTIE M., [b. Feb. 16, 1849; m. William Blanchard, Nov. 4, 1868.]
2. HENRY P., [b. April 3, 1854; d. July 21, 1874.]
3. WILLIE L., [b. Dec. 8, 1860.]

## STARRETT.

WILLIAM STARRETT was son of Dea. William (who was deacon of the church in Francestown forty-eight years, and one of those who signed a petition to Gov. Wentworth in 1773, for a land-tax to build a meeting-house and settle a minister) and Abigail (Fisher) Starrett, and grandson of William and Mary (Gamble) Starrett, which last-named William came over from Scotland with his brother's family and settled in Warren, Me., in the early part of the eighteenth century. William, who came here, was born in Francestown, Nov. 4, 1771, being the second of thirteen children, all of whom are now dead. He came to Antrim from Francestown in 1793; was a tanner by trade, and put up the tannery long owned by George Duncan. He married Lucy Baldwin of Antrim (sister of Capt. Isaac Baldwin), Sept. 22, 1797; built and occupied the house now Isaac Fletcher's. He moved to Warren, Me., in 1803, and died in Putnam, that State, Aug. 25, 1817. His wife died in Warren, Me., Feb. 18, 1821, aged forty-five. Their children, except one that died here at the age of two, were : —

1. CHARLES HAMMOND, [b. in Antrim, July 6, 1800 ; was a blacksmith ; lived awhile in Francestown, then in Nashua, then moved to Gray, Me., and d. there in 1869; m. Betsey Hopkins of Francestown. No children.]
2. CYRUS, [b. in Antrim, Feb. 21, 1802 ; started to join the Mormons but changed his mind and settled in Warren, Penn. He m. a Miss Philbrook of Appleton, Me. They are still living.]
3. LOE, [b. in Warren, Me., March 13, 1804 ; m. Johnson Thurston of Franklin, Mass. ; settled in Appleton, Me. ; now lives, a widow, in North Union, that State.]
4. WILLIAM, [b. in Warren, Me., Sept. 26, 1806 ; was a blacksmith ; moved from Francestown to East Douglas, Mass., where he d. in 1848.]
5. MARK, [b. in Putnam, Me., January, 1809 ; was a blacksmith ; unm. ; d. at Douglas, Mass., at the age of 29.]
6. FANNY, [b. in Putnam, Me., Nov. 5, 1810 ; m. John Miller of that place ; had nine children ; moved to Lawrence, Mass. She d. there in 1855, and her husband in 1859.]
7. HARRIET, [b. July 24, 1814 ; m. William Perkins of Kennebunkport, Me. He d. young, leaving but one child, Philip Perkins, who graduated at Cornell and is now a lawyer in Wisconsin.]
8. ABIGAIL, [b. Sept. 25, 1817 ; went at the age of fourteen to Cincinnati, Ohio, as a teacher.]

JOHN STARRETT, son of John Starrett and Betsey Day, was born in Antrim, in 1807, and lived here until 1829. He now lives in Stoneham, Mass. Has been successful in business, and is placed among the most worthy that have gone out from Antrim. He married, first, Nancy Richardson of Hillsborough, who left one child, now Mrs. Ann O. Chase of

Winchester, Mass. He married, second, Adeline White of Deering, who died childless. He married, third, Minerva H. Cheney of Weare. Their daughter, Sarah E., married George J. Childs.

DAVID STARRETT, son of John and Anna (Love) Starrett of Francestown, married Sarah A. Bixby of Hillsborough, and came here in 1852, on to the Daniel Lowe, or Dea. Worthley place, which he soon sold and bought the Jonathan Carr place. This he sold to Dea. H. B. Newman in 1855, and now lives in Greenfield, having but one child born in this town: —

1. RANSOM B., [b. in Antrim, April 21, 1853.]

## STEELE.

SAMUEL STEELE came here from Lyndeborough in 1782, and located on the Benjamin Kidder farm. It is not certain that his log cabin was on the site of the present house. His name appears in the transcript of a road July 9, 1783, " along Marked trees to Sam¹ Steels house." He and his wife were warned out of town Oct. 22, 1783. This was only a legal formality, but it seems that they moved away in the following year. Whither they went, and what became of them, we have no means of knowing.

JAMES STEELE (son of Thomas, who was born in Ireland in 1694, married Martha Morrison in 1715, and became one of the first sixteen settlers of Londonderry) came here in 1780, being then fifty-five years of age, and began the clearing of the farm now Franklin Perry's. Two sons, Alexander, aged about seventeen, and Samuel, aged about fourteen, were left to clear the place, and boarded with Widow James Dickey, where the large brick house now stands. They worked every day until, in early twilight, they heard the wolves howl in the meadows below, when they started by marked trees to find the house. Mr. Steele married, first, Peggy Ramsay, daughter of Hugh Ramsay of Londonderry, who seems to have died near the close of 1757. He married, second, Mrs. Margaret (Parker) Cochran, and died here Feb. 19, 1819. Two children, one by the first, and one by the second wife, are supposed to have died in infancy. The following obituary, copied from the "Cabinet" of March 13, 1819, gives still further notice of his life and character: —

" In Antrim, on the 19th ult. [February, 1819], Mr. James Steele, aged ninety-five, wanting but a few weeks. From his extreme age, and the vicissitudes through which he passed, it may be proper to give a biographical sketch of his life. His parents were one of the first sixteen families which settled in Londonderry in 1719. He was born in March, 1724. He was twice married. By his first wife he had six children, and after her death he entered the army in the old French war, under Generals Amherst and Broadstreet, and was marched from Albany, by the way of Oswego and the lakes, into Canada, as far as Montreal. At the close of the campaign, in 1758, he returned to Londonderry. In 1761 he married his second wife, by whom he had seven children. After his second mar-

riage, he lived five years in Londonderry, and then moved to Haverhill, Mass., where he lived seven years, and carried on the potter's business. He then moved to Bedford, this State, and carried on his wife's farm till her first husband's children came of age. In 1780 he moved to Antrim, where he ended his days. He retained his mental faculties to a great age, though for several of his last years he was much superannuated and childish; but was carefully and tenderly used by an affectionate son and daughter-in-law with whom he lived, and no doubt they will receive their reward for performing the duty required in the fifth commandment. He was a professor of religion for above seventy years, and has left a numerous offspring. His last illness was short but severe. He lost his speech for some days, until within a few hours of his death, when he revived and made an appropriate prayer, to the astonishment of the beholders — then died — the good old man; and we trust he has made a happy change, and is now at rest. The memory of the just is blessed."

Children of James Steele are as follows : —

1. MARTHA, [m. Daniel McFarland ; d. April 25, 1831, aged 79.]
2. SARAH, [m. Dea. James Fisher, and lived in Francestown.]
3. MARGARET, [m. Hugh Jameson of Antrim; d. June, 1848, aged 95.]
4. MOLLY, [m. Thomas Jameson ; d. June 5, 1831, aged 71.]
5. JAMES, [m. Alice Boyd, and settled where William Curtis now lives (the Asa Goodell farm). He built the large square house now standing there; also the Steele mills (now Esty and McIlvaine's stand), next below the Branch. He d. March 5, 1825, aged 67. His children were : —

*Lettice*, (b. Oct. 21, 1786 ; d. unm. aged 60.)

*Margaret*, (b. Nov. 3, 1788 ; m. John Ramsay, and settled in Hancock.)

*Alice*, (b. Aug. 12, 1791 ; m. Jesse Cheney of Antrim, Nov. 25, 1813, and was mother of Benjamin P. Cheney, the proprietor of Cheney's Express. She d. July 28, 1849.)

*James*, (b. Oct. 7, 1793 ; m. Submit R. Tuttle, Dec. 21, 1824 ; lived on the Flint place at the Branch, and d. in 1831, leaving one son, Jacob P., who was b. Nov. 19, 1827, and is now living in Boston.)

*Mary*, (b. April 7, 1796 ; m. George Dascomb of Hillsborough, Feb. 26, 1822, and is the mother of Rev. A. B. Dascomb of Winchendon, Mass.)

*Anne*, (b. May 6, 1800 ;. m. Nathaniel M. Wright of Concord, Mass., and now lives in Manchester.)

*Isaac B.*, (b. April 19, 1803 ; m. Clarissa J. Stickney, Jan. 31,

1833; lived on his father's place, where he d. in 1846, leaving children as follows: Adeline M., who was b. April 24, 1836, and is now a teacher in Boston; Frances M., who was b. Jan. 8, 1839, and is now a teacher in Boston; George E., who was b. March 4, 1841, and d. June 11, 1844; James A., who was twin-brother of George, and d. Feb. 10, 1843; Georgianna, who was b. May 1, 1844, and is now a teacher in Boston.)

*Thomas*, (b. May 20, 1806; m. Diadeema Huse; went to Hillsborough, thence to Manchester, where he d. in 1869, leaving no children.)]

6. THOMAS, [first child by second wife; went to South Carolina in early life, and but little is known of him.]

7. ALEXANDER, [went South with his brother, and his descendants all live there.]

8. SAMUEL, [m. Nancy McKeen of Deering. Her father, Robert McKeen, settled in Cherry Valley, N. Y., and being on a sick-bed when that place was destroyed by Indians Nov. 11, 1778, rose and fled with his family to the woods. At night, driven by cold to seek shelter, they crept to a house which the Indians had spared, built a fire and warmed themselves, then all crept back again to the woods, not daring to stay in the house. After this was over, they came at once to New Hampshire, and settled in Deering, where his brother, Dea. William McKeen, had already settled. Samuel Steele lived on the old homestead, and d. June 21, 1845, aged 79. His wife d. Feb. 15, 1841, aged 74. His children were: —

*Dea. Robert*, (b. Dec. 25, 1791; m. Betsey Temple, sister of Zenas Temple, Dec. 26, 1815, and lived on the old homestead. He was appointed deacon in the Presbyterian Church in 1825, and was an able and good man. He sold his place to Dea. Shattuck in 1856, and, to the regret of all his townsmen, moved to Geneseo, Ill., where he d. in 1867, leaving four children, as follows: Mary, who m. John E. Bryant of Francestown, who carried on the shoe business in the Amos Holt house and thence went to New York, where she d. in 1873; Lizzie, who m. John M. Taylor of Geneseo, Ill., Oct. 6, 1852; Samuel, who m. Mary Fairchild of Ogdensburg, N. Y., went to Geneseo, and d. there in 1874; and Hon. Robert F., who m. Eliza Hardy and lives in Geneseo, Ill., having been promoted to many offices of trust in that place, and being one of the most worthy of Antrim's scattered sons.)

*Margaret*, (b. Sept. 25, 1793; m. John Taylor, Dec. 7, 1815; d. in Geneseo, Ill., in 1862.)

*Mary*, (b. Oct. 31, 1795; m. Anson S. Slosson, Oct. 16, 1827; after his death she followed her sons to Albany, Kan., where she d. in 1867.)

*James*, (b. Feb. 26, 1798; d. Aug. 22, 1800.)

*Nancy*, (b. Jan. 25, 1800; d. Aug. 29, 1800.)

*James*, (b. April 8, 1802; m. Susan Manahan of Francestown in 1831, and moved on to the N. C. Ferry place; after some years he moved on to the Cram place, and thence to Nashua in 1852, where he d. in May, 1866, leaving eight children, thus: Nancy A., who m. Frank B. Simonds in 1852 and lives in Greenfield; David, who m. 1st, Ellen Ford of Bristol. Vt., and 2d, Elvira Hewlit of New York, and d. in Nashua in 1872, aged 33; Samuel, who m. Orient Turner of Canada, and d. in 1867, aged 28, leaving no children; James, who m. Jennie P. Chamberlain of Portland, Me., and lives in Nashua; Mary L., who m. Alfred Davis of Londonderry, Vt., and lives in Nashua; John A., who m. Lucy Greeley of Londonderry, and lives at Springfield, Vt.; Ella F., who d. in 1850, aged 4 years; Almon, who d. in 1862, aged 11 years.)

*Nancy J.*, (b. May 20, 1809; m. Edmond Sawyer of Antrim, Nov. 19, 1835.)]

9. JENNETT, [b. 1772; m. Charles Wood, and was mother of Dea. Samuel Wood.]

10. SUSANNA, [m. 1st, Dea. James Robinson of Bow, Nov. 24, 1812, and after his death m. Dea. Jacob Spalding of Hillsborough, whom she survived, and d. in good old age, leaving generous sums of money for religious purposes.]

11. ROBERT, [b. in Bedford, April 13, 1774; m. Sally Carson of Francestown, Dec. 31, 1801; lived some years in a house on what was then part of his father's estate, now Franklin Perry's pasture. The house stood on the west side of Cochran brook. About 1807 he moved with three children to Hebron, N. Y. He d. Nov. 11, 1848, in Oberlin, Ohio. His wife d. in the same place, Jan. 25, 1864. Children were: —

*Dr. Alexander*, (b. here, Oct. 25, 1802; m. Maria Whedon of Hebron, N. Y., July 12, 1831; d. in Oberlin, Ohio, April

6, 1872. Had six children. John, the second son, was a lieutenant-colonel in the war, was on staff of Gen. Thomas, and at close of the war was judge-advocate of the interior. Another son, George W., was one of the founders of "Oberlin Conservatory of Music," is an organist of note, lives in Hartford, Conn., and is professor of music in Smith College, Northampton, Mass. Charlotte, daughter of Dr. Alexander Steele, has charge of the music in Mt. Holyoke Seminary. Dr. Steele graduated at Castleton, Vt., in 1829, and went at once into practice, but moved to Oberlin in 1836. Was among the first settlers in that place. Lived in a log house, but survived to pursue an extensive practice for thirty-six years, amass wealth, and die with the respect and veneration of a large and most intelligent community. Was a philanthropist and Christian. a pleasant man, but always faithful to his convictions. Filled many places of trust. His record is an honor to his native town.)

*Dr. John*, (b. here, Aug. 19, 1804; m. Mary Snell of Plainfield, Mass., Nov. 11, 1836; d. in Dondegal. India, October, 1842. Left no children. Went to the Madura Mission as physician and secretary in 1836. After six years of faithful labor in this missionary work, he fell a victim to fever, and d. in the midst of increasing usefulness.)

*Nancy C.*, (b. here, June 22, 1806; m. Joseph W. Butler of Volney, N. Y., March 10, 1836, and d. in that place Jan. 2, 1858. Two of her sons lost their lives in the army. One, Jay S. Butler, is an editor in Oswego, N. Y.)

*Rev. James*, (b. in Hebron, N. Y., Nov. 24, 1808; m. 1st, Frances Cochran; 2d, Minerva McConoughey. He d. in Oberlin in 1859. Was a student in Lane Seminary; was one of the "thirty anti-slavery rebels," as they were then called, who left that institution. He graduated at Oberlin Theological Seminary in 1840. Was appointed to the Madura Mission in 1841. Was a devoted missionary. Left three children, one of whom is Rev. Edward S. Steele, pastor of the Congregational Church at Joy Prairie, Ill.)

*Mary Jane*, (d. March 21, 1818, aged 8.)

*Rev. Calvin*, (b. in Rupert, Vt., Feb. 1, 1813; m. 1st, Amorette Eells; 2d, Amelia Ferry. He d. in Oberlin, Feb. 23, 1851. Was a graduate of Oberlin Theological Seminary, 1844. Was an energetic minister, most of his work being the help and organization of churches on the frontier. Left but two children.)

*Martha A.*, (d. in infancy.)

*Samuel*, (b. in Hebron. N. Y., Feb. 3, 1817. Graduate of Oberlin Theological Seminary, in class of 1843. Never went into the ministry. Was out in the Union army three years. Is now an extensive farmer in Ionia, Ill. He m. Elizabeth Kedzie, Jan. 4, 1844.)

*Susannah*. (b. April 30. 1819; d. in Oberlin in 1855, unm.)]

## STICKNEY.

WILLIAM STICKNEY and his wife Elizabeth, with three children, Samuel, Amos, and Mary, were among the first settlers of Rowley, Mass. He was born in Frampton, England, in 1592, and died in Rowley, Mass., in 1665. His wife survived him several years. They had ten children. the eldest of whom. Samuel Stickney, was born in England in 1633 and came to America with his father when five years of age. He married, first, Julian Swan of Rowley in 1653; second, Mrs. Prudence (Leaver) Gage of Bradford, April 6. 1674. This Samuel had a *son* Samuel, by his first wife. Julian Swan. born in Rowley in 1663. This second Samuel married Mary Heseltine. who was born April 30, 1672. and they had among other children a son Abraham, born in Bradford, Oct. 16. 1703. Abraham married Abigail Hall of Dracut, Feb. 20, 1727-8. They lived in Billerica and afterwards in Tewksbury, where he was deacon of the Congregational Church. He died in that place, Aug. 23, 1783, leaving seven children. Abraham, son of Dea. Abraham and Abigail (Hall) Stickney, mentioned above, was born in Billerica, Mass., Nov. 28. 1733; married Sarah Kittredge of Tewksbury, Mass., Dec. 9, 1755, by whom he had ten children, and died in Tewksbury March 19, 1803. He was lieutenant in the Revolutionary service during the years 1776 and 1778.

DR. JEREMIAH STICKNEY of Antrim, the youngest child of Abraham and Sarah (Kittredge) Stickney. was born in Tewksbury, Mass., April 21, 1783. At the age of sixteen, he went to Mont Vernon to live with Dr. Zephaniah Kittredge (who was his brother-in-law, having married his sister Elizabeth). There he attended school awhile, and then went to Hancock to school, boarding in the family of Dr. Stephen Kittredge, brother of Zephaniah. He studied Latin with Rev. Dr. Church of Pelham, and also in Westford Academy. In 1803, he commenced the study of medicine with Dr. A. P. Grosvenor of Pelham, and married Susannah Atwood of that town, Feb. 9, 1807. Equipped now, with horse and saddle-bags, he started in pursuit of a location. Arrived at Mont Vernon, he heard of the death of Dr. Cleaves, and came to Antrim at once (April 21, 1807). He engaged board with Dr. Cleaves's widow, and at once found himself in good practice. In July of the same year he brought his wife here, taking rooms in the Dea. Weston house (Oliver Swett's), then new, and the best in the place. In 1809 he moved and fitted up the

Champney house, which he occupied thirteen years, and there most of his children were born. In 1819, he went to Bradford under an urgent call, and every man in Antrim signed a petition to have him return, which he accordingly did. In 1822, he built the Moody McIlvaine house, and there spent the remainder of his days. He was a man of extensive influence; genial and social: was disabled many years by a shock of palsy. He united with the Center Church in his old age, and died in Christian peace, Aug. 24, 1865. His wife died in 1854, aged seventy. Their large family of children, all born in Antrim, are as follows: —

1. DR. AUGUSTUS GROSVENOR, [b. Sept. 7. 1807; studied medicine with his father, and at Williams College; m. Louisa Wilson of Hancock, June 10, 1834; settled in West Townsend, Mass.; had a large practice; d. in 1862.]
2. MOSES WHITING, [b. Dec. 7, 1810; m. Susan S. Carr of Antrim, Feb. 25, 1834, who d. in 1848 : m. 2d, Mary A. Plank of Lowville, N. Y. He went to Boston as a clerk in 1826, but afterwards was in business many years in Albany, N. Y., having the largest spice and coffee establishment in America. He was one of the donors of the organ and vestry to the Center Church. A genial and good man. He d. Feb. 5, 1877. Left but one child : —

   *Milton Whiting*, (b. Jan. 4, 1852; m. Rosa A. Hobbs, Dec. 26, 1878.)]
3. ALFRED, [b. Jan. 6, 1812; d. May 23, 1819.]
4. DR. JAMES MILTON, [b. Nov. 24, 1813; studied medicine with his father, graduated at Vermont Medical College, and has long been in practice in Pepperell, Mass. He m. Mary Eaton of Townsend, Mass., but has no children.]
5. LEANDER, [b. Nov. 12, 1815; m. Fanny Rogers in 1841, who d. in 1851; m. 2d, Mary E. Dowlin, in 1853. He is in company with his brother, Whiting Stickney, in the spice business at Albany, N. Y.]
6. MARY WHITING, [b. July 2, 1818; m. Moody B. McIlvaine, Oct. 29, 1835, and lives on the homestead at North Branch.]
7. EMILY, [b. Sept. 27, 1820; m. James Templeton of Peterborough, in 1844, and now lives, a widow, in that town.]
8. CAROLINE, [b. Nov. 28, 1822; m. Robert C. Stuart of Antrim, Oct. 1, 1844.]
9. SYLVESTER, [b. Dec. 12, 1824; d. Dec. 26, 1824.]
10. LOUISA TUTTLE, [b. Dec. 2, 1825; m. Harrison G. O. Whittle, Nov. 25, 1845, and resides in North Chelmsford, Mass.]

11. ALMIRA, [b. Nov. 8, 1827; m. Stephen W. Flint in 1848, and lives at Bellows Falls, Vt.]

## STORY.

Ambrose, Daniel, Simon, and Hiram Story, four brothers, sons of William and Lois (Lowe) Story of Goffstown, were all born in that town. William Story's father moved there in 1777. He was of English origin, the son of Dea. William Story, whose father is believed to have been one of three brothers who came over and settled in Essex, Mass., and were probably the ancestors of all the Storys in New England. Two of these brothers were once out hunting and were surrounded by Indians, when one of them was killed and the other saved his life by hiding in a hollow log.

AMBROSE STORY was born in 1806. He came to Antrim in 1832, and boarded with his uncle, Daniel Lowe, while he built the house and mill now occupied by his brother, Daniel Story. In 1833 he married Rachel Smith, daughter of Dea. Thomas Smith of New Boston. In 1835 he sold his house and mill to his brother Daniel, and moved to Goffstown. He came back to Antrim in 1851, and sometime after bought the Dr. Whiton place at the Center, where his wife died in 1868. In April, 1869, he married Mrs. Almira Travis, and died in 1875, aged sixty-nine, leaving no children and devising part of his property as a fund for the Center Church.

DANIEL STORY was born May 8, 1807. He came to Antrim in 1833, to work for his brother, Ambrose Story, mentioned above; bought him out in 1835, and has since been engaged there in manufacturing bedsteads and similar wares. Sept. 24, 1835, he married Almira Parmenter, who died in 1846, leaving two children. Mr. Story married, second, Hannah M. Gregg, Sept. 10, 1847. He is one of the purest of men, peaceable and Christian, without deception and above reproach. He was appointed deacon in the Presbyterian Church in 1860, but declined.

1. WILLIAM W., [b. June 16, 1837; m. Lizzie, daughter of Hon. R. B. Cochrane of New Boston, Nov. 6, 1870; built his house in Clinton in 1872, and has children as follows: —
   *Anna G.*, (b. March 8, 1872.)
   *Myra F.*, (b. May 9, 1874.)
   *John Parker*, (b. April 15, 1878.)]
2. CHARLES H., [b. July 20, 1841; m. Margaret J. Holt in 1862; entered the army, and d. in service at Milldale, Miss., July 24, 1863, leaving one child: —
   *Charles F.*, (b. Nov. 23, 1862; now lives in Lowell.)]

HIRAM STORY, a younger brother, was born in 1824. He came to Antrim in 1849, and worked some years for his brother Daniel. He married Keziah Wellman of Lyndeborough, May 8, 1855; and bought the Cummings place (now Dea. E. C. Paige's) and mill, where he manufactured bedsteads until he died, much lamented, in the prime of life, June 22, 1866, aged forty-two. He had two children, both of whom died before him. The widow married Henry W. Austin, Feb. 6, 1872, and lives in Milford.

SIMON STORY, another brother, was born in 1815. He married Mindwell Smith, and came to Antrim from Mont Vernon in 1860, and lives in "Happy Valley," so called. They have but one child living : —

1. WILLIAM, [b. Feb. 13, 1846, in Mont Vernon; m. Nellie Brooks, and lived in Greenfield several years. Has recently moved to Antrim.]

## STOWELL.

JOSHUA P. STOWELL, son of Moses and Mary (Chessmore) Stowell of Ashburnham, Mass., and grandson of John and Susanna (Todd) Stowell of Temple, was born in Leominster, Mass., May 10, 1837. He married, first, Eunice L. Whipple of Ashburnham, Mass.; was out in the army in the Twenty-fifth Mass. Volunteers (October, 1861), and in September, 1862, was discharged on account of an injury received in the service, by which he was disabled. Mr. Stowell married, second, Elvira L. Green of Antrim, Dec. 29, 1874, having come here the same year on to the Caleb Clark place, owning one-half of the same. His children are: —

1. ELMER F., [b. in Ashburnham, Oct. 11, 1861.]
2. IRVING E., [b. in same town, June 17, 1865.]
3. EDGAR A., [b. in Antrim, Oct. 30, 1875.]

## STUART.

CAPT. THOMAS STUART came here from Merrimack and settled the Flint place at the Branch in 1775; married Sarah McCauley, a most excellent woman; was called a Revolutionary soldier. Was chairman of the first board of selectmen, though but twenty-nine years of age, and was ten years selectman. He died Dec. 9, 1803, aged fifty-four. He and his wife were among the founders of the church in 1788. She died July, 1817, aged sixty-seven. Their children having all died, their property was inherited by Capt. David McCauley, a nephew, whose brief history will be found on another page. John, only son of Capt. Thomas Stuart, died December, 1785, aged eight years. His only daughter, Molly, died May 30, 1800, aged twenty. This family were of Scotch race. A Mr. "John Stewart" was one of the proprietors of Londonderry, 1722. This name, once common in Antrim, long since disappeared. A John Stuart lived on the Dimon Dodge place in 1804, possibly being one of the old gentlemen named below.

FRANCIS STUART, brother of Thomas, married Susannah Swan of Peterborough, and moved on to the English Hill northeast of the Branch in 1777. After two years he went on to the Stacey place. The house stood in the field south of William Stacey's. He went to Canada, in after years, thence to Grand Isle, Vt., and died there. His children were: —

1. ANN H., [m. Robert Carr, and d. Jan. 24, 1856, aged 73.]
2. ELIZABETH, [m. Brewer Dodge; went to Montreal, and d. there.]
3. SUSAN, [m. Silas Gear of Canada.]
4. NANCY, [m. Silas Carr, and went to Canada, thence to Franklin, Vt., where she d.]
5. THOMAS, [m. Sally Combs, May 31, 1814; lived in various places in town, then went to Canada, thence to Ohio, where he lived many years a sort of hermit life, accumulated property, and d. in 1860. After his departure Mrs. Sally (Combs) Stuart lived many years in a small house which stood on the south side of the road at the corner just east of Reed Carr's. Nearly opposite and close by, on land now Mr. Pelsey's, stood another small house remembered as occupied by a Widow Blanchard. Thomas and Sally had two children: —

    *Harriet*, (m. Alvin Glover of Berkshire, Canada, and raised up fifteen children.)

    *Robert C.*, (was brought up from a babe by his uncle, Robert Carr; m. Caroline Stickney, daughter of Dr. Jeremiah Stickney, Oct. 1, 1844, and lived some years at the Branch. Afterwards, his father, who had never seen him, wrote to him to come to Ohio and receive his property and care for him in his old age. He first wrote to the postmaster of Antrim, inquiring if such a young man were living. The son immediately started for the place (Peru, Ohio), took care of his father in his last sickness, and remained in that vicinity till his own family was broken up by death. His wife d. Feb. 12, 1876, in Ashley, Ohio. He d. very recently in Palmyra, Mich. The children of Robert C. Stuart and Caroline Stickney, the three oldest of whom were b. in Antrim, were: Emma, who d. at the age of thirteen; Albert J., who lives in Palmyra, Mich.; Frank Carr, who m. Lillie Julian and lives in Ashley, Ohio; Carrie, who m. Willis Julian, and lives in Ashley, Ohio; Henry L.; and Mary E.)]
6. FRANCIS, [m. in Canada, but left and went to Ohio and lived with his brother Thomas, where he d. in 1850.]

7. JANE, [m. Silas Durgee, and has always lived in Canada.]

JOHN STUART, cousin of Capt. Thomas and Francis Stuart, was born in Haverhill, Mass., in 1727. He came here from Londonderry in 1778; lived a year or so on the Wallace place, south of William Stacey's, then some years out northeast of the Branch. He moved to Unity in 1816, where he died in 1818, aged ninety-one. His wife was Abigail Phipps, born in Cape Ann, Mass., and was said to be a great-granddaughter of Sir William Phipps, the royal governor of Massachusetts. She was probably a remote connection, but Gov. Phipps is understood to have left no children. Mrs. Stuart was always called "Granny Stuart." She was a woman of great endurance, was excellent in sickness, and frequently took the place of a doctor in the new settlement, being always ready for many years to start at any hour of the day or night in service to the suffering. She died in 1800, aged seventy-five. She was said to be a second wife, and to have left no children. She was marked with negro blood; and this surely may be said of her, that she did a great deal of good in her day. I can learn nothing positive about the descendants of this John Stuart; but he seems to have gone in old age to live with some of them, and I think they are still living in Unity and Goshen.

JOHN STUART and Jean Stuart were "published" in Antrim, Jan. 14, 1781. I think this John was son of the preceding John by a former wife, but cannot be sure. He had his leg taken off, after having been lame many years. Was a shoemaker; lived in a house that stood at or near the place now occupied by Grafton Curtis; afterwards lived at the Branch, but became poor and died on the town farm some forty-five years ago. He had a sister Lydia that married David Stevens of Bedford and lived and died with him there. Another sister, Sarah, was a great spinner and weaver, and used to go from house to house to carry on this work; lived many years in New Boston, but died here, unmarried, on the town farm about 1845, aged about eighty. The children of John and Jean (Stuart) Stuart were as below, though perhaps in different order:—

1. JOHN, [was out in the war of 1812; was several years after the war in the United States service; came back and d. here on the town farm, unm., March, 1856.]
2. WILLIAM, [m. Betsey Hall; lived some years in the Dea. Alexander house at the Branch, and in other places in town; subsequently went to Washington, and d. there Jan. 21, 1845, aged 56. His son, James Stuart, lives in Walpole.]
3. SARAH, [m. John Pettingill, and d. in 1855.]
4. MARY, [m. John Elliot of Mont Vernon, and d. in that town very aged, 1879.]
5. ABIGAIL, [called "Nabby," unm.]
6. HANNAH, [m. Joseph Derush.]

## SUMNER.

SYLVANUS SUMNER owned and run the clothing-mill at the Branch a short time. He married a daughter of Samuel Gove of Weare. Little is known of him.

## SWAIN.

JEREMIAH SWAIN, first of this family known in America, was in Charlestown, Mass., in 1638, and soon after moved to Reading, Mass. His son, Maj. Jeremiah Swain of Reading, was born in 1643. Was a physician by profession. Was commander-in-chief of all the forces raised in the colony against the Eastern Indians, and had his headquarters for some time in Berwick, Me. Was in many battles and skirmishes with the red men, and is described as "an able and brave officer." Benjamin Swain, son of Maj. Jeremiah, was a physician, selectman of his town, and lieutenant in the army. John Swain, son of Dr. Benjamin, was a captain in the army. Rev. Joseph Swain, son of Capt. John, was born in 1723; was graduated at Harvard College in 1744, and was pastor of the Congregational Church in Wenham forty-two years. He married Mrs. Elizabeth (Chipman) Warren, widow of his predecessor, Rev. John Warren, and daughter of Rev. John Chipman, who was pastor of the church in North Beverly, Mass., sixty years. Rev. Joseph Swain had six children, and died June 27, 1792. It must not escape our notice that he was the author of several of the most beautiful hymns in our language. Some of these may be found in almost any collection. The hymns commencing, "O thou in whose presence my soul takes delight," and "I stand on Zion's mount," are worthy of note. Few hymns have been more admired than that we sing so often:—

"How sweet, how heavenly is the sight
When those who love the Lord,
In one another's peace delight,
And so fulfill his word!

"When each can feel his brother's sigh,
And with him bear a part!
When sorrow flows from eye to eye,
And joy from heart to heart!"

Daniel, the fourth child of Rev. Joseph Swain, was born Sept. 19, 1756. He went to New Ipswich in 1780 and set up business as a hatter, which he continued till his death by spotted fever about 1808. Was a man of wit and considerable ability. The first page of his account-book dated "Nov. ye 3ᵈ 1780" is headed thus: —

"Daniel Swain is my name,
English is my nation;
The hatter's trade my choice —
An honest occupation."

He married Hittie Stickney of New Ipswich, April 25, 1782, and had nine children. The widow died in Antrim, June, 1847, aged eighty-nine.

GILMAN SWAIN, eighth child of Daniel, was born June 6, 1800, and came to Antrim to work at the age of fourteen. He married Betsey Combs, April 19, 1825; lived on the B. F. Dustin place in the west part of the town, and died April 5, 1862. His widow reached the ripe age of eighty-two. They had children thus: —

1. ROANSA F., [b. Jan. 28, 1826; m. Alonzo Dimond of Antrim in 1850, and d. July 20, 1854. Left no children.]
2. ADNA T., [b. April 1, 1828; m. Alice Lonergan of Boston, April 12, 1863, and lives in that city.]
3. CHARLES, [b. Sept. 8, 1830; d. in infancy.]
4. SARAH M., [b. Aug. 27, 1833; m. Charles W. Abbott of Lowell, Mass., Oct. 23, 1858. They now live in Reading, Mass. They have one child, Frank P., who was born at Salmon Falls, this State, Jan. 11, 1860. Mrs. Abbott has furnished much information concerning this family and others, and in most welcome and scholarly shape.]
5. ANSON T., [b. Sept. 13, 1836; m. Mary —— in New York City in 1864, and d. there April 12, 1865. The widow soon after m. and went to California. They had one child, Sarah Louise.]
6. HENRY E., [b. Sept. 15, 1838; m. Mary A. Upton of Stoddard, Sept. 15, 1862. Was a cavalry soldier in the war against the rebels. Has been a life-long student in phrenology and kindred sciences. Is abroad on lecturing tours most of the time, with noteworthy success. Is described as an easy and agreeable speaker, and as one having marked proficiency in the line of his subject. Resides at the Branch. Has children: —

*Helen R.*, (b. March 14, 1864.)
*Mary A.*, (b. April 6, 1866.)
*Henry E.*, (b. July 8, 1868.)
*Gracie A.*, (b. Oct. 11, 1870.)
*Sarah B.*, (b. April 23, 1873; d. July 30, 1878.)]

## SWETT.

Three brothers, Henry B., Daniel, and Oliver, came here from Windsor. Their grandfather, Jonathan, settled in that town in 1779, coming there from Nottingham. This Jonathan was son of John Swett; and John's father, Jonathan, came from England and was among the early settlers of Portsmouth.

HENRY B. SWETT, son of Samuel and Mary (Dresser) Swett, and grandson of Jonathan and Lydia (Huntress) Swett, was born in Windsor

GENEALOGIES.   701

June 26, 1810; married Sarah B. McIlvaine of Antrim, and lived in Windsor many years. After the death of his son he came to North Branch, where he now resides. He was selectman in 1862. His children are: —

1. DANIEL M., [b. in Windsor, Dec. 19, 1834; d. Dec. 7, 1861.]
2. MARY E., [b. April 11, 1839; m. David M. Stacey, Nov. 27, 1862, and lives at North Branch.]

DANIEL SWETT, brother of Henry B. Swett, was born in Windsor in 1812; married Roxah Boutwell of Antrim, June 18, 1840, and came here from Windsor in 1857. He bought the Webster place. The house once stood on the north declivity of Meeting-House Hill, and was there occupied by Abraham McNiel. It was moved to its present locality in 1832. The old Webster house stood on the opposite side of the road, so high on the bank that they had to have stairs to get up to it. Daniel Swett's wife died Aug. 26, 1875, aged sixty. Their children are: —

1. MARTHA A., [b. in Windsor, March 27, 1841; m. Charles D. Sawyer of Antrim, Nov. 5, 1863.]
2. ANSON, [b. in Windsor, Feb. 2, 1845; m. Alice C. Wilkins, March 15, 1877.]
3. FRANK, [b. March 31, 1848; leader of Center choir; lived on the homestead with his father; m. Lizzie J. Goodwin, Feb. 4, 1879; d. June 7, 1880; a young man universally loved, and of great value in the community.]
4. MARTIN, [b. Nov. 22, 1855.]

OLIVER SWETT, another brother, was born July 16, 1818; married Mahala Perkins in 1845, and came to Antrim in 1860 and bought the Dustin, or Dea. Weston place at North Branch. They have two children: —

1. LUMAN A., [b. Aug. 5, 1847; m. Alma A., daughter of Benjamin Swett, Dec. 2, 1874, and lives at the Branch, having one child: —
*Edward H.*, (b. Aug. 8, 1876.)]
2. LAURA J., [b. July 13, 1850; d. Oct. 24, 1868, aged 18.]

LANGDON SWETT, son of John and Mary (Preston) Swett, and cousin of the brothers Henry B., Daniel, and Oliver Swett, was born in Windsor in 1805; married Sarah Allds, April 25, 1833; came here in 1863 and bought what was called the Cooledge place at North Branch (house built by Joel Jones in 1807). His wife has become totally blind. She is a devoted Christian and,wonderfully sustained in this affliction by the grace of God. Have no children.

BENJAMIN SWETT, son of Daniel and Jane Swett, was born in Perry, Me., Feb. 5, 1805; married Elsie J. Shannon of Gilmanton, and came to Antrim in 1869. Mrs. Swett died April 10, 1874. Their children are: —

1. CELESTIA A., [b. in 1833; m. William Eaton; lives in Weare.]
2. ELIZA J., [b. in 1836; m. Edward F. Beals, and lives in Augusta, Me.]
3. DANIEL E., [b. Dec. 4, 1838; m. Mrs. Ellen (Smith) Lazelle; lived in Boston, but moved back to Antrim in 1877, now occupying the Chapin place.]
4. NATHANIEL F., [b. Dec. 4, 1840; m. Lucy W. Annis of Goffstown, May 5, 1858; moved to Antrim in 1872, and occupies the William Wilkins place, having two children: —
    *Willie N.*, (b. in Goffstown, July 3, 1859.)
    *Florence E.*, (b. in Sanbornton, June 27, 1872.)]
5. ELLA M., [b. Nov. 8, 1849; m. Marshall J. Wood, Feb. 10, 1870, and went to Brooklyn, N. Y.]
6. ALMA A., [b. in 1852; m. Luman A. Swett, Dec. 2, 1874.]
7. FRANK, [b. Aug. 3, 1853; m. Lizzie Early in 1874, and now lives in Nashua.]

NAHUM B. SWETT, son of Bela M. and Persis (Brown) Swett, was born in Henniker in 1822; married Ruth I. Stearns of Bradford, Me., in 1851 (both mutes), and came here from Henniker on to the Thomas Barker place, at the foot of sand-hill, in 1870. Mrs. Swett died Aug. 10, 1872, aged forty-eight. Their children are: —

1. MARY J., [b. in Henniker, Jan. 6, 1857; m. Andrew J. Stevens of Bennington, Aug. 24, 1879.]
2. CHARLOTTE E., [educated mute, b. April 2, 1861.]
3. MITCHELL S., [educated mute, b. Oct. 2, 1862.]
4. MARGARET S., [educated mute, b. Jan. 12, 1866.]

## TAYLOR.

JAMES TAYLOR, named below, came here, a young, unmarried man, to succeed Benjamin Sargent as a clothier. The following advertisement appears in the Amherst paper: —

### "CLOTHING BUSINESS.

" The subscriber takes this method to inform the public that he carries on the clothing business at the Fulling mill in Antrim lately occupied by Mr. Benjamin Sargent, where he proposes dying deep blue, crimson, scarlet, and other good durable colors. Those who will favor him with their custom may depend upon having their work done with fidelity and dispatch. Constant attendance will be given, and any favor gratefully received.

"JAMES TAYLOR.

" Antrim, July 25, 1796."

In this business he continued several years. The mill stood on the site of the Breed mill, just below the blacksmith's shop of Locke Hill in South Village. James Taylor was son of James Taylor. His mother's name was Elizabeth Center. He came here from Dunstable in 1795, and married Rachel Duncan, daughter of Hon. John Duncan, in 1801. He was once licensed as a hotel-keeper here, was quite a military man, and a long time captain of one of the companies of this town. He lived in several places in town, was a short time in Lyndeborough, and after a return went to New Boston, thence to Herkimer, N. Y., in 1814, where he died July 1, 1834, aged sixty-seven. His widow died May 7, 1852. Their children were : —

1. WILLIAM T., [b. June 24, 1802 ; d. in infancy.]
2. JOHN MOOR, [b. Jan. 7, 1804, in Antrim ; went West in early life and d. unm.]
3. ADELINE, [b. in Lyndeborough, Dec. 5, 1806 ; d. in 1822.]
4. ELIZABETH C., [b. in Antrim, Oct. 20, 1807 ; m. William Tubbs of Herkimer, N. Y., Feb. 22, 1831.]
5. KATHERINE McF., [b. in Antrim in 1810 ; d. unm. Feb. 14, 1863.]
6. JAMES B., [b. in New Boston, Feb. 17, 1812. He was last heard of in California, about 1850 ; was shot in the street while having his boots blacked. One son, Charles B., lives at Mohawk, N. Y.]
7. THERESA A., [b. in Lawrence, N. Y., Sept. 17, 1815 ; m. Michael Schaffner of Herkimer, N. Y., Nov. 18, 1840, and lived in New York City till 1861. He was a wholesale confectioner ; went into the army in 1861, thence retired, in poor health, to Herkimer, N. Y., where they now reside.]

NATHAN TAYLOR moved here from Amherst in 1780, and subsequently succeeded John Gordon on the Dea. Weston place at the Branch (now Oliver Swett's), and died about 1808, after great suffering. Nothing more can be learned of him. He seems to have lived on the Gordon place only a short time before Dea. Weston. But he was in town as early as 1776, though probably without his family, having a log house somewhere in the vicinity of the Branch. His name appears to the Association Test in the summer of 1776. The town voted him "six cord of good fire wood" at the March meeting of 1802, and continued the same by annual vote for five years. As they voted March 10, 1807, "not to supply the wood," it is supposed he was understood to be near his end so as not to need it.

DEA. JOHN TAYLOR came here from Beverly in 1800, and lived where Raymond afterwards lived, at the corner below the Nesmith place. He was appointed deacon in the Presbyterian Church in 1816; went to New York in 1824, and died in Newark, N. Y., in 1837, aged seventy-five.

He married, first, Hannah Woodbury, who died in 1819, aged fifty-seven; married, second, Mrs. Judd of Newark. His children, all by the first wife, were as follows: —

1. POLLY, [b. in 1784; m. James, son of Dea. Jonathan Nesmith; lived on a farm now George Brown's some years, then moved to Cortland, N. Y., where she d. in 1845.]
2. JOHN B., [b. in Beverly in 1787; m. Margaret Steele, sister of Dea. Steele, Dec. 7, 1815; built southeast of the Thomas Brown place, now Andrew Cochran's pasture, in 1812; went West in 1821; then his house fell to pieces. He was noted as a musician, being for some years a leader of church music. He d. in Geneseo, Ill., in 1839. The children of John B. Taylor were: —

    *Nancy S.*, (b. in Antrim in 1816; m. Sperry S. Howard in 1832, and now lives, a widow, in Edgerton, Wis.)

    *John*, (b. in Antrim in 1818; d. in infancy.)

    *Harriet N.*, (b. in 1820 in Antrim; m. 1st, John T. Nesmith in 1842; 2d, William T. Crosier in 1854, and lives in Sharon, Ill.)

    *Mary A.*, (b. after her father moved West; m. Charles B. Miner of Weathersfield, Ill.)

    *Samuel S.*, (m. Rosaltha M. Bliss of Sharon, Ill.)

    *John M. W.*, (m. Lizzie T. Steele of this town, Oct. 6, 1852, and d. in Brooklyn, N. Y., in 1873.)

    *Jane C.*, (m. George I. Bliss, and lives in Geneseo, Ill.)]

3. ANDREW, [b. in Beverly, Jan. 17, 1789; m. Polly Brown, Oct. 11, 1814, who d. in 1828; went to Union County, N. Y., in 1825; m. 2d, Rebecca Butterfield, and d. Oct. 26, 1843. His children, all by the first wife, were: —

    *John B.*, (b. Nov. 7, 1815; d. in infancy.)

    *Nathan W.*, (b. July 28, 1817; m. Elizabeth Coleman in 1844, and d. July 4, 1875.)

    *James N.*, (b. June 17, 1819; m. Sarah Decker in 1842, and d. March 26, 1866.)

    *John*, (b. Aug. 16, 1821; m. Elizabeth Ogden, Nov. 15, 1849, and lives in Atkinson, Ill.)

    *Mary E.*, (b. March 4, 1823; m. James S. Hamilton, March 4, 1840, and lives in Florence, Io.)

    *Sarah A.*, (b. May 18, 1827, in Union, N. Y., and d. in infancy.)]

4. HANNAH, [b. in 1791; m. John McCoy, Jr., April 13, 1813,

GENEALOGIES. 705

and d. in Bennington, Sept. 5, 1847; several of her descendants reside in Lowell.]
5. ABIGAIL, [b. in 1793; m. Isaac Barker of Antrim, Dec. 25, 1817; lived in Somerville, Mass., where she d. in 1846.]
6. NANCY, [b. in Ipswich, Mass., in 1795; m. Thomas Barker, Dec. 8, 1825, and d. in Bennington in 1849.]

## TEMPLE.

ZENAS TEMPLE, son of Jonathan and Hepsibah (Parker) Temple, was born in Reading, Mass., Feb. 17, 1786. He came to Antrim in 1805, and with his father bought the then-called Alexander Jameson place, where he lived sixty-six years. He married Margaret J., daughter of Thomas Jameson, Dec. 23, 1813. He was a member of the Presbyterian Church forty years.—the father, mother, and daughter uniting at the same time. His wife died Aug. 4, 1870, aged eighty-three. He died April 7. 1871. His father died here Jan. 1, 1842, aged eighty-two; and his mother, Jan. 27, 1837, aged sixty-three. His children were:—

1. JANE M., [b. in 1814. She was a dressmaker, and d. here Nov. 11, 1861.]
2. HARRIET N., [b. Sept. 21, 1815; d. of brain fever, March 27, 1836, at the age of 20.]
3. JONATHAN E., [b. May 15, 1818; m. Lucy Damon of Reading, Mass., and d. Jan. 1. 1869. They had six children, only two of whom are now living: Lucy E., now Mrs. A. G. Patch of Boston, and John F., who lives with his sister.]
4. MARGARET A., [b. March 12, 1820; m. Simon A. Peaslee of Nashua, Oct. 8, 1850, and had two daughters and a son, all of whom d. in infancy. Mr. Peaslee lived largely in Nashua, but spent the last few years of his life in South Village on the spot where Dea. Aiken built. He was foreman in the knife-factory till failing health compelled him to give up business; was a genial, generous, and good man, and d. in the summer of 1877. His widow survives.]
5. SOPHIA J., [b. in 1822; d. in childhood.]
6. THOMAS, [b. in 1824; d. in childhood.]
7. MARY J., [b. Feb. 4, 1827; m. William A. Ober of Nashua, Oct. 8, 1850. The two sisters, Margaret and Mary, with their husbands, were united in marriage by Dr. Whiton in one ceremony. She has no children and resides in Nashua.]

## TEMPLETON.

There was a Matthew Templeton in the French war, who was discharged Oct. 27, 1758. This was, without question, the settler in Antrim.

He was son of Adam and Margaret (Lindsay) Templeton, and was born in Ireland, though of Scotch race. He came over to Windham with his parents when a small boy. There he married Jennie Harkness. He came from that town to Antrim in 1775 (though he lived in Peterborough part of several previous years), and began the Isaac Cochran place. He was constable in Windham before coming here. The name of his father, Adam Templeton, appears on the town record of Windham in 1753, and occasionally until the fall of 1776. Adam Templeton's wife, Margaret (Lindsay) Templeton, died in Windham, April 5, 1784, aged sixty-five; and after her death he followed his son to Antrim, died here in 1795, aged eighty-four, and was buried in the old cemetery on the hill. They had other children, as John, who was the father of Isaac Templeton of this town; Daniel Templeton of Hillsborough; James, who settled in Peterborough; and others. Matthew Templeton's wife died in Antrim in 1780, aged forty-three. He moved from this town to Peterborough in 1784, where he died May 30, 1809, aged seventy-three. He was an odd mortal, strictly pious, a rigid Presbyterian, and terribly bitter against all innovations. His cuts and thrusts against new fashions became by-words, and probably helped along what he opposed, as is often the case. He considered the use of instrumental music in church an invention of the devil, and left the church in indignation when a bass-viol was first introduced. While living in Peterborough, he thought to get rid of the offensive music by going to Greenfield to meeting; and accordingly he started one Sabbath morning, but, he says, " When I got in sight of the meeting-house, there was a man with a goon [bassoon], and Dagon [bass-viol] was there too, and I jist got on to mee ould meer and cum home." The pitch-pipe he called the " whastle." On one occasion when the chorister, John Smith, gave the key with the pitch-pipe, the choir broke down and stopped, when Mr. Templeton called out in an audible voice, " Ah ! Johny Smith, ye maun blaw your whastle again!" If the old gentleman had lived in these days of operatic performances in church music, he might think the devil rather active, and, perhaps, not get far from the truth. His children were: —

1. BETSEY, [b. in Windham in 1770 ; m. John Holmes of Peterborough, and went to Montpelier, Vt.]
2. SAMUEL, [b. in Windham in 1772 ; m. Jane Miller, and settled on his father's farm in Peterborough. He d. in 1832, and of his children his daughter Catherine (b. Oct. 22, 1811) alone survived him. She m. Caleb F. Wilder, and occupies the homestead.]
3. JEAN, [called " Jane," b. in 1774 ; m. Hugh Miller of Peterborough in 1795, and d. June 9, 1845.]
4. SALLY, [b. in Antrim in 1776 ; m. Reuben Robbe, but didn't succeed in living with him.]
5. JENNIE, [b. in Antrim in 1778 ; d. unm. Feb. 19, 1849.]

GENEALOGIES. 707

ISAAC TEMPLETON, son of John and Mary (Mayhew) Templeton of Windham, grandson of Adam and Margaret (Lindsay) Templeton, and nephew of Matthew Templeton, mentioned above, was born in Windham in 1795; married Mary Ross, March 15, 1814; came here from Hillsborough in 1817, lived here and there in town, and after several years moved to Deering, thence back to Hillsborough, where he died April 19, 1869, aged seventy-four. His wife died in 1874, aged eighty-three. Their children were : —

1. ———, [b. in Hillsborough in 1815; d. in infancy.]
2. MARY J., [b. in Hillsborough, April 21, 1816; m. Robert B. Austin of Deering, who was a mechanic and worked at making organs, and d. in Worcester, Mass., in 1875. She now lives, a widow, at Hillsborough Bridge.]
3. JAMES R., [b. in Antrim, May 4, 1818; m. Emily Stickney, daughter of Dr. Stickney of Antrim; was a tailor; lived several years at the Branch, thence moved to Peterborough, where he d. April 8, 1876. Their children are : —
    *Harry H.*, (b. Oct. 8, 1846; m. Mary Ella, daughter of Frederick Livingston of Peterborough, Jan. 2, 1870, and is engaged in business as a merchant-tailor in Peterborough.)
    *Frank G.*, (b. in Nashua, Nov. 9, 1853; m. Mattie J. Hubbard, Nov. 27, 1876; is assistant in clothing-store of Marshall Nay, Peterborough.)
    *Carrie*, (b. Dec. 10, 1855; d. in infancy.)]
4. MARGARET, [twin-sister of James R.; d. in infancy.]
5. JOHN, [b. in Antrim, July 31, 1822; m. Mary J. Nichols of Hillsborough; d. in 1848.]
6. ISAAC, [b. Sept. 22, 1824; m. Sarah A. Brooks of Bennington; d. in the army at Hilton Head.]
7. LINDA E., [twin-sister of Isaac; m. William Pritchard, and lives at Hillsborough Bridge.]
8. LUTHER, [b. in Antrim; d. at the age of 4.]
9. MADISON, [one of triplets, b. April 22, 1830; m. Mary A. Newton of Bennington; d. in Worcester, Mass., in 1868.]
10. MILTON, [one of triplets mentioned above; d. in infancy.]
11. MARIA, [one of triplets, sister of Madison and Milton; d. in infancy.]
12. EMILY, [b. in June, 1835; m. Rodney Clark, and lives in Deering, near Hillsborough Bridge.]
13. EMELINE, [twin-sister of Emily; m. Edward Cotter, and lives at Hillsborough Bridge.]

## TENNANT.

ROBERT TENNANT came here from Deering in 1795, or before, and bought, of John Gilmore, the Whitney place, which he occupied many years, and was appointed by the selectmen of Antrim to keep tavern and sell rum at that place in 1795. He married Elizabeth Alcock, daughter of Judge Robert Alcock of Deering. His name was Hogg, but just before his marriage he had it changed to Tennant. Probably she didn't want to be called " a Hogg ! " She died Oct. 30, 1839. He lived awhile on the Charles Appleton place, where he died May 26, 1843, aged eighty-two. They had but one child: —

1. JOHN, [m. Elizabeth Houston of Antrim, who d. April 18, 1823, aged 31. He was drowned in the Contoocook River, not far from George Thompson's, Oct. 12, 1839. He walked off the bank into the river, it being a dark night, and thus perished, being the last of the family. They had three children, as follows : —

    *Moses B.*, (d. Jan. 3, 1832, aged 17.)
    *Elizabeth*, (d. Oct. 20, 1829, aged 13.)
    *Aura Ann*, (d. Oct. 10, 1829, aged 10.)]

## TENNEY.

In the year 1638, Rev. Ezekiel Rogers and twenty families of his people came over from Rowley, in Yorkshire, England, and settled a township in Massachusetts which they called " Rowley," for their old home. Among these families were Thomas Tenney and his wife Ann. The next year, William Tenney, a younger brother of Thomas, came over with forty families. In 1667 this William was chosen deacon of the church. His only son died young. Thomas had four sons and two daughters. One son, Daniel, by his wife Mary had six sons and two daughters. William, fourth son of Daniel and Mary, had two wives, Abigail and Mehitable. The first wife died young, leaving one daughter and no sons. The second wife left four sons and two daughters. William, second son of William and Mehitable, married Ann Jewett, moved to Hollis in 1750, and died in 1783, leaving children: Martha, Benjamin, William, Ann, and Oliver. The second of these, Benjamin, born Oct. 28, 1746, married Ruth Blanchard and settled in Temple. He died at the age of forty-three, leaving children: William, Benjamin, Lucy, Amos, Samuel, Solomon, and John. The widow afterwards married Darius Hudson of Temple, and died April 13, 1831, aged seventy-nine.

JOHN TENNEY, youngest son of Benjamin and Ruth (Blanchard) Tenney, was born in Temple in 1787; came to Antrim in 1815; bought the Nathaniel Griffin place, now J. F. Tenney's, and married Betsey Wright of Concord, Mass. He died in 1820, aged thirty-three. Children : —

1. BETSEY CAROLINE, [b. in Temple, March 19, 1812 ; became

second wife of John S. Parmenter, April 5, 1832; d. suddenly, Dec. 31, 1867.]
2. LUCY ELVIRA, [b. in Temple, Oct. 1, 1813; m. Luke Nichols, April 21, 1836; d. very suddenly, Jan. 30, 1856.]
3. RUTH MERRIAM, [b. June 30, 1815; d. at age of 20.]
4. JOHN W., [b. June 8, 1817; m. Louisa Hills, April 18, 1844; lived on the old homestead, and d. March 10, 1851, leaving children: —
*Lizzie S.*, (b. March 8, 1845.)
*John E.*, (b. March 25, 1850.)]
5. ABNER SPOFFORD, [b. Feb. 8, 1819; d. in childhood.]
6. BENJAMIN B., [b. Feb. 10, 1821; m. Tryphena Putnam of Lyndeborough; came on to the old homestead at the death of his brother John, and d. there Jan. 1, 1866, leaving children: —
*John F.*, (b. May 30, 1851; m. Julia L. Richardson of Dublin, Dec. 14, 1876, and lives on the old homestead; has one child, Lucy Anabel, b. Dec. 4, 1878.)
*Amy T.*, (b. Sept. 7, 1854; d. March 10, 1871.)]

JAMES E. TENNEY, son of Stillman and Roxanna (Smith) Tenney, was born in Hancock in 1840; came to Antrim in 1866, and bought the John Robinson place; is engaged in the lumber business; married Leona A. Dutton of Greenfield, March 7, 1864, and they have one child: —
1. NETTIE L., [b. Dec. 1, 1871.]

## THAYER.

CHARLES THAYER came into possession of the mill on the old Aiken stand, South Village, after Abijah Whitcomb. He married a Miss Mayo from Cape Cod, from which vicinity he came. He lived here and carried on the mill about eight years.

## THOMPSON.

JOHN THOMPSON was actively engaged in the war of the Revolution, being out at sea in privateers. He was twice taken prisoner by the British, once being taken to Halifax, and once to the Island of Bermuda, where he was charged with desertion from the British, and his life threatened. The officer who examined him being a Tory, and having some knowledge of the town from whence he came, confirmed his statement of being an American, and he was accordingly liberated or exchanged. He married, first, Esther Redington, and came to Antrim from Beverly in 1793. They lived in a log house at the corner of the roads east of the Artemas Brown place, where they had seven children, only one of whom, James C. Thompson of Illinois, now survives. Several years after the death of his first wife, Mr. Thompson was in the United States navy; but returned about 1810, married Betsey Day, July 25, 1811, and lived on the mountain southeast of Samuel Dinsmore's. About 1830, he bought land of John C. Flint, and built on it the house recently occupied by Henry D. Chapin. After a few years he sold that and moved into the stone house by the pond, where he died in 1842, aged eighty-one. By the last marriage there were the following children: —

8. THOMAS, [b. May 11, 1812; m. Elizabeth M. Buswell in 1842, and lived on the Dea. Bond place, from whence he moved to Francestown, remaining there four years. He came from thence into the stone house in Antrim, and in 1850 he built over what had been the tin-shop of his brother Luke into the house he now occupies in Clinton. He is a humble, modest, and godly man, well versed in the sacred Word, and was appointed deacon in the Presbyterian Church in 1860. His children are: —

*Augusta M.*, (b. Aug. 6, 1843; m. James Thompson of Fall River in 1872; d. in Antrim Feb. 10, 1878.)

*Daniel W.*, (b. Nov. 19, 1844; cabinet-maker by trade; lives in Melrose, Mass.)]

9. SARAH, [b. May 1, 1813; m. Aaron Morse of Lynn, Mass., and has since lived there.]

10. BETSEY, [d. at the age of 13.]

11. LUKE, [b. May 30, 1817; m. Sabra A. Muzzey, April 18, 1844, and went to Nashua. He afterwards came to Clinton, where he had a tin-shop some years. In 1862 he built the tin-shop at South Village, and did a good business for ten years, when he sold out to Squires Forsaith, the present occupant. In 1863 he built the house he last occupied. Built the lower mills in 1868, where, in connection with his son, he carried on manufacturing business of various kinds. He d. suddenly, Nov. 16, 1878. His children are: —

*Edward J.*, (b. Feb. 11, 1846; m. Flora Goodell, Oct. 15, 1868; is a printer by trade; was for a time editor of "Hillsborough Messenger." Published the "Antrim Home News" for a time. Has a good job-printing business at South Village, and does highly creditable work.)

*Emma F.*, (b. Oct. 31, 1848; m. Stephen Trask of Lynn, Nov. 27, 1869.)

*Charles W.*, (b. May 5, 1851; m. Mary E. Richardson, Oct. 7, 1875.)]

ALEXANDER THOMPSON, an emigrant from Perth, Scotland, was of a family of wealthy land-holders there. His father had six sons, and some of them, according to the English law, must be given to the army. The lot fell on Alexander to go, and he served in the British army several years. He began the farm now occupied by his son, George Thompson, about 1796. He descended from a daughter of the Scottish chief Robert Bruce. Was born in 1761. Married Elisabeth Nutt, and died in 1827. His wife died May 27, 1840, aged seventy-eight. Their children were: —

1. MARY M., [b. May 27, 1790, in Londonderry; m. 1st, John McCoy of Francestown, March 10, 1814; 2d, Israel Gillingham of Newbury, Oct. 20, 1838. She d. in the last-named town, Dec. 26, 1876.]
2. ALEXANDER, [b. in 1792; m. Matilda Richardson; moved to Newbury, Vt., and d. there.]
3. LEVI, [b. in 1793; left town when a young man, and never subsequently heard from.]
4. ISABEL, [b. in 1794; m. Benjamin Durant, Jan. 19, 1815; went to Stowe, Vt., and d. there.]
5. DEA. DANIEL, [b. in 1796; m. Persis Ladd of Haverhill; was a blacksmith many years in Francestown; was deacon in the Congregational Church there; now lives in Lancaster.]
6. ELISABETH, [b. in 1798; m. Ephraim Stearns, Dec. 19, 1823; d. in this town many years ago. Her husband m. again, and is now living in Nashua.]
7. SAMUEL, [b. in 1801; m. Rachel Kingsbury; lived and d. in Roxbury, Mass.]
8. GEORGE, [b. July 26, 1803; m. Melita Gillingham of Bradford, in the spring of 1839; lives on the farm settled by his father, and is among the largest land-owners of this vicinity. His wife d. May 20, 1852. Their children were: —

*George E.*, (b. Sept. 11, 1840.)
*Helen M.*, (b. June 25, 1842; m. Marcus M. Bailey, April 18, 1867, and lives in Nelson.)
*Eveline M.*, (b. Dec. 16, 1843.)
*Addie E.*, (b. March 9, 1845; m. Alvin Sheldon, June 4, 1871, and lives in Hancock.)
*Samuel M.*, (b. Aug. 9, 1848; m. Sophia Chaney of Bennington, Oct. 29, 1878; lives on the McCoy or Reuben Boutwell place.)
*Mary J.*, (d. in infancy.)]

## TODD.

SOLOMON TODD, a connection of Col. Andrew Todd named below, was born in the north of Ireland, and came over to Londonderry in 1740. He is said to have been nineteen years old on his arrival. He married Elisabeth, daughter of John and Janet (Steele) Wallace. He was an officer in the Revolutionary army, serving through the war with distinction; but the exposure and hardship told upon him, and he died soon after the close of the war. Not long subsequent to his death, in the year 1787, his widow and her five children came here. Samuel Gregg, who was then wealthy and lived at the Center, and whose wife Margaret was a sister to Mrs. Todd, built a house for the widow and her children. It stood on the west side of the old road a few rods above the town-house. Here they had a home many years. The children were "put out" at one place and another in town and served till "twenty-one." Mrs. Elisabeth Todd subsequently married a Kinnard, whom she also survived; was a useful and noble old lady, known as "Grandmother Kinnard;" and died at the age of ninety-six. The children of Solomon and Elisabeth Todd were: —

1. HENRY, [m. Sarah McIlvaine, who d. in childbirth, leaving a babe, b. Nov. 2, 1802. He was named Robert M., and on coming of age went below. m. Elisabeth M. Hodgkins of Gloucester, Mass., and is now one of the leading and most worthy citizens of Milton, Mass. Henry Todd, soon after the death of his wife, went off into the State of Maine, and d. in Knox, that State, in 1820.]

2. JOHN, [b. Feb. 17, 1777; m. Dolly Hood of Boxford, Mass., Nov. 3, 1806; lived in Salem, Mass., where he d. Jan. 15, 1831. Left five sons and four daughters. Two sons, John and Benjamin, d. in Africa. Most of this large family are now gone. One son, Charles, now lives in Salem, Mass., after years of life on the sea.]

3. DEA. SAMUEL C., [b. in Peterborough during a brief sojourn of his parents in that town. In August, 1808, he m. Lydia Gould, who is now living, at the age of ninety-one. He was brought up by James Steele, his mother's uncle, in the east part of Antrim. In 1803, he went to Topsfield, Mass., and learned the trade of making fishermen's boots, which trade he followed most of his life. He d. Dec. 31, 1858, aged 75 years and 8 months. Was deacon in the Orthodox Church of Topsfield, more than forty years. Left a family of eleven children. Prof. A. C. Perkins of Exeter, a native of Topsfield, speaks of him as his "first Sabbath-school teacher, and a godly man, whose good name will live

forever in the Topsfield church." His oldest son, Samuel Todd, Esq., b. Oct. 15, 1812, is one of the leading men of Topsfield at the present time, honored in every possible way by his native town.]

4. ALEXANDER, [went to Belfast, Me., quite young, to live with a person for whom he was named. Two sons, Samuel and Alexander, were in the lumber business in the city of Belfast a few years ago.]

5. MARGARET, [went with her bróther to the State of Maine. She was b. about 1781. It is not known that she was ever married, though a report has it that she entered the sacred bonds somewhat late in life, spent her days in Belfast, and d. without children.]

COL. ANDREW TODD, ancestor of the other Todds of Antrim, was born in Ireland in 1697. His parents, James Todd and Rachel Nelson, were both born in Scotland. He was married in Ireland to Beatrix Moore, daughter of John Moore who was murdered in the massacre of Glencoe, Scotland, in 1692. Andrew Todd was not one of the first settlers, but arrived in Londonderry in the year 1720. He soon became a leading man in town; was often moderator of their public meetings; was fourteen years a selectman; was representative of the town in the provincial legislature; was an officer in the French war of 1744, and again in the war of 1755, in the course of which he was promoted to the rank of colonel. His military reputation was of the best. In his old age he went to live with his daughter in Peterborough, but survived there less than a year, dying Sept. 15, 1777. Of his eight children we have only room to say, that they were as follows: Samuel, who was born in Londonderry, June 3, 1726, married, first, Hannah Morrison, and second, Ann Cochran, and, settling in Peterborough, was killed by the fall of a tree, March 30, 1765; Rachel, who married Moses Morrison and lived in Hancock; John, who was drowned at Amoskeag Falls at the age of twenty-four; James. who inherited the homestead of his father in Londonderry, but died soon after; Jane, who married William Miller of Peterborough; Andrew, who was called " Uncle Andrew" by everybody, led a wandering life, never married, was full of jokes and stories, and loved a " drop of spirit " a little too well. At one time he stopped over night with Samuel Duncan of Hancock, carrying his faithful jug. In the morning he went out in the woods where Duncan was chopping, and lay down to sleep near by, having his jug beside his head. A large hemlock-tree fell the wrong way, and the limbs crashed down on to the sleeping man. Duncan ran and pulled him out, crying " Uncle Andrew, are you dead? Uncle Andrew, are you dead?"—" I can't tell, Sam; but hand us the jug; we'll na part wi' dry lips !" Todd lived to wet his lips a good many times after that. The other child of Col. Andrew was Capt. Alexander, who was born Jan. 2, 1731; married Letitia Duncan; lived on a beautiful farm in Hooksett, and died in Londonderry at the age of seventy. He was a captain in the French war; was taken prisoner by the Indians, and after due time they prepared to burn him, according to their custom. When all was ready, they stripped him naked; but just as they got his shirt off over his head, he sprang away and ran for his life. He was hotly pursued but managed to escape, was three days and nights naked in the woods, and succeeded in reaching his camp in safety. Capt. Alexander Todd left several children, one of whom was Andrew, who married Margaret Duncan and was father of Josiah D. Todd and George Todd of Antrim.

JOSIAH D. TODD, son of the last-named Andrew, was born in Hancock, May 26, 1817. At the death of his father in 1826, he came here to live with his uncle, Dea. Robert Duncan. There he grew up to manhood, and has spent most of his life in Antrim. Is unmarried, a carpenter by trade, and lives in Hancock at this writing.

GEORGE TODD, brother of Josiah D., was born March 25, 1819, and was brought up by Giles Newton of Antrim. Married, Dec. 9, 1858, Mrs. Silvia N. Todd, widow of his brother, John Todd. He died in Peterborough, July 10, 1878.

JOHN TODD, brother of Josiah D. and George, was born June 28, 1809; lived some years with Dea. Josiah Duncan; married Sylvia Knowlton of Nelson, and settled in Hancock, where he died Jan. 3, 1858. His children are mostly in Peterborough.

It may be added to the above that it is believed Col. Andrew Todd had a younger daughter whose birth is not recorded, that she was born about 1744, and married Dea. Robert Duncan of Hancock.

CAPT. JOSHUA TODD married Mrs. Sarah (Parker) Fletcher, mother of Dea. Samuel Fletcher, and came here in old age to die with him, but did not survive many years. His death occurred April 23, 1815, at the age of ninety. His wife died Dec. 25, 1825, at the age of eighty-five.

## TOMB.

REV. SAMUEL TOMB was born in Wallkiln, N. Y., in 1766. Was of the Scotch-Irish race, and hence was introduced in Antrim. Was son of Dea. David Tomb. Studied for the most part at Columbia College; was licensed to preach by the Associate Reformed Synod of New York in 1789; came here early in May, 1792, and stayed till November. The people were greatly pleased with him and gave him a call, which he declined. But so much were the people desirous of him that they sent for him the next spring and renewed their call (1793). It was a matter of sad disappointment to them when he declined a second time. He was settled in Newmarket in July, 1793. After four years he was called to Newbury, Mass. From that place he was soon called to Salem, N. Y., where he was settled in 1806. In this field he continued to labor till 1832, when he resigned his charge on account of bodily infirmities. He died a few weeks after. Tall, slim, of dark complexion, long hair, flash-

ing eye, and strong voice, he made an impressive appearance in the desk. He was a man of accurate scholarship, peculiarly gifted in prayer, fluent without notes ; and it is no wonder the people sought after him. He used to keep his finger in his vest-pocket when he prayed, so an old person remembers hearing it said : " Mr. Tomb, we always know when we are to have a good prayer by how deep you dig in your pocket."

## TRAVIS.

LEVI TRAVIS came from Deering, but lived in Washington, and came here from that town about 1840; lived in various places in town, being a shoemaker by trade. He married Almira Hall of New Boston, and died here (Clinton) May 6, 1866, aged nearly fifty-nine. Children were as follows : —

1. LUTHER C., [d. Dec. 4, 1852, aged nearly 23.]
2. JAMES H., [d. Nov. 5, 1850, aged 16.]
3. SARAH, [m. Henry W. Tuttle, June 14, 1868; d. Nov. 26, 1871, aged 23.]

## TRUE.

MARK TRUE, A. M., son of John and Lucy (Dole) True, and grandson of Reuben and Hannah (Osgood) True, was born in Francestown, Nov. 1, 1815. His grandfather was born June 26, 1732, and married April 19, 1758. He was early noted for a desire to obtain an education, taught his first school at the age of sixteen, and worked his way to the accomplishment of his design in the face of great obstacles, graduating at Dartmouth College in 1845. He immediately devoted himself to the profession of teaching, which he followed for twenty-five years with unusual zeal and success. He came to Antrim in 1860, and was a great force in the business of Clinton Village. He was a deacon in the Baptist Church, of which he was a stanch supporter with heart and hand. He was a thorough Christian, one of stout convictions, great humility, and unflagging zeal. He was always ready to acknowledge wrong when he saw it in his own course, and always ready to see the virtues of others as well as his own. Fearless, manly, honest, devoted, and full of work, his influence will long be felt for good, and his memory long be dear. The long services of Mr. True as teacher, during twenty-five years, were at New Hampton, Hancock, Brewster, Mass., Winchester, Mass., and New London. He was an enthusiastic educator ; was up with the times, stirring, and wide-awake ; was superintending school committee of the town at the time of his death, and often before. He was at times moderator of town meetings ; was representative in 1864 and 1867. I append some just words of another : —

"He had a quick, nervous spirit, which could not brook inactivity. He kept abreast of his time. I do not know that he ever shrank from any task on account of its difficulty, or because it was unpleasant. Indeed, I am assured that he was accustomed to pursue, with the same industry and patience and perseverance, whatever devolved upon him, whether disagreeable in itself, or more to his taste. He *loved* work, and he worked fast. His life was comparatively short — at least, not long; but if we take into account what he accomplished, we shall feel that he lived much longer than thousands of men whose years have greatly outnumbered his.

"His spiritual perception was quick and discriminating, and he had a sound judgment. Error did not easily escape his detection, though dressed in the semblance of something better. A half truth, in his view, was no better, and, if anything, a little less respectable, than a straightforward, ungarnished lie. Strict with himself, of simple, unpretending life, he made no attempt to conceal his dislike for everything bordering upon the artificial, the pharisaical, and the extravagant. He loved justice. Indeed, I have met very few men who had such a keen sense of right, and who so despised everything that was low and mean and false and unfair among his fellows. Having a somewhat extensive knowledge of men and things, his opinions, ripe with experience and observation, were just and accurate. Nothing could induce him to violate his sense of right and his love for the truth. It was on this account that his counsel was often esteemed of the greatest value.

"He was also a man of very strong convictions. His ideas did not suffer change with every wind and tide. Naturally cautious and somewhat conservative, yet when his judgment was formed and the path of duty lay open before him, he acted with great warmth and energy. In a cause of righteousness he was fearless of consequences and careless of popular opinion. He was decisive in the principles which he embraced. He knew what he believed, and held nothing with a loose hand. At the same time he would not measure other men by his standard. Though firm, he yet knew how to be charitable. He judged no man harshly for not accepting his opinions. When he differed from you, it was always with a kind and Christian spirit."

Mr. True married, first, Laura A. Fiske of Dublin, in May, 1846. She died April 16, 1851, leaving one child. In 1852 he married, second, Mary H. Crocker of Brewster, Mass.; and she died in April, 1861, also leaving one child. In 1862 he married, third, Hannah S. Neal of Meredith, who survives him. He died of apoplexy, Feb. 13, 1875. Children were as follows: —

1. ABBOTT F., [b. April 4, 1852; built in South Village in 1876; m. Mary Brant of Stoddard, Aug. 28, 1877; superintending school committee of the town in 1876 and 1877; was member of Brown University at the death of his father, but did not finish the college course; bought the lower crib and bedstead factory of Dea. E. C. Paige, which he now occupies, employing several hands.]
2. HERBERT O., [b. May 30, 1859; graduate of Exeter Academy; member of Brown University, class of 1884.]

## TURNER.

CALEB TURNER was born in Harvard, Mass., Oct. 27, 1785. His mother's name was Martha Conn. He married Sally Conn of the same place. She was born Oct. 5, 1788, and died in the summer of 1868. Mr. Turner came here from Milford in 1834, on to the Dea. Daniel Nichols place, into the large house built by Dea. Nichols in 1803. He died in 1864. Most of his large family of children were born in Milford.

1. BETSEY, [b. July 27, 1810; d. Nov. 2, 1814.]
2. SALLY, [b. Oct. 27, 1812; d. April 8, 1841.]
3. GRANVILLE, [b. Oct. 5, 1815; m. Martha Marcy of Hillsborough; lives in Milford.]
4. GEORGE, [d. in infancy.]
5. AVERILL, [b. March 21, 1819; drowned in Contoocook River, June 9, 1837.]
6. MARY S., [b. Feb. 21, 1820; d. July 12, 1839.]
7. CALEB, [b. March 14, 1823; drowned in Contoocook River, July 18, 1841.]
8. RACHEL G., [b. Dec. 25, 1826; m. James S. Ellenwood of Deering, Nov. 25, 1851.]
9. GEORGE, [b. Aug. 17, 1828; m. Caroline E. Duncan, Jan. 1, 1863; occupies the homestead of his father; has one child: *Anna M.*, (b. May 4, 1865.)]
10. CHARLES, [b. Jan. 14, 1831; m. Geraldine Kennedy; was some years in manufacturing business at Clinton. Is cabinet-maker and carpenter by trade. Now lives in Hancock.]

## TUTTLE.

HON. JACOB TUTTLE, a man very prominent in Antrim for half a century, was born Feb. 6, 1767. His father, Sampson Tuttle, was born Aug. 29, 1738, and died at the age of seventy-seven. His mother, Submit Warren, was born March 12, 1742, and died at the age of fifty-five. Samuel Tuttle, the father of Sampson Tuttle, was born in 1709, and in 1729 married Martha, daughter of Rev. Benjamin Shattuck, the first minister of Littleton, Mass. The Hon. Jacob came here from that place in 1795, and bought the McClary farm, now the home of his grandson, James A. Tuttle. At once he opened a store, and for a long time carried on a heavy business, both in trade and in farming. In 1818 he moved his store and residence to the Branch village, where he continued business many years. He built the store now occupied by Almus Fairfield, and the large house now Hiram Griffin's. Few men in town have been kept in office so long as he. He was known as "Judge Tuttle," having been a judge in the court of common pleas. He was three years moderator, three years selectman, three years town clerk, and sixteen years representative. Was state senator, councilor, and presidential elector. He died Aug. 20, 1848, aged eighty-one. He married Betsey Cummings of Westford, Mass. She was daughter of Isaac and Elizabeth (Trowbridge) Cummings, and was born May 25, 1778. She united with the church in 1801; was intelligent and highly esteemed; and died Jan. 28, 1852, aged seventy-three. They had a large family of children. They buried three children in one month in the dysentery of 1800, and were left childless; but eleven were afterwards born to them. All the names were as follows: —

1. BETSEY, [b. June 13, 1796; d. Sept. 13, 1800.]
2. JACOB, [b. Feb. 4, 1798; d. Sept. 3, 1800.]
3. NANCY, [b. Jan. 17, 1800; d. Sept. 25, 1800.]
4. BETSEY, [b. July 13, 1801; d. Feb. 15, 1814.]
5. NANCY. [b. April 9, 1803; d. May 6, 1805.]
6. SUBMIT R., [b. April 21, 1805; m. James Steele, Jr., Dec. 21, 1824; d. on the Flint place, Aug. 3, 1833.]
7. LUCETTA, [b. March 23, 1807; m. John Sargent, Sept. 29, 1829, and went to Cambridgeport, Mass. She d. Aug. 1, 1855.]
8. LOUISA, [b. June 3, 1809; m. Andrew C. Cochran of Hancock, Dec. 11, 1828; d. Jan. 11, 1849.]
9. LYDIA S., [b. June 1, 1811; m. Hiram Griffin of Antrim, Oct. 27, 1835, and now lives on her father's place at the Branch.]
10. JAMES M., [b. July 6, 1813; m. Hannah Shedd of Hillsborough, Sept. 8, 1836, and lived on the original homestead. He d. Dec. 5, 1861. His widow d. March 5, 1873, aged 62. Her mother closed her life with her at the age of 91. The children of James M. and Hannah (Shedd) Tuttle were: —
*Mary E.*, (b. Dec. 27, 1838; d. unm. July 24, 1877.)
*James A.*, (b. Sept. 1, 1841; lives on old homestead.)]
11. SUSAN, [b. July 17, 1815; m. Henry D. Pierce of Hillsborough, Nov. 11, 1841; d. Oct. 20, 1874.]
12. HARRIET, [b. Aug. 3, 1817; m. David W. Grimes, May 30, 1844; moved to Boston, and d. Sept. 2, 1848.]
13. ISAAC C., [b. Sept. 11, 1820; m. Louisa J. Lowe, Nov. 11, 1846, and lives in Pecatonica, Ill.]
14. MARY E., [b. May 15, 1823; m. John S. Shedd of Antrim, May 20, 1846.]

CHARLES TUTTLE, a Revolutionary soldier, was born in Hamilton, Mass., March 11, 1749. His father, Charles Tuttle, was born in that town, Dec. 1, 1708; married Anne Jewett; and died on his birthday, 1788. They were of English descent. Charles Tuttle who came here was collector of Hamilton, his native town, in 1794, and, it seems, moved here in 1796. He married Lucy Dodge, sister of Ammi Dodge of New Boston. All his children were born in Hamilton, Mass. Several of them were buried there; and the oldest came here with a family of his own. They settled on the north side of Tuttle Mountain, south of the Dinsmore place. The buildings have been gone many years, but the mountain bears his name to this day. On this spot he died, Oct. 29, 1820. His wife subsequently went to New Boston, and died there June 9, 1843. The children were: —

1. CAPT. WILLIAM T., [b. Feb. 1, 1773; came here with his father, or soon after, and built on the same tract of land, their houses being but a few rods apart. He had m. Mary Woodbury in his native town. Here he remained till 1812, or a little later. when he moved to where is now the city of Cleveland, Ohio, and thence to Ashtabula, Ohio, where he d. in 1853. His sons are said to be all dead; but several daughters, who m. and settled near Cleveland, yet survive. The names of his children were Charles, William, Sarah, Barnet, Annie, Martha, John, and Mary, — all b. in Antrim. They settled in the West in a line, — so that their land reached seven miles, and were all wealthy people.]
2. SETH, [m. Elisabeth Poland of Hamilton, Mass., in 1811; was a carpenter; d. on the passage from New York to South America in 1825.]
3. JEDEDIAH, [m. Jane Warren of New Boston, Dec. 26, 1809; lived here and there awhile, then built a small house on the old road next east of Samuel Dinsmore's, but after some years moved to New Boston, and d. there in 1845. He had five children, all but the last b. here : —

*Lucy J.*, (b. Nov. 6, 1810; m. Jonathan G. Leach of New Boston; d. December, 1855.)

*Daniel M. C.*, (d. in childhood.)

*Charles*, (d. in infancy.)

*Josiah W.*, (b. Jan. 10, 1818; went into the Mexican war under Gen. Pierce, and lost his life in battle, in May, 1847.)

*James M.*, (b. in New Boston, Nov. 8, 1821; lives in that town and is a most respectable and good man; m. 1st, Esther Warren of Goffstown, his cousin, daughter of Dea. Ephraim Warren; 2d, Rachel McNiel of New Boston, daughter of Dea. Peter McNiel.)]

4. DANIEL, [d. Dec. 16, 1798.]
5. HEPSABETH, [d. Jan. 30, 1799.]
6. ANNE, [d. Jan. 29, 1799. This one was taken suddenly ill,

and while they were working over her a messenger came saying that Hepsabeth, who had gone a few miles on a visit, was also very sick. But the parents stayed with Anne till she died, — then started to aid the other, and found her also dead. One was 18, and the other 20 years of age.]

7. CHARLES, [b. Jan. 25, 1777; m. Sarah Austin of Salem, Mass., Feb. 5, 1803; was a cabinet-maker; d. in Cambridge, Mass., April 30, 1843, leaving a large and respectable family.]
8. SARAH, [m. 1st, Isaac Warden; 2d, John Allds, 1803; d. Feb. 18, 1853, aged 79.]
9. ELISABETH, [m. her cousin, James Tuttle of Hopkinton.]

SAMUEL TUTTLE, son of Samuel and Betsey (Baker) Tuttle of Acton, Mass., and a connection of Hon. Jacob Tuttle it is believed, came to Antrim from Temple in 1816, and bought the farm in High Range cleared by Alexander Witherspoon. This Witherspoon set out the old orchard of sixty-six trees, now mostly gone, with his own hands, then walked to Francestown, — twelve miles, — got two gallons of rum and brought it back on his shoulder, — all in the same day! It may be added that all the trees lived! Mr. Tuttle married Mary W. Wright of Concord, Mass., September, 1805, and they lived on this farm until their death, when it was occupied several years by their son, William N. Tuttle. The parents of Samuel Tuttle came to live with him, and were here several years before their death. His father, Samuel Tuttle, Sen., died Feb. 25, 1829, aged seventy years; and his mother, Mrs. Betsey Tuttle, died Sept. 29, 1834, aged seventy-two. Samuel Tuttle, Jr., died Sept. 10, 1854, aged seventy-three, and his widow died Dec. 2, 1859, aged seventy-five. Their children are as follows : —

1. HORACE, [b. in Acton, Mass., April 11, 1806; m. Mrs. Almira (Brown) Handly of Carlyle, Mass., in 1832, and lived on the farm now occupied by Jackson Boutelle. Before that this place is said to have been drunk out three times in sixteen years. He d. Nov. 16, 1859, and his wife August, 1877, leaving children : —

*Almira E.*, (b. Oct. 18, 1833. She was driven into fits and insanity by a fall at the age of three years, and d. April 5, 1877.)

*Mary J.*, (b. Feb. 28, 1835; became third wife of Edward Z. Hastings of Antrim, Aug. 21, 1860.)

*Lucy A.*, (b. Aug. 22, 1837; m. George L. Herrick of Antrim, Jan. 1, 1865; d. June 20, 1870.)

*Horace Brown*, (b. March 1, 1840; m. Martha J. Shattuck, daughter of Dea. Shattuck of Antrim, in 1870, and lives in this town on the Shattuck farm, having one child, Otis Henry, b. Oct. 25, 1875.)

*Henry W.*, (b. April 29, 1846; m. Sarah Travis of Antrim; was a blacksmith in Clinton, and d. June 28, 1870. His widow d. Nov. 26, 1871.)]

2. JONAS W., [b. in Acton, Mass., Dec. 31, 1807; m. Mary Dinsmore of Antrim, Feb. 20, 1834, and moved to Newbury, Vt., in 1840, where he is now a prominent citizen. Their children were b. first three in Antrim and last three in Newbury: —

*Edwin*, (b. Oct. 3, 1834; m. 2d, Mary Temple, and lives in Newbury, Vt. His first wife was Ruth Whitcher.)

*Mary E.*, (b. Jan. 22, 1838; m. William Buchanan, March 12, 1857, and lives in Boston.)

*Susan D.*, (b. Dec. 19, 1839; m. Walter Buchanan, Nov. 30, 1858, and lives in Newbury, Vt.)

*Samuel*, (b. Oct. 26, 1841; m. Rebecca Caruth, and lives in Newbury, Vt.)

*Clarissa*, (b. Aug. 19, 1844; m. Nathan A. Hunter; d. recently in her native town.)

*Silas M.*, (b. Jan. 16, 1851; m. Ella M. Maloon, and lives in Grinnell, Io.)]

3. MARY A., [b. in Temple, July 9, 1811; m. Samuel P. Chase, Feb. 16, 1837, and lives in Biddeford, Me.]

4. GEORGE F., [b. in Temple, Jan. 19, 1813; m. Lucy Kendall of Tyngsborough, Mass.; d. in 1850.]

5. SAMUEL E., [b. in Temple, July 14, 1815; m. Abby F. Demerett of Nottingham, April, 1844; lived here some years, and now lives in Harrisville, having children as named below, all b. in Antrim save two: —

*Josephine S.*, (b. April 12, 1846; m. Thomas E. Colby of Henniker, March, 1869.)

*Charles D.*, (b. in Lancaster, Mass., Nov. 16, 1849; d. in infancy.)

*Mary A.*, (b. July 24, 1851; m. William W. Applin of Marlborough, January, 1876.)

*Samuel W.*, (b. June 11, 1853; m. Lovella J. Lewis of Stoddard, August, 1874.)

*Selden P.*, (b. Dec. 9, 1855; m. Laura F. Tufts, Nov. 3, 1878.)

*John D.*, (b. June 30, 1857.)

*George*, (b. Aug. 11, 1860; d. in infancy.)

*Horace C.*, (b. in Stoddard, Sept. 4, 1861.)]
6. ELIZABETH, [b. in Antrim, Aug. 7, 1817 ; m. Horace Gillis, Oct. 6, 1842.]
7. ALMIRA, [b. in Antrim, Jan. 19, 1820 ; d. in 1826.]
8. WILLIAM N., [b. Feb. 11, 1822 ; m. Almira B. Frost of Madison, Jan. 11, 1848, and lived on the old homestead until 1870, when he sold to Gardiner Wallace and moved to South Antrim, where he now resides. The old house was burned in 1873. His townsmen have repeatedly honored him with the highest offices within their gift. He has but one child : —

*Emily F.*, (b. Dec. 31, 1851 ; m. William E. Downes, a native of Francestown, son of Samuel D. Downes, Esq., March 11, 1875. Mr. Downes is now a merchant in Bennington, and they have one child, Nellie S., b. July 20, 1876.)]
9. SARAH J., [b. September, 1829 ; became the second wife of Edward Z. Hastings of Antrim, Nov 8, 1855 ; d. May 1, 1860.]

ISAAC M. TUTTLE, son of Benjamin and Ann (McAllister) Tuttle, grandson of Sampson and Submit (Warren) Tuttle, and nephew of Hon. Jacob Tuttle, previously mentioned, was born in Hillsborough in 1813. He married Sophronia Chase of Hillsborough, came to Antrim in 1840, and bought the Houston and McAllister places, where he settled and has remained till now. The new house he now occupies was built in 1871. Their children are : —

1. MILES BENTON, [b. June 22, 1845 ; m. Lizzie A. Marshall of Hillsborough in 1868, and lives on the Houston place ; was selectman in 1875 and 1876.]
2. LUCY A., [b. Oct. 24, 1849 ; m. Scott Moore of Hillsborough in 1867.]
3. ANNA L., [b. Sept. 1, 1855.]

## TWISS.

DIMON C. TWISS was only child of Daniel and Rebecca (Creasy) Twiss of Marblehead, and grandson of Daniel Twiss, who came over with his brothers, Robert and Nathan. Dimon C. was born Sept. 4, 1773. His father, Daniel Twiss, was a minute-man in Revolutionary days ; was at work in the field when the signal-gun was fired ; carried his boy to the house, and started, and was killed at Bunker Hill. This boy, Dimon C., on growing up, married, first, Mary Woodbury of Beverly, September, 1793, who died in childbed, 1795, and was buried with her little one. In 1798, he married, second, Sarah Ireson of Marblehead, who died in Hudson in 1815, leaving eight children. He afterwards married, third, Mary

Jones of Hillsborough, July, 1817. He came here from Hudson in 1818, and bought of Nathan Pierce, who lived there a short time, the place now Luther Campbell's. There he lived about thirty years, when he sold to Jonathan Carr, moved to Amherst, and died in Mont Vernon, January, 1861, aged eighty-eight.

2. FANNY C., [b. in Beverly, Mass., Oct. 18, 1799; m. Jesse Carr, Dec. 3, 1833; d. in Antrim, Nov. 30, 1858.]
3. POLLY, [b. in Beverly, Nov. 22, 1800; d. in 1814.]
4. THOMAS D., [b. in Marblehead, Mass., Dec. 23, 1801; m. Betsey H. Brackett, Jan. 30, 1834, and the same year erected the buildings which he occupied until his death, March 21, 1876. The children are: —

*Alfred C.*, (b. April 25, 1837; m. Sarah E. Goodwin of Thornton's Ferry, Aug. 25, 1863; was a machinist; moved to Lawrence, Mass., where he held a position of responsibility, and d. greatly respected, in the prime of life, July 21, 1875.)

*Sarah E.*, (b. June 23, 1840; m. Charles J. Davis of Hancock, Feb. 23, 1865; d. Jan. 20, 1870.)

*Hannah A.*, (b. July 12, 1843; m. Nathan D. Curtis Dec. 4, 1866, and lives in Stoddard.)]

5. DIMON, [b. August, 1803; m. 1st, Harriet Parmenter, Oct. 30, 1834. He was a blacksmith, and built him a shop just below the bridge, on the brook, south of his father's house. One day in August of 1832, Dea. Parmenter, who was a live man, asked him how he would like to go on if his shop were in Clinton. He replied favorably, and accordingly the neighbors went up and the shop went down. It is said that buildings are not often known to move so quickly as that did. On the new stand in Clinton he followed his trade more than thirty years. At the time the shop was moved, the only houses in Clinton were Edward Hastings's and Daniel Story's. Mrs. Harriet (Parmenter) Twiss d. in 1844. Mr. Twiss m. 2d, Mehitable Hills, June 10, 1845. They moved to Mont Vernon in 1868, where she d. June 4, 1874, and he still resides there. His first wife left children as follows: —

*Harriet M.*, (b. Jan. 29, 1836; m. Dr. William H. Hines of Milford, Aug. 23, 1861, and d. in that place Feb. 7, 1871.)

*Mary E.*, (b. June 20, 1838; m. Daniel Richardson, May 9, 1857, and lives in Mont Vernon.)

*Hannah M.*, (b. Oct. 17, 1840; m. Elbridge F. Trow, Jan. 1, 1863, and lives in Mont Vernon.)]
6. SARAH, [b. Aug. 23, 1811; d. in infancy.]
7. GEORGE, [b. Dec. 10, 1804, in Hudson; m. Mary Flagg of Boston, 1831, and d. in that city July 26, 1852.]
8. DANIEL, [b. Dec. 18, 1806; painter by trade; m. a Nova Scotia lady; lives in East Boston.]
9. JAMES, [b. Aug. 27, 1809; unm.; d. Sept. 14, 1859.]
10. ABRAHAM G., [b. in Hudson, May 19, 1818; m. Sabra G. Carr of Antrim, 1841; was a machinist; d. in Manchester, April 8, 1876.]
11. MARY W., [b. in Hudson, Oct. 26, 1819; m. Mark Putnam, Dec. 10, 1839; now lives in Amherst.]
12. JOHN W., [b. in Antrim, May 2, 1822; m. 1st, Hannah McIlvaine; 2d, Margaret Price of Plattsburg, N. Y.; d. March 6, 1876.]
13. MARK, [b. in Antrim, Feb. 5, 1827; m. Mrs. Caroline Crosby of Milford, 1852; lives in Providence, R. I.; iron-molder by trade.]
14. CHARLES CUMMINGS, [b. in Antrim, Aug. 8, 1829; m. 1st, Harriet Glover of Franklin, Vt., March 4, 1857; 2d, Mrs. Ellen Jaquith, September, 1876; lives in Nashua.]
15. CATHERINE J., [b. in Antrim, Dec. 21, 1824; m. Freeman C. Bills of Amherst, March 12, 1845.]
16. ADONIRAM JUDSON, [b. in Antrim, March 21, 1832; m. Mary Gibson of Nashua; lives in Chelsea, Mass.; is foreman in a stove-foundry.]

## VARNUM.

ANDREW J. VARNUM came here from Amherst when a boy to live with James Wood. Married Susan E. Keyes of Antrim. Moved to Ashland and lived there several years, but came back insane in 1871, and wandered off and hanged himself on the top of Tuttle Mountain. He had concealed himself so cunningly, that, despite a general hunt of the people, the search was given up. The body was found many weeks afterwards, by accident, hanging in a state of shocking decay. His age was thirty-nine. He left three children: —

1. CHARLES A., [b. in 1860.]
2. MARY F., [b. in 1864; these two oldest were drowned in Bridgewater, July 19, 1871; were fishing on the banks of the stream, when the little girl fell in, and the boy springing in to save her, both perished.]
3. JOHN L., [b. in 1869.]

## VOSE.

The Voses came to this town from Bedford. They emigrated from Lancashire, England, to Dorchester, Mass., in 1638. Robert Vose, the original settler there, lived to a great age and left two sons, Edward and Thomas. Edward remained on the homestead, and his posterity kept the name on that spot for nearly two hundred years. From him descended Col. Elijah Vose and Col. Joseph Vose, who each commanded a regiment in the Revolution. Col. Joseph Vose was grandfather of Rev. Thomas Savage of Bedford. Thomas, the younger son, settled near the homestead of his father, locating in that part of Dorchester now Milton; was a farmer, smart, and locally distinguished, and seems to have left but one son, Henry. This Henry left a numerous family, several sons being among them, one of whom was Robert, who inherited the homestead and was father of Samuel Vose of Bedford, and his brother Lieut. James Vose of Bedford. The Voses now living in Bedford are descended from Lieut. James. It is not known when Samuel Vose came from Dorchester (Milton), Mass., and settled in Bedford; probably, however, it was not later than 1755, as he married in Bedford, and his fifth son, Hon. John Vose, was born there in 1766. Samuel Vose was on the "Committee of Safety" in Bedford in 1778. He married Phebe Vickery. She seems to have been daughter of Thomas Vickery (then spelled "Vickere"), a sturdy Presbyterian, whose name appears on a petition to Gov. Wentworth in behalf of that denomination, May 10, 1750. The Vickeres were among the early settlers of Bedford, which town was settled in 1737, as their names appear — Thomas Vickere and Thomas Vickere, Sen. — appended to a petition from that place (Sow-Hegon) for protection against the Indians, June 12, 1744. "Old Thos. Vickery departed this life Feb. 27, 1767, about 10 o'clock forenoon." (Matthew Patten's Diary.) The children of Samuel Vose and Phebe Vickery were: Thomas V., born Aug. 5, 1757; Samuel (of Antrim); Robert (of Antrim); Francis; Hon. John Vose (of Atkinson; Dartmouth College, 1795; gave Phi Beta Kappa oration, 1805; published several books on astronomy; state senator, 1816; deacon Congregational Church; died in 1840, aged seventy-four); Roger; Mercy; and Phebe. The last-named married Capt. John Worthley of this town. Roger went with a family of ten children to Spencer, N. Y.

DEA. SAMUEL VOSE of Antrim was born in Bedford, May 23, 1759; came here in 1788, and began the farm west of the pond long occupied after him by Rodney Sawyer. Lived many years in a log house, in which most of his children were born. He lived in his rude cabin upwards of two years alone. At one time during his absence a bear broke in, ate up his provisions, and upturned things in a careless way. Dea. Vose was for many years a leading spirit in the town; was a man of marked ability, and ready for every call. The good Dr. Whiton says of him that he kept the Sabbath so sacredly that he would not answer a man who spoke to him of secular business on the holy day. He married Mary Saltmarsh. Was appointed elder in the Presbyterian Church in

1816. He died Aug. 8, 1830, aged seventy-one. His wife died April 21, 1848, aged eighty-one. Their children were : —

1. DR. SAMUEL, [b. Aug. 2, 1792. After the best use of the limited opportunities of his native town, he studied with Dr. Nathan Smith of Hanover. He graduated from the Maine Medical School in 1823, and immediately commenced practice in New Portland, that State, where he was an active and successful physician till his death, which occurred Nov. 14, 1860. He was a very modest and retiring man, of genuine ability and personal excellence, and held in the very highest esteem. Was out for a time in the war of 1812. He m. Ruth D. Hanson. His children were : —

    *Mary E.*, (b. March 3, 1832; m. Sylvester Little, March 27, 1860.)
    *Harriet E.*, (b. Aug. 12, 1834; m. B. F. Walton in 1857.)
    *Ruth A.*, (b. in 1836; m. E. W. McIntosh, and lives in Peterborough.)
    *Sarah H.*, (b. in 1845; m. James M. Nay, Oct. 26, 1867, and lives in Quincy, Mass.)
    *Samuel*, (d. in childhood.)
    *Samuel*, (lives in New Portland, Me.; m. Etta M. Buckley of that place.)
    *John T.*, (lives in New Portland, Me.; unm.)]

2. THOMAS, [twin-brother of Dr. Samuel; built in 1822, on the west part of his father's farm, at the end of the road. He m. 1st, Sally Muzzey of Weare, May 20, 1823; 2d, Isabella Waldron, July 1, 1847. The first wife d. Dec. 9, 1845, aged 47. Thomas Vose d. March 22, 1849. His children were : —

    *Almeda*, (b. April 30, 1824; d. aged 7.)
    *Col. Samuel I.*, (b. Dec. 31, 1825; m. Sarah J. Nay of Sharon, Oct. 21, 1850; lived in Peterborough; was distinguished far and near as an auctioneer; his much-applauded response on Centennial Day has already greeted the reader's eye; was an exceedingly pleasant and kind man, making friends everywhere; went to Milford as proprietor of the hotel there, in 1878, where he d. suddenly, Aug. 31, 1880.)
    *Nancy B.*, (b. April 12, 1828; m. Samuel Nay, May 13, 1845.)
    *Julia H.*, (b. Aug. 17, 1831; m. Isaac Pettengill of Peterborough, Nov. 26, 1857.)
    *Thomas J.*, (b. July 11, 1834; m. Anna Finn of Boston. Was

out in the army. Was sick and started for home on a furlough. The morning he started his trembling hand wrote in his diary, " Thank God, I'm going home." But he d. on the way, May 10, 1862. He left one child, Nellie Frances, now Mrs. Frank P. Steel of Peterborough.)

*Mary H.*, (d. March 22, 1852, aged 15.)]
3. POLLY, [b. Sept. 26, 1795 ; m. Philip Averill of Antrim, Sept. 25, 1834 ; d. in 1838. No children.]
4. ISAAC. [b. June 10, 1797 ; d. in childhood.]
5. DEBBY. [b. May 15, 1799 ; d. in childhood.]
6. DEA. JOHN, [b. Aug. 28, 1801 ; m. 1st, Julianna Hunt, daughter of Dea. Timothy Hunt of Peterborough ; m. 2d, Maria Poor. The first wife d. here Dec. 23, 1831, aged 29. He sold to Rodney Sawyer and moved to Peterborough in 1835, and d. there June 4, 1867. Was appointed elder in the Presbyterian Church here in 1830, which office he declined, but accepted a similar one in the Congregational Church at Peterborough, which he held till death. His children were : —

*John Hazen*, (son of first wife, b. here Feb. 2, 1830 ; m. Alice Cragin ; lives in Peterborough.)

*Samuel W.*, (son of second wife, b. Jan. 27, 1840 ; m. Hannah M. Cragin, sister of Alice ; inherited homestead of his father in Peterborough.)

*Harriet M.*, (d. at age of 10.)

*Mary Frances*, (b. Aug. 2, 1844 ; unm.)]
7. HAZEN S., [b. July 12, 1804 ; d. Sept. 16, 1828.]
8. EDWARD L., [known as " Luke " Vose, b. Aug. 16, 1806 ; m. Aurelia Wilson of Stoddard, Oct. 28, 1835, and lived in that town a short time succeeding his marriage. She was daughter of Capt. Joel Wilson. Her parents both d. here at great age and were buried in the Center yard. Mr. Vose was in trade at the Center in 1834 and 1835, and probably somewhat earlier. In 1846 he bought of Baker Pratt the place known in recent years as the Luke Vose farm. There was on it a large, two-story house, probably built by Samuel Caldwell. At one time Zaccheus Fairbanks, successor of Caldwell, kept tavern in this great house ; and also for a short time had a store in it. Singing-schools and dancing-schools were kept in the great hall overhead. This house Mr. Vose at once took down and replaced with the present

structure. Here he resided till his death, May 1, 1868. Mr. Vose was often called to places of trust by his townsmen; served as superintending school committee; was often selectman, and was chairman of the board at the time of his death. Was a thinking man, enjoyed the highest respect of all, and d. in a Christian hope. Was very plain in speech, keen in sarcasm, witty, full of jokes, and ready to turn back a hit in the shrewdest way. At a meeting of the selectmen at the Branch, the question arose and was warmly discussed, whether Mr. Edmund Sawyer spelled his first name with a *u* or an *o* in the last syllable. Mr. Vose declared it was spelled with an *o*. In the height of the discussion Mr. Sawyer happened to come in, and said it was spelled with a *u*. But as the laugh began to roll upon Mr. Vose he drawled out: "Well, I'm not to blame if he don't know how to spell his own name!" Mr. Vose left but one child, now Prof. James E. Vose of Cushing Academy, Ashburnham, Mass. He was b. July 18, 1836. He was an invalid and sufferer through all his youth, yet by indomitable courage and patience he pursued his studies until he stands in the very front rank of the scholars and educators in New England. It is within bounds to say that he is one of the clearest thinkers and keenest writers to be found. He is what is called a self-made man, and that in spite of constant sickness and frailty. His admirable oration will be found among the Centennial papers. Has published an excellent treatise on grammar. He m. Mary Neville of New Boston. She was a brilliant scholar, a sweet Christian, and a most amiable woman. The writer, who knew her from childhood, counts it a privilege to say that hers was the most remarkable mind he ever met with, and that she was among the best of girls and saintliest of women. She d. Jan. 6, 1875, and her body rests in Maplewood cemetery. She departed at the early age of 28. Her only child, Edward, was b. in Albany, Kan., Aug. 1, 1870. Prof. Vose m. 2d, Mrs. Lois E. (Stickney) Rockwood of Ashburnham, Mass., a native of Townsend, that State.]

9. HARRIET, [b. March 19, 1810; unm.; d. at Dea. John Vose's in Peterborough, of consumption, about 1840.]

ROBERT VOSE, brother of Dea. Samuel, came here from Bedford in 1790, or a little earlier, and began the old Gates farm at the foot of Holt's

Hill. Here he lived in a log house several years, and then moved to some town in Vermont. His wife's name was Mehitable. This is all I can learn of him. He had two children born here : —

1. POLLY, [b. Oct. 27, 1796.]
2. PRISSY, [b. March 25, 1799.]

## WALKER.

JAMES WALKER was son of Andrew Walker of New Boston. The latter came from Londonderry in 1753 and began a contract to build a grist-mill for the people of New Boston, for which he was to receive five hundred acres of land, provided he kept the mill in order and was fair in tolls. But he managed to get the intense ill-will of the people of that town, by hard tolls or otherwise, so that the proprietors sent a committee to get redress, or eject him. Thus driven to the test, he gave some satisfaction to them, improved his dealings, retained his mills, and died there in ripe years. He had two sons in the Revolutionary army: Alexander, who lost his life in 1776, and James, who came to this town. The latter settled in New Boston and had a family of six children there. His first wife was Hannah Woodbury of that town. Soon after his return from the army, probably not far from 1800, he left New Boston, and after a time located here; married, second, Lucinda Bowen; built a log house in the woods a half-mile west of Ira Holmes's, to which there never was any road, though one was vainly petitioned for several times. On this spot he spent the rest of his days. He was frozen to death on his way home from the Branch Feb. 17, 1837, aged seventy-seven. His children were as follows, the three last being children of the second woman and natives of this town : —

1. ALEXANDER, [went when a young man to Cherry Valley, N. Y.; came back on a visit, was taken sick with small-pox in Acworth, and d. many years ago. He was unm.]
2. BENJAMIN, [went to Cherry Valley, N. Y.]
3. SIMEON, [m. Martha Ring; settled and d. in Cherry Valley.]
4. JACOB, [went to Cherry Valley.]
5. JAMES, [m. Sally Curtis of Windsor in 1813, but soon ran away and was never again heard of.]
6. RACHEL, [m. Joshua E. Woodbury of New Boston, and was mother of Hammon Woodbury, a graduate of Dartmouth College.]
7. ELVIRA C., [m. John L. Tewksbury, and lives at Weeping Water, Neb.]
8. MARGARET A., [lived here and there many years; then m. James Towns of Hancock, and d. in that town in 1869.]
9. ISAAC F., [b. Jan. 16, 1820; is a very respectable citizen of North Weare at the present time. He m. Nancy J. Rich-

ardson of this town, and lived several years in the Herrick house, adjacent to Loveren's mills. Left Antrim in 1858. Three children were b. in this town, whose names are Jenness M., Leona J., and Julia E.]

## WALLACE.

JOHN WALLACE came over from Coleraine, county of Antrim, Ireland, in 1719, and was one of the most active settlers of Londonderry, occupying from time to time many important offices. He married Annis Barnett, May 18, 1721, they being the first couple married in Londonderry. They had eight children, of whom John, the fourth child, born April 12, 1727, married Sarah Woodburn, daughter of John Woodburn who came from Ireland to Londonderry a few years after its settlement. They settled in Bedford in 1756, and had four sons and five daughters. Their sons were: James, who settled in Antrim; John, who settled in Antrim; Thomas, who married Mercy Frye, settled in Bedford, and was the father of Rev. Cyrus W. Wallace, D. D., of Manchester; and Josiah, who settled in Antrim. The three brothers who settled here will now be noticed in order.

JAMES WALLACE, son of John and Sarah (Woodburn) Wallace of Bedford, and grandson of John and Annis (Barnett) Wallace of Londonderry, was born in Bedford. Aug. 8, 1760. He was in the Revolutionary army, being enrolled as a soldier at the age of seventeen, and was under Gen. Stark at Bennington. He married Jennet Walker, daughter of James Walker of Bedford, and came to Antrim in 1784 or earlier, being among the early settlers. He settled where William Stacey now lives, and had a store there, the first opened in town. His first log house was a little west of the present house, and on the opposite side of the road. Soon after his settlement he was driven up a tree by a bear. Bruin sat and watched him, as a cat watches a mouse, for about two hours, and then walked off, sour and hungry! Mr. Wallace lived to a great age; was much honored by his townsmen, being called "Judge," on account of his soberness and good sense. James Wallace died in May, 1848. His wife died in March, 1834. Their children were:—

1. BETSEY, [b. April 1, 1786; m. Francis Reed, Dec. 23, 1817; lived at North Branch some years, when they moved to Manchester, where she d.]
2. JOHN, [b. June 5, 1789; m. Sally Paige of this town, Feb. 24, 1824; built the house now Samuel S. Sawyer's, where he d. July 20, 1861. His widow d. Jan. 22, 1864, aged 67. Their children were: —

*Ira P.*, (b. Jan. 6, 1825; lives in Chicago, Ill.; unm.)

*John M.*, (b. Feb. 18, 1829; m. Frances A. Holmes, Nov. 14, 1853; lives in Fairfax, Io.)

*Miles N.*, (b. May 20, 1830; was clerk in McKeen's store, and d. Oct. 21, 1850.)

*Sarah E.*, (b. March 18, 1835.)]

3. JAMES, JR., [b. Aug. 2, 1792; m. Naomi Cochran, granddaughter of Dea. Isaac Cochran, Feb. 5, 1818; built the east house on Stacey hill, but moved to Bedford in 1837, thence to Manchester in 1839, and d. March 19, 1859. She d. May 19, 1877, aged 83. They had children as follows: —

*Sarah J.*, (b. Dec. 19, 1818; m. Frederick Mitchell of Claremont; d. at Manchester, Nov. 29, 1849.)

*Col. Andrew C.*, (b. Oct. 26, 1820; m. Olive Sturtevant of Meredith, and lives in Manchester. He has often been representative from Manchester, been honored with many offices, both civil and military, and is a man of great business capacity, being the largest individual manufacturer of lumber in the State. His children are Clara A., and Andrew C., Jr.)

*James M.*, (b. Nov. 24, 1822; m. 1st, Nancy Tebbets of Lee; 2d, Laura Dunham of Hooksett; 3d, Mrs. Susan (Tebbets) Drew, and now lives in Manchester.)

*Charlotte W.*, (b. March 10, 1825. She lives in Manchester, unm., being a book-keeper on the Amoskeag corporation.)

*Betsey A.*, (b. May 10, 1827; m. Charles White of Concord, where she recently d.)

*Luther C.*, (b. Oct. 24, 1829; d. Aug. 20, 1831.)

*Harriet M.*, (b. March 18, 1832; now lives in Manchester; is a book-keeper on the Amoskeag corporation.)

*Elwin C.*, (b. Oct. 20, 1834; d. November, 1835.)

*Luther C.*, (b. Nov. 15, 1836; m. Frances O. Tufts; was a book-keeper, and d. in Manchester Feb. 21, 1877.)]

4. SALLY W., [b. July 27, 1794; m. Dr. James A. Gregg, Sept. 27, 1810, and d. March 3, 1812.]

5. IRA, [b. June 13, 1798. He volunteered in the war of 1812, to take the place of a drafted man in Windsor, and d. in service at Portsmouth.]

6. BENJAMIN F., [b. Oct. 8, 1802; m. 1st, Marion Shattuck of Amherst; had a large family of children by his first wife, who d. in 1847, and he m. 2d, Mary Butler. He d. in this town, May 5, 1864. Mr. Wallace was for a time editor of the " Manchester Saturday Messenger," which had been an independent paper, but was at once made by him an ardent

advocate of Whig principles. He was an outspoken, ardent, pious, and useful man. The writer remembers him as a teacher and was under his instruction for a term in Piscataquog Academy, now Manchester. Of this last-named academy he was principal several years prior to 1851, when he became editor. Perhaps his best success in his long experience as a teacher was at Francestown Academy, of which he was principal in 1832, 1833, 1834, 1835, and again in 1838. Of these five years the historian of the institution says: —

> The academy flourished under the instruction of Mr. Benjamin F. Wallace, and even went so far as to publish a catalogue each year. We find there recorded over one hundred pupils, who seem to have been as congenial a band of young people as ever were thrown together. One, Clark B. Cochrane, rose to be a prominent member of Congress, and others have held, and in the prime of life still hold, some of the most honorable places in the nation. Mr. Wallace had attended school here to Dr. Bard; was a man of medium height, strongly built, and was, especially when excited, a terrible stammerer. His scholars will recall the "hem! hem!" which always preceded the rebuke of an offender, and they had a saying among them that after three droppings of his chin, they must look out for a storm.]

7. ACHSAH, [b. May 19, 1806; d. in 1829.]

JOHN. WALLACE, brother of James, before mentioned, was born in Bedford, May 12, 1764; came to Antrim not long after his brother, and settled on the Wilson farm, now Reed Carr's. He married Tryphena Abbott, and of their children little has been ascertained. They moved to Westmoreland in 1813, with their five children, where one of them died. The next year they moved to Putney, Vt., where he died in 1834. His wife died in June, 1836. Names of children are: —

1. JOHN W., [d. young.]
2. SARAH, [d. young.]
3. POLLY, [m. David Carpenter, and d. in Greenfield, Mass.]
4. HANNAH, [m. Elisha Wilbur, and d. Nov. 16, 1836, aged 42. Her son, John Wilbur, Esq., is superintendent of the railroad, Staten Island, N. Y. The other son is Lewis Wilbur, Esq., of Norfolk, N. Y.]
5. CYRUS, [d. young.]
6. MOSELY, [d. young.]
7. FREEMAN, [d. young.]
8. MARGARET, [d. unm.]

GENEALOGIES. 733

JOSIAH WALLACE, brother of James and John, mentioned above, was born in Bedford in 1769. He married Polly Goffe of Bedford, and came to Antrim in 1804. He lived at North Branch, built the three-story house there, and, in connection with his brother James, built a clothing-mill just opposite Parkhurst's mill. After running it many years, he sold to Francis Reed. It was subsequently moved down to the dam below, made into a bobbin-factory, and burned. Josiah Wallace died April 6, 1843. His widow died Oct. 25, 1854, aged eighty-three years. Their children were: —

1. ROXANNA, [b. in Bedford, Sept. 25, 1791; m. Moses Davis, Sept. 19, 1811, and moved to Manchester.]
2. THEODORE G., [b. in Bedford, Jan. 31, 1795; m. Mrs. Ann (Dustin) Holmes of Francestown, Nov. 10, 1835. He was in the war of 1812; built the Sewall Preston house at the Branch, where he d. April 7, 1852. His widow d. Dec. 12, 1853, aged 66. He had no children.]
3. BARTLETT, [b. in Bedford, Aug. 6. 1797; m. Lucy K. Little, sister of Dea. Little, and lived on the McNiel place. now Hiram Eaton's, finishing both houses there. He was sheriff many years, and d. June 2, 1855. His wife d. July 11, 1855, aged 55 years. Their children were: —

   *Hiram L.*, (b. April 4, 1824; m. Elizabeth Putnam of Lyndeborough, November, 1847, and moved West some years ago. He was a photographer in California, and d. in Oakdale, Cal., June, 1877. He had two children. His son Edward was b. in Antrim, Dec. 11, 1853, m. Laura Glover of Boscabel, Wis., and is a merchant in Oakland, Cal. The daughter, Charlotte, b. Dec. 11, 1854, is a public reader, highly successful and popular. She has filled most acceptably the office of superintendent of schools in Lyndeborough.)

   *Henry*, (never m.; went West, and was murdered in Minnesota, at the age of 27.)

   *Charlotte M.*, (b. Nov. 9, 1827; d. Dec. 25, 1849.)]
4. SAMUEL G., [b. in Bedford, Sept. 1, 1799; m. Sarah Crandall of Homer, N. Y., and went to Michigan.]
5. ELVIRA, [b. in Bedford, Jan. 31, 1802; m. Judge Elkanah Richardson of Ohio.]
6. JOHN W., [b. in Antrim, July 15, 1804;. m. Ann C. Brackett, and lived in the Robert Carr house (moved from opposite Reed Carr's and put up where it now stands in 1859), where he d. April 13, 1878. The children are: —

*Oliver M.*, (b. Feb. 12, 1833; m. Hattie Adams, and lives in Revere, Mass.; painter by trade.)

*Silas G.*, (b. Oct. 25, 1834; m. 1st, Sarah E. Roach, July 4, 1860, who d. Nov. 20, 1864, aged 27. He m. 2d, Eliza J. Whitmore of Salisbury, and lives at South Village; house built in 1870. His children are: Sarah A., b. Nov. 9, 1866; Flora J., b. Feb. 13, 1868; Mary L., b. Feb. 23, 1870; Abbie S., b. Nov. 12, 1871; George W., b. Dec. 29, 1873; Emma F., b. Nov. 29, 1875; and Charles G., b. Dec. 14, 1877.)

*Caroline A.*, (b. June 27, 1837; m. Daniel S. Fuller, Nov. 27, 1859, and lives in Revere, Mass.)

*Edgar A.*, (b. June 7, 1843; m. Gertrude E. Lightcap. He graduated at Harvard Law School in 1867, and went into the practice of law in Havana, Ill.)]

7. NANCY, [b. May 1, 1806; m. Dr. John Scoby, and now resides in Shellrock, Io.]
8. MARY E., [b. Nov. 14, 1809; m. Judge Luke Woodbury, June 10, 1834, and now resides at South Village.]
9. JOSEPH G., [b. Feb. 11, 1813; d. March 4, 1815.]

## WALTON.

AMOS WALTON, son of Josiah Walton, was born in Temple. He married Eunice Oakes of Oakham, Mass., Jan. 18, 1825, and came to Antrim from New Ipswich in 1827. He lived here a few years, in the Gregg house by the pond, and manufactured hand-bellows; then went to Lowell, Mass., thence to Iowa, and died there. Children:—

1. JOSIAH, [b. in New Ipswich; settled in the West.]
2. JOHN WARREN, [b. in Antrim, March 4, 1828; went West with his father. Beyond this we do not trace any of them. They settled in Muscatine County, Mich.]

## WARD.

DR. WILLIAM WARD came here probably as early as 1787, and remained about five years, when he seems, like Drs. Frye and Adams, to have sought a better field. It is not known where he lived in town, but probably it was on the Knights place (Harold Kelsea's), or in a little house that stood about on the spot now Mr. Corey's. A tract of land in that vicinity, which it would be difficult now to define, was in after years designated as the "Ward Land," as appears in a transcript of a road changing the north end of the street to its present locality. Dr. Ward left town about the close of 1792. Nothing more is known of him.

A hundred years ago there was a William Ward in New Boston, near my father's, who was a somewhat noted character, a Scotchman, a blacksmith, full of fun, and engaged in various practical jokes, characteristic of that day. He printed over the door of his shop in rude, plain letters:—

"Now pay me down upon the board,
Your humble servant, William Ward."

## WARREN.

JOHN WARREN lived here about twenty-seven years. He came here as early as 1774, and that year built his cabin on what is now S. S. Sawyer's farm at the Branch. In 1776 he built the first saw-mill in town. It stood eight or ten rods below the bridge in Branch Village, and a little below the Wallace or Parkhurst mills, and the remnants of it may still be found. Subsequently he seems to have built another log house to go with his mill, and to have disposed of the first one. This second log house stood a little south of the mill, on a knoll back of the Sylvester Preston place. Here he lived a dozen years or more, when this property passed into other hands, and Warren moved on to Meeting-House Hill. Thence, about 1802, he went to Canada. He was noted for telling great stories,— of the kind so great that nobody would believe them. Hence, anything doubtful used to be called one of "John Warren's stories." As an instance of his exceedingly vigorous talent in setting things strong, we may notice his distinguished shot at wild geese. He saw the flock coming, and, telling his wife to watch them, he hurried in to load his gun. He poured in one-quarter of a pound of powder and two pounds of shot, when his wife shouted, "They're right over the house !" Without taking out the ramrod, he fired up the chimney, and brought down eleven of the flock all skewered on the ramrod ! Of course it was very thoughtful in him to save the ramrod in this way ! John Warren of Antrim was born in Chelmsford, Mass., Sept. 14, 1733; was son of Ephraim and Esther (Parker) Warren, and grandson of Joseph and Ruth (Wheeler) Warren ; and was said to be akin to Gen. Joseph Warren, of Bunker-Hill fame. He was brother of Capt. Josiah Warren of New Boston, and, therefore, great-great-uncle of the writer. He was also own uncle of Mrs. William Duncan and Mrs. Samuel Christie of Antrim. This latter fact accounts for his going to live near Samuel Christie on Meeting-House Hill after the death of his wife and the sale of his property at the Branch. It is to be regretted that so little can be learned concerning this pioneer of the town. He was constable of Antrim in 1784. Sold his pew, Sept. 2, 1801, to Asahel Cram. His wife seems to have died at the Branch about 1800. A grandson, Eben Warren of New Boston, thinks that John Warren died in Antrim, but it is certain that he left Antrim in the year 1802, going to the northern part of Vermont, or to Canada. He probably followed his son Moses to that region. His wife was a Dimond. Their children, so far as known, were : —

1. MOSES, [probably b. as early as 1770; is said to have owned a slate-quarry in Vermont.]

2. POLLY, [went to Vermont with Moses and settled there.]
3. DIMOND, [settled in Amherst, about a mile north of the village, and d. there about thirty years ago, in good old age. Eben Warren of New Boston was his son, and he left several other children.]
4. JONATHAN, [b. April 15, 1788. He settled in Canada, and d. in Portland, Province of Ontario, in April, 1854. He was known as "John Warren," though he wrote his name "Jonathan." He m. Mrs. Mary Jaquith, Feb. 6, 1834. One child of Jonathan survives, Mrs. Elizabeth Trickey of Oso, Fontenac County, Ont. Her son, John Warren Trickey, Esq., is a business man in Oso.]

## WEBBER.

BROOKS K. WEBBER, son of Maximilian J. and Clarissa (Sweet) Webber, and grandson of Jeremiah and Lydia Webber of Boscawen (now Webster), was born in the above place in 1837. He studied law in Newport, and in Woodstock, Vt., and was admitted to the bar in 1859. Opened a law-office in South Antrim in May, 1862, but after return from the army he moved to Hillsborough Lower Village, and thence, after a few years, to the Bridge, where he now resides, having a large practice and enjoying the confidence of the community. Mr. Webber enlisted from Antrim in August, 1862, and was promoted to first lieutenant. Was representative of Hillsborough in 1868 and 1869, and was a member from that town of the constitutional convention of 1876. He married, first, Francelia E. Gage of Washington; second, Louisa L. Brigham of Lempster; third, Annie L. Merrill of Deering. Has children : —

1. NED DOUGLAS, [b. in Washington, Jan. 19, 1865.]
2. CLARA SOPHIA, [b. in Hillsborough, Oct. 6, 1872.]

## WEBSTER.

ISAIAH WEBSTER, son of Nathan (who was killed by the falling of a tree in 1787) and Hannah (Bailey) Webster of Salem, Mass., was born in 1766. He married Abigail Heath of Pelham in 1790, and came to Antrim from Salem, N. H., in 1794, lived a few years on the Jonas White place, and went to Salem, Mass., in 1811. He was out during the war of 1812, and at the close of the same, on his way home, stopped here at his brother Nathan's, where he suddenly died, aged forty-four. His children were : —

1. HEMAN, [m. Mary Eaton of Andover, Mass., in 1807, and settled in Methuen.]
2. PHŒBE, [b. in Antrim, Jan. 22, 1795; m. Edward Perry of Danvers, Mass., in 1817.]

3. RHODA, [became second wife of John Frye, and went to Java, N. Y.]
4. MARY G., [b. in 1806; m. John Frye of Salem, Mass., in 1823, but lived only a few years.]

NATHAN WEBSTER, brother of Isaiah, mentioned above, was born in Salem, N. H., in 1771; married Anna Bayls of his native town, came here in 1798, settled on the place now Daniel Swett's, and died Aug. 4, 1845. His widow died May 14, 1854, aged eighty-three. Their children were : —

1. PAMELIA, [b. in 1797; m. Lemuel Curtis of Windsor, Feb. 28, 1822, and d. in 1857.]
2. JONATHAN, [b. Nov. 4, 1798; d. Feb. 5, 1814.]
3. ENOS, [b. Nov. 28, 1800; m. Elizabeth Keyes, Jan. 20, 1831; lived on the homestead with his father, but sold in 1855. He lived some years on the Ambrose Story place; went West in 1867, and now lives in Antrim, Minn. His children are : —

    *Fanny M.*, (b. Jan. 5, 1832; d. April 6, 1858.)
    *Jonathan E.*, (b. July 16, 1833; m. Cynthia J. H. Cram of Bennington, Nov. 23, 1851, and d. in that town, July 14, 1856.)
    *Elizabeth A.*, (b. March 21, 1835; m. 1st, Orren D. Parker of Hillsborough, March 26, 1851, and lived in this town several years, where they had four children. He d. in Stoddard in 1862, and she m. James P. Wood in 1866, and now lives in Antrim, Minn.)
    *Orlando T.*, (b. Sept. 23, 1836; enlisted in the Union army, Ninth Illinois Regiment, and d. in service, Dec. 15, 1861.)
    *Loammi H.*, (b. July 30, 1838; entered the army and starved to death in a Southern prison, dying March 23, 1864.)
    *Anna B.*, (b. May 11, 1840; d. April 10, 1859.)
    *Jason K.*, (b. April 12, 1842; m. Lizzie A. Fisher, Jan. 1, 1867, and is now postmaster in Madelia, Minn.)
    *Ulyssa H.*, (b. Oct. 10, 1845; m. Luther M. Wilkins, Nov. 8, 1860, and d. in 1861.)
    *Mary E.*, (d. in infancy.)
    *Enos B.*, (b. May 5, 1857.)]
4. NATHAN, [b. Sept. 14, 1802; m. Martha Hurd of Maine, and went to Charlestown, Mass., where he d. in 1865.]
5. BENAIAH, [b. Jan. 1, 1806; d. April 1, 1806.]

6. BENAIAH, [b. June 8, 1807; m. Katherine Godfrey of Charlestown, Mass., and d. in that place Oct. 31, 1864.]
7. FANNY, [b. Oct. 3, 1809; d. Oct. 10, 1831.]
8. HANNAH, [b. Jan. 12, 1812; m. Loammi S. Hurd of Maine, April 10, 1834, and moved to Charlestown, Mass., where she d. August, 1843.]
9. KIMBALL E., [b. March 5, 1814; d. in infancy.]

SAMUEL WEBSTER built, in 1806, a large three-story house on the west side of the old common on the hill. He was a shoemaker by trade, and had a shop for that purpose in the basement of the lower story. In the upper part he intended to keep tavern; but he probably did not count the cost, inasmuch as he never finished the building, and moved away about three years afterwards, greatly in debt. Nothing is known of whence he came or whither he went. The house stood awhile, unfinished, being occupied by transient parties, several dying there of spotted fever, but was finally taken down and used for the frame of the Appleton house, now standing in the west part of Deering, and known as "Appleton Tavern."

## WEEKS.

SAMUEL WEEKS was born in 1764; married Sarah Wadleigh of Londonderry, and came from that town to Antrim; lived in a long, low, wooden house where the brick house, now Samuel M. Thompson's, stands. He was a drover, and brought large flocks of sheep and hogs from Vermont. He seems to have lived awhile about 1812 on the Shattuck place; was an active, energetic man; moved to Chelmsford, Mass., and kept tavern awhile, then came back and settled in Bennington, just over the river from his old home, where he died in 1816, aged fifty-two. His wife died in 1813, aged fifty-three. Their children were:—

1. MARTHA, [m. Thomas D. Nesmith, March 30, 1813, and d. in Antrim, June 17, 1828.]
2. JOHN, [m. Hannah Hunkins, and d. in Poplin, now Fremont.]
3. HANNAH, [m. Josiah Roach, and d. in Bennington.]
4. SARAH, [m. 1st, a Mr. Lowe; 2d, George Gibson, and went to Fremont, where she d.]
5. SAMUEL. JR., [lived some six years with Capt. Thomas D. Nesmith; went to Charlestown, Mass., where he d. about 1825, a young man.]
6. MARY, [m. Jonathan Atwood; moved to Haverhill, and d. there.]

## WELLMAN.

ISRAEL WELLMAN was born in Lyndeborough in 1829; married Orra A. Dutton of Greenfield in 1855; came here in 1873, lived in various places about town, and has recently moved to Stoddard. His children are Henry P., George W., Ida A., Nellie O., John R., and Charles.

## WESTON.

DEA. SUTHERIC WESTON, son of Ebenezer and Mehitable (Sutheric) Weston, grandson of Thomas and Elizabeth Weston, and great-grandson of John and Sarah (Fitch) Weston of Reading, Mass. (which John came from England to Salem, Mass., in 1644, at the age of thirteen, and settled in Reading, Mass., in 1652, where he married Sarah Fitch), was born Nov. 19, 1751. Judge Weston of Augusta, Me., and Ex-Gov. Weston of Manchester are of the same stock. The "Weston coat of arms" being identical with that of the "Earl of Portland," it is claimed that their descent can be traced from him. The parents of Dea. Sutheric Weston moved to Amherst, N. H., in 1752. He was out in the Revolutionary war, and suffered much from hardship and starvation. At the battle of the Cedars in Canada he was taken prisoner by the Indians and nearly starved, when they decided to give him and others a chance to run for their lives. The deacon, being a man of great muscular power and endurance, made for the woods, rushed into a dense swamp, and managed to escape pursuit after a time. He was finally discovered by a scout of his regiment, his flesh torn and bleeding, his clothes hanging in fragments about him, and in a nearly famished condition. He is also said to have been once regularly exchanged, in company with Lemuel Curtis and others, for British prisoners. He went from Amherst to Bunker Hill, and was one of those who went across and shared in the last part of that battle. Jan. 20, 1779, Dea. Weston married Mary DeLancy ; came from Amherst to Antrim in 1786; and succeeded John Gordon at North Branch on the place now owned by Oliver Swett, building, in connection with his son, Capt. Sutheric Weston, the large house on that place, in 1807. He was appointed deacon in the Presbyterian Church in 1800; was a faithful, able, and good man, and died May 11, 1831, aged over seventy-nine years. His wife died Aug. 4, 1838, aged eighty-two. Their children are as follows : —

1. MARY L., [b. Nov. 12, 1780 ; m. Daniel Moore of Bedford, and had a large family ; d. in Montpelier, Vt., at great age.]
2. CAPT. SUTHERIC, [b. March 8, 1783 ; m. Sally S. McCauley in 1808 ; was familiarly called "Captain," holding that commission in the cavalry in 1819 ; lived for some time with his father, afterward moved into a house then standing northeast of J. G. Flint's, (built by Francis Stuart just within the town line, because he wanted the honor of living in Antrim, — wise man !) moved thence to Whitney place, and from there to Nashua in 1836, where he d. May 30, 1850. His widow d. in Holyoke, Mass., in 1854. Their children were : —

*Esther M.*, (b. June 24, 1809 ; m. Joseph Atwood of Bedford,

Feb. 11, 1834, and lives in Hamilton, Ill. One old resident says : " She was as smart a woman as was ever raised in Antrim." She was a fine scholar and teacher.)

*Sarah*, (b. Dec. 14, 1811 ; d. at the age of 3 months.)

*David*, (b. in 1813 ; d. at the age of 5 months.)

*Mary D.*, (b. April 25, 1815 ; d. in Nashua, Oct. 26, 1836.)

*Sutheric J.*, (b. July 28, 1816 ; m. Elizabeth Porter of Manchester, and now resides in San Francisco.)

*David M.*, (b. May 22, 1818 ; m. Mary Jane Carter of Hollis, and now lives in Boston. Was one of the donors of the Center vestry; is a man of large means. and a generous giver to all the charities. Is a man full of faith and full of good works. Mr. Weston is the inventor of the machine for drying sugar in process of manufacture, now used all over the world. This invention is simply the application of centrifugal motion to useful purposes. The same principle appears in his " laundry-machine," " centrifugal clothes-wringer," and in his " cream-machine." The latter effects the mechanical separation of cream from the milk in less time than is occupied in milking, and promises to revolutionize the dairy business in all large establishments. Mr. Weston holds several patents, both in the United States and Great Britain, of inventions highly useful to the world and profitable to himself. He is a thinking, practical man, — one of the ablest and best that have gone out from Antrim ; a Christian, enjoying the confidence of men and living in the fear of God.)

*Rebecca J.*, (b. April 8, 1820 ; m. Lawson E. Russell of Bethel, Me.; d. in that place, Sept. 10, 1855.)

*Harriet N.*, (b. April 2, 1822 ; m. Sidney Alden of Troy, N. Y., in 1838, and now lives in that city.)

*Eliza A.*, (b. May 15, 1824 ; m. Hon. Charles Williams of Easton, Mass., in 1846. They now reside in Nashua. She is a woman widely known, gifted, devoted, charitable, and a leader in the missionary work of the N. H. Woman's Board. Mr. Williams has been several times mayor of the city, — is a man affable, efficient, and with hosts of friends. Their son, Dr. Seth W. Williams, just dead at the age of 30, was a graduate of Yale, a young man of most finished education and most noble character, and had begun life's work with much promise in New York City. He was under appoint-

ment to a position of heavy responsibility in Bellevue Hospital, but was taken down suddenly with congestion of the brain and d. on his way home from an excursion, at Portland, Me.)

*Leonard*, (b. April 28, 1826. Graduated at Phillips Academy, class of 1846. Was a talented young man, from whom the family had many hopes. He entered Dartmouth College with the intention of studying for the ministry, but d. in his Freshman year, Sept. 1, 1848. Thus dying at the age of 22, the work which his piety prompted* was not done, but its reward was reached early and triumphantly.)

*Sarah J.*, (b. July 7, 1833; m. Benjamin P. Crocker of Cambridge, N. Y., and lives in that place.)]

3. REBECCA, [b. April 24, 1785; d. unm. in Hancock, Dec. 25, 1841.]

4. LEONARD, [b. Oct. 10, 1791; went to Phelps, N. J.; m. Alma Wright in, 1818; moved to Michigan in 1840, where he d. in 1855.]

5. SOPHIA, [b. Oct. 20, 1794; m. Capt. William Gregg of this town, Feb. 7, 1814; went to Nashua in 1837, where she d. June 29, 1844.]

6. LANCY, [b. Nov. 11, 1800; m. Elizabeth Moore of Bedford in 1831; lived many years on the Taylor place, east of the Jonathan Nesmith place; went thence to Bedford in 1847, but moved to Mount Clemens, Mich., in 1850, and d. there December, 1877. His children, all of whom are believed to have been b. here, were : —

*Nathaniel H.*, (b. July 21, 1833; m. 1st, Miss H. P. Hoyt of Weare; 2d, Mrs. Laura Moore of New Boston; lives in Oscada, Mich., winters in Detroit.)

*Clinton H.*, (b. Dec. 7, 1839; m. Martha Ketchum, May 1, 1873, and lives at Au Sable, Mich.)

*W. Clark*, (b. Dec. 8, 1842; was out in the Ninth Michigan Regiment, and d. in service at West Point, Ky., Dec. 4, 1861.)

*George W.*, (b. Aug. 7, 1846; m. Jennie Bowman, Dec. 29, 1875, and lives in Richmond, Mich.)]

SAMUEL WESTON came here from Stoddard, married Mary Dunlap, and lived on the old Burns place near the first High-Range schoolhouse, where he died Dec. 10, 1836, aged forty. Their children were : —

1. MEHITABLE B., [b. May 8, 1824; m. Amos Dodge, April 18, 1844.]
2. HANNAH, [b. March 9, 1826; m. Veranus Atwood, and lives in Nelson.]
3. SAMUEL, [b. March, 1828; d. in Sanbornton, aged 24.]
4. SARAH, [b. April, 1830; m. Orrel Atwood of Nelson, and d. in that town June 27, 1856.]

WILLIAM WESTON was grandson of Timothy and Esther (Lampson) Weston of Concord, Mass., and son of Ephraim and Elisabeth (Nay) Weston of Peterborough, and was born in that town April 15, 1798. His father was born Aug. 19, 1767, and died Sept. 8, 1829, in this town. Buried in Stoddard. He came here in 1820, and settled on the Andrew Robb place as known at the present day, on a tract of wild land belonging to "Squire James Wilson" of Keene, father of Gen. Wilson. This land, and other large tracts with it, Mr. Weston soon acquired. He became an extensive raiser of stock, at one time owning a thousand sheep and many cattle, and having in charge also large flocks that were owned below. He was a man of many virtues, and was honest as the daylight. It used to be said that "Bill Weston's word was as good as his note." His removal to Hancock in 1834 was a matter of general regret in Antrim. In that town he died June 24, 1848. He married Harriet Hall, Dec. 17, 1822, who died May 9, 1831, aged thirty-one. He married, second, Mrs. Mary D. (Copeland) Fisher in 1833. She was born in Stoddard, July 19, 1803, and died in Hancock, Aug. 28, 1853. The children of William Weston were as follows, all but the youngest born in Antrim:—

1. CAPT. EPHRAIM, [b. Nov. 9, 1823. Was a man of good education, of great agility and strength, and of marked nobleness and manliness of character. He was one whose bearing compelled the respect of others. Always took great interest in military affairs, and was among the very first to enlist in his country's service on the breaking-out of the rebellion. Was captain in the Second N. H. Regiment; was in the first battle of Bull Run; lost his life in the service, coming home to die,— which event took place in Hancock, Dec. 9, 1861. He is justly placed among the most worthy of the sons of Antrim. His wife was Elvina H. Gates. They settled in Hancock, and he enlisted from that town. His children were: William Henry, who was b. Aug. 8, 1849; Clara Elvina, who was b. June 16, 1851, and m. Alfred Barber, Feb. 5, 1868; George F., who was b. Oct. 3, 1853, and graduated at Brown University in 1878; Mary E., who was b. July 1, 1856, and d. at the age of three; Harriet E., who was b. Oct. 6, 1858; and Ephraim, Jr., who was b. May 23, 1861.]

2. WILLIAM, JR., [b. May 4, 1825; m. Sarah A. Wilder of Stoddard, April 17, 1859; was the last owner that lived on Robb Mountain; now lives in Hancock, having moved there in 1868. Four of his children were b. in Antrim. His children are: —
*James T.*, (b. May 25, 1860.)
*Harriet E.*, (b. June 25, 1862.)
*Sarah F.*, (b. June 26, 1864.)
*Mary Annabel*, (b. Sept. 2, 1866.)
*William*, (b. March 3, 1869.)
*Ephraim*, (b. Aug. 7, 1872.)]
3. HARRIET H., [b. Nov. 24. 1826; m. Oliver Messer, who has been a leading citizen of Clinton, Io., more than twenty years. He was b. in Bow, May 19, 1823. Is superintendent of the gas and water works in the city of Clinton.]
4. JAMES T., [b. Sept. 24, 1829; d. on the ship "Richmond" off Cape Horn, in February, 1850, and was buried at sea. He d. in his berth at night, and it was claimed that no one knew of it till morning. There was a mystery about it never cleared up. With many others, he was on his way to California at the time of the gold excitement. Was a promising young man. Many will remember his handsome form and pleasant disposition, and how there were a host of friends that mourned his early death.]
5. JOHN C., [b. Oct. 26, 1834; was weak and feeble in his early years, but was stirred with a great desire to travel, and so went round the world as a "sailor before the mast." He sailed from Boston on the ship "John Wade" Sept. 5, 1851, being less than seventeen years of age, and returned Aug. 5, 1852. The next year he went again to California and remained fifteen years, mostly among the mines of that State and Oregon. He then settled in Clinton, Io., where he still resides. Is cashier of Clinton National Bank and director of Clinton Savings Bank. Is also secretary and treasurer of Clinton Gas Company and of Clinton Water-works, and is identified with most of the public interests and improvements of the place. He m. Jennie Sibley in Sailor Diggings, Ore., June 23, 1860; m. 2d, Carrie F. White in Norwood, Mass., Jan. 14, 1870. She is a descendant of Peregrine White, b. on the "Mayflower," in the harbor of Cape Cod.]

6. GEORGE W., [b. in Hancock, Feb. 24, 1837; was two years in the mines of California when quite young, then settled in Iowa. Was a vigorous abolitionist and stockholder in the underground railway, and personally helped fourteen slaves to gain their freedom. So when the war broke out he entered the Union army from principle, was lieutenant in the Twenty-sixth Iowa Volunteers, and d. in the service Aug. 18, 1863. He m. Emelia J. Marshall of Dublin. She d. in Low Moor, Io., in 1866, aged 30.]

TIMOTHY WESTON, brother of William, Sen., named above, was born Dec. 7, 1805. He married his cousin, Matilda Nay of Peterborough, April 8, 1830; succeeded his brother on the Robb Mountain, but afterwards sold to William Weston, Jr., and went to Nauvoo, Ill., to join the Mormons. He soon became disgusted with their practices, and, with lost health and lost property, he returned to Hancock and died Sept. 29, 1855. His widow became the second wife of Abisha Tubbs of Peterborough. They had one child, Sarah A. Weston, who died July 9, 1849, aged sixteen; and four others that died very young. The second husband, in company with his brother, Joseph Tubbs, was for many years a manufacturer of cotton yarn, batting. etc., in Peterborough. He was born in Marlow, May 21, 1791.

The brothers and sisters of Timothy Weston all lived together in the family on the mountain for a short time, and were as follows: Ephraim, Jr., who died in Cambridge, Mass., June 22, 1828; second, Elizabeth, who died unmarried, Feb. 26, 1865; third, William, noticed above; John, who married Sophronia Farwell and died in Washington, June 4, 1873, aged sixty-nine; fifth, Esther, who married Robert McClure of Antrim, 1828, and died July 15, 1835; sixth, Timothy, noticed above; and seventh, Sarah Ann, who died unmarried Feb. 12, 1836, aged twenty-two, and was buried on the plain in Antrim. At the time this family lived together on the mountain, and down as late as 1840, there were four farm-houses on the land of William Weston, with large families, full barns, and large stocks of cattle and sheep. Now every house is gone, the road is thrown up, and one hardly sees an indication that human habitations once were there!

## WHITCOMB.

ABIJAH WHITCOMB came here from Swanzey in 1846 and lived about two years. He built the mill on the site of the Aiken or Volney Johnson mill, now Goodell's lower mill. His son Frank married a Miss Nichols of Peterborough, and lived here about a year with his father. They all moved to Peterborough. Thence the older couple moved to Claremont and died there. There was an Abijah Whitcomb in the Revolutionary army from Swanzey, probably father of above.

## WHITE.

HENRY WHITE, son of William and Polly (Griffin) White of New Boston, was born in 1771; married Elizabeth Dustin, sister of Zaccheus Dustin's wife; came to Antrim from Weare in 1798, and lived on what was afterward known as the Dea. Sawyer place, just north of the old cemetery on Meeting-House Hill. It is not known who commenced this place. Mr. White returned to Weare in 1809, where he died in 1853. His children were: —

1. POLLY G., [b. in Weare in 1796; m. Jesse Walker and lives in Whitefield.]
2. DUSTIN, [b. in Weare in 1798; m. Polly Colby of Weare and settled in that town, where he now lives.]
3. JAMES, [b. in Antrim in 1800; m. Lydia Bradford of Marlow, and lived in Hudson, Wis., until his death in 1855.]
4. TRISTRAM S., [b. in Antrim in 1802; d. in childhood.]
5. HENRY S., [b. in Antrim, May 4, 1804; d. in Dunstable, Mass., in 1830.]
6. RHODA, [b. in Antrim in 1806; m. Jonathan Flanders of Bradford.]
7. ALICE B., [b. in Antrim in 1808; m. Levi Watson of Weare.]
8. WILLIAM, [b. in Weare in 1810; m. Mary Colby of Mont Vernon, and lives in Wilton.]
9. ELIZA, [b. in 1812; m. Alhanon Codman of Hillsborough, and d. in 1869.]

JONATHAN WHITE, son of Silas and Sarah (George) White, was born in Greenwich, N. Y., in 1814, and was brought here by his widowed mother when two years of age. He began as an apprentice with Dea. Isaac Baldwin in 1834; married Laura Lord of Woodstock, Vt., and was in business at the South Village under the firm-name of Eaton and White, and afterwards alone. He held the patent for the welded shovel, which was sold to the Ames Company. He built and lived where John Shedd now lives, and died July 7, 1864. The children are thus: —

1. HORACE P., [now lives in California.]
2. CHARLES F., [now lives in California.]
3. GEORGE H., [was in N. H. Sharp-shooters, and was killed at the battle of Gettysburg, July 3, 1863.]

JAMES WHITE, son of James and Susannah (Flint) White (who was the daughter of Lieut. Miles Flint, who was out during the whole of the Revolutionary war), was born in Methuen, Mass., in 1802. He married, first, Abigail Coburn of Boston, and settled in Deering. He came to Antrim in 1840, and built the house on the river next east of William Duncan's the same year. He was a carpenter, did business in Manchester, and moved to that city in 1846, where he is an influential man. His first wife died in 1847, and he married, second, Mahala Lord of Bow, 1849. His children are as follows: —

1. OLIVE A., [b. in Deering; m. John G. Richardson of Hooksett; now lives in Woburn, Mass.]
2. ELIZA S., [b. in Deering; d. Sept. 17, 1849.]
3. CHARLES A., [b. in Deering; m. Cora P. Foster of Boston; now lives in Greeley, Col.]
4. R. AMANDA, [b. in Deering; m. John Fickett.]
5. JOSEPH W., [b. in Antrim, Feb. 25, 1843; entered the army and was killed at Fort Wagner, July 18, 1863.]
6. J. EDWARD, [b. in 1856; now resides in Manchester.]

NATHAN WHITE, son of Nathan and Dorcas (Wilson) White, came here from Deering in 1842. He married Jane B. Smith of Milford, and lived in the Starrett house (now Fletcher's), South Village. He was a cooper by trade, and died in 1852 aged thirty-five, leaving children: —

1. GEORGE H., [b. Nov. 30, 1846; now lives in Boston.]
2. MARY J., [b. April 16, 1851; m. Edward Horne in 1872 and lives in Rochester, N. Y.]
3. ANNIE M., [b. Nov. 1, 1843; m. E. P. Gilman and lives in Nashua.

JONAS WHITE, son of John and Lucy (Tucker) White of Nelson, was born in 1802; married Margaret Clark of Bellingham, Mass., and came to Antrim in 1849. He bought the Dea. Benjamin Nichols place in 1858, where he lived until 1874, when he moved into the Paige house. His children are: —

1. JOHN W., [b. in Brandon, Vt., Nov. 25, 1826; m. 1st, Laura A. Foss of Concord, Jan. 7, 1850, who d. Nov. 8, 1850; m. 2d, Emily A. Sargent of Concord, Sept. 11, 1851. He is a marble worker and carver, and has resided chiefly in Concord, but in 1874 he bought the Nichols place of his father and moved to Antrim. He moved back to Concord after about two years. Children are: —

*Frank A.*, (b. in Concord, July 3, 1852; m. Mary A. Green of Concord, April 1, 1876, and resides in that city, having two children.)
*Walter E.*, (b. in Antrim, May 1, 1854.)
*Laura A.*, (b. in Antrim, Nov. 3, 1855.)
*Willie*, (b. in Lawrence, Mass., Feb. 5, 1858; d. in infancy.)
*Willie A.*, (b. in Lawrence, Mass., Jan. 21, 1859; d. in November of same year.)

*Nellie M.*, (b. in Lawrence, Mass., Dec. 21, 1860.)
*Fred E.*, (b. in Peterborough, April 17, 1863.)
*John W.*, (b. in Peterborough, Aug. 29, 1865.)
*Mabel*, (b. in Concord, Feb. 17, 1868; d. Aug. 3, 1877.)
*Jennie*, (b. in Concord, Sept. 20, 1869; d. in infancy.)
*Julia*, (twin-sister of Jennie; d. in infancy.)
*Bennie B.*, (b. in Concord, Sept. 28, 1870; d. Aug. 30, 1877.)
*Abbie C.*, (b. in Concord, Feb. 8, 1874.)]

2. HARVEY, [b. April 18, 1828; entered the army in the Seventy-fourth Ohio Volunteers, and d. in service in 1863.]
3. ELIZA J., [b. July 8, 1832; m. 1st, Rev. William W. Lovejoy, July 31, 1855, who d. in 1862, leaving children: Antoinette E., Etta, and Flora. In 1868 Mrs. Lovejoy m. Charles I. Wright, son of Dea. Imla Wright, and now lives in Demascoville, Ohio.]
4. MARIA, [b. Aug. 28, 1834; m. Prentiss W. Clark.]
5. CHAUNCEY, [b. June 30, 1837; m. Melissa L. Carleton of Hancock, in 1870, and now lives in the Paige house. He has one child: —
*William C.*, (b. Oct. 9, 1875.)]
6. FRANCIS, [b. Oct. 18, 1839; m. Emily Smith, Nov. 7, 1865, and lives in Cambridge, Mass. He was a member of the First N. H. Regiment, and afterwards of the Seventh N. H. Regiment, in the late war, and was promoted to first lieutenant. His children are: —
*Albert E.*, (b. Nov. 5, 1866.)
*William H.*, (b. June 20, 1870.)]

DAVID O. WHITE, son of David (a Revolutionary soldier) and Sarah (Dutton) White of Peterborough, grandson of Patrick (who studied for a Catholic priest in Ireland, but fled to this country on renouncing that doctrine) and Jane (White) White, and great-grandson of John and Elizabeth White of Ireland, — was born Nov. 18, 1809; married Mary Ann Carr of Antrim, Dec. 13, 1838, and came on to the homestead of her father, William Carr, in 1850. Their children are: —

1. NANCY A., [b. Aug. 23, 1841; m. George Sanders of Epsom in 1875.]
2. ANDREW D., [b. Nov. 4, 1845; m. Clara Ann Appleton, April 4, 1877, and lives on the homestead with his father.]

WILLIAM WHITE, son of William White of Stoneham, Mass., was born in 1797; married Mary Wilson in Deering, April 22, 1823, and came to Antrim from that town on to the Kendall or John Gibson place in

1851. After living here about fifteen years he moved over the line into Hillsborough, and there died Jan. 16, 1869, aged seventy-two. His widow survives. Their children are: —

1. LAWSON A., [b. in Greenfield, Aug. 18, 1825; m. Caroline C. Gould of Deering, and lives on the place next west of the Gibson place, having children thus: —
   *Ellen F.*, (b. Dec. 1, 1851; m. Frank E. Lovering and lives at Hillsborough Bridge.)
   *Leonard P.*, (b. Oct. 10, 1853.)
   *Martha A.*, (b. in 1855; d. Dec. 27, 1870.)
   *Alma S.*
   *Mary T.*, (b. Dec. 25, 1860.)
   *Charles F.*, (b. Oct. 20, 1864.)
   *Harvey A.*, (b. July 20, 1867.)]
2. LOEL F., [b. in Deering, May 22, 1828; m. Zoa L. Ward of Ashby, Mass., and lives in Hillsborough.]
3. HARVEY L., [b. Dec. 29, 1830; lives unm. in Hillsborough near Antrim line.]
4. CAROLINE L., [b. May 5, 1832; is unm.]
5. REBECCA S., [b. March 7, 1835; m. Samuel D. Hastings, May 5, 1853, and lives at Hillsborough Bridge.]

## WHITELEY.

EDWARD WHITELEY, son of William H. and Louise (Jury) Whiteley, and grandson of William and Lydia (Garfitt) Whiteley of Morley, Yorkshire, England, was born in Islington, near London, Nov. 11, 1824; married Betsey H. Blanchard of this town in Boston, Sept. 15, 1853. He lives on the Miltimore or Blanchard place, but does business in Boston. Is a thinking man, a machinist and inventor, having taken out nine patents in this country, chiefly for heating and cooking apparatus. Some of these inventions are highly useful, as well as creditable. Was one of the donors of the Center vestry. Has children: —

1. M. LOUISE, [b. July 23, 1854; m. Charles F. Belcher of Cambridge, Mass., Jan. 27, 1876.]
2. MARY E., [b. July 12, 1856.]
3. NELLIE M., [b. Dec. 21, 1858.]
4. ALBERT E., [b. Dec. 26, 1861.]

## WHITNEY.

CYRUS J. WHITNEY, son of Jonah and Jane (Stone) Whitney, was born in Henniker, April 26, 1812; married Mary J. Morrison of Warner in 1836; moved to Antrim in 1843, and has since lived on the then-so-called Weston place. Their children are: —

1. SUSAN C., [b. Feb. 28, 1837 ; d. in Manchester, Oct. 4, 1856.]
2. ELIZA J., [b. Oct. 30, 1838 ; m. David W. Boutelle.]
3. GEORGE G., [b. Feb. 6, 1840; m. Elizabeth Bowl of Louisville, Ky., and now resides in that place, or vicinity.]
4. MARY M., [b. Dec. 2, 1842; m. Samuel A. Holt, Aug. 15, 1861.]
5. CYRUS J., [b. Sept. 27, 1844; m. Louisa E. Allds, Oct. 17, 1875, and lives on the Prescott Parmenter or Cram place. They have one child : —
   *Roscoe.* (b. March 18, 1877.)]
6. CHARLES F., [b. Sept. 20, 1847 ; lives with his father.]
7. JULIA E., [b. July 9, 1850 ; m. Almus T. Rogers of Antrim in 1873.]
8. CLARA ELLA, [b. Jan. 25, 1853 ; m. Henry A. Rogers of Antrim. Nov. 27, 1872.]
9. EMMA C., [b. Oct. 18, 1855 ; d. June 27, 1861.]
10. JOSEPHINE N., [b. May 31, 1860 ; m. George H. Rogers, Oct. 18, 1879.]
11. FREDERICK A., [b. Jan. 4, 1864.]

## WHITON.

JAMES WHITON, the first of the name in America, came over from Hingham, England, and settled in Hingham, Mass., in 1647, and married Mary Beals Dec. 30, 1647. His house was burned by Indians, April 20, 1676. He died in 1710, aged ninety years, leaving a large family.

James Whiton, second son of the preceding, was born in 1651, leading a life of quiet industry in Hingham, where he died at the age of seventy-four, leaving a large family. His wife's name is not known.

Joseph Whiton, son of second James, was born in 1687 ; married Martha Power in 1713 ; moved to Ashford, Conn., in 1730 ; was a cooper by trade ; died in 1777 in his ninety-first year, leaving seven children.

Elijah Whiton, son of Joseph, was born in Hingham in 1714. He learned the cooper's trade of his father. He married, first, Priscilla Russ in 1741, who died about 1755 leaving nine children. He married, second, Hannah Crocker, by whom he also had nine children.

Dr. Israel Whiton, son of Elijah and Priscilla (Russ) Whiton, was born in Ashford, Conn., in 1754. He commenced the study of medicine in 1773, enlisted as surgeon's mate in the army in 1776, was a short time orderly sergeant to Gen. Putnam at Boston, and was in the disastrous campaign and retreat at New York in 1776. He began the practice of medicine in April, 1777, in Winchendon, Mass. He made a profession of religion the next year ; married Dorothy Crosby, Oct. 28, 1784 ; was engaged in extensive practice forty-two years ; was deacon in the church ; often representative of the town ; was widely known and largely esteemed. He died in 1819. His widow, Mrs. Dorothy Whiton, died in

Antrim, Oct. 7, 1826. The new bell first tolled for her. Alas, how many since!

REV. JOHN MILTON WHITON, D. D., son of Dr. Israel and Dorothy (Crosby) Whiton, was born in Winchendon, Mass., Aug. 1, 1785; studied at New Ipswich, and Leicester, Mass., and entered Dartmouth College in September, 1801. At his father's wish, he took up his connection at Dartmouth in 1804, and spent his last year at Yale, graduating there in 1805. He was then engaged one year as assistant of James Morris, in his academy at Litchfield, Conn., where he made the acquaintance of Abby Morris, whom he afterwards married. In the fall of 1806, he went to Hanover to attend medical lectures, having in view the physician's profession, on the ground that his voice was not sufficient for public speaking; but, on arriving at Hanover, after some struggle of mind, he concluded to commence theological studies under the direction of Prof. Shurtleff. He finished the same under Rev. Samuel Austin, D. D., of Worcester, Mass., and preached here awhile during the summer of 1807. A call was voted him by the town, Sept. 21, 1807, which he declined; but the call being renewed the next spring he accepted it, and was ordained Sept. 28, 1808. He continued pastor, in active service, until Jan. 1, 1853, being settled at the age of twenty-three and vacating at the age of sixty-eight. He at once removed to Bennington, and was acting pastor there until his death, Sept. 27, 1856. The degree of D. D. was conferred upon him by Princeton College. Mr. Whiton married Abby Morris of Litchfield, Conn., Oct. 18, 1808. Her grandfather, Dea. James Morris, was born in New Haven, Conn., in 1722. Her father, James Morris, Esq., was a graduate of Yale College; a captain in the Revolutionary army, being some time on Gen. Washington's staff; and for a long series of years a teacher of distinguished success. He married Elizabeth Hubbard of Middleton, Conn., in 1781, and their daughter, Abby Morris, was born in 1783. Mr. Whiton moved into the old Butler house Dec. 5, 1808, built the Bass house on the same spot in 1812, built the Clark house in 1831, sold his farm in 1835, and moved up to the Center in 1843. Mrs. Whiton survived her husband, and died April 10, 1865, aged eighty-one.

John M. Whiton was a man of complete and rounded character. He had no salient points. He had no extreme endowments. There was nothing that could be called brilliant about him. Yet he was so finished and capable in every respect, that he left good impressions of himself everywhere, and the public generally both admired and loved him. Splendid things cannot be written of him; noble and blessed things without number can be. If he was great, it was the greatness of symmetry. People felt that he was a safe man. He commanded their respect. There was a peculiar grace about him everywhere, which attracted regard and reverence, and seemed as winning by the wayside as in the pulpit. Prof. Baldwin, than whom none knew him better, thus writes of him: "For most other great men, my reverence has diminished with near approach; but *he* so combined dignity and gentleness, that in the most familiar intimacy he ever commanded respect, reverence, and love. All were drawn toward him, and, being in his presence, were not in haste to leave. His life was a gospel of peace to all who were acquainted with him!"

Mr. Whiton was a very scholarly man. He had what might be called a balanced education. We do not find in him any engrossing admiration of a particular branch. He was not carried away by music, or poetry, or philology; but he had a clear, strong understanding of all the branches. In common conversation with him, one could see that he was a scholar. He was very clear in his knowledge of the Bible. The whole field of history was familiar ground to him. His language, whether he spoke or wrote, was singularly pure and tasteful. He shunned all colloquial expressions, and never was sharp at the expense of elegance; but, on the other hand, there was nothing heavy or tiresome in his careful sentences. He was a student to the close of life; and his last sermon, written but a few days before his death, is suggestive of a mind that was a treasury of rich things! Mr. Whiton had great charity of opinion. He respected the thoughts of others, and, though he cherished his own opinions somewhat strongly, he always held his dissent from others in abeyance as long as possible. If he expressed a different view, he did it with such gentleness as many times to carry the opposite opinions with him!

Theologically, Mr. Whiton was a man of moderate views. He was a Calvinist, but his presentation of that faith was in exceedingly cautious and gentle terms. Born and brought up a Congregationalist, he is said to have leaned that way during all his ministerial service; yet he was truly loyal to the Presbyterian body, and came to love its character and influence so much, that, in his riper years, he prepared a history of "Presbyterianism in New Hampshire," which he left behind him in manuscript. He preached a full provision of grace in Christ for every soul, and urged the largest meanings of "Whosoever will." He honored the Holy Ghost, and again and again declared if any were lost, it must be from refusal to come to Christ. His theology and his preaching all centered in Jesus as a Savior from sin. He always wrote good sermons. They had solid meat in them, and there was a plan and a framework in all. The writer has examined many of them; always to find a marked unity and system. The sermon grew out of the text. It was always clear, plain, simple in form, straightforward, and had a definite end. He never ran away from his text. He never spread it out so thin that it lost its force. There must be an application in every sermon. He was called an instructive preacher. He was not an orator, but in some way he gained people's attention. He made almost no gestures, but his eye and the expression of his face made tender enforcement of his words. With feeble voice, he could generally be heard in his large house of worship. His eyes were often open in prayer, as though he were looking round, yet, at the same time, everybody seemed to realize that his soul was with God. As a reader, he made beautiful rendering of Scripture and hymn. In short, his whole appearance in the pulpit was so refined and affectionate as to impress every heart! The boldest and plainest warnings were couched in such terms of love, and spoken in so tender a manner, as to take hold of men without offending them. He was dignified, agreeable, faithful, and affectionate in the sacred desk. Few men, probably, have excelled Dr. Whiton as a pastor. He visited his people, — knew them, — was familiar with their troubles, and had a kind word for every one! He knew how to adapt himself to any circumstances, and was at home anywhere. Everybody confided in him, and he was welcome at every fireside. He visited the sick without being sent for; and the sorrowing found in him a most wise comforter. He bent tenderly over the dying bed, and in his long pastorate directed many a closing eye to the " Lamb of God." He was said to be excellent at funerals; having just the prudent, comforting, guiding words it was best to say! Often he was called out of town to say the last words of earthly tenderness and farewell.

Dr. Whiton was a man of *rare prudence*. It was this that gave him so generally the reputation of a peace-maker. He seemed to foresee difficulties, and avoid them. His long pastorate began with some opposition; had some stormy seasons; personal feuds occasionally were bitter among his flock; a few dissatisfactions arose with regard to his course: but he outlived them all, and left with the affection of a united people. He tried no experiments, and was careful not to touch uncertain things. There was a peculiar thoughtfulness and caution in what he said. Exceedingly conscientious and open-hearted, he had a charming faculty of making people attribute these qualities to him. He would have made an admirable judge. Various difficulties were referred to him for settlement, because all parties agreed that Mr. Whiton would do right. It was this *visible fairness* which made him so successful in settling ecclesiastical disputes. He never attempted to manage a case, but his quiet and considerate advice generally prevailed. This thoughtful, careful spirit characterized the humblest acts of his ministry; wise, even in the words and methods of his farewell! The one word that would better describe Dr. Whiton than any other, is this word, — prudent. I find that ministers of the olden days characterized Dr. Whiton as a *modest* man. He was exceedingly courteous, easy-mannered, and unruffled when called upon, and it is said that the first time he was overcome, was when he parted with his people. Nobody ever saw in him any forwardness, or ambition to get noticed. He was qualified for a high place, but he always chose a lowly one. He was no front-seat minister. He wasn't one of the clique that manage the public religious bodies, — always doing the talking and making the motions! He was content to stand back, and let all the airing and small talk fall to the lot of the weaker brethren! Who ever heard of his getting into the newspapers if he could help it? Did he once leave these obscure valleys of Antrim to candidate in the city? It was said of him that he always had his own way, — and probably it was true; yet it was not because of any self-assertion, or forward determination of his, but because his demands were so few and just, so well calculated for, and so modestly asked, that everybody felt like yielding to him. His unpretending ways suited the people.

Mr. Whiton was a man very precisely honest. His honesty was of the conscientious, Christian kind, that reached everything. He kept his word exactly. He was a punctual man. He never took any advantage of another. When hay was selling for twenty-five dollars per ton,—equivalent to forty dollars now,—he happened to have a little left, and sold a ton to a neighbor for fifteen dollars. *That*, he said, was all it was worth, and he couldn't take any more! He was once offered one hundred dollars for a horse. "No," said he, "that is too much; if you'll give me seventy-five dollars you may have it!" Wouldn't a little of this sort of honesty work well among us now? There is an honesty about at this time, very popular in the world and in the church,—an honesty that goes according to law. It pays its notes on time, and never gets beyond the statute; but it takes all sorts of legal advantages, waits for exorbitant prices, will help a poor man for a big bonus, and gives just as little as it can for charitable and religious purposes. Mr. Whiton's honesty was the honesty of principle. He wanted to *do right!* He was shrewd and cunning in calculation, but never to the disadvantage of anybody else!

Mr. Whiton, like other ministers, grew absent-minded. That word is only a wicked form of saying that when a man is thinking of the Bible's great themes all the time, he can't be thinking of everything else! Wrong hours of study, bad habits of study, mental carelessness, and sometimes the pressure of calls that forces a man to do his thinking on the road, or when he wakes up in the night,—have all helped to make us absent-minded. All clergymen that are vigorous students are charged, more or less, with this great sin of forgetting something; and the careful Mr. Whiton was no exception, though he was not so guilty as some of us! On one occasion, being called to a wedding which was a little more than common, he told his wife he must dress up to the best advantage and would wear his black silk stockings. She gave them to him, and he proceeded to put them on, probably thinking all the time of the dignified words the occasion would demand of him. Having dressed one foot, he asked for the other stocking. Not finding it, they both searched the room, the bureau, and every possible place without avail, and finally gave it up. Taking a common pair to put on, he drew off the silk one, when, to his great astonishment, he found he had got them both on one foot!

Mr. Whiton was a man of sly humor and wit. No man enjoyed a good hit better than he. He was exceedingly cautious and sweet about it at the same time that he was running over. Many, judging from his dignified bearing, might have thought he could never *give* or *take* a *joke;* but he was a master at both! At one time there was a great excitement in town on the subject of temperance. Mr. Whiton held the old-fashioned, conservative views, not quite up to the standard of the church now. John R. Abbott, then worshiping at the Center, was the leader of the radical temperance men. Being on the best of terms, Mr. Whiton called down at Mr. Abbott's one Monday afternoon, and they talked and argued and quoted Scripture a long time. As the doctor rose to leave, Mr. Abbott (playfully alluding to the question in the Sunday-school the day before, whether there were any irony in the Bible) asked: "Well, Mr. Whiton, do you think there is any irony in the Bible?"—"Yes, yes," he replied, I do think of one passage. It is in Job: 'No doubt but ye are the people, and wisdom will die with you!'" Sometimes the witty, pleasant parson got a hit back. He had one parishioner that always paid his minister tax with a skim-milk cheese. On one occasion of receiving it the doctor blandly told the man about the solid and lasting qualities of the preceding cheese, and added: "I trust *this* one will be good."—"I guess it's as good as the preaching," said the man, as he drove away master of the situation! Fearlessly calm was Mr. Whiton in all repartee. No appearance of anger ever spoiled it. Nobody could very well be angry with him. It was hard to get him off his balance. You couldn't frighten him into being disconcerted. Once, in the later years of his ministry, one of his neighbors thought he would try the good doctor's pork-barrel. He took a hand with him, one passing the pork out the cellar-window, the other putting it in a basket outside. The doctor heard the noise, and slipped out-doors and round the house, when the man outside ran off without speaking! Silently the doctor took his place and piled the pork into the basket for him. "Would you take it all?" asked the man in the cellar.—"Perhaps you'd better leave a little for them," quietly replied the doctor, in his well-known and pleasant voice! The man, seeing he was caught, at once asked for mercy, and begged that he might not be exposed,—all which the doctor readily granted, on his promising that he would never again steal anything as long as he lived. That promise was never known to have been broken, and the criminal's name was never made public. This story has gone everywhere, and has been credited to other parties; it may be found thus credited in one of Dr. Hall's popular books. But the real hero was Dr. Whiton; the time, it is believed, the fall of 1846; and the house was that now occupied by the writer!

Mr. Whiton should not pass unnoticed as an author. He published a history of New Hampshire in 1834, which was considered, at the time, a valuable work. He also published an account of the ministers of Hillsborough County. His "History of Antrim" is certainly remarkable for the amount of information compressed within small compass. Several published sermons are worthy of being perpetuated; and it is believed that out of his manuscript sermons, volumes might be culled that would compare favorably with known literature of that kind. It has already been stated that he had nearly completed a history of Presbyterianism in New Hampshire; and it may not be generally known that Mr. Whiton occasionally indulged in musical composition. One beautiful piece entitled "Farewell," printed in the "Boston Sacred Harmony," was sung at his funeral.

Mr. Whiton, with the usual vicissitudes of his position, workfully and patiently held on his way,—called upon for all ministries of counsel and love, till, after forty years of service, he began to feel heavily the burdens of age, and several times conferred with the session with regard to resigning his pastoral charge. But they would not hear a word to it, until some four years later, May, 1852, taking the matter in his own hands, he read his resignation to the people. In my opinion, the grandest thing in Mr. Whiton's pastorate was its close. His self-surrender, his wise counsel, his fatherly affection, the tender and universal regard of the people, and their long, united experience of his care,—all tended to impart glory to the parting scene! The men who had welcomed him here were in heaven, and their children were bidding him farewell! Solemn, blessed, tender scene! But when his service in Antrim was over, the good man felt that he must work on in some smaller field. Immediately, in the dead of winter, he went to North Ashburnham and preached two months; receiving an urgent call to continuous labor with that church, and coming home near the close of February to visit his family and ask their consent, he received the call to Bennington, and went there at once, because it was in sight of the town and the home he loved. Then he made frequent visits here; he lingered among these hills; he visited the aged and the sick; and it touches our hearts to know that his last sickness was occasioned by a visit of this kind, at Mr. Buswell's, Sept. 3, 1856. Sabbath evening, Sept. 14, after prayer, his wife and children, at his request, stood round his bed to hear his parting counsel. He could only whisper; and Morris Whiton bent his ear down to his lips, and repeated his words aloud, — part of which were these: " Your mother and I have kept house nearly forty-eight years, and during that period there has not been a death in the family. . . . I have thought I saw the shadows of coming changes. . . I trust I feel submissive to the divine will. . . It has been my earnest wish that you might all become pious. . . I trust you will all so live as to meet at last in heaven. I am not able to say more, but I want you all to pray for me, that whatever may be the result of my present sickness, it may be for the glory of God!" These were his last words to his family. How calm and unexcited, and like himself to the last! In a few days he passed peacefully away. Oct. 1, there was a funeral service at Bennington in the morning, sermon by Mr. Bates; then the long procession started for Mr. Whiton's old church here; all business was given up in both towns; the bell in Bennington tolled till the bell here returned the sound; and the slow-moving reverent multitude entered this house of God. Rev. Thomas Savage of Bedford preached from John xxi. 20: "The disciple whom Jesus loved." After other impressive services and reverent gaze upon the peaceful face of the dead, "Devout men carried him to his burial," and when the coffin was lowered nearly to its bed, they sang these words the good man had used so often for others : —

> " Unveil thy bosom, faithful tomb;
>   Take this new treasure to thy trust,
>   And give these sacred relics room
>     To slumber in the silent dust !
>
> " Nor pain, nor grief, nor anxious fear
>   Invade thy bounds. No mortal woes
>   Can reach the peaceful sleeper here !
>     While angels watch the soft repose."

This notice of one man is allowed to be thus lengthy, because this one man had so much to do with shaping the character of this town; coming here at the age of twenty-three, growing up with this people, having so wide an influence over their social, educational, and religious affairs, being a marked man for counsel in all this part of the State, being favorably known in New England, and leaving impressions that are good and strong to this hour, — it is proper that he have unusual space and notice. Let it not, however, be inferred from this honest praise, that Mr. Whiton was a *faultless* man. He felt and deplored his imperfections. He spoke of them with sadness, on the bed of death. But they were not conspicuous. People saw his virtues rather. In him, the good was overwhelmingly in the majority. In purity and saintliness, he was, at least, a leader among men! Mr. Whiton's work in Antrim was a great work. It will stand grandly in the day of God. There was no noise about it, and not much glory of this world. He labored under many geographical difficulties, and his field was one that demanded vigorous thought and earnest effort. It was no place for ease or dreams. To be sure, he was backed by noble men and godly women. He commanded a strong army, — but he must be at the head! Brave, faithful, patient, undiscouraged, he led the way for forty-five years! Another generation has grown up since his departure; but his memory is sacred and precious to us all! Many aged people, in all parts of the land, once living here, speak to-day of Dr. Whiton with reverent love! His praise is everywhere! And now he and his flock are together; wherever the good are, there are they. And it is fitting that the last public tribute he may receive on earth should close with the memorial lines of his gifted daughter, Mrs. Richards: —

"Sainted father! now no longer
 Will thy counsel and thy prayer
Guide our lonely, weary footsteps
 O'er life's pilgrim way of care.
Oh, the loss! how much we feel it!
 That thy voice, so mild and sweet,
Now no more will call upon us
 Blessings from the mercy-seat!

"Now the insatiate grave encloses
 Thee — dear father — shepherd, guide —
And thy form in peace reposes,
 With thy flock on either side!
Near, thy dear old church is standing,
 Pointing to thy home of rest;
While its shadow almost presses
 On the turf above thy breast!

"Here thy warning voice has echoed,
 Here thy welcome face appeared;
Beds of death and hearts of sorrow
 Often comforted and cheered!
But no more upon these hill-tops
 Will thy beauteous feet appear;
Never more thy hand so gentle
 Wipe away the falling tear!

"But, instead, thy song of rapture
  Through immortal arches thrills;
And thy crown with gems is sparkling,
  Gathered from these rock-bound hills.
Father, — all thy toil is over,
  Life's rude conflict now is past;
All earth's griefs and cares and watchings
  End in heavenly rest at last!"

Mrs. Whiton, his honored wife, was born Aug. 2, 1783. She was a feeble child and had fits, for which her parents tried everything without avail, and finally small-pox was recommended. She had that disease in a mild form, and never had a fit afterwards! Mrs. Whiton thus alludes to it in her reminiscences written in 1856: —

"Accordingly, when I was thirteen and a half years old, I was inoculated for it; . . was carried to a log house, father having secured the attendance of a physician who took his family in; also Mrs. Chace, the minister's wife, who took her children; also an excellent nurse, who was *pious*, as the physician said the small-pox would kill or cure."

The following from the same source speaks of her life in Antrim: —

"October, 1808, the 18th of the month, we were married and set off for Antrim. . . . The first person to whom I was introduced was good old Dea. Aiken, who was standing on the brow of the hill near his house. . . . The South Village, at that time, was small, houses low, but three or four two-story houses in it. One of the number was Esquire Hopkins's [Arthur Miller's], where we boarded six weeks. . . . . On the 5th of December, we went to our house [Eben Bass place]. . . . I rode up behind Mr. Whiton. . . . At nine o'clock I walked up to Stephen Paige's and asked for lodging. . . . I then took a hemlock-broom and went down to sweep my house. . . . We slept on a bed on the floor in the chamber where I could look out through the crevices of the roof and see stars. . . . When night came my goods had not arrived, but supper must be got. I set out a new wash-form for a table, boiled some pork, made a cup of tea, spread my rude table with the best I had, and we thus partook of our first meal. . . .

"Here my trials commenced. I was a minister's wife, the first that had ever resided in the town. Of course I was a mark to be shot at. Every minute action was noticed and remarked upon. Some thought I was too dressy. I wore white and prints, while the dress of my neighbors was of home manufacture. One remarked I was a *mighty lady* but she would not knuckle to me! . . . The first winter I spent in Antrim (1808) we were treated with much attention after the farmers 'went below,' as they called it, and procured their stores for the year. Our invitations to visit were frequent. I was a stranger to the customs in town. . . . Their practice was to invite their neighbors, — a sort of party; when assembled, a waiter was passed round filled with tumblers, each one containing raw rum and brown sugar, with tea spoons to eat the sugar. The afternoon would be spent socially, and before nine o'clock, or perhaps a little later, the guests would be invited to take their seats at a loaded table, — roast turkey, fowls, potatoes, onions, pickles, apple-sauce, toast, various kinds of pies, doughnuts, and cake, with a good cup of tea. Being unaccustomed to Thanksgiving dinner in the evening, my stomach not strong enough to bear it, I went home almost every night about sick. . . . We had no wood except green hemlock, no stoves used in that day, and of course an open fire-place. . . . It was then the practice for ministers to keep a sort of tavern for their brethren in the ministry. They would go two or three miles out of their way to pass the night with a minister to whom they were entire strangers. . . . In the spring of 1812 we put up the front part of our house [Eben Bass house], which stood a year without a room finished. In the spring of 1813 the lower rooms and front entry were finished and furnished. . . . I found it more difficult to rock the cradle of age than infancy. . . . My immediate family were all spared to me, — no break for forty-eight years; we lived in Antrim for forty-four years with much harmony. . . . Mr. Whiton [at the close of his pastorate, Jan. 1, 1853] urged them to settle a gospel minister, and by all means keep united, and do it immediately after his dismission took effect. He was then applied to to go to North Ashburnham, and he labored there till the latter part of February, . . . came home for a visit, — . . . received an invitation from Bennington to labor there, . . . commenced in Bennington the first Sabbath in March. . . . The inhabitants [of Antrim] were pious, intelligent, and well calculated to make a minister comfortable in his profession; some of them being so well read, that they could and often did *volunteer* their advice to their youthful pastor. It seemed strange to me, having been taught to look up with great reverence and confidence to a minister of the gospel. When I was a child you could not appeal to higher authority: but, alas! at the present day, the hat is not raised, the bow and courtesy not made; and if you can get by a child without its running against you, esteem yourself fortunate. While I was boarding at Esquire Hopkins's (1808), they made a party on our account. Their front room was well filled with guests, — men and their wives. The men came in, dressed in plain homespun cloth, with a colored silk handkerchief on the neck for a cravat, every one of them except Dea. Baldwin's father, who wore a white one. But little attention was paid to dress, by male or female. The object was to work for a living."

Mrs. Whiton was a most excellent woman, and was greatly loved by the people, and, indeed, by all that knew her; yet she was generally understood to stand a little on her dignity, when she first came to this town. This arose from the fact that she was diffident, and was unacquainted with the ways and manners of a country place. In the first year of Mr. Whiton's ministry they were invited to a remote part of the town to marry a couple. They found a large company of guests, and, all being in readiness, the ceremony was soon over. Mrs. Whiton happened, just then, to notice one woman who seemed to be quite alone, so she went and sat down by her, and commenced conversation; spoke of the pleasant occasion, the large company, the pleasant looks of the bride, etc. The woman, not knowing to whom she was speaking, responded very freely, and then added: "They say Mr. Whiton has just brought his wife to town. I've never seen her, but they say she is a *mighty lady;* why, she wouldn't speak to common folks like you and me!" Mrs. Whiton *was a lady* in the best sense of that word. In her place, her success was not less than her husband's in his place. She was prudent, genial, lively, a good scholar, full of sympathy for the afflicted, attractive in person, and an earnest Christian, — in short, a model wife for a minister. She took great interest in every good work, and deserves great praise. Her life was of the kind not to be written in history, but there are few who have fulfilled their mission with more dignity and more success, — all which the records of another world will show clearer than those of earth. But this much is written of her, as the preceding sketch is of him, as a tribute, which their long and useful lives seemed to require at our hands.

The children of Rev. Dr. John M. and Abby (Morris) Whiton are as follows: —

1. JAMES MORRIS, [b. Nov. 9, 1809; m. Mary E. Knowlton of Boston, and was many years a merchant in that city, being called a "Christian merchant." He was an energetic member of the old South Church. On retiring from successful mercantile pursuits he moved to Plymouth and became superintendent of the Boston, Concord, and Montreal Railroad, and in that place and office suddenly d. March 22, 1857, but a few months after his father, leaving children: —

    Rev. James Morris, Ph. D., (b. in Boston, April 11, 1833; graduated at Yale College in 1853; m. Mary E. Bartlett of Brooklyn, N. Y., May 1, 1855; taught Worcester High School one year, was rector of Hopkins Grammar School, New Haven, ten years, pastor at Lynn, Mass., ten years, and principal of Williston Academy, Easthampton, two years. Is now pastor of Congregational Church, Newark, N. J. He received the degree of Ph. D. from Yale College in 1861. He is distinguished as a writer and author, the following being among his publications: "Hand-book of Latin Lessons," published in 1860; "First Lessons in Greek," 1861; "Is Eternal Punishment Endless?" 1876; "Six Weeks' Preparation for Reading Cæsar," published 1877. He has children: Mary Bartlett, James Bartlett, and Helen Isabel.)

    Mary E., (m. Charles F. Washburne of Worcester, Mass.)

*Charlotte,* (wife of Rev. Walcott Calkins of Buffalo, N. Y., now of Newton, Mass.)

*Miriam B.,* (wife of Henry B. Opdyke of New York City.)

*John M.,* (of Plainfield, N. J.)

*Grace,* (wife of Rev. Washington Choate, late of Manchester.)]

2. ELIZABETH D.. [b. March 7, 1811; m. Rev. Josiah Ballard of Carlyle, Mass.. in 1835. Mr. Ballard was b. in Peterborough, graduated at Yale in 1833, was settled in Nelson, and afterwards in Carlyle, Mass., where he d. Dec. 12, 1863, aged 57. Mrs. Ballard d. Aug. 10, 1862, and their bodies were among the first buried in our lovely Maplewood cemetery. She was a woman of rare abilities, and ever cherished a great love for her native Antrim. She left two children : —

*Edward Otis,* (b. in Nelson, April 19, 1837, and is now a merchant in Boston.)

*Catherine S.,* (now Mrs. Emery B. Smith of Melrose, Mass.)]

3. HELEN D., [b. July 8, 1814; m. Prof. Cyrus S. Richards of Meriden, and d. in 1860. She was a woman of dignity and grace and a devoted Christian. Her children are : —

*Helen M.,* (wife of Rev. Geo. P. Herrick, missionary at Constantinople.)

*Rev. Charles H.,* (b. in 1839; settled as pastor of the Congregational Church in Madison, Wis.)

*Abby.* (wife of Rev. Frank Woodbury of Rockford, Ill.)

*Willie H.,* (now living in Texas.)]

4. ABBY M., [b. May 31, 1817; m. Charles P. Whittemore of . Bennington, July 29, 1841, who d. in 1874.]

5. MARY C., [b. Feb. 20, 1819; m. 1st, George C. Duncan of this town, Nov. 3, 1841, who d. in 1855. She m. 2d, John M. Taylor, son of Andrew Taylor, and nephew of Dea. John Taylor, May 14, 1857; and d. Nov. 10 of the same year, aged 38.]

6. JOHN MILTON, [b. March 7, 1821; m. 1st, Fidelia Wilson of Nelson, who d. in 1860, leaving five children. He m. 2d, Mary J. Hartshorn of Franklin, Conn., in 1862. He was in trade awhile in Stoddard, also at Antrim Center, and now resides in Norwich, Conn. His children are as follows, all but the last two being the children of his first wife : —

*Henry Albin,* (b. in Stoddard, June 25, 1845.)

*John M.,* (b. same place, June 4, 1848.)

*Helen M.*, (b. same place. Jan. 9. 1852; m. Edward B. Woodworth of Concord, September, 1875.)
*Frank H.*, (b. in same town, May 26, 1854.)
*Mary Fidelia*, (b. in Warren. July 10, 1859.)
*George Morris*, (b. in Marlborough, Mass., Dec. 4, 1863.)
*Abby Morris*, (b. June 13, 1866, in Boston.)]

## WHITTEMORE.

The name has been spelled in a variety of ways, as Whytemere, Whitmore, Whitmere, Whitamor, Whatmore, Whittemore, etc. There is ample proof that these are all of one stock. It is said that Shakspeare's name was spelled ten different ways while he was living; and it would take a man of numbers to count up the variations since the poet's death! An individual called "John" was knighted on the field for valorous conduct in England in the year 1230, and received a tract of land called "Whytemere," or "white meadow." Hence he was called "Lord John de [of] Whytemere." The "de" (or of) was dropped about 1475. The family lived in Hitchin, Hertfordshire, England, though branches appear elsewhere, as in Shropshire, etc. An old record found in London in 1871 makes the line as follows: —

1. John de Whytemere.
2. Philip de Whytemere; died in 1300.
3. John de Whytemere; died in 1365.
4. Richard de Whytemere; died in 1386.
5. Richard de Whytemere.
6. Richard de Whytemere; died in 1442.
7. Thomas Whytemere; died in 1483.
8. Richard Whytemere; died in 1504.
9. Richard Whitmore; died in 1595.
10. William; and Thomas, who died in 1617, leaving, among others, a son Thomas. This last-named was the ancestor of the Whittemores of America. He was born about 1594 and died in 1660. He and his wife Hannah were married in England, and they had five children when they came over in 1642. He settled in Charlestown, Mass. (that part now Malden), and had in all twelve children. His will was proved June 25, 1661. The second, or nearly the oldest child, was John, baptized in Hitchin, England, Feb. 11, 1638; married, first, Mary Upham of Weymouth, Mass.; second, Mary Miller. From these descended the Whittemores of Pembroke, Lexington, Mass., Rindge, and many others. Nathaniel, another son who came over with his father, Thomas, settled in Spencer, Mass., and was ancestor of the Peterborough Whittemores. A younger brother was ancestor of Hon. E. S. Whittemore of Sandwich, Mass., and others. Many branches of this large family have come to honor. The parish register of Hitchin, England, speaks of the father of the American Thomas thus: "Apr. 26, 1617 was buried Thomas *Whitemore* Sen. widower, who by his will dated the 5th of May 1613 gave £20 to trustees for the best sort of poor people in Hitchin."

## GENEALOGIES.

The Whittemores of Greenfield and Antrim descended from Daniel Whittemore, another son of the first Thomas this side the water. He was two or three years old when his father settled in Charlestown, Mass. This Daniel married Mary, daughter of Richard Mellen of Charlestown, March 7, 1662. They had five children, of whom one was John Whittemore, born Feb. 12, 1664-5. This John married Ruth Bassett and had nine children. Benjamin, a son of John and Ruth, married Sarah Kendall in Boston, Dec. 10, 1723. She came from Woburn, Mass. They had eight children, one of whom was Benjamin, Jr., who was born Oct. 9, 1724, married Hannah Collins April 28, 1746, and died in Greenfield, Jan. 10, 1798. The oldest child of Benjamin and Hannah (Collins) Whittemore was Maj. Amos, who was born near the close of 1746. We have no record of the place or date of his birth. He settled in Greenfield in 1771, or earlier, but did not get the deed of his land there till early in 1772. Maj. Amos Whittemore married Molly Taylor of Milford. Was perhaps the leading man in Greenfield for fifty years. His descendants are numerous. Some of them occupy the old first settlement of the major to the present day. His wife was aunt to Mrs. Ira Cochran of Antrim. She died Nov. 27, 1837, aged ninety-two. Maj. Amos died Aug. 18, 1827, aged eighty-one. They had a large family of children. Those who reached mature years were as follows : Collins, who married Mehitable Fuller, and settled on the place in Hancock where his son, Hiram Whittemore, recently died ; Asa, who married Hannah Burnham of Greenfield, and lived and died in Hancock ; Amos, who married Polly Savage, lived in Greenfield, and was father of Amos, Alfred, and John of Bennington ; Benjamin, who married Deborah Perry, lived and died in Bennington, and was father of Charles P., Timothy of Boston, Emily, Francis M. Whittemore, and others ; Polly, who married Paul Cragin of Greenfield ; Betsey, who married Dr. Moses Marsh ; Jacob, of Antrim ; William, noticed below ; and Abram, who married Martha Marshall and died on the old homestead in Greenfield. His son, Marshall Whittemore, Esq., now occupies the same. Maj. Amos came to Greenfield from Nottingham. He held the rank of major in the Revolutionary army ; but I am not able to learn much concerning his military record. On one occasion he received orders to march the next morning. But he was wofully short of pantaloons at that time, and knew not what to do. Nevertheless, after consultation with his blessed wife, Molly Taylor, he went to the barn, though now three o'clock in the afternoon, and sheared a sheep ; and from the wool his wife carded, spun, wove, and made up a pair of pants, ready for the morning's march ! Who says that woman isn't equal to anything ?

Hon. JACOB WHITTEMORE, son of Maj. Amos and Molly (Taylor) Whittemore, was born in Greenfield, Oct. 12, 1780, and died in Antrim, Oct. 14, 1860. The name Jacob appears occasionally in the family, there being one or two among the grandchildren of Thomas who came over. Jacob who came here married Rebecca Bradford of Hancock. She was a sister of Rev. E. P. Bradford of New Boston. He came here and located on the Philip Riley place in 1809, and remained there till death. Was a vigorous and able man. He had all manner of town offices year after year. Was representative of Antrim in 1818, 1819, 1838, 1839, and 1840. Was also high sheriff under Gov. Pierce. Was one of the judges of the court of common pleas. Was a man of good address, smooth, genial, and having a multitude of friends. His children were: —

1. DR. JACOB P., [b. May 16, 1810. After the district school, he was under the instruction of B. F. Wallace at the Branch, and then pursued his studies at Hopkinton Academy. Began the study of medicine at the age of twenty, but failing health compelled the relinquishing of it for a time, and he went into a store in Amherst. Afterwards he went into trade for himself at Hillsborough Bridge. But failing in business, he again took up the study of medicine, and received his degree at Dartmouth College in 1844, being thirty-four years of age. He then took the practice of a physician in Gilmanton one year, and in the autumn of 1845 he settled in Chester. There he had a large and laborious practice for nineteen years, and had a great hold upon the esteem and affection of the community and the adjoining towns. He then, for the sake of an easier practice, sold out and moved to Haverhill, Mass., where he continued an active and "beloved physician" till his sudden death, June 17, 1873. He was a genial, pious, and noble man, and had many friends. All that was mortal of him was laid in Maplewood cemetery, Antrim. Dr. Whittemore m. Eliza Cochran of Antrim, Oct. 29, 1835. He left three children: —

*Frances M.*, (b. Dec. 16, 1836, in Hillsborough; m. Charles E. Robinson of Concord, and resides in Jamaica Plain, Mass.)

*Dr. James H.*, (b. in Hillsborough, June 15, 1839; studied medicine with his father, and with Prof. Dixi Crosby of Hanover. Took his degree of M. D. from Dartmouth College in 1862, after which he studied in the hospitals of London and Vienna. On return he was connected several years with the McLean Asylum, Somerville, Mass. He is now the resident physician and head of the Mass. General Hospital, Boston. Has risen fast and has a very honorable record in his profession.)

*Mary T.*, (b. in Chester, April 12, 1849.)]

2. MARY T., [b. Dec. 12, 1811; m. Charles D. Robbins of Hillsborough in 1861.]

3. WILLIAM B., [b. May 22, 1814; m. 1st, Lucretia Dinsmore of Francestown; 2d, Fanny Mills of Deering. The first wife d. February, 1861, leaving three children, named below. Mr. Whittemore lived chiefly at Hillsborough Bridge, and d. there May 9, 1876 Was often put in the highest offices by the people of that town. A genial and upright man.

*William H.*, (b. in Antrim. June 5, 1845; d. in Hillsborough, May 25. 1865.)

*Capt. Jacob B*. (b. Dec. 9, 1851: was chosen captain of the Carter Guards, Hillsborough; has just been promoted to paymaster of the regiment; lives on the farm of his grandfather, Hon. Jacob Whittemore.)

*Mary Ellen*, (b. Nov. 4, 1853.)]

4. REED PAIGE, [b. Sept. 4, 1816; m. Sarah E. Dodge, daughter of John and Betsey (Dinsmore) Dodge of Bennington, Feb. 10. 1842. Received the homestead from his father. Has filled many places of trust at the call of his townsmen. Was representative in 1857 and 1858. Has been ten years selectman. His children are thus: —

*Charles A*, (b. Jan. 23. 1843; m. Anna Woodbury, granddaughter of Dr. P. P. Woodbury of Bedford, and lived on the farm with his father some years; has children, all b. in Antrim: Arthur P., b. Oct. 27, 1870; Edwin J., b. June 22, 1874; and William R., b. April 19, 1877.)

*George R*, (b. May 21, 1845; m. Helen Grimes of Hillsborough; moved with one child, Henry E., to Boston, where he is now in business.)

*Maria C*., (b. March 19. 1848; m. Rodney Smith of Hillsborough. They lived in Boston some years, but now live in Hillsborough.)]

5. HENRY D., [d. Aug. 24, 1825, aged 5.]
6. JOHN B., [d. Aug. 14, 1825, aged 2.]

WILLIAM WHITTEMORE, brother of Hon. Jacob, came to Antrim about 1807, and put up a store (now Gibson house, South Village) in which he traded for a few years, was succeeded by Miller and Caldwell, and moved back to Greenfield, where he died in 1876, aged ninety-four. His memory was remarkable, and he was a model of a genial, cheery, oldstyle gentleman. He married Lydia Collins Day. His adult children were: —

1. WILLIAM H., [m. Sylvia Hayward, and lives in Peterborough.]
2. MICHAEL A., [unm.]

GENEALOGIES. 765

3. LEONA C., [m. Horace Hopkins of Francestown.]
4. GEORGE J., [m. Lizzie Clement, and lives in Greenfield.]
5. ALMIRA P.. [m. J. B. Dane, and lives in Hancock.]
6. CORNELIA E.. [m. Henry H. Duncklee. proprietor of Greenfield Hotel.]

COLLINS WHITTEMORE, son of Collins and Mehitable (Fuller) Whittemore of Hancock, and grandson of Maj. Amos, was born Dec. 27, 1794, and died March 31, 1868, after great and long-continued suffering. He married Ruth Jacobs of Carlyle, Mass., May 25, 1820; came here on to the Amos Blanchard place in 1841, where he resided till death. His children were : —

1. FRANKLIN J , [d. in childhood.]
2. SARAH R., [b Jan. 31, 1828 ; m. E. R. Russell of Nashua, May 19, 1846 ; d. Sept. 20, 1847.]
3. HELEN M., [b. July 27, 1832; became second wife of E. R. Russell of Nashua, Nov. 16, 1848.]
4. JOHN J.. [b. Aug. 5, 1835 ; m. Sarah G. Spalding of Nashua, Oct. 3, 1872 ; is a druggist in that city ; was one of the donors of the vestry at the Center.]
5. MARY C., [b. Nov. 20, 1840 ; m. John B. Woodbury of Antrim, May 28, 1861.]

## WIER.

JEREMIAH WIER came here from Chelmsford, Mass., at what time it is impossible to tell, but not far from 1778. He built a small house on the north side of the road between Benjamin Kidder's and the Dustin Barrett place. — which house has been gone more than half a century; and the cellar, if there ever was any, is nearly filled up. Wier was, no doubt, of Scotch descent. A "Robert Weir," probably same name, was chairman of the selectmen of Londonderry, 1737-38. With different spellings the name appears often in the old Scotch records of that town. Adam and William "Wiar" signed the Association Test there. Jeremiah Wier married Esther Kidder of Chelmsford. They had five children, two or three of whom were brought with them here. Jeremiah was a soldier from Antrim in the Revolution for several years. He was at home on a furlough when peace was declared. He remained here the following winter and then returned to New York for his arrears of pay. The money could not be obtained till fall (1784), and, therefore, Wier let himself to work in the vicinity for the summer. In the autumn he received pay in full for his military service, making, together with the earnings of the summer, a handsome sum of money for those days. With this, he started for home. But he was never again heard from. It has always been supposed that he was robbed, and murdered to put him out of the way. There can't be much doubt of this. The widow subsequently married Thomas Miller, moved to Hillsborough, and died on the Scott Moore place there about 1824, quite aged. It must not be inferred from Dr. Whiton's narrative that Wier was only here during the winter of 1783-84, though probably this was the only entire winter that he ever spent here. The children, soon after the loss of their father, seem to have returned to Chelmsford for a time. On coming back to Antrim, they were all save the youngest warned out of town, Nov. 29, 1788. The names are now given : —

1. LYDIA, [d. on town farm, unm., about 1858, aged 83.]
2. JEREMIAH, JR., [used to live with Dr. Cleaves. When the town farm was bought, he went at once there, and stayed through life. Was a cripple and had fits, but was a clever, kind-hearted man ; was a great worker, and when the county took the older paupers, the town would not let him go, but supported him till death, which occurred about 1864, at the age of 80 years. He never m.]
3. STEPHEN, [m. Susan Hathaway of Hillsborough. Soon after went to Greenwich, Mass., thence to the adjoining town of Enfield, where he d.]
4. ESTHER, [m. 1st, James Tolbert; 2d, Joseph Moore. Lived chiefly in Hillsborough. They lived in old age a year or two in this town, thence went to the county farm, where she d. in 1872, aged about 90.]
5. MOSES PARKER, [was out in the war of 1812; afterwards served five years in the regular army. On return he m. Maria Cowdry of Hillsborough. Subsequently he went to Louisiana, and again entered the army. He d. in that place in the regular service in the year 1833.]

## WILCOX.

GEORGE WILCOX, son of Thomas and Mary (McDougal) Wilcox, was born in Sherbrooke, Canada, in 1806; married Mary A. Morrison of Peterborough, and came to Antrim from Peterborough, on to the Thomas Flint place, in 1873. They have two children: —

1. CHARLES F., [b. in Hancock in 1849 ; m. Thirsa Blake of that town, and now lives in Ipswich, Mass.]
2. NELLIE M., [b. in Peterborough in 1854.]

## WILDER.

JAMES W. WILDER, son of Abel and Hannah (Green) Wilder, was born in Dublin in 1799; married, first, Mary R. Crombie of New Boston, and settled in that town, but after her death in 1832 he came to Antrim, and the next year, March 19, 1833, he married, second, Betsey Boyd. After some years he moved to Providence, Penn., where he died Dec. 14, 1876. By the first marriage there were three children, and by the second, seven.

1. JOHN C., [b. in New Boston in 1825; m. Annie V. Pearson of Boston, and d. in New York in 1869.]
2. JAMES W., [is now living unm. in California.]
3. CHARLES S., [m. Lydia Wilson of Nashua, and lives in Lawrence, Kan.]
4. MARY E., [d. in childhood.]
5. SAMUEL N., [d. in 1868, aged 33.]
6. HARRIET N., [d. in 1853, aged 16.]
7. EVELINE M., [m. Henry Heermans in 1853, and lives in Providence, Penn.]
8. CAROLINE F., [d. in infancy.]
9. GEORGE W., [b. in 1843; now lives in Providence, Penn.]
10. FRANCES C., [d. in 1875, aged 20.]

## WILKINS.

Three brothers, William, James, and Enoch Wilkins, were sons of Abial and Amy (Howard) Wilkins, which Abial Wilkins was son of William Wilkins of English descent, whose mother, an excellent woman, lived in Salem, Mass. She was accused, when a girl, of being a witch; went home from church, and, when they followed her, her father fought them off with pitch fire-brands and saved his child. They came here from Mont Vernon, near the close of the last century.

WILLIAM WILKINS came to Antrim in 1798; settled at the foot of the sand-hill, living some years in a log house, and put up the present buildings a few rods north of it. He married, first, Sarah Whipple of Hamilton, Mass., who died May 13, 1826, aged forty-six. He married, second, Elizabeth Hopkins, July 20, 1826. Mr. Wilkins died May 15, 1837, aged sixty-three. His second wife, Mrs. Elizabeth Wilkins, died in 1856, aged sixty-nine. His children were as follows, all but the last two being the children of his first wife: —

1. BETSEY, [b. July 8, 1798; d. in 1800.]
2. BETSEY, [b. July 28, 1801; m. Dea. Joel Wilkins, Dec. 21, 1820; d. Sept. 9, 1855.]
3. WILLIAM, [b. March 29, 1804; m. Zilpha Whittemore of Woodstock, Vt., and is now living in Alden, N. Y.]
4. LYDIA, [b. March 21, 1807; d. July 13, 1812.]
5. MELINDA F., [b. Feb. 2, 1819; m. William B. Curtis of Antrim, Nov. 17, 1842.]

6. MORRIS B., [b. in 1828; was a cripple, and d. April 21, 1858.]
7. MARIA E., [m. Mr. John Kidder, Sept. 8, 1857, and lives in Nashua.]

ENOCH WILKINS, brother of William, before mentioned, settled above the school-house in the extreme west of this town, some thirty rods north of the road now leading to Stoddard Box. Buildings are now gone. He married Sally Case. They had no children, but brought up the following: Hiram Fairfield, who married Fanny Peabody of Lyndeborough, moved from here to Stoddard in 1850, and then went West; and Jane P. Town, who came here from Lyndeborough in 1830, married Caleb Greene of Woonsocket, R. I., in 1847, and now lives in Lewiston, Me. Enoch Wilkins died very suddenly, June 13, 1851. His wife died Oct. 2, 1852. Each died at the age of seventy-five.

JAMES WILKINS, brother of William and Enoch, came here in 1799. He married Lydia Whipple, and on coming here they moved into a little hovel, built by Michael George, then standing a little toward the west of the subsequent site, while he put up the present house (Luther Wilkins's), which he completed in 1801. He died in 1803, in early life, just after his buildings were completed and part of his land cleared, leaving three children. His widow died Oct. 2, 1852, aged seventy. Children were three: —

1. JAMES, [b. in 1792, probably; m. Mariam Harper, Sept. 8, 1818; moved to Reading, Vt., in November, 1820; was some time a school-teacher; afterwards settled in Weston, Vt. He d. in September, 1832. Left children: George, James, Joel, William, Manly, Clark, Margaret, Sarah, and Walter.]
2. POLLY, [b. Aug. 27, 1796; m. Peter C. Atwood, Feb. 13, 1816, and moved, 1820, to Londonderry, Vt., where she d. Oct. 8, 1847.]
3. DEA. JOEL, [b. March 18, 1800; m. 1st, Betsey Wilkins, his cousin, Dec. 21, 1820, and lived on the homestead. She d. in 1855. Mr. Wilkins was appointed deacon in the Presbyterian Church in 1831, and was an excellent and popular man. In 1856, he m. 2d, Mrs. Hannah B. Crombie of New Boston, and d. Nov. 28, 1865, leaving children as follows, the youngest by the second wife: —

*Prynthia*, (d. July 29, 1834, aged 9.)
*Mark*, (b. Jan. 2, 1822; m. 1st, Esther Robb of Stoddard. In 1861 he m. 2d, Marietta Tyler of Westford, Vt., a deaf-mute. He was also a deaf-mute, made so by scarlet fever in childhood. He lived on the Stephen Butterfield place, which he

and his brother, J. G. Wilkins, owned together. He d. Aug. 29, 1875, aged 53, leaving one child by the second wife, Betsey M., b. Jan. 12, 1866.)

*Sarah E.*, (d. Feb. 18, 1844, at the age of 17.)

*Joel N.*, (b. June 9, 1828; m. Mary E. Wright of Antrim; is a mechanic, and lives in Clinton, having one child, George H., b. June 7, 1861.)

*Mary E.*, (d. May 28, 1849, aged 18.)

*James Grosvenor*, (b. June 25, 1832. He is a deaf-mute and was educated at Hartford, Conn.; m. Mary E. Pratt of Cambridge, Vt., who is also a deaf-mute, educated at Hartford. They live on the Stephen Butterfield place, having children: Gilmore G., b. March 15, 1864, drowned June 17, 1878; Mary Augusta, b. Oct. 16, 1868; Maria Belle, b. Sept. 21, 1874. He is a cabinet-maker by trade. Is a smart, intelligent, and good man.)

*Lydia Sophia*, (d. June 19, 1847, at the age of 13.)

*Dr. George A.*, (b. March 9, 1836; studied at New Hampton, graduated at Albany Medical College, and settled in Hillsborough, where he d. very suddenly Nov. 1, 1856, during the first year of his practice. Was a young man of much promise.)

*Luther M.*, (b. Oct. 4, 1838; m. Cathie C. Barney, April 4, 1870; is a shoemaker and lives on the old homestead, having one child, Eda M., b. Feb. 3, 1871.)

*Henry E.*, (b. April 1, 1840; m. Henrietta Eaton of Wakefield, Mass., and is a druggist in Stoughton, Mass.)

*Ida F.*, (b. Jan. 8, 1859.)]

MOSES WILKINS, son of Darius and Sarah (Dodge) Wilkins, came here and worked as an apprentice in building the Center Church. He married Sarah Miller of Peterborough, and put up the Capt. Smith buildings, where he lived till 1834; then moved to the Cram place and lived there till 1846, when he went to Peterborough, where he died in 1868, aged sixty-two. She died Feb. 15, 1852, aged forty-six. Their children were: —

1. SARAH, [b. in 1831; d. in childhood.]
2. SARAH JANE, [b. in 1834; m. George Howe of Peterborough, Oct. 9, 1851, and lived in Lynn, Mass., where she d. May 4, 1860.]
3. RUTH E., [b. in 1835; d. in 1852.]
4. CATHERINE M., [b. in 1837; d. at Peterborough in 1850.]

5. CHARLOTTE M., [b. in 1843. She became second wife of Col. Charles Scott of Peterborough, Sept. 7. 1863. Col. Scott's first wife was drowned in the Potomac River, by the collision of the steamer "West Point" with the "George Peabody," Aug. 13, 1862, being on her return from a visit to her husband then in the army.]

DR. LEVI W. WILKINS, son of Levi and Ann (McColley) Wilkins, was born in Merrimack in 1823; studied with Dr. Graves of Nashua, and took the degree of M. D. at Berkshire Medical College. He married Elissie Wakefield of Reading. Mass., in 1851, and came to North Branch in 1852, where he practiced eight years, living where David Stacey now lives. He afterwards went to Milford. where he had a large practice, but died of quick consumption in 1864. Two children survive, as follows: —

1. FRANK P., [b. June 12, 1854; now lives in Boston.]
2. EVELYN E., [b. in 1857; now lives in Reading, Mass.]

## WILLEY.

ROBERT WILLEY, an emigrant from Ireland, came here as early as 1784, and was the first settler on the John Robinson farm west of the pond. He and his wife were among the original members of the Presbyterian Church. He left town in 1801. Nothing further can be learned about him; but it is believed that his descendants are now living in Rochester, Vt. I find by records of New Boston that Robert Willey married Nabby Campbell in that town, Jan. 15, 1795. This was probably a second wife.

## WILSON.

The ancestor of the Antrim Wilsons was Rev. John, who came over with Gov. Winthrop in 1630. He had a grandson, Joseph Wilson, whose son James was born in 1703. James had a son, Capt. Jesse, a Revolutionary soldier, born Jan. 20, 1729. Capt. Jesse married Abigail Gage, settled in Pelham, and was father of Jesse of Antrim. This latter was born Feb. 24, 1768; came here in 1798, and bought the place then occupied by James Hall, a blacksmith, whose stand was a few rods north of where the East meeting-house was afterwards built. He married Patty Hall, who first came from Pelham to Antrim on horseback and waded across the Contoocook River, there being no bridge at that time. Mr. Wilson died of spotted fever, March 21, 1812, aged forty-two. His wife died Dec. 13, 1833, aged sixty-two. Their children are as follows: —

1. PATTY, [b. June 28, 1797; is still living unm. on the homestead.]
2. SOPHIA, [b. June 22, 1799; d. in infancy.]
3. SOPHIA, [b. April 5, 1801; m. Samuel Hosley of Hancock,

April 13, 1824, and d. in 1871. She was mother of Hon. John Hosley of Manchester.]
4. JESSE, [b. March 12, 1803 ; d. of spotted fever in 1812.]
5. LYDIA R., [b. June 20, 1805 ; m. Hon. Henry Parkinson of New Boston, Nov. 2, 1843, and afterwards moved to Nashua. He was recently killed by the cars. A trusted and good man.]
6. ABIGAIL G., [b. June 13, 1807 ; d. Oct. 13, 1863.]
7. JAMES MERRILL, [b. June 16, 1809 ; m. 1st, Achsah Boutwell, Dec. 25, 1834, who d. July 25, 1863, aged 49. and he m. 2d, Mrs. Eliza (Bullard) Burtt of Bennington, Nov. 28, 1865. He inherited the homestead, originally bought, together with the Ladd place on which his father lived many years, situated some twenty rods west of the first. The buildings are now all gone, but Mr. Wilson, while living recent years on what was then the Dea. Barachias Holt place. adjoining. still retains the whole, which he has greatly improved. His children, all by his first wife, are thus: —

*Jesse W.*, (b. June 30, 1837 ; d. June 23, 1859.)
*Martha A.*, (b. July 11, 1839 ; d. July 8, 1840.)
*Charlotte A.*, (b. July 26, 1841 ; m. Allen L. Skinner, Dec. 31, 1868, and lives in Springfield, Mass., having children, Arthur J. and Henry J.)
*James H.*, (b. July 18, 1844 ; is now living in Buffalo, N. Y. Is railroad engineer.)
*Abby S.*, (b. July 28, 1847 ; m. James M. Gove of this town, Oct. 11, 1877.)
*Frank J.*, (b. March 13, 1850 ; m. Junia E. Barker, Sept. 14, 1880 ; occupies the farm with his father.)
*George C.*, (b. Nov. 1, 1854 ; now of Springfield, Mass. ; is engaged in mercantile pursuits.)]

ZADOK P. WILSON, son of James and Lucinda (Paige) Wilson, grandson of Capt. Jesse and Abigail (Gage) Wilson, and nephew of Jesse Wilson mentioned above, was born in Pelham, June 17, 1800 ; married Anna Richardson of Hudson, April 13, 1826, who died in that town in 1840. He married, second, Mrs. Abigail (Smith) Martin of Bedford, daughter of John Smith of Hudson, and came here, on to the Charles Wood place (now Levi Curtis's), in 1850 ; moved to Lempster in 1862, and thence to Sanbornton in 1871. Mr. Wilson died in 1879. He had children as follows, the youngest by the second marriage : —

1. FOSTER, [b. July 5, 1827 ; m. 1st, Maria Lovejoy ; 2d, Martha Trow. Is superintendent of mills, Holyoke, Mass.]

GENEALOGIES.

2. KIMBALL J., [b. Jan. 12, 1829; m. 1st, Marion Piper of Weston, Vt.; 2d, Laura Fales of New York, 1868. Is superintendent of asylum for poor, Tewksbury, Mass.]
3. GEORGE L., [b. Nov. 5, 1831; m. a Miss Foster of Bristol; lives in Rosemont, Minn.]
4. HENRY P., [b. Nov. 25, 1833; m. 1st, Mary F. Bailey of Manchester. Dec. 12, 1858; 2d, Augusta A. Philbrook of Concord, 1871; lives in Sanbornton.]
5. ANNA R., [b. July 1. 1836; m. James McClintock of Hillsborough. They live in Manchester.]
6. ALLEN, [d. in 1840 in infancy.]
7. ABI, [b. in Hudson, Oct. 16, 1843; m. Dr. William Donol, and lives in Kansas.]

SAMUEL WILSON was son of Robert and Nancy (Gregg) Wilson, and grandson of Robert. They were of the old Londonderry stock. Samuel came here from New Boston in 1817, put up a set of buildings (now gone) on the south part of the Caleb Clark farm, and lived there many years. Afterward moved on to the old John Wallace farm near Reed Carr's, where he died April 4, 1855, aged eighty-eight. He married Sally Reed, daughter of Zadok Reed, who died Nov. 4, 1844, and their children were: —

1. ROBERT, [b. March 17, 1798; d. November, 1815.]
2. ALMIRA, [b. March 1, 1801; m. Andrew Silloway, 1840; moved to Canaan, where she d. December, 1863.]
3. LUCY REED, [b. July 2, 1809; m. Dea. Erastus Nesmith, April 22, 1830, and lives in Enfield.]
4. SAMUEL, [b. April 29, 1814; m. 1st, Rhoda Paige, who d. Aug. 3, 1859; 2d, Mrs. Persis Perrington, Feb. 21, 1861. Has no children.]
5. ALBERT, [b. June 1, 1817; first called "Robert," but had his name changed to "Albert;" m. Elizabeth Bowers; lived in Somerville, Mass.; d. December, 1872.]
6. SABRINA, [b. Aug. 9, 1824; m. Lyman Bowers; lived and d. in Worcester, Mass. Her death was in January, 1859.]
7. ROXANNA, [b. June 26, 1829; m. Horace D. Northrop of Vermont; moved to Iowa, and d. January, 1857.]

JONAS WILSON came here from Carlyle, Mass. He built a house, probably in 1825, about forty rods southeast of school-house No. 6; was a shoemaker; after several years moved back to Massachusetts. He married Lydia Kidder, Dec. 31, 1818, and their children born here all died young except one: —

1. WILLARD H., [settled in Bedford, Mass., where he d. in 1860.]

## WITHERSPOON.

ALEXANDER WITHERSPOON was born in Chester in 1761; married Jane Starrett of Francestown, March 20, 1788, who died March 28, 1810; settled on the Samuel Tuttle place in 1787, but in a few years moved on to the Artemas Brown place, and died in 1848, aged eighty-seven. His children were: —

1. POLLY. [b. Aug. 2, 1789: m. David Paige, Dec. 11, 1812, and had a large family; d. in 1873.]
2. JOHN. [b. Jan. 11, 1791. He enlisted in the war of 1812. It was said that he deserted; but this is by no means certain. His fate was never known. The report that he "settled after the war in Maine, and raised a large and respectable family," lacks confirmation.]
3. ISABEL, [b. July 3, 1793; d. Oct. 6, 1800.]
4. JOSEPH S., [b. March 17, 1796; d. Oct. 8, 1800.]
5. ABIGAIL S., [b. Dec. 26, 1799; d. Oct. 2, 1800.]
6. ACHSAH. [b. Feb. 8, 1801; m. Charles Guild and lives in Concord.]
7. CHARLOTTE P., [b. April 16, 1803; m. Robert Todd of New London; d. Oct. 16, 1875.]
8. LOUVICY R., [b. Feb. 6, 1805; d. June 10, 1824.]
9. JANE S., [b. Sept. 12, 1807; lives unm. in Nashua; name changed to "Atherton."]
10. JOSEPH S., [b. March 8, 1810; had his name changed to "Atherton;" m. Hilenia C. Houston of Hillsborough, March 7, 1837, and lived with his father. He was a peculiarly pious and promising man, and d. greatly lamented in 1845, in the prime of life. His widow m. Joshua Chamberlain and moved to Nashua in 1849, where she still lives. Mr. Atherton's children were: —

*Lorenza Anna*, (b. in 1837; m. Charles B. Wright of Boston.)
*Hilenia J.*, (b. in 1839; m. Hiram F. Barney of Nashua.)
*Emily Frances*, (b. in 1841.)
*John Mason*, (b. in 1843; m. Martina L. Greeley, and d. in 1872.)]

## WOOD.

CHARLES WOOD, son of Samuel and Hannah (Webster) Wood of Methuen, was born in that town in 1770; came to Antrim in 1789 or earlier; married Jennette Steele, daughter of James Steele, Sen., and began the Henry Barker farm, which he exchanged for the Levi Curtis farm the next year. This latter farm he cleared, and he lived there until his death, Jan. 16, 1848. He was a strong man, but had forty fevers. His wife died May 1, 1846, aged seventy-four. Their children were: —

1. DEA. SAMUEL, [b. Aug. 17, 1801; m. Margaret Bell, Dec. 24, 1833, and settled on the Daniel Brown place (house built in 1827), where he lived until his death, Nov. 24, 1876. He was appointed deacon in the Presbyterian Church in 1852. Dea. Wood was a man of the old style, simple in his habits, a great worker, firm in his convictions, having an opinion of his own but modest and manly in the expression of it, a stout Presbyterian, and a straightforward member of the session for twenty-four years. It would be hard to find a better man. Was very lame for many years, but was active in business till near the end. His children are: —

   *Margaret Jane.* (b. Oct. 29, 1834; m. Daniel J. Parkhurst.)
   *Mary Eliza.* (b. Dec. 15, 1837; m. Chester A. Appleton of West Deering.)]

2. ELIZA, [b. March 4, 1805; m. Lyman Dow, Feb. 11, 1836, and d. Aug. 16, 1842.]

3. JAMES, [b. Sept. 11, 1811; m. Harriet J. Taft of Weld, Me., June 14, 1856, who d. in 1872, leaving no children. March 13, 1873, Mr. Wood m. Mrs. Margaret (Boyce) Goodwin, and they have one child: —

   *Harriet J.* (b. April 15, 1874.)

   Mrs. Margaret (Goodwin) Wood has children by her previous marriage as follows: Millie J. Goodwin, who m. W. A. Barker, and lives in Nashua; Nelson O., now of this town; Charles A.; William B; and Lilla M., who lives with her mother. James Wood moved on to the Campbell place in 1850, and still occupies the same.]

CHARLES A. WOODS, son of Asa and Polly (Laton) Woods, and grandson of Jonas and Lydia (Hobart) Woods of Hollis, was born in Nashua, Nov. 19, 1831. He married Adeline R. Barker of Antrim, July 3, 1854, and lived awhile in Nashua; came here in 1859, and lived two or three years in South Village; moved to Windsor in May, 1862; thence, in 1869, to Hillsborough, in which last town they still reside. Their children are as follows: —

1. ADDIE E., [b. in Antrim, April 25, 1859.]
2. CHARLES O., [b. in Windsor, April 7, 1863.]

## WOODBRIDGE.

GEORGE B. WOODBRIDGE, son of Osgood and Hannah (Stevens)

Woodbridge, was born in Andover, Mass., in 1820 ; married his cousin, Elizabeth Woodbridge of that town, and came here from Greenfield on to the Dea. Baldwin place in 1872. Has recently moved to Bennington. They have but one child : —

1. GEORGE, [b. in Francestown in 1861.]

## WOODBURY.

JOHN WOODBURY was the first of the name who came (1624) to America. In 1627, he brought over his son Humphrey. About 1631 his brother William came over. A deposition of Humphrey, taken fifty years after, states that when his father first came over to Cape Ann, in 1624, he traveled up with him from Somersetshire to Dorchester ; but how long John had lived in Somersetshire is not certain. The earliest notice of the family describes them seated in the parish of Woodbury, hundred of East Budleigh, county of Devon. The exchequer records, "Testa de Nevill," covering A. D. 1216 to 1308, record William de Wodeberie as holding lands in "Wodebere," in "Esse and Brigeford." We also find the name of Roberto de Wodeberie (knight) as the witness to a deed A. D. 1241; and in the reign of Edward, David de Wodeberie as a grand juror. In the following century, the tax-lists disclose the names of John, Nicholas, Alicia, and Walter in the same neighborhood. A later William was lord prior of Worcester in 1515. The name, before this, ceases to be found around Woodbury, and appears in Burlescombe, in the hundred of Bampton, Devon, where, in 1543, we find John and Nicholas Wodbeire taxed on their lands, and Jacob Wodbeire on his goods. This John had a son, John Woodbury, Jr., who, according to the records of that parish, "intermarred with Jane Humffrys June 2, 1596." They had two daughters born in that parish and in that century. The age of this John, Jr., and several other probabilities, concur to identify him with the emigrant to New England, and, unless positive proof shall be found in Somerset of his birthplace elsewhere, it may be conclusively assumed. The name Woodbury is derived from the Danish *woden*, and in the Anglo-Saxon is a compound of *wode*, meaning "mad or furious," and *bury*, or *byrig*, equivalent to German *burgh* or our *borough*. Woodbury castle is an old Danish earthwork, extant, on a hill in the parish to which it gave its name long before the Norman conquest. The spelling of the name, whether indicating the parish or the family, has curiously varied with the fashion, in each century, but has been spelled substantially alike at every epoch.

John Woodbury came to Cape Ann in the year 1624, in the employment of a company for settling, fishing, and trading in New England, called the "Dorchester Company," of which the Rev. John White of Dorchester, England, was an active instrument. Lord Sheffield, within whose limits Cape Ann lay, agreed, under seal, with Messrs. Winslow and Cushman and their associates, known as the "Dorchester Company," to permit them to settle certain lands in Gloucester Harbor, and, when he got his own title, to convey the same to the actual settlers. On this foundation, the "Dorchester Company" sent out vessels with settlers and cattle to carry on agriculture and fishing. The site, however, proved unfavorable to each branch of the enterprise, and in 1626 a greater part of the adventurers retired. Rev. John White with a few others resolved to continue the enterprise, and offered to procure for the old planters, Conant, Woodbury, Balch, and Palfrey, grants of land at Naumkeag, now Salem, and to send them such men, provisions, and goods, as they desired, to trade with the Indians. They accordingly removed to Naumkeag with their stock, in 1626, and in the autumn of 1627 sent John Woodbury to England to complete arrangements with the new company for carrying on the plantation. He remained in England about six months, and returned the following June with his son Humphrey, "bringing a comfortable answer." In 1630 the general court of the company made a general levy of taxes. Not having made any county or town government, it created the office of constable, the duties of which were to assess, collect, and disburse taxes, record deeds, bounds of land, etc. John Woodbury of Salem, and Stoughton of Dorchester, were selected for this office. It is uncertain how long he occupied the office, but when the town record begins, in 1634, he appears, trusted in many local affairs. In May, 1635, he was sent to the general court as deputy for Salem, and again in September. He was also one of the overseers to lay out and make grants of land. In November of 1635, Salem granted two hundred acres of land each to the old planters, Woodbury, Conant, Balch, and Palfrey of Naumkeag, to be laid out at "Bass river head," in what is now Beverly. Woodbury, with Balch, surveyed this land, part of which is still in the possession of his descendants. In 1636 he was one of the selectmen, and was on a committee regarding the site of a college, then meditated by Salem. In 1637, he was again a selectman, and one of the deputies to the general court. In 1638 he was again deputy, was on the committee of valuation and distribution of rates and taxes, and on a committee of contract to build a church in Salem, which church is now in existence. He and his wife Agnes were both members of the first church. From this time until his death his name is prominent in various offices, but Dec. 3, 1641, was his last appearance at the meeting of the board of selectmen. Essex Institute's Collections, Vol. I., p. 150, title "The Old Planters," has the following: "Mr. Woodbury, after a life of energy and faithfulness to the interests of the Colony, died in 1641. We do not know his age, but probably not much above sixty years. He was called 'Father Woodbury,' however, as early as 1635, which may have been a title due him as one on whom many leaned for counsel and advice."

None of John Woodbury's children, born in England, came here, except his son Humphrey, who was born in 1608. In the first church record, at its beginning in 1629, his wife's name is given as Agnes; but when he died he left a wife Ann, who sold the house in Salem Village to George Curwin in 1660. The records of the first church in Salem give dates of baptism of three children: Hannah (1636), Abigail (1637), and Peter (1640).

Peter Woodbury, son of John and Ann Woodbury, was born in 1640; married, first, Abigail Batchelder, who left a son Peter, born Dec. 12, 1666 (the ancestor of the wife of Peter Woodbury of Francestown). He married, second, Sarah Dodge, and their children were Josiah and seven daughters. He died July 5, 1704.

Josiah Woodbury, son of Peter and Sarah (Dodge) Woodbury, was born June 15, 1682; married Lydia Herrick in 1708, and had one son, Josiah, and four daughters.

Josiah Woodbury, Jr., son of Josiah and Lydia (Herrick) Woodbury, was born Feb. 15, 1709; married Hannah Perkins of Ipswich, who died in 1761, aged forty-six years. He died in 1773. They had two sons, Peter and Josiah, and four daughters.

PETER WOODBURY, son of Josiah, Jr., and Hannah (Perkins) Woodbury, was born in Beverly, Mass., March 28, 1738; married Mrs. Elizabeth (Dodge) Rea (a great-granddaughter of Richard Dodge, Esq., of Beverly, Mass., and widow of James Rea, Esq., being then seventeen years of age with one child), in 1760. She is described as "a woman of shrewdness and energy." His cousins, Josiah and James of Francestown, served several campaigns in the French war. A tradition in the family is that Peter was also out at Lake George during one campaign. In his youth he passed some years as a sea-faring man. In 1773 he went to Amherst, N. H., and settled in what is now Mont Vernon. He was several years on the board of selectmen, representative to the general court in 1776 and 1777, and member of the convention which framed the first constitution of New Hampshire. When the Revolution became imminent, a declaration of association to resist with arms the encroachments of the English Parliament, started in Amherst, April 10, 1776, was sent through the State for signatures. The fifth signature in Amherst was Peter Woodbury. His name occurs several times on the records after Mont Vernon was set off. It was probably about 1800 that he moved to Antrim and took up his abode with his son, Mark Woodbury, then a flourishing merchant here. He seems to have been taxed subsequently in Mont Vernon as a non-resident. He died Oct. 11, 1817, aged seventy-nine years and six months. His wife died in Antrim, April 19, 1812, aged sixty-nine years. They were buried on Meeting-House Hill. The children of Peter and Elizabeth Woodbury were: First, Levi, who was born Jan. 20, 1761; entered the privateer service in the Revolution, was captured in the armed ship "Essex," and died in prison at Plymouth. Second, Jesse, who was born Oct. 2, 1763; went to Mexico, where he procured large grants in Western Texas, and died, it is said, about the time of the Texan Revolution. The third child of Peter and Elizabeth was Peter, who was born Jan. 17, 1767; settled in Francestown, and married his second cousin, Mary Woodbury (daughter of James Woodbury, whose ancestor was the Peter Woodbury born in 1666). He was a prominent citizen of Francestown, being representative about fifteen years and senator two years in the state legislature, besides holding many minor offices. His children were Peter P., who was born Aug. 8, 1791, and was a physician in Bedford during a long life; Hon. Levi Woodbury, LL. D., who was born Dec. 22, 1789, was judge of our state court at the age of twenty-eight, was twice United States senator, was associate justice of the United States supreme court, was secretary of state under Jackson and Van Buren, and, at the time of his death, a leading candidate for the office of President of the United States, with every prospect of election; Rev. James T. Woodbury, of Acton, Mass.; Jesse Woodbury, Esq., now living in Francestown; George W. Woodbury, M. D., of Yazoo County, Miss.; Mary, who married Dr. Luke How of Jaffrey; Anstess, who married Hon. Nehemiah Eastman, formerly member of congress; Martha, who married Thomas Grimes, a merchant of Windsor, Vt.; Hannah T., who married Hon. Isaac O. Barnes of Boston; Harriet, who married Hon. Perley Dodge of Amherst; and Adeline, who married Edwin F. Bunnel, a merchant of Boston. The fourth child of Peter and Elizabeth was Betsey, who was born Feb. 9, 1770, and married Peter Jones, Esq., of Amherst. The fifth was Hannah, who was born Feb. 14, 1772, and died young. The sixth was Mark of Antrim, who is further noticed below.

ESQ. MARK WOODBURY, youngest child of Peter and Elizabeth Woodbury of Beverly, Mass., was born in Amherst (now Mont Vernon), Jan. 1, 1775. When quite young he started out for himself, opening a store in Hancock as early as 1793. Came here from the last-named place and opened a store in 1794. His store for four years was in one end of the house, leaving only one room to live in. The store was moved across the road to its present site in 1800. The house was enlarged in subsequent years according to necessity and ability. He married Alice, daughter of Dea. Joseph Boyd. Was vigorously engaged in trade and farming for many years. He was justice of the peace and representative, and died March 17, 1828, leaving a large property. His widow died April 15, 1858, aged seventy-eight. She was a noble woman, — one of piety, and great strength of character. Their children were as follows: —

1. HON. LUKE, [b. Dec. 25, 1800; graduated at Dartmouth College in 1820; was for many years judge of probate for Hillsborough County, and at the time of his death was the Democratic candidate for governor of New Hampshire. He m. Mary E. Wallace of Antrim, June 10, 1834. Built his fine residence in South Village in 1849, and d. Aug. 27, 1851; no children. Was a very honest and truthful man. His schoolmates used to say, "You can't trust any deviltry with Luke!" Was a man extremely diffident and self-distrustful, but capable of filling any office with credit. His death was universally deplored.]

2. SABRINA, [b. Feb. 4, 1804; she was called the "best-educated girl in town;" m. George W. Hill, May 20, 1828, and d. May 8, 1856. Of her children three survive: Alice R.; Susie S., who is the wife of Morris Christie, M. D.; and John R., who is a prominent citizen of Johnson, Vt.]

3. MARY, [b. Dec. 8, 1805; m. Joshua C. Dodge, Oct. 23, 1828, and d. May 3, 1836.]

## GENEALOGIES.

4. BETSEY, [b. May 8, 1808 ; d. in infancy.]
5. BETSEY B., [b. May 8, 1809 ; m. Benjamin B. Muzzey, Oct. 6, 1834, and d. March 20, 1849.]
6. MARK B., [b. May 9, 1811 ; m. Emily Wilson of Stoddard, in 1837 ; was in trade on the Woodbury stand many years; was a genial, social man. His wife d. June 30, 1872, aged 57. He d. Oct. 24, 1874. Marion E. Woodward had her home with them several years. She was daughter of Franklin and Sarah (Bradford) Woodward of Francestown. She m. Eugene G. Bullard, Nov. 12, 1865, and after living here a few years, moved to Woburn Mass. Mark B. Woodbury left but one child : —

*Frank B.*, (b. Jan. 28, 1849.)]

7. FANNY, [b. Nov. 14, 1813 ; d Oct. 15, 1858.]
8. NANCY, [b. Oct. 28, 1817 ; m. 1st, A. N. Moore in 1837, who d. in 1844, and she m. 2d, George C. Trumbull, Oct. 21, 1855, and now resides in Boston.]
9. LEVI, [b. Feb. 18, 1820 ; m. Anna M. Baldwin of Bennington, May 21, 1856 ; was in trade at the old stand, did much to improve the village, and d. much lamented, Aug. 10, 1865. His widow now occupies the fine residence at the South Village ; has no children ; is always ready with heart and hand to aid in every good work, and has generously aided in procuring the illustrations of this book. Levi Woodbury was genial and popular, a man of genuine worth.]
10. JOHN B., [b. Oct. 13, 1823 ; m. 1st, Mary F. Pattee, daughter of Hon. L. N. Pattee, March 6, 1849, who d. Oct. 15, 1858, leaving three children ; m. 2d, Mary C. Whittemore of Antrim, May 28, 1861. He continues in trade at the old stand, where the family have done business for more than eighty years. His children by second marriage are the four last named : —

*John N. P.*, (b. Oct. 31, 1850 ; m. Ella L. Carr of Antrim, Feb. 12, 1873 ; was in business with his father some years ; now owns the stage-line from Hillsborough to Greenfield. They have one child, Nannie Blanche, b. June 19, 1877.)

*Levi*, (b. Jan. 14, 1854 ; m. Ida M. Whittle of Hillsborough Bridge, Aug. 26, 1873, and now lives in that place.)

*Mary Alice*, (b. Oct. 8, 1858. After the death of her mother she went to Goffstown to live with her grandfather, L. N. Pattee, and there m. William A. Parker, Aug. 23, 1876.)

*Helen C.*, (b. Aug. 7, 1863.)
*George T.*, (b. Sept. 18, 1865.)
*Arthur W.*, (b. Feb. 14, 1868 ; d. April 12, 1869.)
*Ralph B.*, (b March 4, 1879.)]

STEPHEN WOODBURY came here from Vermont in 1802. He lived a few rods southeast of Linn Parker's, a short distance from the present road, remaining here about twelve years, when he moved back to Vermont. The house (built by Nathan Cole, Jr., in 1795) was afterwards occupied by various parties, and was taken down in 1847. Mr. Woodbury was at one time selectman. He was frequently in disagreement with those around him, and engaged in several lawsuits. He claimed a tract of land on the river now Mr. Holton's, which to this day is called the "battle-ground," because here he had so many severe fights in trying to drive other claimants off. He had three sons and one daughter. The name of the latter cannot be found.

1. STEPHEN, JR., [m. —— Holden of Hillsborough ; went into the tanning business in the Center of that town about 1825.]
2. WILLIAM.
3. JOHN.

## WOODCOCK.

JOHN WOODCOCK came here from Peterborough about 1788 and succeeded Dea. James Nesmith on the Chandler Boutwell place. His wife was Dorothy Brackett, an older sister of James Brackett of Antrim. She was born in Peterborough, Oct. 7, 1772. They moved to Hillsborough in 1804. While there they had their name changed to "Bertram." Thence they moved to Newport, where he died, Sept. 19, 1854, aged ninety-seven. His wife died in Enfield, this State, 1864, aged ninety-two. They were married in Peterborough, 1785. They had nine children, five of whom died with consumption : —

1. JOHN, [studied medicine ; took degree of M. D. from Dartmouth College ; was associated in practice with Dr. Gregg of Unity and Dr. Farley of Francestown two or three years, but began practice for himself in Townsend, Mass., in 1827. Had a large practice and was a worthy and promising physician. He d. of consumption, Dec. 8, 1846, in Townsend. Left no children. He m. 1st, Ann Gilman of Unity ; 2d, Mary Adams of Townsend, Mass., April 13, 1831.]
2. SALLY, [b. in Antrim ; m. Elesson Emerson ; lived in Lempster, Newport, and Enfield, and d. in the last-named town in the fall of 1862.]
3. SAMUEL, [m. Lydia Wilkins of Unity ; was a hotel-keeper ; moved to Cambridge, N. Y. ; d. in Rome, that State, 1869.]

GENEALOGIES. 781

4. ELIZA, [b. in Antrim; m. Hiram Smith; lives in Champlin, Minn. He was a comb-manufacturer, but went West in 1854 and settled down at farming.]
5. CALISTA, [m. Oren D. Thompson: lived in Newport, Springfield, and Grantham, and d. in the last-named town February, 1876.]
6. DOROTHY, [d. young.]
7. REBECCA, [b. in Antrim; d. unm., aged 30.]
8. WILLIAM, [b. in Antrim; d. in infancy.]
9. BELINDA, [b. in Hillsborough; d. there, aged 15.]

## WORTHLEY.

CAPT. JOHN WORTHLEY, son of Timothy and Molly (Johnson) Worthley, was born May 20, 1769; married Phœbe Vose, daughter of Samuel Vose of Bedford, and lived west of the pond, clearing his farm himself. He lived to a good old age, obtained a large estate, was an influential, hard-working man, and the last survivor of those who cleared their own farms. Was selectman seven times. Was chairman of the committee to build the Center Church. He died Feb. 3, 1853. His wife died Nov. 29, 1835, aged seventy. Their children were as follows: —

1. DEA. JOHN, [b. Oct. 31, 1795; m. Betsey Templeton, March 23, 1819, who d. May 4, 1823, leaving two children, twins, as follows: —

*Samuel N.*, (b. in Unity, April 21, 1823; m. Nancy Crawford of Plattsburg, N. Y., in 1845. He is a carpenter; built his house in 1866, in Clinton. Their children now living are Mary H., b. Nov. 13, 1855, and Alice E., b. Aug. 22, 1870. Their son, John L., was b. March 10, 1849, and d. Jan. 22, 1869. Was a soldier in the Union army.)

*Thomas S.*, (twin-brother of Samuel N.; m. 1st, Mary R. Robinson, Aug. 31, 1847, who d. June 15, 1857, leaving children as follows: Frank S., b. April 12, 1851, m. Lizzie Bowker and lives in Charlestown, Mass.; Edwin T., b. Sept. 30, 1854, m. Lottie Ritchie July 27, 1873, lived awhile in Lowell, and bought the Lovejoy place in 1876, and has children, George A., b. Aug. 8, 1874, and Eva J., b. Oct. 31, 1877; and Mary Ella, b. June 13, 1857, adopted by Frank Robinson. In 1859, Thomas S. Worthley m. Mrs. Emily J. Merrill, and they have one child, Flora A., b. Oct. 20, 1864.)

After the death of his first wife, Dea. Worthley m. Polly Harwood of Unity, and they had children as follows: —

*Mary E.*, (b. June 19, 1825; m. Franklin Robinson, Nov. 8, 1853.)

*John O.*, (b. April 29, 1823; went to California in 1849, where he d. in 1851. Had accumulated quite an amount of gold, and, for possession of it, is supposed to have been helped out of the world.)

*Martha J.*, (b. May 31, 1831; m. Charles Bruce and moved to Winchendon, Mass., where she d. in 1857, aged 26.)

*Mariam*, (b. Feb. 22, 1834; m. Henry E. French of Jaffrey, and they live on her father's farm.)

Dea. John Worthley lived some years in Unity, but moved back to Antrim in 1841, on to the old place, which he sold in 1854, and bought the Daniel Lowe farm, where he d. June, 1877. His second wife d. in 1861. He was deacon of the Congregational Church in Unity; was a person of some peculiarities, but a good man, enjoying the confidence of the entire community.]

2. DANIEL, [b. Dec. 7, 1797; m. Elizabeth Smallcorn, and lived in Brookline, Mass., where he d. in 1875.]

3. PHŒBE. [b. Feb. 22, 1800; d. in infancy.]

4. MARY, [b. Jan. 8, 1802; m. John R. Hills, April 6, 1830, and lives in this town.]

5. MIRIAM, [b. May 16, 1804; d. in 1831.]

6. MARK, [b. Jan. 20, 1807; m. Catherine Durgin, and d. in Charlestown, Mass., in 1861.]

7. LUKE, [b. June 27, 1809; m. Elizabeth Poor, June 2, 1835, and lives in Andover, Mass.]

## WRIGHT.

DEA. IMLA WRIGHT, son of Ephraim and Mary (Blodgett) Wright of Westford, Mass., and grandson of Abram and Abigail (Trowbridge) Wright, was born in Littleton, Mass., July 13, 1799. He tended store awhile at Westford, Mass., then was clerk several years in Swanzey, after which he went to Westford to learn the carpenter's trade; worked at his trade for a time in New Ipswich. He married Rachel McMaster of Bennington, July 7, 1823; and in 1824, went to Shirley, Mass., to run a factory, which he did for six years. At the same time that he was engaged there, he moved his family to Antrim, in 1828, and built a cotton-mill right in the woods, on the spot now occupied by E. Z. Hastings's shop. There was, at that time, no building of any kind in the vicinity, the nearest house being Dea. Parmenter's, and that could not be seen, on account of the woods. He built the Hastings house the same year. After several years, Dea. Wright sold out to a company (incorporated as the Clinton Company in 1831). DeWitt Clinton was then very popular, and they, being in search of a name, took a fancy to this, and adopted it. Dr. Stickney proposed to call the village, then growing up, "Wrightsville," in honor of Dea. Wright; but the deacon objected, and proposed that they call the place, as they had the company, "Clinton," by which name it has ever since been known. In the panic of 1837 this company went down. Dea. Wright, as owner or agent, run the mill till 1841. In 1844 he built the Dodge mill, where he made batting and twine till 1854, when he sold his machinery to a man in Bunker Hill, Ill., where he spent the succeeding year in setting it at work. He has been, for many years, engaged in probate business, and has been a counselor to all in trouble. Men of better heart or clearer head than Dea. Wright are hard to be found. He was appointed deacon in the Presbyterian Church in 1860. His children are as follows, the three oldest born in Shirley, Mass., the rest here : —

1. ABRAHAM W., [b. March 18, 1824; m. 1st, Sarah R. Whitcomb of Waldo, Me., Feb. 4, 1854, and built the house now J. N. Wilkins's, which he moved from Nahor Hill. His first wife d. in 1860, and he m. 2d. Margaret Stockton of Gillespie, Ill., and is now engaged in teaching here and there in the West, being a very faithful and successful teacher. His first wife left one child : —

    Sarah A., (b. in Antrim, January, 1855.)]
2. LOUISA M., [b. July 15, 1825; d. in infancy.]
3. GEORGE W., [b. Feb. 29. 1828; d. aged 3.]
4. CHARLES I., [b. Aug. 14, 1829; m. 1st, Maria A. Corey of Stoddard; moved to Bunker Hill, Ill., thence to Pittsburg, Penn., where she d. In 1868 he m. 2d. Mrs. Eliza Lovejoy, and moved to Damascoville, Ohio, where he d. at the age of 48.]
5. MARY E., [b. Oct. 3, 1831; m. J. N. Wilkins, Sept. 27, 1857, and lives at Clinton Village.]
6. JACOB H., [b. April 30, 1834; d. aged 3.]
7. SARAH A., [b. Dec. 13, 1838; m. 1st, Dr. Albert R. Sawyer in 1856, and lived in Bunker Hill, Ill., where he d. in 1868. March 8, 1871, she m. 2d, Thomas Collier, and now lives in Dover, N. Y.]

## WYMAN.

IPS WYMAN, son of Jonathan and Ruby (Richardson) Wyman, was born in Greenfield in 1810; married Lydia A. Ward of Berkshire, Vt., and came here from Stoddard on to the Butters place in 1867. Their children are : —

1. AMOS A., [b. in Glenville, N. Y., in 1840; m. Francelia A. Eaton, and is in business at Hillsborough Bridge.]
2. RUBY B., [b. in Glenville in 1842; m. Albert O. Cutter.]
3. RODNEY D., [b. in Hancock in 1844; m. Lizzie J. Boutelle, and d. in Nelson in 1866.]
4. HIRAM E., [b. in Hancock; d. in 1863 aged 17.]
5. LYDIA A., [d. at the age of 3 years.]
6. ARMENDA O., [b. in Hancock in 1851; m. George F. Mellen of Stoddard.]
7. SARAH C., [b. in Hancock in 1855; m. William H. Shoults, Feb. 13, 1879.]

## YOUNGMAN.

JABEZ YOUNGMAN, JR., son of Jabez and Susannah (Powers) Youngman of Hollis, was born in Hollis in 1786, and was the eldest of twelve children. The elder Jabez Youngman, with three brothers, was in the Revolutionary army, and Ebenezer, one of the brothers, was killed at Bunker Hill. He and his wife lived together fifty-four years, and died in Lempster (whither they had removed from Hollis) so near together that they were both buried at one funeral and in one grave. Jabez Youngman, Jr., married Emma Baldwin of this town, March 14, 1809, and moved here on to the William Parker place. He moved to Wilmot in 1812, thence after many years to Dorchester, where he died in 1863. The children were: —

1. DAVID S., [b. in Antrim in 1809; d. in 1835.]
2. ISAAC B., [b. in Antrim in 1811; m. Mrs. Hannah (Thompson) Langley, and lives in Wilmot Center.]
3. FANNY B., [b. in 1814; m. Wells Currier in 1835, and lives in Danbury.]
4. NAHUM B., [b. in 1817; m. Elsie Hadley, and lives in Wentworth.]
5. EMMA B., [b. in 1819; m. 1st, Wells Robbins of Antrim, who d. in 1860; 2d, Ezra Alden. and lives in Lyme.]
6. MARY B., [b. in 1822; m. Thomas Parsons, and d. at Wilmot in 1850.]
7. MILTON B., [b. in 1824; m. Susan Leavitt of Dorchester, and d. in that town in 1860.]
8. HARRIET B., [b. in 1826; m. Nathaniel Burnham, and resides in Dorchester.]
9. JANE, [b. in 1828; m. Washington Perkins of Londonderry, where they now reside.]
10. WALTER S., [b. in 1830; d. in 1847.]

11. ALDEN, [b. in 1832; m. Maria Smith of New Boston and lives in Dorchester.]
12. BERTHA P., [b. in 1840; m. 1st, Samuel Roberts, who d. in the army in 1862; 2d, George E. Patterson, and moved to South Merrimack, where she d. in 1875.]

NOAH YOUNGMAN, brother of Jabez Youngman, Jr., mentioned above, was born in Hollis in 1788; married Sarah Field, daughter of John Field, Sen., of Peterborough, in 1812, and came here on to the Zadok Dodge place early in the year 1813, he and his wife uniting with the church here that year. Afterwards he lived on the Dea. Worthley place. He moved to Lempster in the fall of 1818. Mrs. Youngman died March 24, 1854, aged sixty-three years. He died in Newbury in 1867. Their children were : —

1. JOHN F., [b. in Peterborough; was an infant when his father came here; m. Roxanna Bailey in 1830, lived in Lempster, and d. in 1838.]
2. LOUISA S., [b. in Antrim in 1815; m. Elliot Wright of Swanzey in 1834, who d. in the army in 1862, leaving a large family.]
3. SARAH F., [b. in Lempster, November, 1818; d. unm. in 1852.]
4. HARRIET S., [b. in 1823; m. David McIndoe in 1850, and lives in Windsor, Vt.]
5. NOAH E., [b. in 1827; d. at the age of 5.]

## ADDENDA.

ISAAC EATON, son of James and Martha (McClure) Eaton, lived some years in Antrim, here and there, chiefly in the house next east of Maplewood Cemetery. His wife's name was Lorinda, and she was a Francestown girl. He died Feb. 4, 1866. He buried a daughter, Lorinda, Sept. 15, 1855, aged twenty-one years. His son, John H. Eaton, of the Fifth N. H. Regiment, lost his life in the war, Sept. 9, 1862, aged twenty years.

www.ingramcontent.com/pod-product-compliance
Lightning Source LLC
Chambersburg PA
CBHW071432300426
44114CB00013B/1402